Handbook of Conceptual Modeling

T0135162

David W. Embley · Bernhard Thalheim
Editors

Handbook of Conceptual Modeling

Theory, Practice, and Research Challenges

 Springer

David W. Embley
Department of Computer Science
Brigham Young University
Provo, Utah 84602
USA
embley@cs.byu.edu

Bernhard Thalheim
Universität Kiel
Inst. Informatik
Olshausenstr. 40
24098 Kiel
Germany
thalheim@is.informatik.uni-kiel.de

ISBN 978-3-642-43049-7   ISBN 978-3-642-15865-0 (eBook)
DOI 10.1007/978-3-642-15865-0
Springer Heidelberg Dordrecht London New York

Cover design: Integra, Puducherry, India

Printed on acid-free paper

Springer is part of Springer Science+Business Media (www.springer.com)

Preface

The Handbook of Conceptual Modeling: Theory, Practice, and Research Challenges
is about the challenges faced by conceptual-modeling researchers and their successes in meeting these challenges by formalizing underlying theory and showing
how to put conceptual modeling into practice. Conceptual modeling is about describing the semantics of software applications at a high level of abstraction. Specifically, conceptual modelers (1) describe structure models in terms of entities, relationships, and constraints; (2) describe behavior or functional models in terms of
states, transitions among states, and actions performed in states and transitions; and
(3) describe interactions and user interfaces in terms of messages sent and received,
information exchanged, and look-and-feel navigation and appearance.

In their typical usage, conceptual-model diagrams are high-level abstractions that
enable clients and analysts to understand one another and enable analysts to communicate successfully with application programmers. It is a challenge to successfully
provide the right set of modeling constructs at the right level of abstraction to enable
this communication. It is an added challenge to formalize these modeling abstractions so that they retain their ease-of-communication property and yet are able to
(partially or even fully) generate functioning application software. It is also a challenge to push conceptual modeling toward serving as analysis and development tools
for exotic applications such as modeling the computational features of DNA-level
life or modeling the ability to read and extract information from free-form text.

A central challenge of conceptual modeling is to facilitate the long-time dream
of being able to develop information systems strictly by conceptual modeling. The
handbook begins with a manifesto stating that this dream is becoming reality and
asserting that applications amenable to conceptual modeling should be programmed
abstractly, at the level of conceptual modeling. It thus asserts that "conceptual modeling is programming" and that "the model is the code." Subsequent chapters support
the manifesto's assertions by showing not only how to abstractly model complex information systems but also how to formalize abstract specifications in ways that let
developers complete programming tasks within the conceptual model itself. In addition to addressing this central challenge, several chapters concern demanding challenge areas for conceptual modeling. These include system evolution and migration,

spatial modeling, information integration, conceptual-model-based information extraction, and biological conceptual modeling. The handbook ends with a chapter reflecting on the theoretical foundations of conceptual modeling and addresses both a theory of conceptual modeling (how it is practiced) and a theory of conceptual models (how it is formalized).

Taken together, the chapters selected for inclusion nicely serve the purpose of a handbook by collecting in a single volume many of the best conceptual-modeling ideas and techniques, as well as the challenges that drive research in the field. The handbook is thus suitable as a text for graduate students. It provides a firm foundation for the field of conceptual modeling, and it points toward interesting challenges and puts researchers on a path toward contributing to the conceptual-modeling discipline.

Structurally, the handbook consists of five sections, each with two or more chapters. The first section directly explores the central challenge of conceptual modeling – making conceptual models serve both as high-level abstractions and as executable code. The second section focuses on structure modeling, while the third and fourth sections add material whose main focus is process modeling and user-interface modeling. The final section includes several special challenge-area chapters and ends with central directions for future work both in the theory of conceptual modeling (its practice) and the theory of conceptual models (its formalization).

Section I: *Programming with Conceptual Models*

Chapter 1: Conceptual-Model Programming: A Manifesto. The manifesto expounds upon the vision that all programming activities can and should be carried out completely at the abstract level of conceptual modeling. It asserts that for applications amenable to conceptual-model designs, software developers should never need to write a line of traditional code.

Chapter 2: Model-Driven Software Development. The essence of model-driven software development is the idea that software models can go beyond being mere blueprints: they can constitute the basis for automatically or semiautomatically generating the software system itself. This chapter surveys various major approaches to model-driven software construction and illustrates how model-driven development works in practice.

Section II: *Structure Modeling*

Chapter 3: The Entity-Relationship Model – Toward a Unified View of Data. To provide historical context, this first chapter in the structure-modeling section is a reprint of Peter P. Chen's 1976 article, which originally appeared as the first article in the first volume of *ACM Transactions on Database Systems*. The publication of this article propelled the ER Model into its place as the foundation for conceptual modeling. No conceptual-modeling handbook would be complete without this historical perspective.

Chapter 4: UML and OCL in Conceptual Modeling. This chapter explains how the Unified Modeling Language (UML) and its accompanying Object Constraint Language (OCL) support structure modeling for information systems. UML class diagrams allow information-system-developers to model databases in terms of classes and associations and more advanced features such as part–whole relationships. OCL allows developers to enrich UML diagrams with textual constraints that cannot otherwise be expressed.

Chapter 5: Mapping Conceptual Models to Database Schemas. Automated generation of database schemas from conceptual data models has been a mainstay of conceptual modeling from its earliest beginnings. This chapter generalizes schema-generation rules for use with all kinds of conceptual data models and several types of target databases.

Chapter 6: The Enhanced Entity-Relationship Model. The Enhanced Entity-Relationship Model (EERM) described in this chapter extends the ER Model with complex attributes, cluster or generalization types, and relationship types of higher order. Even with these more complex abstractions, the EERM retains its formal mapping to database schemas and predicate-logic-based integrity constraints. Further, the described EERM extends ER modeling beyond structure modeling to include functionality in terms of queries, transactions, and workflows. The EERM thus facilitates codesign of structure and behavior.

Section III: *Process Modeling*

Chapter 7: Object-Process Methodology for Structure-Behavior Co-Design. Emphasizing both structure modeling and behavior modeling, this chapter asserts that architecting a software system is best approached by codesign using a single model. The chapter describes the Object-Process Methodology (OPM). OPM enables system architects and designers to freely express the tight, inseparable relationships and interactions between a system's static and dynamic components.

Chapter 8: Business-Process Modelling and Workflow Design. Business-process models and workflows provide invaluable understanding of organizational operations. They support process management from modeling and design to execution, monitoring, optimization, and reengineering. This chapter explains basic terms and concepts of process modeling and workflow design and gives details of the three most extensively described process perspectives: the control flow perspective, the organizational perspective, and the data perspective. The chapter also explores some areas of research: problem detection and avoidance in control flow, correctness and generation of process views, and exploitation of temporal information to improve performance.

Chapter 9: BPMN Core Modeling Concepts: Inheritance-Based Execution Semantics. This chapter defines an abstract model for the dynamic semantics of the core process modeling concepts in the Business Process Modeling Notation (BPMN). Each flow element has a rigorous behavior definition, formalized in terms of a basic class inheritance hierarchy that includes sequence flow, flow nodes, gateways, events, and activities. Developers can use the model to test reference implementations and to verify properties of interest for certain classes of BPMN diagrams.

Section IV: *User Interface Modeling*

Chapter 10: Conceptual Modelling of Interaction. Just specifying the structure and behavior of an information system is insufficient – it is also necessary to specify how end users will interact with the system. This chapter presents a practical approach to conceptually specifying end-user interaction. The approach is embedded in a model-driven engineering method, called the OO-Method, which allows full functional systems to be generated from conceptual models. The focus of the chapter, however, is on how the OO-Method supports interaction modeling.

Chapter 11: Conceptual Modelling of Application Stories. The development of complex software systems requires an understanding of how the system is to be used – how actors are to navigate through the system and which actions they are to execute to perform certain tasks. This chapter explains how conceptual models describe navigation paths that correspond to "telling stories" about system usage. The chapter highlights key concepts of storyboarding such as actors, scenarios, and tasks, as well as composed action schemes called "plots." The chapter also addresses the pragmatics of conceptual storyboards and discusses a development methodology for storyboarding.

Section V: *Special Challenge Areas*

Chapter 12: Evolution and Migration of Information Systems. The management of evolution, migration, refinement, and modernization is an essential component of information-system development. Typical problems include management of evolution and migration; versioning; changes to metadata; system upgrades; modernization in time and space; and change detection, monitoring, and mining. A key challenge is to minimize service disruption and down time and maximize the availability of data and applications. This chapter provides insight into several of these problems from a conceptual-modeling point of view.

Chapter 13: Conceptual Geometric Modelling. This chapter presents a geometrically enhanced ER Model (GERM), which preserves the key principles of ER modeling while at the same time introducing bulk constructions and types that support geometric objects. GERM distinguishes between a syntactic level of types and an explicit internal level, in which types give rise to polyhedra defined by algebraic varieties. GERM further emphasizes the stability of algebraic operations by means of a natural modeling algebra that extends the usual Boolean operations on point sets.

Chapter 14: Data Integration. Data integration is about combining data residing in different sources (virtually or actually) and providing users with a unified view of the data. At the heart of data integration is conceptual matching and mappings, making conceptual modeling of one sort or another central to data integration. This chapter presents an overview of the relevant research activities and ideas in data integration, and it discusses as an example the MOMIS system – a framework to perform information extraction and integration from both structured and semistructured data sources.

Chapter 15: Conceptual Modeling Foundations for a Web of Knowledge. The first-generation web is a web of pages. This chapter shows how conceptual modeling can play a central role in turning the web of pages into a web of knowledge to be superimposed over the current web of pages. Success in this endeavor would enable the web to become a gigantic, queriable database.

Chapter 16: A Conceptual Modeling Approach to Improving Human Genome Understanding. The main purpose of conceptual modeling is to represent knowledge in some application domain – usually for the purpose of developing and maintaining information systems. In a slight paradigm shift, it is possible to imagine the human body as an information system – highly complex, but ultimately built on biological information-processing molecules. This paradigm shift allows for exciting possibilities: just like acquiring the source code of a manmade system allows for postproduction modifications and easy software maintenance, the same could very well apply to the human body. Acquiring the source code to the human information system begins with the first step in any information system development – creation of a comprehensive and correct conceptual model of the human genome. This chapter aims at this objective.

Chapter 17: The Theory of Conceptual Models, the Theory of Conceptual Modelling, and the Foundations of Conceptual Modelling. This final chapter aims at the heart of conceptual modeling itself. It not only summarizes the foundations of conceptual modeling, but it also goes beyond this toward the development of both a theory of conceptual models and a theory of the practice of conceptual modeling. A remaining challenge for conceptual modeling is to harness its foundations in terms of a theoretical perspective that leads to better usage by practitioners and pushes researchers to meet its challenges head-on and resolve them.

Provo, Utah, USA   *David W. Embley*
Kiel, Germany   *Bernhard Thalheim*
August 2010

Contents

Part III Process Modelling

Part I
Programming with Conceptual Models

Chapter 1
Conceptual-Model Programming: A Manifesto

David W. Embley, Stephen W. Liddle, and Óscar Pastor

1.1 Preamble

In order to promote conceptual-model programming (CMP), we present these *CMP articles*. We hold these articles to be the defining principles for model-complete software development.

Essentially, this CMP manifesto asserts that programming activities are to be carried out via conceptual modeling. For applications amenable to conceptual-model designs, software developers should never need to write a line of traditional code. Thus, programming is actually conceptual-model programming.

To accommodate CMP, conceptual-modeling languages must be executable. They must also be capable of completely deploying both databases and user interfaces and conceptually expressing database access and user interaction. To enable CMP, a conceptual-model compiler must exist to generate underlying code, which could be, but is not necessarily, high-level language code that itself needs further compilation. Important, however, is that model-compiled code is beyond the purview of CMP programmers – both for initially creating the application system being developed and for enhancing or evolving the application system. Thus, application-system development becomes entirely model-driven, and CMP constitutes model-complete software development.

David W. Embley
Brigham Young University, Provo, Utah 84602, USA, e-mail: embley@cs.byu.edu

Stephen W. Liddle
Brigham Young University, Provo, Utah 84602, USA, e-mail: liddle@byu.edu

Óscar Pastor
Valencia University of Technology, 46022 Valencia, Spain, e-mail: opastor@dsic.upv.es

D. W. Embley and B. Thalheim (eds), *Handbook of Conceptual Modeling.*
DOI 10.1007/978-3-642-15865-0, © Springer 2011

1.2 CMP Articles

Conceptual modeling is programming. The conceptual-model instance is the code, i.e., instead of "the code is the model," the phrase now becomes "the model is the code." A conceptual-model compiler assures that program execution corresponds to the conceptual specification, thus making the conceptual-model instance directly executable.

The conceptual model, with which modelers program, must be:

- **complete and holistic.** The conceptual model must provide a holistic view of all application components. It must include all necessary aspects of data (structure), behavior (function), and interaction (both component interaction and user interaction).
- **conceptual but precise.** The conceptual-modeling elements must be precisely defined and must be based on an ontological agreement that fixes the concepts and their associated notation. Parsimony should guide, but not rule, both the modeling elements and the notation.

Application evolution occurs at the level of the model. Conceptual-model programmers should evolve an application through the model instance, not through generated, lower-level code.

1.3 Exposition

The principles of the CMP articles are tenable only if (1) a conceptual-model instance is executable (Sect. 1.3.1) and (2) programmers can do all their development work by specifying a conceptual-model instance for their application (see Sect. 1.3.2).

1.3.1 Executable Conceptual Models

Conceptual-model programming (CMP) is about precisely capturing an application in the language of an executable conceptual model that is sufficient for all storage, functional, and interaction requirements of an application. Precisely capturing an application as a conceptual-model instance *is* programming, i.e., it is conceptual-model programming (known as CM programming, or CMP).

To illustrate CMP, Figs. 1.1–1.8 show some sample conceptual-model specifications. These sample specifications consider a free-lance photography agency. Free-lance photographers register with the agency. They then submit annotated pictures. An evaluator for the agency determines which pictures to syndicate. Customers use syndicated pictures and pay royalties. The company pays free-lance photographers a percentage of the royalties and keeps the rest.

The particular notation of the conceptual-modeling language is not important, except that it is conceptual. What is important is that a collection of conceptual-model specifications provides all the information needed to generate a fully executable application.

Figures 1.1–1.4 show some generic samples covering the full range of development activities from specifying database storage structures, through stipulating behavior and component interaction, to describing user-interface data exchange. They represent a coherent collection in which cross-diagram objects and components have the same name. Together, they constitute, along with additional diagrams needed to complete the full specification, a CM program for the free-lance photography agency.

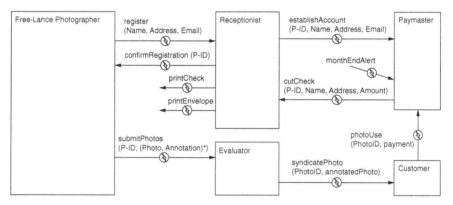

Fig. 1.1 Sample CMP component interaction

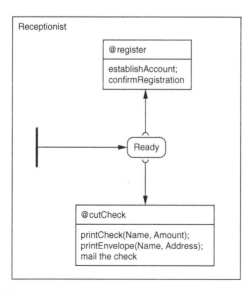

Fig. 1.2 Sample CMP behavior

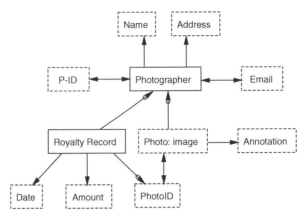

Fig. 1.3 Sample CMP database structure

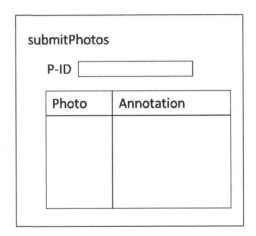

Fig. 1.4 Sample CMP conceptual user-interface specification

Figures 1.5–1.8 illustrate alternative graphical notation and also serve to indicate that the collection of conceptual-model diagrams constituting a CM program need not all be of the same genre. Figure 1.5 is a UML communication diagram that corresponds to the interaction diagram in Fig. 1.1. Figure 1.6 is a statechart that corresponds to the behavior diagram in Fig. 1.2. Figure 1.7 is an entity-relationship (ER) diagram that is semantically equivalent to the structure diagram in Fig. 1.3. Additionally, Fig. 1.8 is an OlivaNova user-interface specification that not only establishes the data to be exchanged, as expressed in Fig. 1.4, but also establishes the appearance of the interface a user of the free-lance photography sees when submitting photos for potential syndication.

Observe that in all diagrams fundamental constructs have two-dimensional, graphical representations. Behavior diagrams express control flow graphically; interaction diagrams express sending and receiving actions graphically; database

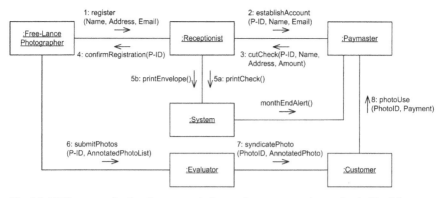

Fig. 1.5 UML communication diagram equivalent to the component interaction in Fig. 1.1

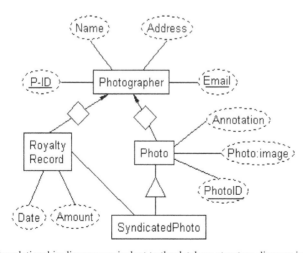

Fig. 1.6 Statechart diagram equivalent to the behavior diagram in Fig. 1.2

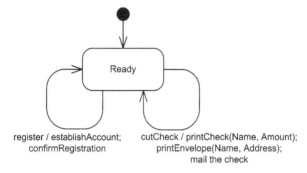

Fig. 1.7 Entity-relationship diagram equivalent to the database structure diagram in Fig. 1.3

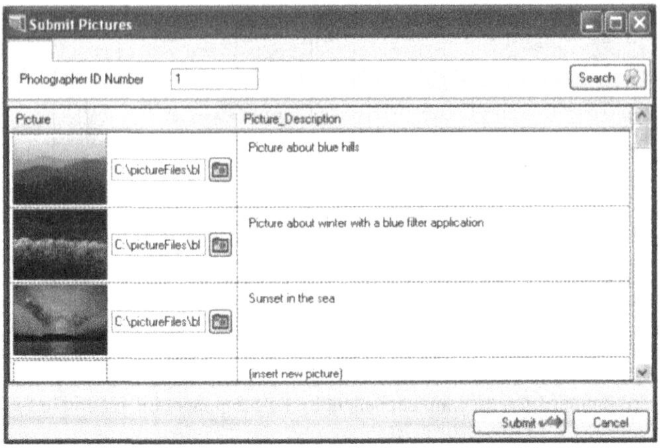

Fig. 1.8 OlivaNova user-interface specification equivalent to the user-interface specification in Fig. 1.4. (Note: an additional conceptual specification exists that associates the external names "Submit Pictures", "Photographer ID Number", "Picture", and "Picture_Description", respectively, with the internal names "submitPhotos", "P-ID", "Photo", and "Annotation". Also, an additional top-level conceptual specification exists to allow a photographer to navigate to this "Submit Pictures" interface.)

structure diagrams express entities, relationships, and constraints graphically; and user-interaction diagrams express data exchange and the look-and-feel of a user interface graphically. Text associated with graphical constructs provides names for objects and components, expressions that naturally appear as text, and connecting syntax.

Although the ability to render fundamental conceptualizations graphically is a requirement, actually rendering them graphically is not. CM programmers may express conceptualizations in purely textual languages, so long as the languages are *model-equivalent*. In a model-equivalent language each fundamental construct has

```
...
Photographer [1] P-ID [1];
Photographer [1] Name [1:*];
...
@initialize Receptionist
enter Ready
end;

when Ready new thread
@register(Name, Address, Email) then
...
end;
...
```

Fig. 1.9 Model-equivalent textual representation

an isomorphic correspondence to a graphical representation. Figure 1.9 shows some examples. *Photographer [1] Name [1:*]* in Fig. 1.9 corresponds to the functional edge between the nodes *Photographer* and *Name* in the database-structure graph in Fig. 1.3. The *[1]* and the *[1:*]* are participation constraints; thus, each *Photographer* object associates with exactly one *Name* object, making the relationship functional. In Fig. 1.2, the circled *Ready* denotes the potential for an object to be in the ready state – *when Ready* in Fig. 1.9 denotes the same; both the arrows whose tails are disconnected from the *Ready* state in Fig. 1.2 and *new thread* in Fig. 1.9 denote spawning new threads of control; and the event-condition-action (ECA) box with the event *@register* in Fig. 1.2 matches through its name with the interaction *register(Name, Address, Email)* in Fig. 1.1. Allowing experienced CM programmers to express conceptual-model instances textually provides for economy of expression without loss of conceptualization. Ideally, CM programmers and analysts can be at either extreme (no graphics/all graphics), or at a comfortable place in between.

To see that conceptual-model instances can be fully executable, consider the diagrams in Figs. 1.1–1.3. In Fig. 1.1, message passing is executable if in the code the point of initiation of the message is known, the information to be passed is known, and the point of reception of the message is known. An interaction such as *establishAccount(P-ID, Name, Address, Email)* in Fig. 1.1 specifies the information to be passed and provides a name for reference within specified origin and destination active objects. The tail side of the interaction arrow specifies the origin (*Receptionist* for *establishAccount*), and the head side specifies the destination (*Paymaster* for *establishAccount*). Within the behavior diagram of active objects, an appropriate reference to the name specifies the point of initiation in the originating behavior diagram and the point of reception in the receiving behavior diagram. In the behavior diagram in Fig. 1.2, for example, *establishAccount* in the ECA box initiates the interaction *establishAccount(P-ID, Name, Address, Email)* in Fig. 1.1, and *@register* is the point of reception for the interaction *register(Name, Address, Email)*, also in Fig. 1.1.

Behavior diagrams require a full specification of the control flow. The behavior diagram in Fig. 1.2, for example, consists fundamentally of a collection of ECA rules: when events (marked by @) occur, if an object's thread is in a prior state and specified conditions (if any) hold, the ECA rule fires. Thus, for example, when a thread of control is in the *Ready* state in Fig. 1.2 and a *Receptionist* receives an *@register* message, the ECA rule fires, spawning a thread of control to establish an account and confirm the registration. The new thread of control then dies, but the original thread of control remains active in the *Ready* state. In addition to full specification of control flow, the events, conditions, and sequence of statements in ECA rules must be formal enough to be compilable into code. In Fig. 1.2, the *@register* ECA rule is fully formal: both the event and the actions reference fully specified messages in the interaction diagram in Fig. 1.1. The *@cutCheck* ECA rule is also fully formal if the actions are all primitive or provided in a library. Alternatively, if the *Receptionist* is actually a human user of the system, all the ECA rules are sufficient as instructions. Further, each fully specified message implicitly has a corresponding interface form (e.g., Fig. 1.4 for the *submitPhotos* message in Fig. 1.2),

```
CREATE TABLE Photographer (
    P-ID VARCHAR(30) PRIMARY KEY,
    Email VARCHAR(30) NOT NULL UNIQUE,
    Name VARCHAR(30) NOT NULL,
    Address VARCHAR(30) NOT NULL
    );

CREATE TABLE Photo (
    PhotoID VARCHAR(30) PRIMARY KEY,
    Annotation VARCHAR(30) NOT NULL,
    P-ID VARCHAR(30) NOT NULL REFERENCES Photographer
    );

CREATE TABLE PhotoFile (
    PhotoID VARCHAR(30) PRIMARY KEY REFERENCES Photo,
    Photo BLOB
    );

CREATE TABLE RoyaltyRecord (
    RoyaltyRecordID INT PRIMARY KEY,
    Date DATE NOT NULL,
    Amount VARCHAR(30) NOT NULL,
    PhotoID VARCHAR(30) NOT NULL REFERENCES Photo,
    P-ID VARCHAR(30) NOT NULL REFERENCES Photographer
    );
```

Fig. 1.10 Generated database schema

which can be directly implemented (as-is) or visually enhanced to be more pleasing with an improved user-interface specification (e.g., Fig. 1.8).

Structure diagrams must fully specify the database schema. From the conceptual-model instance either in Fig. 1.3 or in Fig. 1.7 the CM compiler can infer the SQL schema in Fig. 1.10. From Fig. 1.7, for example, the mapping algorithm generates each entity as a table with its associated attributes and foreign-key references. Then, since the attribute *Photo:image* for the entity *Photo* is an image, which is to be implemented with the type *BLOB*, the mapping algorithm generates the attribute *Photo:image* as a weak entity and thus as the table *PhotoFile*, which is dependent on the table *Photo*. Additional constraints, such as check constraints and alternative-type constraints, can be added to the conceptual database structure diagram and propagated into a formal schema specification. The type specification *image* in Fig. 1.3 is an example; specifying *Amount:smallmoney* in place of *Amount* in Fig. 1.3 would be another example.

1.3.2 Conceptual Modeling and CMP

CMP development work includes analysis, specification, design, implementation, deployment, enhancement, and evolution. CM programmers work through every stage conceptually, writing all descriptions in a conceptual-modeling language. Typically, initial stages are informal – progressing through the stages is a process of formalizing the CM descriptions until in the implementation stage they are fully formal and ready for deployment. Subsequent enhancement and evolution makes direct use of CM descriptions, which are kept for this purpose. CM programmers should never discard deployed conceptual-model instances (the executable conceptual-model instances are the code), and CM programmers should neither enhance nor evolve deployed applications by altering compiled code, but rather always by altering and recompiling conceptual-model instances.

The notion of "tunable formalism" plays an interesting role in CMP. The idea is that formalism in conceptual-model descriptions can be "tuned" "down" or "up" depending on the needs of the development team. When tuned down, clients, who contract with software-development teams to produce application software and who are typically untrained in CMP, can usually read and understand informal conceptual-model descriptions. Thus, CM analysts can directly use conceptual-model descriptions, whose formalism is tuned down, to enhance communication between clients and CM programmers. When tuned up all the way, the application is fully implemented. In between, CM programmers can read and understand the developing application abstractly and can begin to see various parts of the system execute as they become formal enough for emulation or compilation.

CMP accommodates various development strategies. CM developers need not complete one stage of the process before moving on to the next, and various parts of the application can be at different development stages at the same time. CM developers can forge ahead with the development of a kernal for the application and then treat the remaining development as enhancement and evolution.

At each stage of development CMP offers abundant opportunities for managing software development and for enhancing communication among development team members and between team members and clients. We offer a few insights:

- **Analysis** is about understanding an application and documenting that understanding. A strength of conceptual modeling is its ability to promote a common understanding within a heterogeneous development team. Conceptual modeling serves analysts well in their role of a "go-between" – it facilitates precise and concise communication with both clients and programmers. Clients can understand abstract conceptual models with the formalism tuned down; programmers tune up the formalism to make the application executable. Clients, analysts, and programmers all use the same CM notation, which results in better communication.
- **Specification** is about producing a detailed and precise proposal for a system. A difficulty with specification is that clients often do not really know what they want until they see it. Prototyping helps alleviate this concern, and CMP facilitates prototyping. Conceptual models with tuned up formalism can execute fully, but even with the formalism tuned down, they are still executable. Every CM diagram is executable as a prototype. When an emulator encounters an informal statement, it can explain its state and display the informal statement it is "executing," and it can accept user input to allow it to continue to operate and show in

mock-up style how the application works. Mock-ups of end-user interfaces can be real since their specification automatically allows them to execute as part of the CM application. One view of CM programming is that it is about quickly developing a prototype and then enhancing the prototype until it becomes the deployed application.

- **Design** is about organizing a software system to achieve its goals, e.g., efficiency, maintainability, extensibility, and similar properties. An example of design is database normalization; a CM designer can use standard conceptual-modeling techniques to canonicalize a structure-model diagram to guarantee that a CM compiler's database-schema generator produces a normalized schema. A CM compiler should, as a matter of course, optimize the code it generates, but when optimization depends on "proper" conceptualization, as it does for database normalization, the CM designer should organize conceptual-model instances so that the CM compiler generates optimal code. CMP naturally promotes maintainability and extensibility. Conceptual-model diagrams are the high-level code. Because CMP compiles models into executable systems, the models cannot, as so often is the case with conceptual diagrams, be either summarily discarded or left in a disheveled state not synchronized with nor updated to match the deployed application.

- **Implementation** is about faithfully translating a design into code. For CMP, this translation is automatic. Thus, implementation requires zero effort. This does not mean, however, that application development is effortless. Rather, it means that the effort is shifted upstream. The emphasis is on analysis and specification, rather than on translating designs to programming-language syntax. Significantly, software created via CMP is "defect-free" with respect to the implementation layer. If the model compiler faithfully translates higher level specifications into lower-level code, then the only defects that can occur in a CMP-generated system are either design, specification, or analysis issues or problems with standard libraries. Thus, by avoiding implementation-layer defects, CMP promotes early detection of design-level defects.

- **Deployment** is about delivering the application system for client use. Because CM programs are immediately executable, at least in prototype fashion, pre-alpha, alpha, and beta releases follow naturally as CM programmers proceed through analysis and specification. Eventual deployment is a natural consequence of fully formalizing and properly organizing conceptual-model instances in accordance with client requirements.

- **Enhancement and evolution** are about making deployed applications better serve end users. In one sense, enhancing and evolving a deployed CMP application is no different from enhancing and evolving an application coded in a high-level language, except that CM programmers continue to work at a conceptual level rather than at the syntax level of the high-level language. Often, however, when evolving code written in a high-level language, enhancement and evolution require re-conceptualizing some parts of the application to serve as a starting place for improvements – either through reverse engineering or by updating and synchronizing conceptual-model instances. Although this step is often both necessary and costly when programming in a high-level language, it is never necessary and never costs anything in CMP application development because the code is already the model, which renders re-conceptualization unnecessary.

Appendix

1. Principles similar to CMP expounded by others:

Others have set forth principles similar to CMP. In 2004, Brown, Iyengar, Rumbaugh, and Selic published *The MDA Manifesto* expounding the principles of Model-Driven Architecture [1]. The MDA Manifesto has three tenets:

1. **Direct representation**: reduce distance between problem domain and software representation
2. **Automation**: mechanization of facets of software development that do not depend on human ingenuity and, especially, mechanization of bridging the gap between problem-domain representation and software representation
3. **Open standards**: open-source development and accepted industry standards

The CMP Manifesto harmonizes well with the MDA Manifesto. The CMP Manifesto, however, takes automation a step further. It insists that conceptualizations are to be fully executable so that there is no gap between a conceptualization and a software representation. A CMP conceptualization is a software representation. Although not opposed to domain-specific modeling languages, generic, all-purpose conceptual-modeling languages must be among the languages available for application development. Ideally, CM programmers should have a variety of notational choices. Domain-specific notation is acceptable, and perhaps even preferable, but to be a CMP conceptualization, a domain-specific conceptualization must be executable.

2. Cautions about CMP:

In 2008, Selic wrote *MDA Manifestations* [27], a commentary on the MDA Manifesto. Selic's commentary includes cautions about Model-Driven Development (MDD). He asserts that MDD likely requires the following:

1. **Education** (shift in view to understanding clients and users and especially an increase in the introduction of MDD methods in software-engineering education)
2. **A comprehensive and systematic theory of MDD** (modeling language semantics and design, model transformations, model analysis of safety and liveness properties, model-based verification, model management, MDD methods and processes, and tools)
3. **Standards** (the key to success of any widely used technology)

Selic believes that the shift to MDD is likely to be gradual. He also believes that it will be tough to see the MDA Manifesto – and by implication the CMP Manifesto – through to adoption. This does not mean, however, that we should not hold CMP as a goal and work toward its realization and general acceptance. The benefits appear to be worth the costs.

3. Extreme non-programming:

We sometimes refer to CMP as XNP (eXtreme Non-Programming). Like XP (eXtreme Programming), programmers begin to code early in the development process, and the code is the model. Unlike XP, CM programmers do no programming at all – at least, they do not program in the traditional sense. Instead, the model is the code. XNP retains the advantages of XP and overcomes its disadvantages. A primary advantage of XP is that it allows clients, analysts, and programmers to begin to see the application run immediately. XNP has this same advantage. XNP also retains other advantages typically attributed to XP, including responsiveness to changing client requirements, short development cycles resulting in improved productivity, and frequent client checkpoints and continuous client involvement. Primary disadvantages of XP are that it lacks overall analysis and has no overall design specification. XNP overcomes these disadvantages because the process focuses directly on analysis and specification, and the result of XNP is a design specification.

4. CMP in current practice:

Model-driven engineering (MDE), which is also referred to as model-driven development (MDD) or model-driven architecture (MDA), advocates the creation of software systems by model specification. As is the case for CMP, the models are abstract conceptualizations of particular domain concepts, rather than algorithmic specifications written in a high-level language, and conceptual modeling is the primary means of software production. In MDE, CASE tools generate code skeletons or, when enough detail is provided, they generate complete, deployable systems. Usually, however, only parts of the deployed system are fully generated. CMP requires full automation, including the full automation of enhancements and system evolution. Full automation avoids the prevalent pitfall of having conceptual diagrams that are not synchronized with deployed systems. To the extent that MDE supports full automation, MDE and CMP are the same.

5. CMP status and outlook:

CMP is not just an academic dream. There are numerous commercially available model compilers, such as IBM Rational Rhapsody, the OlivaNova tool suite from CARE Technologies, Netfective Technology Group's Blu Age, Obeo's Acceleo, the UWE UML Web Engineering platform, and WebRatio from Web Models to name just a few. As a specific example, consider the OlivaNova technology, developed by *CARE Technologies* [3], S.A. OlivaNova implements the OASIS approach to CMP [21, 22]. OASIS has a conceptual model with a precisely defined semantics that allows for a formal specification of all functionality needed for a final application. The conceptual model has four views that together completely specify an application for a management information systems: a static view, a dynamic view, a functional view, and a presentation view. A conceptual-model compiler translates modeling primitives into their corresponding software representations. The OlivaNova technology automatically generates the final application from the specification of an OASIS model. The technology has two main components: a modeling tool called *OlivaNova Modeler* and a model compiler called *OlivaNova Transformation Engine*. The *Modeler* is a support tool that allows its users to specify an OASIS conceptual model and to verify that the conceptual model functions as expected. Then, when ready, the developer sends an XML representation generated by the *Modeler* to the *OlivaNova Transformation Engine*, indicating the target implementation platform and some configuration parameters according to the selected platform. The *Transformation Engine*'s compiler automatically generates the source code of final applications, which is implemented for the selected platforms in a three-tier software architecture.

6. Additional readings:

Books by Dori [6], by Embley [8], by Embley and Thalheim [10], by Mellor and Balcer [17], by Morgan [19], by Pastor and Molina [22], by Raistrick et al. [25], and by Rossi, Pastor, Schwabe, and Olsina [26] directly advocate CMP and explain how it works. Articles by

Liddle, Embley, and Woodfield [15, 16] describe model-equivalent languages and their role in CMP.

Books by Olivè [20], by Papazoglou, Spaccapietra, and Tari [23], and by Thalheim [28] focus more on conceptual modeling itself, but have a strong component that leads to CMP. A book by Harel and Politi [13] describes a CMP-styled approach to creating executable systems via statecharts. Another book by Ceri et al. [5] describes WebML, a CMP-styled approach to creating data-intensive web applications.

Many published articles discuss, argue for, and explain various aspects of CMP: formal specification of active objects along with rapid prototyping and object reification [21], tunable formalism [4], seamlessly combining multiple kinds of conceptual models [7], prototyping with conceptual models [14], user-interface modeling patterns [18, 24], and statecharts, both early work [12] and from a historical perspective [11].

Conceptual modeling itself has a long history. The book edited by Brodie, Mylopoulos, and Schmidt [2] contains several articles that together provide an early look at the overall process leading to CMP. Proceedings of the International Conference on Conceptual Modeling [9] contain many articles that describe the research and development of the field of conceptual modeling. An article by Thalheim [29] summarizes and explains the conceptualization process in terms of an overall theory of conceptual modeling.

References

1. Booch G, Brown A, Iyengar S, Rumbaugh J, Selic B (2004) An MDA manifesto. MDA J, May 2004:133–143
2. Brodie ML, Mylopoulos J, Schmidt JW (eds) (1984) On conceptual modelling: perspectives from artificial intelligence, databases, and programming languages. Springer, Berlin Heidelberg New York
3. CARE-technologies (2010) http://www.care-t.com/. Accessed October 2010
4. Clyde SW, Embley DW, Woodfield SN (1992) Tunable formalism in object-oriented systems analysis: meeting the needs of both theoreticians and practitioners. In: Proceedings of the 1992 Conference on Object-Oriented Programming Systems, Languages, and Applications (OOPSLA'92), pp 452–465, Vancouver, October 1992
5. Ceri S, Fraternelli P, Bongio A, Brambilla M, Comai S, Matera M (2003) Designing data-intensive web applications. Morgan Kaufmann, San Francisco
6. Dori D (2009) Object-process methodology: a holistic systems paradigm. Springer, Berlin Heidelberg New York
7. Embley DW, Jackson RB, Liddle SW, Woodfield SN (1994) A formal modeling approach to seamless object-oriented systems development. In: Proceedings of the Workshop on Formal Methods for Information System Dynamics at CAiSE'94, pp 83–94, The Netherlands, June 1994
8. Embley DW (1998) Object database development: concepts and principles. Addison-Wesley, Reading
9. Entity relationship (ER) (2010) http://conceptualmodeling.org/. Accessed October 2010
10. Embley DW, Thalheim B (eds) (2011) The handbook of conceptual modeling: its usage and its challenges. Springer, Berlin Heidelberg New York
11. Harel D (2009) Statecharts in the making: a personal account. Comm ACM 52(3):67–75
12. Harel D, Gery E (1997) Executable object modeling with statecharts. IEEE Comput 30(7):31–42
13. Harel D, Politi M (1998) Modeling reactive systems with statecharts: the statemate approach. McGraw-Hill, New York
14. Jackson RB, Embley DW, Woodfield SN (1995) Developing formal object-oriented requirements specifications: a model, tool and technique. Info Syst 20(4):273–289

15. Liddle SW, Embley DW, Woodfield SN (1995) Unifying modeling and programming through an active, object-oriented, model-equivalent programming language. In: Proceedings of the 14th International Conference on Object-Oriented and Entity-Relationship Modeling (OOER'95), pp 55–64, Gold Coast, Queensland, December 1995
16. Liddle SW, Embley DW, Woodfield SN (2000) An active, object-oriented, model-equivalent programming language. In: Papazoglou MP, Spaccapietra S, Tari Z (eds) Advances in object-oriented data modeling, pp 333–361. MIT Press, Cambridge
17. Mellor SJ, Balcer M (2002) Executable UML: a foundation for model-driven architectures. Addison-Wesley-Longman, Boston
18. Molina PJ, Meliá S, Pastor O (2002) User interface conceptual patterns. In: Proceedings of the 9th International Workshop on Interactive Systems. Design, Specification, and Verification (DSV-IS'02), Rostock, June 2002
19. Morgan T (2002) Business rules and information systems: aligning IT with business goals. Addison-Wesley, Reading
20. Olivè A (2007) Conceptual modeling of information systems. Springer, Berlin Heidelberg New York
21. Pastor O, Hayes F, Bear S (1992) OASIS: an object-oriented specification language. In: Proceedings of the 4th International Conference on Advanced Information Systems Engineering (CAiSE'92), pp 348–363, Manchester
22. Pastor O, Molina JC (2007) Model-driven architecture in practice: a software production environment based on conceptual modeling. Springer, Berlin Heidelberg New York
23. Papazoglou MP, Spaccapietra S, Tari Z (eds) (2000) Advances in object-oriented data modeling. MIT Press, Cambridge
24. Pederiva I, Vanderdonckt J, España S, Panach JI, Pastor O (2007) The beautification process in model-driven engineering of user interfaces. In: Proceedings of the 11th IFIP TC 13 International Conference on Human-Computer Interaction (INTERACT 2007), Rio de Janeiro September 2007
25. Raistrick C, Francis P, Wright J, Carter C, Wilkie I (2004) Model driven architecture with executable UML. Cambridge University Press, Cambridge
26. Rossi G, Pastor O, Schwabe D, Olsina L (eds) (2008) Web engineering: modelling and implementing web applications. Springer, Berlin Heidelberg New York
27. Selic B (2008) MDA manifestations. Eur J Info Prof IX(2):12–16
28. Thalheim B (2000) Entity-relationship modeling: foundations of database technology. Springer, Berlin Heidelberg New York
29. Thalheim B (2009) Towards a theory of conceptual modeling. In: Advances in Conceptual Modelling: Challenging Perspectives (ETheCoM 2009 – First International Workshop on Evolving Theories of Conceptual Modeling), pp 45–54, Gramado, November 2009

Chapter 2
Model-Driven Software Development

Stephen W. Liddle

Abstract Software development is a complex and difficult task that requires the investment of significant resources and carries major risk of failure. For decades now, researchers have proposed "model-driven" approaches to improve the state of the art in software engineering. Software models are intended to improve communication among stakeholders and aid in the overall understanding both of a problem space and a proposed software solution that satisfies given requirements. As with architectural blueprints or miniature 3D models, software models make it possible to explore and test a design and its ramifications before investing in the actual build-out. The traditional approach to software development involves a modeling process – analysis, requirements specification, design – followed by an implementation process. In the traditional approach, programmers manually write software that conforms (more or less) to specifications described in software models; this process involves transformations that are often incomplete, awkward, and informal. The essence of model-driven software development is the idea that software models can go further than being mere blueprints, and constitute the basis for automatically or semiautomatically generating the software system itself. In this chapter, we survey various major approaches to model-driven software construction and illustrate how model-driven development works in practice.

2.1 Introduction

Software development is a complex and difficult task that requires the investment of significant resources and carries major risk of failure. According to its proponents, *model-driven* (MD) software development approaches are improving the way we build software. Model-driven approaches putatively increase developer productivity, decrease the cost (in time and money) of software construction, improve software

Stephen W. Liddle
Brigham Young University, Provo, Utah 84602, USA, e-mail: liddle@byu.edu

D. W. Embley and B. Thalheim (eds), *Handbook of Conceptual Modeling.*
DOI 10.1007/978-3-642-15865-0, © Springer 2011

reusability, and make software more maintainable. Likewise, model-driven techniques promise to aid in the early detection of defects such as design flaws, omissions, and misunderstandings between clients and developers. The promises of MD are rather lofty, and so it is only natural to find many skeptics.

As Brooks famously described [27], software engineering will not likely deliver the sort of productivity gains we experience in hardware engineering where we see "Moore's law"-styled doublings every 24 months [121]. Thus, if we accept Brooks' premise, nobody should expect any innovative approach to software development to be a "magical silver bullet" that will increase productivity by an order of magnitude within a decade. Unfortunately, the amount of hyperbole surrounding the various flavors of MD sometimes makes it seem like advocates believe MD to be a silver bullet. Model-driven development is no panacea. However, we believe that *model-driven* is a superior approach to software construction. This chapter examines the current state of the art in model-driven software development.

We begin by characterizing the various approaches to model-driven development (Sect. 2.2). Then we examine what modeling is and why we engage in modeling (Sect. 2.3). Next, we explore the history of software modeling that has led to current model-driven approaches and discuss what is required to make our models formal and executable (Sect. 2.4). With this background laid out, we explore the details of various model-driven approaches to software development. We commence with a reference model (Sect. 2.5) and then examine MDA (Sect. 2.6), giving special attention to the Executable UML variant of MDA (Sect. 2.6.3). In Sect. 2.7 we describe the OO-Method approach to MD and the comprehensive OlivaNova tool that implements this approach. We next explore MD in the context of web engineering (Sect. 2.8) and then examine the argument for an agile approach to MD (Sect. 2.9). We conclude by summarizing available tools, arguments for and against, and directions for future research (Sect. 2.10).

2.2 Overview of Model-Driven Approaches

There are numerous ideas that come under the umbrella of *model-driven approaches*. We take an expansive view of what "model-driven" means. *Model-driven engineering* (MDE) and *model-driven development* (MDD) are generic terms describing an approach where we represent systems as models that conform to metamodels, and we use model transformations to manipulate the various representations (see, for example, [15, 28, 90, 132]). We use the terms MDD and MDE interchangeably.

Although the phrase "model-driven" has been used for decades with respect to software development, one of the earliest mentions of a "model-driven approach" comes from the work done by Embley et al. on object-oriented systems modeling (OSM) (see [53]; the book's subtitle is "A Model-Driven Approach"). Object-oriented methodologies were a topic of lively discussion in the early 1990s, and OSM eschewed any specific software process methodology in favor of letting model creation drive the development process. This is analogous to the idea of maps and directions: when someone needs help driving to an unfamiliar destination, we can either give turn-by-turn instructions on how to drive from their current location, or we can give them the address of the destination and let them use their own map to determine a route. If the path is relatively straightforward and there are no unexpected delays or impediments along the way, the *instructions* approach may be superior. But when exceptions occur, the *map* approach may be superior. In practice, a hybrid approach often gives the best of both worlds: expert guidance based on local knowledge can help travelers avoid common pitfalls, but their ability to read maps provides an improved mental model of the travel process, and makes them more resilient in the face of unexpected challenges. By taking a model-driven approach to software development, OSM focuses developers on creating models as central artifacts of interest, and remains independent of, and neutral with respect to, any particular software process methodology.

A notable MDD initiative is the Object Management Group (OMG) Model Driven Architecture (MDA) [111, 112, 155]. MDA can be viewed as an instance of MDD where the core standards and tools are the OMG standards – Unified Modeling Language (UML), MetaObject Facility (MOF), XML Metadata Interchange (XMI), and the Common Warehouse Metamodel (CWM). Because OMG is an influential industry consortium, MDA has gathered considerable attention. However, just as UML is not the only object-oriented modeling language, so also MDA is not the only model-driven approach. There are numerous non-MDA initiatives – commercial and academic – that continue to advance the state of the art in MDD.

Metaprogramming, where a program manipulates itself or another program, often leads to forms of programming that are arguably model-driven, or at least model-based. One class of metapgrogramming, template-based generic programming, starts with a modeling process to create a template from which programs can be generated. The related field of *domain-specific languages* is also inherently a model-based approach. A domain-specific language, in contrast with a general-purpose programming language, models aspects of a particular problem domain and provides special-purpose constructs tailored to the needs of that domain.

Similarly, in the field of modeling, *domain-specific modeling* (DSM) uses a modeling language customized to a particular domain to represent systems, and often includes the ability to generate code for corresponding software systems. CASE tools are forerunners of DSM languages and tools, but they are not the same. A CASE tool is created by a vendor to address a class of software engineering problems, whereas DSM tools let clients create custom domain-specific models and generate code using models and concepts that are specific to the client's particular needs.

Another closely related area is *generative programming*, which seeks to model families of software systems so that they can be created assembly-line style; the central idea is to generate code for each of the desired systems in an automated way from a *generative domain model* [34]. Many researchers have seen a need to industrialize software production. The *software factories* work gives an excellent description of this perspective [70, 71]. Research in software architecture has demonstrated that we can increase productivity by developing families of software systems as a product line rather than as one-off creations [34, 44].

MD is also a potential solution to the problem of integrating inherently heterogeneous systems whose development requires the multi-disciplinary talents of workers who are experts in widely differing domains [156]. Consider, for example, the software required in a modern automobile. Physical control systems may manage the engine, brakes, and passenger-restraint systems in a mostly automatic and hidden manner, while an in-dash touch-driven display may give access to a more traditional information system that offers satellite navigation and mapping features, media playback, and the viewing of statistical information. The field of *model-integrated computing* [156, 161, 168] brings MD techniques to the problem of engineering these types of systems.

As models become increasingly important, so too does the management of models and particularly of transformations or mappings between models. Research on *generic model management* addresses techniques for treating models and mappings as first-class objects that have high-level operations to simplify their management [18]. The Rondo project provides a working prototype of a programming platform for generic model management [113, 123].

If a model is a representation of a system, then in some sense, programming in any language involves some kind of model. A C++ programmer thinks about the subject domain in terms of C++ classes and instances. A SQL programmer views the subject domain through the lens of tables that have rows and typed columns. Whether we explicitly create artifacts we call models – especially *conceptual models* – or whether we implicitly map between our internal mental models of the world and the systems we produce, we are nonetheless involved in a modeling process as we construct software. And so MD is more about raising the level of abstraction of our programming models rather than introducing models into the process in the first place.[1]

Indeed, as Brown points out [28], there is a spectrum of modeling from code-only solutions to model-only solutions (see Fig. 2.1). As we have argued, even in the code-only scenario, developers still create mental models and informal models, but the system representation is entirely in the code. In the second scenario, the developer uses models primarily as a means for visualizing the code; a reverse engineering tool reads the code and displays a corresponding model view of what is captured in the code. In the round-trip engineering scenario, a tool maintains tight correspondence between model and code; changes made to the code are immediately reflected in the model and vice versa. In the model programming scenario, the model is the code, and the lower level of code is simply generated and compiled behind the scenes; all changes to the system happen at the model level[2] (see Chap. 1

---

[1] Our argument is a special case of the assertion in [15] that "[m]odeling is essential to human activity because *every* action is preceded by the construction (implicit or explicit) of a model" (emphasis added).

[2] This is analogous to compiling a FORTRAN program by translating it to assembly language, which is then assembled and linked. The assembler version is to "code" as the FORTRAN version is to "model".

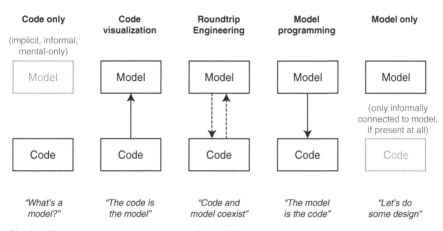

Fig. 2.1 The modeling spectrum (adapted from [28])

for a detailed discussion of *conceptual model programming*). The final scenario is what happens when either we model without creating an operational system, or we develop models that are never formally tied to the operational system; perhaps we start by creating an ER diagram to generate an initial database schema, but then we evolve the schema independently of the model so that they become disconnected. We view the round-trip engineering and model programming scenarios as *model-driven*, while the others are at best *model-based* or *model-aware*.

2.3 Modeling

To understand model-driven software development, it is helpful to review some background on models and modeling. What is a model, and why do we as humans and as software developers build models?

The term *model* is heavily overloaded. A model may be "a set of designs ... for a projected building or other structure," or "a three-dimensional representation" of such a building or structure [131]. In the mathematical logic sense, a *model* is a "set of entities that satisfies all the formulae of a given formal or axiomatic system" [131]. Within software development, we also overload the term. In this chapter, when we say "model" without an adjective we mean a diagram or model instance that conforms to a particular modeling language.

Models come in many forms. Three useful categories of models include graphical, mathematical, and textual. A graphical model is a two-dimensional diagram that graphically depicts concepts using a combination of lines, shapes, symbols, and (usually) some text (e.g., an ER diagram). A mathematical model describes some aspect of a system as a formula (e.g., $A = \pi r^2$ is a model for the area of a circle). A textual model describes a portion of a system using narrative and prose (e.g., we can view a "scenario" description as a textual model of a process).

No matter the particular form, common to all models is that they represent some aspect of a system that the modeler is studying or creating [150]. To be useful, such a representation abstracts (separates or summarizes) some aspect of the underlying system. Abstractions are helpful because they let us focus on specific aspects of a system without needing to simultaneously consider the complexity of the full system.

Implicit in our definition of "model" is the fact that it is a written artifact. As humans we form abstractions of the world around us – we classify, generalize, associate, and otherwise construct purely mental models. It is in the writing down of our models that we make it possible to share, discuss, revise, and implement software systems that conform to those models [28].

Software engineers create models for many of the same reasons architects and engineers create blueprints and 3D miniatures:

- Models help us communicate more effectively with the many stakeholders who need to participate in the software development process. For example, a client usually finds it easier to understand a graphical class diagram than, say, C++ source code. Improved communication leads to increased understanding, more reasonable expectations, and a better overall work product.
- Models let us visualize the finished product without requiring its full construction first. By examining the model we can discover design flaws that are far less expensive to resolve up-front rather than after construction has begun (or worse, been completed). In the same way a 3D model of an automobile can be examined in a wind tunnel to tune its aerodynamic performance, a model of a graphical user interface can be placed in front of typical users early on to test usability characteristics.
- Models constitute precise specifications of work to be done. They provide an accurate roadmap of the work, thus allowing project managers to estimate, schedule, and otherwise plan the construction phase.

The value of models and abstractions in software is substantial, as the history of programming languages and operating systems demonstrates [106]. The history of computing is a study in layers of abstraction. Programming progressed from hard-wired computers to stored-program machines, to assembly languages, to high-level languages, CASE tools, object-oriented systems, and domain-specific languages. Operating systems were introduced to manage the complexities of interfacing with the hardware. "Device drivers" abstracted out the challenges of interfacing to storage devices, printers, and other peripherals so developers could concentrate on application development, not low-level hardware control. The abstraction of "processes" introduced multi-tasking in a way that allowed software developers to avoid dealing with most of the associated complexity. Each step in the evolution of programming languages and operating systems has introduced higher level abstractions into our tools.

Programmers today commonly think in terms of software objects rather than 0s and 1s stored in a particular location. Software developers can focus on the application domain much more readily because the abstractions they use to build their products are conceptually much closer to that application domain. Today's programmers often develop to highly virtualized platforms – whether it be a Java virtual machine or a web-browser environment that uses HTML, CSS, and JavaScript. And not coincidentally, software development today is also a study in reuse. Developers commonly leverage large libraries – both built-in and external – in their software projects. An underlying reason for these improvements in the state of software development is that models and abstractions have improved significantly over the years.

2.4 Software Modeling

Since modeling in general has so many uses and benefits, we should expect modeling to be a major research topic in computing, and indeed this is the case. The decade of the 1970s saw the development of formal approaches to data modeling. Abrial [1] and Senko [154], among others, explored binary relationships as an abstraction for data modeling. Falkenberg built on this work and developed the "object-role model" (ORM) framework that used n-ary relationships as a fundamental data modeling construct [56]. Meanwhile, Chen proposed the highly successful entity-relationship (ER) model [42] that has become nearly synonymous with database design. Tsichritzis and Lochovski [175] and Brodie [21] describe much of the early work on data models and conceptual modeling well.

During the 1980s, researchers studied how to improve data models and experimented with so-called semantic data models that introduced additional constructs with more semantic richness than the earlier, simpler models [79, 140, 177]. Richer constructs came with more complex notation, and the results were not always an improvement over the simpler predecessor data models.[3] However, research on semantic data models gave way to work on object-oriented (OO) models [24, 53, 144, 159], which researchers debated hotly in the early-to-mid 1990s.

The so-called OO *method wars* led to the proposal of a unified OO model, and the Unified Modeling Language (UML) emerged in 1995 (as the Unified Method version 0.8) and was subsequently standardized by OMG. The latest version, UML 2.2 [181], defines fourteen different diagram types (see Fig. 2.2), including seven that are structural and seven that are behavioral in nature. As with the work on semantic data models, researchers often criticize UML for its complexity, among other complaints [57, 83, 96, 165, 174]. However, UML has become not quite universal, but perhaps ubiquitous, in spite of the criticisms.

Where modeling has worked especially well is in the design of database schemas. From an ER or OO schema, it is straightforward to generate a corresponding normalized relational database schema. Many practitioners equate *conceptual modeling* with *database design* because the early conceptual models only addressed structural

---

[3] Bolchini and Garzotto discovered this in the domain of MDWE as well [16]; see Sect. 2.8.

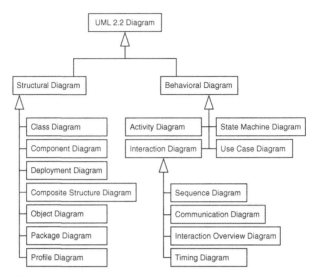

Fig. 2.2 UML 2.2 diagram types (structural and behavioral)

aspects of information systems. ER and ORM, for example, do not attempt to model behavior.

In contrast, the OO models have been especially helpful in capturing behavioral aspects of systems. Note that fully half of the diagram types in UML 2.2 address these behavioral aspects (see Fig. 2.2). Generally, the OO paradigm describes *behavior* in terms of the lifecycles of objects (often represented as a state machine) and their interactions with other objects.

When we include system behavior in the model, it becomes possible to generate more than just the system schema from the model; thus we can generate source code for the system, whether in the form of code skeletons, or in the form of fully operational code that compiles into a deployable application.

If we make the behavioral model formal, then it becomes executable. OSM is an example of a modeling language that supports the creation of fully executable models [100, 102]. The OSM metamodel is itself expressed formally in OSM [43, 53, 54, 102]. Given a formal metamodel, it is a straightforward process to interpret any particular model instance formally. OSM model instances can be executed simulation-style in a prototyping tool [89] or translated automatically to a model-equivalent language and executed directly [102].

Many other researchers have also advocated software development approaches that begin with executable models. Notable examples include the work of (1) Harel et al. on the Statecharts, STATEMATE, and Rhapsody research line [66, 74–76, 78, 82], (2) Pastor et al. on the OASIS, OO-Method, and OlivaNova group of projects [138, 139, 141], and (3) Mellor et al. on the executable UML line of research [108, 126, 145, 188]. We address these in subsequent sections of this chapter.

What is different about executable conceptual models is that they include behavior and interaction, not just structural components. Furthermore, executable models generally must conform to a precisely, formally specified metamodel so that the model semantics are clear. We explore this concept further by introducing OSM as a reference model.

2.5 OSM: Making Conceptual Models Formal and Executable

Object-oriented systems modeling (OSM) views the software development process as a set of activities with different concerns: analysis, specification, design, implementation, and evolution [52–54, 102]. The OSM philosophy is that all these activities should share a single core conceptual modeling language, and shifts in lifecycle phases merely constitute shifts in perspective. Analysis is the study of system, which can be existing or planned; typical analysis-phase activities center around gathering and documenting information regarding user requirements and current system characteristics. Implementation, on the other hand, involves creating a running system that delivers required functions. In OSM, a single core model serves as the basis for all development activities.

OSM has three major views (*diagram types* in UML parlance) for describing object and relationship structure, behavior, and interaction, but all three can be combined in a single seamless model. Figures 2.3 through 2.6 give an example. Figure 2.3 shows a simple object-relationship model instance for the banking domain. Figure 2.4 shows a simple state net that describes at a high level the behavior of *Account* objects. Figure 2.5 shows how customers and banks can interact. Figure 2.6 shows all three views in a single diagram.

OSM notation is fairly consistent with other object-oriented modeling languages. Rectangles represent object sets and lines represent relationship sets. Lexical object sets may either have a dashed border or (as Fig. 2.3 shows) no border at all. *Min:max* numbers near a relationship-set connection indicate participation constraints (e.g., *0:4* near account means that an account can be associated with at most four customers). Names and reading arrows indicate relationship-set names (e.g., *Bank manages Account* and *Customer owns Account* are the two explicit relationship-

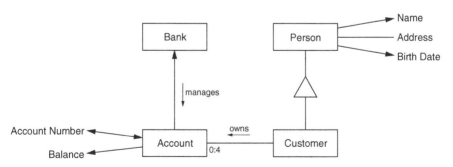

Fig. 2.3 Banking example object-relationship model instance

Fig. 2.4 Banking example object behavior model instance (state net)

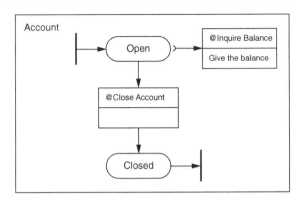

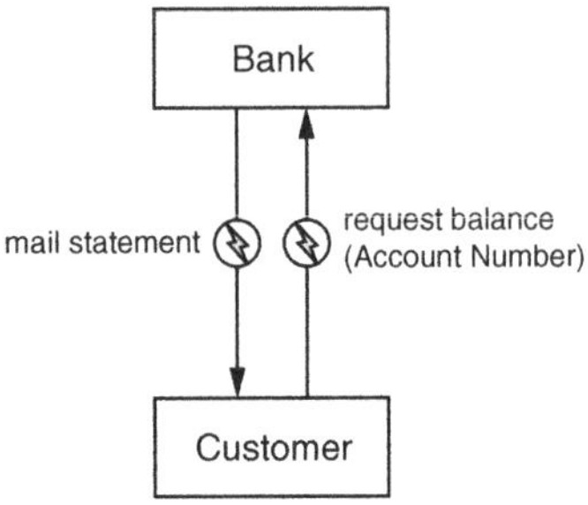

Fig. 2.5 Banking example object interaction model instance

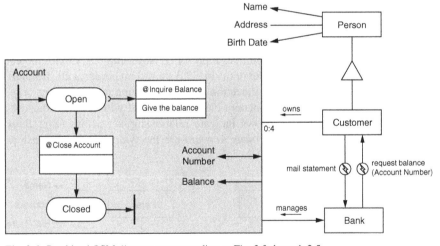

Fig. 2.6 Combined OSM diagram corresponding to Fig. 2.3 through 2.5

set names in Fig. 2.3). Arrow heads on relationship-set lines indicate functional relationships (e.g., a person has exactly one name and birth date; an account has exactly one account number and vice versa), while no decoration on the line together with no participation constraint indicates no limit on the number of associations (we can also write this as the participation constraint *0:**). An open triangle represents generalization/specialization (e.g., customer is a person).

A state net (see Fig. 2.4) describes the behavior of an object – its lifecycle from creation to destruction. We write states as rounded rectangles (e.g., *Open* and *Closed*), and transitions as divided rectangles with a transition *trigger* written in the upper portion, and an *action* written in the lower portion of the transition rectangle. A trigger is a boolean expression, and an "@" sign on a trigger indicates the occurrence of an event. When the prior state(s) for a transition are all on, we say that the transition is *enabled*, and it can *fire* when the trigger is true. When a transition fires, it (1) turns off prior states, (2) executes the transition action (if any), and (3) turns on any subsequent states. Arrows between states and transitions identify prior and subsequent states, and indicate flow of control. When the tail of an arrow leaving a state has a half circle slightly separated from the state, this indicates that the state is not turned off when the transition fires (i.e., a new, concurrent thread of control can begin when the transition fires). For example, when a balance inquiry transition executes, the corresponding account still remains in the *Open* state, and the *Give the balance* action executes on its own thread. A transition with no prior states indicates an *initial transition* that creates an object, while a transition with no subsequent states indicates a *final transition* that destroys an object. Initial and final transitions may be written as vertical bars as in Fig. 2.4.

An object interaction model instance documents communication or interaction between objects, as Fig. 2.5 shows. In this example, banks mail statements to customers and customers request account balances from banks. When a customer requests an account balance, he or she also indicates the corresponding account number. An arrow with a lightning-bolt symbol at the center of a circle indicates an interaction; the tail of the arrow indicates the interaction origin, while the head indicates the destination.

Figure 2.6 shows a unified version of Figs. 2.3 through 2.5. The primary difference is that in Fig. 2.6 we have represented *Account* as a high-level object set with *Account Number*, *Balance*, and two relationship sets nested inside. OSM has fully-reified high-level constructs, meaning that high-level object sets, relationship sets, states, transitions, and interactions are first-class elements that can be treated just like their non-high-level forms. High-level components are helpful for organizing a model and displaying simplified views (see Fig. 2.7, for example).

OSM has a number of features that make it well suited to model execution. As we observed earlier, OSM has a precise formal foundation; notably, the OSM metamodel is itself expressed in OSM and translates directly to first-order predicate calculus [53, 54]. Figure 2.8 shows the layers of OSM's modeling hierarchy. The metamodel (level M2) contains constructs such as *Object Set, Relationship Set,*

Fig. 2.7 Collapsed high-level view corresponding to a portion of Fig. 2.6

Fig. 2.8 OSM three-tier seamless model

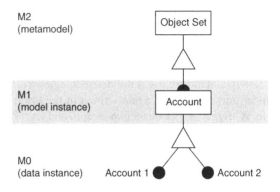

State, and *Transition*. The model instance (level M1) contains domain constructs, such as *Bank*, *Customer*, and *Account* in our running example. The data instance (level M0), contains objects and relationships such as particular accounts, their balances, customers, and relationships among these objects. This three-tier model is *seamless* because a single underlying formalism expresses them all, and elements at one level are directly connected by is-a relationships with elements at the next level (*Account 1* and *Account 2* are instances of *Account*, and *Account* is an instance of *Object Set*). Constraints and expressions in OSM can refer to elements within any of the three levels as needed. Furthermore, OSM is computationally complete [102], and so can directly model any algorithm or data structure.

Additionally, OSM embraces a concept called *tunable formalism* [37], allowing users to work at levels ranging from informal to mathematically rigorous. Formal models generally do not provide enough expressiveness or allow the varying levels of detail and completion that practitioners need to build real systems. On the other hand, model execution cannot be built on informal models. Because of OSM's precise formal foundation, we can interpret any model instance uniformly both at a summary level and at a detailed level. For example, the model instance in Fig. 2.7 has a completely consistent formal interpretation regardless of whether we include or ignore the details nested within the high-level *Account* object set. Similarly, triggers associated with transitions could be written in a natural language at first. In this form the statements are merely incomplete w.r.t. model execution: they represent propositional statements whose truth cannot be computed automatically. If we desire automatic computation (as opposed to consulting an external oracle), we simply replace the incomplete statements with an executable refinement.

For example, the natural-language action description *Give the balance* in Fig. 2.6 could be refined to an executable construction by specifying for the interaction a return parameter named *balance* and then replacing the natural-language phrase with the statement `balance := self.Balance`. The right-hand side of the assignment statement is a query that finds the *Balance* object associated with the current *Account* object. Assigning that object to the return parameter completes the action.

OSM has a rapid prototyping tool, IPOST, that allows developers to begin with an analysis-oriented model instance, and then gradually refine it with formal expressions for the various triggers and actions [89]. Using IPOST, a developer can initially populate a model instance with objects and relationships, and then as the system executes, the developer can successively refine it. IPOST automatically generates graphical dialogs to simulate interactions and the firing of transitions. IPOST can simulate the model instance in Fig. 2.7, but it must ask the user (the external oracle) to interpret the effect of the natural-language expression *Give the balance*, whereas we can directly execute the statement `balance := self.Balance` automatically.

OSM was designed to address the poor integration of OO systems across several dimensions, including the following:

1. the software development lifecycle and the models, languages, and tools used to develop software;
2. the so-called *impedance mismatches* between the semantics of persistent objects and behavioral protocols for objects, between declarative and imperative programming paradigms, and between visual and textual styles of programming; and
3. the reification of abstract objects, particularly meta-information and high-level abstractions of low-level modeling components.

OSM addresses the lifecycle issues by using a single modeling and development environment for all activities; changes in development phases or activities are merely shifts in perspective for OSM. Furthermore, the concept of *model-equivalent language* addresses the impedance mismatch issues. In essence, a language L is model-equivalent with respect to a model M if each progam written in L has a corresponding model instance M whose semantics are one-to-one with the program, and vice versa [100, 101]. The executable statement described above is written in OSM's model-equivalent language, OSM-L. Using OSM-L, programming becomes just a shift in perspective to focus on efficient algorithms and structures. A "program" is just an alternative view of a "model", and it is easy to iterate rapidly from one version of the system to another. Also, given OSM's first-class, fully-reified abstract elements (high-level object sets, relationship sets, states, transitions, and interactions), OSM provides the considerable expressiveness and flexibility needed for MDD. OSM does not have high-quality commercial tool support, but it does serve as a complete reference model for MDD.

2.6 Model-Driven Architecture (MDA)

We now give an overview of MDA (Sect. 2.6.1), discuss the MDA Manifesto (Sect. 2.6.2), describe Executable UML (Sect. 2.6.3), and point to further MDA readings (Sect. 2.6.4).

2.6.1 MDA Overview

The Object Management Group (OMG) is an industry consortium established in 1989 with the goal of defining standards for interoperability for distributed object systems. Their initial effort revolved around the Common Object Request Broker Architecture (CORBA) middleware standard. Their next major standard was the Unified Modeling Language (UML), adopted as a standard at UML version 1.1, in 1997. Following adoption of the UML standard, OMG began to work on its model-driven architecture initiative. OMG adopted the Model Driven Architecture (MDA) standard in 2001 [134]. In a nutshell, MDA is model-driven development that uses the core OMG standards (UML, MOF, XMI, CWM).

The three primary goals of MDA are (1) portability, (2) interoperability, and (3) reusability, and the key abstraction for delivering on these goals is "architectural separation of concerns" [112].

MDA describes three main layers of architectural abstraction, called *viewpoints*: computation independent, platform independent, and platform specific. As Fig. 2.9 shows, MDA describes systems using models that correspond to the three viewpoints. A *computation independent model* (CIM) describes a system environment and its requirements using terminology that is familiar to practitioners in the system domain. A *platform independent model* (PIM) describes a system's structure and functions formally, and yet without specifying platform-specific implementation details. At the lowest level of the MDA architecture, a *platform specific model* (PSM) includes details that are important to the implementation of a system on a given platform. By *platform*, MDA means a cohesive set of subsystems and technologies on which a system can execute (such as Sun's Java EE or Microsoft's .NET platforms, for example).

As Fig. 2.9 suggests, model mappings or transformations are a key aspect of MDA. Each arrow in Fig. 2.9 represents a transformation from one model to another. Mappings happen at many levels and for many purposes, and MDA does not try to specify precisely how mappings can occur, but a key aspect of MDA trans-

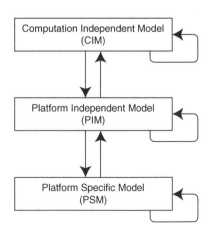

Fig. 2.9 MDA architectural layers and model transformations

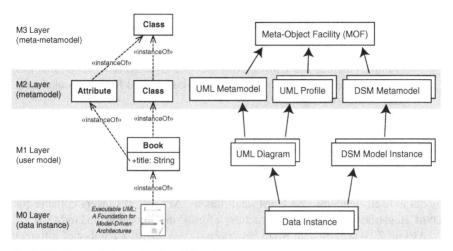

Fig. 2.10 MDA modeling and metamodeling layers

formations is that each mapping may involve the addition of information external to the source model. For example, when mapping from a PIM to a PSM that targets the Java EE platform, the transformation would likely need to combine a sizeable Java EE model that includes formal descriptions of various Java EE abstractions – such as messaging and storage frameworks – with the PIM to generate Java code that implements the PIM abstractions within the Java EE framework. The resulting PSM could then be compiled, deployed, and executed on a Java virtual machine.

Transformations are not merely one way, CIM-to-PIM and PIM-to-PSM. There are mappings between models up and down as Fig. 2.9 suggests. CIM-to-CIM or PIM-to-PIM mappings represent model refinements, such as the transformation that occurs when moving from an analysis phase into a design phase [111]. A PSM-to-PSM transformation may be required in order to configure and package the elements of a PSM for deployment to the desired target environment. A PSM-to-PIM transformation may be required when refactoring or reverse-engineering a system.

MDA does not expect that there will be only one CIM, one PIM, and one PSM for any given system. Each model only captures a single view of the system, and a complete system may consist of many CIM's and PIM's. One of the main benefits of taking a model-driven approach is that the implementation step, PIM-to-PSM transformation, can presumably be done relatively easily for multiple platforms. Thus, there may be many PSM's corresponding to each of the target platforms.

The MDA Guide discusses a wide variety of transformation types, techniques, and patterns [112]. As with MDD in general, the concept of model transformations is central to the MDA philosophy.

Also central to the MDA philosophy is the role of modeling layers and meta-models. Figure 2.10 illustrates some important MDA dimensions. UML, and hence MDA, has four modeling layers:

M3: The *meta-metamodel* layer; describes concepts that appear in the metamodel, such as *Class*. For UML, MOF describes the M3 layer.

M2: The *metamodel* layer; describes concepts that make up a modeling language; examples include the UML metamodel, the Executable UML profile, and a domain-specific metamodel created and customized for a particular company or industry segment.

M1: The *user model* or *model instance* layer; class diagrams, statecharts, and other such artifacts are M1-layer elements.

M0: The *data instance* layer; objects, records, data, and related artifacts exist at this level.

In contrast, recall that OSM has three modeling layers because the OSM metamodel is itself defined using OSM, and thus the M2 and M3 layers collapse for OSM. Regardless of the specific structure, a formal metamodel is vital to MDD.

As Fig. 2.10 suggests, an MDA process may use any of a number of different UML profiles or domain-specific metamodels, rather than using UML exclusively for all modeling activities. While developers usually produce UML diagrams using UML or UML profiles, it is also possible to create an MDA process that uses a MOF-conforming domain-specific metamodel to then perform domain-specific modeling tasks within the MDA framework.

2.6.2 An MDA Manifesto

In 2004, proponents of and major contributors to the MDA initiative working at IBM Rational Software published an "MDA Manifesto" describing the tenets that motivate MDA [10]. Figure 2.11 illustrates the three basic tenets of the MDA Manifesto: (1) direct representation, (2) automation, and (3) open standards. We summarize each of these in turn.

The principle of *direct representation* expresses a desire to shift the focus of software development away from the technology domain and toward the concepts and terminology of the problem domain. The goal is to represent a solution as directly as possible in terms of the problem domain. The expectation is that this will lead

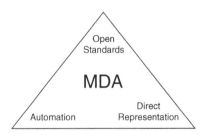

Fig. 2.11 Basic tenets of the MDA manifesto (adapted from [10])

to more accurate designs, improved communication between various participants in the system development process, and overall increased productivity.

The principle of automation endorses the concept of using machines to perform rote tasks that require no human ingenuity, freeing software developers to focus on creative problem-solving work. Just as database developers today give little thought to the implementation of B-trees, so too should MDA developers be able to ignore technological aspects of graphical interfaces, web services, or any of a hundred other elements of an underlying technology platform. It may be nice to know that a database index is implemented using a B-tree or that a particular communication link is implemented via a WSDL/SOAP web service, but dealing directly with the underlying implementation is not productive per se; it is the solving of business problems that creates value and thus constitutes productivity.

Building on open standards is important not only because standards promote reuse, but also because they cultivate the building of an ecosystem of tool vendors addressing the various needs of MDA. Since MDA has such a large vision, it is difficult – perhaps impossible – for a single vendor to provide everything that is required to carry out the vision. According to the manifesto authors, a successful ecosystem requires a few large vendors who can develop comprehensive tools, along with many medium-sized vendors and hundreds of small niche vendors. In order to attract such vendors, the ecosystem must provide standards that form the basis for solid interoperability. This turns out to be one of the points of criticism of MDA, i.e., that vendors have implemented MDA in such a way that even though they conform to the UML and XMI standards, their products are still not interoperable. The manifesto authors point out that this was a downfall of the CASE industry of the 1980s – vendors trying to "go it alone" [10, 60].

The manifesto authors describe the MDA ecosystem as a gradually evolving framework that will improve over time. Indeed, it is clear that an enormous amount of energy has been invested in MDA by a number of vendors, researchers, and practitioners over the years. Much of that work is available as open source, such as the Eclipse Modeling Framework (EMF), which integrates with the popular open source Eclipse IDE [51]. An ecosystem of MDA vendors does exist; what remains to be seen is how effective that ecosystem will be over time.

In a more recent follow-up to the MDA manifesto, one of the authors observes that the slow pace of MDA adoption is the result of challenges in three general areas: (1) technical hurdles such as complex tools, vendor lock-in, and lack of a sound theory of MDD, (2) cultural hurdles such as insufficient practitioner awareness of MDD benefits and enormous inertia for alternative software development tools and techniques, and (3) economic hurdles such as the long-term nature of payback for an investment in MDD. Selic concludes that the way forward for MDA may lie in the areas of education, research, and standardization [153].

2.6.3 Executable UML

One of the most concrete instances of MDA is Executable UML (xUML, also sometimes labeled xtUML for Executable/Translatable UML) [108, 145, 188]. The main idea of Executable UML is to define a UML profile that specifies a well-defined subset of UML that includes a precise *action semantics language* (ASL) [188] that can be used in the procedures associated with states in a model's statechart diagrams. When developers use ASL to specify the underlying state procedures, we can directly compile and execute the full xUML model.

Figure 2.12 shows a portion of an xUML class diagram. Observe that we associate role names and multiplicity constraints with each association connection. In xUML it is also conventional to name each association with a simple label of the form *Rn* so it is easy to refer to associations uniquely. In our example, *R1* refers to the association *Bank manages Account* (or *Account is managed by Bank*), while *R2* refers to the *Customer owns Account* association. Attributes may have an associated tag as shorthand for an OCL uniqueness constraint. In Fig. 2.12, for example, *id* on *Bank* and *Account*, and *email* on *Customer* have the tag *{I}*, which indicates that each corresponding attribute must have a unique value within its class. Additionally, the tag *{I2}* on *accountNumber* indicates that it also must be unique within *Account*.

Figure 2.13 illustrates a small portion of a typical xUML statechart diagram for our running banking example. Notice that the state procedures are all written as formal action-language statements that are straightforward to compile into an executable system. As Fig. 2.13 shows, when an account is created it receives an *openAccount* event with two parameters: a customer who will own the new account, and an initial balance. After connecting itself to the given customer, the account initializes its balance to the given amount and sends itself a *ready* signal, which causes the account to advance to the second state, *Waiting for Activity*. In this state, when a *depositOrWithdraw* event occurs, the account updates its balance by the given amount

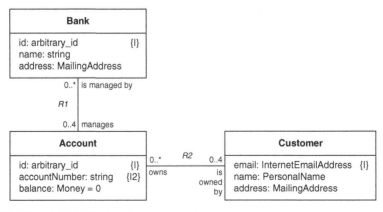

Fig. 2.12 Executable UML class diagram example

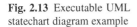

Fig. 2.13 Executable UML
statechart diagram example

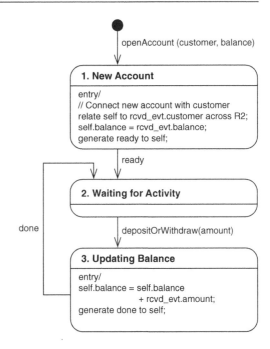

and generates a *done* signal, which causes the account to return to the *Waiting for Activity* state.

As with OSM, it is possible to represent xUML model instances at varying degrees of completion [37]. For example, Fig. 2.13 shows compilable statements in each of the state procedures. However, it is typical in the first version of an xUML statechart to write the procedures informally, as natural-language statements. These can easily be encoded as comments in an action language (e.g., the comment *//Connect new account with customer* in Fig. 2.13). For initial stages of work, it is sufficient to capture this sort of behavior requirement informally; in later stages developers refine the model to the point that all requirements are expressed formally. Significantly, even in the early stages when the model is incomplete, it is still possible to simulate the system as far as it is specified. This ability makes it possible to apply agile software development principles to Executable UML [108, 126].

Since ASL looks so much like ordinary programming, how can Executable UML really claim any advantage over an ordinary high-level language like C# or Java? The answer may seem subtle, but it is key to understanding the benefit of model execution: ordinary code links computation inextricably with data structure, while action models and languages separate the two. As Mellor explains (see [126], p. 95), a common way to find the sum of the last ten transactions is to loop through the transaction history data structure and accumulate the sum with each loop iteration. The action semantics approach to this problem is to divide the problem into (1) retrieving the last ten transaction amounts, and (2) computing their sum. In this way, with action semantics it is possible to change the underlying data structure without affecting the algorithm. This is a key benefit to a model-driven approach: by separating data structures cleanly from algorithms, at translation (or compile) time we can choose different underlying data structures without impacting the algorithmic specifications. Algorithms written according to action semantics are thus written at a higher level of abstraction.

Several tools that support Executable UML include BridgePoint by Mentor Graphics [26], iUML by Kennedy–Carter [86], and Kavanagh Consultancy's OOA Tool [135] (which as of this writing could be downloaded at no charge, but only includes a model editor and not a model compiler).

Executable UML succeeds by narrowing the UML concepts it supports and by focusing on real-time embedded applications. While it is possible to do general-purpose modeling and development with xUML, it excels with applications that have rich and interesting object behavior lifecycles, which is typical in real-time embedded systems.

2.6.4 MDA Readings

There is a large body of literature that describes MDA. In addition to the OMG publications [111, 112, 134, 155], there are a number of helpful books. Kleppe et al. [98] discuss MDA and walk through an extended example of how it actually works. Frankel [63] provides a thorough discussion of strengths and weaknesses of MDA, and especially pays attention to enterprise-scale issues. Mellor et al. [126] give a concise and clear guide to MDA, and advocate an agile approach to MDA that leverages the strengths of model execution. Nolan et al. [128] describe MDA from the perspective of the IBM Rational software group that has invested a significant amount of energy in the MDA initiative, including creating commercial tools and software development methodologies around MDA and related standards. Stahl et al. [166] give comprehensive practical guidance. Olivé gives a useful presentation of the underlying concepts, theory, and formalisms of UML and MDA, along with a practical case study [133].

In *The MDA Journal* [60], Frankel and Parodi capture the lively debate from a number of blog columns originally published on the BP Trends web site that elucidate the discussion of general-purpose versus domain-specific approaches to MDD and respond to various other criticisms of MDA. This book also contains the MDA manifesto [10].

Chapter 4 of [65] gives a nice overview of MDA, paying special attention to metamodeling, UML profiles, and model interchange via XMI. Chapter 16 of [50] gives a good discussion of what it means to be platform independent and offers criticisms of UML and MDA.

Brown et al. have written several excellent summaries of MDA, issues surrounding MDD in general, and the IBM Rational tools that support MDA [19, 28, 29]. Also see [9], which includes two of Brown's MDA papers [13, 14]. Meservy and

Fenstermacher give a concise summary and analysis of MDA [115]. Uhl [179] deals with practicalities of implementing MDD in general at the enterprise level.

A 2003 issue of *IEEE Software* provides a number of helpful articles on MDD and MDA [109]. Selic identifies a number of pragmatic issues surrounding MDD and discusses how tool vendors are addressing them [151]. Seidewitz explores what models mean, and gives a thorough discussion of how we use models and metamodels [150]. Atkinson and Kühne describe the linguistic and ontological dimensions of MDA-style metamodeling and explain how the second version of MDA improves its clarity with respect to these dimensions [4]. Sendall and Kozaczynski describe various kinds of model transformations and call for an executable model transformation language [157] (see [113]). Kulkarni and Reddy propose "template abstraction" as a means for separating concerns at the model and code levels for improved reuse and system evolution. Finally, Uhl and Ambler engage in a point/counterpoint debate over whether MDA is "ready for prime time", with Uhl claiming it is and Ambler expressing skepticism and asserting that agile MDD is a better approach [7, 178]. Similarly, a 2008 issue of the UPGRADE journal provides a number of helpful MDA and MDD articles [32].

Finally, Milicev's work [117] is really about *an* executable UML, not Mellor's Executable UML. Milicev links Java, OQL, and other PSM-specific elements into an end-to-end approach to MDD. It is comprehensive, but more platform-specific than most approaches.

2.7 OO-Method

A significant MDD initiative is OO-Method [141] and its realization as the OlivaNova tool suite [33]. OO-Method builds on the OASIS formal specification language, which is based on dynamic logic and process algebra [139] and supports precise specification of modeling constructs, or *conceptual patterns*. OO-Method emphasizes the specification of conceptual patterns in precise, unambiguous terms, followed by the combination of *architectural patterns* with the system model. As with OSM and xUML, formal underlying semantics in combination with a sufficient execution model give OO-Method the ability to compile and execute models directly. The OlivaNova tool includes two main components: the modeler for developing system models, and the transformation engine, which is a model compiler. The OlivaNova transformation engine is one of the most robust commercially available model compilers, and is able to target a number of platforms and architectures.

OO-Method defines four main model types: object model, dynamic model, functional model, and presentation model. The first three constitute the core with which developers create a *conceptual schema*, and the fourth lets developers model how users can interact with the modeled system.

The OO-Method object model contains primitives for capturing structural information. It uses a mostly UML-like notation, with the notable addition of constructs that capture *agent relationships*. In order to invoke a method, an object must first

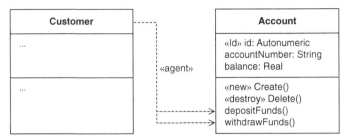

Fig. 2.14 Agent relationships in the OO-Method object model

be classified as an agent for that method. In this way, OO-Method supports non-uniform service availability [130], a key aspect of dynamic OO types that some approaches ignore. Agent relationships add another dimension of richness to the encapsulation structure of a system. Figure 2.14 illustrates the graphical notation for an agent relationship between *Customer* and the *depositFunds* and *withdrawFunds* methods of *Account*.

The OO-Method dynamic model includes fairly typical state transition and object interaction diagrams, but unlike UML statecharts, OO-Method places the specification of service functionality in a separate functional-model layer. Whereas xUML associates procedures with states, OO-Method places these service specifications, which it calls *evaluations*, in the functional model. The functional model specifies how the state of objects can change during their lifecycles. An evaluation has an event that triggers it, an attribute (of some class) that it affects, a condition that may modify when the evaluation can occur, and an evaluation effect that describes the result of performing the evaluation. For example, given the partial class diagram in Fig. 2.14 we may wish to specify an evaluation that automatically issues a service charge when an account that has a negative balance attempts a funds withdrawal. Such an evaluation could specify event *withdrawFunds*, attribute *balance*, evaluation condition *balance <0*, and evaluation effect *balance = balance − 10*.

A distinctive aspect of OO-Method is its presentation model, which specifies and describes how users can interact with the system. The OO-Method presentation model is essentially a collection of patterns that specifies the user interface as an abstract model that has three levels of patterns: (1) system access structure, (2) interaction units, and (3) basic supporting elements. The framework for the presentation model is an *action hierarchy tree* that defines the hierarchical structure through which users access system functions (e.g., it could be implemented as a menu hierarchy in a typical GUI application). Nodes of the action hierarchy tree are *interaction units* that describe scenarios through which users interact with the system to carry out specific tasks. Basic element patterns support further specification of the user interface as we illustrate below.

OO-Method includes four general kinds of interaction units: service, population, instance, and master/detail. A *service interaction unit* (SIU) models human/computer interaction that results in the execution of a service in the system. Figure 2.15 shows a simple SIU for depositing funds into an account. Input fields

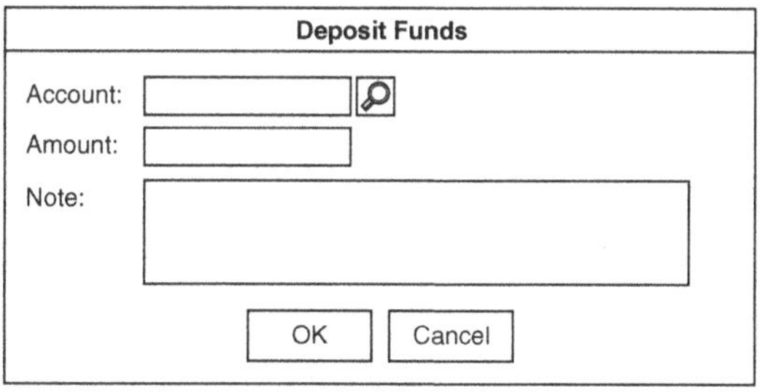

Fig. 2.15 Deposit funds service interaction unit for abstract graphical interface

allow the user to specify the account number, amount to deposit, and an explanatory note. A button next to the account entry field lets the user look up the account
number from a list. Lower level patterns may also be associated with SIU's. For
example, we could add several patterns to the *amount* field in Fig. 2.15, such as (1)
an edit mask ## , ### . ##, (2) a help message *Please enter the amount you want to
deposit*, and (3) an underlying datatype of *Real* for the entered value.

A *population interaction unit* (PIU) specifies patterns for displaying and interacting with collections of objects (such as lists). Figure 2.16 shows an example for
a list of accounts. In addition to displaying the details of an underlying collection
(population), this PIU has a filter pattern that lets the user display only accounts
whose owner name matches some expression ("La*" in the example) and an order
criteria button that allows the user to sort the results according to various terms. The
PIU in Fig. 2.16 also has a set of action buttons that invoke specific SIUs (e.g. to
add or remove an account) and a set of navigation buttons that move from the current dialog to some other interaction unit (e.g. a transaction history PIU). The other
basic-element pattern in Fig. 2.16 is a display-set pattern that indicates which fields
associated with accounts should appear in the user interface.

Instance interaction units specify patterns for displaying and interacting with
individual objects. Instance and population interaction units are similar, with the
exception that the former displays information only about a single object, while
the latter displays information about a collection of similar objects. The fourth major category of interaction unit is the *master/detail interaction unit* (MDIU), which

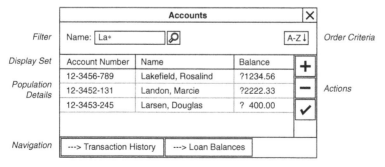

Fig. 2.16 Accounts population interaction unit for abstract graphical interface

models the common scenario where a collection of objects is associated with some other object (e.g., a list of transactions associated with a particular account). Often, the "master" portion of an MDIU is an instance interaction unit and the "detail" portion is a population interaction unit.

With its presentation model, OO-Method is suitable for modeling general-purpose applications that perform typical graphical user interface interactions. Further developing the presentation model to cover additional interaction scenarios is a particularly interesting area of ongoing research [8, 120, 138, 143].

OO-Method constitutes an MDA-like approach to model-driven development. It does not use the OMG standards, and so it is not pure MDA. However, we believe that OO-Method could be recast as a UML profile, and thus become pure MDA should its creators choose such a strategy. CARE Technologies [33] has put a significant amount of resources into commercializing OO-Method and refining the OlivaNova model execution tool. We see this as one of the more promising model-driven software development projects. It is possible to compile models into complete, operational business systems today using the OlivaNova technology.

2.8 Model-Driven Web Engineering (MDWE)

Web engineering is a discipline that is ripe for model-driven development because web applications fall into a fairly small set of typical patterns (such as document-centric, workflow-based, transactional, and so forth [94]) and the architectural concerns of web applications – as opposed to applications in general – are relatively narrow. In response, researchers have created a number of comprehensive approaches to model-driven web engineering (MDWE). Figure 2.17, adapted from [158] and [190], gives a concise history of many prominent MDWE initiatives, showing how web modeling languages have evolved over time. Wimmer and Schwinger et al. identify five major groupings of MDWE methods:

- *Data-oriented* approaches such as RMM [85], WebML [11, 40, 41], and Hera [58, 81, 84, 183] have their origins in database systems, and focus on data-intensive web applications.
- *Hypertext-oriented* methods such as HDM [69], HDM-lite [59], WSDM [171, 176], and W2000 [17] originate from work in hypermedia design, and handle nicely the hypertext nature of web applications.
- *Object-oriented* approaches follow in the tradition of OO modeling, and include such methods as OOHDM [147, 162, 163], UWE [80, 91], OOWS [61, 136], and OO-H [64].
- *Software-oriented* methods take an approach similar to traditional software development. Web Application Extension (WAE) and its WAE2 extension exemplify this approach [45].
- *MDE-oriented* methods explicitly take a model-driven approach to web application development and emphasize the automatic generation of source code

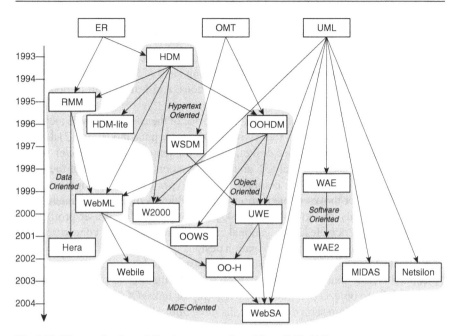

Fig. 2.17 History of web modeling languages, adapted from [158, 190]

from web application models. Examples of this category include Webile [48], WebSA [116], MIDAS [185], and Netsilon [125].

Moreno et al. divide the various MDWE initiatives into two broad groups: those that follow the ER modeling style and those that take an object-oriented approach [124]. In any case, the different categories of MDWE methods reflect diversity both in modeling-language origins and target web application types.

What distinguishes web applications from other types of applications is the prominence of navigation as a construct that should be modeled explicitly and carefully [148]. Navigation modeling essentially consists of describing the information units that users need to navigate along with the structure of the navigation space (which nodes are reachable from which other nodes). It is important to note that the structure of navigation nodes is not the same as the structure of conceptual items in the problem domain. Navigation nodes are likely to consist of views that combine information from parts of multiple domain objects. Furthermore, the navigation space structure is not ideally characterized merely by nodes and links. That works well for simple navigation structures, but typical web applications are more complex and are better modeled by higher-level abstractions such as sets, lists, and navigation chains [146].

There are other distinguishing aspects of web applications as well. For example, personalization is quite common in web applications now, whereas it is less common in traditional application development. Presentation issues tend to be emphasized in web applications, though the same issues also exist for traditional applications.

Web applications typically combine rich media from various sources, and must run properly on a wide variety of different browsers, operating systems, and physical devices. The context within which web applications operate evolves quickly, and so do web applications themselves [127]. A repeating them of MDWE is that there are common patterns associated with web applications, and it is helpful to document and reuse these common patterns [68].

To illustrate MDWE, we examine OOHDM, one of the earliest MDWE methods. The OOHDM method specifies four activities: (1) conceptual modeling, (2) navigation design, (3) abstract interface design, and (4) implementation. After identifying actors, performing use case analysis, and creating a conceptual model of the problem domain – all of which are common to other types of OO development – the OOHDM developer moves to navigation design, which is of particular interest for MDWE. The details are extensive [72, 147], but briefly, for each user profile, the OOHDM developer creates a navigational class schema and then a context schema that describes web application's navigation design.

An OOHDM *navigational class schema* consists of *nodes*, which are views over conceptual classes that contain information we want the user to perceive, and *anchors*, which are objects that allow the triggering of links. OOHDM structures the navigational space into sets of nodes it calls *navigational contexts*. A unique aspect of navigational contexts is that intra-set navigation is often desirable, as so we define each navigational context in terms of (1) its elements, (2) its internal navigational structure (e.g., can the set be accessed sequentially with next/previous links), and (3) its associated access structures, called *indexes*.

Figure 2.18 shows an abbreviated example of an OOHDM navigation context diagram for a part of our running banking example. Rectangles with solid borders indicate navigational contexts, while dashed rectangles denote access structures (indexes). Shaded rectangles represent classes (*Account*, *Summary*, and *Activity* in the example). The arrows with black dots at the origin leading from *Main Menu* indicate *landmarks* that are accessible globally from all contexts (implemented, perhaps, as a global menu of links on the top or side of the page). The small black box on *By Account* is a shorthand notation indicating that there is an associated index for this

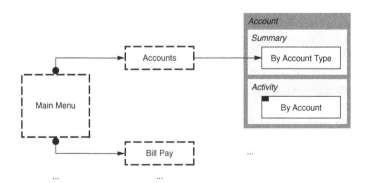

Fig. 2.18 OOHDM navigation context diagram abbreviated example

context. Since *Summary* and *Activity* are nested in the same scope, the user can navigate freely between the two views (if this were not desired, we would draw a dashed line between the two).

The various MDWE methods have different levels of support for model-driven development (see especially [48, 116, 125, 127, 149, 158, 164, 185]). UWE and WebML have some of the more comprehensive tool sets for MDD, though most methods have some tool support. WebRatio Enterprise Edition [189], by Web Models, is an XML and Java-centric tool that integrates with the Eclipse IDE and supports WebML modeling [189]. WebRatio generates Java Enterprise Edition (JEE) code from WebML and BPMN models. UWE has a MagicDraw plugin called MagicUWE and an Eclipse plugin called UWE4JSF, among other tools [182]. VisualWade generates PHP code for OO-H web application models [186], but is a bit dated. The HyperDE tool for OOHDM generates systems for the Ruby on Rails platform, and is suitable for "creating semantic web prototype applications" [77].

As MDWE methods have evolved and matured, researchers have expressed increasing concern over macro-level issues, such as whether new refinements make the method too complex and cumbersome [119, 164]. Some have also expressed concern that MDWE is in a state similar to the OO "method wars" of the 1990s and now call for consolidation and standardization efforts [184, 190]. The MDWEnet initiative [184] is working on responding to some of these concerns, and we anticipate that researchers will continue to work to bring together the various approaches where feasible. Interestingly, some of the researchers behind HDM and W2000 subsequently decided that a simpler approach would be more effective for various aspects of design, and they proposed the significantly simpler IDM [16], which takes a dialog-oriented perspective and advocates conceptual, logical, and page-design activities. We expect that there will be a fair amount of continued refinement and consolidation research in MDWE.

Many workshops and conferences that have published significant MDWE-related work including workshops on the World Wide Web and Conceptual Modeling (WWWCM'99 [36] and WCM2000 [103]), Web-Oriented Software Technology (IWWOST 2001–present), and Model-Driven Web Engineering (MDWE 2005–present), and the International Conference on Web Engineering (ICWE 2001–present), among others. Several books nicely summarize the state of the art in MDWE [94, 118, 146] (note especially that [146] distills the work published in IWWOST and WCM). Furthermore, an extensive survey by Schwinger et al. [164] provides excellent details and analysis of MDWE initiatives.

2.9 Agile MDD

A criticism often leveled against MDD in general, and MDA in particular, is that it is too complex and difficult to use. Ambler argues that the so-called "generative" approaches to MDD, such as MDA, are too complex for the current generation of developers [7]. His argument is that only after a large up-front effort – including a steep learning curve for the chosen modeling languages and tools – can we create the sophisticated models that are required to be able to generate code for the various platforms we want to target.

In contrast, the agile software development movement advocates making customer satisfaction the highest priority, and agilists see early and continuous delivery of useful software as the path to achieving this goal. They value "**individuals and interactions** over processes and tools, **working software** over comprehensive documentation, **customer collaboration** over contract negotiation, and **responding to change** over following a plan" [2]. The whole premise of creating complex models and then generating code from those models seems completely counter to these agile principles.

However, as one of the original signatories to the Agile Manifesto points out, there is no conflict between "agile" and "modeling" per se [114]. The conflict is in how we often use models. If models are not executable, the reasoning goes, then they cannot be agile. If a model is supposed to be a blueprint against which we later build a software system, then we must first go through the effort of creating the blueprint, and then we must go through a second process of construction. This is a heavyweight, non-agile approach. However, if our models are executable, then we can immediately use them in the way we typically use code (prototyping early and often), and thus the same agile principles that apply to programming apply equally well to modeling [108, 114, 126].

Ambler believes that MDA is flawed and will not succeed for most organizations. He takes a pragmatic approach and questions MDA along the following dimensions (among others) [6]:

- It takes a high level of education and training for developers to use MDA tools. UML (and related standards) are overly complex and may not be what the industry really needs anyway. The MDA standards are incomplete and still evolving.
- Tool vendors have historically been unwilling to create truly interoperable model-sharing standards (CORBA, also an OMG standard, suffered from tool vendors who would announce support and then implement the standard in a proprietary way).
- The industry has seen other approaches, like I-CASE in the 1980s and CORBA in the 1990s, that made similar promises but never fully delivered. Why will MDA be any different?
- Business stakeholders do not ask us to develop detailed, sophisticated, platform-independent models using a precise industry-standard modeling language to describe their business. Developing complex models is not what they request – they want working systems that deliver value.

Ambler's answer is to advocate agile MDD, which replaces the task of creating extensive models with agile models that are "just barely good enough" to drive the software development process.

We share most of the concerns Ambler expressed. MDA is built on a complex set of standards, and those standards do indeed continue to evolve. It is difficult to achieve true interoperability between different vendors' products in spite of their implementation of XMI import/export. History is full of failures in this arena. However, it is possible to apply agile techniques in an MDA framework, and indeed it has been done successfully [108]. When we shift from the use of models as sketches or blueprints to the use of models as the executable system itself, many of the difficulties Ambler points out simply go away. Furthermore, we caution readers not to confuse MDA, which Ambler specifically criticizes, with the broader concept of MDD; weaknesses (or strengths) of MDA do not necessarily apply to MDD in general.

2.10 Conclusions

A wide variety of model-driven methods have been proposed over the years and continue to be developed. MDA is certainly one of the more prominent approaches to model-driven software development, but it is by no means the only method. Model-driven techniques have been applied in a range of domains, and have been particularly well accepted in the field of web engineering. Some researchers advocate an agile approach to MDD because the traditional approach to modeling suffers from the same problems as the waterfall approach to software development.

There is an ecosystem of model-driven software development researchers, vendors, and practitioners. IBM Rational has been a major player in this field, creating many research advances and commercial tools for MDD. The Eclipse project has been prominent as well, with the Eclipse Modeling Framework and numerous related plugins. Some types of MDD have better tool support than others. For example, Executable UML has several good tools (BridgePoint, Rhapsody, and iUML), and the OlivaNova suite is an excellent and comprehensive model compiler.

On the other hand, many tool vendors have struggled to make sustainable model-driven tools. OptimalJ by Compuware was recently discontinued by its vendor, Compuware, even though OptimalJ was generally regarded as technically strong. A search of the web for model-driven tools yields many links to projects that are no longer active. Nonetheless, there are a number of active vendors with high quality tools available today. Altova's UModel, Artisan's Studio, Borland's Together, Gentleware's Apollo and Poseidon tools, IBM Rational's various tools (e.g., Rhapsody, Rose, and Software Architect), No Magic's MagicDraw, SparxSystems' Enterprise Architect, and Visual Paradigm's tool suite are some (but not all) of the active vendors with quality tools. We expect to see continued energy and innovation in the MDD tool vendor market in the coming years.

The question remains whether model-driven approaches to software development can deliver on the promise of increased productivity, quality, reusability, and maintainability. The skeptics are abundant, particularly among proponents of agile techniques, and the vast majority of software today is still developed using non-model-driven methods. However, the industry has been moving inevitably toward model-driven approaches, and we expect it will continue to do so. We answer the skeptics by taking an expansive view of what "model-driven" means; the phrase is not owned by any one vendor or consortium, and it does not require cumbersome or unwieldy solutions, even though that is what many early MDD proponents delivered. The move toward model-driven approaches is really the same phenomenon that has been occurring in computing for decades – a move to ever higher levels of abstraction.

In his classic essay on software engineering, "No Silver Bullet – Essence and Accidents of Software Engineering", Fred Brooks observed that there are two kinds of complexity: "essential" and "accidental" [27]. His central point was that some complexity aspects of software systems are intrinsic or inherent (essential), while other aspects are artificially (accidentally) complex. Furthermore, essential complexity cannot be removed from the software development process. Therefore, unless accidental complexity accounts for at least 90 % of the effort required to develop complex systems, we will never see a "silver bullet" that increases productivity be an order of magnitude.

For example, a software system capable of making highly accurate weather forecasts has significant inherent complexity because the environmental model is quite involved, gathering the many necessary inputs is a difficult distributed process, and the algorithms that manipulate that model and its inputs are computationally complex. However, the particular tools we might use today to build such a system have some measure of accidental complexity. Consider the productivity improvement that comes with using an integrated development environment to develop in a modern object-oriented programming language with its extensive libraries of functions as compared to programming in COBOL or FORTRAN on punch cards. By introducing an environment that conveniently speeds up the edit-compile-run-test cycle, we remove some of the accidental programming complexity that software developers of the 1970s and 1980s experienced. Much of that complexity is now removed with graphical toolbar buttons and library objects. We can store our programs on convenient, stable, solid-state storage that fits in our pockets rather than on paper cards and bulky reels of magnetic tape.

Have we seen order-of-magnitude-scale productivity increases over the years? Yes, certainly we have; but Brooks is still correct. First, he limited his prediction to a one-decade timespan, so if the tenfold productivity improvement comes over a period of more than ten years, his thesis holds. Second, because our tools improve dramatically over time, we are able to tackle increasingly difficult and challenging tasks, and so we shift the ratio of essential to accidental complexity gradually and quite naturally. Thus, as our capabilities increase, so too does the essential complexity of the systems we choose to build. As the essential complexity increases, we naturally begin to devise additional mechanisms for dealing with that complexity, and consequently the accidental complexity increases as well. Consider the case of the OMG standards: the UML 2.2 specification [180, 181] is 966 pages long! As many critics have argued, there is certainly considerable accidental complexity in UML and the other standards around which MDA is built.

This is the context in which we should examine today's model-driven software development approaches. Just as with evolution in nature, ideas in the model-driven arena have variable quality, with only a subset leading to improvements. Nevertheless, the industry has been moving inexorably toward improved abstractions, and it will continue to do so. This is the natural arc of evolution for software development.

References

1. Abrial, J-R (1974) Data semantics. In: Klimbie JW, Koffeman KL (eds) IFIP working conference data base management. North-Holland, Amsterdam, pp 1–60
2. Beck K et al (2001) Agile manifesto. http://www.agilemanifesto.org. Accessed 17 June 2010
3. Agrawal A (2003) Graph rewriting and transformation (GReAT): a solution for the model integrated computing (MIC) bottleneck. In: Automated software engineering. Proceedings 18th IEEE international conference, pp 364–368
4. Atkinson C, Kuhne, T (2003) Model-driven development: a metamodeling foundation. IEEE Software, 20(5):36–41
5. Agrawal A, Karsai G, Ledeczi A (2003) An end-to-end domain-driven software development framework. In: OOPSLA '03: Companion of the 18th annual ACM SIGPLAN conference on object-oriented programming, systems, languages, and applications. ACM, New York, pp 8–15
6. Ambler, SW (2003) Examining the model driven architecture (MDA). http://www.agilemodeling.com/essays/mda.htm. Accessed 17 June 2010
7. Ambler, SW (2003) Agile model driven development is good enough. IEEE Software 20(5):71–73
8. Aquino N, Vanderdonckt J, Pastor O (2010) Transformation templates: adding flexibility to model-driven engineering of user interfaces. In: Proceedings of the 2010 ACM symposium on applied computing (SAC), Sierre, Switzerland, 22–26 March 2010, pp 1195–1202
9. Beydeda S, Book M, Gruhn V (eds) (2005) Model-driven software development. Springer, Berlin
10. Booch G, Brown A, Iyengar S, Rumbaugh J, Selic B (2004) An MDA manifesto. The MDA journal: model driven architecture straight from the masters. Meghan-Kiffer Press, Tampa, pp 133–143
11. Brambilla M, Comai S, Fraternali P, Matera M (2008) Designing web applications with WebML and WebRatio In: Rossi et al [146], pp 221–261
12. Batini C, Ceri S, Navathe SB (1992) Conceptual Database Design: An entity-relationship approach Benjamin/Cummings, Redwood City
13. Brown AW, Conallen J, Tropeano D (2005) Models, modeling, and model driven development. In: Beydeda S, Book M, Gruhn V (eds), Model-driven software development. Springer, Berlin, pp 1–17
14. Brown AW, Conallen J, Tropeano D (2005) Practical insights into MDA: lessons from the design and use of an MDA toolkit. In: Beydeda S, Book M, Gruhn V (eds), Model-driven software development. Springer, Berlin, pp 403–432
15. Bézivin J (2005) On the unification power of models. Softw and Syst Model 4(2):171–188
16. Bolchini D, Garzotto F (2008) Designing multichannel web applications as "dialogue systems": the IDM model. In: Rossi et al [146], pp 193–219
17. Baresi L Garzotto F, Paolini P (2001) Extending UML for modeling web applications. Hawaii international conference on system sciences 34(3):3055
18. Bernstein PA, Halevy AY, Pottinger R (2000) A vision of management of complex models. SIGMOD Rec 29(4):55–63
19. Brown AW, Iyengar S, Johnston S (2006) A rational approach to model-driven development. IBM Syst J 45(3):463–480
20. Biskup J (1998) Achievements of relational database schema design theory revisited. In Thalheim B, Libkin L (eds) Semantics in databases; Lecture notes in computer science. vol 1358. Springer, Heidelberg pp. 29–54

21. Brodie ML, Mylopoulos J, Schmidt JW (eds) (1984) On conceptual modelling: perspectives from artificial intelligence, databases, and programming languages. Springer, New York
22. Bailey J, Maier D, Schewe KD, Thalheim B, Wang XS (eds) Web information systems engineering – WISE 2008, Proceedings 9th international conference, Auckland, 1–3 September 2008. Lecture notes in computer science, vol 5175. Springer, Heidelberg
23. Bock C (2003) Uml without pictures. IEEE Software 20(5):33–35
24. Booch G (1991) Object-oriented analysis and design with applications Benjamin/Cummings. Menlo Park
25. Butler MJ, Petre L, Sere K (eds) (2002) Integrated formal methods. In: Proceedings third international conference, IFM2002, Turku, 15–18 May 2002. Lecture notes in computer science Springer, vol 2335. Springer, Heidelberg
26. Mentor Graphics. http://www.mentor.com/products/sm/model_development/bridgepoint. Accessed 17 June 2010
27. Brooks FP (1995) The mythical man-month: essays on software engineering. Addison-Wesley, Boston
28. Brown AW (2004) Model driven architecture: principles and practice. Softw and Syst Model 3(4):314–327
29. Brown AW (2008) MDA redux: practical realization of model driven architecture. In: Seventh international conference on composition-based software systems ICCBSS 2008. IEEE Press, Washington DC, pp 174–183
30. Bunge MA (1977) Treatise on basic philosophy: Ontology I: the furniture of the world, vol 3. Reidel, Boston
31. Bunge MA (1979) Treatise on basic philosophy. Ontology II: a world of systems, vol 3. Reidel, Boston
32. Bézivin J, Vallecillo-Moreno A, García-Molina J, Rossi G (2008) Editor's introduction: MDA at the age of seven: past, present and future. Eur J Informat Prof 9(2):4–6
33. CARE-technologies web site. http://www.care-t.com. Accessed 17 June 2010
34. Czarnecki K, Eisenecker U (2000) Generative programming: methods, tools, and applications. Addison-Wesley Professional, Boston
35. Chen PP, Embley DW, Kouloumdjian J, Liddle SW, Roddick JF (eds) (1999) Advances in conceptual modeling: Proceedings ER '99 workshops on evolution and change in data management, reverse engineering in information systems, and the world wide web and conceptual modeling, Paris, 15–18 November 1999; Lecture notes in computer science, vol 1727, Springer, Heidelberg
36. Chen PP, Embley DW, Kouloumdjian J, Liddle SW, Roddick JF (eds) (1999) Advances in conceptual modeling: Proceedings ER '99 workshops on evolution and change in data management, reverse engineering in information systems, and the world wide web and conceptual modeling, Paris, 15–18 November 1999; Lecture notes in computer science, vol 1727. Springer, Heidelberg
37. Clyde SW, Embley DW, Woodfield SN (1992) Tunable formalism in object-oriented systems analysis: Meeting the needs of both theoreticians and practitioners. In: Proceedings of the 1992 conference on object-oriented programming systems, languages, and applications (OOPSLA'92), Vancouver, October 1992, pp 452–465
38. Clyde SW, Embley DW, Woodfield SN (1996) Improving the quality of systems and domain analysis through object class congruency. In: Proceedings of the international IEEE symposium on engineering of computer based systems (ECBS'96), Friedrichshafen, March 1996, pp 44–51
39. Ceri S, Fraternelli P (1997) Designing database applications with objects and rules: the IDEA methodology. Addison-Wesley, Reading
40. Ceri S, Fraternali P, Bongio A (2000) Web modeling language (WebML): a modeling language for designing web sites. Comput Network, 33(1–6):137–157
41. Ceri S, Fraternelli P, Bongio A, Brambilla M, Comai S, Matera M (2003) Designing data-intensive web applications. Morgan Kaufmann, San Francisco
42. Chen PP (1976) The entity-relationship model – toward a unified view of data. ACM Trans Database Syst 1(1):9–36

43. Clyde SW (1993) An initial theoretical foundation for object-oriented systems analysis and design. PhD thesis, Brigham Young University
44. Clements P, Northrop L (2001) Software product lines: practices and patterns. Addison-Wesley, Reading
45. Conallen J (2003) Building web applications with UML, 2nd edn. Pearson, Boston
46. BYU Data Extraction Group web site. http://www.deg.byu.edu. Accessed 17 June 2010
47. BYU Data Extraction Group demos page. http://www.deg.byu.edu/multidemos.html. Accessed 17 June 2010
48. Di Ruscio D, Muccini H, Pierantonio A (2004) A data-modelling approach to web application synthesis. Int J Web Eng Technol 1(3):320–337
49. Dori D (2009) Object-process methodology: a holistic systems paradigm. Springer, Berlin
50. Draheim D, Weber G (2005) Form-oriented analysis. Springer, Berlin
51. Eclipse project web site. http://www.eclipse.org. Accessed 17 June 2010
52. Embley DW, Jackson RB, Liddle SW, Woodfield SN (1994) A formal modeling approach to seamless object-oriented systems development. In: Proceedings of the workshop on formal methods for information system dynamics at CAiSE'94, June 1994, pp 83–94
53. Embley DW, Kurtz BD, Woodfield SN (1992) Object-oriented systems analysis: a model-driven approach. Prentice-Hall, Englewood Cliffs
54. Embley DW (1998) Object database development: concepts and principles. Addison-Wesley, Reading
55. ER web site. http://conceptualmodeling.org/. Accessed 17 June 2010
56. Falkenberg ED (1976) Concepts for modelling information. In: IFIP working conference on modelling in data base management systems, pp 95–109
57. France RB, Ghosh S, Dinh-Trong T, Solberg A (2006) Model-driven development using UML 2.0: promises and pitfalls. Computer 39(2):59–66
58. Frasincar F, Houben GJ, Vdovjak R (2001) An RMM-based methodology for hypermedia presentation design. In: Advances in databases and information systems, Proceedings 5th East European conference, ADBIS 2001, Vilnius, 25–28 September 2001. Lecture notes in computer science, vol 2151. Springer, Heidelberg, pp 323–337
59. Fraternali P, Paolini P (2000) Model-driven development of web applications: the autoweb system. ACM Trans Inf Syst 18(4):323–382
60. Frankel DS, Parodi J (eds) (2004) The MDA journal: model driven architecture straight from the masters. Meghan-Kiffer Press, Tampa
61. Fons J, Pelechano V, Pastor O, Valderas P, Torres V (2008) Applying the OOWS model-driven approach for developing web applications. The internet movie database case study. In: Rossi et al [146], pp 65–108
62. France RB, Rumpe B (2005) Domain specific modeling. Softw and Syst Model 4(1):1–3
63. Frankel DS (2003) Model-driven architecture: applying MDA to enterprise computing. Wiley, Indianapolis
64. Gómez J, Cachero C, Pastor O (2001) Conceptual modeling of device-independent web applications. IEEE Multimed 8(2):26–39
65. Gašević D, Djurić D, Devedžić V (2006) Model driven engineering and ontology development. Springer, Berlin
66. Gery E, Harel D, Palachi E (2002) Rhapsody: a complete life-cycle model-based development system. In: Butler et al [25], pp 1–10
67. Guizzardi G, Herre H, Wagner G (2002) On the general ontological foundations of conceptual modeling. In: Proceedings of the 21st international conference on conceptual modeling (ER2002), Tampere, Finland, October 2002, pp 65–78
68. Garzotto F, Paolini P, Bolchini D, Valenti S (1999) "Modeling-by-Patterns" of web applications. In: Proceedings of WWWCM'99, Paris, December 1999, Lecture notes in computer science, vol 1727, Springer, Heidelberg
69. Garzotto F, Paolini P, Schwabe D (1993) HDM – a model-based approach to hypertext application design. ACM Trans Inf Syst 11(1):1–26

70. Greenfield J, Short K (2003) Software factories: assembling applications with patterns, models, frameworks and tools. In: OOPSLA'03: Companion of the 18th annual ACM SIGPLAN conference on Object-oriented programming, systems, languages, and applications. ACM, New York, pp 16–27
71. Greenfield J, Short K (2004) Software Factories: Assembling applications with patterns, models, frameworks, and tools. Wiley, Indianapolis
72. Güell N, Schwabe D, Vilain P (2000) Modeling interactions and navigation in web applications. In: Liddle SW, Mayr HC, Thalheim B (eds) Conceptual modeling for E-business and the web, Proceedings ER 2000 workshops on conceptual modeling approaches for E-business and the world wide web and conceptual modeling, Salt Lake City, 9–12 October 2000. Lecture notes in computer science, vol 1921. Springer, Heidelberg, pp 115–127
73. Halpin T (1995) Conceptual schema & relational database design, 2nd edn. Prentice-Hall of Australia, Sydney, Australia
74. Harel D (1987) Statecharts: A visual formulation for complex systems. Sci Comput Program 8(3):231–274
75. Harel D (2001) From play-in scenarios to code: An achievable dream. IEEE Comput, 36(1):53–60
76. Harel D (2009) Meaningful modeling: What's in the semantics of "semantics"? Comm ACM 52(3):67–75
77. HyperDE web site. http://www.tecweb.inf.puc-rio.br/hyperde. Accessed 17 June 2010
78. Harel D, Gery E (1997) Executable object modeling with statecharts. IEEE Comput (7):31–42
79. Hull R, King R (1987) Semantic database modelling: Survey, applications and research issues. ACM Comput Surv 19(3):605–625
80. Hennicker R, Koch N (2000) A UML-based methodology for hypermedia design. In: UML 2000 – The Unified Modeling Language, advancing the standard, In: Proceedings third international conference, York, UK, 2–6 October 2000. Lecture notes in computer science, vol 1939. Springer, Heidelberg, pp 410–424
81. Houben GJ (2000) HERA: Automatically generating hypermedia front-ends. In: engineering federated information systems, pp 81–88
82. Harel D, Politi M (1998) Modeling reactive systems with statecharts: the statemate approach. McGraw-Hill, New York
83. Henderson-Sellers B (2005) UML – the good, the bad or the ugly? perspectives from a panel of experts. Softw and Syst Model 4(1):4–13
84. Houben GJ, van der Sluijs K, Barna P, Broekstra J, Casteleyn S, Fiala Z, Frasincar F (2008) HERA. In: Rossi et al [146], pp 263–301
85. Isakowitz T, Stohr EA, Balasubramanian P (1995) RMM: A methodology for structured hypermedia design Comm ACM, 38(8):34–44
86. iUML. http://www.kc.com/PRODUCTS/iuml/
87. Jackson RB (1994) Object-oriented requirements specification: a model, a tool and a technique. PhD thesis, Brigham Young University
88. Jarzabek S (1993) Domain model-driven software reengineering and maintenance. J Syst Software 20(1):37–51
89. Jackson RB, Embley DW, Woodfield SN (1995) Developing formal object-oriented requirements specifications: a model, tool and technique. Inform Syst 20(4):273–289
90. Kent S (2002) Model driven engineering. In: Butler et al [25], pp 286–298
91. Koch N, Knapp A, Zhang G, Baumeister H (2008) UML-based web engineering. In: Rossi et al [146], pp 157–191
92. Kojarski S, Lorenz DH (2003) Domain driven web development with WebJinn In: OOPSLA '03: Companion of the 18th annual ACM SIGPLAN conference on object-oriented programming, systems, languages, and applications. ACM, New York, pp 53–65
93. Kifer M, Lausen G, Wu J (1995) Logical foundations of object-oriented and frame-based languages. J ACM 42(4):741–843
94. Kappel G, Prýýll B, Reich S, Retschitzegger W (eds) Web engineering: The discipline of systematic development of web applications. Wiley, Hoboken

95. Kulkarni V, Reddy S (2003) Separation of concerns in model-driven development. IEEE Software 20(5):64–69
96. Kühne T (2008) Making modeling languages fit for model-driven development. http://www.mm.informatik.tu-darmstadt.de/~kuehne/publications/papers/making-fit.pdf
97. Koch N, Vallecillo A, Houben GJ (eds) (2007) Model-driven engineering 2007. Proceedings of the 3rd international workshop on model-driven web engineering (MDWE 2007), Como, Italy, July 2007, CEUR workshop proceedings, vol 261. CEUR-WS.org. Accessed 17 June 2010
98. Kleppe AG, Warmer J, Bast W (2003) MDA explained: the model driven architecure: practice and promise. Pearson, Boston
99. Liddle SW, Embley DW, Woodfield SN (1993) Cardinality constraints in semantic data models. Data Knowl Eng 11(3):235–270
100. Liddle SW, Embley DW, Woodfield SN (1995) Unifying modeling and programming through an active, object-oriented, model-equivalent programming language In: Proceedings of the 14th international conference on object-oriented and entity-relationship modeling (OOER'95), Gold Coast December 1995, Lecture notes in computer science, vol 1021, Springer, Heidelberg, pp 55–64
101. Liddle SW, Embley DW, Woodfield SN (2000) An active, object-oriented, model-equivalent programming language. In: Papazoglou MP, Spaccapietra S, Tari Z (eds) Advances in object-oriented data modeling. MIT Press, Cambridge, pp 333–361
102. Liddle SW (1995) Object-oriented systems implementation: a model-equivalent approach. PhD thesis, Brigham Young University
103. Liddle SW, Mayr HC, Thalheim B (eds) (2000) Conceptual modeling for E-business and the web, Proceedings ER 2000 workshops on conceptual modeling approaches for e-business and the world wide web and conceptual modeling, Salt Lake City, 9–12 October 2000. Lecture notes in computer science, vol 1921. Springer, Heidelberg
104. Liu S, Offutt AJ, Ho-Stuart C, Sun Y, Ohba M (1998) Sofl: A formal engineering methodology for industrial applications. IEEE Trans Software Eng 24(1):24–45
105. Liskov BH, Zilles SN (1974) Programming with abstract data types. Proceedings of the ACM symposium on very high level languages. SIGPLAN notices 9(4):50–59
106. Mahoney MS (2004) Finding a history for software engineering. IEEE Ann Hist Comput 26(1):8–19
107. Maier D (1983) The theory of relational databases. Computer Science Press, Rockville
108. Mellor SJ, Balcer M (2002) Executable UML: a foundation for model-driven architectures. Addison-Wesley Longman, Boston
109. Mellor SJ, Clark AN, Futagami T (2003) Model-driven development – guest editor's introduction. IEEE Software 20(5):14–18
110. Mok WY, Embley DW (1998) Using NNF to transform conceptual data models to object-oriented database designs. Data Knowl Eng 24(3):313–336
111. Miller J, Mukerji J (eds) (2001) Model driven architecture (MDA) http://www.omg.org/cgi-bin/doc?ormsc/01-07-01.pdf. Accessed 17 June 2010
112. Miller J, Mukerji J (eds) (2003) MDA guide version 1.0.1. http://www.omg.org/cgi-bin/doc?omg/03-06-01. Accessed 17 June 2010
113. Melnik S (2004) Generic model management: concepts and algorithms Lecture notes in computer science, no. 2967. Springer, Heidelberg
114. Mellor S (2005) Editor's introduction: adapting agile approaches to your project needs. IEEE Software 22(3):17–20
115. Meservy TO, Fenstermacher KD (2005) Transforming software development: an MDA road map. Computer 38(9):52–58
116. Meliá S, Gómez J (2006) The WebSA approach: applying model driven engineering to web applications. J Web Eng 5(2):121–149
117. Milicev D (2009) Model-driven development with executable UML. Wiley, Indianapolis
118. Mendes E, Mosley N (2006) Web engineering. Springer, Berlin
119. Moreno N, Meliá S, Koch N, Vallecillo A (2008) Addressing new concerns in model-driven web engineering approaches. In: Bailey et al [22], pp 426–442

120. Molina PJ, Meliá S, Pastor O (2002) User interface conceptual patterns. In: Proceedings of the 9th international workshop on interactive systems. Design, specification, and verification (DSV-IS'02)

121. Moore's law. http://en.wikipedia.org/wiki/Moore's_law, May 2010. Accessed 17 June 2010

122. Morgan T (2002) Business rules and information systems: aligning IT with business goals. Addison-Wesley, Reading

123. Melnik S, Rahm E, Bernstein PA (2003) Rondo: A programming platform for generic model management. In: Proceedings of the ACM international conference on management of data (SIGMOD'03), San Diego

124. Moreno N, Romero JR, Vallecillo A (2008) On overview of model-driven web engineering and the MDA In: Rossi et al [146], pp 353–382

125. Muller PA, Studer P, Fondement F, Bézivin J (2005) Platform independent web application modeling and development with Netsilon. Softw Syst Model 4(4):424–442

126. Mellor SJ, Scott K, Uhl A, Weise D (2004) MDA Distilled: principles of model-driven architecture. Addison-Wesley, Boston

127. Murugesan S (2008) Web application development: Challenges and the role of web engineering. In: Rossi G, Pastor O, Schwabe D, Olsina L (eds) Web engineering: modelling and implementing web applications. Springer, Berlin, pp 7–32

128. Nolan B, Brown B, Balmelli L, Bohn T, Wahli U (2008) Model driven systems development with rational products. IBM Redbooks, Armonk

129. Nečaský M (2006) Conceptual modeling for XML: a survey. In: Proceedings of the annual international workshop on databases, texts, specifications and objects (DATESO 2006), Desna, 2006, pp 45–53

130. Nierstrasz O (1993) Regular types for active objects. In: Proceedings of the 1993 conference on object-oriented programming systems, languages, and applications (OOPSLA'93), pp 1–15

131. Oxford english dictionary. http://www.oed.com/. Accessed 17 June 2010

132. Olivè A (2005) Conceptual schema-centric development: A grand challenge for information systems research. In Pastor O, Cunha JF [137], pp 1–15

133. Olivè A (2007) Conceptual modeling of information systems. Springer, Berlin

134. Object Management Group home page. www.omg.org. Accessed 17 June 2010

135. OOA Tool. http://www.ooatool.com/OOATool.html. Accessed 17 June 2010

136. Pastor O, Abrahão SM, Fons J (2001) An object-oriented approach to automate web applications development. In: Electronic commerce and web technologies. Proceedings of second international conference, EC-Web 2001 Munich, 4–6 September 2001. Lecture notes in computer science, vol 2115. Springer, Berlin, pp 16–28

137. Pastor O, Falcão J, Cunha (eds) (2005) Advanced Information Systems Engineering, Proceedings 17th International Conference, CAiSE 2005, Porto, 13–17 June 2005. Lecture notes in computer science, vol 3520. Springer, Heidelberg

138. Pastor O, España S, Panach JI, Aquino N (2008) Model-driven development. Inform Spektrum 31(5):394–407

139. Pastor O, Hayes F, Bear S (1992) OASIS: An object-oriented specification language. In: Proceedings of international conference on advanced information systems engineering (CAiSE'92), Manchester, pp 348–363

140. Peckham J, Maryanski F (1988) Semantic data models. ACM Comput Surv 20(3):153–189

141. Pastor O, Molina JC (2007) Model-driven architecture in practice: a software production environment based on conceptual modeling. Springer, New York

142. Papazoglou MP, Spaccapietra S, Tari Z (eds) (2000) Advances in object-oriented data modeling. MIT Press, Cambridge

143. Pederiva I, Vanderdonckt J, España S, Panach JI, Pastor O (2007) The beautification process in model-driven engineering of user interfaces. In: Proceedings of the 11th IFIP TC 13 international conference on human-computer interaction (INTERACT 2007), Rio de Janeiro, September 2007

144. Rumbaugh J, Blaha M, Premerlani W, Eddy F, Lorensen W (1991) Object-oriented modeling and design. Prentice-Hall, Englewood Cliffs

145. Raistrick C, Francis P, Wright J, Carter C, Wilkie I (2004) Model driven architecture with exectuable UML. Cambridge University Press, Cambridge
146. Rossi G, Pastor O, Schwabe D, Olsina L (eds) (2008) Web engineering: modelling and implementing web applications. Springer, London
147. Rossi G, Schwabe D (2008) Modeling and implementing web applications with OOHDM. In: Rossi et al [146], pp 109–155
148. Rossi G, Schwabe D, Lyardet F (1999) Web application models are more than conceptual models. In: Chen et al [35], pp 239–253
149. Schmid HA, Donnerhak O (2005) OOHDMDA – an MDA approach for OOHDM. In: Web engineering, proceedings 5th international conference, ICWE 2005, Sydney, 27–29 July 2005. Lecture notes in computer science, vol 3579. Springer, Heidelberg, pp 569–574
150. Seidewitz E (2003) What models mean. IEEE Software 20(5):26–32
151. Selic B (2003) The pragmatics of model-driven development. IEEE Software 20(5):19–25
152. Selic B (2007) From model-driven development to model-driven engineering. Euromicro conference on real-time systems, Pisa, 4–6 July 2007, p 3
153. Selic B (2008) MDA manifestations. Eur J Informat Profess 9(2):12–16. http://www.upgrade-cepis.org
154. Senko ME (1975) Information systems records, relations, sets, entities, and things. Inform Syst 1(1):3–13
155. Soley R, OMG Staff Strategy Group (2003) Model driven architecture. http://www.omg.org/cgi-bin/doc?omg/00-11-05. Accessed 17 June 2010
156. Sztipanovits J, Karsai G (1997) Model-integrated computing. Computer 30(4):110–111
157. Sendall S, Kozaczynski W (2003) Model transformation: the heart and soul of model-driven software development. IEEE Software 20(5):42–45
158. Schwinger W, Koch N (2006) Modeling web applications. In: Kappel G, Prýýll B, Reich S, Retschitzegger W (eds) In: Web engineering: The discipline of systematic development of web applications. Wiley, Hoboken, pp 39–64
159. Shlaer S, Mellor SJ (1988) Object-oriented systems analysis: modeling the world in data. Prentice-Hall, Upper Saddle River
160. Spyns P, Meersman R, Jarrar M (2002) Data modeling versus ontology engineering. SIGMOD Record 31(4):12–17
161. Sprinkle J (2004) Model-integrated computing. IEEE Potentials 23(1):28–30
162. Schwabe D, Rossi G (1995) Building hypermedia applications as navigational views of information models. In: Proceedings of 28th Hawaii international conference on system sciences (Hawaii international conference on system sciences '95), vol 3, pp 231–240
163. Schwabe D, Rossi G (1995) The object-oriented hypermedia design model. Comm ACM 38(8):45–46
164. Schwinger W, Retschitzegger W, Schauerhuber A, Kappel G, Wimmer M, Pröll B, Cachero C, Casteleyn S, De Troyer O, Fraternali P, Garrigós I, Garzotto F, Ginige A, Houben GJ, Koch N, Moreno N, Pastor O, Paolini P, Pelechano V, Rossi G, Schwabe D, Tisi M, Vallecillo A, van der Sluijs K, Zhang G (2008) A survey on web modeling approaches for ubiquitous web applications. IJWIS 4(3):234–305
165. Singh Y, Sood M (2009) Model driven architecture: A perspective. In: Advance computing conference, IACC 2009. IEEE International, pp 1644–1652
166. Stahl T, Voelter M, Czarnecki K (2006) Model-driven software development: technology, engineering, management. Wiley, New York
167. Sengupta A, Wilde E (2006) The case for conceptual modeling for XML. Technical report, Wright State University (WSU) and Swiss Federal Institute of Technology (ETH)
168. Sztipanovits J (2001) Advances in model-integrated computing. In: Proceedings of the 18th IEEE instrumentation and measurement technology conference, IMTC 2001, vol 3, pp 1660–1664
169. Sztipanovits J (2005) Model integrated computing: foundations and applications. In: Proceedings of 12th IEEE international conference and workshops on the engineering of computer-based systems, ECBS '05. p xii

170. Thomas D, Barry BM (2003) Model driven development: the case for domain oriented programming. In: OOPSLA '03: Companion of the 18th annual ACM SIGPLAN conference on Object-oriented programming, systems, languages, and applications. ACM, New York, pp 2–7
171. De Troyer O, Casteleyn S, Plessers P (2008) WSDM: Web semantics design method. In: Rossi et al [146], pp 303–351
172. Thalheim B (2000) Entity-relationship modeling: foundations of database technology. Springer, Berlin
173. Thalheim B (2009) Towards a theory of conceptual modeling. In: Advances in conceptual modelling – challenging perspectives ETheCoM 2009 – First international workshop on evolving theories of conceptual modeling. Gramado, November 2009, pp 45–54
174. Thomas D (2004) MDA: revenge of the modelers or UML utopia? IEEE Software 21(3):15–17
175. Tzichritzis D, Lochovski FH (1982) Data models. Prentice-Hall, Englewood Cliffs
176. De Troyer O, Leune CJ (1998) WSDM: A user centered design method for web sites. Comput Netw 30:85–94
177. Teorey TJ, Yang D, Fry JP (1986) A logical design methodology for relational databases using the extended entity-relationship model. ACM Comput Surv 18(2):197–222
178. Uhl A (2003) Model driven arcitecture is ready for prime time. IEEE Software 20(5):70–72
179. Uhl A (2008) Model-driven development in the enterprise. IEEE Software 25(1):46–49
180. Object Management Group (2009) OMG Unified Modeling Language (OMG UML), infrastructure: Version 2.2. http://www.omg.org/spec/UML/2.2/. Accessed 17 June 2010
181. Object Management Group (2009) OMG Unified Modeling Language (OMG UML), superstructure: Version 2.2. http://www.omg.org/spec/UML/2.2/, Feb. 2009. Accessed 17 June 2010
182. UWE web site. http://uwe.pst.ifi.lmu.de
183. Vdovjak R, Frasincar F, Houben GJ, Barna P (2003) Engineering semantic web information systems in Hera. J Web Eng 2(1–2):3–26
184. Vallecillo A, Koch N, Cachero C, Comai S, Fraternali P, Garrigós I, Gómez J, Kappel G, Knapp A, Matera M, Meliá S, Moreno N, Pröll B, Reiter T, Retschitzegger W, Eduardo Rivera J, Schauerhuber A, Schwinger W, Wimmer M, Zhang G (2007) MDWEnet: A practical approach to achieving interoperability of model-driven web engineering methods. In: Koch et al [97]
185. Vela B, Acu na CJ, Marcos E (2004) A model driven approach to XML database development. In: Proceedings of the 23rd international conference on conceptual modeling (ER2004), Shanghai, November 2004, pp 273–285
186. Visualwade. http://www.visualwade.com
187. Wand Y (1989) A proposal for a formal model of objects. In Kim W, Lochovsky FH (eds) Object-oriented concepts, databases, and applications, ACM Press, New York, pp 537–559
188. Wilkie I, King A, Clarke M, Weaver C, Raistrick C, Francis P (2003) UML ASL Reference Guide: ASL Language Level 2.5. Kennedy Carter, Guildford
189. Webratio. http://www.webratio.com. Accessed 17 June 2010
190. Wimmer M, Schauerhuber A, Schwinger W, Kargl H (2007) On the integration of web modeling languages: Preliminary results and future challenges. In: Koch et al [97]

Part II
Structure Modelling

The Entity-Relationship Model—Toward a Unified View of Data

PETER PIN-SHAN CHEN

Massachusetts Institute of Technology

A data model, called the entity-relationship model, is proposed. This model incorporates some of the important semantic information about the real world. A special diagrammatic technique is introduced as a tool for database design. An example of database design and description using the model and the diagrammatic technique is given. Some implications for data integrity, information retrieval, and data manipulation are discussed.

The entity-relationship model can be used as a basis for unification of different views of data: the network model, the relational model, and the entity set model. Semantic ambiguities in these models are analyzed. Possible ways to derive their views of data from the entity-relationship model are presented.

Key Words and Phrases: database design, logical view of data, semantics of data, data models, entity-relationship model, relational model, Data Base Task Group, network model, entity set model, data definition and manipulation, data integrity and consistency
CR Categories: 3.50, 3.70, 4.33, 4.34

1. INTRODUCTION

The logical view of data has been an important issue in recent years. Three major data models have been proposed: the network model [2, 3, 7], the relational model [8], and the entity set model [25]. These models have their own strengths and weaknesses. The network model provides a more natural view of data by separating entities and relationships (to a certain extent), but its capability to achieve data independence has been challenged [8]. The relational model is based on relational theory and can achieve a high degree of data independence, but it may lose some important semantic information about the real world [12, 15, 23]. The entity set model, which is based on set theory, also achieves a high degree of data independence, but its viewing of values such as "3" or "red" may not be natural to some people [25].

This paper presents the entity-relationship model, which has most of the advantages of the above three models. The entity-relationship model adopts the more natural view that the real world consists of entities and relationships. It

A version of this paper was presented at the International Conference on Very Large Data Bases, Framingham, Mass., Sept. 22–24, 1975.
Author's address: Center for Information System Research, Alfred P. Sloan School of Management, Massachusetts Institute of Technology, Cambridge, MA 02139.
ACM Transactions on Database Systems, Vol. 1, No. 1, March 1976, Pages 9–36.

incorporates some of the important semantic information about the real world (other work in database semantics can be found in [1, 12, 15, 21, 23, and 29]). The model can achieve a high degree of data independence and is based on set theory and relation theory.

The entity-relationship model can be used as a basis for a unified view of data. Most work in the past has emphasized the difference between the network model and the relational model [22]. Recently, several attempts have been made to reduce the differences of the three data models [4, 19, 26, 30, 31]. This paper uses the entity-relationship model as a framework from which the three existing data models may be derived. The reader may view the entity-relationship model as a generalization or extension of existing models.

This paper is organized into three parts (Sections 2–4). Section 2 introduces the entity-relationship model using a framework of multilevel views of data. Section 3 describes the semantic information in the model and its implications for data description and data manipulation. A special diagrammatic technique, the entity-relationship diagram, is introduced as a tool for database design. Section 4 analyzes the network model, the relational model, and the entity set model, and describes how they may be derived from the entity-relationship model.

2. THE ENTITY-RELATIONSHIP MODEL

2.1 Multilevel Views of Data

In the study of a data model, we should identify the levels of logical views of data with which the model is concerned. Extending the framework developed in [18, 25], we can identify four levels of views of data (Figure 1):

(1) Information concerning entities and relationships which exist in our minds.

(2) Information structure—organization of information in which entities and relationships are represented by data.

(3) Access-path-independent data structure—the data structures which are not involved with search schemes, indexing schemes, etc.

(4) Access-path-dependent data structure.

In the following sections, we shall develop the entity-relationship model step by step for the first two levels. As we shall see later in the paper, the network model, as currently implemented, is mainly concerned with level 4; the relational model is mainly concerned with levels 3 and 2; the entity set model is mainly concerned with levels 1 and 2.

2.2 Information Concerning Entities and Relationships (Level 1)

At this level we consider entities and relationships. An *entity* is a "thing" which can be distinctly identified. A specific person, company, or event is an example of an entity. A *relationship* is an association among entities. For instance, "father-son" is a relationship between two "person" entities.[1]

---

[1] It is possible that some people may view something (e.g. marriage) as an entity while other people may view it as a relationship. We think that this is a decision which has to be made by the enterprise administrator [27]. He should define what are entities and what are relationships so that the distinction is suitable for his environment.

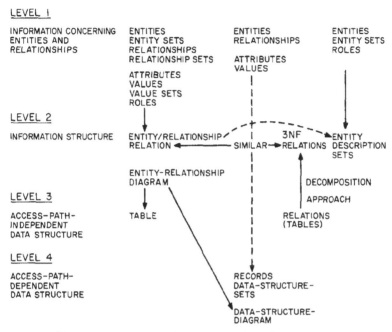

LEVELS OF LOGICAL VIEWS   MODELS

ENTITY-RELATIONSHIP NETWORK RELATIONAL ENTITY-SET

Fig. 1. Analysis of data models using multiple levels of logical views

The database of an enterprise contains relevant information concerning entities and relationships in which the enterprise is interested. A complete description of an entity or relationship may not be recorded in the database of an enterprise. It is impossible (and, perhaps, unnecessary) to record every potentially available piece of information about entities and relationships. From now on, we shall consider only the entities and relationships (and the information concerning them) which are to enter into the design of a database.

2.2.1 Entity and Entity Set. Let e denote an entity which exists in our minds. Entities are classified into different *entity sets* such as EMPLOYEE, PROJECT, and DEPARTMENT. There is a predicate associated with each entity set to test whether an entity belongs to it. For example, if we know an entity is in the entity set EMPLOYEE, then we know that it has the properties common to the other entities in the entity set EMPLOYEE. Among these properties is the afore-mentioned test predicate. Let E_i denote entity sets. Note that entity sets may not be mutually disjoint. For example, an entity which belongs to the entity set MALE–PERSON also belongs to the entity set PERSON. In this case, MALE–PERSON is a subset of PERSON.

2.2.2 Relationship, Role, and Relationship Set. Consider associations among entities. A *relationship set*, R_i, is a mathematical relation [5] among n entities, each taken from an entity set:

$$\{[e_1, e_2, \ldots, e_n] \mid e_1 \in E_1, e_2 \in E_2, \ldots, e_n \in E_n\},$$

and each tuple of entities, $[e_1, e_2, \ldots, e_n]$, is a *relationship*. Note that the E_i in the above definition may not be distinct. For example, a "marriage" is a relationship between two entities in the entity set PERSON.

The *role* of an entity in a relationship is the function that it performs in the relationship. "Husband" and "wife" are roles. The ordering of entities in the definition of relationship (note that square brackets were used) can be dropped if roles of entities in the relationship are explicitly stated as follows: $(r_1/e_1, r_2/e_2, \ldots, r_n/e_n)$, where r_i is the role of e_i in the relationship.

2.2.3 Attribute, Value, and Value Set. The information about an entity or a relationship is obtained by observation or measurement, and is expressed by a set of attribute-value pairs. "3", "red", "Peter", and "Johnson" are values. Values are classified into different *value sets*, such as FEET, COLOR, FIRST-NAME, and LAST-NAME. There is a predicate associated with each value set to test whether a value belongs to it. A value in a value set may be equivalent to another value in a different value set. For example, "12" in value set INCH is equivalent to "1" in value set FEET.

An *attribute* can be formally defined as a function which maps from an entity set or a relationship set into a value set or a Cartesian product of value sets:

$$f : E_i \text{ or } R_i \to V_i \text{ or } V_{i_1} \times V_{i_2} \times \cdots \times V_{i_n}.$$

Figure 2 illustrates some attributes defined on entity set PERSON. The attribute AGE maps into value set NO-OF-YEARS. An attribute can map into a Cartesian product of value sets. For example, the attribute NAME maps into value sets FIRST-NAME, and LAST-NAME. Note that more than one attribute may map from the same entity set into the same value set (or same group of value sets). For example, NAME and ALTERNATIVE-NAME map from the entity set EMPLOYEE into value sets FIRST-NAME and LAST-NAME. Therefore, attribute and value set are different concepts although they may have the same name in some cases (for example, EMPLOYEE-NO maps from EMPLOYEE to value set EMPLOYEE-NO). This distinction is not clear in the network model and in many existing data management systems. Also note that an attribute is defined as a function. Therefore, it maps a given entity to a single value (or a single tuple of values in the case of a Cartesian product of value sets).

Note that relationships also have attributes. Consider the relationship set PROJECT-WORKER (Figure 3). The attribute PERCENTAGE-OF-TIME, which is the portion of time a particular employee is committed to a particular project, is an attribute defined on the relationship set PROJECT-WORKER. It is neither an attribute of EMPLOYEE nor an attribute of PROJECT, since its meaning depends on both the employee and project involved. The concept of attribute of relationship is important in understanding the semantics of data and in determining the functional dependencies among data.

2.2.4 Conceptual Information Structure. We are now concerned with how to organize the information associated with entities and relationships. The method proposed in this paper is to separate the information about entities from the infor-

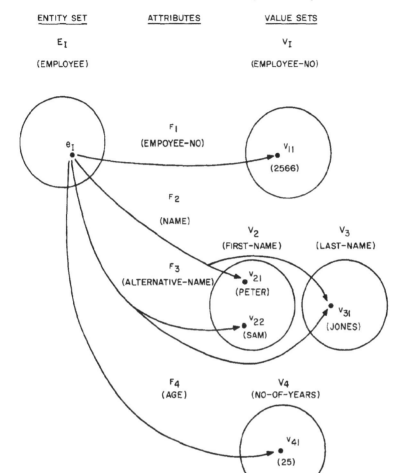

ENTITY SET   ATTRIBUTES   VALUE SETS

E_I V_I

(EMPLOYEE)   (EMPLOYEE-NO)

Fig. 2. Attributes defined on the entity set PERSON

mation about relationships. We shall see that this separation is useful in identifying functional dependencies among data.

Figure 4 illustrates in table form the information about entities in an entity set. Each row of values is related to the same entity, and each column is related to a value set which, in turn, is related to an attribute. The ordering of rows and columns is insignificant.

Figure 5 illustrates information about relationships in a relationship set. Note that each row of values is related to a relationship which is indicated by a group of entities, each having a specific role and belonging to a specific entity set.

Note that Figures 4 and 2 (and also Figures 5 and 3) are different forms of the same information. The table form is used for easily relating to the relational model.

14   ·   **P. P.-S. Chen**

ENTITY SETS   RELATIONSHIP SETS   ATTRIBUTE   VALUE SET

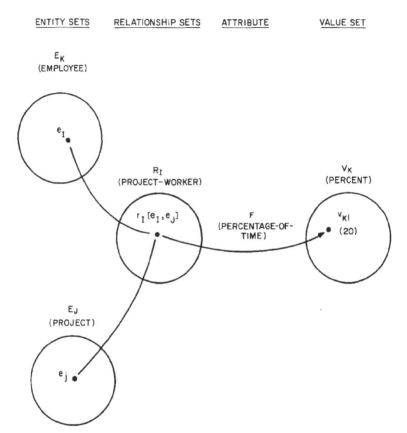

Fig. 3. Attributes defined on the relationship set PROJECT–WORKER

2.3 Information Structure (Level 2)

The entities, relationships, and values at level 1 (see Figures 2–5) are conceptual objects in our minds (i.e. we were in the conceptual realm [18, 27]). At level 2, we consider representations of conceptual objects. We assume that there exist direct representations of values. In the following, we shall describe how to represent entities and relationships.

2.3.1 Primary Key. In Figure 2 the values of attribute EMPLOYEE–NO can be used to identify entities in entity set EMPLOYEE if each employee has a different employee number. It is possible that more than one attribute is needed to identify the entities in an entity set. It is also possible that several groups of attributes may be used to identify entities. Basically, an *entity key* is a group of attributes such that the mapping from the entity set to the corresponding group of value sets is one-to-one. If we cannot find such one-to-one mapping on available data, or if simplicity in identifying entities is desired, we may define an artificial attribute and a value set so that such mapping is possible. In the case where

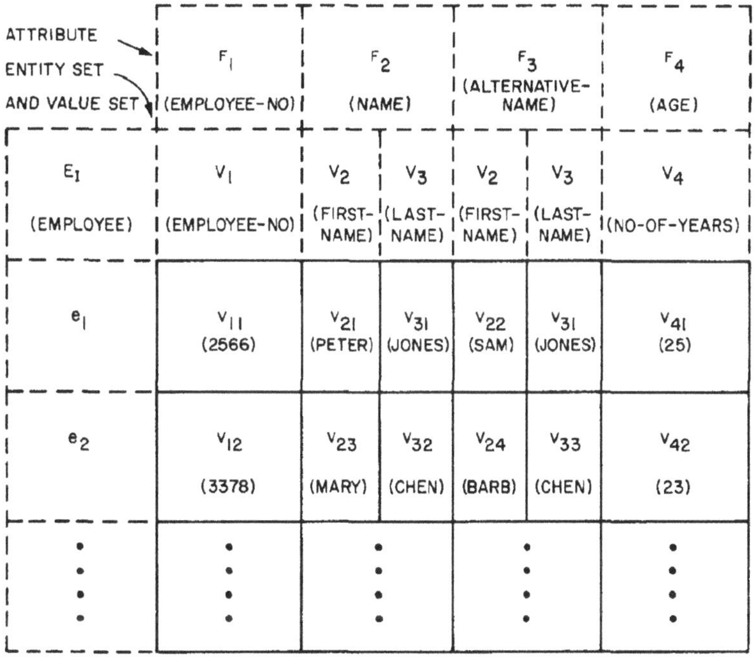

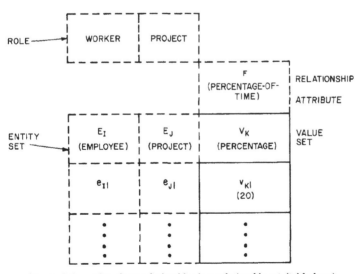

Fig. 4. Information about entities in an entity set (table form)

Fig. 5. Information about relationships in a relationship set (table form)

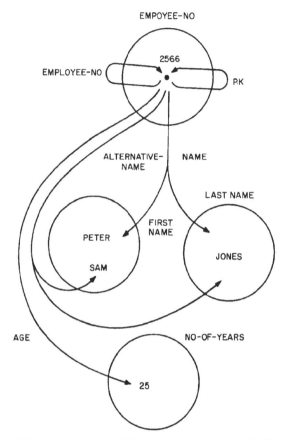

Fig. 6. Representing entities by values (employee numbers)

several keys exist, we usually choose a semantically meaningful key as the *entity primary key* (PK).

Figure 6 is obtained by merging the entity set EMPLOYEE with value set EMPLOYEE–NO in Figure 2. We should notice some semantic implications of Figure 6. Each value in the value set EMPLOYEE–NO represents an entity (employee). Attributes map from the value set EMPLOYEE–NO to other value sets. Also note that the attribute EMPLOYEE–NO maps from the value set EMPLOYEE–NO to itself.

2.3.2 Entity/Relationship Relations. Information about entities in an entity set can now be organized in a form shown in Figure 7. Note that Figure 7 is similar to Figure 4 except that entities are represented by the values of their primary keys. The whole table in Figure 7 is an *entity relation*, and each row is an *entity tuple*.

Since a relationship is identified by the involved entities, the *primary key of a relationship* can be represented by the primary keys of the involved entities. In

ATTRIBUTE	EMPLOYEE-NO	NAME		ALTERNATIVE-NAME		AGE
VALUE SET (DOMAIN)	EMPLOYEE-NO	FIRST-NAME	LAST-NAME	FIRST-NAME	LAST-NAME	NO-OF-YEARS
ENTITY (TUPLE)	2566	PETER	JONES	SAM	JONES	25
	3378	MARY	CHEN	BARB	CHEN	23
	⋮	⋮	⋮	⋮	⋮	⋮

Fig. 7. Regular entity relation EMPLOYEE

Figure 8, the involved entities are represented by their primary keys EMPLOYEE-NO and PROJECT-NO. The role names provide the semantic meaning for the values in the corresponding columns. Note that EMPLOYEE-NO is the primary key for the involved entities in the relationship and is not an attribute of the relationship. PERCENTAGE-OF-TIME is an attribute of the relationship. The table in Figure 8 is a *relationship relation*, and each row of values is a *relationship tuple*.

In certain cases, the entities in an entity set cannot be uniquely identified by the values of their own attributes; thus we must use a relationship(s) to identify them. For example, consider dependents of employees: dependents are identified by their names and by the values of the primary key of the employees supporting them (i.e. by their relationships with the employees). Note that in Figure 9,

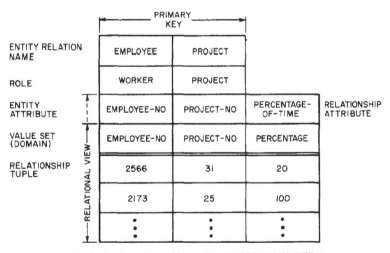

ENTITY RELATION NAME	EMPLOYEE	PROJECT		
ROLE	WORKER	PROJECT		
ENTITY ATTRIBUTE	EMPLOYEE-NO	PROJECT-NO	PERCENTAGE-OF-TIME	RELATIONSHIP ATTRIBUTE
VALUE SET (DOMAIN)	EMPLOYEE-NO	PROJECT-NO	PERCENTAGE	
RELATIONSHIP TUPLE	2566	31	20	
	2173	25	100	
	⋮	⋮	⋮	

Fig. 8. Regular relationship relation PROJECT-WORKER

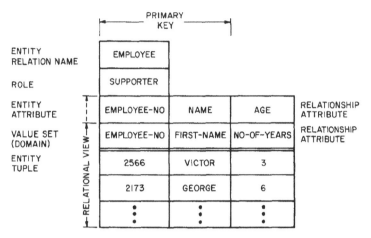

Fig. 9. A weak entity relation DEPENDENT

EMPLOYEE–NO is not an attribute of an entity in the set DEPENDENT but is the primary key of the employees who support dependents. Each row of values in Figure 9 is an entity tuple with EMPLOYEE–NO and NAME as its primary key. The whole table is an entity relation.

Theoretically, any kind of relationship may be used to identify entities. For simplicity, we shall restrict ourselves to the use of only one kind of relationship: the binary relationships with $1:n$ mapping in which the existence of the n entities on one side of the relationship depends on the existence of one entity on the other side of the relationship. For example, one employee may have n ($= 0, 1, 2, \ldots$) dependents, and the existence of the dependents depends on the existence of the corresponding employee.

This method of identification of entities by relationships with other entities can be applied recursively until the entities which can be identified by their own attribute values are reached. For example, the primary key of a department in a company may consist of the department number and the primary key of the division, which in turn consists of the division number and the name of the company.

Therefore, we have two forms of entity relations. If relationships are used for identifying the entities, we shall call it a *weak entity relation* (Figure 9). If relationships are not used for identifying the entities, we shall call it a *regular entity relation* (Figure 7). Similarly, we also have two forms of relationship relations. If all entities in the relationship are identified by their own attribute values, we shall call it a *regular relationship relation* (Figure 8). If some entities in the relationship are identified by other relationships, we shall call it a *weak relationship relation*. For example, any relationships between DEPENDENT entities and other entities will result in weak relationship relations, since a DEPENDENT entity is identified by its name and its relationship with an EMPLOYEE entity. The distinction between regular (entity/relationship) relations and weak (entity/relationship) relations will be useful in maintaining data integrity.

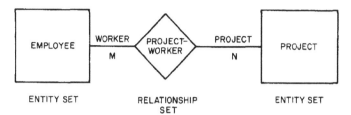

ENTITY SET   RELATIONSHIP   ENTITY SET
                                 SET

Fig. 10. A simple entity-relationship diagram

3. ENTITY-RELATIONSHIP DIAGRAM AND INCLUSION OF SEMANTICS IN DATA DESCRIPTION AND MANIPULATION

3.1 System Analysis Using the Entity-Relationship Diagram

In this section we introduce a diagrammatic technique for exhibiting entities and relationships: the entity-relationship diagram.

Figure 10 illustrates the relationship set PROJECT–WORKER and the entity sets EMPLOYEE and PROJECT using this diagrammatic technique. Each entity set is represented by a rectangular box, and each relationship set is represented by a diamond-shaped box. The fact that the relationship set PROJECT–WORKER is defined on the entity sets EMPLOYEE and PROJECT is represented by the lines connecting the rectangular boxes. The roles of the entities in the relationship are stated.

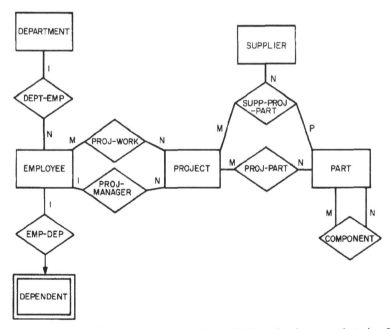

Fig. 11. An entity-relationship diagram for analysis of information in a manufacturing firm

Figure 11 illustrates a more complete diagram of some entity sets and relationship sets which might be of interest to a manufacturing company. DEPARTMENT, EMPLOYEE, DEPENDENT, PROJECT, SUPPLIER, and PART are entity sets. DEPARTMENT–EMPLOYEE, EMPLOYEE–DEPENDENT, PROJECT–WORKER, PROJECT–MANAGER, SUPPLIER–PROJECT–PART, PRO-JECT–PART, and COMPONENT are relationship sets. The COMPONENT relationship describes what subparts (and quantities) are needed in making super-parts. The meaning of the other relationship sets need not be explained.

Several important characteristics about relationships in general can be found in Figure 11:

(1) A relationship set may be defined on more than two entity sets. For example, the SUPPLIER–PROJECT–PART relationship set is defined on three entity sets: SUPPLIER, PROJECT, and PART.

(2) A relationship set may be defined on only one entity set. For example, the relationship set COMPONENT is defined on one entity set, PART.

ˊ(3) There may be more than one relationship set defined on given entity sets. For example, the relationship sets PROJECT–WORKER and PROJECT–MANAGER are defined on the entity sets PROJECT and EMPLOYEE.

(4) The diagram can distinguish between $1:n$, $m:n$, and $1:1$ mappings. The relationship set DEPARTMENT–EMPLOYEE is a $1:n$ mapping, that is, one department may have n $(n = 0, 1, 2, \ldots)$ employees and each employee works for only one department. The relationship set PROJECT–WORKER is an $m:n$ mapping, that is, each project may have zero, one, or more employees assigned to it and each employee may be assigned to zero, one, or more projects. It is also possible to express $1:1$ mappings such as the relationship set MARRIAGE. Information about the number of entities in each entity set which is allowed in a relation-ship set is indicated by specifying "1", "m", "n" in the diagram. The relational model and the entity set model[2] do not include this type of information; the network model cannot express a $1:1$ mapping easily.

(5) The diagram can express the *existence dependency* of one entity type on another. For example, the arrow in the relationship set EMPLOYEE–DEPEND-ENT indicates that existence of an entity in the entity set DEPENDENT de-pends on the corresponding entity in the entity set EMPLOYEE. That is, if an employee leaves the company, his dependents may no longer be of interest.

Note that the entity set DEPENDENT is shown as a special rectangular box. This indicates that at level 2 the information about entities in this set is organized as a weak entity relation (using the primary key of EMPLOYEE as a part of its primary key).

3.2 An Example of a Database Design and Description

There are four steps in designing a database using the entity-relationship model: (1) identify the entity sets and the relationship sets of interest; (2) identify semantic information in the relationship sets such as whether a certain relationship

---

[2] This mapping information is included in DIAM II [24].

set is an $1:n$ mapping; (3) define the value sets and attributes; (4) organize data into entity/relationship relations and decide primary keys.

Let us use the manufacturing company discussed in Section 3.1 as an example. The results of the first two steps of database design are expressed in an entity-relationship diagram as shown in Figure 11. The third step is to define value sets and attributes (see Figures 2 and 3). The fourth step is to decide the primary keys for the entities and the relationships and to organize data as entity/relationship relations. Note that each entity/relationship set in Figure 11 has a corresponding entity/relationship relation. We shall use the names of the entity sets (at level 1) as the names of the corresponding entity/relationship relations (at level 2) as long as no confusion will result.

At the end of the section, we illustrate a schema (data definition) for a small part of the database in the above manufacturing company example (the syntax of the data definition is not important). Note that value sets are defined with specifications of representations and allowable values. For example, values in EMPLOYEE-NO are represented as 4-digit integers and range from 0 to 2000. We then declare three entity relations: EMPLOYEE, PROJECT, and DEPENDENT. The attributes and value sets defined on the entity sets as well as the primary keys are stated. DEPENDENT is a weak entity relation since it uses EMPLOYEE.PK as part of its primary key. We also declare two relationship relations: PROJECT-WORKER and EMPLOYEE-DEPENDENT. The roles and involved entities in the relationships are specified. We use EMPLOYEE.PK to indicate the name of the entity relation (EMPLOYEE) and whatever attribute-value-set pairs are used as the primary keys in that entity relation. The maximum number of entities from an entity set in a relation is stated. For example, PROJECT-WORKER is an $m:n$ mapping. We may specify the values of m and n. We may also specify the minimum number of entities in addition to the maximum number. EMPLOYEE-DEPENDENT is a weak relationship relation since one of the related entity relations, DEPENDENT, is a weak entity relation. Note that the existence dependence of the dependents on the supporter is also stated.

DECLARE	VALUE-SETS	REPRESENTATION	ALLOWABLE-VALUES
	EMPLOYEE-NO	INTEGER (4)	(0,2000)
	FIRST-NAME	CHARACTER (8)	ALL
	LAST-NAME	CHARACTER (10)	ALL
	NO-OF-YEARS	INTEGER (3)	(0,100)
	PROJECT-NO	INTEGER (3)	(1,500)
	PERCENTAGE	FIXED (5.2)	(0,100.00)

DECLARE   REGULAR ENTITY RELATION EMPLOYEE
<u>ATTRIBUTE/VALUE-SET</u>:
      EMPLOYEE-NO/EMPLOYEE-NO
      NAME/(FIRST-NAME, LAST-NAME)
      ALTERNATIVE-NAME/(FIRST-NAME,LAST-NAME)
      AGE/NO-OF-YEARS
<u>PRIMARY KEY</u>:
      EMPLOYEE-NO

<u>DECLARE</u>   <u>REGULAR ENTITY RELATION</u> PROJECT
            <u>ATTRIBUTE/VALUE-SET</u>:
                PROJECT-NO/PROJECT-NO
            <u>PRIMARY KEY</u>:
                PROJECT-NO

<u>DECLARE</u>   <u>REGULAR RELATIONSHIP RELATION</u> PROJECT-WORKER
            <u>ROLE/ENTITY-RELATION.PK/MAX-NO-OF-ENTITIES</u>
                WORKER/EMPLOYEE.PK/m
                PROJECT/PROJECT.PK/n   (m:n mapping)
            <u>ATTRIBUTE/VALUE-SET</u>:
                PERCENTAGE-OF-TIME/PERCENTAGE

<u>DECLARE</u>   <u>WEAK RELATIONSHIP RELATION</u> EMPLOYEE-DEPENDENT
            <u>ROLE/ENTITY-RELATION.PK/MAX-NO-OF-ENTITIES</u>
                SUPPORTER/EMPLOYEE.PK/1
                DEPENDENT/DEPENDENT.PK/n
            <u>EXISTENCE OF DEPENDENT DEPENDS ON</u>
            <u>EXISTENCE OF SUPPORTER</u>

<u>DECLARE</u>   <u>WEAK ENTITY RELATION</u> DEPENDENT
            <u>ATTRIBUTE/VALUE-SET</u>:
                NAME/FIRST-NAME
                AGE/NO-OF-YEARS
            <u>PRIMARY KEY</u>:
                NAME
                EMPLOYEE.PK <u>THROUGH</u> EMPLOYEE-DEPENDENT

3.3 Implications on Data Integrity

Some work has been done on data integrity for other models [8, 14, 16, 28]. With explicit concepts of entity and relationship, the entity-relationship model will be useful in understanding and specifying constraints for maintaining data integrity. For example, there are three major kinds of constraints on values:

(1) Constraints on *allowable values* for a value set. This point was discussed in defining the schema in Section 3.2.

(2) Constraints on *permitted* values for a certain attribute. In some cases, not all allowable values in a value set are permitted for some attributes. For example, we may have a restriction of ages of employees to between 20 and 65. That is,

$$\text{AGE}(e) \in (20,65), \text{ where } e \in \text{EMPLOYEE}.$$

Note that we use the level 1 notations to clarify the semantics. Since each entity/relationship set has a corresponding entity/relationship relation, the above expression can be easily translated into level 2 notations.

(3) Constraints on *existing values* in the database. There are two types of constraints:

(i) Constraints between sets of existing values. For example,

$$\{\text{NAME}(e) \mid e \in \text{MALE-PERSON}\} \subseteq \{\text{NAME}(e) \mid e \in \text{PERSON}\}.$$

(ii) Constraints between particular values. For example,

$$\text{TAX}(e) \leq \text{SALARY}(e), \ e \in \text{EMPLOYEE}$$

or

$$\text{BUDGET}(e_i) = \sum \text{BUDGET}(e_j), \text{ where } e_i \in \text{COMPANY}$$
$$e_j \in \text{DEPARTMENT}$$
$$\text{and } [e_i, e_j] \in \text{COMPANY-DEPARTMENT}.$$

3.4 Semantics and Set Operations of Information Retrieval Requests

The semantics of information retrieval requests become very clear if the requests are based on the entity-relationship model of data. For clarity, we first discuss the situation at level 1. Conceptually, the information elements are organized as in Figures 4 and 5 (on Figures 2 and 3). Many information retrieval requests can be considered as a combination of the following basic types of operations:

(1) Selection of a subset of values from a value set.

(2) Selection of a subset of entities from an entity set (i.e. selection of certain rows in Figure 4). Entities are selected by stating the values of certain attributes (i.e. subsets of value sets) and/or their relationships with other entities.

(3) Selection of a subset of relationships from a relationship set (i.e. selection of certain rows in Figure 5). Relationships are selected by stating the values of certain attribute(s) and/or by identifying certain entities in the relationship.

(4) Selection of a subset of attributes (i.e. selection of columns in Figures 4 and 5).

An information retrieval request like "What are the ages of the employees whose weights are greater than 170 and who are assigned to the project with PROJECT-NO 254?" can be expressed as:

$\{\text{AGE}(e) \mid e \in \text{EMPLOYEE}, \text{WEIGHT}(e) > 170,$
$[e, e_j] \in \text{PROJECT-WORKER}, e_j \in \text{PROJECT},$
$\text{PROJECT-NO}(e_j) = 254\};$

or

$\{\text{AGE}(\text{EMPLOYEE}) \mid \text{WEIGHT}(\text{EMPLOYEE}) > 170,$
$[\text{EMPLOYEE}, \text{PROJECT}] \in \text{PROJECT-WORKER},$
$\text{PROJECT-NO}(\text{EMPLOYEE}) = 254\}.$

To retrieve information as organized in Figure 6 at level 2, "entities" and "relationships" in (2) and (3) should be replaced by "entity PK" and "relationship PK." The above information retrieval request can be expressed as:

$\{\text{AGE}(\text{EMPLOYEE.PK}) \mid \text{WEIGHT}(\text{EMPLOYEE.PK}) > 170$
$(\text{WORKER}/\text{EMPLOYEE.PK}, \text{PROJECT}/\text{PROJECT.PK}) \in \{\text{PROJECT-WORKER.PK}\},$
$\text{PROJECT-NO } (\text{PROJECT.PK}) = 254\}.$

To retrieve information as organized in entity/relationship relations (Figures 7, 8, and 9), we can express it in a SEQUEL-like language [6]:

```
SELECT      AGE
FROM        EMPLOYEE
WHERE       WEIGHT > 170
```

Table I. Insertion

level 1	level 2
operation: insert an entity to an entity set	*operation:* create an entity tuple with a certain entity-PK *check:* whether PK already exists or is acceptable
operation: insert a relationship in a relationship set *check:* whether the entities exist	*operation:* create a relationship tuple with given entity PKs *check:* whether the entity PKs exist
operation: insert properties of an entity or a relationship *check:* whether the value is acceptable	*operation:* insert values in an entity tuple or a relationship tuple *check:* whether the values are acceptable

```
AND          EMPLOYEE.PK =
             SELECT    WORKER/EMPLOYEE.PK
             FROM      PROJECT-WORKER
             WHERE     PROJECT-NO = 254.
```

It is possible to retrieve information about entities in two different entity sets without specifying a relationship between them. For example, an information retrieval request like "List the names of employees and ships which have the same

Table II. Updating

level 1	level 2

operation:
• change the value of an entity attribute
	operation:
	• update a value
	consequence:
	• if it is not part of an entity PK, no consequence
	• if it is part of an entity PK,
	  •• change the entity PKs in all related relationship relations
	  •• change PKs of other entities which use this value as part of their PKs (for example, DEPENDENTS' PKs use EMPLOYEE'S PK)

operation: • change the value of a relationship attribute	*operation:* • update a value (note that a relationship attribute will not be a relationship PK)

Table III. Deletion

level 1	level 2
operation: • delete an entity *consequences:* • delete any entity whose existence depends on this entity • delete relationships involving this entity • delete all related properties	*operation:* • delete an entity tuple *consequences* (applied recursively): • delete any entity tuple whose existence depends on this entity tuple • delete relationship tuples associated with this entity
operation: • delete a relationship *consequences:* • delete all related properties	*operation:* • delete a relationship tuple

age" can be expressed in the level 1 notation as:

$$\{(\text{NAME}(e_i),\text{NAME}(e_j)) \mid e_i \in \text{EMPLOYEE}, e_j \in \text{SHIP}, \text{AGE}(e_i) = \text{AGE}(e_j)\}.$$

We do not further discuss the language syntax here. What we wish to stress is that information requests may be expressed using set notions and set operations [17], and the request semantics are very clear in adopting this point of view.

3.5 Semantics and Rules for Insertion, Deletion, and Updating

It is always a difficult problem to maintain data consistency following insertion, deletion, and updating of data in the database. One of the major reasons is that the semantics and consequences of insertion, deletion, and updating operations usually are not clearly defined; thus it is difficult to find a set of rules which can enforce data consistency. We shall see that this data consistency problem becomes simpler using the entity-relationship model.

In Tables I–III, we discuss the semantics and rules[3] for insertion, deletion, and updating at both level 1 and level 2. Level 1 is used to clarify the semantics.

4. ANALYSIS OF OTHER DATA MODELS AND THEIR DERIVATION FROM THE ENTITY-RELATIONSHIP MODEL

4.1 The Relational Model

4.1.1 The Relational View of Data and Ambiguity in Semantics. In the relational model, *relation*, R, is a mathematical relation defined on sets $X_1, X_2, \ldots, X_n$:

$$R = \{(x_1, x_2, \ldots, x_n) \mid x_1 \in X_1, x_2 \in X_2, \ldots, x_n \in X_n\}.$$

The sets $X_1, X_2, \ldots, X_n$ are called *domains*, and $(x_1, x_2, \ldots, x_n)$ is called a *tuple*. Figure 12 illustrates a relation called EMPLOYEE. The domains in the relation

---

[3] Our main purpose is to illustrate the semantics of data manipulation operations. Therefore, these rules may not be complete. Note that the consequence of operations stated in the tables can be performed by the system instead of by the users.

ROLE		LEGAL	LEGAL	ALTERNATIVE	ALTERNATIVE	
DOMAIN	EMPLOYEE-NO	FIRST-NAME	LAST-NAME	FIRST-NAME	LAST-NAME	NO-OF-YEARS
TUPLE	2566	PETER	JONES	SAM	JONES	25
	3378	MARY	CHEN	BARB	CHEN	23

Fig. 12. Relation EMPLOYEE

are EMPLOYEE-NO, FIRST-NAME, LAST-NAME, FIRST-NAME, LAST-NAME, NO-OF-YEAR. The ordering of rows and columns in the relation has no significance. To avoid ambiguity of columns with the same domain in a relation, domain names are qualified by *roles* (to distinguish the role of the domain in the relation). For example, in relation EMPLOYEE, domains FIRST-NAME and LAST-NAME may be qualified by roles LEGAL or ALTERNATIVE. An *attribute name* in the relational model is a domain name concatenated with a role name [10]. Comparing Figure 12 with Figure 7, we can see that "domains" are basically equivalent to value sets. Although "role" or "attribute" in the relational model seems to serve the same purpose as "attribute" in the entity-relationship model, the semantics of these terms are different. The "role" or "attribute" in the relational model is mainly used to distinguish domains with the same name in the same relation, while "attribute" in the entity-relationship model is a function which maps from an entity (or relationship) set into value set(s).

Using relational operators in the relational model may cause semantic ambiguities. For example, the join of the relation EMPLOYEE with the relation EMPLOYEE-PROJECT (Figure 13) on domain EMPLOYEE-NO produces the

PROJECT-NO	EMPLOYEE-NO
7	2566
3	2566
7	3378

Fig. 13. Relation EMPLOYEE-PROJECT

		LEGAL	LEGAL	ALTERNATIVE	ALTERNATIVE	
PROJECT-NO	EMPLOYEE-NO	FIRST-NAME	LAST-NAME	FIRST-NAME	LAST-NAME	NO-OF-YEARS
7	2566	PETER	JONES	SAM	JONES	25
3	2566	PETER	JONES	SAM	JONES	25
7	3378	MARY	CHEN	BARB	CHEN	23

Fig. 14. Relation EMPLOYEE–PROJECT' as a "join" of relations EMPLOYEE and EMPLOYEE–PROJECT

relation EMPLOYEE–PROJECT' (Figure 14). But what is the meaning of a join between the relation EMPLOYEE with the relation SHIP on the domain NO-OF-YEARS (Figure 15)? The problem is that the same domain name may have different semantics in different relations (note that a role is intended to distinguish domains in a given relation, not in all relations). If the domain NO-OF-YEAR of the relation EMPLOYEE is not allowed to be compared with the domain NO-OF-YEAR of the relation SHIP, different domain names have to be declared. But if such a comparison is acceptable, can the database system warn the user?

In the entity-relationship model, the semantics of data are much more apparent. For example, one column in the example stated above contains the values of AGE of EMPLOYEE and the other column contains the values of AGE of SHIP. If this semantic information is exposed to the user, he may operate more cautiously (refer to the sample information retrieval requests stated in Section 3.4). Since the database system contains the semantic information, it should be able to warn the user of the potential problems for a proposed "join-like" operation.

4.1.2 Semantics of Functional Dependencies Among Data. In the relational model, "attribute" B of a relation is *functionally dependent* on "attribute" A of the same relation if each value of A has no more than one value of B associated with it in the relation. Semantics of functional dependencies among data become clear

SHIP-NO	NAME	NO-OF-YEARS
037	MISSOURI	25
056	VIRGINIA	IO

Fig. 15. Relation SHIP

in the entity-relationship model. Basically, there are two major types of functional dependencies:

(1) Functional dependencies related to description of entities or relationships. Since an attribute is defined as a function, it maps an entity in an entity set to a single value in a value set (see Figure 2). At level 2, the values of the primary key are used to represent entities. Therefore, nonkey value sets (domains) are functionally dependent on primary-key value sets (for example, in Figures 6 and 7, NO–OF–YEARS is functionally dependent on EMPLOYEE–NO). Since a relation may have several keys, the nonkey value sets will functionally depend on any key value set. The key value sets will be mutually functionally dependent on each other. Similarly, in a relationship relation the nonkey value sets will be functionally dependent on the prime-key value sets (for example, in Figure 8, PERCENTAGE is functionally dependent on EMPLOYEE–NO and PROJECT–NO).

(2) Functional dependencies related to entities in a relationship. Note that in Figure 11 we identify the types of mappings $(1:n, m:n,$ etc.) for relationship sets. For example, PROJECT–MANAGER is a $1:n$ mapping. Let us assume that PROJECT–NO is the primary key in the entity relation PROJECT. In the relationship relation PROJECT–MANAGER, the value set EMPLOYEE–NO will be functionally dependent on the value set PROJECT–NO (i.e. each project has only one manager).

The distinction between level 1 (Figure 2) and level 2 (Figures 6 and 7) and the separation of entity relation (Figure 7) from relationship relation (Figure 8) clarifies the semantics of functional dependencies among data.

4.1.3 3NF Relations Versus Entity-Relationship Relations. From the definition of "relation," any grouping of domains can be considered to be a relation. To avoid undesirable properties in maintaining relations, a normalization process is proposed to transform arbitrary relations into the first normal form, then into the second normal form, and finally into the third normal form (3NF) [9, 11]. We shall show that the entity and relationship relations in the entity-relationship model are similar to 3NF relations but with clearer semantics and without using the transformation operation.

Let us use a simplified version of an example of normalization described in [9]. The following three relations are in first normal form (that is, there is no domain whose elements are themselves relations):

EMPLOYEE (EMPLOYEE–NO)
PART (PART–NO, PART–DESCRIPTION, QUANTITY–ON–HAND)
PART-PROJECT (PART–NO, PROJECT–NO, PROJECT–DESCRIPTION,
            PROJECT–MANAGER–NO, QUANTITY–COMMITTED).

Note that the domain PROJECT–MANAGER–NO actually contains the EMPLOYEE–NO of the project manager. In the relations above, primary keys are underlined.

Certain rules are applied to transform the relations above into third normal form:

EMPLOYEE' (EMPLOYEE–NO)
PART' (PART–NO, PART–DESCRIPTION, QUANTITY–ON–HAND)

PROJECT' (PROJECT-NO, PROJECT-DESCRIPTION, PROJECT-MANAGER-NO)
PART-PROJECT' (PART-NO, PROJECT-NO, QUANTITY-COMMITTED).

Using the entity-relationship diagram in Figure 11, the following entity and relationship relations can be easily derived:

entity relations	PART''(PART-NO, PART-DESCRIPTION, QUANTITY-ON-HAND)
	PROJECT''(PROJECT-NO, PROJECT-DESCRIPTION)
	EMPLOYEE''(EMPLOYEE-NO)

| relationship relations | PART-PROJECT''(PART/PART-NO, PROJECT/PROJECT-NO, QUANTITY-COMMITTED) |
| | PROJECT-MANAGER''(PROJECT/PROJECT-NO, MANAGER/EMPLOYEE-NO). |

The role names of the entities in relationships (such as MANAGER) are indicated. The entity relation names associated with the PKs of entities in relationships and the value set names have been omitted.

Note that in the example above, entity/relationship relations are similar to the 3NF relations. In the 3NF approach, PROJECT-MANAGER-NO is included in the relation PROJECT' since PROJECT-MANAGER-NO is assumed to be functionally dependent on PROJECT-NO. In the entity-relationship model, PROJECT-MANAGER-NO (i.e. EMPLOYEE-NO of a project manager) is included in a relationship relation PROJECT-MANAGER since EMPLOYEE-NO is considered as an entity PK in this case.

Also note that in the 3NF approach, changes in functional dependencies of data may cause some relations not to be in 3NF. For example, if we make a new assumption that one project may have more than one manager, the relation PROJECT' is no longer a 3NF relation and has to be split into two relations as PROJECT'' and PROJECT-MANAGER''. Using the entity-relationship model, no such change is necessary. Therefore, we may say that by using the entity-relationship model we can arrange data in a form similar to 3NF relations but with clear semantic meaning.

It is interesting to note that the decomposition (or transformation) approach described above for normalization of relations may be viewed as a bottom-up approach in database design.[4] It starts with arbitrary relations (level 3 in Figure 1) and then uses some semantic information (functional dependencies of data) to transform them into 3NF relations (level 2 in Figure 1). The entity-relationship model adopts a top-down approach, utilizing the semantic information to organize data in entity/relationship relations.

4.2 The Network Model

4.2.1 Semantics of the Data-Structure Diagram. One of the best ways to explain the network model is by use of the *data-structure diagram* [3]. Figure 16(a) illustrates a data-structure diagram. Each rectangular box represents a record type.

---

[4] Although the decomposition approach was emphasized in the relational model literature, it is a procedure to obtain 3NF and may not be an intrinsic property of 3NF.

30   ·   P. P.-S. Chen

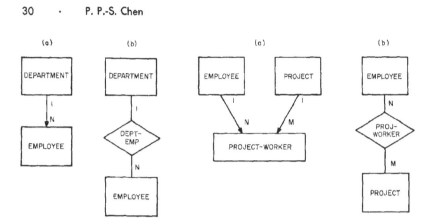

Fig. 16. Relationship DEPART-
    MENT-EMPLOYEE
    (a) data structure diagram
    (b) entity-relationship diagram

Fig. 17. Relationship PROJECT-WORKER
    (a) data structure diagram
    (b) entity-relationship diagram

The arrow represents a data-structure-set in which the DEPARTMENT record is the *owner-record*, and one owner-record may own n ($n = 0, 1, 2, \ldots$) *member-records*. Figure 16(b) illustrates the corresponding entity-relationship diagram. One might conclude that the arrow in the data-structure diagram represents a relationship between entities in two entity sets. This is not always true. Figures 17(a) and 17(b) are the data-structure diagram and the entity-relationship diagram expressing the relationship PROJECT-WORKER between two entity types EMPLOYEE and PROJECT. We can see in Figure 17(a) that the relationship PROJECT-WORKER becomes another record type and that the arrows no longer represent relationships between entities. What are the real meanings of the arrows in data-structure diagrams? The answer is that an arrow represents an $1:n$ relationship between two *record* (not entity) types and also implies the existence of an access path from the owner record to the member records. The data-structure diagram is a representation of the organization of records (level 4 in Figure 1) and is not an exact representation of entities and relationships.

4.2.2 Deriving the Data-Structure Diagram. Under what conditions does an arrow in a data-structure diagram correspond to a relationship of entities? A close comparison of the data-structure diagrams with the corresponding entity-relationship diagrams reveals the following rules:

1. For $1:n$ binary relationships an arrow is used to represent the relationship (see Figure 16(a)).

2. For $m:n$ binary relationships a "relationship record" type is created to represent the relationship and arrows are drawn from the "entity record" type to the "relationship record" type (see Figure 17(a)).

3. For k-ary ($k \geq 3$) relationships, the same rule as (2) applies (i.e. creating a "relationship record" type).

Since DBTG [7] does not allow a data-structure-set to be defined on a single record type (i.e. Figure 18 is not allowed although it has been implemented in [13]), a "relationship record" is needed to implement such relationships (see

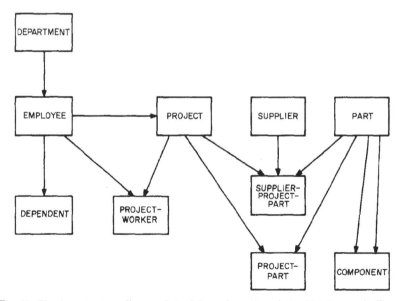

Fig. 18. Data-structure-set defined on the same record type

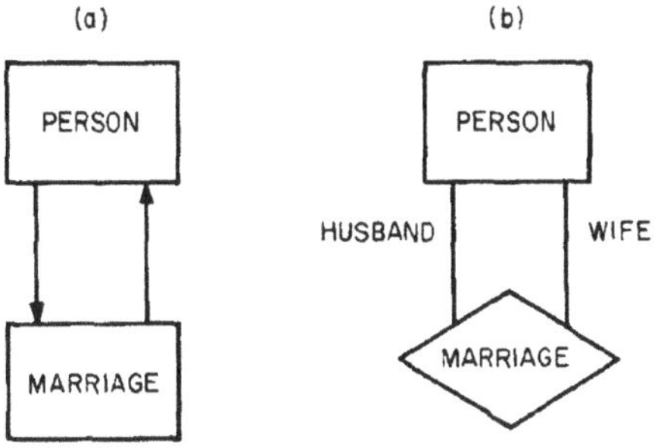

Fig. 19. Relationship MARRIAGE (a) data structure diagram (b) entity-relationship diagram

Figure 19(a)) [20]. The corresponding entity-relationship diagram is shown in Figure 19(b).

It is clear now that arrows in a data-structure diagram do not always represent relationships of entities. Even in the case that an arrow represents a $1:n$ relationship, the arrow only represents a unidirectional relationship [20] (although it is possible to find the owner-record from a member-record). In the entity-relationship model, both directions of the relationship are represented (the roles of both entities are specified). Besides the semantic ambiguity in its arrows, the network model is awkward in handling changes in semantics. For example, if the relationship between DEPARTMENT and EMPLOYEE changes from a $1:n$ mapping to an $m:n$ mapping (i.e. one employee may belong to several departments), we must create a relationship record DEPARTMENT-EMPLOYEE in the network model.

Fig. 20. The data structure diagram derived from the entity-relationship diagram in Fig. 11

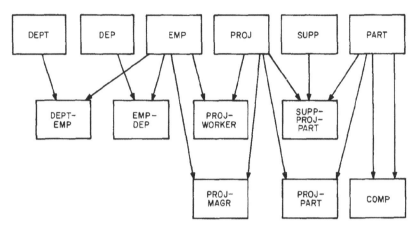

Fig. 21. The "disciplined" data structure diagram derived from the entity-relationship diagram in Fig. 11

In the entity-relationship model, all kinds of mappings in relationships are handled uniformly.

The entity-relationship model can be used as a tool in the structured design of databases using the network model. The user first draws an entity-relationship diagram (Figure 11). He may simply translate it into a data-structure diagram (Figure 20). using the rules specified above. He may also follow a discipline that every entity or relationship must be mapped onto a record (that is, "relationship records" are created for all types of relationships no matter that they are $1:n$ or $m:n$ mappings). Thus, in Figure 11, all one needs to do is to change the diamonds to boxes and to add arrowheads on the appropriate lines. Using this approach three more boxes—DEPARTMENT-EMPLOYEE, EMPLOYEE-DEPENDENT, and PROJECT-MANAGER—will be added to Figure 20 (see Figure 21). The validity constraints discussed in Sections 3.3–3.5 will also be useful.

4.3 The Entity Set Model

4.3.1 The Entity Set View. The basic element of the entity set model is the entity. Entities have names (*entity names*) such as "Peter Jones", "blue", or "22". Entity names having some properties in common are collected into an *entity-name-set*, which is referenced by the *entity-name-set-name* such as "NAME", "COLOR", and "QUANTITY".

An entity is represented by the entity-name-set-name/entity-name pair such as NAME/Peter Jones, EMPLOYEE-NO/2566, and NO-OF-YEARS/20. An entity is described by its association with other entities. Figure 22 illustrates the entity set view of data. The "DEPARTMENT" of entity EMPLOYEE-NO/2566 is the entity DEPARTMENT-NO/405. In other words, "DEPARTMENT" is the role that the entity DEPARTMENT-NO/405 plays to describe the entity EMPLOYEE-NO/2566. Similarly, the "NAME", "ALTERNATIVE-NAME", or "AGE" of EMPLOYEE-NO/2566 is "NAME/Peter Jones", "NAME/Sam Jones", or "NO-OF-YEARS/20", respectively. The description of the entity EMPLOYEE-

NO/2566 is a collection of the related entities and their roles (the entities and roles circled by the dotted line). An example of the *entity description* of "EMPLOYEE–NO/2566" (in its full-blown, unfactored form) is illustrated by the set of role-name/entity-name-set-name/entity-name triplets shown in Figure 23. Conceptually, the entity set model differs from the entity-relationship model in the following ways:

(1) In the entity set model, everything is treated as an entity. For example, "COLOR/BLACK" and "NO–OF–YEARS/45" are entities. In the entity-relationship model, "blue" and "36" are usually treated as values. Note treating values as entities may cause semantic problems. For example, in Figure 22, what is the difference between "EMPLOYEE–NO/2566", "NAME/Peter Jones", and "NAME/Sam Jones"? Do they represent different entities?

(2) Only binary relationships are used in the entity set model,[5] while *n*-ary relationships may be used in the entity-relationship model.

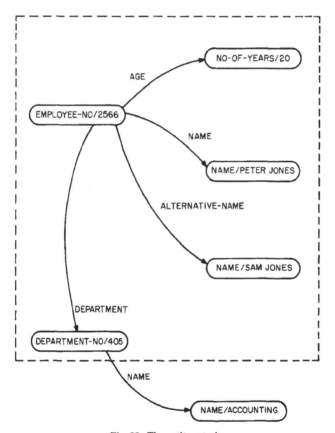

Fig. 22. The entity-set view

---

[5] In DIAM II [24], *n*-ary relationships may be treated as special cases of identifiers.

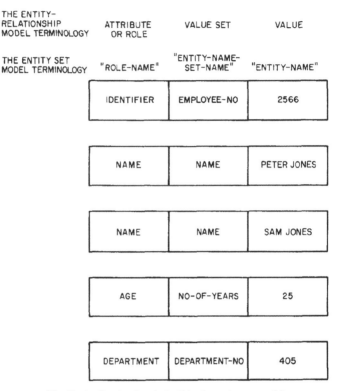

THE ENTITY-RELATIONSHIP MODEL TERMINOLOGY	ATTRIBUTE OR ROLE	VALUE SET	VALUE
THE ENTITY SET MODEL TERMINOLOGY	"ROLE-NAME"	"ENTITY-NAME-SET-NAME"	"ENTITY-NAME"
	IDENTIFIER	EMPLOYEE-NO	2566
	NAME	NAME	PETER JONES
	NAME	NAME	SAM JONES
	AGE	NO-OF-YEARS	25
	DEPARTMENT	DEPARTMENT-NO	405

Fig. 23. An "entity description" in the entity-set model

4.3.2 Deriving the Entity Set View. One of the main difficulties in understanding the entity set model is due to its world view (i.e. identifying values with entities). The entity-relationship model proposed in this paper is useful in understanding and deriving the entity set view of data. Consider Figures 2 and 6. In Figure 2, entities are represented by e_i's (which exist in our minds or are pointed at with fingers). In Figure 6, entities are represented by values. The entity set model works both at level 1 and level 2, but we shall explain its view at level 2 (Figure 6). The entity set model treats all value sets such as NO-OF-YEARS as "entity-name-sets" and all values as "entity-names." The attributes become role names in the entity set model. For binary relationships, the translation is simple: the role of an entity in a relationship (for example, the role of "DEPARTMENT" in the relationship DEPARTMENT-EMPLOYEE) becomes the role name of the entity in describing the other entity in the relationship (see Figure 22). For n-ary ($n > 2$) relationships, we must create artificial entities for relationships in order to handle them in a binary relationship world.

ACKNOWLEDGMENTS
The author wishes to express his thanks to George Mealy, Stuart Madnick, Murray Edelberg, Susan Brewer, Stephen Todd, and the referees for their valuable sug-

gestions (Figure 21 was suggested by one of the referees). This paper was motivated by a series of discussions with Charles Bachman. The author is also indebted to E.F. Codd and M.E. Senko for their valuable comments and discussions in revising this paper.

REFERENCES

1. ABRIAL, J.R. Data semantics. In *Data Base Management*, J.W. Klimbie and K.L. Koffeman, Eds., North-Holland Pub. Co., Amsterdam, 1974, pp. 1–60.
2. BACHMAN, C.W. Software for random access processing. *Datamation 11* (April 1965), 36–41.
3. BACHMAN, C.W. Data structure diagrams. *Data Base 1*, 2 (Summer 1969), 4–10.
4. BACHMAN, C.W. Trends in database management—1975. Proc., AFIPS 1975 NCC, Vol. 44, AFIPS Press, Montvale, N.J., pp. 569–576.
5. BIRKHOFF, G., AND BARTEE, T.C. *Modern Applied Algebra*. McGraw-Hill, New York, 1970.
6. CHAMBERLIN, D.D., AND RAYMOND, F.B. SEQUEL: A structured English query language. Proc. ACM-SIGMOD 1974, Workshop, Ann Arbor, Michigan, May, 1974.
7. CODASYL. Data base task group report. ACM, New York, 1971.
8. CODD, E.F. A relational model of data for large shared data banks. *Comm. ACM 13*, 6 (June 1970), 377–387.
9. CODD, E.F. Normalized data base structure: A brief tutorial. Proc. ACM-SIGFIDET 1971, Workshop, San Diego, Calif., Nov. 1971, pp. 1–18.
10. CODD, E.F. A data base sublanguage founded on the relational calculus. Proc. ACM-SIG-FIDET 1971, Workshop, San Diego, Calif., Nov. 1971, pp. 35–68.
11. CODD, E.F. Recent investigations in relational data base systems. Proc. IFIP Congress 1974, North-Holland Pub. Co., Amsterdam, pp. 1017–1021.
12. DEHENEFFE, C., HENNEBERT, H., AND PAULUS, W. Relational model for data base. Proc. IFIP Congress 1974, North-Holland Pub. Co., Amsterdam, pp. 1022–1025.
13. DODD, G.G. APL—a language for associate data handling in PL/I. Proc. AFIPS 1966 FJCC, Vol. 29, Spartan Books, New York, pp. 677–684.
14. ESWARAN, K.P., AND CHAMBERLIN, D.D. Functional specifications of a subsystem for data base integrity. Proc. Very Large Data Base Conf., Framingham, Mass., Sept. 1975, pp. 48–68.
15. HAINAUT, J.L., AND LECHARLIER, B. An extensible semantic model of data base and its data language. Proc. IFIP Congress 1974, North-Holland Pub. Co., Amsterdam, pp. 1026–1030.
16. HAMMER, M.M., AND McLEOD, D.J. Semantic integrity in a relation data base system. Proc. Very Large Data Base Conf., Framingham, Mass., Sept. 1975, pp. 25–47.
17. LINDGREEN, P. Basic operations on information as a basis for data base design. Proc. IFIP Congress 1974, North-Holland Pub. Co., Amsterdam, pp. 993–997.
18. MEALY, G.H. Another look at data base. Proc. AFIPS 1967 FJCC, Vol. 31, AFIPS Press, Montvale, N.J., pp. 525–534.
19. NIJSSEN, G.M. Data structuring in the DDL and the relational model. In *Data Base Management*, J.W. Klimbie and K.L. Koffeman, Eds., North-Holland Pub. Co., Amsterdam, 1974, pp. 363–379.
20. OLLE, T.W. Current and future trends in data base management systems. Proc. IFIP Congress 1974, North-Holland Pub. Co., Amsterdam, pp. 998–1006.
21. ROUSSOPOULOS, N., AND MYLOPOULOS, J. Using semantic networks for data base management. Proc. Very Large Data Base Conf., Framingham, Mass., Sept. 1975, pp. 144–172.
22. RUSTIN, R. (Ed.). Proc. ACM-SOGMOD 1974—debate on data models. Ann Arbor, Mich., May 1974.
23. SCHMID, H.A., AND SWENSON, J.R. On the semantics of the relational model. Proc. ACM-SIGMOD 1975, Conference, San Jose, Calif., May 1975, pp. 211–233.
24. SENKO, M.E. Data description language in the concept of multilevel structured description: DIAM II with FORAL. In *Data Base Description*, B.C.M. Dougue, and G.M. Nijssen, Eds., North-Holland Pub. Co., Amsterdam, pp. 239–258.

25. SENKO, M.E., ALTMAN, E.B., ASTRAHAN, M.M., AND FEHDER, P.L. Data structures and accessing in data-base systems. *IBM Syst. J. 12*, 1 (1973), 30–93.
26. SIBLEY, E.H. On the equivalence of data base systems. Proc. ACM-SIGMOD 1974 debate on data models, Ann Arbor, Mich., May 1974, pp. 43–76.
27. STEEL, T.B. Data base standardization—a status report. Proc. ACM-SIGMOD 1975, Conference, San Jose, Calif., May 1975, pp. 65–78.
28. STONEBRAKER, M. Implementation of integrity constraints and views by query modification. Proc. ACM-SIGMOD 1975, Conference, San Jose, Calif., May 1975, pp. 65–78.
29. SUNDGREN, B. Conceptual foundation of the infological approach to data bases. In *Data Base Management*, J.W. Klimbie and K.L. Koffeman, Eds., North-Holland Pub. Co., Amsterdam, 1974, pp. 61–95.
30. TAYLOR, R.W. Observations on the attributes of database sets. In *Data Base Description*, B.C.M. Dougue and G.M. Nijssen, Eds., North-Holland Pub. Co., Amsterdam, pp. 73–84.
31. TSICHRITZIS, D. A network framework for relation implementation. In *Data Base Description*, B.C.M. Douge and G.M. Nijssen, Eds., North-Holland Pub. Co., Amsterdam, pp. 269–282.

Chapter 4
UML and OCL in Conceptual Modeling

Martin Gogolla

Abstract The development of the entity-relationship (ER) model is one of the cornerstones for conceptual modeling of information systems. The Unified Modeling Language (UML) and the Object Constraint Language (OCL) take up central ideas from the ER model and put them into a broad software development context by proposing various graphical sublanguages and diagrams for specialized software development tasks and by adding more precision through textual constraints. The first section of this contribution will introduce the correspondence between basic ER modeling concepts and their UML counterparts. The next part will explain how more advanced conceptual modeling concepts can be formulated in UML. In the following section we will use OCL for features not expressible in diagrammatic form. Then we turn to the description of relational databases with UML. Before we conclude, we will show how to metamodel conceptual modeling features with UML itself and discuss further relevant work from the literature.

4.1 Introduction

The development of the entity-relationship (ER) model is probably one of the cornerstones for conceptual modeling of information systems. The Unified Modeling Language (UML) takes up central ideas from the ER model and puts them into a broad software development context by proposing various graphical sublanguages and diagrams for specialized software development tasks. It is said that the most commonly used UML diagram form is the class diagram. Entities and relationships have their counterparts there and are called classes and associations. Additionally, UML class diagrams allow the developer to include behavior in the form of operations.

Martin Gogolla

Department of Computer Science, Database Systems Group, University of Bremen, 28334 Bremen, Germany, e-mail: gogolla@informatik.uni-bremen.de

D. W. Embley and B. Thalheim (eds), *Handbook of Conceptual Modeling.* 85
DOI 10.1007/978-3-642-15865-0, © Springer 2011

The first versions of UML were developed in the mid-1990s. UML has changed since then and is still under development. For many years UML has included a textual language, the Object Constraint Language (OCL), whose main task is to enrich UML diagrams by textual constraints that cannot be expressed otherwise. However, apart from constraining, OCL can be used for querying UML models as well.

The rest of this chapter is structured as follows. The first section will introduce the correspondence between basic ER modeling concepts and their UML counterparts. The next section will explain how more advanced conceptual modeling concepts can be formulated in UML. The following section will use OCL for features not expressible in diagrammatic form. Then we turn to a description of relational databases with UML. Before we conclude, we will show how to metamodel conceptual modeling features with UML itself.

4.2 Basic Conceptual Modeling Features in UML

This section introduces the central features of UML [19, 20], namely class and object diagrams, and the Object Constraint Language (OCL) [18, 21, 25] which is part of UML.

4.2.1 Class and Object Diagrams

The main purpose of class diagrams within UML is to capture the basic static structures and operations of a system. In this subsection we will briefly explain the most important features in class diagrams such as classes and associations. In later sections we discuss more advanced features.

Classes: A class is a descriptor for a set of objects sharing the same structure and behavior. In the database context, we concentrate on the structural aspect, although the behavioral aspect may be represented in UML as well. Object properties can be described by attributes classified by data types like String or Boolean. Later we will see that properties can also stem from roles in associations that connect classes.

Example: Figure 4.1 follows the example from Chen's original paper [6] on the ER model and shows the classes Supplier, Project, and Part together with some basic attributes including their data types, e.g., we identify Supplier:: Name:String and Project::Budget:Integer. In this contribution, the general scheme for denoting properties (attributes and roles) is Class:: Property:PropertyType. Most names for entities, relationships, and attributes are taken from Chen's original article. Our UML and OCL examples have been realized in the tool USE [11, 12]. USE supports the development of information systems with UML and OCL by testing, validation, and verification techniques.

Associations: An association represents a connection between a collection of classes and may be given a name. An association is manifested by a set of object

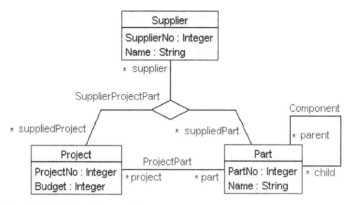

Fig. 4.1 Example UML class diagram 1

connections, so-called links, sharing the same structure. A binary association can be defined between two different classes. Objects of the respective classes play a particular role in the association. A binary association can also be defined on a single class; then objects of the class can play two different roles. Such a binary association is called reflexive. A ternary association involves three roles. The notion n-ary association refers to a ternary or higher-order association. Binary associations are shown with a simple line and an n-ary association with a small rhomb-shaped polygon.

Example: In Fig. 4.1, we identify the binary association `ProjectPart` with roles `project` and `part`, the ternary association `SupplierProjectPart` with roles `supplier`, `suppliedProject`, and `suppliedPart`, and the reflexive association `Component` with roles `parent` and `child`.

Objects and links: Structural aspects in UML can also be represented in an object diagram showing objects, links, and attribute values as manifestations of classes, associations, and attributes. An object diagram shows an instantiation of a class diagram and represents the described system in a particular state. Underlining of objects and links is used in object diagrams in order to distinguish them clearly from class diagrams.

Example: Figure 4.2 shows an object diagram for the class diagram from Fig. 4.1. Objects, links, and attribute values fit to the classes, associations, and attributes. The object identity is shown in the top part of the object rectangle to the left of the class to which the object belongs. Formally, there is no connection between the object identity and attribute values. For the example classes `Supplier` and `Part`, we have chosen object identities that are close to but not identical with the attribute `Name`, but for the class `Project` the object identities have no connection to the attribute values. There are two `Project` objects, two `Supplier` objects, and five `Part` objects. Each `Part` object represents a piece of software realizing controller (`Ctrl`) code that is responsible for a particular portion of a car. The `Component` links express part–whole relationships, for example, the `Engine Code` (`engineCtrl`) includes the `Battery Code` (`batteryCtrl`) and the `Motor Code` (`motorCtrl`).

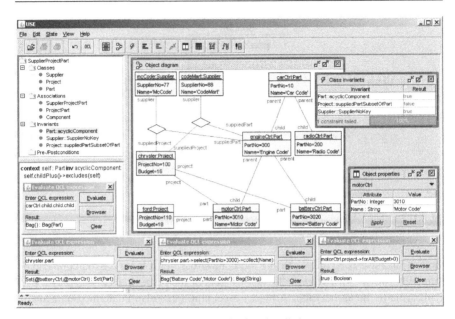

Fig. 4.2 Example object diagram 1 (and other USE functionality)

Roles: Proper roles must be specified on a class diagram in order to guarantee unique navigation, in particular in the presence of reflexive associations or when two or more associations are present between two classes. Navigation in a class diagram means fixing two classes and considering a path from the first class to the second class using associations. The roles on the opposite side of a given class in an association determine also properties of the given class by navigating via the roles. Therefore, in UML and OCL the opposite-side roles must be unique. Recall that properties can also come from attributes.

Example: On links, also the roles are captured. This is necessary in reflexive associations and in other situations, for example, if two associations are present between two given classes. For example in Fig. 4.2, if we consider the link between `carCtrl` and `engineCrtl`, without roles we could not tell which object played the `parent` role and which one the `child` role. In the class diagram in Fig. 4.1, the class `Project` has two direct navigation possibilities with respect to class `Part`: one via association `ProjectPart` and the other via association `SupplierProjectPart`. One obtains, therefore, two properties in class `Project` returning `Part` objects: `Project::part:Set(Part)` from association `ProjectPart` and `Project::suppliedPart:Set(Part)` from association `SupplierProjectPart`. In the object diagram we obtain, for example, that `ford.part` evaluates to `Set{motorCtrl}` and `ford.suppliedPart` gives `Set{}`.

Class diagram versus database schema: In the database context, it is interesting to remark that the connection between a class diagram and its object diagrams resembles the connection between a database schema and its associated database states: The class diagram induces a set of object diagrams and the database schema determines a set of database states; object diagrams and database states follow the general principles formulated in the class diagram and database schema, respectively. Because example object diagrams have to be displayed on screen or paper, they tend to show less information than proper, large database states. They may, however, explain the principles underlying a class diagram pretty well if the examples are well chosen.

4.2.2 Object Constraint Language

UML includes a textual language that allows the developer to navigate in class diagrams and to formulate queries and restricting integrity constraints for the class diagram: the Object Constraint Language (OCL). Roughly speaking from a practical perspective, OCL may be viewed as an object-oriented version of the Structured Query Language (SQL) originally developed for the relational data model. Roughly speaking from a theoretical perspective, OCL may be viewed as a variant of first-order predicate logic with quantifiers on finite domains only. The central language features in OCL are navigation, logical connectives, collections, and collection operations.

Navigation: The navigation features in OCL allow you to determine connected objects in the class diagram by using the dot operator " . ". Starting with an expression `expr` of start class `C`, one can apply a property `propC` of class `C` returning, for example, a collection of objects of class `D` by using the dot operator: `expr.propC`. The expression `expr` could be a variable or a single object, for example, or a more complicated expression. The navigation process can be repeated by writing `expr.propC.propD`, if `propD` is a property of class `D`.

Examples: Given the object diagram in Fig. 4.2, the following navigation expressions are syntactically valid in OCL and yield the stated return values and return types. OCL uses the convention that types are denoted by parentheses ( ) and values by braces { }:

```
chrysler.part ==
  Set{batteryCtrl,motorCtrl}:Set(Part)                (1)
batteryCtrl.project.supplier ==
  Bag{codeMart,mcCode}:Bag(Supplier)                  (2)
carCtrl.child ==
  Set{engineCtrl,radioCtrl}:Set(Part)                 (3)
carCtrl.child.child ==
  Bag{batteryCtrl,motorCtrl}:Bag(Part)                (4)
carCtrl.child.child.child ==
  Bag{}:Bag(Part)                                     (5)
```

Expressions (3) and (4) are similar insofar as expression (3) employs the dot in one place and expression (4) in two places. The difference in the result type, namely `Set(Part)` vs. `Bag(Part)`, will be explained below.

We have used above the notation `LEFT == RIGHT` with double use of the equals sign. This indicates that the OCL term `LEFT` evaluates to `RIGHT`, which represents also an OCL term optionally equipped with its type. The OCL equality check introduced below is written with a single equality symbol, e.g., we will have `42=43 == false`.

Logical connectives: OCL offers the usual logical connectives for conjunction `and`, disjunction `or`, and negation `not`, as well as the implication `implies` and a binary exclusive or `xor`. An equality check `=`, an inequality check `<>`, and a conditional `if then else endif` is provided on all types.

Examples: If we consider the objects `ford` and `chrysler` from Fig. 4.2, repeated in Fig. 4.3 for ease of tracing the resulting values, an OCL engine will deliver the following results:

```
ford.Budget>16 and chrysler.Budget>16
  == false:Boolean
ford.Budget>16 or chrysler.Budget>16 == true:Boolean
not(ford.Budget>16) == false:Boolean
ford.Budget>16 implies chrysler.Budget>16
  == false:Boolean
ford.Budget>16 xor chrysler.Budget>16 == true:Boolean
ford=ford == true:Boolean
ford=chrysler == false:Boolean
if ford.Budget>16 then 42 else 43 endif == 42:Integer
if chrysler.Budget>16 then mcCode else codeMart endif
  == codeMart:Supplier
```

Collections: In the original OCL there were three kinds of collections: sets, bags, and sequences. Later ordered sets were added, which we do not discuss here because they are similar to sequences; a discussion of OCL collections can be found in [3]. A possible collection element can appear at most once in a set, and the insertion order in the set does not matter. An element can appear multiple times in a bag, and the order in the bag collection does not matter. An element can appear multiple times in a sequence in which the order is significant.

Examples: The following expressions state the characteristic features of OCL collections:

```
Set{11,22}        =Set{22,11}        == true
Bag{11,22}        =Bag{22,11}        == true
Sequence{11,22}   =Sequence{22,11}   == false
```

Fig. 4.3 Objects `ford` and `chrysler` from Example Object Diagram 1

```
- - - - - - - - - - - - - - - - - - - - - - - - - - - - - - - - - - - - - - -
Set{11,22}           =Set{11,22,11}          == true
Bag{11,22}           =Bag{11,22,11}          == false
Sequence{11,22}      =Sequence{11,22,11}  == false
- - - - - - - - - - - - - - - - - - - - - - - - - - - - - - - - - - - - - - -
Set{11,11,22}        =Set{11,22,11}          == true
Bag{11,11,22}        =Bag{11,22,11}          == true
Sequence{11,11,22}=Sequence{11,22,11}  == false
```

We use terms of type `Set(Integer)` to demonstrate these features. However, we could have used terms of type `Set(Project)` as well, e.g., `Set{ford, chrysler}`, instead of `Set{11, 22}`. Sets are insensitive to insertion order and insertion frequency. Bags are insensitive to insertion order but are sensitive to insertion frequency. Sequences are sensitive to insertion order and insertion frequency.

Conversions: OCL collections can be nested and converted to each other. Bags and sequences can be converted to sets with `->asSet()`, sets and sequences to bags with `->asBag()`, and sets and bags to sequences with `->asSequence()`. The conversion to sequences assumes an order on the elements. The arrow notation will be explained in more detail below.

Examples: The following evaluations give an impression of how the conversions work:

```
Sequence{11,22,11}->asBag() ==
   Bag{11,11,22}:Bag(Integer)
Sequence{11,22,11}->asSet() ==
   Set{11,22}:Set(Integer)
Bag{11,22,11}->asSet() ==
   Set{11,22}:Set(Integer)
```

Special type `OclAny`: Collection terms in OCL possess a type as in the following examples:

```
Sequence{ford,chrysler,ford}: Sequence(Project)
Set{42,41,40}: Set(Integer)
```

However, the special type `OclAny` is a supertype of all other types, and `OclAny` can be used for collections. Therefore, the following expressions are valid in OCL:

```
Set{'Talking Heads', 3.14, 42, false}: Set(OclAny)
Bag{Set{8, 9}, Set{ford, carCtrl}}: Bag(Set(OclAny))
```

Collection operations: There is a large number of operations on collections in OCL. A lot of convenience and expressibility is based upon them. The most important operations on all collection kinds are `forAll`, `exists`, `select`, `collectNested`, `collect`, `size`, `isEmpty`, `includes`, and `including`. Table 4.1 gives an overview on the functionality of the operations.

There are also special operations available only on particular collections, e.g., the operation `at` on sequences for retrieving an element by its position. All collection operations are applied with the arrow notation already mentioned above. Roughly

Table 4.1 Important collection operations

Operation	Functionality
forAll	Realizes the universal quantification
exists	Formulates existential quantification
select	Filters elements with a predicate
collectNested	Applies a term to each collection element
collect	Applies a term to each collection element, flattening the result
size	Determines the number of collection elements
isEmpty	Tests on emptiness
includes	Checks whether the collection includes a possible element
including	Returns a collection that includes an element

speaking, the dot notation is used when a property follows, i.e., an attribute or a role follows, and the arrow notation is used when a collection operation follows.

Variables in collection operations: Most collection operations allow variables to be declared (possibly including a type specification), but the variable may be dropped if it is not needed.

Example: The following expressions are equivalent:

```
motorCtrl.project->forAll(Budget<120) == true
motorCtrl.project->forAll(p|
   p.Budget<120) == true
motorCtrl.project->forAll(p:Project|
   p.Budget<120) == true
```

Another important possibility is a feature that allows one to retrieve the finite set of all current instances of a class by appending .allInstances to the class name. In order to guarantee finite results, .allInstances cannot be applied to data types like String or Integer.

Examples: With regard to collection operations, an OCL evaluator would obtain the following results in the above object diagram:

```
motorCtrl.project->forAll(Budget<120) == true:Boolean
chrysler.supplier->exists(s|s.SupplierNo=99) ==
   false:Boolean
Part.allInstances->select(PartNo>=300) ==
   Set{batteryCtrl,engineCtrl,motorCtrl}:Set(Part)
chrysler.part->collect(p|p.Name) ==
   Bag{'Battery Code','Motor Code'} : Bag(String)
chrysler.part->collectNested(p|p.parent) ==
   Bag{Set{engineCtrl},Set{engineCtrl}}:Bag(Set(Part))
chrysler.part->collect(p|p.parent) ==
   Bag{engineCtrl,engineCtrl}:Bag(Part)
chrysler.part->collectNested(p|p.parent)->size() ==
   2:Integer
ford.supplier->isEmpty() == true:Boolean
```

Table 4.2 Result types of collection operations

Argument collection	Collection operation	Result type
Set/Bag/Sequence(T)	forAll	Boolean
Set/Bag/Sequence(T)	exists	Boolean
Set/Bag/Sequence(T)	select	Set/Bag/Sequence(T)
Set/Bag/Sequence(T)	collectNested	Bag/Bag/Sequence(T')
Set/Bag/Sequence(T)	collect	Bag/Bag/Sequence(T')
Set/Bag/Sequence(T)	size	Integer
Set/Bag/Sequence(T)	isEmpty	Boolean
Set/Bag/Sequence(T)	includes	Boolean
Set/Bag/Sequence(T)	including	Set/Bag/Sequence(T)

```
chrysler.part->includes(carCtrl) == false:Boolean
chrysler.part->including(carCtrl) ==
  Set{batteryCtrl,carCtrl,motorCtrl}:Set(Part)
```

Result types in collection operations: The result types of collection operations are shown in Table 4.2. Most notably, the operations collectNested(...) and collect(...) change the kind of argument collection Set(T) to a Bag(T') collection. The reason for this is that the term inside the collect may evaluate for two different collection elements to the same result. In order to reflect that the result is captured for each collection element, the result appears as often as a respective collection element exists. This convention in OCL resembles the same approach in SQL: SQL queries with the additional keyword distinct return a set; plain SQL queries without distinct return a bag. In OCL, the convention is similar: Plain collect(...) expressions return a bag; using the conversion asSet() as in collect(...)->asSet() returns a set.

Example: With respect to return types in collection operations, we see the following evaluation in which collect(...) is applied to a set, but it properly returns a bag:

```
Set{radioCtrl,motorCtrl}->
  collect(p|p.Name.substring(7,10)) ==
    Bag{'Code','Code'}:Bag(String)
```

In the above examples, we also saw this result for a collectNested term:

```
chrysler.part ==
  Set{batteryCtrl,motorCtrl} : Set(Part)
chrysler.part->collectNested(p|p.parent) ==
  Bag{Set{engineCtrl},Set{engineCtrl}}:Bag(Set(Part))
```

Thus the collectNested(...) operation applied to Set(Part) with the inner term p.parent, which returns Set(Part), yields Bag(Set(Part)). In this example, a bag is needed in order to capture the result correctly.

Operation flatten(): In OCL, collections can be nested. For example, one can build bags whose elements are sets. In order to flatten nested collections to unnested ones, the operation `flatten()` is available. The kind of the result collection is determined by the outermost collection. For example, bags of sets of something would be flattened to bags of something. For building sequences, an implementation-dependent order is chosen.

Example: The following expressions demonstrate the effect of `flatten()`:

```
Set{Set{10,20},Set{30,40}}->flatten() ==
   Set{10,20,30,40}:Set(Integer)
Set{Set{10,20},Set{20,30}}->flatten() ==
   Set{10,20,30}:Set(Integer)
Bag{Bag{10,20},Bag{30,40}}->flatten() ==
   Bag{10,20,30,40}:Bag(Integer)
Bag{Bag{10,20},Bag{20,30}}->flatten() ==
   Bag{10,20,20,30}:Bag(Integer)
Bag{Set{10,20},Set{30,40}}->flatten() ==
   Bag{10,20,30,40}:Bag(Integer)
Bag{Set{10,20},Set{20,30}}->flatten() ==
   Bag{10,20,20,30}:Bag(Integer)
```

Dot shortcut: Another convenient OCL feature is the dot shortcut, which allows the developer easy navigation through a class diagram using multiple roles. Speaking technically, a property `propD` may follow a dot as in the term `expr.propC.propD`, although the left part `expr.propC` yields a collection and only a collection operation and not a property (attribute or role) would be expected. However, the term `expr.propC.propD` is understood as a shortcut for `expr.propC->collect(x|x.propD)`. The aim of this shortcut is to avoid explicitly writing calls to `collect(...)` and to simply navigate with properties (attributes or roles), as for example in `expr.propC.propD.propE`. The dot shortcut is on the one hand very convenient because it allows the developer easy navigation through a class diagram. On the other hand, it blurs the distinction between a single object and an object collection insofar as a property can be applied with the dot shortcut to a collection as if the collection were an object.

Examples: The following examples illustrate the dot shortcut and the effects of `flatten()` in the context of the above object diagram:

```
chrysler.part->collectNested(p|p.parent)
   == Bag{Set{@engineCtrl},Set{@engineCtrl}}:
      Bag(Set(Part))
chrysler.part->collectNested(p|p.parent)->flatten()
   == Bag{@engineCtrl,@engineCtrl}:Bag(Part)
chrysler.part->collect(p|p.parent)
   == Bag{@engineCtrl,@engineCtrl}:Bag(Part)
chrysler.part->collectNested(p|p.parent)->flatten()->
   collect(p|p.Name)
   == Bag{'Engine Code','Engine Code'}:Bag(String)
chrysler.part.parent.Name
   == Bag{'Engine Code','Engine Code'}:Bag(String)
```

Example: Above we mentioned the term `carCtrl.child` with the type `Set(Part)` and the term `carCtrl.child.child` with the type `Bag(Part)`. This difference in the type is essentially a consequence of a combination of the dot shortcut and the fact that `collect` returns a bag when applied to a set: `carCtrl.child.child` is short for `carCtrl.child->collect(child)`, which is a term having the type `Bag(Part)`.

Operation definitions with OCL: OCL may be used to define side-effect-free operations. You may associate a correctly typed OCL term with an operation name. The term may use the declared parameters. The operation definition may be recursive.

Example: In the class `Project` one could define an operation `partCompetitors()` returning type `Set(Project)`. This operation should yield the set of those projects needing at least one common part with the considered project. The OCL operation `excluding` (used below) eliminates an element from a collection:

```
Project::partCompetitors():Set(Project) =
   self.part.project->excluding(self)->asSet()
```

The operation is formulated within the class `Project`. Therefore, the variable `self` references the current object on which the operation is called.

As an example of a recursive operation, we define in the class `Part` the transitive closure `childPlus()` of the role `child` with the help of an auxiliary recursive operation.

```
Part::childPlus():Set(Part)=childPlusAux(self.child)
Part::childPlusAux(aPartSet:Set(Part)):Set(Part)=
   let oneStep:Set(Part)=aPartSet.child->asSet() in
   if oneStep->exists(p|aPartSet->excludes(p))
     then childPlusAux(aPartSet->union(oneStep))
     else aPartSet endif
```

The last example uses the following OCL features not mentioned yet: `let` allows the developer to define subexpressions to be used in various places; `union` is another collection operation with the obvious meaning. We emphasize that the operation `childPlus` defined in the above manner is well defined and terminating for all possible object diagrams. Recall that the class `Part` (as any other class) has only finitely many instances in each system state. Therefore, the recursion finally terminates. The maximal set that can be computed is `Part.allInstances`. Analogously to the transitive closure `childPlus()`, one could define the transitive and reflexive closure `childStar()`.

4.3 Advanced Conceptual Schema Elements in UML

This section shows how to describe conceptual schemas in UML class diagrams without using any OCL features. In the first part, those UML class diagram features are introduced that are relevant for conceptual schema representation. In the second part, we discuss how to represent standard ER modeling concepts with these UML features.

4.3.1 Class Diagram Features for Conceptual Schemas

The language features in UML class diagrams introduced above are classes, data-valued attributes, associations, and roles. We now turn to describe object-valued, collection-valued, and compound attributes, role multiplicities, association classes, generalizations, aggregations, compositions, and invariants.

Object-valued attributes: Attributes in UML may not only be data-valued as above, but the attribute type may be a class as well that leads to object-valued attributes. Like associations, object-valued attributes also establish a connection between classes. The object-valued attribute is, however, only available in the class in which it is defined. The information from that attribute is not directly present in the attribute type class. Thus an object-valued attribute may be regarded as a unidirectional association without an explicit name and where only one role is available.

Examples: The examples in this section will be discussed in the context of the class diagram in Fig. 4.1 and the class diagram in Fig. 4.4, which extends the former one by introducing the new classes Employee, Dependent, and Project-Worker and the associations EmployeeDependent, ProjectManager, and ProjectWorker. The fact that ProjectWorker is mentioned as a class as well as an association will be explained below. The object diagram in Fig. 4.5 shows an example state for the class diagram from Fig. 4.4. As a forward reference we remark that we will come back later to the fact that ada's project participation sums up to 110 %.

As an example of an object-valued attribute and as an alternative to the association ProjectManager, we could extend the class Project by an at-

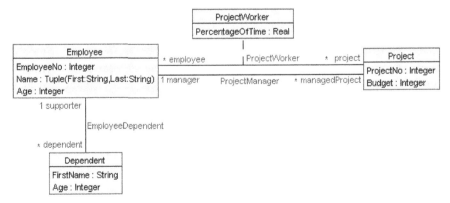

Fig. 4.4 Example UML class diagram 2

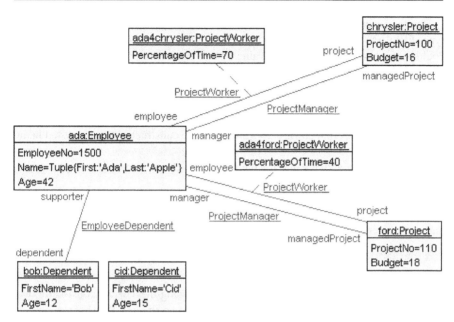

Fig. 4.5 Example UML object diagram 2

tribute `manager` with type `Employee`. This could be represented altogether as
`Project::manager:Employee`.

Collection-valued attributes: We have already introduced the collection kinds
set, bag, and sequence. These collection kinds can be used as type constructors on
data types and classes. For building attribute types, the constructors may be nested.

Examples: An attribute could possess a type like `Set(Project)`. As an
alternative to the association `ProjectManager` we could have one attribute
`managedProject:Set(Project)` in the class `Employee` and another attribute `manager:Employee` in the class `Project`. There is, however, an important difference between the model with the association `ProjectManager`, including the roles `manager` and `managedProject`, and the model with the two
attributes `manager` and `managedProject`. In the model with the association,
we would always have that the roles `managedProject` and `manager` represent
the same set of object connections, i.e., the following two OCL expressions will
evaluate to true in that model:

```
Employee.allInstances->forAll(e|
    e.managedProject.manager->includes(e))
Project.allInstances->forAll(p|
    p.manager.managedProject->includes(p))
```

These two OCL expressions are not always true in the model possessing the two
attributes. In this case the two attributes `managedProject` and `manager` are
independent of each other and may represent different sets of object connections.

Another useful application of collection-valued types are collections over data types like `Set(Sequence(String))`. A value for an attribute typed in that way could be, for example, the complex value `Set{Sequence{'Rome', 'Euro'}, Sequence{'Tokyo', 'Yen'}}`.

Compound attributes: Apart from using the collection constructors `Set`, `Bag`, and `Sequence` for attributes, one can employ a tuple constructor `Tuple`. A tuple has a set of components each possessing a component discriminator and a component type. The collection constructors and the tuple constructor may be nested in an orthogonal way.

Examples: The above value for the type `Set(Sequence(String))` could be represented also with the type

```
Set(Tuple(Town:String,Currency:String))
```

and with the corresponding value

```
Set{Tuple{Town:'Rome', Currency:'Euro'},
    Tuple{Town:'Tokyo', Currency:'Yen'}}.
```

As a further example of a compound attribute using the `Tuple` constructor, we see in the class diagram in Fig. 4.4 the attribute `Name` in class `Employee`, which is a compound attribute with type `Tuple(First:String, Last:String)`.

Role multiplicities: Associations may be restricted by specifying multiplicities. In a binary association, the multiplicity on the other side of a given class restricts the number of objects of the other class to which a given object may be connected. In a simple form, the multiplicity is given as an integer interval `low..high` (with `low≤high`), which expresses that every object of the given class must be connected to at least `low` objects and at most `high` objects of the opposite class. The `high` specification may be given as `*`, indicating no higher bound. A single integer `i` denotes the interval `i..i`, and `*` is short for `0..*`. The multiplicity specification may consist of more than one interval.

Examples: The multiplicity `1` on the role `supporter` indicates that an object of the class `Dependent` must be linked to exactly one object of the class `Employee` via the association `EmployeeDependent`.

Association classes: Associations may be viewed again as classes, leading to the concept of an association class. Association classes are shown with a class rectangle and are connected to the association (represented by a line or a rhomb) with a dashed line. Association classes open the possibility of assigning attributes to associations.

Examples: The association `ProjectWorker` is modeled also as a class: `ProjectWorker` is an association class. This makes it possible to assign the attribute `PercentageOfTime` to the association `ProjectWorker`. In the class diagram, `ProjectWorker` can be found redundantly as the class name and as the association name. The specification as the class name would be sufficient.

Generalizations: Generalizations [23] are represented in UML with directed lines having an unfilled small triangle pointing to the more general class. Usually the more specific class inherits the properties from the more general class. Generalizations are known in the database context also as ISA (IS-A) hierarchies. In the

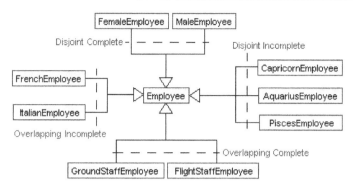

Fig. 4.6 Different example generalizations and specializations in UML

programming language context often the notion of inheritance shows up. Viewed from the more general class, its more specific classes are its specializations. In general, a class may have many specializations, and a class may have many generalizations. A set of generalizations may be restricted to being disjoint and a set of generalizations may be classified as complete. The classification disjoint means that no two specific classes are allowed to have a common instance. The label complete means that every instance of the general class is also an instance of at least one more specific class. The explicit keywords overlapping and incomplete may be attached to sets of generalizations for which no respective restriction is made.

Examples: Figure 4.6 shows different specializations of the class Employee. The subclasses FemaleEmployee and MaleEmployee represent a disjoint and complete classification. The subclasses CapricornEmployee, Aquarius Employee, and PiscesEmployee classify employees according to their birthday (December 22–January 20, 21 January–19 February, 20 February–20 March, respectively). This classification is disjoint but incomplete. The subclasses Ground StaffEmployee and FlightStaffEmployee in the context of an airline company are labeled overlapping and complete because each airline employee either works on the ground or during a flight and, for example, a steward is allowed to work on the ground during boarding and of course during the flight. The subclasses FrenchEmployee and ItalianEmployee are overlapping because employees may have two citizenships, but it is incomplete because, e.g., Swiss employees are not taken into account.

Special care must be devoted to the classifications overlapping and incom plete. As already stated, they represent the general case and no restriction is made by these classifications. But the wording could improperly suggest that an overlap *must* exist and the incompletion *must* occur, although this is not the case. Altogether, overlapping and incomplete in the class diagram would accept an object diagram that is disjoint and complete, but disjoint and complete in the class diagram would not accept an object diagram being overlapping or incomplete.

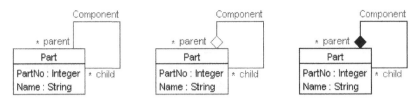

Fig. 4.7 Component as association, aggregation, and composition

Aggregations: Part–whole relationships [23] are available in UML class diagrams in two forms. The first form represents a loose binding between the part and the whole, while the second form realizes a stronger binding. Both forms can be understood as binary associations with additional restrictions. The first form, called aggregation, is drawn with a hollow rhomb on the whole side and is often called a white diamond. The second form, called composition, is drawn with a filled rhomb on the whole side and is often called a black diamond. The links in an object diagram belonging to a class diagram with a part–whole relationship must be acyclic if one regards the links as directed edges going from the whole to the part. This embodies the idea that no part can include itself as a subpart. Such cyclic links are allowed, however, for arbitrary associations. Part objects from an aggregation are allowed to be shared by two whole objects, whereas this is forbidden for composition.

Examples: The class diagrams in Fig. 4.7 show on the left the association `Component` already introduced and on the right two alternatives in which the association is classified as an aggregation with a white diamond and as a composition with a black diamond, respectively. Recall that roles are essential in reflexive as-

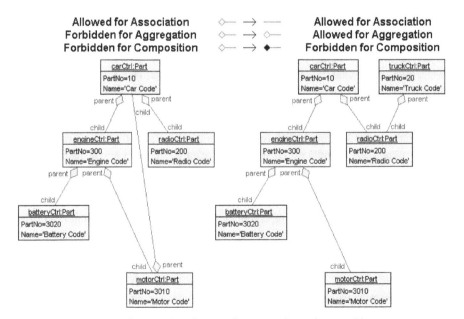

Fig. 4.8 Forbidden and allowed object diagrams for aggregation and composition

sociations and therefore in reflexive part–whole relationships. Here the `parent` objects play the whole role and the `child` objects play the part role. The two object diagrams in Fig. 4.8 explain the differences between association, aggregation, and composition. The diamonds are shown as gray diamonds, a symbol that does *not* exist in UML. We will discuss what happens if the gray diamond is substituted by a white or black one. If the gray diamond is replaced by a white diamond, the left object diagram is forbidden because there is a cycle in the part–whole links that would mean that the object `carCtrl` is a part of itself. This would also hold for the other two objects in the cycle. Recall that if we were to have a simple association instead of the gray diamond, this object diagram would be allowed. If the gray diamond were replaced by a white diamond, the right object diagram would be an allowed object diagram. Here, the object `radioCtrl` is shared by the objects `carCtrl` and `truckCtrl`. Naturally, if the gray diamond became an association, the right object diagram would be allowed as well.

Compositions: Compositions pose further restrictions on the possible links in addition to the required acyclicity. Part objects from a composition cannot be shared by two whole objects. Table 4.3 gives an overview of association, aggregation, and composition properties.

Table 4.3 Overview of properties of associations, aggregations, and compositions

	Acyclicity	Prohibition of sharing
Association	−	−
Aggregation	+	−
Composition	+	+

Examples: Let us now discuss what happens in Fig. 4.8 if the gray diamond is substituted in order to represent compositions. If the gray diamond is replaced by a black diamond, the left object diagram is again forbidden because there is a cycle in the part–whole links. If the gray diamond is replaced by a black diamond, the right object diagram is a forbidden object diagram for compositions because the sharing of objects is not allowed in that case. To show also a positive example of composition and aggregation, we state that, if we remove the link from `motorCtrl` to `carCtrl` in the left object diagram, we get a valid object diagram for composition and aggregation.

Data types and enumeration types: UML offers a collection of predefined data types with common operations on them. The data types include `Integer`, `Real`, `String`, and `Boolean`. Application-dependent enumeration types can also be defined in a class diagram. The enumeration type name is followed by the list of allowed enumeration literals. Enumeration types can be used as attribute, operation parameter, or operation return types.

Examples: Figure 4.9 shows two enumeration types useful in the context of our example. The type `Gender` may represent the gender of an employee and the type `CivilStatus` his or her civil status.

Fig. 4.9 Enumerations in UML

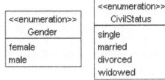

Invariants: OCL allows the developer to specify invariants, i.e., conditions that must be true during the complete lifetime of an object (or perhaps more precisely, at least, in moments when no activity in the object takes place). Such invariants are implicitly or explicitly universally quantified OCL formulas introduced with the keyword `context`.

Example: In order to require that employees have an age of at least 18, one could state the following invariant:

```
context Employee inv EmployeeAreAtLeast18: Age>=18
```

That constraint has an implicit variable `self` of type `Employee` and is equivalent to

```
context self:Employee inv EmployeeAreAtLeast18:
  self.Age>=18
```

Instead of `self` we could have used any other name for the variable, e.g., the variable e. The invariant corresponds to the following OCL formula, which must be true in all system states:

```
Employee.allInstances->forAll(self|self.age>=18)
```

4.3.2 Representation of Standard ER Modeling Concepts

This section explains how those basic ER modeling concepts that do not need OCL can be expressed in UML class diagrams. Some more advanced ER modeling concepts needing OCL, e.g., primary keys or computed attributes, are explained later when OCL is also used.

The main concepts from the ER model have a direct representation in UML class diagrams. The ER diagram in Fig. 4.10 shows the ER representation of what has been shown in the UML class diagram in Fig. 4.4.

- Standard entities are represented in the ER notation and in the UML as rectangles. In the ER notation, single lines are used for ordinary entities and double lines for dependent entities.
- In the ER approach, binary relationships and n-ary relationships are shown as rhombs with the relationship name within the rhomb. Binary relationships are pictured as lines in the UML. N-ary relationships in UML are shown with small

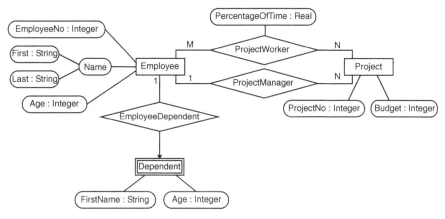

Fig. 4.10 Example ER diagram

rhombs. The relationship respectively association name is given close to, but not inside, the rhomb.

- Simple ER cardinalities (called multiplicities in UML) as in the example diagram can equivalently be shown with the UML multiplicities 0..* and 1. But be warned: The ER notation with intervals as in (0,*) is placed differently in the ER approach and UML.

  In the context of relationships, we emphasize that relationship names are usually mandatory in the ER approach. Association names are, however, optional in the UML in general. This fact shows that relationships play a more important role in ER than associations in the UML. One reason for this may be seen in the fact that one generates relational schemas from relationships and one needs names for these schemas.
- Standard attributes have an extra symbol in ER, but the attributes are integrated into the class rectangle in UML.
- Roles are shown in a similar way in ER and UML, although we have not explicitly shown them in the ER approach.
- Weak entities depicted in ER as double-lined rectangles do not have an explicit notation in UML but may be expressed with a 1..* multiplicity. In addition, the owning entity could indicate ownership with a black diamond. Additional OCL constraints that are discussed in the next section will govern the object identification.
- ISA hierarchies [23] from ER may be represented in UML with generalizations and additional constraints. Union, disjoint, overlapping, and partitioned ISA hierarchies as discussed in the ER literature correspond to generalizations with constraints, as shown in Table 4.4.
- Compound and multivalued attributes are realized in UML with the Tuple and collection constructors Set, Bag, and Sequence.
- Mandatory or optional participation in relationships is expressed in UML with multiplicities.

Table 4.4 Correspondence between ISA hierarchies and UML constraints

ISA notion	UML notion
Union	Complete and overlapping
Disjoint	Complete and disjoint
Overlapping	Incomplete and overlapping
Partitioned	Incomplete and disjoint

- Part–whole relationships [23] have been proposed in the ER approach with several notations. Part–whole relationships are represented in UML with a white or black diamond.

4.4 Employing OCL for Conceptual Schemas

This section will explain the use of UML extension concepts like constraints and stereotypes for standard ER concepts such as keys and derived and computed attributes. The section will also show how to utilize queries that are executed on sample database states during database schema development.

4.4.1 Standard ER Concepts Expressed with OCL

Keys: An identification mechanism for objects is probably a very fundamental application of OCL within conceptual modeling. In databases, objects often possess a set of attributes that identify an object uniquely.

Example: In the running example, we assume `Employee` objects are identified by the attribute `EmployeeNo`. This is expressed in OCL as follows.

```
context e1:Employee inv EmployeeNoIsKey:
  Employee.allInstances->forAll(e2|
    e1<>e2 implies e1.EmployeeNo<>e2.EmployeeNo)
```

Alternatively and equivalently, we could state the implication the other way around:

```
context e1:Employee inv EmployeeNoIsKey:
  Employee.allInstances->forAll(e2|
    e1.EmployeeNo=e2.EmployeeNo implies e1=e2)
```

We emphasize that within the context of an object-oriented data model like the one from UML, there is a difference between specifying no keys at all and designating the set of all attributes as the key. Assume `Part` objects are identified by the combination of the part number and the name. Recall that name and part number are the only attributes of the class `Part`.

```
context p1:Part inv NamePartNoIsKey:
  Part.allInstances->forAll(p2|
    p1<>p2 implies
      (p1.Name<>p2.Name or p1.PartNo<>p2.PartNo))
```

Requiring this invariant is different from giving no key specification, because with this invariant it is not possible to have two different `Part` objects with the same `PartNo` and `Name`. But this is possible in a model where no keys are specified.

In order to represent the identification of `Dependent` objects in the spirit of the ER model, the key restriction for class `Dependent` would look as follows:

```
context d1:Dependent inv FirstNameEmployeeNoIsKey:
  Dependent.allInstances->forAll(d2| d1<>d2 implies
    (d1.FirstName<>d2.FirstName or
    d1.supporter.EmployeeNo<>d2.supporter.EmployeeNo))
```

As a variation, a similar requirement could be stated using an inequality on `Employee` objects.

```
context d1:Dependent inv FirstNameEmployeeNoIsKey:
  Dependent.allInstances->forAll(d2| d1<>d2 implies
    (d1.FirstName<>d2.FirstName or
    d1.supporter<>d2.supporter))
```

Further possibilities for conceptual modeling of keys are discussed in [9].

Derived or computed attributes: We have discussed compound and multivalued attributes above. Another variation for attributes are so-called derived or computed attributes. Derived respectively computed attributes can be realized in OCL with an invariant or with a derivation rule within an operation.

Example: Assume we want to record for `Part` objects the number of direct (not indirect) children the respective `Part` object has with respect to the `Component` association. This could be realized with an invariant assuming the class `Part` has an additional attribute `NumOfChildren` or as a definition of an additional operation `NumOfChildren()`:

```
context Part inv NumOfChildrenDerived:
  NumOfChildren=self.child->size()
Part::NumOfChildren()=self.child->size()
```

4.4.2 Constraints and Stereotypes

General OCL invariants may be employed for conceptual modeling in order to describe integrity constraints for a conceptual schema. UML makes it possible to denote such invariants in explicit form or the constraints may be indicated as a shortcut by using stereotypes.

Keys as stereotypes: Because certain kinds of constraints appear frequently in conceptual modeling, it makes sense to indicate this recurring structure by indicating the constraints only with stereotypes. A very good example for this are keys. At least two alternative notations for key stereotypes can be conceptualized: (1) indicating for each attribute separately whether it contributes to the key or (2) indicating the set of key constituents as a whole.

Example: For the running example, key specifications for selected classes could look as shown in Fig. 4.11. In the class `Employee` the key consists of the attribute `EmployeeNo`. For `Part`, the key is made of `PartNo` and `Name`. The key for `Dependent` consists of `FirstName` and the reference to the key of the supporter.

Alternative keys could be indicated similar to the above-mentioned key stereotype notation (2) in which the complete set of alternative key attributes would be indicated as a whole. As a side remark, we mention that the underlining of attributes in UML class diagrams, which is used in some ER notations to indicate keys, already has a fixed, different meaning in UML: Underlined attributes indicate class attributes that, in contrast to ordinary object attributes, describe properties of the class and not properties of the single instances belonging to the class.

Stereotypes for general invariants: Due to UML's and OCL's flexibility, apart from keys, various useful patterns for invariants could be provided by stereotypes, e.g., attribute restrictions, commutativity restrictions, and existence dependencies.

• Attribute restrictions could be an alternative for enumeration types with the additional advantage that respective operations would be applicable then as well. For example, an attribute `month:Integer` could be restricted by a stereotype «`1..12`».
• Commutativity restrictions could indicate that two paths in the class diagram are commutative in the sense that the two paths either yield the same result or that the result of one path is included in the other. Given the context of a particular class and appropriate roles, for example, `self.role1.role2=self.role3` would require that the results of the two expressions involving the roles coincide. Instead of requiring equality, one could allow that one specifies an inclusion with the stereotype «`subset`». For example, within the context of the class

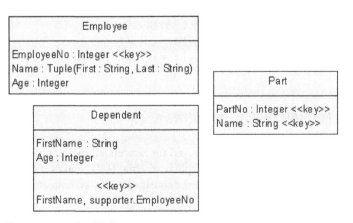

Fig. 4.11 Keys represented as UML stereotypes

Employee, the requirement `self.managedProject «subset» self.project` would express that a manager works on her or his projects.

- Existence dependencies, like that for `Dependent` objects, could be specified by providing a term indicating the master object the slave object depends on. For example, within the context of the class `Dependent` the term `self.supporter` within the class rectangle in a special section labeled «dependency» could indicate that for each `Dependent` object, a supporting employee must exist. In easy cases like the one above, dependencies can also be shown with a multiplicity specification.

- Apart from these application-specific constraints, the UML provides a standard constraint for requiring that two or more associations exclude each other with the keyword `xor` and a standard constraint expressing that one association is included in the other by using the keyword `subset`.

Transitive closure: By means of appropriate operations it is possible in UML and OCL to define the transitive closure as a built-in language. Any property `C::prop:Set(C)` for a class `C` can be extended to `C::propPlus:Set(C)` for yielding the transitive closure and to `C::propStar:Set(C)` for yielding the transitive and reflexive closures. One would automatically extend the model with appropriate operations as indicated below:

```
C::propPlus():Set(C)=propPlusAux(self.prop)
C::propPlusAux(aSet:Set(C)):Set(C)=
   let oneStep:Set(C)=aSet.prop->asSet() in
   if oneStep->exists(p|aSet->excludes(p)) then
      propPlusAux(aSet->union(oneStep)) else aSet endif
C::propStar():Set(C)=propPlus()->including(self)
```

This notation can be generalized to bags and sequences.

Example: The requirement that no `Part` object can be connected to itself with a chain of `Component` links in the `child` direction could be stated as follows:

```
context p:Part inv ComponentNotReflexive:
   not(p.childPlus->includes(p))
```

General constraints: Apart from constraints indicated with stereotypes, one can naturally employ the invariant mechanism of OCL and define special, application-dependent invariants.

Examples: Above we discussed what would happen if the association `Project Manager` were to be replaced by two object-valued attributes in the participating classes. In order to only allow similar object diagrams as in the model with the association, one would need then the following two invariants:

```
context Employee inv ManagerManagesOwnProjects:
   managedProject->forAll(p|p.manager=self)
context Project inv ProjectManagedByProjectManager:
   manager.managedProject->includes(self))
```

Note that, in general, both directions of the constraint, and not only one direction, have to be stated.

Another example of a general constraint concerns the attribute `Percentage OfTime` in the relationship `ProjectWorker`. The sum of percentages for a single employee should not be more than 100%:

```
context Employee inv SumPercentageOfTimeLessEqual100:
   self.projectWorker.PercentageOfTime->sum()<=100
```

With respect to this constraint, the object diagram from Fig. 4.5 is invalid because the sum of ada's project participation is 110%.

The above example also shows one OCL feature that we have not covered yet: In the context of association classes it is possible to navigate from a participating class to the association class and also from the association class to the participating classes. Above, the role `projectWorker` is a property within the class `Employee` having the result type `Set(ProjectWorker)`.

4.4.3 Queries

OCL also supports the formulation of queries. Ordinary SQL following the select-from-where pattern would be formulated in OCL obeying an allInstances-select-collect pattern.

Example: Find the employee numbers of employees having at least two dependents.

```
select EmployeeNo
from   Employee
where  exists
          (select *
           from   Dependent d1, Dependent d2
           where  d1.EmployeeNo=d2.EmployeeNo and
                  d1.EmployeeNo=Employee.EmployeeNo and
                  d1.FirstName<>d2.FirstName)

Employee.allInstances->
  select(dependent->
    exists(d1,d2|d1.FirstName<>d2.FirstName))->
      collect(EmployeeNo)

Employee.allInstances->
  select(e:Employee|e.dependent->
    exists(d1,d2|d1.FirstName<>d2.FirstName))->
      collect(EmployeeNo)
```

The SQL query, which is formulated on a relational database schema, uses a subquery to filter the result and a select clause to indicate which attributes are wanted.

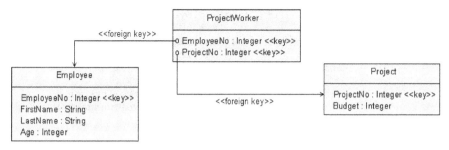

Fig. 4.12 Foreign keys represented graphically with UML stereotypes

In OCL, one starts with an `allInstances` expression, then filters the objects with a select expression, and finally obtains the desired attributes with a collect expression.

4.5 Describing Relational Schemas with UML

This section will show how relational schemas are represented in UML. Constraints and stereotypes will represent primary keys and foreign keys.

4.5.1 Relational Schemas

Relational schemas in UML: There are radically different alternatives for representing relational schemas in UML. (1) One might represent each entity and each relationship from the conceptual schema as a separate class, or (2) one could use the type constructors offered by OCL (like `Tuple` and `Set`) and represent the entire database as a single complex value. There are other solutions that lie between these extreme points. We will further follow an alternative in which a relational schema is represented by a class; however, we will briefly also explain the other extreme.

   Example: Let us consider only the two entities `Employee` and `Project` together with their relationship `ProjectWorker`, and let us further assume that we translate this into three relational schemas. If we give a separate class for each entity and each relationship, we achieve the representation in Fig. 4.12. If we represent the three relational schemas with a complex value, we achieve the structure in Fig. 4.13. Primary and foreign keys would have to be formulated additionally as OCL invariants.

```
DB:Tuple(Employee:Set(Tuple(EmployeeNo:Integer,
                             FirstName:String,
                             LastName:String,
                             Age:Integer)),
         Project:Set(Tuple(ProjectNo:Integer,
                           Budget:Integer)),
         ProjectWorker:Set(Tuple(EmployeeNo:Integer,
                                 ProjectNo:Integer)))
```

Fig. 4.13 Relational schemas as complex value

4.5.2 Constraints for Primary and Foreign Keys

Representing primary keys and foreign keys: Primary keys in a relational schema can be shown with a stereotype as primary keys in the conceptual schema. For the representation of foreign keys there are again two alternatives, a graphical one and a textual one. (1) In the graphical solution, the relational schema possessing the foreign key would point to the relational schema in which the referenced primary key occurs. Technically, this *pointing to* would be a UML dependency pictured in graphical form using a stereotype. (2) In the textual solution, the relational schema possessing the foreign key would indicate the relational schema in which the referenced primary key occurs. On the technical level, this would again be a UML dependency, but this time displayed in textual form.

Example: Figures 4.12 and 4.14 show the graphical and textual alternatives for the example. The graphical alternative has the advantage of visually showing the connection between the relational schemas. But the graphical representation also has the disadvantage that it becomes more complicated, and even not understandable, if the foreign key consists of more than one attribute and if additionally the foreign key references attributes in the same relational schema.

Stereotypes for primary keys and foreign keys are only shortcuts for more involved OCL invariants not explicitly shown, but being present behind the visual representation. In our example, we would have that the stereotypes are shortcuts for the following OCL invariants:

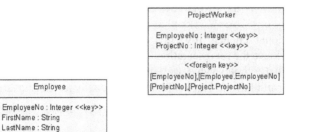

Fig. 4.14 Foreign keys represented textually with UML stereotypes

```
context e1:Employee inv EmployeeNoIsKey:
  Employee.allInstances->forAll(e2 |
    e1<>e2 implies e1.EmployeeNo<>e2.EmployeeNo)
context p1:Project inv ProjectNoIsKey:
  Project.allInstances->forAll(p2 |
    p1<>p2 implies p1.ProjectNo<>p2.ProjectNo)
context pw1:ProjectWorker inv EmployeeProjectNoIsKey:
  ProjectWorker.allInstances->forAll(pw2 |
    pw1<>pw2 implies
      (pw1.EmployeeNo<>pw2.EmployeeNo or
       pw1.ProjectNo<>pw2.ProjectNo))
context pw:ProjectWorker inv EmployeeNoIsForeignKey:
  Employee.allInstances->exists(e |
    pw.EmployeeNo=e.EmployeeNo)
context pw:ProjectWorker inv ProjectNoIsForeignKey:
  Project.allInstances->exists(p |
    pw.ProjectNo=p.ProjectNo)
```

As a final remark, we emphasize that foreign keys are *not* associations because an association would imply that it will be manifested by links, which is not true for foreign keys. Foreign keys are dependencies and can be represented by stereotypes. We also emphasize that we represent relational schemas as classes. In this UML representation, there are no associations or relationships, only dependencies.

4.6 Metamodeling Data Models with UML

This section studies a UML metamodel for the ER and the relational data model. UML is well suited for the description of metamodels. We start by describing the syntax of the ER data model through the introduction of classes for ER schemas, entities, and relationships. We also describe the semantics of the ER data model by introducing classes for ER states, instances, and links. The connection between syntax and semantics is established by associations explaining that syntactical objects are interpreted by corresponding semantical objects. Analogously this is done for the relational data model. The CWM metamodel from [17] is, to a certain extent, comparable to our approach. However, there only the syntax of data models is treated, not the interpretation of database schemas as in our approach.

4.6.1 Class Diagram

Consider the class diagram in Fig. 4.15. It shows four *packages*: in the left part a solid gray and a solid black package, in the right part a dashed gray and a dashed black package. The two solid left packages model the syntax of the data models,

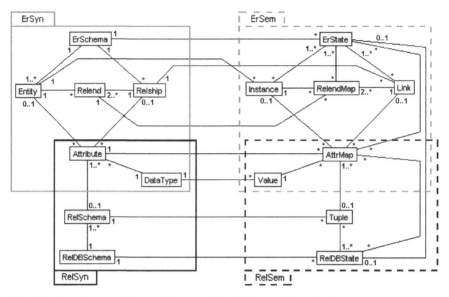

Fig. 4.15 Class Diagram Metamodeling the ER and Relational Data Model

the two dashed right packages the semantics; the upper two packages describe the ER data model, the lower two packages the relational data model. The ER and relational data models share some concepts, namely, the parts in the middle specifying data types, attributes, and their semantics. We have indicated the multiplicities in the class diagram. All role names are identical to the respective class, with the first letter of the class name converted to a lower case letter, e.g., we have the role names `dataType` and `relDBSchema`. The various parts of this class diagram will be explained below with the scenario from Fig. 4.16 and the object diagrams in Figs. 4.17–4.20.

Syntax of the ER data model: This part introduces the classes `ErSchema`, `Entity`, `Relship`, `Relend`, `Attribute`, and `DataType`. `ErSchema` objects consist of `Entity` and `Relship` objects, which in turn may possess `Attribute` objects typed through `DataType` objects. `Relend` objects represent the connection points between the `Relship` objects and the `Entity` objects.

Semantics of the ER data model: In this part we set up the classes `ErState`, `Instance`, `Link`, `RelendMap`, `AttrMap`, and `Value`. The interpretation is as follows. An `ErSchema` object is interpreted by possibly many `ErState` objects. An `Entity` is given semantics by a set of `Instance` objects, and a `Relship` by a set of `Link` objects. `DataType` objects are given life through a set of `Value` objects. `Relend` and `Attribute` objects are interpreted by a set of `RelendMap` objects and `AttrMap` objects, respectively.

Syntax of the relational data model: Here the classes `RelDBSchema`, `Rel Schema`, `Attribute`, and `DataType` are needed. `RelDBSchema` objects

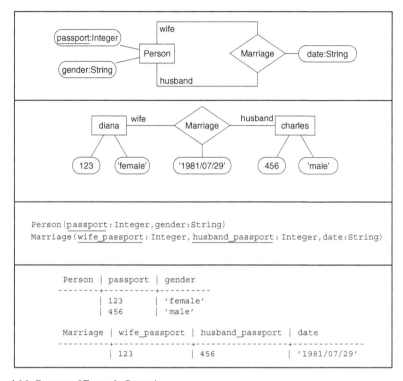

Fig. 4.16 Content of Example Scenario

consist of `RelSchema` objects that possess `Attribute` objects typed through `DataType` objects.

Semantics of the relational data model: The last part utilizes the classes `Rel-DBState`, `Tuple`, `AttrMap`, and `Value`. `RelDBSchema` objects are interpreted by a set of `RelDBState` objects. Each `RelDBState` object consists of a set of `Tuple` objects that are typed by a `RelSchema`. `Tuple` objects in turn consist of a set of `AttrMap` objects assigning a `Value` object to an `Attribute` within the `Tuple`.

Let us briefly mention the attributes and operations that are relevant for the class diagram but not displayed. All classes in the (left) syntax part possess an attribute name of data type `String`. The class `Attribute` has an additional boolean-valued attribute `isKey` indicating whether this attribute contributes to the key of the `Entity` or the `RelSchema`. The class `Value` possesses the attribute `content` of data type `String`, indicating the actual content of the `Value` object.

Concerning operations, the classes `Instance`, `Link`, and `Tuple` have an operation `applyAttr()` with a `State` and an `Attribute` parameter returning the actual `Value` object of the `Attribute`. The class `Link` has an operation `applyRelend()` with an `ErState` and a `Relend` parameter returning the ac-

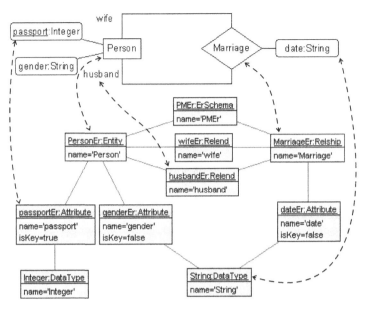

Fig. 4.17 Viewing the example scenario as an ER schema

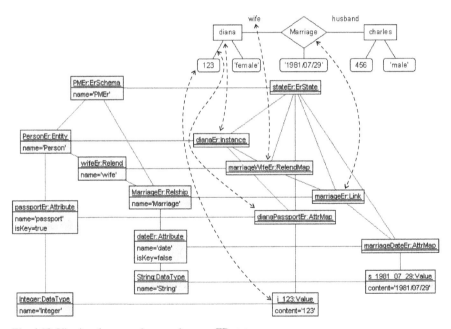

Fig. 4.18 Viewing the example scenario as an ER state

tual `Instance` of the `Relend`. The classes `Entity` and `RelSchema` possess an operation `key()` returning the set of its key attributes.

4.6.2 Object Diagrams

The modeling is best explained by an example. Figure 4.16 shows an example scenario that is represented in Fig. 4.17 as an ER schema, in Fig. 4.18 as an ER state, in Fig. 4.19 as a relational schema, and in Fig. 4.20 as a relational state.

Syntax of the ER data model: Figure 4.17 shows the metamodel representation of the example ER schema. There is one `ErSchema` object connected to one `Entity` and one `Relship` object. The two `Relend` objects connect the `Relship` with the `Entity`. The three attributes stand in connection with the `Entity` resp. `Relship` on which they are defined and with the `DataType` of the respective attribute. We regard the upper representation as the concrete syntax of the ER schema and the lower representation in the form of an object diagram as the abstract syntax.

Semantics of the ER data model: Figure 4.18 displays on the left a part of the ER schema and on the right semantic objects instantiating the objects from the ER schema on the left. The semantic objects are typed by horizontal links going to the left. The `ErState` is typed by an `ErSchema`, the `Instance` by an `Entity`, the `Link` by a `Relship`, the `RelendMap` object by a `Relend` object, each `AttrMap` object by an `Attribute` object, and each `Value` object

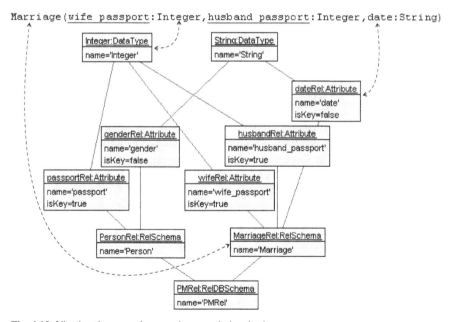

Fig. 4.19 Viewing the example scenario as a relational schema

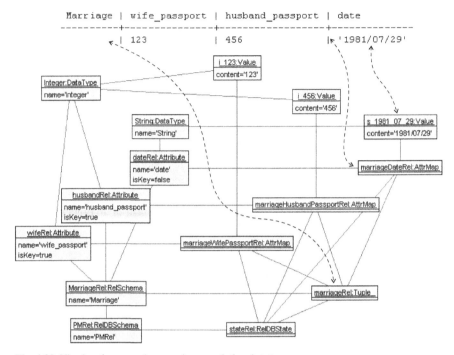

Fig. 4.20 Viewing the example scenario as a relational state

by a `DataType` object. In order to be comprehensible, this left part does not show the complete ER state, but only a part of it.

Syntax of the relational data model: Figure 4.19 represents the relational database schema with two relational schemas. The first relational schema has two attributes, and the second one three attributes. All five attributes are typed by appropriate data types.

Semantics of the relational data model: Figure 4.20 gives a part of the relational database state. Only one tuple with three components, i.e., with three `AttrMap` objects, is shown. The three `Value` objects are typed with links into the left syntax part. For example, the two `Value` objects `i_123` and `i_456` are connected to the `DataType` object `Integer`.

4.6.3 Constraints

The multiplicities in the class diagram constrain the valid object diagrams and are so-called model-inherent constraints. Apart from these constraints, all parts in the class diagram must be restricted by appropriate explicit constraints. In total we obtain about 50 constraints. We do not go into the details here, which can be found in [10], but show only one typical example from each of the four parts.

Syntax of the ER data model: Within one `Entity`, different `Attributes` have different names.

```
context self:Entity inv uniqueAttributeNamesWithinEntity:
  self.attribute->forAll(a1,a2 |
    a1<>a2 implies a1.name<>a2.name)
```

Thus we would obtain an invalid ER schema if we changed the `name` attribute of the `genderEr` object from `'gender'` to `'passport'` in Fig. 4.17.

Semantics of the ER data model: Two different `Instances` of one `Entity` can be distinguished in every `ErState` (where both `Instances` occur) by a key `Attribute` of the `Entity`.

```
context self:Instance inv keyMapUnique:
  Instance.allInstances->forAll(self2 |
    self<>self2 and self.entity=self2.entity
    implies
    self.erState->intersection(self2.erState)->forAll(s |
      self.entity.key()->exists(ka |
        self.applyAttr(s,ka)<>self2.applyAttr(s,ka))))
```

One would achieve an invalid ER state if we changed the `content` attribute of the `i_123` object from `'123'` to `'456'`, because there is another `Instance` object (not shown in Fig. 4.18), namely, `charlesEr`, with `passport` number `'456'`, and `passport` is the only key attribute in the example ER schema.

Syntax of the relational data model: The set of key `Attributes` of a `Rel-Schema` is not empty:

```
context self:RelSchema inv relSchemaKeyNotEmpty:
  self.key()->notEmpty
```

We would get an invalid relational schema if we changed the `isKey` attribute of the `passportRel` object from `true` to `false`, because then the relational schema named `Person` would not have any key attributes.

Semantics of the relational data model: As shown in Fig. 4.21, the `Attributes` connected to the `RelSchema` of a `Tuple` are identical to the `Attributes` connected to the `AttrMap` of the `Tuple`. In other words, there are attribute assignments for all `Attributes` of a `Tuple` (and for only those).

```
context self:Tuple inv commutativityAttribute:
  self.relSchema.attribute=self.attrMap.attribute->asSet
```

We would obtain an invalid relational state if we deleted the `marriage-WifePassportRel` object. Then there would exist an `Attribute` with the name `wife_passport`, which is present in the relational schema named

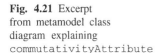

Fig. 4.21 Excerpt from metamodel class diagram explaining `commutativityAttribute`

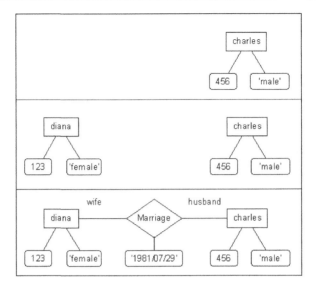

Fig. 4.22 Three consecutive ER states

`Marriage`, but one tuple for this relational schema would miss the attribute assignment for the attribute `wife_passport`, i.e., there would be no corresponding `AttrMap` object.

Our example scenario included only one ER state, namely, an ER state where two entities and one relationship connection are present. The metamodel is, however, more general in the sense that not only can one ER state be described, but it is possible to link several ER states to a single ER schema. For example, the three ER states displayed in Fig.4.22, together with the corresponding ER schema, could be represented as a single object diagram in the metamodel.

Apart from describing the data models, it is also possible to give a metamodel for the transformation of ER schemas into relational database schemas. We will not go into details here but only refer to the detailed metamodel, which can be found in [10]. By characterizing the syntax and semantics of the data models and also the transformation itself within the same (meta-)modeling language, one can include equivalence criteria on the syntactic and semantic levels for the transformation. In particular, one can give a semantic equivalence criterion requiring that the ER states and the corresponding relational states carry the same information.

4.7 Further Related Work

Relevant related work has been mentioned already in the respective chapters. In addition, we want to point to the following books and papers relating on the one hand UML and conceptual modeling and on the other hand UML and constraint development. Further relevant literature can be found by using the "Complete Search'; facility on DBLP by searching with "Conceptual UML Model" or "UML Database Design," for example.

An early approach to developing databases with object-oriented design techniques is given in [4]. Comparisons between designing (database) schemas and class diagrams with UML and with ORM are discussed in [13, 14]. Object-oriented and object-relational schemas described with UML and other object-oriented techniques are studied in [2, 15, 24]. The work in [1] proposes a UML profile for database design, whereas in [26] a UML profile for conceptual modeling in connection with data warehouses is worked out.

Constraints and OCL have been used for conceptual modeling since the early days of UML. [8] treats the transformation of OCL constraints into relational database requirements. The textbook [16] uses OCL and UML in a radical way for all facets of conceptual modeling. [22] discusses the impact of MOF on developing database schemas. [5] is a further approach using OCL for conceptual modeling that proposes special treatment of typical, schematic integrity constraints. [7] emphasizes the incremental development of OCL constraints.

4.8 Conclusions

This contribution has explained how UML can be employed for conceptual modeling of information systems. On the one hand, UML supports all classical features of the ER model, and on the other hand, more advanced features like part–whole relationships are expressible as well. Within UML, the textual constraint and query language OCL is available. OCL has many similarities to SQL.

However, support for conceptual modeling within UML can be improved in a number of ways. Proposals have been advanced for a UML profile for data modeling, but an overall accepted solution is still missing. Such a profile should take into account data modeling on various abstraction levels, e.g., the conceptual, the logical, and the physical levels. Complete metamodeling of these data models respecting syntactic and semantic aspects is another open issue. One reason for the success of the relational model is probably the well-studied relationship between descriptive languages like tuple or domain calculus and operationally effective languages like relational algebra. OCL as a central ingredient for conceptual modeling and as a descriptive language within UML would benefit from a clear relationship to an operationally effective UML execution language.

Appendix A: Original ER Diagram from Chen's Paper

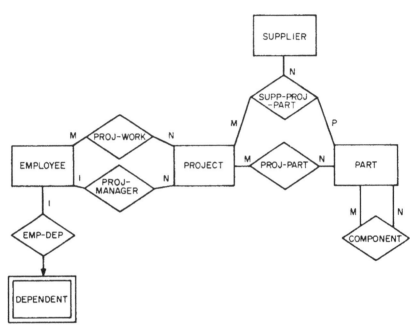

Fig. 4.23 Original ER diagram from Chen's paper

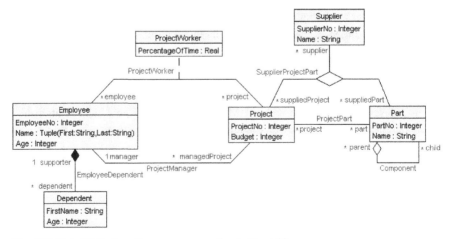

Fig. 4.24 Plain UML class diagram corresponding to Fig. 4.23

```
context e1:Employee inv EmployeeNoIsKey:
  Employee.allInstances->forAll(e2|
    e1<>e2 implies e1.EmployeeNo<>e2.EmployeeNo)
-- above invariant analogously for other classes
context d1:Dependent inv FirstNameEmployeeNoIsKey:
  Dependent.allInstances->forAll(d2| d1<>d2 implies
    (d1.FirstName<>d2.FirstName or
    d1.supporter.EmployeeNo<>d2.supporter.EmployeeNo))
```

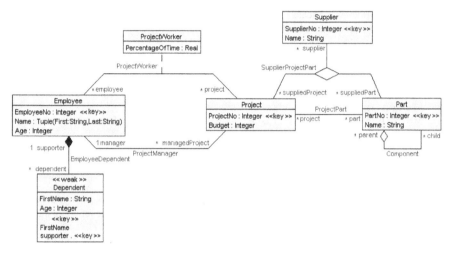

Fig. 4.25 Stereotyped UML class diagram corresponding to Fig. 4.23

References

1. Ambler SW (2009) A UML profile for data modeling. Technical report, AgileData.org. www.agiledata.org/essays/umlDataModelingProfile.html
2. Abrahão SM, Poels G, Pastor O (2006) A functional size measurement method for object-oriented conceptual schemas: design and evaluation issues. Softw Syst Model 5(1):48–71
3. Büttner F, Gogolla M, Hamann L, Kuhlmann M, Lindow A (2010) On better understanding OCL collections *or* an OCL ordered set is not an OCL set. In: Ghosh S (ed) Workshops and symposia at the 12th international conference on model-driven engineering languages and systems (MODELS'2009). Lecture notes in computer science, vol 6002. Springer, Berlin, pp 276–290
4. Blaha M, Premerlani W (1998) Object-oriented modeling and design for database applications. Prentice-Hall, Englewood Cliffs
5. Costal D, Gómez C, Queralt A, Raventós R, Teniente E (208) Improving the definition of general constraints in UML. Softw Syst Model 7(4):469–486
6. Chen PP (1976) The entity-relationship model – toward a unified view of data. ACM Trans Database Syst 1(1):9–36

7. Cabot J, Teniente E (2009) Incremental integrity checking of UML/OCL conceptual schemas. J Syst Softw 82(9):1459–1478
8. Demuth B, Hussmann H, Loecher S (2001) OCL as a specification language for business rules in database applications. In: Gogolla M, Kobryn C (eds) Proceedings of the 4th international conference on Unified Modeling Language (UML'2001), 2001. Lecture notes in computer science, vol 2185. Springer, Berlin, pp 104–117
9. Gogolla M (1999) Identifying objects by declarative queries. In: Papazoglou MP, Spaccapietra S, Tari Z (eds) Advances in object-oriented data modeling. MIT Press, Cambridge, pp 255–277
10. Gogolla M (2005) Tales of ER and RE syntax and semantics. In: Cordy JR, Lämmel R, Winter A (eds) Transformation techniques in software engineering. IBFI, Schloss Dagstuhl. Dagstuhl Seminar Proceedings 05161. 51 pp
11. Gogolla M, Bohling J, Richters M (2005) Validating UML and OCL models in USE by automatic snapshot generation. J Softw Syst Model 4(4):386–398
12. Gogolla M, Büttner F, Richters M (2007) USE: a UML-based specification environment for validating UML and OCL. Sci Comput Programm 69:27–34
13. Halpin TA (2002) Metaschemas for ER, ORM and UML data models: a comparison. J Database Manag 13(2):20–30
14. Halpin TA, Bloesch AC (1999) Data modeling in UML and ORM: a comparison. J Database Manag 10(4):4–13
15. Marcos E, Vela B, Cavero JM (2003) A methodological approach for object-relational database design using UML. Softw Syst Model 2(1):59–75
16. Olive A (2007) Conceptual modeling of information systems. Springer, Berlin
17. OMG (ed) (2003) Common Warehouse Metamodel (CWM) Specification V 1.1. www.omg.org
18. OMG (ed) (2010) Object Constraint Language (OCL) Specification V 2.2. www.omg.org
19. OMG (ed) (2010) Unified Modeling Language (UML) Specification V 2.3. www.omg.org
20. Rumbaugh J, Booch G, Jacobson I (2005) The Unified Modeling Language reference manual, 2nd edn. Addison-Wesley, Reading
21. Richters M, Gogolla M (1998) On formalizing the UML Object Constraint Language OCL. In: Ling T-W, Ram S, Lee ML (eds) Proceedings of the 17th international conference on conceptual modeling (ER'98). Lecture notes in computer science, vol 1507. Springer, Berlin, pp 449–464
22. Raventós R, Olive A (2008) An object-oriented operation-based approach to translation between MOF metaschemas. Data Knowl Eng 67(3):444–462
23. Smith JM, Smith DCP (1977) Database abstractions: aggregation and generalization. ACM Trans Database Syst 2(2):105–133
24. Urban SD, Dietrich SW (2003) Using UML class diagrams for a comparative analysis of relational, object-oriented, and object-relational database mappings. In: Grissom S, Knox D, Joyce D, Dann W (eds) Proceedings of the 34th SIGCSE technical symposium on computer science education (2003). ACM, New York, pp 21–25
25. Warmer J, Kleppe A (2003) The Object Constraint Language: precise modeling with UML, 2nd edn. Addison-Wesley, Reading
26. Zubcoff JJ, Trujillo J (2007) A UML 2.0 profile to design association rule mining models in the multidimensional conceptual modeling of data warehouses. Data Knowl Eng 63(1):44–62

Chapter 5
Mapping Conceptual Models to Database Schemas

David W. Embley and Wai Yin Mok

Abstract From the beginning, a primary objective of conceptual modeling has been to generate good database schemas. This chapter surveys and explains the principles and practices of algorithmically mapping conceptual models to database schemas. An important unifying theme is that the underlying principles are independent of conceptual-modeling languages and notation. Although illustrated mainly in terms of the entity-relationship model, the chapter explains and illustrates the application of the mapping principles to extended entity-relationship models, the unified modeling language, and generic conceptual-model hypergraphs. Besides explaining conceptual-model-independent mapping rules, the chapter also addresses normalization issues, explaining both the map-then-normalize approach and the normalize-then-map approach to schema normalization. In addition to mapping conceptual models to flat relations for standard relational databases, the chapter also shows how to map conceptual models to nested relations applicable for object-based and XML storage structures.

5.1 Introduction

The mapping of a conceptual-model instance to a database schema is fundamentally the same for all conceptual models. A conceptual-model instance describes the relationships and constraints among the various data items. Given the relationships and constraints, the mappings group data items together into flat relational schemas for relational databases and into nested relational schemas for object-based and XML databases.

David W. Embley
Brigham Young University, Provo, Utah 84602, USA, e-mail: embley@cs.byu.edu

Wai Yin Mok
Economics and Information Systems, University of Alabama in Huntsville, Huntsville, Alabama 35899, USA, e-mail: mokw@uah.edu

D. W. Embley and B. Thalheim (eds), *Handbook of Conceptual Modeling.*
DOI 10.1007/978-3-642-15865-0, © Springer 2011

Although we are particularly interested in the basic principles behind the mappings, we take the approach of first presenting them in Sects. 5.2 and 5.3 in terms of mapping an entity-relationship (ER) model to a relational database. In these sections, for the ER constructs involved, we (1) provide examples of the constructs and say what they mean, (2) give rules for mapping the constructs to a relational schema and illustrate the rules with examples, and (3) state the underlying principles. We then take these principles and show in Sect. 5.4 how to apply them to the unified modeling language (UML). This section on UML also serves as a guide to applying the principles to other conceptual models. In Sect. 5.5 we ask and answer the question regarding the circumstances under which the mappings yield normalized relational database schemas. In Sect. 5.6 we extend the mappings beyond flat relations for relational databases and show how to map conceptual-model instances to object-based and XML databases. We provide pointers to additional readings in Sect. 5.7. Throughout, we use an application in which we assume that we are designing a database for a bed-and-breakfast service. To illustrate all conceptual-modeling features of interest, we take the liberty of poetic license in imagining what features might be of interest to the application.

This chapter assumes a solid understanding of several other chapters in this handbook: the entity-relationship model (Chap. 3), the enhanced entity-relationship model (Chap. 6), the unified modeling language (Chap. 4), and the theory of functional dependencies and normalization (as introduced in many database text books, e.g., [11, 13, 15]). We do not extensively discuss any of these topics. We do, however, add enough commentary about these topics to make this chapter reasonably self contained. This chapter also assumes a minimal understanding of the relational data model, SQL, object-oriented databases, object-relational databases, and XML Databases. We make no explanatory comments about these topics.

5.2 Entity-Relationship Model Mappings

5.2.1 Basic Mappings

We give an ER diagram in Fig. 5.1 a and the database schema generated from the ER diagram in Fig. 5.1b. In our bed-and-breakfast application, as modeled in Fig. 5.1, registered guests occupy rooms and are signed up for activities such as golf, tennis, and horseback riding. Although there may be other occupants of a room in a registered guest's party, in this initial example, we only capture each registered guest (presumably the ones who are paying the bill). Further, in this example we only allow a registered guest's party as a whole to sign up for various activities.

Notationally, each box in Fig. 5.1a represents an entity set, e.g., *Room*, *Guest*, and *Activity*. The diamonds with lines connected to entity sets represent relationship sets among the connected entity sets, e.g., *occupies* and *is signed up for*. The ovals

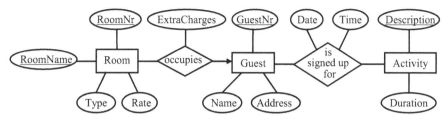

Fig. 5.1 Basic mappings. ER diagram and Generated schemas

represent attributes, e.g., *RoomNr*, *Date*, and *Duration*, which may be connected with either entity sets (boxes) or relationship sets (diamonds).

Cardinality constraints for binary relationship sets are one of the following:

1. *many–many*, indicated by the absence of arrowheads on the lines connecting entity sets and relationship sets, e.g., *is signed up for*;
2. *many–one*, indicated by an arrowhead on the *one* side, e.g., *occupies* is many–one from *Room* to *Guest*, and thus there can be only one registered guest's party occupying a room, although the registered guest's party may occupy one or more rooms;
3. *one–many*, which is the same as many–one, only in the opposite direction, e.g., *occupies* is one–many from *Guest* to *Room*; and
4. *one–one*, indicated by arrowheads on both sides, e.g., *occupies* would be one–one if the bed and breakfast had the policy that a guest's party could occupy at most one room.

Cardinality constraints for attributes are many–one from entity set to attribute or from relationship set to attribute. If an entity-set attribute is a key, however, as indicated by underlining of the attribute name, then the cardinality is one–one. Thus, for example, *Type* is many–one from *Room* to *Type* so that many rooms can be of the same type (e.g., the bed and breakfast can have several single rooms, several double rooms, and several suites). *RoomNr*, on the other hand, is a key attribute for *Room*, and thus each room has one room number and each room number designates one room. *RoomName* is also a key for *Room* (each room has a name such as the "Gold Room" or the "Penthouse Suite"). Although rare, relationship sets may also have keys designated by an underline (e.g., a guarantee number for a guest's room reservation). Relationship sets, of course, have keys, often a composite of the keys for its related entity sets (e.g., {*GuestNr*, *Description*}, which is a composite key[1] for the relationship set *is signed up for*). The standard ER model, however, provides no way to directly designate composite keys for relationship sets.

ER Mapping Rule #1. An entity set E with n key attributes $A_1, \ldots, A_n$ and m nonkey attributes $B_1, \ldots, B_m$ maps to the relational schema $E(\underline{A_1}, \ldots, \underline{A_n}, B_1, \ldots, B_m)$. The underlines designate keys for the relational schema. If there is only one

---

[1] Here and throughout the chapter "composite key" always designates a minimal key, so that if any of the attributes of the key is removed, the remaining attribute(s) no longer provide the unique identification property of a key.

key, it is the primary key; if there are several keys, one is designated as the primary key. ER Mapping Rule #1 applies when E is a regular entity set (i.e., not a weak entity set) and has no entity set E' connected to E by a relationship set that is one–one or is many–one from E to E'.

ER Mapping Rule #1 applies to *Activity* in Fig. 5.1a. *Activity* is a regular entity set (as are all entity sets in Fig. 5.1a), and its only connected relationship set is many–many. When we apply ER Mapping Rule #1 to *Activity*, since *Description* is a key attribute and *Duration* is a nonkey attribute, we obtain *Activity(Description, Duration)*, which is the first relational schema in Fig. 5.1b. ER Mapping Rule #1 also applies to *Guest*, yielding the second relational schema in Fig. 5.1b. ER Mapping Rule #1 does not apply to *Room* because the connected relationship set *occupies* is many–one from *Room* to *Guest*.

ER Mapping Rule #2. Let E be a regular entity set with n key attributes $A_1, \ldots, A_n$, m nonkey attributes $B_1, \ldots, B_m$, and p many–one-connected entity sets whose primary keys are $C_1, \ldots, C_p$, and that have q attributes $D_1, \ldots, D_q$ associated with the p many–one relationship sets. Assuming E has no one–one-connected entity sets, E maps to $E(\underline{A_1}, \ldots, \underline{A_n}, B_1, \ldots, B_m, C_1, \ldots, C_p, D_1, \ldots, D_q)$.

ER Mapping Rule #2 applies to *Room* in Fig. 5.1a. *Room* has two key attributes (*RoomNr* and *RoomName*), two nonkey attributes (*Type* and *Rate*), and one many–one-connected entity set with a primary key (*GuestNr*) and with an attribute (*Extra-Charges*) on its connecting relationship set (*occupies*). Thus, applying ER Mapping Rule #2 to *Room*, we obtain *Room(RoomNr, RoomName, Type, Rate, GuestNr, ExtraCharges)*, the third relational schema in Fig. 5.1.[2]

ER Mapping Rule #3. Let E and E' be two regular entity sets connected by a single one–one relationship set R between them. Let E have n key attributes $A_1, \ldots, A_n$, m nonkey attributes $B_1, \ldots, B_m$, and p many–one-connected entity sets whose primary keys are $C_1, \ldots, C_p$ and that have q attributes $D_1, \ldots, D_q$ associated with the p many–one relationship sets. Let E' have n' key attributes $A'_1, \ldots, A'_{n'}$, m' nonkey attributes $B'_1, \ldots, B'_{m'}$, and p' many–one-connected entity sets whose primary keys are $C'_1, \ldots, C'_{p'}$ and that have q' attributes $D'_1, \ldots, D'_{q'}$ associated with the p' many–one relationship sets. And let R have r attributes $R_1, \ldots, R_r$. Then, E, E', and R together map to the single relational schema $R(\underline{A_1}, \ldots, \underline{A_n}, \underline{A'_1}, \ldots, \underline{A'_{n'}}, B_1, \ldots, B_m, B'_1, \ldots, B'_{m'}, C_1, \ldots, C_p, C'_1, \ldots, C'_{p'}, D_1, \ldots, D_q, D'_1, \ldots, D'_{q'}, R_1, \ldots, R_r)$.

ER Mapping Rule #3 does not apply to the ER model instance in Fig. 5.1. It would apply if *occupies* were one–one, which would mean that a guest's party would occupy one room and could only occupy one room. If *occupies* were one–one, then we would map *Room*, *Guest*, and *occupies* together to *occupies(RoomNr, RoomName, GuestNr, Type, Rate, Name, Address, ExtraCharges)*. Furthermore, there would be no separate schemas for *Room* and *Guest* schema since both would be entirely included in this *occupies* schema.

---

[2] Unless otherwise explicitly stated, the first key listed in a relational schema is the primary key – *RoomNr* in this example.

It becomes unwieldy to formally specify further generalizations of ER Mapping Rule #3. Furthermore, these generalizations seldom arise in practice. The generalizations involve adding more and more entity sets in a one-to-one correspondence with the entity sets already in a one-to-one correspondence. In principle, we just combine together into a single relational schema all the attributes of these entity sets, of their connecting one–one relationship sets, and of their connecting many–one relationship sets (but not their connecting one–many and many–many relationship sets), and all the primary-key attributes of their connecting many–one relationship sets. Unfortunately, however, we have to be careful. Basically the connected one–one relationship sets must all have mandatory participation; and if there are cycles in the set of entity sets in the one-to-one correspondence, the one–one relationship sets must all be semantically equivalent.[3]

ER Mapping Rule #4. Let R be a many–many binary relationship set with attributes $A_1, \ldots, A_n$. Let E and E' be the entity sets connected by R, and let P be the primary-key attribute of E and P' be the primary-key attribute of E'. Then R maps to $R(\underline{P, \ P'}, A_1, \ldots, A_n)$.

ER Mapping Rule #4 applies to *is signed up for*, a many–many relationship set whose attributes are *Date* and *Time*. Its connected entity sets are *Guest* and *Activity*, whose primary keys are, respectively, *GuestNr* and *Description*. Thus, when we apply ER Mapping Rule #4, we obtain *IsSignedUpFor(GuestNr,Description, Date, Time*, which is the last relational schema in Fig. 5.1b.

General Principle #1. In general, mappings of conceptual models to relational schemas are about finding key attributes and composite key attributes and grouping these attributes together into relational schemas along with attributes that directly depend on them. Finding key attributes and composite key attributes is about observing cardinality relationships among attributes (one–one, one–many, many–one, and many–many). Finding directly dependent attributes is about finding attributes that functionally depend on keys, but only on keys within the group of attributes mapped together into a relational schema (i.e., never on some nonkey attribute or attribute group, never on a proper subset of a composite key, and never on a combination of a proper subset of a composite key and nonkey attributes). Functional dependency arises from cardinality constraints – an attribute B functionally depends on another attribute A if there is a many–one (or one–one) relationship from A to B. More generally, an attribute B functionally depends on a set of attributes $A_1 A_2 \ldots A_n$ if there is a many–one (or one–one) relationship from the n-tuples in $A_1 A_2 \ldots A_n$ to B.

General Principle #2. Graphical instantiations of conceptual models dictate cardinality relationships among attributes. Sometimes the graphical instantiations of conceptual models are insufficient to express all needed cardinality relationships. In this case, we express the missing cardinality constraints we need using a formal constraint language when one is defined for the conceptual model or notes in the absence of a defined formal constraint language.

---

[3] We refer the interested reader to the additional readings in Sect. 5.7 for these esoteric mappings.

General Principle #3. The following algorithm generally applies to all conceptual models.

Step 1   Group keys, which may be single-attribute keys or composite-attribute keys, into sets in which the keys in a set are all in a one-to-one correspondence with each other. (In practice, these key sets will often be singleton sets.)

Step 2   In each key set, designate one of the keys (or the only key) as the primary key for the key set.

Step 3   To each key set add all directly dependent nonkey attributes, plus, from among other key sets, the attributes of all directly dependent primary keys.

Step 4   For each group of attributes formed in step 3, select a name and form a relational schema. (Name selection is often obvious. Since keys are for entity sets or relationship sets, we typically use the entity-set name or the relationship-set name.)

If we apply general principle #3 to the ER diagram in Fig. 5.1a, step 1 yields the following set of key sets: {{*Description*}, {*GuestNr*}, {*RoomNr, RoomName*}, {*GuestNr Description*}}.[4] In step 2 we designate *RoomNr* as the primary key for the key set {*RoomNr, RoomName*}. All other key sets are singleton sets, and thus each key in these singleton sets is a primary key. In step 3 we group attributes, and in step 4 we select names for these attribute groups and form relational schemas. For the key set {*Description*}, the only directly dependent attribute is *Duration*. Hence, we add it, yielding (*Description, Duration*). Based on the diagram in Fig. 5.1a, the obvious name for this attribute group is *Activity*. Thus, *Activity(Description, Duration)* becomes the relational schema for the key set {*Description*}. This is the first relational schema in Fig. 5.1b. The key set {*GuestNr*} has two directly dependent attributes: *Name* and *Address*. Thus, with the addition of the obvious schema name, *Guest(GuestNr, Name, Address)* becomes the relational schema for the key set {*GuestNr*}. This is the second relational schema in Fig. 5.1b. The key set {*RoomNr, RoomName*} has three directly dependent non-key attributes: *Type* and *Rate* from the entity set *Room* and *ExtraCharges* since it is an attribute of *occupies*, the many–one relationship set from *Room* to *Guest*. From among the other key sets, *GuestNr* is the only primary key directly dependent on *RoomNr*.[5] Thus, with the addition of the obvious schema name, *Room(RoomNr, RoomName, Type, Rate, GuestNr, ExtraCharges)* becomes the relational schema. This is the third relational schema in Fig. 5.1b. Finally, for {*GuestNr Description*}, which is the key set for the relationship set *is signed up for*, the only directly

---

[4] Here we make use of the common set notation in the relational database literature that lets a sequence of attribute names designate a set. Thus, {*GuestNr Description*} is a key set with a single composite key consisting of two attributes, whereas {*RoomNr, RoomName*} is a key set with two keys.

[5] Note that although *Name* and *Address* functionally depend on *RoomNr* and also on *RoomName*, they do not directly functionally depend on either *RoomNr* or *RoomName* because they functionally depend on *GuestNr*, which is not a key attribute for the key set {*RoomNr, RoomName*} for which we are building a relational schema.

dependent attributes are *Date* and *Time*.[6] Thus, with the addition of the obvious schema name, *IsSignedUpFor(GuestNr, Description, Date, Time)* becomes the relational schema.

Observe that ER Mapping Rules #1–4 are simply special cases of the general principles written specifically for the ER model. ER Mapping Rule #1 gathers together key attributes and nonkey attributes from a single regular entity set that has no connecting functionally dependent entity sets. ER Mapping Rule #2 gathers together key attributes and nonkey attributes from a single regular entity set along with directly functionally dependent attributes that are not keys and the attributes of a primary key from each entity set functionally dependent on the single regular entity set for which we are constructing the relational schema. ER Mapping Rule #3 and its generalizations gather together all attributes from all entity sets in a one-to-one correspondence, plus all attributes connected to any of the relationship sets forming the one-to-one correspondence, plus all primary-key attributes of all the entity sets connected by a many–one relationship set from any one of the entity sets in a one-to-one correspondence, plus all attributes of these many–one relationship sets. ER Mapping Rule #4 identifies the special case where the composite key for a relationship set consists of primary key attributes of its connecting entity sets. The attributes from these two primary keys, along with any attributes connected to the relationship set, form the relational schema.

5.2.2 Complex Key Attributes

Key identification is a central component of mapping conceptual models to database schemas. Conceptual models commonly provide a direct way to identify keys via diagramming conventions. For the ER model, it is common to underline key attributes for entity sets, as shown by Fig. 5.1a. This convention, along with cardinality constraints imposed over relationship sets, provides sufficient information for identifying many keys for entity and relationship sets – indeed most keys in practice.

ER diagramming conventions, however, are not sufficient to allow us to identify all keys. Two common cases are (1) composite keys for entity sets and (2) keys for relationship sets not derivable from information about entity-set keys coupled with relationship-set cardinality constraints. The ER diagram in Fig. 5.2 a gives examples of these two cases.

1. The entity set *Guest* in Fig. 5.2a has no key attribute. Neither *Name* alone nor *Address* alone uniquely identifies a guest. Many different people with the same name may make reservations, and we may wish to make it possible for different people with the same address to make reservations. *Name* and *Address* together, however, may uniquely identify *Guest*, and we may designate that this must

---

[6] Note that *Duration* functionally depends on *Description*, but since *Description* is a proper subset of *GuestNr Description*, we exclude *Duration*. Similarly, we exclude *Name* and *Address* since *GuestNr* is a proper subset of *GuestNr Description*.

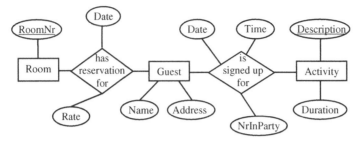

Name Address → Guest
RoomNr Date → Name Address Rate
Name Address Date Time → Description NrInParty

(a) ER Diagram.

Room(RoomNr)
Guest(Name, Address)
Activity(Description, Duration)
HasReservationFor(RoomNr, Date, Name, Address, Rate)
IsSignedUpFor(Name, Address, Date, Time, Description, NrInParty)

(b) Generated Schemas.

Fig. 5.2 Mappings for complex key attributes. ER diagram and Generated schemas

hold in our database so that *Name Address* becomes a composite key. If no
diagramming convention or other formal convention provides a way to designate
composite keys for an entity set,[7] it is best to record this information in a note. In
our notes here, we use standard functional dependency (FD) notation, allowing
both attribute names and entity-set names to appear as components of left-hand
and right-hand sides of FDs. To say that *Name Address* is a key for *Guest*, we
write the FD *Name Address → Guest* as shown in Fig. 5.2a.

2. Since only one guest's party can occupy a room on any given date, *RoomNr* and
Date uniquely identify a reservation. Thus *RoomNr* and *Date* constitute the composite key for the many–many relationship set *has reservation for*. This is contrary to the usual convention, which would have the key consist of the primary
keys from the connecting entity sets. It is easy to see, however, that *RoomNr
Name Address* cannot be the key because it would allow multiple parties to occupy the same room on the same day. We designate the key for a relationship
set by including all the primary-key attributes of all connecting entity sets and
all the attributes of the relationship set in an FD. Thus, for example, we write
RoomNr Date → Name Address Rate as shown in Fig. 5.2a. Similarly, we write
Name Address Date Time → Description NrInParty to designate *Name Address
Date Time* as a composite key for *is signed up for*, i.e., a guest's party can only
sign up for one activity at a given time on a given date.

---

[7] There are many ER variants, and some have conventions to designate composite keys for entity
sets (e.g., a connecting line among underlined attributes of an entity set).

Figure 5.2b shows the relational schemas generated from Fig. 5.2a. We obtain these relational schemas by following the algorithm in general principle #3. In step 1 we generate keys for each of the entity sets and each of the many–many relationship sets. This step yields the set of key sets {{*Name Address*}, {*Description*}, {*RoomNr Date*}, {*Name Address Date Time*}, {*RoomNr*}}. Since each key set has only one key, it becomes the primary key called for in step 2. Next we add all directly dependent nonkey attributes and needed directly dependent primary-key attributes as called for in step 3 and select names as called for in step 4. The result consists of the relational schemas in Fig. 5.2b.[8]

ER Mapping Rule #1′, **ER mapping rule #2′**, and **ER mapping rule #3′**. The mapping rules for entity sets with possible composite keys are straightforward generalizations of ER Mapping Rules #1–3. Their formal statement, however, is quite complex. Basically, instead of just simple single-attribute keys, we must also allow for composite keys. Thus, for example, for ER mapping rule #1′ (the generalization of ER Mapping Rule #1), we include all attributes that are keys, all attributes that are parts of composite keys, and all nonkey attributes in the generated relational schema. It is possible, though rare, for composite keys to overlap. For example, if we had kept *RoomName* from Fig. 5.1a in our example for Fig. 5.2a, we would also have the composite key *RoomName Date* grouped with the composite key *RoomNr Date*. In this case, the mapping rule should only generate three attributes (not four) for these two composite keys. The single occurrence of *Date* in the relational schema would be part of both composite keys.

ER Mapping Rule #4′. For any relationship set, we gather together all attributes constituting primary keys of all related entity sets plus all attributes of the relationship set. We then determine, from among these attributes, which attributes and attribute sets are keys. This becomes the relational schema for the relationship set, except in two special cases having to do with ER Mapping Rules #2′ and #3′. If the primary key of one and only one of the connected entity sets E of relationship set R is a key for R, then as part of mapping rule #2′, all the attributes of the relational schema for R become part of the relational schema for E; there is no separate relational schema for R. If the primary keys of two or more of the connected entity sets $E_1, \ldots, E_n$ of relationship set R is each a key for R, then as part of ER Mapping Rule #3′, all the attributes from the relational schemas for $E_1, \ldots, E_n$, and R are all combined to form a single relational schema for the database.

5.2.3 Recursive Relationship Sets and Roles

To be understood, recursive relationship sets require roles. Figure 5.3a shows an example. The role *Connecting Room* helps us understand that the relationship set

---

[8] Whether we should keep a relation for *Room* here is an interesting question. Observe that its data may be completely recorded in the relation *HasReservationFor*. If so, we can discard it. In our application, however, it is possible (even likely) that there is no current reservation for some of the rooms. Thus, to preserve all room numbers in our database, we keep it.

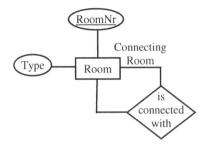

(a) ER Diagram.

Room(<u>RoomNr</u>, Type)
IsConnectedWith(<u>RoomNr, ConnectingRoomNr</u>)

(b) Generated Schemas.

Fig. 5.3 Mappings for roles. ER diagram and Generated schemas

denotes adjoining rooms with a doorway between them: a *Room* is connected with a *Connecting Room*.

Roles also help us choose attribute names for recursive relationship sets. We map a recursive relationship set to a relational schema in the same way we map regular relationship sets to a relational schema. One–one and many–one recursive relationship sets become part of the relational schema for the entity set, and many–many recursive relationship sets become relational schemas by themselves. In all cases, however, there is one difference – we must rename one (or both) of the primary-key attributes. Because the regular mapping for a recursive relationship set would make the primary key of the entity set appear twice, and since a relational schema cannot have duplicate attribute names, we must rename one (or both) of them. The role helps because it usually gives a good clue about what one of the names should be. As Fig. 5.3b shows, we map the many–many recursive relationship set to the relational schema with attribute names *RoomNr* and *Connecting-RoomNr*.

We can also use roles in this same way even when a relationship set is not recursive. For example, we could have added a role *Occupied Room* to the *Room* side of *occupies* in the ER diagram in Fig. 5.1a. In this case we could have generated *Room(OccupiedRoomNr, OccupiedRoomName, Type, Rate, GuestNr, ExtraCharges)* in which *OccupiedRoomNr* replaces *RoomNr* and *OccupiedRoomName* replaces *RoomName* in the relational schema in Fig. 5.1b. Using the role name in this way is optional but may be useful for distinguishing the roles attributes play when we have more than one relationship set between the same two entity sets. For example, we could have also had *has reservation for* in addition to *occupies* as a relationship set between *Room* and *Guest* in Fig. 5.1a.

5.2.4 Weak Entity Sets

A weak entity set is an entity set with no key among its directly associated attributes.
If we augment our bed-and-breakfast example to a chain of bed-and-breakfast establishments as shown in Fig. 5.4a, the room number no longer uniquely identifies
a room. Every bed and breakfast in the establishment likely has a room #1 and
a room #2 and probably more. Thus, *Room* has no key among its directly associated
attributes, and it becomes a weak entity set.

In an ER diagram, we designate a weak ·entity set by enclosing the name of
the weak entity set in a double box. In addition, we add a special relationship
set connecting the weak entity set to the entity set on which the weak entity set
depends for its key. We designate these special relationship sets by a double diamond and by adding an arrowhead on the side connecting to the entity set on
which the weak entity set depends. Adding the arrowhead is appropriate since
there is always a many–one relationship from the weak entity set to the entity set

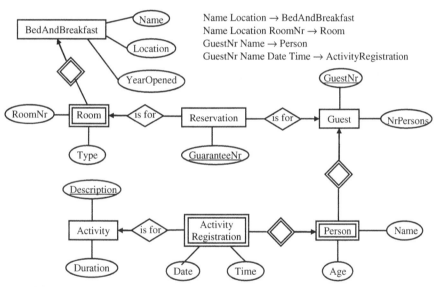

(a) ER Diagram.

    BedAndBreakfast(Name, Location,YearOpened)
    Room(Name, Location, RoomNr, Type)
    Reservation(GuaranteeNr, Name, Location, RoomNr, GuestNr)
    Guest(GuestNr, NrPersons)
    Person(GuestNr, Name, Age)
    Activity(Description, Duration)
    ActivityRegistration(GuestNr, Name, Date, Time, Description)

(b) Generated Schemas.

Fig. 5.4 Mappings for weak entity sets. ER diagram and Generated schemas

on which the weak entity set depends. The ER model does not, by the way, preclude an entity set on which a weak entity set depends from itself being a weak entity set.

Figure 5.4a is an ER diagram showing the three situations in which we normally find weak entity sets. Weak entity sets typically arise (1) when there is an organizational subdivision (e.g., *Room* is an organizational division of the *BedAndBreakfast* chain), (2) when one entity depends on the existence of another (e.g., for the bed-and-breakfast database, *Person* depends on the existence of a registered *Guest*), and (3) when we wish to view relationship sets as entity sets (e.g., an *Activity Registration* rather than just a relationship set between *Person* and *Activity*).[9]

The general principles tell us how to map weak entity sets to relational schemas. We first identify keys. In every case in which we find a weak entity set, the identity of entities in the weak entity set depends on the key for some other one or more entity sets. The identity of a room depends on the bed and breakfast in which the room is located. The key for *BedAndBreakfast*, which for our example is the composite key *Name Location*,[10] plus a *RoomNr* uniquely identify a room. Thus, the key for *Room* is the composite of all three attributes, namely, *Name Location RoomNr*. For *Person*, names are not unique identifiers, but are usually unique within a family, which often constitutes a registered guest's party. In our example, we require unique names within a registered guest's party, and thus the key for the weak entity set *Person* is the composite of *GuestNr* and *Name* (of *Person*). A person can sign up for only one activity at a given time on a given date. Thus, to uniquely identify an *ActivityRegistration*, we need the key of *Person*, which is *GuestNr Name*, as well as *Date* and *Time*, to all be part of the key. Thus, the composite key for *ActivityRegistration* is *GuestNr Name Date Time*.

After identifying keys for a weak entity set (and designating one as the primary key in case there are several), we add all directly dependent nonkey attributes and directly dependent primary-key attributes. We then choose a name – usually the name of the weak entity set – and form a relational schema. Figure 5.4b shows the result for the ER diagram in Fig. 5.4a. For the weak entity set *Room*, the only directly dependent attribute is *Type*. Thus, since the key is the composite *Name Location RoomNr*, the relational schema is *Room(Name, Location, RoomNr, Type)*, the second relational schema in Fig. 5.4b. Similarly, for *Person*, since *Age* is the only directly dependent attribute, the relational schema for the weak entity set is *Person(GuestNr, Name, Age)*. For the weak entity set *Activity Registration, Description* is a directly dependent primary-key attribute. Thus, since the composite key is *GuestNr Name Date Time*, we generate the last relational schema in Fig. 5.4b.

---

[9] Note, by the way, that the entity set *Reservation* is not weak, even though it is certainly a relationship set we view as an entity set. When we turned it into an entity set, we gave it a key, *GuaranteeNr*, so that it did not become a weak entity set.

[10] *Location* is meant to be a simple city or town or other designated place. Several bed-and-breakfast establishments can be in the same location (e.g., Boston), but each establishment in the same location must have a different name. Thus, *Name Location* → *BedAndBreakfast*.

ER Mapping Rule #5. Let W be a weak entity set, let E be an entity set on which W depends (E may itself be weak), and let $F_1, \ldots, F_m$ be the m other entity sets (if any) in a many–one relationship from W to F_i ($1 \le i \le m$). Form a relational schema called W with attributes consisting of all the attributes of W, the primary-key attribute(s) of E, all the primary-key attributes of $F_1, \ldots, F_m$, and all the attributes (if any) of the many–one relationship sets from W to each F_i ($1 \le i \le m$). From among the attributes, determine the keys for W and designate one as the primary key. Each key of W is formed by adding one or more attributes of W to the primary key for E.[11]

5.3 Extended Entity-Relationship Model Mappings

Extended ER models include generalization/specialization or ISA hierarchies, with possible union, disjoint, overlapping, partition, and intersection constraints. They also include compound attributes, multivalued attributes, computed attributes, and designations for mandatory and optional participation. In this section, we consider mappings for each of these extensions.

5.3.1 ISA Mappings

Figure 5.5a shows an ER diagram with several ISA constructs. Graphically, triangles denote ISA constructs, which fundamentally designate entity sets as subsets and supersets.[12] An entity in a subset entity set is also an entity in its superset entity set – thus the "ISA" designation. The apex of a triangle connects to superset entity sets, and the base connects to subset entity sets. In Fig. 5.5a, both *CurrentGuest* and *FutureGuest* are subsets of *Guest*, and *ReturningGuest* is a subset of both *CurrentGuest* and *FutureGuest*. We can constrain the subsets by placing symbols in the triangles: $\cap$ for intersection, $\cup$ for union, $+$ for mutual exclusion, and $\uplus$ for partition. An intersection constraint requires that the subset entity set be exactly the intersection of the superset entity sets (e.g., in Fig. 5.5a *ReturningGuest* is exactly the intersection of *CurrentGuest* and *FutureGuest*). Without the intersection constraint (triangle with no special constraint inside it) the subset entity set could be a proper subset of the intersection. Union requires that the superset be exactly the union of the subsets (e.g., *Guest* is defined to be exactly the union of those guests who are currently at the bed and breakfast and those who will be future guests). Mutual exclusion requires that the subsets pairwise have an empty intersection (e.g., *High-*

---

[11] Typically, as in our examples here, W has only one key. But, for example, if we also had *RoomName* for the weak entity set *Room*, we would have a second key for *Room*, namely, *Name Location RoomName*.

[12] In this context, we call subset entity sets "specialization entity sets" or just "specializations" and superset entity sets "generalization entity sets" or just "generalizations."

CostActivity and *FreeActivity* have an empty intersection). Partition requires both union and mutual exclusion (e.g., a room must be a single room, a double room, or a suite).

Figure 5.5b shows the relational schemas generated from the ER diagram in Fig. 5.5a. For ISA hierarchies, there are three basic mappings, which we label as ER Mapping Rules #6.1–6.3. (Combinations over multiple-level hierarchies are also possible.)

ER Mapping Rule #6.1. *Make a relational schema for all entity sets in the hierarchy.* Although not always best, this is the most straightforward mapping for ISA hierarchies. The mapping for an entity set in an ISA hierarchy that has no generalization is the same as the mapping for any entity set. The mapping for a specialization is also the same except that the primary-key attribute(s) of the generalization(s)[13]

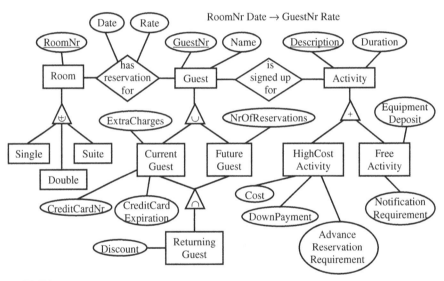

(a) ER Diagram.

Room(RoomNr, RoomType)
Guest(GuestNr, Name, ExtraCharges?, CreditCardNr?, CreditCardExpiration?,
    NrOfReservations?, Discount?)
Activity(Description, Duration)
HighCostActivity(Description, Cost, DownPayment, AdvanceReservationRequirement)
FreeActivity(Description, EquipmentDeposit, NotificationRequirement)
HasReservationFor(RoomNr, Date, GuestNr, Rate)
IsSignedUpFor(GuestNr, Description)

(b) Generated Schemas.

Fig. 5.5 Mappings for ISA hierarchies. ER diagram and Generated schemas

---

[13] Since all specializations in an ISA hierarchy are subsets of their generalizations, entities in the specializations inherit their identity from their generalization(s). In most common cases there is only one generalization. When a specialization has more than one generalization, it inherits its

are also added to the relational schema. In general any key for the specialization can be the primary key. Normally, however, there will be only one key, the inherited primary key. In Fig. 5.5 we map the ISA hierarchy rooted at *Activity* in this way. The relational schema for *Activity* in Fig. 5.5b is the same as it would be without the ISA hierarchy. *HighCostActivity* and *FreeActivity*, however, both inherit the primary key *Description* from *Activity* and include it as the primary key for their relational schemas along with all directly dependent attributes.

ER Mapping Rule #6.2. *Make a relational schema for only root entity sets.* For this mapping, we collapse the entire ISA hierarchy to the entity set of the root generalization,[14] so that all attributes of specializations become attributes of the root and all relationship sets associated with specializations become relationship sets associated with the root. We then map this single entity set to a relational schema in the usual way. After doing the mapping, we determine which attributes are nullable. All attributes that would not have been in the mapping if we had not collapsed the ISA hierarchy are nullable. In our relational schemas, we mark nullable attributes with a question mark. When we transform generic relational schemas to SQL *create* statements for implementation, we allow nullable attributes to have the value NULL; nonnullable attributes may not have the value NULL. In Fig. 5.5 we map the ISA hierarchy rooted at *Guest* in this way. When collapsing the ISA hierarchy, the attributes of the three specializations all become nullable attributes of *Guest*. As Fig. 5.5b shows, these five attributes all have an appended question mark.

We might wonder if this mapping causes us to lose track of which guests are current guests, which are future guests, and which are returning guests. For this example we do not lose the information. According to the semantics of the ER model instance in Fig. 5.5a, only returning guests will have *Discount* values, whereas current and future guests who are not returning guests will not have *Discount* values. Future guests will have a value for *NrOfReservations*, whereas current guests will not. Similarly, current guests will have extra charges, credit card numbers, and credit card expirations, whereas future guests will not. Sometimes, however, it is not possible to know the specialization categories based on attribute values, and even when it is possible, we may wish to have a way to record the specialization categories. The following two additions to mapping rule #6.2 show us how we can provide attributes in which we can record this information about specializations.

- **ER Mapping Rule #6.2a.** *Add a new attribute for each specialization.* When mapping the generalization entity set to a relational schema, generate an additional attribute for every specialization entity set. Values for these attributes are Boolean, saying for each record of the relational schema whether the entity the record represents is or is not in the specialization. If we were to add these ad-

---

identity from all generalizations. Often, however, all generalizations have the same identifying attribute inherited from some root generalization. *ReturningGuest* in Fig. 5.5 a inherits its identity from both *CurrentGuest* and *FutureGuest*, but these entity sets, in turn, both inherit their identity from *Guest*. Thus, *GuestNr* becomes the one and only key attribute that identifies returning guests.

[14] Although rare, if there are multiple roots, we collapse the hierarchy to all roots. Any entity set that is the specialization of multiple roots collapses to all of them.

ditional attributes for *Guest*, the relational schema for *Guest* in Fig. 5.5b would instead be:

> *Guest(GuestNr, Name, ExtraCharges?, CreditCardNr?,*
>   *CreditCardExpiration?, NrOfReservations?, Discount?,*
>   *CurrentGuest, FutureGuest, ReturningGuest).*

If we wish, we could omit *ReturningGuest* and just compute its value for a record as *yes* if both values for *CurrentGuest* and *FutureGuest* are *yes* and as *no* otherwise.

- **ER Mapping Rule #6.2b.** *Add only one new attribute representing all specializations.* This mapping only applies when the specializations are mutually exclusive. If so, when mapping the generalization entity set to a relational schema, we only need to generate one additional attribute to represent all specializations. The specialization entity-set names can be the values for this new attribute. In Fig. 5.5a, *Room* has three mutually exclusive specializations that designate the room type. We therefore generate a new attribute, *RoomType*, for the generalization entity set *Room*. The values for this attribute can be the names of the specialization entity set. The generated relational schema for *Room* in Fig. 5.5b has the attributes *RoomNr* and *RoomType*. Values for *RoomType* would be "*Single,*" "*Double,*" and "*Suite*" or any other designating value to say that the room is a single room, a double room, or a suite.

ER Mapping Rule #6.3. *Make a relational schema for only the leaves in the hierarchy.* The leaf entity sets inherit all attributes and all relationship sets from parents along a path all the way back to the root.[15] This mapping only applies when union constraints are present along all paths. If a union constraint were missing, there could be members of the entity sets in the hierarchy that would not appear in the leaf entity sets and thus would be lost in the implementation. Further, we usually only apply this mapping when mutual exclusion is also present along all paths. If not, then members of the entity sets could appear in more than one leaf entity set and thus would appear as duplicates in the implementation, once for each leaf entity set in which a member appears. As an example, assume that there are only high-cost activities and free activities and thus that the constraint for the ISA hierarchy rooted at *Activity* in Fig. 5.5 a is a partition (⊎) constraint rather than a mutual-exclusion (+) constraint. Applying the mapping in which we only represent the leaves of the ISA hierarchy, we would replace the three relational schemas *Activity*, *HighCostActivity*, and *FreeActivity* in Fig. 5.5b by the following two relational schemas:

> *HighCostActivity(Description, Duration, Cost, DownPayment,*
>   *AdvanceReservationRequirement)*
> *FreeActivity(Description, Duration, EquipmentDeposit,*
>   *NotificationRequirement.)*

Observe that both *HighCostActivity* and *FreeActivity* include the attribute *Duration* as well as *Description* and that the connection to the *IsSignedUp*

---

[15] If there are multiple roots, the leaves inherit from all roots.

For relational schema is accounted for through the *Description* attributes. When we make a relational schema for only the leaves in an ISA hierarchy, we must account for all attributes and relationship-set connections of all ancestors of each leaf entity set.

General Principle #4. Map ISA hierarchies to relational schemas by choosing to make a relational schema for (1) all entity sets in an ISA hierarchy, (2) only root entity sets, or (3) only leaf entity sets. Although there are guidelines that typically indicate which of the three mappings to use, making the best choice is often application dependent. Deciding among the possibilities depends on the ISA constraints and the number of attributes involved. Designers use the following rule-of-thumb guidelines.

- Select (1) when the generalizations and specializations all have many attributes.
- Select (2) when the specializations collectively have few attributes.
- When the specializations have no attributes, select (2a) either for an ISA union constraint or for an ISA with no constraint.
- When the specializations have no attributes, select (2b) either for an ISA partition constraint or for an ISA mutual-exclusion constraint.
- Select (3) for an ISA partition constraint, especially when there are many attributes for the specializations and few for the generalizations.

Often there is no obvious best choice. In this case the developer must choose one. Furthermore, in some complex cases, especially with large hierarchies, it may be best to make a separate choice for each individual ISA configuration in the hierarchy. In the end the mappings must account for representing all possible entities in every entity set in the ISA hierarchy and all possible relationships and attributes of these entities.

5.3.2 *Mappings for Complex Attributes*

Extended ER models allow for several types of complex attributes. Figure 5.6a includes examples for each type.

- A *multivalued attribute* is an attribute whose values are sets of values. In an extended ER diagram, we denote a multivalued attribute by a double oval. In Fig. 5.6, *ActivityInterest* is a multivalued attribute. Guests may be interested in several activities – one guest may be interested in the set of activities {golf, horse-back riding, canoeing}, while another guest may be interested in the set of activities {chess, hiking, canoeing}. *View* is also a multivalued attribute whose sets might be {Ocean, CityOverlook} or just {Ocean} depending on what can be seen by looking out the window(s) of a room in the bed-and-breakfast establishment.
- A *compound attribute* is an attribute with component parts each of which is also an attribute. In an extended ER diagram, we denote compound attributes by attaching component attributes directly to the compound attribute. In Fig. 5.6a, *NameAndAddress* is a compound attribute whose component attributes are *Name*

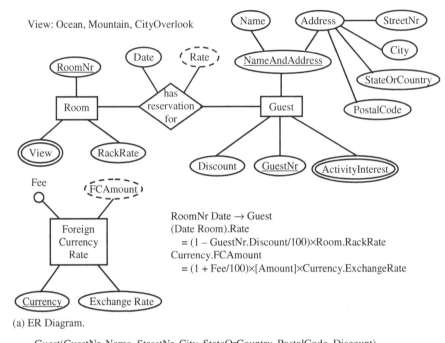

RoomNr Date → Guest
(Date Room).Rate
   = (1 − GuestNr.Discount/100)×Room.RackRate
Currency.FCAmount
   = (1 + Fee/100)×[Amount]×Currency.ExchangeRate

(a) ER Diagram.

Guest(GuestNr, Name, StreetNr, City, StateOrCountry, PostalCode, Discount)
GuestActivityInterest(GuestNr, ActivityInterest)
Room(RoomNr, RackRate, Ocean, Mountain, CityOverlook)
HasReservationFor(RoomNr, Date, GuestNr, Rate)
ForeignCurrencyRate(Currency, ExchangeRate)
Fee(Fee)

(b) Generated Schemas.

Fig. 5.6 Mappings for complex attributes. ER diagram and Generated schemas

and *Address*. The component attribute *Address* is also compound; its component attributes are *StreetNr*, *City*, *StateOrCountry*, and *PostalCode*.

- A *computed attribute* is an attribute whose value can be computed. In an extended ER diagram, we denote a computed attribute by a dashed oval. In Fig. 5.6a, *FCAmount* and *Rate* are computed attributes.
- An *entity-set attribute*, called in other contexts a *class attribute*, is an attribute whose value is the same for all entities in the entity set and thus can be thought of as applying to the entire set of entities rather than each individual entity in the set. In an extended ER diagram, we denote an entity-set attribute by a small circle. In Fig. 5.6a, *Fee* is an example. It is a percentage and is meant to be the fee collected by the bed-and-breakfast establishment for accepting payment in a foreign currency.

Figure 5.6b shows how we map the various complex attributes in Fig. 5.6 a to relational schemas. Basically, the mappings are straightforward applications of the general principles. The cardinality constraints for multivalued attributes make them have the properties of many–many relationship sets. The collapsing of compound-attribute trees make the leaves of these trees have the properties of directly dependent attributes. Computed attributes are the same as regular attributes except we may not need to store them. Although entity-set attributes could be treated as regular attributes, their singleton property makes them amenable to a different kind of mapping, making entity-set attributes an exception to the general principles.

ER Mapping Rule #7. Fundamentally, multivalued attributes are in a many–many relationship with the entity set to which they are connected. Each entity in an entity set E with a multivalued attribute A relates to n values $v_1, \ldots, v_n$ of A, and each value of A relates to m entities $e_1, \ldots, e_m$ in E. Thus, unless the number of values in A, $|A|$, is fixed and small, we treat A as if it were another entity set E' in a many–many relationship with E; E''s only attribute, and therefore its primary-key attribute, is A. When $|A|$ is fixed and small, it is possible to treat it as $|A|$ attributes $v_1, \ldots, v_{|A|}$ of E whose values are Boolean stating whether an entity e relates to that value or does not relate to that value.

- **ER Mapping Rule #7a.** *If entity set E has a multivalued attribute A, then if P is the primary key of E, generate the relational schema $N(\underline{P, A})$. If the primary key of E happens to be composite, P represents the attribute list for the composite primary key. N is a chosen name – often a concatenation of the name of E and the name of A.* The relational schema *GuestActivityInterest* in Fig. 5.6b is an example. A guest can be interested in may different activities, and an activity can be of interest to many different guests. Thus, since *GuestNr* is the primary key of *Guest*, we generate *GuestNr* and *ActivityInterest* as the attributes and as the composite key for the relational schema.

- **ER Mapping Rule #7b.** *As an exception to ER Mapping Rule #7a, if entity set E has a multivalued attribute A, n is the size of A, and n is fixed and small, then if $A = \{V_1, \ldots, V_n\}$, add $V_1, \ldots, V_n$ as Boolean attributes to the relational schema formed for E.* The relational schema *Room* in Fig. 5.6b is an example. As specified in a note in the diagram, a room can have only up to three views (*Ocean*, *Mountain*, or *CityOverlook*). Thus, for the multivalued attribute *View* of *Room*, we add these three view names, *Ocean*, *Mountain*, and *City*, as attributes to the relational schema. Values for these attributes are Boolean: if a front corner room has all three views, all three attribute values would have the value *yes*, and if a back center room looks out only on the mountains, the *Mountain* value would be *yes* and the *Ocean* and *cityOverlook* values would be *no*.

ER Mapping Rule #8. *Treat each leaf attribute of a compound attribute tree T of an entity set E as an attribute of E; then map E in the usual way. In addition, if any nonleaf node N of T is a key for E, form a composite key from the leaf attributes of the subtree rooted at N.* In Fig. 5.6a *Guest* has a compound attribute *NameAndAddress*. Its leaf attributes are *Name*, *StreetNr*, *City*, *StateOrCountry*, and *PostalCode*. Thus, for *Guest* we form a relational schema with these attributes along with the regular attributes *GuestNr* and *Discount*. (Being multivalued, *ActivityInterest* is not a regular attribute and is not included – nor are the nonleaf attributes of the com-

pound attribute tree, *NameAndAddress* and *Address*.) Further, since the nonleaf attribute   *NameAnd
Address* is a key for *Guest*, we form a composite key from all its leaf attributes, as shown in Fig. 5.6b.

ER Mapping Rule #9. *If a computed attribute is to be stored in the database, treat it as a regular attribute for the purpose of mapping it to a relational schema.* When values for attributes are computed, we may or may not want to store their values in the database. If computed values serve to initialize a field and the field value may later change, we store the values. In this case, there must be an attribute for it in the generated relational schema. On the other hand, if the value is computed from other existing values whenever we need it, we need not store it. In this case, we ignore it when generating relational schemas. In our example in Fig. 5.6a, *Rate* is an initial value, which depends on a guest's discount and the room's rack rate but which can be set to another value. Thus, we generate an attribute for *Rate* in the relational schema for *HasReservationFor*, the place it would go if it were a regular attribute. *FCAmount*, however, is only computed when a guest wants to know how much to pay if the amount owed is to be paid in a foreign currency. Thus, we do not generate an attribute for *FCAmount* in any relational schema.

ER Mapping Rule #10. *For an entity-set attribute A, we either ignore it or map it to a single-attribute, single-valued relation A(A).* Values for entity-set attributes may be constants established in the program code, may be values accepted as input values when needed, or may be stored in the database and updated occasionally. In our example, we store the fee value as a percentage number in the database and thus need the relational schema *Fee(Fee)*, as Fig. 5.6b shows.

5.3.3 Mappings for Mandatory/Optional Participation

Figure 5.7a illustrates mandatory and optional participation in an ER diagram. We designate optional participation by placing a small "o" near a connection for attributes and relationship sets, and we designate mandatory participation by the absence of an "o." Optional participation for an attribute *A* means that an entity in an entity set need not have a value for *A*; mandatory participation means that an entity must have a value. In Fig. 5.7 a a *Guest* need not provide an *Address* when registering (i.e., the database system will allow the *Address* field in a record for a *Guest* to be null). Optional participation for a relationship set *R* means that an entity in an entity set need not participate in the relationship set; mandatory participation means that it must participate. For example, a *Room* in Fig. 5.7a need not be occupied, need not be anyone's favorite, and need not be reserved by anyone. Similarly, someone recorded as a *Guest* in the database need not have a reservation, need not occupy a room, and need not have a favorite room. The database would allow, for example, a record to be kept for someone who had been a guest but is not currently occupying a room, has no reservation, and has no particular favorite room.

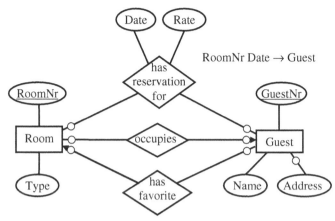

(a) ER Diagram.

RoomAndOccupant(<u>RoomNr</u>, Type, GuestNr?)
GuestAndFavoriteRoom(<u>GuestNr</u>, Name, Address?, RoomNr?)
HasReservationFor(<u>RoomNr, Date,</u> GuestNr, Rate)

(b) Generated Schemas.

Fig. 5.7 Mappings for mandatory/optional constructs. ER diagram and Generated schemas

Figure 5.7b shows how we consider optionality when we map to relational schemas. As before, the question mark means that an attribute is nullable. When attributes are optional, they are nullable; when they are mandatory, they are not nullable. Thus, for example, *Address* has an appended question mark in *GuestAnd-FavoriteRoom* whereas *Name* does not. When attributes of a relationship set plus the primary-key attributes of the associated entity sets are mapped into a relational schema for an entity set, if participation in the relationship set is optional, these imported attributes are all nullable. When participation is mandatory, these attributes are not nullable. Thus, for example, *GuestNr* is nullable in *RoomAndOccupant*. Because *occupies* is many–one from *Room* to *Guest*, the primary key for *Guest*, which is *GuestNr*, becomes one of the attributes of *RoomAndOccupant*, and because participation of a *Room* in the *occupies* relationship set is optional, *GuestNr* is imported as a nullable attribute. Similarly, *RoomNr* is nullable in *GuestAndFavoriteRoom* since the *has favorite* relationship set is many–one from *Guest* to *Room* and *Guest* optionally participates in *has favorite*. Observe that the relationship set *has reservation for* is many–many and is not imported into either *Room* or *Guest*. Thus, there is no special mapping based on the optionality of reservations for rooms and guests.

ER Mapping Rule #11. *Mark all nullable attributes in generated relational schemas. Attributes that are the primary key of a relational schema or that are in the composite primary key of a relational schema are never nullable. All other attributes may be nullable and should be so marked if their value for a record can be NULL.*

This rule is a little different from all other rules. It is written with respect to generated schemas. Thus, it does not say how to generate schemas, nor does it say exactly how to decide which attributes are nullable. Rather, it says which attributes are and are not potentially nullable, and it says that among those that are potentially nullable the database designer should decide which ones should allow null values. The reason for writing the rule this way is twofold:

1. Many ER diagrams never specify mandatory/optional participation (sometimes because the notation does not allow it, and sometimes just because it is not commonly done). Thus the nullable properties of attributes in relational schemas are often not derivable from an ER diagram.
2. When mandatory/optional participation can be specified in an ER diagram, even if someone specifies that an attribute that turns out to be part of the primary key of some relational schema should be nullable, it cannot be nullable. Relational database systems do not allow nulls in primary keys.

To illustrate reason #1, we can consider the ER diagrams in Figs. 5.1–5.6 in which no optional participation explicitly appears. One view we can take for all these diagrams is that there is no optional participation. In this case, all generated relational schemas remain as they are. This point of view, however, does say something about the semantics of the schemas. For example, in the *Room* schema in Fig. 5.1b, we can only record room numbers, type, and rate for occupied rooms. If we want to store this information for unoccupied rooms, we would be forced to enter some bogus *GuestNr* (e.g., −1) and some bogus value for *ExtraCharges* (e.g., 0). It may be better to simply allow these attributes to be nullable. The same is true for the address of a guest in the *Guest* schema in Fig. 5.1b. Even if the guest is in the process of moving and has no address to give, or if the guest refuses to give an address, something (e.g., "none") must be entered.

To illustrate reason #2, consider what it would mean if *RoomNr* for *RoomAnd-Occupant* in Fig. 5.7b were marked as optional and thus allowed to be nullable. This means that some rooms would have no identifier – no room number. Suppose we try to store information about several no-number double rooms that currently have no occupants. Even if the database would let us store the room number as null, we would have trouble since we could not distinguish the rooms from one another. We would not even know how many unoccupied double rooms we had. This motivates the rule: *attributes of primary keys in a relational schema may not be null.* Note that this rule does not say that key attributes cannot be null, only that primary-key attributes cannot be null. Suppose, for example, that a guest can have a guarantee number (*GuaranteeNr*) that uniquely identifies the guest in addition to a guest number (*GuestNr*). We could then add *GuaranteeNr* as a key attribute to the attributes already in *GuestAndFavoriteRoom* in Fig. 5.7b and let it be nullable so that not all guests would have to have a guarantee number. Note also that this rule does not say that primary-key attributes imported into a relational schema cannot be null. Indeed, *GuestNr* is nullable in *RoomAndOccupant*, where it is not the primary key, even though it is the primary key for *GuestAndFavoriteRoom*.

General Principle #5. Make attributes nullable if they can have NULL as their value. Attributes of primary keys in a relational schema are not nullable.

5.4 UML Mappings

In this section, we explain how to generate relational schemas from UML class diagrams. We base our procedure on the general principles, and thus this explanation serves as an example of how to develop mapping rules to map any conceptual model to relational schemas. In general, we first need to understand the syntactic features of the conceptual model and determine which corresponding ER features or extended ER features they denote. We can then map them to relational schemas in the same way we map ER features to relational schemas.

We illustrate our UML mappings using the class diagram in Fig. 5.8 as an example. We begin by pointing out several syntactic features of this class diagram and explain how they correspond to (extended) ER features. First, UML does not provide a graphical notation for specifying keys.[16] UML does, however, provide an *Object Constraint Language (OCL)*, in which we can express FDs. Figure 5.9 shows an example of how to specify the FD *name location → BedAndBreakfast*. Thus, to derive keys of classes in a class diagram, we consult the OCL expressions associated with the class diagram. Second, we can use attribute multiplicity in class diagrams to specify optional attributes and multivalued attributes. In Fig. 5.8, *age* is an optional attribute and *activityInterest* is a multivalued attribute. Third, UML allows the definition of a class to rely on the definition of another class. This allows us to specify compound-attribute groups. For example, *MailingAddress* is a compound attribute group on which the class *Guest* depends. Fourth, UML allows operations to be defined in class diagrams. For example, *rate*, a computed attribute for the association *Reservation*, takes on the result of the operation *calcRate()* as its initial value.

Based on the general principles, we now present a high-level algorithm that generates relational schemas from a UML class diagram. As an example, we show how the UML diagram in Fig. 5.8 along with the OCL constraints in Fig. 5.9 map to the relational schemas in Fig. 5.10.

Step 1   *Based on General Principles #1 and #2, identify keys for each class.* In our example, the UML OCL provides us with these keys. The left-hand side of each FD in Fig. 5.9 is the key for the class on the right-hand side of the FD.

Step 2   *Based on General Principles #1 and #2, identify keys for each association.* Usually multiplicity constraints of associations, along with keys for classes, determine these additional FDs. For example, if A is an n-ary association that connects n classes $C_1, \ldots, C_n$ whose primary keys are, re-

---

[16] UML does not use underlines to denote keys for classes; rather it uses underlines to denote static attributes – attributes that belong to classes, not attributes applicable to instances of classes.

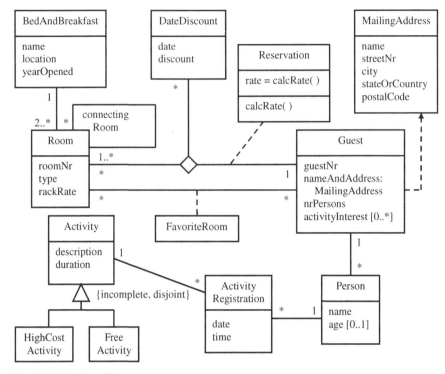

Fig. 5.8 UML class diagram

context BedAndBreakfast
inv: BedAndBreakfast.allInstances()-> forAll(b1, b2 |
    b1.name = b2.name and b1.location = b2.location implies b1 = b2)
        -- *name location → BedAndBreakfast*
...   -- *roomNr name location → Room*
...   -- *guestNr → Guest*
...   -- *date → DateDiscount*
...   -- *name guestNr → Person*
...   -- *description → Activity*
...   -- *name guestNr date time → ActivityRegistration*

Fig. 5.9 OCL for an FD plus other FDs declared for classes in Fig. 5.8

spectively, $P_1, \ldots, P_n$ and the maximum value of the multiplicity for C_n in this association is 1, then the FD $P_1 \ldots P_{n-1} \rightarrow P_n$ holds for A. In our example, we have *roomNr name location date → GuestNr* for the ternary association *Reservation* in Fig. 5.8. When an association has no max-1 multiplicity constraints, the key is the composite of the primary keys for all associated classes. For example, *roomNr name location guestNr* is the key for *FavoriteRoom*.

Step 3 *Based on General Principle #4, determine how generalization/ specialization should be mapped.* Since the ISA constraints for the only generalization/specialization in Fig. 5.8 are *incomplete* and *disjoint*, and since there are no associations for the specializations, we choose to introduce one new attribute, *costLevel*, representing all specializations as suggested by ER Mapping Rule #6.2b.

Step 4   *Based on General Principle #3, map classes to relational schemas.* We generate a relational schema R for a class C as follows. R has the following attributes:

- All the attributes of C except (1) those whose multiplicity is greater than one (e.g., *activityInterest* in Fig. 5.8) and (2) those compound attributes that reference another class (e.g., *nameAndAddress* in Fig. 5.8);
- All leaf attributes of compound attributes (e.g., *name, streetNr, city, stateOrCountry,* and *postalCode* are all included in the relational schema for *Guest*);
- All attributes included in the primary key for C, if not already included (e.g., *name* and *location* from the class *BedAndBreakfast* are included in the relational schema for *Room*); and
- For each association A, if a key of A is also a key of R, then (1) all attributes of A, if any, and (2) for each class C' connected to C by A, the primary-key attributes of C' (e.g., *description*, the primary key of *Activity*, belongs in the relational schema for *ActivityReservation*).

Step 5   *Based on General Principle #3, map the remaining associations to relational schemas.* An association remains after step 4 only if it is not one–one and not one–many or many–one. We generate a relational schema R for each remaining association A as follows. For each class C connected by A, R includes the primary-key attributes of C. *FavoriteRoom* and *Reservation* in Fig. 5.10 are examples.

Step 6   *Based on General Principle #3, map multivalued attributes to relational schemas.* For each multivalued attribute M in a class C, generate a relational schema that includes M and the primary-key attributes of C. The multivalued attribute *activityInterest* in *Guest* in Fig. 5.8 is an example that yields the relational schema *GuestActivityInterest* in Fig. 5.10.

BedAndBreakfast(name, location, yearOpened)
Room(roomNr, name, location, type, rackRate)
ConnectingRoom(roomNr, name, location, connectingRoomNr)
Guest(guestNr, name, streetNr, city, stateOrCountry, postalCode, nrPersons)
GuestActivityInterest(guestNr, activityInterest)
FavoriteRoom(roomNr, name, location, guestNr)
DateDiscount(date, discount)
Reservation(roomNr, name, location, date, guestNr, rate)
Person(name, guestNr, age?)
Activity(description, duration, costLevel?)
ActivityRegistration(name, guestNr, date, time, description)

Fig. 5.10 Schemas generated from Figs. 5.8 and 5.9

Step 7   *Based on General Principle #5, identify nullable attributes.* In our example, *age* is nullable because it is a single-valued, optional attribute of *Guest*,
and *costLevel* is nullable because the ISA hierarchy in Fig. 5.8 has an *incomplete* constraint.

Once we have relational schemas for the database, like those in Fig. 5.10, we
can derive SQL DDL for a relational database. We illustrate here[17] how to turn
generated relational schemas into SQL table creation statements. Figure 5.11 shows
our SQL DDL for the first three relational schemas in Fig. 5.10. The translation is
straightforward.

1. Obtain the name and basic attribute structure for the tables to be created directly
    from the generated schemas. As Fig. 5.11 shows, the *BedAndBreakfast* table
    has the attributes *name, location*, and *yearOpened*. We can rename attributes to
    make them more understandable. *BandBname* and *BandBlocation* are preferable
    to *name* and *location* in *Room* (otherwise most people would read *name* in *Room*
    as the name of the room and *location* as the location of the room).
2. Represent the constraints captured in the diagram and generated schemas. The
    primary-key constraints come directly from the relational schemas, as do other
    uniqueness constraints. The foreign-key constraints come indirectly from the
    relational schemas. An attribute or attribute group that is not a key in a rela-
    tional schema *R* but is a key in a relational schema *S* is a foreign key for *R* that

```
create table BedAndBreakfast(name varchar(20),
      location varchar(20),
      yearOpened number(4) not null,
      primary key (name, location));
create table Room(roomNr number,
      BandBname varchar(20),
      BandBlocation varchar(20),
      type varchar(10) not null,
      rackRate money not null,
      primary key (roomNr, BandBname, BandBlocation),
      foreign key (BandBname, BandBlocation) references BedAndBreakfast (name, location));
create table ConnectingRoom(roomNr number,
      BandBname varchar(20),
      BandBlocation varchar(20),
      connectingRoomNr number,
      primary key (roomNr, BandBname, BandBlocation, connectingRoomNr),
      foreign key (roomNr, BandBname, BandBlocation) references Room,
      foreign key (connectingRoomNr, BandBname, BandBlocation)
          references Room (roomNr, BandBname, BandBlocation)),
      check (roomNr != connectingRoomNr));
...
```

Fig. 5.11 SQL for generated schemas

---

[17] We could have illustrated the derivation of SQL DDL for all earlier generated schemas as well
as this one, but we only illustrate this derivation once.

references S. *BandBname* and *BandBlocation*, for example, constitute a composite foreign key in *Room* that references the composite key *name* and *location* in *BedAndBreakfast*. If desired, we also add *check* constraints, such as *roomNr != connectingRoomNr*. These constraints, however, are not derivable from the relational schemas we generate.

3. Add type declarations, which are usually only implicit in the conceptual-model instance. The types *varchar, number*, and *money* are examples.
4. Reflect the null properties of the relational schemas in the SQL DDL. Primary-key attributes are *not null* by default. All other attributes are nullable unless otherwise specified by a *not null* constraint.

5.5 Normal-Form Guarantees

When mapping conceptual models to database schemas, the question of normalization naturally arises. Are generated relational schemas fully normalized? By "fully normalized" we mean they are in PJNF – Project-Join Normal Form – which also implies that they are in 4NF, BCNF, 3NF, 2NF, and 1NF. Interestingly, we can answer "yes" for conceptual-model diagrams that are *canonical*.

Although circular, the easiest way to define *canonical* is that when mapped according to the mapping rules or algorithms, every relational schema is fully normalized. In practice, many (if not most) diagrams are canonical.[18] Giving a general statement that characterizes canonical for all types of conceptual models (or even for one type of conceptual model) is difficult especially if the characterization is to be given in the least constraining way. Many conceptual-model instances, however, satisfy stronger than necessary conditions, and it is easy to see that they are canonical. We can see, for example, that an ER model instance is canonical by checking the following criteria.

1. Each attribute is atomic (i.e., not decomposable into component attributes we wish to access in the database).
2. Each entity set has one or more keys (possibly inherited if the entity set is weak or in an ISA hierarchy) but has no other FDs among attributes with left-hand sides that are not keys.
3. Each many–many relationship set has one or more keys, but no other FDs among attributes with left-hand sides that are not keys.
4. Every n-ary relationship set ($n \geq 3$) is fully reduced (i.e., we cannot losslessly decompose it into two or more relationship sets).
5. There are no relationship-set cycles, or if there are cycles, then every path from one entity set to another is nonredundant in the sense that we cannot compute any relationship set as combinations of joins and projections of other relationship sets.

---

[18] Many argue that if conceptual-model diagrams are not canonical, they are not good quality diagrams.

All the earlier ER diagrams in Sects. 5.2 and 5.3 are canonical. Thus, all the generated relational schemas are fully normalized. Based on a similar set of criteria for UML, we can see that the UML diagram in Sect. 5.4 is also canonical and that its generated database schema is thus fully normalized.

To see that not all diagrams are canonical, consider Fig. 5.12. This ER diagram violates the conditions listed above for being canonical. Supposing that we wish to access the first name and last name of the registered guest, *Name* is not atomic and thus is an example of a violation of condition #1. The diagram violates condition #2 because of the FD *Type* → *RackRate*, whose left-hand side is not a key for *Room*. The diagram violates condition #3 because the left-hand side of the FD *Date* → *Discount* is not a key for the relationship set *has reservation for*. (We are assuming for this example that the discount amount depends on the date – i.e., whether it is a weekend, weekday, holiday, during the off season, etc.) The diagram violates condition #4 because we can losslessly decompose *has reservation for* into three relationship sets: one between *Package Deal* and *Guest* (which also happens to be equivalent to the *has* relationship set), one between *Guest* and *Activity* (which also happens to be equivalent to the *is signed up for* relationship set), and one between *Room* and *Guest*. (Perhaps this original quaternary relationship set in Fig. 5.12 arose because a designer was told that when guests make reservations they always also sign up for a package deal that includes certain activities.) The diagram violates condition #5 because of the cycle through the relationship sets *has*, *includes*, and *is*

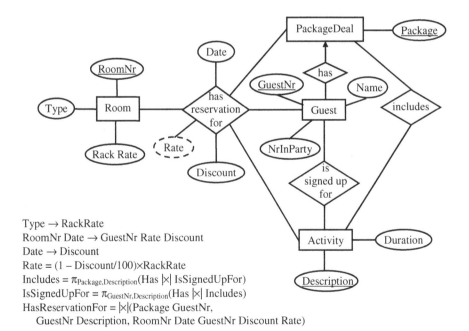

Type → RackRate
RoomNr Date → GuestNr Rate Discount
Date → Discount
Rate = (1 – Discount/100)×RackRate
Includes = π_{Package,Description}(Has |×| IsSignedUpFor)
IsSignedUpFor = π_{GuestNr,Description}(Has |×| Includes)
HasReservationFor = |×|(Package GuestNr,
    GuestNr Description, RoomNr Date GuestNr Discount Rate)

Fig. 5.12 ER diagram with constraints whose standard mapping will yield normal-form violations

signed up for, in which *includes* and *is signed up for* are computable from the other two relationship sets in the cycle.

As we shall see in Sect. 5.5.1, if we use standard schema-generation procedures, we would generate relational schemas that are not normalized. We should then normalize them using standard normalization techniques. We will also see in Sect. 5.5.2, however, that we can rearrange the diagram so that it has the same semantics but is canonical. If we then use standard schema-generation procedures, the resulting relational schemas will be fully normalized. We will thus see that there are two approaches to ensuring that generated relational schemas are fully normalized. (1) We can first generate relational schemas and then normalize using standard normalization techniques. (2) We can first canonicalize a conceptual-model diagram and then generate relational schemas.

5.5.1 Map – Then Normalize

Figure 5.13 shows the relational schemas we would generate according to the standard ER Mapping Rules in Sects. 5.2 and 5.3. We must now recognize the normalform violations and fix them.

- *Guest* is not in 1NF because *Name* is not atomic. We replace *Name* by *First-Name* and *LastName* in *Guest*, which yields *Guest(GuestNr, FirstName, Last-Name, NrInParty, Package)*.
- *HasReservationFor* is not in 2NF because of *Date* → *Discount*. We decompose *HasReservationFor*, which yields *HasReservationFor(RoomNr, Date, GuestNr, Rate, Package, Description)* and a new relational schema *DateDiscount(Date, Discount)*.
- *Room* is not in 3NF because of *Type* → *RackRate*. We decompose *Room*, which yields *Room(RoomNr, Type)* and a new relational schema *RoomType(Type, Rack-Rate)*.
- The relationship set *HasReservationFor* is not in 4NF/PJNF because of the join dependency ⋈*(Package GuestNr, GuestNr Description, RoomNr Date GuestNr Rate)*. (Note that *Discount* is missing because we have already decomposed *HasReservationFor* in a step above.) We thus decompose *HasReservationFor* according to the join dependency, which yields three relational schemas: *HasReservationFor(RoomNr, Date, GuestNr, Rate)*, one whose schema is *(GuestNr,*

Room(RoomNr, Type, RackRate)
Guest(GuestNr, Name, NrInParty, Package)
Activity(Description, Duration)
HasReservationFor(RoomNr, Date, GuestNr, Rate, Discount, Package, Description)
IsSignedUpFor(GuestNr, Description)
Includes(Package, Description)

Fig. 5.13 Generated relational schemas – not normalized

Fig. 5.14 Normalized relation schemas

Room(<u>RoomNr</u>, Type)
RoomType(<u>Type</u>, RackRate)
Guest(<u>GuestNr</u>, FirstName, LastName, NrInParty, Package)
Activity(<u>Description</u>, Duration)
HasReservationFor(<u>RoomNr, Date</u>, GuestNr, Rate)
DateDiscount(<u>Date</u>, Discount)
Includes(<u>Package, Description</u>)

Description), and one whose schema is (<u>*GuestNr, Package*</u>). Since (<u>*GuestNr, Description*</u>) is the same as *IsSignedUpFor*, we discard it, keeping only *IsSignedUpFor*, and since (<u>*GuestNr, Package*</u>) is embedded in *Guest*, we discard it, keeping only *Guest*.

- Finally, we observe that the schema *IsSignedUpFor* is redundant because *IsSignedupFor* $= \pi_{GuestNr,Description}(Has \bowtie Includes)$. Note that although *Includes* is also redundant because *Includes* $= \pi_{Package,Description}(Has \bowtie IsSignedUpFor)$, *IsSignedUpFor* and *Includes* mutually depend on each other. Thus, we can only remove one of them.

Normalizing the relational schemas as described results in the database schema in Fig. 5.14.

5.5.2 Normalize – Then Map

In the alternative approach to normalization, we first make the conceptual-model diagram canonical. We then map it to relational schemas. Because the conceptual-model instance is canonical, the generated relational schemas will be normalized.

To make a conceptual-model instance canonical, we check for and ensure compliance with the basic criteria for characterizing canonical model instances presented earlier. We illustrate this process for ER model instances by making the diagram in Fig. 5.12 canonical.

1. *Nonatomic attributes.* Assuming we wish to have *FirstName* and *LastName* for *Guest*, *Name* is not atomic. We add these attributes, making *Name* a compound attribute, as Fig. 5.15 shows.
2. *FDs whose left-hand sides are not keys.* Recognizing the FD *Type* → *RackRate* as an FD whose left-hand side is not a key, we create a new entity set, *Room Type*, as Fig. 5.15 shows. *Type* is a key attribute for *RoomType*, and *Rack Rate* is a regular attribute. Further, as Fig. 5.15 shows, because the FD *Date* → *Discount* is another FD whose left-hand side is not a key, we create another new entity set, *DateDiscount*. Its attributes are *Date* and *Discount*, with *Date* being a key attribute.
3. *Reducible n-ary relationship sets.* We can losslessly decompose the relationship set *has reservation for*. After adding the new entity set *DateDiscount* to this relationship set, the relationship set *has reservation for* has become a 5-ary

relationship set. We can decompose it losslessly into two binary relationship sets and one ternary relationship set. Since the two new binary relationship sets equate to the existing relationship sets *has* and *is signed up for*, we discard them. This leaves us with the ternary relationship set *has reservation for* in Fig. 5.15.

4. *Reducible cycles*. The cycle of relationship sets from *Guest* to *PackageDeal* to *Activity* and back to *Guest* is a reducible cycle. We can remove either *includes* or *is signed up for* because either is computable from the other two relationship sets. We cannot remove both, however, because we need each one to compute the other. We choose to remove *is signed up for*, as Fig. 5.15 shows.

Figure 5.15 shows the resulting canonical ER diagram, and Fig. 5.14 shows the relational schemas generated from the canonical ER diagram. It should not be a surprise that we obtain the same results whether we first generate relational schemas and then normalize or we first canonicalize the diagram and then generate relational schemas.

An alternative way to do conceptual-model-diagram canonicalization is to (1) transform the conceptual-model diagram to a hypergraph whose nodes are attributes and whose edges are relationship sets,[19] (2) transform the hypergraph to a canonical hypergraph, and (3) map the canonical hypergraph to relational schemas. There are several advantages of this approach. (1) Transforming a conceptual-model diagram to a hypergraph lets us explicitly add all connections among attributes. In particular, it lets us add the troublesome FD connections among attributes that are only implicit in diagrams that force attributes to be attached only to entity sets (e.g., ER) or classes (e.g., UML).[20] (2) Since all the constraints needed for normalization appear directly in the diagram, the canonicalization process proceeds entirely with

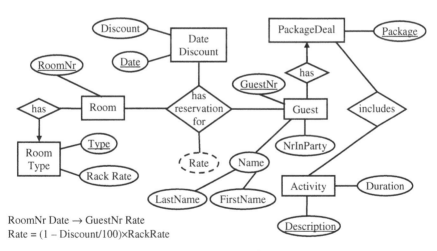

RoomNr Date → GuestNr Rate
Rate = (1 − Discount/100)×RackRate

Fig. 5.15 ER diagram transformed to generate normalized relational schemas

---

[19] Any ISA hierarchies remain intact without alteration.

[20] Some conceptual models (e.g., ORM [9] and OSM [8]) are directly based on hypergraphs and already include all connections among attributes. These conceptual models need no transformation

the diagram alone. (3) Finally, this approach leads to more straightforward mapping algorithms and, as we shall see in Sect. 5.6, leads to mapping algorithms for object-based schemas and XML schemas.

We illustrate this approach beginning with the noncanonical ER diagram in Fig. 5.12, which we first convert to the noncanonical hypergraph in Fig. 5.16. We convert an ER diagram to a hypergraph as follows.

1. Make every attribute be a lexical node in the hypergraph. Lexical refers to readable/writable data; lexical nodes represent the data we store in a database. We represent lexical nodes by dashed boxes, as Fig. 5.16 shows.
2. Make every entity set be a nonlexical node in the hypergraph. Nonlexical refers to real-world objects that, if represented in a database, would be represented by object identifiers. We represent nonlexical nodes by solid boxes; *Room*, *Guest*, *PackageDeal*, and *Activity* are the nonlexical nodes in Fig. 5.16.
3. Make every relationship set be an edge in the hypergraph. The relationship set *has reservation for*, for example, connects the four nonlexical nodes that were originally entity sets and the three lexical nodes that were originally attributes, as Fig. 5.16 shows. If there is a functional relationship among all the nodes of the relationship set, we represent this functional relationship set by marking the functionally determined nodes with arrowheads. The *has* relationship set between *Guest* and *PackageDeal* is an example. If there are other functional

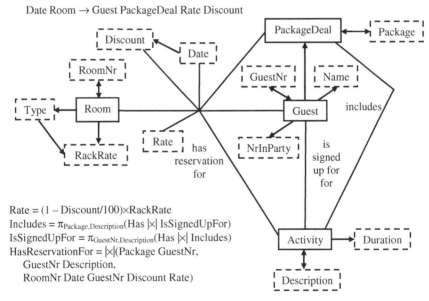

Fig. 5.16 Hypergraph generated from ER diagram in Fig. 5.12

---

to hypergraphs. For these hypergraph-based conceptual models, the canonicalization and mappings to relational schemas proceed as we describe here.

relationships among some or all the nodes, we add an edge for each one. To keep the diagram from becoming too cluttered, we may visually add these additional edges as FDs (but they are nevertheless edges in the hypergraph). Figure 5.16 includes the FD *Date Room* → *Guest PackageDeal Rate Discount*, which is a functional edge relating all nodes of the 7-ary relationship set except *Activity*.

4. Make every connection between an entity set and its attributes be an edge in the hypergraph. For multivalued attributes, the edge is many–many (nonfunctional). For compound attributes, the edge is functional from entity set to leaf attribute, one edge for every leaf attribute. (Nonleaf attributes are discarded.) For all other attributes, the edge is functional from entity set to attribute. The functional edge from *Activity* to *Duration* in Fig. 5.16 is an example. For singleton key attributes we also add a functional edge from attribute to entity. When we have a functional edge between an entity set and an attribute in both directions, we combine them as a single, bidirectional, one–one edge. In Fig. 5.16, *RoomNr* for *Room*, *GuestNr* for *Guest*, *Package* for *PackageDeal*, and *Description* for *Activity* are all examples. For each composite key consisting of n attribute nodes, we add an $(n + 1)$-ary functional edge from the n attribute nodes constituting the composite key to the entity-set node. We also combine the $(n + 1)$-ary functional edge with the n functional edges from the entity set to these attribute nodes to form a single, one–one edge between the entity-set node and the n attribute nodes constituting the composite key.

5. For every FD among lexical nodes, add an edge. For our example, we add the edges *Type* → *RackRate* and *Date* → *Discount*, as Fig. 5.16 shows.

We next make a noncanonical hypergraph canonical in three main steps.[21] We illustrate these steps by converting the noncanonical hypergraph in Fig. 5.16 to the canonical hypergraph in Fig. 5.17.

1. Decompose all hyperedges that can be losslessly decomposed. In Fig. 5.16 we decompose the 7-ary edge along with the edge represented by the FD to a 4-ary functional edge *Room Date* → *Guest Rate* plus several other edges, all of which eventually turn out to be redundant. Fiure 5.17 shows this 4-ary edge, but none of the redundant edges.

2. Remove all redundant edges and all redundant hyperedge components. In addition to the redundant edges just generated and ignored, we also remove the *Room–RackRate* edge and the *Guest–Activity* edge.

---

[21] Usually these three main steps are enough. Exceptions arise when (1) the hypergraph is cyclic after redundancies have been removed and (2) optional participation interferes with our ability to capture all element values. An example of the first would be an additional edge between *Description* and *Duration* where one means the average duration for an activity and the other means the maximum allowable duration. In this case, we need to qualify *Duration* to be, say, *AveDuration* and *MaxDuration*, and generate the relational schema for *Activity* with three attributes, *Duration*, *AveDuration*, and *MaxDuration*. An example of the second would be optional participation for *Name* where we might want to keep all names of guests even if they have no guest number. In this case, we need a separate table for *Name* alone since we cannot capture all names in the *Guest* relational schema, which demands a *GuestNr* for every *Guest*. We can resolve both of these issues by adding roles. See [4] for details.

3. Merge each nonlexical node with its key (any one key, if there is more than one choice). For example, we merge *Room* with its primary key *RoomNr*, which, as Fig. 5.16 shows, are in a one-to-one correspondence. The result of this merge is the lexical node *RoomNr*, which has been merged with *Room* as Fig. 5.17 shows. Similarly, we merge *Package* with *PackageDeal*, *GuestNr* with *Guest*, and *Description* with *Activity*.

Once we have a canonical hypergraph, the conversion to a relational database schema is straightforward. With one mapping rule, we can obtain a set of normalized relational schemas:

> *Every edge becomes a relational schema. If the edge is functional in only one direction, the tail attribute(s) constitute the key. If the edge is functional in both directions [from tail(s) to head(s) and from head(s) to tail(s)], the head attribute(s) constitute a key as well as the tail attribute(s). If the edge is not functional, all the connected attributes constitute the key.*

For example, *RoomNr* → *Type* is a functional edge whose generated relational schema is (<u>*RoomNr, Type*</u>), and *RoomNr Date* → *GuestNr Rate* is another functional edge whose generated relational schema is (<u>*RoomNr, Date*</u>, *GuestNr, Rate*). The edge between *Package* and *Description* is a nonfunctional edge, and thus its generated relational schema is (<u>*Package, Description*</u>). We have no edge that is functional in both directions. To illustrate a bidirectional edge, suppose, as in Fig. 5.1, that in addition to room numbers, rooms in a bed-and-breakfast establishment also have identifying names. We would then have another attribute *RoomName* in a one-to-one correspondence with *RoomNr*. In this case, we would generate the relational schema (<u>*RoomNr*</u>, <u>*RoomName*</u>) in which both *RoomNr* is a key and *RoomName* is a key.

Although this single rule generates relational schemas that are all normalized, it fragments the database into more relational schemas than necessary. Thus, to finalize the relational schemas for the database, we merge as many as we can without violating any normal form using the following simple rule:

> *Merge schemas that have a common key.*

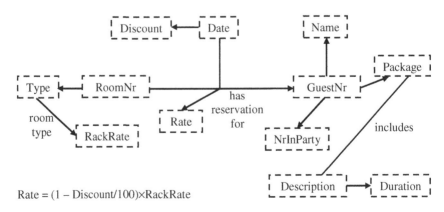

$$Rate = (1 - Discount/100) \times RackRate$$

Fig. 5.17 Canonical hypergraph

For example, we would merge (*GuestNr, Name*), (*GuestNr, Package*), and (*Guest Nr, NrInParty*) because they all have the key *GuestNr*. We also add a name as we merge so that we have a standard relational schema. We would thus obtain *Guest*(*GuestNr, Name, Package, NrInParty*). Note that we would *not* merge (*RoomNr, Type*) and (*RoomNr, Date, GuestNr, Rate*) because they do not have a common key – *RoomNr* is not the same as the composite key *RoomNr Date*. Forming the relational schemas from Fig. 5.17 and then merging those that have a common key results in the relational schemas in Fig. 5.14, except that *Name* appears in place of *FirstName* and *LastName* since we started with *Name* rather than *FirstName* and *LastName* in Fig. 5.12.

Note that we have said nothing about ISA hierarchies. This is because there is no change in the way we map ISA hierarchies to relational schemas. There is a change, however, when we convert noncanonical hypergraphs to canonical hypergraphs. When we merge a nonlexical node with its key, we propagate this merge all the way down the hierarchy. Thus, for example, when we convert the ER diagram in Fig. 5.5 to a canonical hypergraph, every node in the ISA hierarchy rooted at *Guest* becomes a lexical node with the name *GuestNr*.[22] If we choose to have a relational schema for every node in the ISA hierarchy, we simply do not merge relational schemas in the ISA hierarchy that share a common key. If we choose to have a relational schema only for the root of the ISA hierarchy, we merge in the usual way. If we choose to have relational schemas only for the leaves of the ISA hierarchy, we merge along every path from the root to each of the leaves.

5.6 Mappings for Object-Based and XML Databases

In this section, we show how to generate generic hierarchical structures, called *scheme trees*, from a canonical hypergraph. Since scheme trees are generic hierarchical structures, it is straightforward to map scheme trees to database schemas that support hierarchical data. As an example, we show how to map scheme trees to object-relational database schema instances and XML schema instances. Since object-oriented databases are similar to object-relational databases, our example for object-relational databases serves for object-oriented databases as well.

The central idea of generating scheme trees is to ensure that each instance of a hyperedge in a canonical hypergraph only appears once in a scheme-tree instance. To do so, our scheme trees observe the many–one and one–one constraints in the hypergraph. We capture the essence of the idea in the following algorithm.[23]

---

[22] To keep the various nodes straight, we should add comments to the diagram. Unless these comments help us keep the nodes conceptually straight and may help us choose names for relational schemas, we can ignore these comments.

[23] The algorithm is a simplified version of the heuristic *n*-ary algorithm in [12], which generates scheme trees from a canonical hypergraph.

While there is an unmarked hyperedge, do:
> Select a subset V of vertices in an unmarked hyperedge E
> > as the root node of a new scheme tree T.
> While we can add an unmarked hyperedge E to T, do:
> > (We can add an unmarked edge E if the following conditions hold:
> > E must have a nonempty intersection S of vertices with T.
> > A node N must exist in T such that the set S is contained in
> > the union of the nodes above or equal to N and S functionally
> > determines the union of the nodes above or equal to N.)
> > Add E to T as follows:
> > > If S functionally determines $E - S$
> > > > Add the vertices in $E - S$ to node N.
> > > Else
> > > > Make a node consisting of the vertices in $E - S$ and add it to
> > > > the tree as a child node of N.
> > Mark E as used.

If we select *Package* (a subset of the vertices in the edge *GuestNr* $\rightarrow$ *Package*) as the root node, this algorithm generates the scheme tree in Fig. 5.18a. Having selected {*Package*} as the root for T and $E = \{Package, GuestNr\}$ as the edge we are considering, we see that all conditions of the while loop trivially hold (as they always do for the initial selection of a root and an edge). Since $S = \{Package\}$ does *not* functionally determine $E - S = \{GuestNr\}$ (it is actually the other way around), we add {*GuestNr*} as a child node of the node {*Package*}. Continuing, we next consider the edge *GuestNr* $\rightarrow$ *Name*. Here, the conditions of the while loop also hold with $S = \{GuestNr\}$, $N = \{GuestNr\}$, and *GuestNr* $\rightarrow$ *GuestNr Package*. Since S functionally determines $E - S = \{GuestNr, Name\} - \{GuestNr\} = \{Name\}$, we add *Name* to the node containing *GuestNr*. Similarly, we add *NrInParty* to this node, thus completing the second node in Fig. 5.18a. We next consider the edge *RoomNr Date* $\rightarrow$ *GuestNr Rate*. The intersection of S with T is {*GuestNr*}, which is contained in node N we just created. Further, *GuestNr* $\rightarrow$ *GuestNr Name NrInParty Package* so that it functionally determines the union of N and the node above N (the root). Since S does not functionally determine $E - S$ (i.e., {*GuestNr*} does not functionally determine {*RoomNr, Date, Rate*}), we make a new node consisting of {*RoomNr, Date, Rate*} and place it below N as Fig. 5.18a shows. Continuing, we next consider the nonfunctional edge {*Package, Description*}. The nonempty intersection S with the scheme tree T we have built so far is {*Package*}. Since {*Description*} does not functionally determine {*Package*}, we form a new node consisting only of {*Description*} and add it as another child node of {*Package*}, resulting in the scheme tree T in Fig. 5.18a. Of the remaining four edges, *Type* $\rightarrow$ *RackRate* has an empty intersection with T, and the rest (*Date* $\rightarrow$ *Discount, RoomNr* $\rightarrow$ *Type*, and *Description* $\rightarrow$ *Duration*) do not satisfy the functional-dependency condition of the while loop for the scheme tree in Fig. 5.18a.

Figure 5.18b shows the textual representation for the scheme tree in Fig. 5.18a. In the textual representation, each node appears within parentheses with a star to indi-

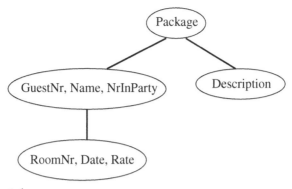

(a) Tree Representation.

(Package, (GuestNr, Name, NrInParty, (RoomNr, Date, Rate)*)*, (Description)*)*

(b) Textual Representation.

Fig. 5.18 Scheme-tree representations. Tree representation and Textual representation

cate repetition; parenthesized nodes appear in line according to their nested position in the scheme tree.

Choosing the best starting place to run the algorithm depends on the semantics of the application. In our example, starting with *Package* is probably not best. The main point of the application is to rent rooms to guests, not the activity packages they may choose. Thus, most of the processing is likely to be about looking up guests. Hence, a likely better starting place for our scheme-tree algorithm is to choose *GuestNr* as the root. When we start with *GuestNr* as the root of the first tree and run the algorithm repeatedly until all edges are in some scheme tree, we obtain the scheme trees in Fig. 5.19.

In Fig. 5.19 we have marked keys in the usual way. In our example, *GuestNr*, *Date*, *Type*, and *Description* values must all be unique in the usual way we expect key values to be unique. Since *RoomNr Date* → *GuestNr*, *RoomNr-Date* value pairs must be unique in the nested relation in which they appear. Similarly, since *RoomNr* → *Type*, *RoomNr* values must also be unique in the nested relation in which they appear.

Figure 5.20 shows an object-relational database schema instance derived from the first scheme tree in Fig. 5.19. The main idea of this derivation is to scan a scheme tree bottom up and generate object types and collection types as we go up the scheme tree. Specifically, consider a leaf node v whose parent is u. We generate an object

(GuestNr, Name, NrInParty, Package, (RoomNr, Date, Rate)*)*
(Date, Discount)*
(Type, RackRate, (RoomNr)*)*
(Description, Duration, (Package)*)*

Fig. 5.19 Generated scheme-tree forest

```
create type reservation as object (
      roomNr                integer,
      reservationDate       date,
      rate                  number,
      static function createReservation(roomNo integer, resDate date, rate number)
            return reservation,
      static function createReservation(roomNo integer, resDate date) return reservation);
create type body reservation is
      static function createReservation(roomNo integer, resDate date, rate number) return reservation is
            begin
                  return reservation(roomNo, resDate, rate);
            end;
      static function createReservation(roomNo integer, resDate date) return reservation is
            begin
                  return reservation(roomNo, resDate, (1-discount.getDiscountRate(resDate)/100)*
                        roomType.getRackRate(roomNo)));
            end;
end;
create type collectionOfReservation as
      varray(200) of reservation;
create type guest as object (
      guestNr               integer,
      name                  varchar2(30),
      nrInParty             integer,
      package               varchar2(40),
      reservations          collectionOfReservation);
create table tableOfGuest of guest;
```

Fig. 5.20 Derived object-relational database schema instance

type t_v for v such that t_v has all the attributes in v. Then, we create a collection type of t_v. Afterwards, we generate an object type t_u for u such that t_u has all the attributes in u and a field whose type is the collection type of t_v. We then continue this process up to the root node of the scheme tree. Thus, for example, for the first scheme tree in Fig. 5.19, we create an object type called *reservation* that includes three fields: *roomNr, reservationDate,* and *rate.* We then create a collection type called *collectionOfReservation,* which is a variable-length array that stores *reservation* objects. Finally, we create an object type called *guest* for the root node. Note that there is a field called *reservations* in *guest* whose type is *collectionOfReservation.* To store *guest* objects, we create *tableOfGuest* – a table of this type. Unfortunately, declared key constraints are not typically provided by object-relational databases. Thus, as for any constraint we wish to enforce that is not directly supported by the database, we must provide our own code to check and enforce it.

Figure 5.21 shows the first and last parts of a derived XML schema instance for the generated scheme-tree forest in Fig. 5.19. Several derivations are possible; Fig. 5.21 shows one derived as follows. For each nesting of a scheme tree we provide two names – one for describing the group and one for describing an individual in the group. Thus, for the scheme tree (Type, RackRate, (RoomNr)*)* we introduce the name *RoomTypes* for the group, *RoomType* for the individuals in the group, *Rooms* for the nested group, and *Room* for the individuals in the nested group. We nest these

```
< ?xml version="1.0" encoding="UTF-8"?>
< xs:schema xmlns:xs="http://www.w3.org/2001/XMLSchema" elementFormDefault="qualified">
  < xs:element name="Document">
    < xs:complexType>
      < xs:sequence>
        < xs:element ref="Guests" minOccurs="0"/>
        < xs:element ref="Activities" minOccurs="0"/>
        < xs:element ref="DateDiscounts" minOccurs="0"/>
        < xs:element ref="RoomTypes"/>
      </xs:sequence>
    </xs:complexType>
  </xs:element>
...
  < xs:element name="RoomTypes">
    < xs:complexType>
      < xs:sequence>
        < xs:element name="RoomType" maxOccurs="unbounded">
          < xs:complexType>
            < xs:sequence>
              < xs:element name="Rooms">
                < xs:complexType>
                  < xs:sequence>
                    < xs:element name="Room" maxOccurs="unbounded">
                      < xs:complexType>
                        < xs:attribute ref="RoomNr"/>
                      </xs:complexType>
                    </xs:element>
                  </xs:sequence>
                </xs:complexType>
              </xs:element>
            </xs:sequence>
            < xs:attribute name="Type" type="xs:ID"/>
            < xs:attribute name="RackRate" type="xs:double"/>
          </xs:complexType>
        </xs:element>
      </xs:sequence>
    </xs:complexType>
    < xs:key name="RoomNrKey">
      < xs:selector xpath="./RoomType/Rooms/Room"/>
      < xs:field xpath="@RoomNr"/>
    </xs:key>
  </xs:element>
  < xs:attribute name="RoomNr" type="xs:integer"/>
  < xs:attribute name="Date" type="xs:date"/>
  < xs:attribute name="Package" type="xs:string"/>
</xs:schema>
```

Fig. 5.21 Derived XML schema instance

names appropriately, as shown by Fig. 5.21. We then put the attributes in their proper place – we nest *Type* and *RackRate* under *RoomType* and *RoomNr* under *Room*. The type for *Type* is *xs:ID*, making it unique throughout the document. Since *Type* appears nowhere else in the scheme-tree forest in Fig. 5.19, this simple declaration is sufficient. For *RoomNr*, which does appear in one other scheme tree, we scope the extent of uniqueness to be within *RoomTypes* and make a key declaration as shown by Fig. 5.21. Further, when an attribute appears in more than one scheme tree, we use *ref* to reference a single declaration for its type. *RoomNr* is an example; its type declaration along with the type declarations for *Date* and *Package*, which also appear in more than one scheme tree, appear globally at the end of the XML schema instance in Fig. 5.21. In the first part of the XML schema instance in Fig. 5.21, we have declarations for the roots of each of the scheme trees, *Guests*, *Activities*, *DateDiscounts*, and *RoomTypes*, all under the ultimate root, *Document*. We allow each of them to be optional except *RoomTypes*. (Although there may be no guests, activities, or date discounts, if there are no rooms, there is no bed-and-breakfast establishment.)

5.7 Additional Readings

From the beginning, mappings from conceptual-model instances to database schemas have been an important part of the conceptual-modeling literature. Peter Chen's seminal article on the ER model includes an extensive discussion of mapping the ER model to various database models [2]. Ever since the appearance of this article, discussions of mapping conceptual-model instances to database schemas have continued. Notable, along the way, are an *ACM Computing Surveys* article [14] and a foundational book on conceptual database design [1]. Most current database textbooks (e.g., [11, 13, 15]) contain chapters on mapping conceptual models to database schemas.

Normalization concerns have also always been a part of mapping conceptual-model instances to database schemas. Chen's seminal article [2] addressed normalization, and his mappings did yield relations in 3NF under his assumptions. Along the way other researchers have added insights about normalization. Researchers have suggested both the map-then-normalize approach [14] and the normalize-then-map approach [3, 10]. In [1] the authors take the point of view that ER diagrams are not of good quality unless they are canonical, and they talk about canonicalizing ER diagrams as one way to help create high-quality diagrams. The hypergraph approach to normalization appeared initially in [5]; full details appeared later in [4].

Only recently have articles appeared that describe the process of mapping conceptual models for object-based, object-oriented, and XML databases. Some initial thoughts appeared in [4, 6]. Proofs that generated scheme trees have no redundancy appeared later [12].

References

1. Batini C, Ceri S, Navathe SB (1992) Conceptual database design: an entity-relationship approach. Benjamin/Cummings, Redwood City
2. Chen PP (1976) The entity-relationship model – toward a unified view of data. Trans Database Syst 1(1):9–36
3. Chung I, Nakamura F, Chen PP (1981) A decomposition of relations using the entity-relationship approach. In: Proceedings of the 2nd international conference on entity-relationship approach to information modeling and analysis (ER'81), Washington, October 1981, pp 149–171
4. Embley DW (1998) Object database development: concepts and principles. Addison-Wesley, Reading
5. Embley DW, Ling TW (1989) Synergistic database design with an extended entity-relationship model. In: Proceedings of the 8th international conference on entity-relationship approach modeling (ER'89), Toronto, October 1989, pp 118–135
6. Embley DW, Mok WY (2001) Developing XML documents with guaranteed 'good' properties. In: Proceedings of the 20th international conference on conceptual modeling (ER2001), Yokohama, Japan, November 2001, pp 426–441
7. Embley DW, Mok WY (2003) Producing XML documents with guaranteed 'good' properties. In: Proceedings of the 7th world multiconference on systemics, cybernetics and informatics (SCI 2003), vol IX, Orlando, FL, July 2003, pp 195–198
8. Embley DW, Kurtz BD, Woodfield SN (1992) Object-oriented systems analysis: a model-driven approach. Prentice Hall, Englewood Cliffs
9. Halpin T (1995) Conceptual schema and relational database design, 2nd edn. Prentice Hall, Sydney, Australia
10. Ling TW (1985) A normal form for entity-relationship diagrams. In: Proceedings of the 4th international conference on entity-relationship approach (ER'85), Chicago, October 1985, pp 24–35
11. Elmasri R, Navathe SB (2004) Fundamentals of database systems, 4th edn. Addison-Wesley, Boston
12. Mok WY, Embley DW (2006) Generating compact redundancy-free XML documents from concptual-model hypergraphs. Trans Knowl Data Eng 18(8):1082–1096
13. Silberschatz A, Korth H, Sudarshan S (2002) Database system concepts, 5th edn. McGraw-Hill, Boston
14. Teorey TJ, Yang D, Fry JP (1986) A logical design methodology for relational databases using the extended entity-relationship model. ACM Comput Surv 18(2):197–222
15. Ullman JD, Widom J (2002) A first course in database systems, 2nd edn. Prentice Hall, Upper Saddle River

Chapter 6
The Enhanced Entity-Relationship Model

Bernhard Thalheim

Abstract This chapter introduces an extended entity-relationship model. Structural extensions are complex attributes, cluster or generalisation types, and higher-order relationship types. These extensions still allow a hierarchical construction of schema items. Therefore, a layered predicate logic can be defined. Classical integrity constraints are thus definable on the basis of this logics. The structuring of a database consists of a schema together with a set of static integrity constraints. Database design is nowadays based on the co-design of structuring and functionality. Therefore, extended entity-relationship model languages are supported by explicit functionality. The relational algebra and aggregation functions are generalised for extended entity-relationship models. Therefore, queries, transactions and workflows can directly be defined within the model. Additionally, views can be defined in a more general setting. This extension also supports a novel and sophisticated simple definition of the OLAP cube and its treatment. Semantics generalises the entire theory of relational integrity constraints in such a way that constraint handling and specification can be entirely managed at the conceptual level. Finally, we show how constraint specification can be supported.

6.1 Database Design

6.1.1 Database Design and Development

The problem of information system design can be stated as follows:

Design the logical and physical structure of an information system in a given database management system (DBMS) (or for a database paradigm), so that it contains all the informa-

Bernhard Thalheim

Department of Computer Science, Christian-Albrechts University Kiel, 24098 Kiel, Germany,
e-mail: thalheim@is.informatik.uni-kiel.de

D. W. Embley and B. Thalheim (eds), *Handbook of Conceptual Modeling.*
DOI 10.1007/978-3-642-15865-0, © Springer 2011

tion required by the user and required for the efficient behaviour of the whole information system for all users. Furthermore, specify the database application processes and the user interaction.

The implicit goals of database design are:

- to meet all the information (contextual) requirements of the entire spectrum of users in a given application area;
- to provide a 'natural' and easy-to-understand structuring of the information content;
- to preserve the designers' entire semantic information for a later redesign;
- to meet all the processing requirements and also achieve a high degree of efficiency in processing;
- to achieve logical independence of query and transaction formulation on this level;
- to provide a simple and easy-to-understand user interface family.

These requirements must be related to database models. We distinguish between relational database models, hierarchical and other graphical database models, object-oriented database models, and object-relational models. The enhanced ER model discussed in this chapter is the only database model that supports mappings to all kinds of database models.

Over the past few years database structures have been discussed extensively. Some of the open questions have been satisfactorily solved. Modelling includes, however, additional aspects:

Structuring of a database application is concerned with representing the database structure and the corresponding static integrity constraints.

Functionality of a database application is specified on the basis of processes and dynamic integrity constraints.

Distribution of information system components is specified through explicit specification of services and exchange frames that specify the architecture and the collaboration among components.

Interactivity is provided by the system on the basis of foreseen stories for a number of envisioned actors and is based on media objects which are used to deliver the content of the database to users or to receive new content.

This understanding has led to the **co-design approach** to modelling by specification **structuring, functionality, distribution** and **interactivity**. These four aspects of modelling have both syntactic and semantic elements.

There are numerous database specification languages. Most of them are called database models. The resulting specification is called a database schema. Simple database models are the relational model and the entity-relationship (ER) model. In this chapter we introduce extensions of the ER model which are consistent, easy to use and have a translation to relational, object-relational and XML database models.

The specification of databases is based on three interleaved and dependent parts:

Syntactics (syntax): **Inductive specification of databases** is based on a set of base types, functions and predicates, a collection of constructors and a theory of construction limiting the application of constructors by rules or by formulas in deontic logic. In most cases, the theory may be simplified to the usage of canonical rules for construction and interpretation. **Structural recursion** is the main specification vehicle.

Semantics: **Specification of admissible databases** on the basis of static and dynamic integrity constraints describes those database states and those database sequences which are considered legal. If structural recursion is used, then a variant of hierarchical first-order predicate logic may be used for the description of integrity constraints.

Pragmatics: **Description of context and intension** is based either on explicit reference to the enterprise model, to enterprise tasks, to enterprise policy and environments or on intensional logic used for relating the interpretation and meaning to users depending on time, location and common sense.

Specification is often restricted to the description of syntactical elements. This restricted approach can only be used for simple applications with simple structuring. However, most applications require the analysis of data, integration or federation of data, advanced aggregation of data, and advanced basic data types.

6.1.2 Implicit Assumptions and Inherent Constraints of Database Specification Languages

Each language used should be based on a clear definition of structure, semantics, operations, behaviour and environment. At the same time, languages presuppose implicit assumptions and constraints. The enhanced or extended ER (EER) model might, for instance, use the following assumptions:

Set semantics: The default semantics of entity and relationship types are set semantics. If extended type constructors are used, then their semantics are explicitly defined.

Identifiability: Each entity type is identifiable. Each component type needs to be labelled whenever it cannot be distinguished from other components. In relationship types, components are ordered. Their labels can be omitted whenever there is an identification. Set semantics implies the identifiability of any element in the database.

Partial unique name assumption: Attribute names are unique for each entity and relationship type. Entity type names and relationship type names are unique for the ER schema.

Referential integrity: If a type is based on component types, then each value for this type can only use such values in components which *exist* as values in the component instance.

Monotonicity of semantics: If integrity constraints Φ are added to a given set of integrity constraints Σ, then the set of possible instances which satisfy the extended set of constraints $\Sigma \cup \Phi$ is a subset of the set of instances which satisfy Σ.

We do not use the entity integrity assumption. The database can use null values in keys as well [24]. The entity integrity assumption can be enforced by the profile used during mapping schema specifications to logical database languages.

6.1.3 Storage and Representation Alternatives

The classical approach to objects is to store them based on strong typing. Each real-life thing is thus represented by a number of objects which are either coupled by the object identifier or by specific maintenance procedures. This approach has led to a variety of types. Thus, we might consider two different approaches.

Class-wise, strongly identification-based representation and storage: Real things may be represented by several objects. Such choice increases maintenance costs. For this reason, we couple things under consideration and objects in the database by an injective association. Since we may be not able to identify things by their value in the database due to the complexity of the identification mechanism in real life, we introduce the notion of the *object identifier* (OID) in order to cope with identification without representing complex, real-life identification. Objects can be elements of several classes. In the early days of object orientation it was assumed that objects belonged to one and only one class. This assumption has led to a number of migration problems which have not been satisfactorily resolved. The association among facets of the same thing that are represented by several objects is maintained by the object identifier.

Object-wise representation and storage: Graph-based models which have been developed in order to simplify the object-oriented approaches [3] display objects by their sub-graphs, i.e. by the set of nodes associated to a certain object and the corresponding edges. This representation corresponds to the representation used in standardisation.

Object-wise storage has a high redundancy which must be maintained by the system, thereby decreasing performance to a significant extent. Besides performance problems, such systems also suffer from low scalability and poor utilisation of resources. The operation of such systems leads to lock avalanches. Any modification of data requires a recursive lock of related objects.

Therefore, objects-wise storage is applicable only under a number of restrictions:

- The application is stable and the data structures and the supporting basic functions necessary for the application do not change during the lifespan of the system.
- The data set is almost free of updates. Updates, insertions and deletions of data are only allowed in well-defined restricted 'zones' of the database.

A typical application area for object-wise storage is archiving or information presentation systems. Both systems have an update system underneath. We call such systems **play-out systems**. The data are stored in such a way so that they are transferred to the user. The data modification system has a **play-out generator** that materialises all views necessary for the play-out system.

Two implementation alternatives are already in use, albeit more on an intuitive basis:

Object-oriented approaches: Objects are decomposed into a set of related objects. Their association is maintained on the basis of OIDs or other explicit referencing mechanisms. The decomposed objects are stored in corresponding classes.

XML-based approaches: The XML description allows one to use null values without notification. If a value for an object does not exist, is not known, is not applicable or cannot be obtained, etc., the XML schema does not use the tag corresponding to the attribute or the component. Classes are hidden. Thus, we have two storage alternatives for XML approaches which might be used at the same time or might be used separately:

Class-separated snowflake representation: An object is stored in several classes. Each class has a partial view on the entire object. This view is associated with the structure of the class.

Full-object representation: All data associated with the object are compiled into one object. The associations among the components of objects with other objects are based on pointers or references.

We may use the first representation for our **storage engine** and the second representation for our **input engine** and our **output engine** in data warehouse approaches. The input of an object leads to the generation of a new OID and to a bulk insert into several classes. The output is based on views.

The first representation leads to an object-relational storage approach which is based on the ER schema. Thus, we may apply translation techniques developed for ER schemata [25].

The second representation is very useful if we want to represent an object with all its facets. For instance, an *Address* object may be presented with all its data, e.g. geographical information, contact information, acquisition information, etc. Another *Address* object is only instantiated by geographical information. A third one has only contact information. We could represent these three objects by XML files on the same DTD or XSchema.

6.1.4 The Higher-Order Entity-Relationship Model

The ER model has been extended by more than three-score proposals. Some extensions contradict other extensions. In this chapter we use the higher-order (or hierarchical) entity-relationship model (HERM). It is a special case of an extended entity-relationship (EER) model (e.g. [9, 11, 15, 25]).

The HERM used in this chapter has the following basic and extended modelling constructs:

Simple attributes: For a given set of domains there are defined attributes and their corresponding domains.

Complex attributes: Using basic types, complex attributes can be defined by means of the tuple and the set constructors. The tuple constructor is used to define complex attributes by Cartesian aggregation. The set constructor allows construction of a new complex attribute by set aggregation. Additionally, the bag, list, and variant constructors can be used.

Entities: Entity types are characterised by their attributes. Entity types have a set of attributes which serve to identify the elements of the type class. This concept is similar to the concept of the key in relational databases.

Clusters: A disjoint union $\dot\cup$ of types whose identification type is domain compatible is called a cluster. Cluster types (or variant types) are well known in programming languages but are often overlooked in database models, where this absence creates needless fragmentation of the databases, confusing mixing of generalisation and specialisation and confusion over null values.

First-order relationships: First-order relationship types are defined as associations between single entity types or clusters of entity types. They can also be characterised by attributes.

Higher-order relationships: The relationship type of order i is defined as an association of relationship types of order less than i or of entity types and can also be characterised by attributes.

Integrity constraints: A corresponding logical operator can be defined for each type. A set of logical formulas using this operator can define the integrity constraints which are valid for each instance of the type.

Operations: Operations can be defined for each type.

*   The generic operations `insert`, `delete`, and `update` are defined for each type.
*   The algebra consists of classical set operations, such as union, intersection, difference and restricted complement, and general type operations, such as selection, map [particular examples of this operation are (tagged) nest, unnest, projection, renaming], and pump (particular examples of this operation are the classical aggregation functions). The fixpoint operator is not used.

- Each type can have a set of (conditional) operations.
- Based on the algebra, query forms and transactions can be specified.

The extensions of the ER model should be **safe** in the sense that appropriate semantics exist. There is a large variety of proposals which are not safe. Some reasons for this include higher-order or function types, such as those used for the definition of derived attributes, or the loss of identification.

It can be observed that higher-order functions can be attached to the type system. However, in this case types do not specify sets, although their semantics can be defined by topoi [12, 21]. This possibility limits simplicity for the introduction of constraints and operations. Furthermore, these semantics are far too complex to be a candidate for semantics. The ER model is simpler than OO models.

6.2 Syntax of EER Models

6.2.1 Structuring Specification

We use a classic three-layered approach to inductive specification of database structures. The first layer is the data environment, called the basic data type scheme, which is defined by the system or is the assumed set of available basic data. The second layer is the schema of a given database. The third layer is the database itself representing a state of the application's data and knowledge.

The second layer is treated differently in most database models. Nevertheless, there are common features, especially type constructors. A common approach in most models is the generic definition of operations according to the structure of the type. The inductive specification of structuring is based on **base types** and **type constructors**.

A **type constructor** is a function from types to a new type. The constructor can be supplemented with

- A *selector* for retrieval (like *Select*) with a retrieval expression and *update functions* (like *Insert, Delete*, and *Update*) for value mapping from the new type to the component types or to the new type;
- *Correctness criteria* and rules for validation;
- *Default* rules;
- One or several *user representations*; and
- A *physical representation* or properties of the physical representation.

A **base type** is an algebraic structure $B = (Dom(B), Op(B), Pred(B))$ with a name, a set of values in a domain, a set of operations and a set of predicates. A class B^C on the base type is a collection of elements from $Dom(B)$. Usually, B^C must be set. It can also be a list (denoted by $< . >$), multiset ($\{|.|\}$), tree, etc. Classes may be changed by applying operations. Elements of a class may be classified by the predicates.

The value set can be discrete or continuous, finite or infinite. We typically assume discrete value sets. Typical predicates are comparison predicates such as $<, >, \leq,$ $\neq, \geq, =$. Typical functions are arithmetic functions such as $+, -,$ and $\times$.

The set of integers is given by the IntegerSet, e.g. integers within a 4-byte representation and basic operations and predicates:

$$\text{integer} := (IntegerSet, \{0, s, +, -, *, \div, \}, \{=, \leq\}) \ .$$

The base type is extended to a **data type** by explicit definition of properties of the underlying value sets:

Precision and accuracy: Data can be precise to a certain extent. Precision is the degree of refinement in the calculations. Accuracy is a measure of how repeatable the assignment of values for properties is.

Granularity: Scales can be fine or coarse. The accuracy of data depends on the granularity of the domain which has been chosen for the representation of properties.

Ordering: The ordering of values of a given domain can be based on ordering schemes such as lexicographic, geographic or chronological ordering or on exact ordering such as orderings on natural numbers. The ordering can also be based on ontologies or categories. Scales have a range with lowest values and highest values. These values can be finite or infinite. If they are finite, then overflow or underflow errors might be the result of a computation.

Classification: The data can be used for representation of classifications. The classification can be linear, hierarchical, etc. The classification can be mono-hierarchical or poly-hierarchical, mono-dimensional or poly-dimensional, analytical or synthetical, monotetical or polytetical. The classification can be based on ontologies and be maintained with thesauri.

Presentation: The data type can be mapped to different representation types depending on several parameters. For instance, in Web applications, the format chosen for presentation types of pictures depends on the capacity of the channel, on the compression, etc. The presentation might be linear or hierarchical and can be layered.

Implementation: The implementation type of the attribute type depends on the properties of the DBMS. The implementation type also influences the complexity of computations.

Default values: During the design of databases, default values can be assigned in order to store properties regarding the existence of data such as 'exists but not at the moment', 'exists but not known', 'exists but under change', 'at the moment forbidden/system defined/wrong', 'not reachable', 'until now not reachable', 'not entered yet', 'not transferrable/transferred', 'not applicable to the object'. Usually, only one default value is allowed. An example of a specific default value is the *null value*.

Casting functions: We assume that type systems are (strongly) typed. In this case we are not able to compare values from different domains and to compute new values from a set of values taken from different domains. Casting functions can be used to map the values of a given domain to values of another domain.

Table 6.1 Data types and their main canonical assumptions

Kind of data type	Natural order	Natural zero	Predefined functions	Example
Extension based				
Absolute	+	+/−	+/−	*Number of boxes*
Ratio	+	+/−	+ (type dependent)	*Length, weight*
Intension based				
Nominal	−	−	(−) (except concatenation)	*Names of cities*
Ordinal	+	−	−	*Preferences*
Rank	+	+	−	*Competitions*
Interval	+	−	(+) (e.g. concatenation)	*Time, space*

It should be noted [16, 17] that the data type restricts the operations which can be applied. Databases often store *units of measure* which are measured using a scale of some sort. *Scales* can be classified [6] according to a set of properties such as the following: a natural origin point of scale represented usually by a meaningful 'zero' which is not just a numeric zero; applicability of meaningful operations which can be performed on the units; existence of natural orderings of the units; the existence of a natural metric function on the units. Metric functions obey a triangular property, are symmetric and map identical objects to the origin of the scale. For instance, adding weights is meaningful, whereas adding shoe sizes looks odd. The plus operation can be different if a natural ordering exists. Metric values are often relative values which are perceived in different ways, e.g. the intensity of light.

Typical kinds of data types are compared in Table 6.1.

We thus specify basic data types by the **extended data type** that extends the data type by description Υ of precision and accuracy, granularity, order, classification, presentation implementation, special values, null, default values, casting functions, and scale.

This extended specification approach avoids pitfalls of aggregation. Aggregation functions can be applied to absolute and ratio values without restriction. Additive aggregation and min/max functions can be applied to interval values. The average function can only be applied to equidistant interval values. The application of aggregation functions such as summarisation and average to derived values is based on conversions to absolute or ratio values. Comparison functions such as min/max functions can be applied to derived values only by attribution to ratio or absolute values. The average function can only be applied to equidistant interval values. Aggregation functions are usually not applicable to nominal values, ordinal values, and rank values.

Given a set of (extended) base types $\mathcal{T}$ and a set of names U, a **data scheme** ($DD = (U, \mathcal{T}, dom)$) is given by a finite set U of *type names*, by a set $\mathcal{T}$ of extended base types, and by a *domain function dom* : $U \rightarrow \mathcal{T}$ which assigns to each base type name its 'domain' type.

We denote DD by $\{A_1 :: dom(A_1), \ldots, A_m :: dom(A_m)\}$ in the case where the set of type names $U = \{A_1, \ldots, A_m\}$ of the data scheme is finite. The A_i are called **atomic attributes** or basic attributes.

Given additionally a set of names NA different from U and a set of labels L that is distinct from NA and U, we inductively introduce the set UN of **complex attributes** or complex attribute types:

- Any atomic attribute is a complex attribute, i.e. $U \subseteq UN$.
- If $X \in UN$, then $l : X \in UN$ for $l \in L$ (labelled attribute).
- If $X \in UN$, then $[X] \in UN$ (optional attribute).
- If $X_1, \ldots, X_n \in UN$ and $X \in NA$, then $X(X_1, \ldots, X_n)$ is a (tuple-valued) complex attribute in UN. This attribute type can also be used in the notation X.
- If $X' \in UN$ and $X \in NA$, then $X\{X'\}$ is a (set-valued) complex attribute in UN.
- No other elements are in UN.

Set L is used as an additional naming language. Each attribute can be labelled by names or labels from L. Labels can be used as alias names for attributes. They are useful for shortening expressions of complex attributes. They can carry a meaning but do not carry semantics. They can be omitted whenever it is not confusing.

Additionally, other type constructors can be used for defining complex attributes:

- Lists of values, e.g. $< X >,$;
- Vectors or arrays of values, e.g. $X_{\text{Min}}^{\text{Max}}(Y)$ with an index attribute Y, and minimal and maximal index values; and
- Bags of values, e.g. $\{|X|\}$.

For reasons of simplicity we restrict the model to tuple and set constructors. However, list and bag constructors can be used whenever type constructors are allowed.

Typical examples of complex attributes are as follows:

> *Name : (FirstNames < (FirstName,use) > , FamName, [NameOfBirth,]*
>   *Title:{AcadTitle}$\dot{\cup}$FamTitle)*
> *Contact : (Phone({AtWork}, private), email, …)*
> *DateOfBirth :: date*
> *AcadTitle :: titleType*
> *PostalAddress : (Zip, City, Street, HouseNumber)*
> *for dom(Zip) = String7, dom(City) = VarString, dom(Street) = VarString,*
>   *dom(HouseNumber) = SmallInt.*

Now we can extend the function dom to Dom on UN.

- $Dom(\lambda) = \emptyset$.
- For $A \in U, Dom(A) = dom(A)$.
- For $l : X \in UN, Dom(l : X) = Dom(X)$.
- For $[X] \in UN, Dom([X]) = Dom(X) \cup \lambda$ for the empty word λ.
- For $X(X_1, \ldots, X_n) \in UN, Dom(X) = Dom(X_1) \times \ldots \times Dom(X_n)$, where $M_1 \times \ldots \times M_n$ denotes the Cartesian product of the sets $M_1, \ldots, M_n$.

- For $X\{X'\} \in UN, Dom(X\{X'\}) = Pow(Dom(X))$,
  where $Pow(M)$ denotes the powerset of the set M.

Two attribute types X, Y are called *domain-compatible* if $Dom(X) = Dom(Y)$.
For the data scheme DD the set D_{DD} denotes the union of all sets $Dom(X)$ for
$X \in UN$.

The subattribute A of B is inductively defined in the same manner (denoted by
$A \preceq B$). A is a non-proper subattribute of A but not a proper subattribute of A.
$X(X_{i_1}, \ldots, X_{i_m})$ and $X(X'_1, \ldots, X'_n)$ are subattributes of $X(X_1, \ldots, X_n)$ for subattributes X'_j of X_j $(1 \le j \le j)$. $X\{X''\}$ is a subattribute of $X\{X'\}$ for a subattribute X'' of X'.

A **tuple** (or object) o on $X \subseteq UN$ and on $DD = (U, \underline{D}, dom)$ is a function

$$o : X \longrightarrow D_{DD} \text{ with } t(A) \in Dom(A) \text{ for } A \in X.$$

An **entity type** E is defined by a triple $(attr(E), id(E), \Sigma)$, where

- E is an entity set name,
- $attr(E)$ is a set of attributes,
- $id(E)$ is a non-empty generalised subset of $attr(E)$ called the key or
  identifier, and
- Σ is a set of integrity constraints.

Trivial elements may be omitted. The set of all attributes is the trivial identifier.
The empty set $\emptyset$ is a trivial set of integrity constraints. Let us assume for the moment
that $\Sigma = \emptyset$. We shall introduce integrity constraints below.

The following types are examples of entity types:

Person $\overset{\circ}{=}$ ({*Name, Address, Contact, DateOfBirth, PersNo* : *EmplNo*$\dot{\cup}$ ... , ...})
Course $\overset{\circ}{=}$ ({*CourseNumber, CName*}, {*CNumber*}),
Room $\overset{\circ}{=}$ ({*Building, RoomNumber*}, {*Building, RoomNumber*}),
Department $\overset{\circ}{=}$ ({*DName, Director, Phones*{*Phone*}}, {*DName*}),
Semester $\overset{\circ}{=}$ ({*Year, Season*}, {*Year, Season*}).

The notion of entity types can be extended to entity types with key sets:

$$E \overset{\circ}{=} \big(attr(E), \{id_j(E) \mid 1 \le j \le m\}\big) \text{ with } m \text{ keys}.$$

We assume that attributes are unique in an entity type. Therefore, we can omit the
set brackets. Identifiers may be given by underlining the corresponding attributes.
Entities or objects o of E can now be defined as tuples on $attr(E)$.
An entity of the type *Person* is for instance the object

β : ((< (*Karl, SecondChristian*), (*Bernhard, Christian*) >, *Thalheim*,
    {*Prof., Dr.rer.nat.habil., Dipl.-Math.*}),
    CAU Kiel, (({+49 431 8804472, +49 431 8804054}, _),
    thalheim@is.informatik.uni-kiel.de), 10.3.1952, 637861, ...).

At any fixed moment in time t an **entity class** E^C for the entity type E is

- a set of objects o on $attr(E)$ for which
  - $id(E)$ is a key, i.e. the inequality $o_{id(E)} \neq o'_{id(E)}$ is valid for any two different tuples o, o' from E^C, and
  - the set of integrity constraints Σ is valid.

In some cases, (entity) types may be combined into a union of types or so-called **cluster types**. Since we need to preserve identification, we restrict the union operation to disjoint unions. Clusters based on entity types can be defined by the disjoint union of types. Furthermore, we require that the identification types of the components of a cluster are domain-compatible. Take now the set of types $\{R_1, \ldots, R_k\}$ as given.

These types can be clustered by a "category" or a *cluster type*

$$C \stackrel{\circ}{=} l_1 : R_1 + l_2 : R_2 + \ldots + l_k : R_k.$$

Labels can be omitted if the types can be distinguished.

Examples of cluster types are as follows:

JuristicalPerson $\stackrel{\circ}{=}$ Person $\dot{\cup}$ Company $\dot{\cup}$ Association,
Group $\stackrel{\circ}{=}$ Senate $\dot{\cup}$ WorkingGroup $\dot{\cup}$ Association.

For a cluster type $C \stackrel{\circ}{=} l_1 : R_1 + l_2 : R_2 + \ldots + l_k : R_k$ we can similarly define the **cluster class** C^C as the 'disjoint' union of the sets $R_1^C, \ldots, R_k^C$. If $R_1, \ldots, R_k$ are entity types, then C is a cluster of entity types. The cluster is defined if $R_1^C, \ldots, R_k^C$ are disjoint.

Entity types $E_1, \ldots, E_k$ are now given. A **(first-order) relationship type** has the form $R \stackrel{\circ}{=} (ent(R), attr(R), \Sigma)$, where

- R is the name of the type,
- $ent(R) = l_1 : R_1, \ldots, l_n : R_n$ is a sequence of (labelled) entity types and of clusters of these,
- $attr(R) = \{B_1, \ldots, B_k\}$ is a set of attributes from UN, and
- Σ is a set of integrity constraints.

First-order relationship types which have only one entity type are called *unary*, those with two entity types are called *binary* and those with several labelled occurrences of the same entity type are called *recursive*. Labels can be omitted if the types can be distinguished.

Example of first-order relationship types are as follows:

InGroup $\stackrel{\circ}{=}$ (Person, Group, {Time(From [,To]), Position}),
DirectPrerequisite $\stackrel{\circ}{=}$ (hasPrerequisite : Course, isPrerequisite : Course),
Professor $\stackrel{\circ}{=}$ (Person, { Specialisation }),
Student $\stackrel{\circ}{=}$ (Person, { StudNo }),
Enroll = (Student, CourseHeld, { Result }),

Major $\stackrel{\circ}{=}$ (*Student, Program, Ø*),
Minor $\stackrel{\circ}{=}$ (*Student, Program, Ø*).

If each R_i is an entity type, then a first-order relationship set R^C is a set of relationships, i.e.

$$R^C \subseteq R_1^C \times \ldots \times R_n^C \times dom(B_1) \times \ldots \times dom(B_k).$$

An assumption that is typically made for representations is that relationships use only the identification part of the objects which participate in the relationships.

If R_i is a cluster $R_{i,1} + \ldots + R_{i,k}$, then the relationships in R^C are distinct according to R_i, i.e. for $r, r' \in R^C$ either $r.R_i \neq r'.R_i$ and $R_{i,j}^C \cap R_{i,j'}^C$ for distinct j, j' or $r.R_i$ determines the component $R_{i,j}$ of R_i, i.e.

$$r.R_i \in R_{i,j}^C \setminus \cup_{j' \neq j} R_{i,j'}^C.$$

The latter disjointness can be weakened by labels.

We may generalise the notion of first-order relationship types to relationship types of arbitrary order. Given now entity types $E_1, \ldots E_k$ and relationship and cluster types $R_1, \ldots, R_l$ of orders not higher than i for $i > 0$, an **(i + 1)-order relationship type** has the form

$$R \stackrel{\circ}{=} (compon(R), attr(R), \Sigma),$$

where

- R is the name of the type,
- $compon(R)$ is a sequence of (labelled) entity and relationship types or clusters from $\{E_1, \ldots, E_k, R_1, \ldots, R_l\}$,
- $attr(R) = \{B_1, \ldots, B_k\}$ is a set of attributes from UN, and
- Σ is a set of integrity constraints.

We may also use constructors $\times, \cup, \dot{\cup}, \{.\}, \{\!\|.\|\!\}, < . >$ [Cartesian product, union, disjoint union, powerset, bags (multisets), list] to define complex components.

The disjointness for clusters can be weakened for relationship types.

Examples of higher-order relationship types are as follows:

Has $\stackrel{\circ}{=}$ *(Project, PrimaryInvestigator:Professor + Member:Person, Ø)*,
Supervisor $\stackrel{\circ}{=}$ *(Student, Professor, { Since })*.

Higher-order types allow a convenient description of classes which are based on other classes. Let us consider a course planning application. Lectures are courses given by a professor during a semester and a number of programs. Proposed courses extend lectures by descriptions of who has made the proposal, who is responsible for the course, which room is requested and which time proposals and restrictions are made. Planning of courses assigns a room to a course that has been proposed and assigns a time frame for scheduling. The kind of course may be changed. Courses held are based on courses planned. The room for a course may be changed. We use the following types for the specification:

$$ProposedCourse \triangleq (Teacher : Professor, Course,$$
$$Proposal : Kind, Request : Room,$$
$$Semester, Set4 : \{Program\}, Responsible4Course : Person,$$
$$InsertedBy : Person, \{Time(Proposal, SideCondition)\}),$$
$$PlannedCourse \triangleq (ProposedCourse, [Kind], [Room], \{TimeFrame\}),$$
$$CourseHeld \triangleq (PlannedCourse, [Room]).$$

The last two types use optional components in the case where a proposal or the planning of rooms or kinds is changed.

Assume now a relationship type, $R \triangleq (R_1, \ldots, R_n, \{B_1, \ldots, B_k\})$ and classes $R_1^C, \ldots, R_n^C$. A **relationship** r is an element of the Cartesian product

$$R_1^C \times \ldots \times R_n^C \times Dom(B_1) \times \ldots \times Dom(B_k).$$

The **relationship class** R^C is a set of relationships, i.e.

$$R^C \subseteq R_1^C \times \ldots \times R_n^C \times Dom(B_1) \times \ldots \times Dom(B_k).$$

If R_i is a cluster $R_{i,1} + \ldots + R_{i,k}$, then the relationships in R^C are distinct according to R_i, i.e. for $r, r' \in R^C$ either $r.R_i \neq r'.R_i$ and $R_{i,j}^C \cap R_{i,j'}^C$ for distinct j, j', or $r.R_i$ determines the component $R_{i,j}$ of R_i, i.e. $r.R_i \in R_{i,j}^C \setminus \cup_{j' \neq j} R_{i,j'}^C$. The last disjointness condition can be weakened by labels. If we use extended relationship types, then identifying subcomponents can be used instead of the full representation.

A set $\{E_1, \ldots E_n, R_1, \ldots, R_m\}$ of entity, cluster and (higher-order) relationship types on a data scheme DD is called **complete** if any relationship types use the types from $\{E_1, \ldots E_n, R_1, \ldots, R_m\}$ as components. A complete set of types is also called **EER schema** S. The EER schema is going to be extended by constraints. The EER schema is defined by the pair (S, Σ).

We can represent a complete set of entity, cluster and relationship types by ER diagrams. One possible kind of diagram is displayed in Fig. 6.1. Entity types are represented graphically by rectangles. Attribute types are associated with the corresponding type. Relationship vertices are represented graphically by diamonds. Clusters are represented by diamonds labelled with a root illustrated $\oplus$ or simply as a common input point to a diamond.

This style of drawing diagrams is one of many variants which have been considered in the literature. The main difference in representation is the style of drawing unary types. Three different styles are depicted in Fig. 6.2. We prefer the compact style in the left diagram.

The notion of subattributes can be extended to **substructures** of an EER structure in a similar form. Substructures use the components of a type. Given two substructures X and Y of a type T, the generalised union $X \sqcup_T Y$ is the smallest substructure of T that has both X and Y as its substructures. The generalised intersection $X \sqcap_T Y$ is the largest substructure of both X and Y.

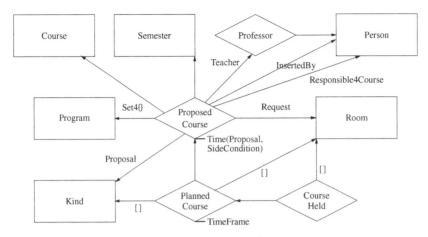

Fig. 6.1 A sample HERM diagram with higher-order relationship types

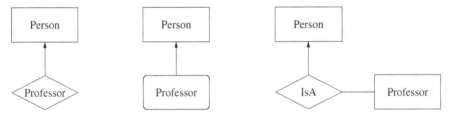

Fig. 6.2 Variants for representation of unary relationship types

We have introduced the essentials of extended ER models. The ER model has attracted a lot of research. A large variety of **extensions** have been proposed. We conclude this subsection with a brief introduction on main extensions.

We do not use so-called **weak types** that use associations among a schema for a definition of their identification. For a discussion on the pitfalls of these types, we refer the interested reader to [25].

A number of domain-specific extensions have been introduced to the ER model. One of the most important extensions is the extension of the base types by **spatial data types** [19] such as point, line, oriented line, surface, complex surface, oriented surface, line bunch, and surface bunch. These types are supported by a large variety of functions such as meets, intersects, overlaps, contains, adjacent, planar operations, and a variety of equality predicates.

We distinguish between **specialisation types** and **generalisation types**. Specialisation is used whenever objects obtain more specific properties, may play a variety of roles, and use more specific functions. Typically, specialisation is specified through *IS-A* associations. Specific relationship types which are used to describe specialisation are as follows: *Is-Specific-Kind-Of, Is-Role-Of, Is-Subobject-Of, Is-Subset-Of, Is-Property-Of, Has-Effect-Of, Has-Function-Of, Is-Partial-Synonym-*

Of, *Entails*, and *Part-Of*. Functions are typically inherited downwards, i.e. from the supertype to the subtype.

Generalisation is used for types of objects which have the same behaviour. The behaviour and some of the components may be *shifted* to the generalisation if they are common for all types which are generalised. Typical generalisations are *Is-Kind-Of*, *Considered-As*, and *Acts-In-Role*. In relationship types generalisation tends to be an abstraction in which a more general (generic) type is defined by extracting common properties of one or more types while suppressing the differences between them. These types are subtypes of the generic type. Thus, generalisation introduces the Role-Of relationship or the Is-A relationship between a subtype entity and its generic type. Therefore, the constructs are different. For generalisation the generic type must be the union of its subtypes. Thus, the subtypes can be virtually clustered by the generic type. This tends not to be the case for specialisation. The specialisation of a role of the subtype can be changed. This is the case for generalisation.

Generalisation is usually defined through a cluster type. The cluster type can be translated to a relational type or to a relational view. Functions are inherited upwards, i.e. from the type to the abstraction. Abstractions typically do not have their own functions.

The distinction into specialisation and generalisation may be based on an introduction of *kernel types*. These types are either specialised or generalised and form a 'centre' of the hierarchy. A pragmatic rule for detection of such types is based on the independent existence of objects. Those object sets that exist (relatively) independently of other object sets are candidates for kernel sets. They form an *existence ridge* within the schema.

Hierarchy abstraction allows one to consider objects in a variety of levels of detail. Hierarchy abstraction is based on a specific form of the general join operator [26]. It combines types which are of high adhesion and which are mainly modelled on the basis of star subschemata. *Specialisation* is a well-known form of hierarchy abstraction. For instance, an *Address* type is specialised to the *GeographicAddress* type. Other forms are *role hierarchies* and *category hierarchies*. For instance, *Student* is a role of *Person*. *Undergraduate* is a category of *Student*. The behaviour of both is the same. Specific properties have been changed. *Variations* and *versions* can be modelled on the basis of hierarchy abstraction.

Hierarchies may be combined and the root types of the hierarchies are generalised to a common root type. The combination may lead to a graph which is not a tree but a forest, i.e. an acyclic graph with one root. The variation of the root type is formed by a number of dimensions applicable to the type. For instance, addresses have a specialisation dimension, a language dimension, an applicability dimension and a classification dimension.

Schemata may have a number of **dimensions**. We observe that types in a database schema are of very different usage. This usage can be made explicit. Extraction of this utilisation pattern shows that each schema has a number of internal dimensions: *specialisation dimension* based on roles objects play or on categories into which objects are separated; *association dimension* through bridging related types and in adding metacharacterisation on data quality; *usage, meta-characterisation or log* *dimension* characterising log information such as the history of database evolution, the association to business steps and rules, and the actual usage; *data quality, lifespan and history dimension*. We may abstract from the last two dimensions during database schema development and add these dimensions as the last step of conceptual modelling. In this case, the schema considered up to this step is concerned with the main facets of the application.

The *metadata* dimension describes the database data. Metadata guide utilisation of evaluation functions. The management of metadata is based on a number of steps:

Creation of meaningful metadata   is based on a proper characterisation of the data by their history, their association to the documents from which the data have been taken, and an evaluation of the quality of the source. Metadata must be appropriate to their use within the model suite. At the same time they must be adequate. Meaningful metadata help to understand the data which are available and provide information on how these data can be used.

Maturing metadata   can be based on adding the context of the data and the metadata, e.g. by a characterisation of time and integrity. Any change in the data must be reflected by changes in the metadata. This change management is based on explicit maintenance of data heritage with respect to the real world at the time the data were initially captured and stored and on data lineage depending on the path taken by the data from initial capture to their present location and how they were altered along that path.

Management of metadata   becomes important whenever the redundancy of data increases, e.g. in data warehouses, in files of data which reuse, aggregate and combine their data from other or their own data. Simple metadata management has been built into data dictionaries and is used in data modelling tools. Extended metadata management has been incorporated into data repositories. Nowadays metadata are becoming an essential source of information and a supporting facility for sophisticated search. Metadata management supports sophisticated storage, concurrent and secured access, and ease of use with browsing, searching, indexing, integration and association facilities.

Maintenance of metadata   must be automated, includes quality assurance and reprocessing, uses intelligent versioning, configuration and combination, and has refreshment cycles.

Migration and sharing of metadata   becomes crucial if data sources are kept distributed and are heterogeneous, if they are shared among different kinds of usage, if interoperability of different data sources is necessary, and if portability requires a change due to different operational uses while maintaining old applications.

Schemata may have a metastructure and may consist of several **components** [27]. These components may be interrelated and may intersect. Some of them are independent. Some of them are interrelated through specific associations by connector types. This metastructure is captured by the *skeleton* of the schema. This skeleton consists of the main modules without capturing the details within the types. The skeleton structure allows one to separate some parts of the schema from others.

The skeleton displays the structure at a large. At the same time, schemata have an internal *meta-structure*.

Component-based ER modelling does not start with the singleton type. First, a skeleton of components is developed. This skeleton can be refined during the evolution of the schema. Then, each component is developed step by step. Each refinement leads to a component database schema. If components share elements then any change for one component must be harmonised with changes to all related components.

Temporality is described for EER models in a variety of ways.

- Data may be temporal and depend directly on one or more aspects of **time**. We distinguish three orthogonal concepts of time: temporal data types such as instants, intervals or periods, kinds of time, and temporal statements such as current (now), sequenced (at each instant of time) and non-sequenced (ignoring time). Kinds of time are *existence time*, *lifespan time*, *transaction time*, *change time*, *user-defined time*, *validity time* and *availability time*. The first two kinds of time are not considered in databases since they are integrated into modelling decisions. Temporal data are supported by specific temporal functions. These functions generalise Allen's time logic [1].
- The database schema may be temporal as well. The **evolution** covers the aspect of changes in the schema. The best approach to handling evolution is the separation of parts of the schema into those types that are stable and those types of the schema that change. The change schema is a meta-schema on those components that evolve.
- Database systems have to support different temporal **viewpoints** and temporal **scopes** of users. Therefore, the database schema has a temporal representation dimension. Typical large systems such as SAP R/3 support this multi-view concept by providing views on the same data. These views are updateable and are equivalent to each other. Another extension of the ER model which supports multi-scoping is the explicit introduction of multiple representations of each type. The types are enhanced by a controller that supports the generation of the appropriate view on the type.

6.2.2 Functionality Specification

The HERM uses an inductive structuring. This inductive structuring can also be used for the introduction of the functionality. Functionality specification is based on the HERM algebra and can easily be extended to HERM/QBE, query forms and transactions. This framework for functionality specification supports the introduction of some kinds of dynamic integrity constraints and consideration of behaviour. The greatest consistent specification (GCS) approach is used for integrity enforcement instead of rule-triggering pitfalls. Another advantage of this approach is that interactivity may be introduced in integrated form based on dialogue scenes, cooperation, messages and scenarios [23]. The translation portfolio may be used for translation and for compilation of functionality to object-relational, relational and semi-structured languages.

The EER algebra uses type-preserving and type-creating functions. Simple type-preserving functions generalise the classical set-theoretic functions. Let R^{C_1} and R^{C_2} be classes over the same type R.

The *union* $R^{C_1} \cup R^{C_2}$ is the standard set union of R^{C_1} and R^{C_2}.

The *difference* $R^{C_1} \setminus R^{C_2}$ is the standard set difference of R^C and R^{C_2}.

The *intersection* $R^{C_1} \cap R^{C_2}$ is the set intersection of R^{C_1} and R^{C_2}.

Clearly, the types of the union, the intersection and the difference are T.

Type-creating functions on type systems can be defined by *structural recursion* [2, 5, 29]. Given types T and T' and a collection type C^T on T (e.g. set of values of type T, bags, lists) and operations such as generalised union $\cup_{CT}$, generalised intersection $\cap_{CT}$, and generalised empty elements $\emptyset_{CT}$ on C^T. Given further an element h_0 on T' and two functions defined on the types $h_1 : T \rightarrow T'$ and $h_2 : T' \times T' \rightarrow T'$, we define the structural recursion by insert presentation for R^C on T as follows:

$$srec_{h_0,h_1,h_2}(\emptyset_{CT}) = h_0;$$
$$srec_{h_0,h_1,h_2}(|\{|s|\}|) = h_1(s) \text{ for singleton collections } |\{|s|\}|;$$

$$srec_{h_0,h_1,h_2}(|\{|s|\}| \cup_{CT} R^C) = h_2(h_1(s), srec_{h_0,h_1,h_2}(R^C))$$
$$\text{iff } |\{|s|\}| \cap_{CT} R^C = \emptyset_{CT}.$$

All operations of the relational database model and of other declarative database models can be defined by structural recursion.

- *Selection* is defined by $\sigma_\alpha = srec_{\emptyset,\iota_\alpha,\cup}$ for the function

$$\iota_\alpha(\{o\}) = \begin{cases} \{o\} & \text{if } \{o\} \models \alpha \\ \emptyset & \text{otherwise} \end{cases}.$$

  and the type $T' = C^T$.
  Selection is a type-preserving function.
- *Projection* is defined by $\pi_X = T[X] = srec_{\emptyset,\pi_X,\cup}$ for the subtype X of T, the function

$$\pi_X(\{o\}) = \{o|_X\}$$

  which restricts any object to the components of X and the type $T' = C^X$.
- *(Natural) join* is defined by $\bowtie = srec_{\emptyset,\bowtie_T,\cup}$ for the type $T = T_1 \times T_2$, the function

$$\bowtie_T(\{(o_1,o_2)\}) = \{o \in Dom(T_1 \cup T_2) \mid o|_{T_1} = o_1 \wedge o|_{T_2} = o_2\}$$

  and the type $T' = C^{T_1 \cup T_2}$.

The natural join is equal to the Cartesian product of the intersection of T_1 and T_2 is empty and is equal to the intersection if T_1 and T_2 coincide.

The *Cartesian product* $R^C \times S^C$ is a class of the scheme $T = R \circ S$ and equals $\{(r_1, \ldots, r_m, s_1, dots, s_n) | (r_1, \ldots, r_m) \in R^C, (s_1, s_n) \in S^C\}$. The concatenation of types is denoted by $\circ$.

- *Renaming* is defined by $\rho_{X,Y} = srec_{\emptyset, \rho_{X,Y}, \cup}$ for the subtype X of T, for a type Y with $Dom(X) = Dom(Y)$, for the function

$$\rho_{X,Y}(\{(o)\}) = \{o' \in Dom((T \setminus X) \circ Y) \mid o|_{T \setminus X} = o'|_{T \setminus X}, \wedge o|_X = o'|_Y\}$$

and for the type $T' = C^{(T \setminus X) \circ Y}$.

- *Nesting* is defined by $\nu_X = srec_{\emptyset, \rho_{X, \{X\}}, h_2}$ for the subtype X of $T = R$, for the type $T' = C^{(R \setminus X) \sqcup_R \{X\}}$, and for the function

$$h_2(\{o'\}, T'^C) = \{o'\} \cup T'^C \text{ if } o'|_X \notin \pi_X(T'^C)$$
$$h_2(\{o'\}, T'^C) = \{o \in Dom(T') | \exists o' \in T'^C : o|_{R \setminus X} = o'|_{R \setminus X}$$
$$\wedge o(X) = \{o''[X] | o'' \in T'^C \wedge o'|_{R \setminus X} = o''|_{R \setminus X}\}\}$$

in the case where $o'|_X \in \pi_X(T'^C)$.

- *Unnesting* is defined by $\mu_X = srec_{\emptyset, \rho_{X, \{X\}}, h_2}$ for the set subtype $\{X\}$ of $T = R$, for the type $T' = C^{(R \setminus \{X\}) \circ X}$, and for the function

$$h_2(\{o'\}, T'^C) = \{o'\} \cup$$
$$\{o \in Dom(T') \mid \exists o'' \in R^C : o[R \setminus \{X\}] = o''[R \setminus \{X\}] \wedge o|_X \in o''|_X\}.$$

We distinguish aggregation functions according to their computational complexity:

- The simplest class of aggregation functions uses simple (one-pass) aggregation. Typical examples are the simple statistical functions of SQL: *count (absolute frequency), average (arithmetic mean), sum (total), min, max.*

- More complex aggregation functions are used in cumulative or moving statistics which relate data subsets to other subsets or supersets, e.g. growth rates, changes in an aggregate value over time or any dimension set (banded reports, control break reports, OLAP dimensions). Typical examples are queries like:
  "What percentage does each customer contribute to total sales?"
  "Total sales in each territory, ordered from high to low!"
  "Total amount of sales broken down by salesman within territories".

Aggregation functions distinguish between normal values and null values. We use two functions for null values:

$$h_f^0(s) = \begin{cases} 0 & \text{if } s = NULL, \\ f(s) & \text{if } s \neq NULL; \end{cases}$$

$$h_{f(s)}^{undef} = \begin{cases} undef & \text{if } s = NULL, \\ f(s) & \text{if } s \neq NULL. \end{cases}$$

Then we can introduce the main aggregation through structural recursion as follows:

- *Summarisation* is defined by $\text{sum}_0^{\text{null}} = srec_{0,h_{\text{Id}}^0,+}$ or $\text{sum}_{\text{undef}}^{\text{null}} = srec_{0,h_{\text{Id}}^{\text{undef}},+}$.
- The *counting* or *cardinality* function counts the number of objects:
  $\text{count}_1^{\text{null}} = srec_{0,h_1^0,+}$ or $\text{count}_{\text{undef}}^{\text{null}} = srec_{0,h_1^{\text{undef}},+}$.
- *Maximum* and *minimum* functions are defined by

  - $\text{max}_{\text{NULL}} = srec_{\text{NULL},\text{Id},\text{max}}$ or $\text{min}_{\text{NULL}} = srec_{\text{NULL},\text{Id},\text{min}}$,
  - $\text{max}_{\text{undef}} = srec_{\text{undef},\text{Id},\text{max}}$ or $\text{min}_{\text{undef}} = srec_{\text{undef},\text{Id},\text{min}}$.

- The *arithmetic average* functions can be defined by

$$\frac{\text{sum}}{\text{count}} \quad \text{or} \quad \frac{\text{sum}_0^{\text{null}}}{\text{count}_1^{\text{null}}} \quad \text{or} \quad \frac{\text{sum}_{\text{undef}}^{\text{null}}}{\text{count}_{\text{undef}}^{\text{null}}}.$$

SQL uses the following doubtful definition for the average function:

$$\frac{\text{sum}_0^{\text{null}}}{\text{count}_1^{\text{null}}}.$$

One can distinguish between distributive, algebraic and holistic aggregation functions:

Distributive or inductive functions are defined by structural recursion. They preserve partitions of sets for a given set X and a given partion $X = X_1 \cup X_2 \cup \ldots \cup X_n$ of X into pairwise disjoint subsets. Then for a distributive function f there exists a function g such that $f(X) = g(f(X_1), \ldots, f(X_n))$. Functions such as count, sum, min, max are distributive.

Algebraic functions can be expressed by finite algebraic expressions defined over distributive functions. Typical examples of algebraic functions in database languages are average and covariance. The average function, for instance, can be defined on the basis of an expression on count and sum.

Holistic functions are all other functions. For holistic functions there is no limit on the size of the storage needed to describe a subaggregate. Typical examples are mostFrequent, rank and median. Usually, their implementation and expression in database languages require tricky programming. Holistic functions are computable over temporal views.

We use these functions to define the derived elementary modification functions:

Insertion of objects: The *insert* function $\text{Insert}(R^C, o)$ is the union $R^C \cup \{o\}$ for classes R^C and objects o of the same type R.

Deletion/removal of objects: The *delete* function $\text{Delete}(R^C, o)$ is defined through the difference $R^C \setminus \{o\}$ for classes R^C and objects o of the same type R.

Update of objects: The modification $\text{Update}(R^C, \alpha, \gamma)$ of classes R^C uses logical conditions α and replacement families $\gamma = \{(o, R^{C_o})\}$ that specify which objects are to be replaced by which object sets. The *update* function $\texttt{Update}(R^C,$ $\alpha, \gamma)$ is defined through the set

$$R^C \setminus \sigma_\alpha(R^C) \cup \bigcup_{o \in \sigma_\alpha(R^C)} R^{C_o} .$$

We notice that this definition is different from the expression $R^C \setminus \sigma_\alpha(R^C) \cup R^{C'}$ which is often used by DBMSs instead of update operations, e.g. by $\texttt{Delete}(R^C,$ $o)$; $\texttt{InsertUpdate}(R^C, o')$. If, for instance, $\sigma_\alpha(R^C) = \emptyset$ and $R^{C'} \neq \emptyset$, then the effect of the update operation is lost.

Structural recursion on collection types, together with canonical operations, provides us with a powerful programming paradigm for database structures. If collections are restricted to 'flat' relations, then they express precisely those queries which are definable in the relational algebra. By adding a fixed set of aggregate operations such as *sum, count, max, min* to comprehension syntax and restricting the input to 'flat' relations, we obtain a language which has the expressive power of SQL. It should be noted that structural recursion is limited in expressive power as well. Non-deterministic tuple-generating while (or object generating) programs cannot be expressed. The definition of structural recursion over a union presentation uses the separation property since the h_2 function is only defined for disjoint collections. Therefore, programs which are not definable over the disjoint union of parts are not representable. However, most common database operations and all database operations in SQL are based on separation. The *traversal combinator* [10] concept is more general. It captures a large family of type-safe primitive functions. Most functions that are expressed as a sequence of recursive programs where only one parameter becomes smaller at each recursive call are members of this family. However, this restriction excludes functions such as structural equalities and ordering because they require their two input structures to be traversed simultaneously. The uniform traversal combinator generalises this concept by combinators each of which takes functions as inputs and returns a new function as output which performs the actual reduction.

An **EER query** is simply an EER expression of the EER algebra. The expression is defined on the EER types $R_1, \ldots, R_n$ and maps to the target type $S_1, \ldots, S_m$. Any database schema $\mathcal{D}$ which contains $R_1, \ldots, R_n$ is therefore mapped to the schema $S^q = \{S_1, \ldots, S_m\}$. EER queries may be enhanced by parameters. We can consider these parameters as an auxiliary schema $\mathcal{A}$. Therefore, an EER query is a mapping from $\mathcal{D}$ and $\mathcal{A}$ to $\mathcal{S}$, i.e.

$$q : \mathcal{D} \times \mathcal{A} \to \mathcal{S}^q .$$

An EER query for which the schema $\mathcal{S}^q$ consists of a singleton atomic attribute and base type is called a *singleton-value query*.

The relational database model only allows target schemata consisting of one type. This restriction is not necessary for EER models. The target schema of the EER query is an EER schema as well. Therefore, we can build query towers by applying queries to the schemata obtained through query evaluation. Therefore, an EER query is a *schema transformation*.

Transactions combine modification operations and queries into a single program. Following [18], we define a transaction T over $(\mathcal{S}, \Sigma)$ as a finite sequence $o_1; o_2; o_3; \ldots; o_m$ of modification and retrieval operations over $(\mathcal{S}, \Sigma)$. Let $read(T)$ and $write(T)$ be the set of basic read and write operations in T.

Transactions may be applied to the database state $\mathcal{D}^C$ sequentially and form a transition $T(\mathcal{D}^C) = o_m(\ldots(o_2(o_1(\mathcal{D}^C))))$. The **result** of applying the transaction T to a database (state) $\mathcal{D}^C$ is the transition from this database to the database $T(\mathcal{D}^C)$. The transaction semantics is based on two assumptions for a database schema $\mathcal{D} = (\mathcal{S}, \Sigma)$:

Atomicity and consistency: The program is executed entirely and preserves the semantics of the database.

Exhaustiveness: The transaction is executed only once.

The **effect** of applying T to $\mathcal{D}^C$ is defined as an *atomic constraint-preserving transition*

$$T(\mathcal{D}^C) = \begin{array}{ll} T(\mathcal{D}^C) & \text{if } T(\mathcal{D}^C) \models \Sigma , \\ \mathcal{D}^C & \text{if } T(\mathcal{D}^C) \not\models \Sigma . \end{array}$$

We note that atomic constraint-preserving transitions can only be applied *isolated* from each other. Transactions T_1 and T_2 are *competing* if $read(T_1) \cap write(T_2) \neq \emptyset$ or $read(T_2) \cap write(T_1) \neq \emptyset$ or $write(T_2) \cap write(T_1) \neq \emptyset$.

Parallel execution of transactions $T_1 \parallel T_2$ is *correct* if either the transactions are not competing or the effect of $T_1 \parallel T_2(\mathcal{S}^C)$ is equivalent to $T_1(T_2(\mathcal{S}^C))$ or to $T_2(T_1(\mathcal{S}^C))$ for any database $\mathcal{S}^C$. If parallel execution is correct, then transaction execution can be scheduled in parallel.

Exhaustiveness can be implemented by assigning to each transaction two states: inactive (for transactions that are not yet executed) and completed (for transactions that have lead to a constraint-preserving transition).

A large variety of approaches to **workflow** specification has been proposed in the literature. We use **basic computation step algebra** introduced in [28]:

Basic control commands are sequence ; (execution of steps in sequence), parallel split $|^\wedge|$ (execute steps in parallel), exclusive choice $|^\oplus|$ (choose one execution path from many alternatives), synchronisation $|^{sync}|$ (synchronise two parallel threads of execution by an synchronisation condition $sync$, and simple merge $+$ (merge two alternative execution paths). The exclusive choice is considered to be the default parallel operation and is denoted by $\parallel$.

Structural control commands are arbitrary cycles $*$ (execute steps without any structural restriction on loops), arbitrary cycles $^+$ (execute steps without any structural restriction on loops but at least once), optional execution [] (execute the step zero times or once), implicit termination $\downarrow$ (terminate if there is nothing to be done), entry step in the step $\nearrow$ and termination step in the step $\searrow$.

The basic computation step algebra may be extended by **advanced step commands**:

Advanced branching and synchronisation control commands are multiple choice $|^{(m,n)}|$ (choose between m and n execution paths from several alternatives), multiple merge (merge many execution paths without synchronizing), discriminator (merge many execution paths without synchronizing, execute the subsequent steps only once) n-out-of-m join (merge many execution paths, perform partial synchronisation and execute subsequent step only once), and synchronizing join (merge many execution paths, synchronise if many paths are taken, simple merge if only one execution path is taken).

We also may define **control commands on multiple objects** (CMO) such as CMO with a priori known design time knowledge (generate many instances of one step when a number of instances is known at design time), CMO with a priori known runtime knowledge [generate many instances of one step when a number of instances can be determined at some point during the runtime (as in FOR loops)], CMO with no a priori runtime knowledge [generate many instances of one step when a number of instances cannot be determined (as in a while loop)], and CMO requiring synchronisation (synchronisation edges) (generate many instances of one activity and synchronise afterwards).

State-based control commands are deferred choice (execute one of two alternative threads; the choice which thread is to be executed should be implicit), interleaved parallel executing (execute two activities in random order, but not in parallel), and milestone (enable an activity until a milestone has been reached).

Finally, **cancellation control commands** are used, e.g. cancel step [cancel (disable) an enabled step] and cancel case [cancel (disable) the case].

These control composition operators are generalisations of workflow patterns and follow approaches developed for Petri net algebras.

Operations defined on the basis of this general frame can be directly translated to database programs. So far no theory of database behaviour has been developed that can be used to explain the entire behaviour and that explains the behaviour in depth for a run of the database system.

6.2.3 Views in the Enhanced Entity-Relationship Models

Classically, (simple) views are defined as singleton types by which data are collected from the database by some query.

```
create view NAME (PROJECTION VARIABLES) as
   select PROJECTION EXPRESSION
      from DATABASE SUBSCHEMA
      where SELECTION CONDITION
      group by EXPRESSION FOR GROUPING
         having SELECTION AMONG GROUPS
      order by ORDER WITHIN THE VIEW ;
```

Since we may have decided to use the class-wise representation, simple views are not the most appropriate structure for exchange specification. The EER schema allows one to directly specify a **view schema** by

- a schema $\mathcal{V} = \{S_1, \ldots, S_m\}$, an auxiliary schema $\mathcal{A}$ and
- a query $q : \mathcal{D} \times \mathcal{A} \to \mathcal{V}$ defined on $\mathcal{D}$ and $\mathcal{V}$.

Given a database $\mathcal{D}^C$ and the auxiliary database $\mathcal{A}^C$, the view is defined by $q(\mathcal{D}^C \times \mathcal{A}^C)$.

Additionally, views should support services. Views provide their own data and functionality. This object orientation is a useful approach whenever data should be used without direct or remote connection to the database engine.

We generalise the view schema by the following frame:

```
generate MAPPING :   VARS → OUTPUT STRUCTURE
     from DATABASE TYPES
     where SELECTION CONDITION
     represent using GENERAL PRESENTATION STYLE
          & ABSTRACTION (GRANULARITY, MEASURE, PRECISION)
          & ORDERS WITHIN THE PRESENTATION   & POINTS OF VIEW
          & HIERARCHICAL REPRESENTATIONS   & SEPARATION
     browsing definition CONDITION   & NAVIGATION
     functions SEARCH FUNCTIONS   & EXPORT FUNCTIONS   & INPUT FUNCTIONS
          & SESSION FUNCTIONS   & MARKING FUNCTIONS
```

The extension of views by functions seems to be superficial during database design. Since we extensively use views in distributed environments, we save efforts of parallel and repetitive development due to the development of the entire view suite instead of developing each view independently.

Let us consider an *archive view* for the schema in Fig. 6.1. The view may be materialised and used as a read-only view. It is based on a slice that restricts the scope to those courses given in the summer term of the academic year 2000/2001

$Archive.Semester := e(Semester)$ for $e = \sigma_{\text{SemesterShortName}="SS00/01"}$.
The view is given through the expressions

$Archive.Course := e(CourseHeld\ [Course])$,
$Archive.Person := e(CourseHeld[PlannedCourse[ProposedCourse$
$\hspace{4cm} [Responsible4Course : Person]]])$,
$Archive.CourseHeld := e(CourseHeld[PlannedCourse[\ ProposedCourse[Course,$
$\hspace{3cm} Program,\ Teacher:Professor,\ Responsible4Course : Person],\ Kind]])$.
The types *Program, Kind, Professor* are given by similar expressions.

We additionally specify the functions which can be used for the archive view. The type *Semester* consists of one object and thus becomes trivial. This type is denoted by a dashed box. The view schema obtained is displayed in Fig. 6.3. We observe that this view can be used directly for a representation through an XML schema.

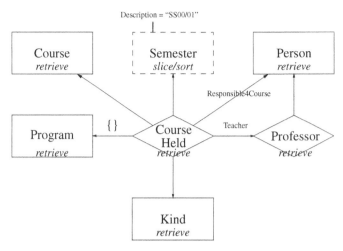

Fig. 6.3 EER view for archiving courses

Views may be used for distributed or collaborating databases. They can be enhanced by functions. **Exchange frames** are defined by

- An *exchange architecture* usually provided by a system architecture integrating the information systems through communication systems,
- A *collaboration style* specifying the supporting programs, the style of cooperation and the coordination facilities, and
- A *collaboration pattern* specifying the data integrity responsibilities, the potential changes within one view and the protocols for exchange of changes within one view.

6.2.4 Advanced Views and OLAP Cubes

The EER model can be used to define an advanced data warehouse model. Classically, the data warehouse model is introduced in an intuitive form by declaring an association or relationship among components of the cube (called dimensions), by declaring attributes (called fact types) together with aggregation functions. Components may be hierarchically structured. In this case, the cube schema can be represented by a *star schema*. Components may be interrelated with each other. In this case the cube schema is represented by a *snowflake schema*. Star and snowflake schemata can be used for computing views on the schemata. View constructors are functions like drill-down, roll-up, slice, dice, and rotate. We demonstrate the power of the EER model by a novel, formal and compact definition of the OLAP cube schema and the corresponding operations.

The data warehouse model is based on **hierarchical data types**. Given an extended base type $B = (Dom(B), Op(B), Pred(B), \Upsilon)$, we may define a number of equivalence relations eq on $Dom(B)$. Each of these equivalence relations defines a partition Π_{eq} of the domain into equivalence classes. These equivalence classes c may be named by n_c. Let us denote named partitions by Π^*. The trivial named partition that only relates elements to themselves is denoted by $\perp^*$. We denote the named partition that consists of $\{Dom(B)\}$ and a name by $\top^*$.

Equivalence relations and partitions may be ordered. The *canonical order* of partitions on $DOM(B)$ relates two partitions Π^*, Π'^*. We define $\Pi^* \preceq \Pi'^*$ iff for all (c, n_c) from Π^* there exists one and only one element $(c', n_{c'}) \in \Pi'^*$ such that $c \subseteq c'$. We also may consider non-classical orderings such as the *majority order* $\preceq_m^{choice}$ that relates two named partitions iff for all (c, n_c) from Π^* there exists one and only one element $(c', n_{c'}) \in \Pi'^*$ such that

either $|c \cap c'| > \max\{|c \cap c''| \,|\, (c'', n_{c''}) \in \Pi'^*, \, c'' \neq c'\}$

or $(c', n_{c'}) \in \Pi'^*$ is determined by a (deterministic) `choice` operator among $\{c^+ \in \Pi'^* \,||\, c \cap c^+| = \max\{|c \cap c''| \,||\,(c'', n_{c''}) \in \Pi'^*\}\}$.

If the last case does not appear, then we omit the choice operator in $\preceq_m^{choice}$.

The *DateTime* type is a typical basic data type. Typical equivalence relations are eq_{hour} and eq_{day} that relate values from $Dom(DateTime)$ which belong to the same hour or day. The partitions $\perp^*$, *Days*, *Weeks*, *Months*, *Quarters*, *Years*, and $\top^*$ denote the named partitions of highest granularity, the named partitions of *DateTime* by days, by weeks, by months, by quarters, by years, and the trivial no-granularity named partition respectively. We observe $\perp^* \preceq \Pi^*$ and $\Pi^* \preceq \top^*$ for any named partition in this list. We note, too, that *Days* $\preceq$ *Months* $\preceq$ *Quarters* $\preceq$ *Years*. *Weeks* $\preceq_m$ *Months* is a difficult ordering that causes a lot of confusion.

This notion of hierarchical data types can be extended to complex attribute types, entity types, cluster types and relationship types. These extended types are also called *hierarchical types*. Aggregation functions are defined for extension-based data types. The cube definition uses the association between attribute types and aggregation functions.

The **grounding schema** of a cube is given by a (cube) relationship type $R = (R_1, \ldots, R_n, \{(A_1, q_1, f_1,), \ldots, (A_m, q_m, f_m)\})$ with

- Hierarchical types $R_1, \ldots, R_n$ which form component (or dimension) types,
- ("Fact") attributes $A_1, \ldots, A_m$ which are defined over extension-based data types and instantiated by singleton-value queries $q_1, \ldots, q_m$ and
- Aggregation functions $f_1, \ldots, f_m$ defined over $A_1, \ldots, A_m$.

The grounding schema is typically defined by a *view* over a database schema.

Given a grounding schema $R = (R_1, \ldots, R_n, \{(A_1, q_1, f_1,), \ldots, (A_m, q_m, f_m)\})$, a class R^C, and partitions Π_i on $DOM(R_i)$ for any component $R_1, \ldots, R_n$. A *cell* of R^C is a non-empty set $\sigma_{R_1 \in c_1, \ldots E_n \in c_n}(R^C)$ for $c_i \in \Pi_i$ and for the selection operation σ_α. Given now partitions $\Pi_1, \ldots, \Pi_n$ for all component types, a **cube** $cube^{\Pi_1^*, \ldots, \Pi_n^*}(R^C)$ on R^C and on Π_i^*, $1 \leq i \leq n$ consists of the set

$$\{\sigma_{R_1 \in c_1, \ldots R_n \in c_n}(R^C) \neq \emptyset | c_1 \in \Pi_1, \ldots, c_n \in \Pi_n\}$$

of all cells of R^C for the named partitions Π_i^*, $1 \leq i \leq n$. If $\Pi_i^* = \top^*$, then we may omit the partition Π_i^*.

Therefore, a cube is a special view which may be materialised. The view may be used for computations. Then each cell is recorded with its corresponding aggregations for the attributes. For instance, $sum(\pi_{\text{PriceOfGood}}(\sigma_{\text{SellingDate}\in Week_x}(R^C)))$ computes the total turnover in week x.

Spreadsheet cubes are defined for sequences $\Pi_1^* \preceq \ldots \preceq \Pi_n^*$ of partitions for one or more dimensional components. For instance, the partitions *Days, Months, Quarters, Years* define a spreadsheet cube for components defined over *DateTime*.

The cube can use another representation: instead of using cells as sets, we may use the names defining the cells as the cell dimension value. This representation is called a **named cube**.

This definition of the cube can be now easily used for a precise mathematical definition of the main operations for cubes and extended cubes. For instance, given a cube with partitions Π^*, Π'^* for a one-dimensional component with $\Pi^* \preceq \Pi'^*$, the drill-down operation transfers a cube defined on Π'^* to a cube defined on Π^*. Roll-up transfers a cube defined on Π to a cube defined on Π'^*. The slice operation is nothing more than the object-relational selection operation. The dice operation can be defined in two ways: either using the object-relational projection operation or using $\top$ partitions for all dimensional components that are out of scope. More formally, the following basic OLAP query functions are introduced for a cube $cube^{\Pi_1^*,\ldots,\Pi_n^*}(R^C)$ defined on the cube schema $R = (R_1,\ldots,R_n,\{(A_1,q_1,f_1,),\ldots,(A_m,q_m,f_m)\})$, a dimension i, and partitions $\Pi_i^* \preceq \Pi_i'^* \preceq \top_i^*$:

Basic drill-down functions map the cube $cube^{\Pi_1^*,\ldots,\Pi_i'^*,\ldots,\Pi_n^*}(R^C)$ to the cube $cube^{\Pi_1^*,\ldots,\Pi_i^*,\ldots,\Pi_n^*}(R^C)$.

Basic roll-up functions map the cube $cube^{\Pi_1^*,\ldots,\Pi_i^*,\ldots,\Pi_n^*}(R^C)$ to the cube $cube^{\Pi_1^*,\ldots,\Pi_i'^*,\ldots,\Pi_n^*}(R^C)$. Roll-up functions are the inverse of drill-down functions.

Basic slice functions are similar to the selection of tuples within a set. The cube $cube^{\Pi_1^*,\ldots,\Pi_n^*}(R^C)$ is mapped to the cube $\sigma_\alpha(cube^{\Pi_1^*,\ldots,\Pi_n^*}(R^C))$. The slice function can also be defined through cells. Let $dimension(\alpha)$ be the set of all dimensions that are restricted by α. Let further

$$\sigma_\alpha^{\sqcap}(c_i) = \begin{cases} \emptyset & \text{if } R_i \in dimension(\alpha) \wedge \sigma_\alpha(c_i) \neq c_i, \\ c_i & \text{otherwise.} \end{cases}$$

Close slice functions restrict the cube cells to those which entirely fulfill the selection criterion α, i.e.

$$\{\sigma_{R_1\in\sigma_\alpha^{\sqcap}(c_1),\ldots R_n\in\sigma_\alpha^{\sqcap}(c_n)}(R^C) \neq \emptyset | c_1 \in \Pi_1,\ldots,c_n \in \Pi_n\}.$$

Liberal slice functions restrict the cells to those which partially fulfill the selection criterion α, i.e. to cells $\{\sigma_{R_1\in\sigma_\alpha(c_1),\ldots R_n\in\sigma_\alpha(c_n)}(R^C) \neq \emptyset | c_1 \in \Pi_1,\ldots,c_n \in \Pi_n\}$. Lazy and eager slice functions apply the selection functions directly to values in the cells.

Basic dice functions are similar to projection in the first-order query algebra. They map the cube $cube^{\Pi_1^*,...,\Pi_i^*,...,\Pi_n^*}(R^C)$ to the cube $cube^{\Pi_1^*,...,\top_i^*,...,\Pi_n^*}(R^C)$. Basic dice functions are defined as special roll-up functions. We also may omit dimension i. In this case we lose the information on this dimension.

Generalising the first-order query algebra, [25] defines additional OLAP operations such as

join functions for mergers of cubes,
union functions for the union of two or more cubes of identical type,
rotation or pivoting functions for rearrangement of the order of dimensions, and
rename functions for renaming of dimensions.

Our new definition of the cube allows us to generalise a large body of knowledge obtained for object-relational databases to cubes. The *integration* of cubes can be defined in a similar way [20].

6.3 Semantics of EER Models

6.3.1 Semantics of Structuring

Each structuring also uses a set of **implicit model-inherent integrity constraints**:

Component-construction constraints are based on the existence, cardinality and inclusion of components. These constraints must be considered in the translation and implication process.

Identification constraints are implicitly used for the set constructor. Each object either does not belong to a set or belongs only once to the set. Sets are based on simple generic functions. The identification property may be, however, only representable through automorphism groups [3]. We shall later see that value representability or weak-value representability leads to controllable structuring.

Acyclicity and finiteness of structuring supports axiomatisation and definition of the algebra. It must, however, be explicitly specified. Constraints such as cardinality constraints may be based on potential infinite cycles.

Superficial structuring leads to the representation of constraints through structures. In this case, implication of constraints is difficult to characterise.

Implicit model-inherent constraints belong to performance and maintenance traps. We distinguish between constraints with a semantic meaning in the application. Either these constraints must be maintained or their validity can be controlled by a controller. Constraints can either be declared through logical formulas or given by four layers:

- Constraints are declared at the *declaration layer* based on logical formulas or constructs and based on the schema declaration.

- Constraints are extended at the *technical layer* by methods for their maintenance, by rules for compensation of their invalidity, and by enactment strategies and auxiliary methods.
- Constraint maintenance is extended at the *technological layer* under explicit consideration of the DBMS programs (e.g. for update in place, in private or in separation) and by transformation to dynamic transition constraints.
- Constraint specification is extended at the *organisational layer* by integration into the architecture of the system, by obligations for users that impose changes in the database, and for components of the system.

Relational DBMS use a constraint specification at the declaration and technical layers. For instance, foreign key constraints explicitly specify which constraint enforcement technics are applied in the case of invalidity of constraint. The systems DB2, Oracle and Sybase use different scheduling approaches for constraint maintenance at the technological layer. Constraints may be maintained mainly through the DBMS or partially maintained through interface programs restricting invalidation of constraints by users.

Implicit language-based integrity constraints are typically based on the mini-semantics of the names used for denotation of concepts. EER modelling is based on a *closed-world approach*. Constructions which are not developed for a schema either do not exist in the application or are unimportant for the database system.

Synonyms form typical implicit constraints. Given two queries q_1, q_2 on $\mathcal{D}$, an empty auxiliary schema $\mathcal{A}$ and the target schema $\mathcal{S}$, a synonym constraint $q_1 \approx q_2$ is valid for the database $\mathcal{D}^C$ iff $q_1(\mathcal{D}^C) = q_2(\mathcal{D}^C)$. *Homonyms* $S \between T$ describe structural equivalence combined at the same time with different meanings and semantics. Homonyms may be simply seen as the negation or inversion of synonymy. *Hyponyms* and *hypernyms* $S \preccurlyeq T$ hint at subtype associations among the types under consideration. Type T can be considered a more general type than S. *Overlappings* and *compatibilites* $S \uplus T$ describe partial similarities.

Exclusion constraints state that two schema types or, in general, two expressions on a schema will not share any values or objects. Given two queries q_1, q_2 on $\mathcal{D}$, an empty auxiliary schema $\mathcal{A}$ and the target schema $\mathcal{S}$, an exclusion constraint $q_1 \| q_2$ is valid for the database $\mathcal{D}^C$ iff $q_1(\mathcal{D}^C) \cap q_2(\mathcal{D}^C) = \emptyset$.

Implicit model-based exclusion constraints exclude common values for basic data types. For instance, the constraint *Semester[Year] $\|$ Room[Number]* is assumed in the schema in Fig. 6.1 without any explicit specification. Implicit language-based exclusion constraints use the natural understanding of names. For instance, the constraint *Course[Title] $\|$ Professor[Title]* is valid in any university application.

Inclusion constraints state that two schema types or, in general, two expressions on a schema are in a subtype association. Given two queries q_1, q_2 on $\mathcal{D}$, an empty auxiliary schema $\mathcal{A}$ and the target schema $\mathcal{S}$, an inclusion constraint $q_1 \subseteq q_2$ is valid for the database $\mathcal{D}^C$ iff $q_1(\mathcal{D}^C) \subseteq q_2(\mathcal{D}^C)$.

Implicit model-based inclusion constraints form the most important class of implicit constraints. The EER model assumes $R_1[R_2[ID]] \subseteq R_2[ID]$ for any relationship type R_1, its component type R_2, and the identification ID of R_2.

The axiomatisation of exclusion and inclusion is rather simple [25]. It may be either based on the logics of equality and inequality systems or on set-theoretic reasoning.

Explicit integrity constraints can be declared based on the B(eeri–)V(ardi) frame, i.e. by an implication with a formula for premises and a formula for the implication. BV constraints do not lead to rigid limitation of expressibility. If structuring is hierarchic, then BV constraints can be specified within the first-order predicate logic. We may introduce a variety of different classes of integrity constraints:

Equality-generating constraints allow one to generate for a set of objects from one class or from several classes equalities among these objects or components of these objects.

Object-generating constraints require the existence of another object set for a set of objects satisfying the premises.

A class $\mathcal{C}$ of integrity constraints is called *Hilbert-implication-closed* if it can be axiomatised by a finite set of bounded derivation rules and a finite set of axioms. It is well known that the set of join dependencies is not Hilbert-implication-closed for relational structuring. However, an axiomatisation exists with an unbounded rule, i.e. a rule with potentially infinite premises.

Functional dependencies are one of the most important class of equality-generating constraints. Given a type R and substructures X, Y of R. The functional dependency $R : X \longrightarrow Y$ is valid in R^C if $o|_Y = o'|_Y$ whenever $o|_X = o'|_X$ for any two objects o, o' from R^C.

A **key dependency**, or simply *key X*, is a functional dependency $R : X \longrightarrow R$. A key is called *minimal* if none of its proper substructures forms a key. The set of all minimal keys of R is denoted by $Keys(R)$. We note that this set may be very large. For instance, an entity type E with n atomic attributes may have $\left(\begin{smallmatrix} n \\ \lfloor \frac{n}{2} \rfloor \end{smallmatrix}\right)$ minimal keys, which is roughly $\frac{2^n}{c\sqrt{n}}$.

The example depicted in Fig. 6.1 uses the following functional dependencies and keys:

Keys(Person) = {{ *PersNo*}, {*Name, DateOfBirth*}}
Keys(PlannedCourse) = {{*Course, Semester*}, {*Semester, Room, Time*},
$\qquad\qquad\qquad$ {*Semester, Teacher, Time*}}
PlannedCourse : {*Semester, Time, Room*} $\longrightarrow$ {{*Program*}, *Teacher, Course*}
PlannedCourse : {*Teacher, Semester, Time*} $\longrightarrow$ {*Course, Room*}
ProposedCourse : {*Semester, Course*} $\rightarrow$ {*Teacher*}

The following axiomatisation is correct and complete for functional dependencies in the EER [14] for substructures X, Y, Z of the EER type R:
Axioms: $R : X \sqcup_R Y \longrightarrow Y$
Rules:

$$\frac{R : X \longrightarrow Y}{R : X \longrightarrow X \sqcup_R Y} \quad \frac{R : X \longrightarrow Y, R : Y \longrightarrow Z}{R : X \longrightarrow Z} \quad \frac{R' : X \longrightarrow Y}{R : R'[X] \longrightarrow R'[Y]} .$$

The type R' denotes a component type of R if R is a relationship type of order i and R' is of order $i - 1$.

Domain constraints restrict the set of values. Given an EER type R, a substructure T' of R, its domain $Dom(T')$, and a subset D of $Dom(T')$, the domain constraint $R : T' \subseteq D$ is valid in R^C if $\pi_{T'}(R^C) \subseteq D$.

For instance, we may restrict the year and the description of semesters by the constraints

Semester.Year $\subseteq \{1980, \ldots, 2039\}$ *and*
Semester.Description $\subseteq \{WT, ST\}$.

Cardinality constraints are the most important class of constraints of the EER model. We distinguish two main kinds of cardinality constraints. Given a relationship type $R \triangleq (compon(R), attr(R), \Sigma)$, a component R' of R, the remaining substructure $R'' = R \setminus R'$ and the remaining substructure $R''' = R'' \sqcap_R compon(R)$ without attributes of R.

The *participation constraint* $card(R, R') = (m, n)$ holds in a relationship class R^C if for any object $o' \in R'^C$ there are at least m and at most n objects o with $o|_{R'} = o'$, i.e. $m \leq |\{o \in R^C | o|_{R'} = o'\}| \leq n$ for any $o' \in \pi_{R'}(R^C)$.

The *lookup constraint* $look(R, R') = [m, n]$ holds in a relationship class R^C if for any object $o'' \in Dom(R'')$ there are at least m and at most n related objects o' with $o|_{R'} = o'$, i.e. $m \leq |\{o' \in \pi_{R'}(R^C) | o \in R^C \wedge o|_{R'} = o' \wedge o|_{R'''} = o'''\}| \leq n$ for any $o''' \in Dom(R''')$.

Lookup constraints were originally introduced by P.P. Chen [7] as cardinality constraints. UML uses lookup constraints. They are easy to understand for binary relationship types without attributes but difficult for all other types. Lookup constraints do not consider attributes of a relationship type. They cannot be expressed by participation constraints. Participation constraints cannot be expressed by lookup constraints. In the case of a binary relationship type $R \triangleq (R_1, R_2, \emptyset, \Sigma)$ without attributes, we may translate these constraints into each other:

$$card(R, R_1) = (m, n) \text{ iff } look(R, R_2) = [m, n].$$

Furthermore, participation and lookup constraints with an upper bound of 1 and a lower bound of 0 are equivalent to functional dependencies for a relationship type R:

$$card(R, R') = (0, 1) \text{ iff } R : R' \longrightarrow R'' \text{ and}$$
$$look(R, R') = [0, 1] \text{ iff } R : R''' \longrightarrow R'.$$

The lower bounds of lookup and participation constraints are not related to each other. They are, however, related for binary relationship types. The lower bound 1 expresses an inclusion constraint:

$$card(R, R') = (1, n) \text{ iff } R[R'] \subseteq R' \text{ and}$$
$$look(R, R') = [1, n] \text{ iff } R[R'''] \subseteq R'''.$$

Cardinality constraints are restrictions of combinatorics within a schema. Sets of cardinality constraints defined on a subschema S' may be *finitely inconsistent* in the sense that any database on S' has either a class for a type in S' that is empty or that is infinite.

Consider, for instance, the following relationship type:

$$DirectPrerequisite \overset{\circ}{=} (HasPrerequisite : Course,$$
$$IsPrerequisite : Course, \emptyset, \Sigma)$$
$$card(DirectPrerequisite, HasPrerequisite) = (0, 2) \text{ and}$$
$$card(DirektVoraussetz, IsPrerequisite) = (3, 4).$$

These cardinality constraints are only satisfied in a database with either an empty set of courses or an infinite set of courses.

Participation and lookup constraints can be extended to substructures and intervals. Given a relationship type R, a substructure R' of R, the remaining substructure $R'' = R \setminus R'$ and the remaining substructure $R''' = R'' \sqcap_R compon(R)$ without attributes of R. Assume furthermore an interval $I \subseteq \mathbb{N}_0$ of natural numbers including 0.

The *(general) cardinality constraint* $card(R, R') = I$ holds in a relationship class R^C if for any object $o' \in \pi_{R'}(R^C)$ there are $i \in I$ objects o with $o|_{R'} = o'$, i.e.
$$|\{o \in R^C | o|_{R'} = o'\}| \in I \text{ for any } o' \in \pi_{R'}(R^C).$$

A participation constraint $card(R, R') = (m, n)$ is just a general cardinality constraint with the interval $\{m, \ldots, n\}$. A lookup constraint $look(R, R') = [m, n]$ is just a general cardinality constraint $card(R, R''') = I$ with the interval $\{m, \ldots, n\}$.

General cardinality constraints are necessary whenever we consider sets of cardinality constraints. There are examples of participation constraints for which general cardinality constraints can be inferred which cannot be expressed through lookup or participation constraints.

If $R = R'$, then the general cardinality constraint specifies the cardinality bounds of the relationship class. The definition of general cardinality constraints can be extended to entity types as well.

Cardinality constraints restrict relationships. We are not able to defer equalities. Consider for instance the following relationship type:

$$Spouse \overset{\circ}{=} (IsSpouse : Person, OfSpouse : Person, \{From, To\}, \Sigma).$$

Neither $card(Spouse, IsSpouse\ From) = (0, 1)$ and $card(Spouse, OfSpouse\ From) = (0, 1)$ nor $look(Spouse, IsSpouse) = [0, 1]$ and $look(Spouse, OfSpouse) = [0, 1]$ express the statement of monogamic societies that the spouse of the spouse is the person itself. The lookup constraints are only valid if a person can be married once. The Islamic rule would be that either the spouse of a spouse is the person itself or the spouse of the spouse of the spouse is the spouse.

Cardinality constraints combine equality-generating and object-generating constraints into a singleton construct. This convenience for declaration is paid back by the impossibility of axiomatising these constraints.

Participation cardinality constraints cannot be axiomatised [25]. If axiomatisation is restricted to the upper bound, then an axiomatisation can be based on the following system for one-type derivations [13]:

$$\text{Axioms:}\quad card(R, X) = (0, \infty);$$

$$\text{Rules:}\quad \frac{card(R, X) = (0, b)}{card(R, X \sqcup_R Y) = (0, b)}\quad \frac{card(R, X) = (0, b)}{card(R, X) = (0, b + c)}.$$

Functional dependencies can be defined through generalised cardinality constraints, i.e. the functional dependency $R : X \longrightarrow Y$ is equivalent to $card(R[X \sqcup_R Y], X) = (0, 1)$. The Armstrong axiomatisation provided above can be combined with the axiomatisation for upper bounds of participation constraints and the following system:

$$\frac{R : X \longrightarrow Y, card(R, Y) = (0, b)}{card(R, X) = (0, b)}\quad \frac{card(R, X) = (0, 1)}{R : X \longrightarrow R}.$$

These three systems are complete and correct for the derivation of upper bounds.

We may also conclude rules for many-type derivations [25]. A typical rule is the following one:

$$\frac{card(R, R') = (m, n), card(R', R'') = (m', n')}{card(R, R'') = (m \cdot m', n \cdot n')}.$$

Multi-valued dependencies are best fitted to the ER model and are difficult to define, teach, handle, model and understand within relational database models. Given an EER type R and partition of components of R into X, Y and Z, the multivalued dependency $X \twoheadrightarrow Y | Z$ is ER-valid in a class R^C defined over the type R (denoted by $R^C \models_{ER} X \twoheadrightarrow Y | Z$) if the type can be decomposed into three types representing X, Y and Z and two mandatory relationship types defined on $X \cup Y$ and $X \cup Z$ respectively.

The multi-valued dependency can be represented by a decomposition of the type R displayed in Fig. 6.4.

We may use the more compact schemata given in Fig. 6.5. In this case, the relationship type with the components $_{(x)}Z$ is based on the X-components. It allows us to show the direct decomposition imposed by the multi-valued dependency.

The deductive system in Fig. 6.6 consisting of the trivial multi-valued dependency, the root reduction rule, and the weakening rule is correct and complete for

Fig. 6.4 ER representations of a multi-valued dependency for a first-order relationship type

abbreviated notation for
X-components that form
an entity type of the
relationship type R

Fig. 6.5 Compact representations of a multi-valued dependency

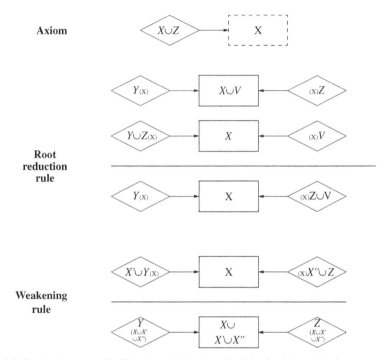

Fig. 6.6 Deductive system for ER schema derivation of multi-valued dependencies

inference of multi-valued dependencies. We observe that the axiomatisation of functional and multi-valued dependencies can be derived in a similar way.

The constraints discussed above can be used for the decomposition of types and restructuring of schemata. **Pivoting** was introduced in [4] and allows one to introduce a higher-order relationship type after factoring out constraints which are applicable to some but not all of the components of the relationship type.

Let us consider the schema depicted in Fig. 6.1. The relationship type *Proposed-Course* has an arity of 8. In the given application, the following integrity constraints are valid:

$$\{Course\} \twoheadrightarrow \{Program\}$$
$$\{Program\} \twoheadrightarrow \{Course\}$$
$$\{Course, Program\} \longrightarrow \{Responsible4Course : Person\} \, .$$

The last functional dependency is a 'dangling' functional dependency, i.e. the right-side components are not elements of any left side of a functional or multi-valued dependency. Considering the axiomatisation of functional and multi-valued dependencies we conclude that right-side components of a dangling functional dependency can be separated from other components. The first two constraints can be used for separation of concern of the type *ProposedCourse* into associations among

$$Course, Program, Responsible4Course : Person$$

and

$$Course, Kind, Semester, Professor, Time(Proposal, SideCondition),$$
$$Room, InsertedBy : Person.$$

According to the decomposition rules we find additional names for the independent component sets in *ProposedCourse*, i.e. in our case *CourseObligation*. We additionally observe that *InsertedBy : Person* can be separated from the last association. This separation is based on *pivoting*, i.e. building a relationship type 'on top' of the 'remaining' type:

$$ProposedCourseRevised \stackrel{\circ}{=} (Teacher : Professor, Course,$$
$$Proposal : Kind, Request : Room, Semester, \{Time(Proposal, SideCondition)\}).$$

Finally, let us consider a constraint on *Course* and *Kind*. In the given application we assume that the selection of the kind for a course is independent of the other components, i.e.

$$ProposedCourseRevised : \{Course, Semester\} \twoheadrightarrow \{Kind\}.$$

This constraint hints at a flaw in modelling. The association between *Course* and *Kind* may vary over semesters for lectures. *Kind* is an enumeration type that categorises the style of how lectures are given. The selection of the kind becomes easier if we develop an abstraction *Applicable* that collects all possible associations between *Course* and *Kind*.

We may also use a pragmatic rule for naming. If a decomposition leads to a separation based on roles, then we may use the role name for the relationship type name.

One of our separation rules allows us to separate optional components of a relationship type by pivoting the type into a new relationship type. We use this rule for pivoting *PlannedCourse* and *CourseHeld*.

Finally we derive the schema displayed in Fig. 6.7. This schema is based on *CourseProposal*, *CoursePlanned* and *Lecture*.

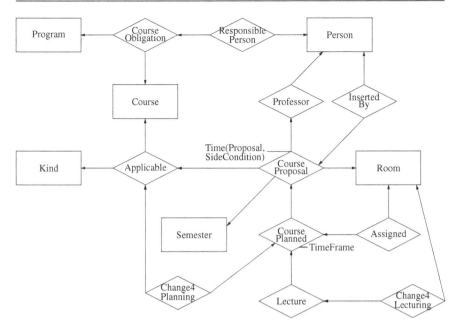

Fig. 6.7 Decomposition of HERM diagram in Fig. 6.1

6.3.2 Semantics of Functionality

Static constraints in a schema (S, Σ) can be transformed into **transition constraints** [25]. A transition constraint $(\Psi_{\text{pre}}, \Psi_{\text{post}})$ defines the preconditions and postconditions for state transitions of databases defined over S. Given a transition τ converting the database S^{C_1} to the database $S^{C_2} = \tau(S^{C_1})$, the transition constraint $(\Psi_{\text{pre}}, \Psi_{\text{post}})$ is valid for the transition $(S^{C_1}, \tau(S^{C_1}))$ if from $S^{C_1} \models \Psi_{\text{pre}}$ it follows that $S^{C_2} \models \Psi_{\text{post}}$.

Static constraints Σ are therefore converted to a transition constraint (Σ, Σ).

Database dynamics is defined on the basis of transition systems. A *transition system* on schema S is a pair $\mathcal{TS} = (S, \{\overset{a}{\rightarrow} \mid a \in \mathcal{L}\})$

where S is a non-empty set of state variables,

$\mathcal{L}$ is a non-empty set (of labels), and

$\overset{a}{\rightarrow} \subseteq S \times (S \cup \{\infty\})$ for each $a \in \mathcal{L}$.

State variables are interpreted by database states. Transitions are interpreted by transactions on S. Database lifetime is specified on the basis of paths on $\mathcal{TS}$. A *path* π through a transition system is a finite or ω length sequence of the form $s_0 \overset{a_1}{\longrightarrow} s_1 \overset{a_2}{\longrightarrow} \dots$ The length of a path is its number of transitions.

For the transition system TS we can introduce now a *temporal dynamic database logic* using the quantifiers $\forall_f$ (always in the future)), $\forall_p$ (always in the past), $\exists_f$ (sometimes in the future), $\exists_p$ (sometimes in the past).

First-order predicate logic can be extended on the basis of temporal operators. The validity function I is extended by time. Assume a temporal class (R^C, l_R). The validity function I is extended by time and is defined on $S(ts, R^C, l_R)$. A formula α is valid for $I_{(R^C, l_R)}$ in ts if it is valid on the snapshot defined on ts, i.e. $I_{(R^C, l_R)}(\alpha, ts) = 1$ iff $I_{S(ts, R^C, l_R)}(\alpha, ts)$.

- For formulas without a temporal prefix the extended validity function coincides with the usual validity function.
- $I(\forall_f \alpha, ts) = 1$ iff $I(\alpha, ts') = 1$ for all $ts' > ts$;
- $I(\forall_p \alpha, ts) = 1$ iff $I(\alpha, ts') = 1$ for all $ts' < ts$;
- $I(\exists_f \alpha, ts) = 1$ iff $I(\alpha, ts') = 1$ for some $ts' > ts$;
- $I(\exists_p \alpha, ts) = 1$ iff $I(\alpha, ts') = 1$ for some $ts' < ts$.

The modal operators $\forall_p$ and $\exists_p$ ($\forall_f$ and $\exists_f$ respectively) are dual operators, i.e. the two formulas $\forall_h \alpha$ and $\neg \exists_h \neg \alpha$ are equivalent. These operators can be mapped onto classical modal logic with the following definition:

$$\Box \alpha \equiv (\forall_f \alpha \wedge \forall_p \alpha \wedge \alpha);$$
$$\Diamond \alpha \equiv (\exists_f \alpha \vee \exists_p \alpha \vee \alpha).$$

In addition, the temporal operators *until* and *next* can be introduced.

The most important class of dynamic integrity constraint are **state-transition constraints** $\alpha O \beta$ which use a precondition α and a postcondition β for each operation O. The state-transition constraint $\alpha O \beta$ can be expressed by the temporal formula $\alpha \xrightarrow{O} \beta$.

Each finite set of static integrity constraints can be equivalently expressed by a set of state-transition constraints $\{\wedge_{\alpha \in \Sigma} \alpha \xrightarrow{O} \wedge_{\alpha \in \Sigma} \alpha) | O \in Alg(M)\}$.

Integrity constraints may be enforced

- either at the procedural level by application of

  - trigger constructs [18] in the so-called active event-condition-action setting,
  - greatest consistent specialisations of operations [21],
  - or stored procedures, i.e. fully fledged programs considering all possible violations of integrity constraints,

- or at the transaction level by restricting sequences of state changes to those which do not violate integrity constraints,
- or by the DBMS on the basis of declarative specifications depending on the facilities of the DBMS,
- or at the interface level on the basis of consistent state-changing operations.

Database constraints are classically mapped to transition constraints. These transition constraints are well understood as long as they can be treated locally. Constraints can thus be supported using triggers or stored procedures. Their global interdependence is, however, an open issue.

The transformation to event-condition-action rules is not powerful enough. Consider the following example [22]:

$$R_1 \stackrel{\circ}{=} (R_3, R_4, \emptyset, \Sigma_1), \quad card(R_1, R_4) = (1, n),$$
$$R_2 \stackrel{\circ}{=} (R_5, R_6, \emptyset, \Sigma_2), \quad card(R_2, R_5) = (0, 1), \quad card(R_2, R_6) = (1, n),$$
$$R_3 \stackrel{\circ}{=} (R_6, \dots, \emptyset, \Sigma_3), \quad card(R_3, R_6) = (0, 1), \quad \text{and } R_4 \| R_5.$$

The greatest consistent specialisation of the operation $\texttt{Insert}\,(R_1, (a, c))$ is the operation

$$\texttt{Insert(R\_1,(a,c))} \Leftrightarrow$$
$$\text{if } c \notin R_2[R_5] \text{ then fail}$$
$$\text{else begin Insert (R\_1,(a,c));}$$
$$\text{if } a \notin R_1[R_3] \text{ then Insert (R\_2,(a,d))}$$
$$\text{where } d \notin R_1[R_4] \cup R_2[R_5] \text{ end;}$$

This operation cannot be computed by trigger constructs. They result in the deletion of a from $R_1[R_3]$ and the deletion of c from $R_2[R_5]$ and thus permit insertion into R_1.

6.4 Problems with Modelling and Constraint Specification

The main deficiency is the constraint acquisition problem. Since we need a treatment for sets, a more sophisticated reasoning theory is required. One good candidate is visual or graphical reasoning that goes far beyond logical reasoning [8].

Most modelling approaches assume *constraint set completeness*, i.e. all constraints of certain constraint classes which are valid for an application must be explicitly specified or derivable. For instance, normalisation algorithms are based on the elicitation of complete knowledge on all valid functional dependencies. Therefore, the designer should have tools or theories on how to obtain all functional dependencies which are independent of the functional dependencies already obtained and which are not known to be invalid.

Excluded functional constraints $X \longrightarrow / Y$ state that the functional dependency $X \longrightarrow Y$ is not valid. Excluded functional constraints and functional dependencies are axiomatisable by the following formal system [25].

Axioms
$$X \cup Y \to Y$$

Rules

$$(1)\frac{X \longrightarrow Y}{X \cup V \cup W \longrightarrow Y \cup V} \qquad\qquad (2)\frac{X \longrightarrow Y, Y \longrightarrow Z}{X \longrightarrow Z}$$

$$(3)\frac{X \longrightarrow Y, X \longrightarrow /Z}{Y \longrightarrow /Z}$$

$$(4)\frac{X \longrightarrow /Y}{X \longrightarrow /Y \cup Z} \qquad (5)\frac{X \cup Z \longrightarrow /Y \cup Z}{X \cup Z \longrightarrow /Y}$$

$$(6)\frac{X \longrightarrow Z, X \longrightarrow /Y \cup Z}{X \longrightarrow /Y} \qquad (7)\frac{Y \longrightarrow Z, X \longrightarrow /Z}{X \longrightarrow /Y}$$

Rules (3) and (7) are one of the possible inversions of rule (2) since the implication $\alpha \wedge \beta \rightarrow \gamma$ is equivalent to the implication $\neg\gamma \wedge \beta \rightarrow \neg\alpha$. Rules (4) and (5) are inversions of rule (1). Rule (6) can be considered the inversion of the following union rule, valid for functional dependencies:

$$(8)\frac{X \longrightarrow Y, X \longrightarrow Z}{X \longrightarrow Y \cup Z}.$$

This rule can be derived from the axiom and rule (2).

Constraint elicitation can be organised by the following approach:

Specification of the set of valid functional dependencies Σ_1: all dependencies which are known to be valid and all those which can be implied from the set of valid and excluded functional dependencies.

Specification of the set of excluded functional dependencies Σ_0: all dependencies which are known to be invalid and all those which can be implied from the set of valid and excluded functional dependencies.

This approach leads to the following simple elicitation algorithm:

1. Basic step: Design obvious constraints.
2. Recursion step: Repeat until the constraint sets Σ_0 and Σ_1 do not change.

- *Find a functional dependency α that is neither in Σ_1 nor in Σ_0.*

  – *If α is valid, then add α to Σ_1.*
  – *If α is invalid, then add α to Σ_0.*

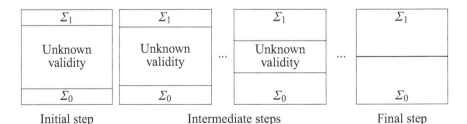

Σ_1	Σ_1		Σ_1		Σ_1
Unknown validity	Unknown validity	...	Unknown validity	...	
Σ_0	Σ_0		Σ_0		Σ_0
Initial step	Intermediate steps				Final step

Fig. 6.8 Constraint acquisition process

• *Generate the logical closures of Σ_0 and Σ_1.*

This algorithm can be refined in various ways. All the known elicitation algorithms are variations of this simple elicitation algorithm.

The constraint acquisition process based on this algorithm is illustrated in Fig. 6.8.

References

1. Allen JF (1984) Towards a general theory of action and time. Artif Intell (6):123–154
2. Beeri C (1992) New data models and languages – the challenge. In: Proceedings of the 11th ACM SIGACT-SIGMOD-SIGART symposium on principles of database systems – PODS'92, San Diego. ACM, New York, pp 1–15
3. Beeri C, Thalheim B (1999) Identification as a primitive of database models. In: Proceedings of FoMLaDO'98. Kluwer, London, pp 19–36
4. Biskup J, Polle T (2000) Decomposition of database classes under path functional dependencies and onto contraints. In: Proceedings of FoIKS'2000. Lecture notes in computer science, vol 1762. Springer, Berlin, pp 31–49
5. Buneman P, Libkin L, Suciu D, Tannen V, Wong L (1994) Comprehension syntax. SIGMOD Rec 23(1):87–96
6. Celko J (1995) Joe Celko's SQL for smarties – advanced SQL programming. Morgan Kaufmann, San Francisco
7. Chen PP (1976) The entity-relationship model: toward a unified view of data. ACM Trans Database Syst 1(1):9–36
8. Demetrovics J, Molnar A, Thalheim B (2004) Graphical and spreadsheet reasoning for sets of functional dependencies. In: Proceedings of ER'2004. Lecture notes in computer science, vol 3255. Springer, Berlin, pp 54–66
9. Elmasri R, Weeldreyer J, Hevner A (1985) The category concept: an extension to the entity-relationship model. Data Knowl Eng 1(1):75–116
10. Fegaras L, Sheard T, Stemple DW (1992) Uniform traversal combinators: definition, use and properties. In: Kapur D (ed) Proceedings of Automated Deduction – CADE'92, 11th international conference on automated deduction, Saratoga Springs, NY. Springer, Berlin Heidelberg New York, pp 148–162
11. Gogolla M (1994) An extended entity-relationship model – fundamentals and pragmatics. Lecture notes in computer science, vol 767. Springer, Berlin
12. Goldblatt R (2006) Topoi: the categorial analysis of logic. Dover, New York
13. Hartmann S (2003) Reasoning about participation constraints and Chen's constraints. In: ADC, volume 17 of CRPIT. Australian Computer Society, pp 105–113
14. Hartmann S, Hoffmann A, Link S, Schewe K-D (2003) Axiomatizing functional dependencies in the higher-order entity-relationship model. Inf Process Lett 87(3):133–137
15. Hohenstein U (1993) Formale Semantik eines erweiterten Entity-Relationship-Modells. Teubner, Stuttgart
16. Lenz H-J, Shoshani A (1997) Summarizability in OLAP and statistical data base. In: Proceedings of the 9th international conference on scientific and statistical database management – SSDBM'97, Olympia, pp 132–143
17. Lenz H-J, Thalheim B (2001) OLAP databases and aggregation functions. In: Proceedings of the 13th international conference on scientific and statistical database management, George Mason University, Fairfax, VA, 18–20 July 2001. IEEE Computer Society, pp 91–100
18. Levene M, Loizou G (1999) A guided tour of relational databases and beyond. Springer, Berlin Heidelberg New York

19. Lipeck UW, Neumann K (1987) Modeling and manipulating objects in geo-scientific databases. In: Proceedings of the 5th Int. ER conference, ER'96, Dijon, France, 17–19 November 1986, 1987. North-Holland, Amsterdam, pp 67–85
20. Molnar A (2007) A general partition data model and a contribution to the theory of functional dependencies. PhD thesis, Eötvös Loránd University, Faculty of Informatics, Budapest
21. Schewe K-D (1994) The specification of data-intensive application systems. Advanced PhD (Habilitation Thesis), Brandenburg University of Technology at Cottbus, Faculty of Mathematics, Natural Sciences and Computer Science
22. Schewe K-D, Thalheim B (1998) Limitations of rule triggering systems for integrity maintenance in the context of transition specification. Acta Cybern 13:277–304
23. Schewe K-D, Thalheim B (2005) Conceptual modelling of web information systems. Data Knowl Eng 54:147–188
24. Thalheim B (1989) On semantic issues connected with keys in relational databases permitting null values. J Inf Process Cybern 25(1/2):11–20
25. Thalheim B (2000) Entity-relationship modeling – foundations of database technology. Springer, Berlin Heidelberg New York
26. Thalheim B (2002) Component construction of database schemes. In: Spaccapietra S, March ST, Kambayashi Y (eds) Proceedings of ER'02. Lecture notes in computer science, vol 2503. Springer, Berlin, pp 20–34
27. Thalheim B (2004) Application development based on database components. In: Kiyoki Y, Jaakkola H (eds) EJC'2004, Information modeling and knowledge bases XVI. IOS Press, Amsterdam
28. Thalheim B, Düsterhöft A (2001) Sitelang: conceptual modeling of internet sites. In: Proceedings of ER'01. Lecture notes in computer science, vol 2224. Springer, Berlin, pp 179–192
29. Wadler PL (1987) List comprehensions. In: Peyton Jones SL (ed) The implementation of functional programming languages. Prentice-Hall, Englewood Cliffs

Part III
Process Modelling

Chapter 7
Object–Process Methodology for Structure–Behavior Codesign

Dov Dori

Abstract Function, structure, and behavior are the three major facets of any system. Structure and behavior are two inseparable system aspects, as no system can be faithfully modeled without considering both in tandem. Object-Process Methodology (OPM) is a systems paradigm and language that combines structure–behavior codesign requirements with cognitive considerations. Based on the formal mathematical foundations of graph grammars and a subset of natural language, OPM caters to human intuition in a bimodal way via graphics and autogenerated natural language text. In a nutshell, OPM processes transform objects by creating them, consuming them, or changing their states. The concurrent representation of structure and behavior in the same, single diagram type is balanced, creating synergy whereby each aspect helps understand the other. This chapter defines and demonstrates the principles and elements of OPM, showing its benefits in facilitating structure–behavior codesign and achieving formal, semantically sound, and humanly accessible conceptual models of complex systems in a host of domains and at virtually any complexity level.

7.1 The Cognitive Assumptions and OPM's Design

Text and graphics are two complementary modalities that our brains process interchangeably. Conceptual modeling, which is recognized as a critical step in architecting and designing systems, is an intellectual activity that can greatly benefit from concurrent utilization of the verbal and visual channels of human cognition. A conceptual modeling framework that employs graphics and text can alleviate cognitive loads [12]. OPM is a bimodal graphics–text conceptual modeling framework that caters to these human cognitive needs. This section argues for the value of the

Dov Dori

Technion, Israel Institute of Technology and Massachusetts Institute of Technology e-mail: dori@ie.technion.ac.il

D. W. Embley and B. Thalheim (eds), *Handbook of Conceptual Modeling.*
DOI 10.1007/978-3-642-15865-0, © Springer 2011

OPM holistic approach in addressing the dual-channel, limited channel capacity, and active processing assumptions. Bimodality, complexity management via hierarchical decomposition, and animated simulation, respectively, address these cognitive needs.

7.1.1 Mayer's Three Cognitive Assumptions

Humans assimilate data and information, converting them into meaningful knowledge and understanding of systems via the simultaneous use of words and pictures. During eons of human evolution, the human brain has been trained to capture and analyze images so it can escape predators and capture food. In contrast, processing of spoken words, let alone text, is the product of a relatively very recent glimpse in the history of mankind. As our brains are hard-wired to process imagery, graphics appeal to the brain more immediately than words. However, words can express ideas and assertions that are far too complex or even impossible to express graphically (try graphing this sentence to get a feeling for the validity of this claim). So while a picture is worth a thousand words, as the saying goes, there are cases where a word, or a sentence, is worth a thousand pictures. A problem with the richness of natural languages is the potential ambiguity that arises from their use. This certainly does not imply that pictures cannot be ambiguous as well, but graphic ambiguity can be greatly reduced, or even eliminated, by assigning formal semantics to pictorial symbols of things and relations among them. Since diagrams usually have fewer interpretations than free text, they are more tractable than unconstrained textual notations.

Mayer [26] found that when corresponding words and pictures are presented near each other, learners can better hold corresponding words and pictures in working memory at the same time, enabling the integration of visual and verbal models. A main contribution of diagrams may be that they reduce the cognitive load of assigning abstract data to appropriate spatial and temporal dimensions. For example, Glenberg and Langston [19] found that where information about temporal ordering is only implicit in text, a flow diagram reduces errors in answering questions about that ordering.

Mayer [26] and Mayer and Moreno [27] proposed a theory of multimedia learning that is based on the following three main research-supported cognitive assumptions.

1. Dual-channel – humans possess separate systems for processing visual and verbal representations [2, 8].
2. Limited capacity – the amount of processing that can take place within each information processing channel is extremely limited [2, 7, 29].
3. Active processing – meaningful learning occurs during active cognitive processing, paying attention to words and pictures, mentally organizing and integrating them into coherent representations. The active-processing assumption is a manifestation of the constructivist theory in education, which puts the construction of

knowledge by one's own mind as the centrepiece of the educational effort [45]. According to this theory, in order for learning to be meaningful, learners must engage in constructing their own knowledge.

7.1.2 Meeting the Verbal–Visual Challenge

As the literature suggests, there is great value in designing a modeling approach and supporting tool that meet the challenges posed by the three cognitive assumptions. While Mayer and Moreno [27] used these assumptions to suggest ways to reduce cognitive overload while designing multimedia instruction, the same assumptions can provide a basis for designing an effective conceptual modeling framework. Indeed, conceptual modeling can be viewed primarily as the active cognitive effort of concurrent diagramming and verbalization of one's thoughts. The resulting diagrams and text together constitute the system's model. A model that is based on a compact set of the most primitive and generic elements is general enough to be applicable to a host of domains and simple enough to express the most complex systems. A sufficiently expressive model can be simulated for detecting design-level errors, reasoning, predicting, and effectively communicating one's design to other stakeholders.

Such a modeling environment would help our brains to take advantage of the verbal and visual channels and to relieve cognitive loads while actively designing, modeling, and communicating complex systems to stakeholders. These were key motivations in the design of OPM [11]. The OPM modeling environment implementation by OPCAT[1] [17] embodies these assumptions. Stateful objects – things that exist in some state – and processes – things that transform objects by changing their state or by creating or destroying them – are the generic building blocks of OPM. Structural and procedural links express static and dynamic relations among entities (objects, object states, and processes) in a system, and a number of refinement/abstraction mechanisms are built into OPM for complexity management.

7.1.3 Dual-Channel Processing and the Bimodality of OPM

Considering the dual-channel assumption, an effective use of the brain is to simultaneously engage the visual and the verbal channels (and hence probably also the two brain hemispheres) for conveying ideas regarding a system's architecture. Indeed, OPM represents knowledge about the system's structure and behavior both pictorially and verbally in a single unifying model. When the user expresses a piece of knowledge in one modality, either graphics or text, the complementary one is automatically updated so the two remain coherent at all times.

---

[1] An academic individual version of OPCAT for modeling small systems can be obtained from opcat.com.

In order to show how the cognitive assumptions have been accounted for, we follow a stepwise example of bread baking. Figure 7.1 depicts OPCAT's graphical user interface, which displays simultaneously the graphic (top) and textual (bottom) modalities for exploiting humans' dual-channel processing. The top pane presents the model graphically in an object–process diagram – OPD, while the one below it lists the same model textually in Object–Process Language – OPL. OPCAT recognizes OPD constructs (symbol patterns) and generates their OPL textual counterparts. OPL is a subset of natural English. Each OPD construct has a textual OPL-equivalent sentence or phrase. For example, **Baking**, the central system's process, is the ellipse in Fig. 7.1. The remaining five things are objects (the rectangles) that enable or are transformed by **Baking**. **Baker** and **Equipment** are the *enablers* of

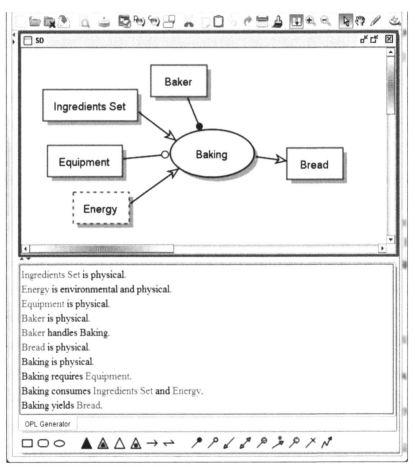

Fig. 7.1 GUI of OPCAT showing the system diagram (SD, top-level diagram) of the Baking system. *Top*: object–process diagram (OPD). *Bottom*: The corresponding, automatically generated Object–Process Language (OPL) paragraph

Baking, while **Ingredients Set**, **Energy**, and **Bread** are its *transformees* – the objects that are transformed by **Baking**. As the direction of the arrows indicates, **Ingredients Set** and **Energy** are the *consumees* – they are consumed by **Baking**, while **Bread** is the resultee – the object created as a result of **Baking**. As soon as the modeler starts depicting and joining things on the graphics screen, OPL sentences start being created in response to these inputs. They accumulate in the OPL pane at the bottom of Fig. 7.1, creating the corresponding OPL paragraph, which tells in text the exact same story that the OPD does graphically.

As the example shows, the OPL syntax is designed to generate sentences in plain natural, albeit restricted, English, with sentences like "**Baking** yields **Bread**." This sentence is the bottom line in Fig. 7.1. An English subset, OPL is accessible to nontechnical stakeholders, and other languages can serve as the target OPL. Unlike programming languages, OPL names can be phrases like **Ingredients Set**.

To enhance the text–graphics linkage, the text colors of the process and object names in the OPL match their colors in the OPD. Since graphics is more immediately amenable to cognitive processing than text, modelers favor modeling the system graphically in the OPD pane, while the textual interpretation is continuously updated in the OPL pane.

The OPL sentences that are constructed or modified automatically in response to linking graphic symbols on the screen provide the modeler and her/his audience with immediate feedback. This real-time humanlike response "tells" the modeler what the modeling environment "thinks" he or she meant to express in the most recent graphic editing operation. When the text does not match the intention of the modeler, a corrective action can be taken promptly. Such immediate feedback is indispensable in spotting and correcting logical design errors at an early stage of the system lifecycle, before they have a chance to propagate and incur costly damage. Any correction of the graphics changes the OPL script, and changes can be applied iteratively until a result that is satisfactory to all the stakeholders from both the customer and the supplier sides is obtained. While generating text from graphics is the prevalent working mode, OPCAT can also generate graphics from text.

The System Diagram (SD, the top-level OPD) is constructed such that it contains a central process, which is the one that carries out the main function of the system, the one that delivers the main value to the beneficiary, for whom the system is built. In our case, **Baking** is the process that provides the value – the **Bread**. This is an example of the application of the *Function as a seed* OPM principle, which states that *modeling of any system starts with specifying the function of the system as the main process in the System Diagram, SD*. Then, objects involved as enablers or transformees are added and both the function and the objects are refined, as described in the sequel. In this system, all the things – objects and processes – are physical, denoted by their shading. **Energy** is also environmental – it is not part of the system, as it is supplied by an external source but is consumed by the system. This is denoted by the dashed contour of **Energy**.

7.1.4 Limited Capacity and the Refinement Mechanisms of OPM

Figure 7.1 is the SD, the bird-eye's view model of the Baking system. This OPD already contains six entities and five links, approaching the limit of the human information processing capacity determined by the "magic number seven plus or minus two" of Miller (1956). However, we have not even started to specify the subprocesses comprising the **Baking** process or the members (parts) of the **Ingredients Set**. To cater to humans' processing limited capacity, OPM advocates keeping each OPD simple enough to enable the diagram reader to quickly grasp the essence of the system by inspecting the OPDs without being intimidated by an overly complicated layout. Overloading the SD with more artifacts will put its comprehension at risk, so showing additional details is deferred to lower-level OPDs, which can be more detailed, as the reader is already familiar with some of their features from upper-level OPDs.

To manage the system's inherent complexity, when an OPD approaches humans' "comprehensibility limit," the model is refined. Refinement in OPD entails primarily the application of the in-zooming refinement mechanism on a process. Figure 7.2 shows a new OPD that resulted from zooming in on the **Baking** process in Fig. 7.1.

This OPD, which is automatically given the name SD1 (**Baking in-zoomed**), elaborates on the SD in several respects. First, **Baking** is inflated, showing within

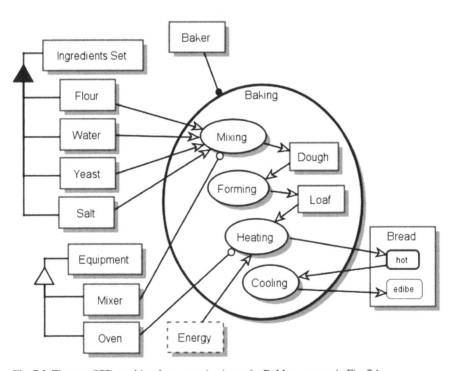

Fig. 7.2 The new OPD resulting from zooming in on the **Baking** process in Fig. 7.1

it the four subprocesses **Mixing**, **Forming**, **Heating**, and **Cooling**, as well as the interim objects **Dough** and **Loaf**. **Bread** is created in the initial state **hot**, and after **Cooling** ends, it is **edible**.

7.1.5 Active Processing and the Animated Simulation of OPM

The active-processing assumption is tacitly accounted for in that each and every modeling step requires complete engagement of the user – the system architect or modeler who carries out the conceptual modeling activity. While modeling, the modeler is active in creating the model, inserting and rearranging elements – entities and links – on the screen. At any time during this process, the modeler can inspect the OPL textual interpretation that is continuously created in response to each new graphic input. At times, he or she needs to rearrange the graphic layout to make it more comprehensible by such actions as grouping entities and moving links to avoid crossings. When the current OPD becomes too busy, it is approaching the limited channel capacity, in which case a new OPD needs to be created via in-zooming or unfolding.

Another aspect of active processing that is unique to OPM is its animated simulation. Humans have been observed to mentally animate mechanical diagrams in order to understand them. Using a gaze tracking procedure, Hegarty [21] found that inferences were made about a diagram of ropes and pulleys by imagining the motion of the rope along a causal chain. Similarly, an active processing aspect of OPCAT is its ability to simulate the system by animating it. The animation enables the modeler to simulate the system and see it "in action" at each point in time during the design. Like a program debugger, the modeler can carry out "design-time debugging" by running the animation stepwise or continuously, back and forth, inserting breakpoints where necessary.

Figure 7.3 is a snapshot of the animated simulation of the **Baking** system, showing it at the point in time when **Heating** just ended, yielding **Bread** at its **hot** state. Currently, as the dots on the arrows to and from **Cooling** indicate, **Cooling** is happening, as indicated by its dark filling. The timeline within an in-zoomed process is from top down, so **Cooling** is the last subprocess of **Baking**, which is therefore dark blue. Rectangular objects (except those with rounded corners) exist at this time point, while white ones (like **Ingredients Set**) are already consumed (or not yet created, but in Fig. 7.3 no such objects exist). The active participation of the modeler in inspecting the system behavior and advancing it step by step has proven highly valuable in communicating action and pinpointing logical design errors, which are corrected early on, saving precious time and avoiding costly troubles downstream.

The ability to animate the system in a simple and understandable manner is yet another benefit of the structure–behavior integration of the OPM model in one type of diagram – the OPD. Splitting the single model into several structural views and several other behavioral views would unnecessarily complicate and obscure the

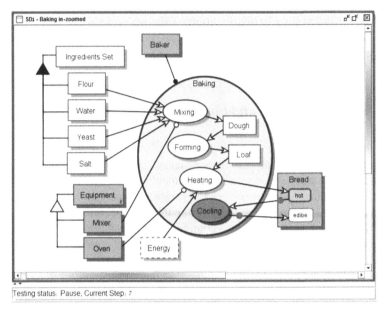

Fig. 7.3 Animated simulation of the OPD in Fig. 7.2

model, preventing it from being amenable to such clear, eye-opening animated simulation.

Having introduced OPM via this simple baking system example, we now define and discuss basic concepts underlying OPM as both a language and a methodology. In parallel, this chapter shows how structure-behaviour codesign is served by the single-model and single-diagram approach of OPM, enabling system architects and designers to freely express the tight, inseparable relationships and interactions between the system's static and dynamic aspects.

7.2 Function, Structure, and Behavior: The Three Major System Aspects

All systems are characterized by three major aspects: function, structure, and behavior. The **function** of an artificial system is its value-providing process, as perceived by the beneficiary, i.e., the person or group of people who gain value from using the system. For example, the function of the organization called hospital is patients' *health level improving*. Each patient is a beneficiary of this system, the customer may be a government or a private entity, and the medical staff constitutes the group of users.

Function, structure, and behavior are the three main aspects that systems exhibit. Function is the top-level utility that the system provides its beneficiaries who use it or are affected by it, either directly or indirectly. The system's function is enabled by its architecture – the combination of structure and behavior. The system's architecture is what enables it to function so as to provide value to its beneficiaries.

Most interesting, useful, and challenging systems are those in which structure and behavior are highly intertwined and hard to separate. For example, in a manufacturing system, the manufacturing process cannot be contemplated in isolation from its inputs – the raw materials, the model, machines, and operators – and its output – the resulting product. The inputs and the output are objects, some of which are transformed by the manufacturing process, while others just enable it. Due to the intimate relation between structure and behavior, it only makes sense to model them concurrently rather than try to construct separate models for structure and behavior, which is the common practice of current modeling languages like UML and SysML. The observation that there is great benefit in concurrently modeling the system's structure and behavior in a single model is a major principle of OPM.

The **structure** of a system is its form – the assembly of its physical and logical components along with the persistent, long-lasting relations among them. Structure is the static, time-independent aspect of the system. The **behavior** of a system is its varying, time-dependent aspect, its dynamics – the way the system changes over time by transforming objects. In this context, transforming means creating (generating, yielding) a new object, consuming (destroying, eliminating) an existing object, or changing the state of an existing object.

With the understanding of what structure and behavior are, we can define a system's architecture.

The **architecture** of a system is the combination of the system's structure and behavior that enables it to perform its **function**.

Following this definition, it becomes clear why codesign of a system's structure and behavior is imperative: they go hand in hand, as a certain structure provides for a corresponding set of system behaviors, and this, in turn, is what enables the system to function and provide value. Therefore, any attempt to separate the design of a system, and hence its conceptual modeling, into distinct structure and behavior models is bound to hamper the effort to arrive at an optimal design. One cannot design the system to behave in a certain way and execute its anticipated function unless the ensemble of the interacting parts of the system – its structure – is such that the expected behavior is made possible and can deliver the desired value to the beneficiary.

It might be interesting to compare our definition of architecture to that used by the U.S. DoD Architecture Framework (DoDAF 2007), which is based on IEEE STD 610.12:

Architecture: the structure of components, their relationships, and the principles and guidelines governing their design and evolution over time.

The common element in both definitions is the system's structure. However, the DoDAF definition lacks the integration of the structure with the behavior to provide the function. On the other hand, the DoDAF definition includes "the principles and guidelines governing the design and evolution of the system's components over time." However, these do not seem to be part of the system's architecture. Rather, principles and guidelines govern the architecting *process*, which culminates in the system's architecture.

7.2.1 Function vs. Behavior

The above definitions lead to the conclusion that the function of a system is identical with its top-level process. Moreover, the architecture of a system, namely its structure–behavior combination, is what enables the system to execute its top-level process, and thereby to perform its function and deliver value to its beneficiary.

The value of the function to the beneficiary is often implicit; it is expressed in process terms, which emphasize what happens, rather than the *purpose* for which the top-level process happens. This implicit function statement can explain why the function of a system is often confused with the behavior or dynamics of the system. However, it is critical to clearly and unambiguously distinguish between function and behavior. Function is the value of the system to its beneficiaries. The function is provided by operating the system, which, due to its architecture – structure–behavior combination – functions to attain this value. Function explicitly coincides with behavior only at the top-most level. At lower levels, behaviors manifested by subprocesses indirectly serve the function. For example, the electric motor of a water pump in a car with an internal combustion engine functions to circulate water, which in turn cools the engine, which in turn drives the car. The function of the car is driving, but processes at various levels of granularity are required to make this happen.

This distinction between function and behavior is of utmost importance since in many cases a system's function can be achieved by different architectures, i.e., different combinations of processes (system behavior) and objects (system structure). Consider, for example, a system for enabling humans to cross a river with their vehicles. Two obvious architectures are ferry and bridge. While the two systems' function and top-level process – river crossing – are identical, they differ dramatically in their structure and behavior. Similarly, a time-keeping system can be a mechanical clock, an electronic watch, or a sundial, to name a few possible system architectures, each with its set of "utilities" (availability, maintainability, precision). Failure to recognize this difference between function and behavior may lead to a premature choice of a suboptimal architecture. In the river-crossing system example above, this may amount to making a decision to build a bridge without considering the ferry option altogether.

Capturing the knowledge about existing systems and the analysis and design of conceived systems requires an adequate methodology, which should be both formal and intuitive. Formality is required to maintain a coherent representation of the system under study, while the requirement that the methodology be intuitive stems from the fact that humans are the ultimate consumers of the knowledge. OPM [10, 11] is an ontology- and systems-theory-based vehicle for codesign via conceptual modeling, as well as for knowledge representation and management, which perfectly meets the formality and intuition requirements through a unique combination of graphics and natural language.

Modeling of complex systems should conveniently combine structure and behavior in a single model. Motivated by this observation, OPM is a comprehensive, holistic approach to the modeling, study, development, engineering, evolution, and lifecycle support of systems. Employing a combination of graphics and a subset of English, the OPM paradigm integrates the object-oriented, process-oriented, and state-transition approaches into a single frame of reference that is expressed in both graphics and text. Structure and behavior coexist in the same OPM model without highlighting one at the expense of suppressing the other to enhance the comprehension of the system as a whole.

A systems modeling methodology and language must be based on a solid, generic ontology. The next section discusses this term as an introduction to presenting the OPM ontology that follows.

7.2.2 Ontology

Ontology is defined as a branch of philosophy that deals with modeling the real world [48]. Ontology discusses the nature and relations of being, or kinds of existence [31]. More specifically, ontology is the study of the categories of things that exist or may exist in some domain [40]. The product of such a study, called ontology, is a catalog of the types of things that are assumed to exist in a domain of interest from the perspective of a person who uses a specific language, for the purpose of talking about that domain.

The traditional goal of ontological inquiry is to discover those fundamental categories or kinds that define the objects of the world. The natural and abstract worlds of pure science, however, do not exhaust the applicable domains of ontology. There are vast, human-designed and human-engineered systems, such as manufacturing plants, hospitals, businesses, military bases, and universities, in which ontological inquiry is just as relevant and equally important. In these human-created systems, ontological inquiry is primarily motivated by the need to understand, design, engineer, and manage such systems effectively. Consequently, it is useful to adapt the traditional techniques of ontological inquiry in the natural sciences to these domains as well [23].

The types in the ontology represent the predicates, word senses, or concept and relation types of the language L when used to discuss topics in the domain D. An uninterpreted logic, such as predicate calculus, conceptual graphs, or Knowledge Interchange Format [22], is ontologically neutral. It imposes no constraints on the subject matter or the way the subject may be characterized. By itself, logic says nothing about anything, but the combination of logic with ontology provides a language about the entities in the domain of interest and relationships among them.

An *informal ontology* may be specified by a catalog of types that are either undefined or defined only by statements in a natural language. In every domain, there are phenomena that the humans in that domain discriminate as (conceptual or physical) objects, processes, states, and relations. A *formal ontology* is specified by a collection of names for concept and relation types organized in a partial ordering by the generalization–specialization (also referred to as the type–subtype or class–subclass) relation. Formal ontologies are further distinguished by the way the subtypes are distinguished from their supertypes. An *axiomatized ontology* distinguishes subtypes by axioms and definitions stated in a formal language, such as logic; a *prototype-based ontology* distinguishes subtypes by a comparison with a typical member or prototype for each subtype. Examples of axiomatized ontologisms include formal theories in science and mathematics, the collections of rules and frames in an expert system, and specifications of conceptual schemas in languages like SQL. OPM concepts and their type ordering are well defined; hence OPM belongs to the family of axiomatized ontologies.

The IDEF5 method [23] is designed to assist in creating, modifying, and maintaining ontologies. Ontological analysis is accomplished by examining the vocabulary that is used to discuss the characteristic objects and processes that compose a domain, developing definitions of the basic terms in that vocabulary, and characterizing the logical connections among those terms. The product of this analysis, ontology, is a domain vocabulary complete with a set of precise definitions, or axioms, that constrain the meanings of the terms sufficiently to enable consistent interpretation of the data that use that vocabulary.

Rather than requiring that the modeler view each of the system's aspects in isolation and struggle to mentally integrate the various views, OPM offers an approach that is orthogonal to customary practices. According to this approach, the structure and behavior system aspects can be inspected in tandem rather than in isolation, providing for better comprehension, as argued above. Complexity is managed by the ability to create and navigate via possibly multiple detail levels, which are generated and traversed through two refinement/abstraction mechanisms: in-zooming/out-zooming and unfolding/folding.

OPM strives to be as generic as possible. Hence its domain is the universe, and its building blocks are things – objects and processes, defined below. Due to its structure–behavior integration, OPM provides a solid basis for representing and managing knowledge about complex systems, regardless of their domain. The remainder of this chapter provides an overview of OPM, its ontology, semantics, and symbols. It then describes applications of OPM in various domains.

7.3 The OPM Ontology

The elements of the OPM ontology, shown in Fig. 7.4, are divided into three groups: entities, structural links, and procedural links.

7.3.1 Entities: Objects, Processes, and Object States

Entities, the basic building blocks of any system modeled in OPM, are of three types: stateful objects, namely, *objects* with *states*, and *processes*. Each entity type stands alone as a concept in its own right, unlike links, which connect two entities. The symbols for these three entities are respectively shown as the first group of symbols on the left-hand side of Fig. 7.4, which contains the symbols in the toolset available as part of the GUI of OPCAT.

Objects are our way of knowing what *exists*, or in other words, the *structure* of systems. To know what *happens*, to understand systems' behavior, a second, complementary type of thing is needed – processes. We know of the existence of an object if we can name it and refer to its unconditional, relatively stable existence, but without processes we cannot tell how this object changes over time.

Objects and processes, collectively referred to as OPM *things*, are the two types of OPM's universal building blocks. OPM views objects and processes as being on equal footing, so processes are modeled as "first-class citizens" that are not subordinate to objects. This is a principal departure from the object-oriented (OO) approach, which places objects as the only major players, and they "own" processes, which in OO jargon are called operations or services or methods.

Major system-level processes can be as important as, or even more important than, objects in the system model. In particular, we already noted that the top-level process of a system is its function, the objective for which the system is built and used. Hence, processes must be amenable to being modeled independently of a particular object class. In OPM, both objects and processes are first-class citizens. They stand on equal footing, such that neither one has supremacy over the other. This OPM *object–process equality principle* enables OPM to model real-world systems in a single model, in which structure and behavior are concurrently represented and can be codesigned. Due to this structure–behavior unification, the single OPM model is simple and intuitive in spite of its formality. The third and last OPM entity, after object and process, which are OPM things, is state. A state, discussed in more detail below, is a situation in which an object can be at some point during its lifetime.

Being able to tell objects and processes apart and use them properly in a model is a key to modeling in OPM. To define these fundamental concepts and to communicate their semantics, we next discuss the concepts of existence and transformation.

Fig. 7.4 The three groups of OPM symbols

7.4 Existence, Things, and Transformations

Webster's New World College Dictionary [50] defines *existence* as the noun derived from exist, which is *be, have being, continue to be*. To exist means to stand out, to show itself, and have an identifiable, distinct uniqueness within the physical or mental realm. A thing that exists in physical reality has "tangible being" at a particular place and time. Because it stands out and shows itself, we can point to it and say: "Now, there it is."

That which we can never identify, or have its identity be inferred in some way, can have no existence for us. In other words, "to stand out" requires a continuous identifiability over an appropriate duration of time, either physically or informatically, as we elaborate below.

When we consider existence along the *time* dimension, there are two modes of "standing out," or existence of things. In the first mode, the "standing out" takes place during a positive, relatively substantial time period. This "standing out" needs to be observable in a form that is basically unchanging, stable, or persistent. We call that which stands out in this mode an *object*.

7.4.1 Physical and Informatical Objects

Webster's 1997 Dictionary [50] defines an object as follows.

[An object is] a material thing; that to which feeling or action is directed; end or aim; word dependent on a verb or preposition.

Webster's 1984 Dictionary [49] provides a different set of relevant definitions for object:

* *Anything that is visible or tangible and is stable in form.*
* *Anything that may be apprehended intellectually.*

These two definitions correspond to our notion of a *physical* object and an *informatical object*. The first definition is the one we normally think of when using the term object in daily usage. The second definition pertains to the informatical, intangible facet of objects. Informatical objects are different from their physical counterparts in that informatical objects have no physical existence and, being intangible, they do not obey the basic laws of physics. However, the *existence* of informatical objects does depend on their being symbolically recorded, inscribed, impressed, or engraved on some tangible medium. This information-carrying medium is a physical object. It can be a stone, papyrus, paper, some electromagnetic medium, or the human brain.

7.4.2 Object Defined

Since OPM uses objects that are physical or informatical, we define object as something that captures these two facets without committing to either one, while including the element of "existence throughout time."

*An **object** is a thing that exists or can exist physically or informatically.*

This definition is quite remote from the classical definitions of object found in the OO literature, which can be phrased as follows: "An object is an abstraction of attributes and operations that is meaningful to a system." For example, in Wikipedia, an object in computer science is defined as a language mechanism for binding data with methods that operate on those data.

A process, on the other hand, is typically a *transient, temporal* thing. It "happens" or "occurs" to an object rather than something that "exists" in its own right. We cannot think of a process independently of at least one object, the one that the process transforms. By their nature, happenings or occurrences involve time. What actually exists as a process is an informatical object that represents the *pattern of behavior*, which the objects that are involved in the interaction exhibit as time goes by. This idea is elaborated on next.

7.4.3 Process as a Transformation Metaphor

There are two perspectives from which a system can be contemplated. One perspective is an instantaneous, snapshotlike, structural one, which views the world at some moment of time. This perspective is timeless; it has no time dimension. The structural perspective represents objects and time-independent relationships that may exist among them. This perspective has no room for processes, as by definition they occur over time, which is not considered in this view. A second perspective is the temporal one, where time is considered as a central theme, such that time-dependent relationships among things are representable. From this temporal viewpoint, the existence of an object is persistent. As long as the object is not involved in a process, it remains unchanged.

We noted that there are two modes of standing out. The first is in space, the second – in time. In the time mode, that which stands out is changing and may have different names as it undergoes its transformation. In particular, the name given to what stands out after the change is complete may be different from the name the thing had before the change occurred. In this case, it is convenient to think of the thing – a process – that has brought about a transformation as some carrier that is "responsible" for this transformation. Hence, the concept of *process* is our abstraction of the thing behind the series of transformations that one or more objects undergo. For the convenience of language or thinking, we associate this patterned changing with the "carrier," to which we mentally assign the "responsibility."

We define *transformation* as a generalization of change, generation, and destruction of an object.

> **Transformation** is the generation (construction, creation) or consumption (destruction, elimination) or change (effect, state transition) of an object.

When we say that the process brought about the creation (or generation or construction) of an object, we mean that the object, which had not existed prior to the occurrence of the process, now exists and is identifiable against its background. Analogously, when we say that the process brought about the elimination (or consumption or destruction) of an object, we mean that the object, which once stood out, has undergone a radical change, due to which it no longer exists. These radical changes of creation and elimination are extreme versions of transformation. Processes are the only things that cause creation and elimination of objects as well as changes in the objects' states. Collectively, creation, elimination, and change are termed transformation.

We call the carrier that causes transformation *process*, and we say that the process is the thing that brings about the transformation of an object. However, that carrier is just a metaphor, as we cannot "hold" or touch a process, although that process may be entirely physical, such as filling a glass of water. What we may be able to touch, see, or measure at given points in time is the object, or one or more of its *attributes*, as the process transforms the object. For example, we can see the glass and the water being poured into it, gradually changing the "fullness" attribute of the glass from empty to full.

At any given point in time before, during, or after the occurrence of the process, the observed object can potentially be different from what it was at a previous point in time. Using our human memory, we get the sense of a process by comparing the present form of the object being transformed to its past form. Hence, we can almost say that *a process is only in a human's mind*, as only through comparing objects or their states at various points in time can we tell that a process took place. Unlike objects, processes do not exist; they happen or occur. The only possible existence of processes is in our minds, where they are recorded as informatical abstract concepts of patterns of object transformations.

7.4.4 Process Defined

According to Webster's 1997 Dictionary [50], a process is "a state of going on, series of actions and changes, method of operation, action of law, outgrowth." The American Heritage Dictionary [1] defines process as "a series of actions, changes, or functions, bringing about a result." Focusing on transformation and the result or effect that it induces, and based on the observations noted above, we adopt the following definition.

*A **process** is a transformation that an object undergoes.*

This definition of process acting on an object immediately implies that no process exists unless it is associated with at least one object, which the process transforms. This is where the symmetry between objects and processes breaks. While we could refer to an object without necessarily using the term "process," the opposite is not possible – the ability to conceive a process depends on the existence of at least one object, which undergoes transformation due to that process. Another asymmetry between an object and a process is related to states. Whereas objects can be stateful, processes do not have states. What can be thought of as states of a process are its possible subprocesses.

The transformation of an object takes place over some time. It may be as minor as moving the object from one location to the other, or as drastic as destroying or creating the object. Without processes, all we can describe are static, persistent structural relations among objects. In a theoretic, frozen, static universe at absolute zero temperature, no processes of interest occur. In a more realistic setting, processes and objects are of comparable importance as building blocks in the description and understanding of systems and the universe as a whole.

As an example, consider Newton's first law, which can be formulated as "Every object persists in a state of rest or uniform motion in a straight line unless compelled by an external force to change that state" [44]. Here, the object is physical, and the "external force" is the process that acts on the object to change its state. The state can be either "moving at constant speed" (including "resting," which amounts to "moving at constant speed that is equal to zero") or "moving at variable speed." As long as no process acts on the object, the object persists in its current state of "moving at constant speed."

7.4.5 Cause and Effect

One insight from investigating the time relationship is *cause* and *effect*. Certain objects, when brought into the right spatial and temporal relationship, enable a process to take place. This is the *preprocess object set* – the *precondition* for the process occurrence. For the process to actually happen, it needs to be triggered. If it is triggered and all the preconditions are met, the process occurs. When the process is over, at least one of the objects involved (as input, output, or both) is transformed (consumed, generated, or changed). The "cause" is the trigger – the event that took place in the concurrent presence of the collection of objects (some of which might need to be in a certain state) that enabled the process – the object transformation. The transformation is the "effect." For example, the process of running an internal combustion engine is contingent upon the presence of the object air–gasoline vapor mixture, at the right pressure and temperature (which are attributes of the mixture), inside the object cylinder, and the concurrent presence of a spark (created by a previous timed process) – the trigger that ignites the mixture. As a result of this process, the gasoline mixture is consumed and the blast increases the pistons' kinetic energy value. If the spark – the trigger – is timed before the mixture is ready or after is has dissipated, no process takes place. In general, the trigger has to be timed such that the process precondition is met; otherwise the trigger has no influence on the system.

7.5 Syntax vs. Semantics

To make it possible to refer to things (both objects and processes) and distinguish among them, natural languages assign names to them. The name of a thing constitutes a primary identifying symbol of that thing, making it amenable to reference and communication among humans. These thing names are known as *nouns*. However, being part of speech, noun is a syntactic term, while objects and processes are semantic terms. We elaborate on this issue next.

7.5.1 Objects to Semantics Is Like Nouns to Syntax

In natural languages, both objects and processes are syntactically represented as nouns. Thus, for example, both "brick" and "construction" are nouns. However, brick is an object, while construction is a process. This can be verified by the fact that the phrase *the construction process* is plausible, while *the brick process* is not. Analogously, the phrase *the object brick* is plausible, while *the object construction* is much less plausible. Natural languages are often even more confusing in this regard. For example, the object building (house, edifice, a noun), which is the outcome of the building (construction) process, is spelled and uttered the same as the process of building (verb). It is only from their context inside a sentence that these two semantically different words – building and building – are distinguishable. These examples demonstrate that we need a semantic, content-based analysis to tell objects from processes.

While in many natural languages nouns primarily represent objects, not every noun is an object, as the examples above demonstrate. Thus, while *construct* is an object, *construction* is a process, yet both are nouns. This is a source of major confusion. We must be aware of this distinction between object and noun and be able to tell apart nouns that are objects from nouns that are processes.

7.5.2 Syntactic vs. Semantic Sentence Analysis

The difficulty we often experience in making the necessary and sufficient distinction between objects and processes is rooted in our education. It is primarily due to the fact that as students in high school we have been trained to think and analyze sentences in syntactic terms of parts of speech: nouns, verbs, adjectives, and adverbs, rather than in semantic terms of objects and processes.

This is probably true for any natural language we study and use, be it our mother tongue or a foreign language. Only through *semantic sentence analysis* can we overcome superficial differences in expression and get down to the intent of the writer or speaker of some text. Nevertheless, the idea of semantic sentence analysis, in which we seek the deep meaning of a sentence beneath its appearance, is probably a relatively less accepted idea. Sentences in Object–Process Language (OPL) are constructed automatically in response to the OPM modeler's graphic input. These sentences have a simple syntax that expresses unambiguous semantics. In OPL, **bold Arial font** denotes nonreserved phrases, while **nonbold Arial** font denotes reserved phrases. In OPCAT, various OPM elements are colored with the same color as their graphic counterparts (by default, objects are rectangular, processes are oval, and states are rectangular with rounded corners).

7.6 The Process Test

To apply OPM in a useful manner, one should be able to tell the difference between an object and a process. The *process test*, defined in this section, has been devised to help identify nouns that are processes rather than objects. Its importance lies in the fact that it is very instrumental in helping analysts to make the essential distinction between objects and processes, a prerequisite for successful system analysis, modeling, and design. Providing a correct answer to the question "Is noun X an object or a process?" is crucial and fundamental to the entire object–process paradigm. The *object–process distinction problem* is simply stated as follows: *Classify a given noun as either an object or a process.*

By default, a noun is an object. To be a process, the noun has to pass the following process test. A noun passes the process test if and only if it meets each of the four *process criteria*:

- Object involvement,
- Object transformation,
- Association with time, and
- Association with verb.

7.6.1 The Preprocess Object Set and Object Involvement

The first process criterion, *object involvement*, implies that in order for the noun in question to be a process, i.e., to happen, a set of one or more nouns, which would be objects, some possibly in certain required states, must be involved.

*The process test **object involvement criterion** is satisfied if the occurrence of the noun in question involves at least one other noun, which would be an object.*

If the noun is indeed a process, the objects that need to exist for the process to happen constitute the *preprocess object set* of that process, as defined below.

*The **preprocess object set** of a process is the set of one or more objects that are required to simultaneously exist, possibly in certain states, in order for that process to start executing once it has been triggered.*

Existence of all the objects in this preprocess object set, possibly in their required states, is the *process precondition* – the condition for the occurrence of the process. As a process, this noun does not exist, but rather occurs, happens, operates, executes, transforms, changes, or alters at least one other noun, which would be an object.

Let us consider two process examples: **Flight** and **Manufacturing**. For **Manufacturing**, the preprocess object set may consist of **Raw Material**, **Operator**, **Machine**, and **Model**, without which no **Manufacturing** can occur. In the **Flight** example, **Airplane**, **Pilot**, and **Runway** are objects in the preprocess object set, since **Flight** cannot occur without them. Moreover, there may be requirements for the state of each of these objects. For **Flight** to take off, it is required that **Airplane** be **operational**, **Pilot** be **sober**, and **Runway** be **open**.

7.6.2 The Postprocess Object Set and Object Transformation

The postprocess object set is defined analogously to the preprocess object set as follows.

*The **postprocess object set** of a process is the set of one or more objects that simultaneously exist, possibly in certain states, after that process has finished executing.*

Existence of all the objects in the postprocess object set, some possibly in specified states, is the *postcondition* of that process.

The preprocess object set and the postprocess object set are not necessarily disjoint; they can be overlapping. In the **Flight** example, all three objects in the preprocess object set, **Airplane**, **Pilot**, and **Runway**, are also in the postprocess object set. However, only **Airplane** and **Pilot** are transformed, as their **Location** attributes change from **source** to **destination**. In the **Manufacturing** example, **Raw Material**, **Operator**, **Machine**, and **Model** are in the preprocess object set, while **Operator**, **Machine**, **Model**, and **Product** are in the postprocess object set. Here, **Raw Material** is transformed by being consumed, while **Product** is transformed by being created.

The second process criterion, *object transformation*, stipulates that a process must transform at least one of the objects in the preprocess object set or in the postprocess object set. In other words, at least one object from the preprocess object set or the postprocess object set must be *transformed* (consumed, created, or change its state) as a result of the occurrence of the noun in question.

> *The process test **object transformation criterion** is satisfied if the occurrence of the noun in question results in the transformation of at least one other noun, which would be an object.*

As noted, the transformed object can belong only to the preprocess object set (if it is consumed), only to the postprocess object set (if it is created), or to both (if it is affected, i.e., if its state changes).

Continuing the two previous process examples, **Flight** transforms **Airplane** by changing its **Location** attribute from **origin** to **destination**. **Manufacturing** transforms two objects: **Raw Material** (by consuming it) and **Product** (by generating it). Here, only **Raw Material** is a member of the preprocess object set, and only **Product** is a member of the postprocess object set.

7.6.3 Association with Time

The third process criterion, *association with time*, is that the process must represent some happening, occurrence, action, procedure, routine, execution, operation, or activity that takes place along the timeline.

> *The process test **association with time** criterion is satisfied if the noun in question can be thought of as happening through time.*

Continuing our example, both **Flight** and **Manufacturing** start at a certain point in time and take a certain amount of time. Both time and duration are very relevant features of these two nouns in question.

7.6.4 Association with Verb

The fourth and last process criterion, *association with verb*, requires that a process be associated with a verb.

*The process test **association with verb** criterion is satisfied if the noun in question can be derived from, or has a common root with, a verb.*

Flying is the verb associated with **Flight**. The sentence "The airplane flies" is a short way of expressing the fact that the **Airplane** is engaged in the process of **Flight**. Similarly, manufacture (produce, yield, make, create, generate) is the verb associated with **Manufacturing**. The sentence "The operator manufactures the product from raw material using a machine and a model" is the natural language short way of saying in OPL that:

Operator handles Manufacturing.
Manufacturing requires Machine and **Model.**
Manufacturing yields Product.

It is not mandatory that the verb be syntactically from the same root as the process name, as long as the semantics is the same. For example, **Marrying** is a process, which is associated with the verb marry. Wed is also a legal verb, albeit less frequently used. Alternatively, we could use **Wedding** to fit it to the verb wed.

Many objects, such as **Apple** and **Airplane**, are not associated with any verb, so they do not fulfill this process criterion. It is easy to verify that both **Apple** and **Airplane** do not meet any one of the previous three process criteria either. As noted, however, failure to fulfill even one of the four criteria results in failure of the entire process test.

7.6.5 Boundary Cases of Objects and Processes

While objects are persistent (i.e., they exhibit static perseverance, or, in other words, the value of their **Perseverance** attribute is **static**) and processes are transient (i.e., they exhibit dynamic perseverance, or, in other words, the value of their **Perseverance** attribute is **dynamic**), boundary examples of persistent processes and transient objects exist.

7.6.5.1 Persistent, State-Preserving Processes

Persistent processes are state-preserving processes. They act to preserve, maintain, or keep a steady state or a status quo of a system. They include such verbs as *holding, maintaining, keeping, staying, waiting, prolonging, delaying, occupying, persisting, preventing, including, containing, continuing, supporting,* and *remaining.* Rather than induce any real change, the semantics of these verbs leaves the state of the object as is, in its status quo, for some more time.

> A ***persistent process*** *is a pseudo process that acts to preserve, maintain, or keep a steady state or a status quo of the system.*

Strictly speaking, these are not real processes, as they fail the object transformation criterion of the process test. Indeed, the static nature of these verbs is contradictory to the definition of process, which requires that it transform some object. In fact, the process test for "**Supporting**" in a system in which a pedestal supports a statue fails because it does not meet the object transformation criterion, as no object is transformed by the support.

Surrounding in the context of a **Highway** that surrounds a **City** is another example. **Surrounding** in this context is not a real process – it too does not meet the object transformation criterion, as no object is transformed by it. Such cases are actually specifications of some structural relation between two objects and are therefore better modeled using tagged structural links, defined and described in the sequel. For example, **surrounds** is a tagged structural relation, from which the OPL sentence "**Highway surrounds City**" is derived.

From another perspective, some of the verbs expressing state preservation can be considered as working against some "force" that would otherwise change some object. For example, a **Pedestal** supporting a **Statue** works against gravity, so we can think of **Supporting** as a "falling-prevention" process, without which the state of the **Statue** would change from **stabilized** to **fallen**.

7.6.5.2 Transient Objects

A *transient object* is a short-lived object that exists only in the context of some subprocess in a system model. Examples of transient physical objects are unstable materials or particles, such as an interim short-lived compound in a chemical reaction or an atom in an excited state that spontaneously decays to the ground state by emission of X-rays and fluorescent radiation [3]. Examples of transient informatical objects are pointers to memory locations in a database system or typed passwords in a Web-based system that are created and immediately deleted after being used.

> A ***transient object*** *is an object that exists only in the context of some process in a system model.*

The context of the transient object is the process within which it is created and consumed. For example, a packet of data in a telecommunications network is a transient informatical object that lives only in the context of the particular instance of a data communication process. Such a packet can reside for a short while at some router on its way and leave no trace of its stay there once the target node has received it and assembled it into a file from which it was derived.

In an OPM model, a transient object that is created by some subprocess within a process and is immediately consumed by a subsequent subprocess can be skipped by using the *invocation link*. This lightening-shaped link is a procedural link that directly connects the two processes, as discussed in the sequel.

7.6.6 Thing Defined

We have seen that objects exist while processes occur. Objects are relatively persistent, static things, while processes are transient, dynamic things. Objects cannot be transformed (generated, affected, or eliminated) without processes, while processes have no meaning without the objects they transform. Hence, objects and processes are two types of tightly coupled complementary *things*. The extent of this coupling is so intense that if we wish to be able to analyze and design systems in any domain as intuitively and naturally as possible, we must consider objects and processes concurrently. While this point has already been made more than once in this chapter, it is worth repeating.

Given a system model in which objects and processes are described in tandem, we are immediately able to tell the set of objects that are transformed by each process and the nature of the transformation of each transformed object – generation, consumption, or state change. Moreover, we are able to tell how refineables – parts, features, or specializations of these objects, discussed later – are involved in subprocesses of these process. This is the extent to which objects and processes are interwoven and the corresponding value of modeling them concurrently.

As we shall see, objects and processes have much in common in terms of relations such as aggregation, generalization, and characterization. The need to talk about a generalization of these two concepts necessitates the advent of a term that is more abstract than an object and a process, and which generalizes the two. As we have already seen, we call this concept simply a "thing."

Thing is a generalization of object and process.

The concept of "thing" enables us to think and to express ourselves in terms of this abstraction and refer to it without the need to repeatedly iterate the words "object or process." The term "thing" is based on the ontology of Bunge [5, 6] and Wand and Weber [46, 47]. Their first premise is that *the world is made of things that have properties*. According to this definition, *thing* seems to be synonymous with the OPM notion of *object*. However, during the last two decades, the term "object" has become deeply rooted, at least in the software engineering community, with the object-oriented concept of object as an encapsulation of attributes and operations. In

SysML, object has been replaced by "block." It therefore seems justified to extend the semantics of *thing* from an object to the generalization of object and process.

7.6.7 States

Objects can be stateful, i.e., they may have one or more states.

> A **state** *is a situation in which an object can exist or a value it can assume at certain time intervals.*

Since a state is always related to or "owned by" an object, it can be found only inside an object. Unlike OPM things – objects and processes – which, as argued, stand on equal footing, a state is a tad lower in this hierarchy, as by definition it is affiliated with the object that owns it.

A stateful object, i.e., an object that has states, can be *affected* by a process. In that case, the affecting process changes the current state of the stateful object.

> **Effect** is a change in the state of an object.

A process that affects an object changes the state of that object from the input (initial) state to the output (final) state.

> **Input state** is the state in which the object being affected is at the beginning of the affecting process.

> **Output state** is the state at which the object being affected is at the end of the affecting process.

An object can be in some of its states (or assume one of its values), but it can also be in transition between two of its states. This is the case when a process is transforming the object, such that the object is no longer in its input state and is not yet at its output state.

Table 7.1 presents the symbols and descriptions of states and values. A value is in principle no different than a state. However, we refer to a situation as a state when there is a small number of discrete situations and they are of an enumerated type. We refer to it as a value when there is a large number of such situations and they are often numeric and continuous.

Table 7.1 Entities of the OPM ontology and **Thing** variants due to different **Essence** and **Affiliation** attributes

ENTITIES			□ ○ ○
Name	**Symbol**	**OPL**	**Definitions**
Things Object	Object A		An object is a thing that exists.
Process	(Process D)		A process is a thing that transforms at least one object.
	B	**B** is physical. *(shaded rectangle)*	
	C	**C** is physical and environmental. *(shaded dashed rectangle)*	Transformation is object generation or consumption, or effect—a change in the state of an object.
	E	**E** is physical. *(shaded ellipse)*	
	F	**F** is physical and environmental. *(shaded dashed ellipse)*	
State	A / s1	**A** is **s1**.	A state is situation an object can be at or a value it can assume.
	B / s1 s1	**B** can be **s1** or **s2**.	States are always within the object that owns them.
	C / s1 s1 s3	**C** can be **s1**, **s2**, or **s3**. **s1** is initial. **s3** is final.	A state can be initial, final, or both.

7.6.8 Things and States Are Entities, Entities and Links are Elements

The word **Thing** may sound too mundane, so one might wish to use the more sophisticated word "entities" instead. However, an entity tends to be interpreted more statically than dynamically, i.e., more as an object than as a process, while we wish to use a word that is as neutral and abstract as possible, so "thing" is preferable. However, we do use "entity" when we wish to refer collectively to things and states. As we have seen, a state is a situation in which an object can be. As such, the semantics it conveys is also static. OPM therefore uses the term **Entity** to generalize a **Thing** and a **State**.[2]

Entity is a generalization of thing and state.

Things (objects and processes) and states are collectively called entities. Since a state can only exist within an object, a stateful object with n distinct states can be thought of as n distinct stateless objects, each with its state name preceding the

---

[2] As we shall see, the meanings of Value and State are very close. In this chapter, we use value and state interchangeably.

name of the stateful object. For example, the stateful object **Car**, which can be in two states, **operational** and **broken**, is equivalent to two stateless objects: **Operational Car** and **Broken Car**.

Climbing one level higher in this hierarchy, links connect entities. Collectively, links and entities are OPM elements.

Element is a generalization of entity and link.

Element is highest in the hierarchy. To specify this hierarchy formally, we use a reflective metamodel, described next.

7.7 A Reflective Metamodel of OPM Elements

We have already defined a substantial part of OPM, but so far we have only done so in text, contrary to the claim that there is great value in formal graphic modeling. This will change right now, as we start modeling the language of OPM. A model-based representation of a modeling language is done via metamodeling it to create a metamodel – a model that specifies the modeling language.

*A language **metamodel** is a specification of a modeling language by a modeling language.*

If the modeling language used to create the metamodel is the same as the modeling language being specified, then the metamodel is a "self metamodel" or a reflective metamodel [34].

*A **reflective metamodel** is a specification of a modeling language by itself.*

7.7.1 An Initial OPM Reflective Metamodel

Figure 7.5 is a portion of a reflective metamodel of the OPM elements hierarchy. At the top of the hierarchy is **OPM Thing**, which, in turn, specializes into **Object** and **Process**. The *generalization–specialization* ("is-a") link, which is a *structural* link, is symbolized graphically as an empty isosceles triangle whose tip is linked to the general thing and whose bottom – to the specialized thing(s).

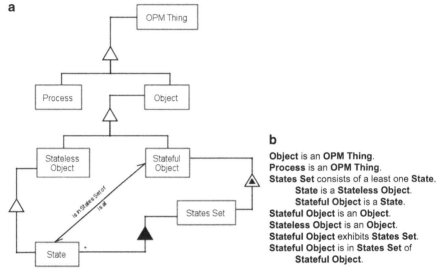

Fig. 7.5 An initial OPM reflective metamodel of the OPM elements hierarchy. **a** Object–process diagram (OPD). **b** Corresponding Object–Process Language (OPL) paragraph

7.7.2 The OPM Graphics–Text Equivalence Principle

Any OPM model is represented concurrently in two modalities: graphics and text. The graphics–text equivalence OPM principle is as follows.

> *In any OPM system model, each OPD – the graphic modality – has an equivalent OPL paragraph – the textual modality, such that both contain exactly the same information and are therefore reconstructible from each other.*

Figure 7.5b contains the OPL paragraph that is the textual representation of the OPD in Fig. 7.5a. The OPM graphics–text principle can be verified here. For example, the first OPL sentence is "**Object is an OPM Thing.**" This is the textual equivalence of the generalization–specialization link from **OPM Thing** to **Object**.

7.7.3 The Five Basic Thing Attributes

Things – objects and processes alike – have five basic attributes: **Perseverance**, **Essence**, **Affiliation**, **Origin**, and **Complexity**. **Perseverance** determines if the thing is an object or a process. **Essence** pertains to whether the thing is **physical** or **informatical**. **Affiliation** concerns the place where the thing belongs – the system or the system's environment. **Origin** describes whether the thing is natural or artificial.

Perseverance is a basic thing attribute that determines whether the thing is **static** (an object) or **dynamic** (a process).

Perseverance enables distinction between objects and processes.

Essence is a basic thing attribute that determines whether the thing is **physical** or **informatical**.

The default **Essence** is **informatical**.

Affiliation is a basic thing attribute that determines whether the thing is **systemic** (part of the system) or **environmental** (external to the system).

The default **Affiliation** is **systemic**.

Origin is a basic thing attribute that determines whether the thing is **artificial** or **natural**.

To define **Complexity**, which can be simple or nonsimple, we need to first define refineables – parts, features, or specializations of a thing.

*A **refineable** of a thing T is a part of T, a feature of T, or a specialization of T.*

The thing being refined is called a refinee.

*A **refinee** is a thing that has one or more parts, features, or specializations.*

According to this definition, a refineable is a generalization of part, feature, and specialization. For example, **Wheel** is a refineable of **Car** since it is a part of **Car**, and **Car** is the refinee. Similarly, **Car** is a refineable of **Vehicle** since it is a specialization of **Vehicle**, and **Vehicle** is the refinee.

Some things have refineables while others do not. For example, an integer does not have refineables. It only has instances, such as 1, 0, 2010, etc. This distinction between things is the basis for the definition of a thing's complexity attribute.

*A thing is **simple** if it has no refineables and **nonsimple**, or compound, otherwise.*

Complexity is a basic thing attribute that determines whether the thing is **simple** or **nonsimple**.

Perseverance, **Essence**, and **Affiliation** have graphical symbols. Table 7.1 shows the entities in the OPM ontology with their graphical symbols. A thing whose perseverance is static – an object – is symbolized by a rectangle, while a thing whose perseverance is dynamic – a process – is symbolized by an ellipse. Both shapes have solid lines with no shading, indicating their default values: **informatical Essence** and **systemic Affiliation**.

A thing whose **Essence** is **physical** is symbolized by a shaded shape (rectangle or ellipse). A thing whose **Affiliation** is **environmental** is symbolized by a dashed contour. As Table 7.1 shows, any combination of a thing's **Essence** and **Affiliation** value is possible.

7.8 OPM Links

OPM links are the mortar that can connect any two OPM entities. Without links, all we could model would be a collection of isolated OPM entities with no ability to say anything about how they relate to each other structurally or procedurally. If entities are the nodes in a graph, the links are the edges. However, an OPD is more expressive than a plain mathematical graph with nodes and edges, since the entities and the links are of several types and any legal entity–link–entity combination conveys a specific defined semantics that is also translated to an English OPL sentence or part of a sentence.

Figure 7.6 extends the reflective metamodel of the OPM elements hierarchy in Fig. 7.5 with links.

At the top level, the metamodel asserts that an **OPM link** connects two **OPM Things**. At the next level, **OPM Link** specializes into **Structural Link** and **Procedural Link**.

7.8.1 Structural Links

*A **structural link** is a link that specifies the long-term, time-independent relations between two things.*

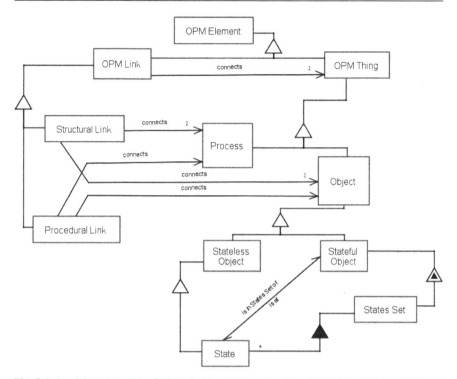

Fig. 7.6 An elaboration of the OPM reflective metamodel of the OPM elements hierarchy from Fig. 7.5 enhanced with the OPM links hierarchy

An example of a structural link in Fig. 7.6 is the generalization–specialization link from **OPM Element** to **OPM Link** and to **OPM Thing**. This generalization–specialization relation between these objects holds true and does not change over time.

As this example shows, structural links usually connect two things that have the same persistence value, namely, either two objects (things whose persistence value is static, as in this example) or two processes (things whose persistence value is dynamic). Two OPL sentences express this:

Structural Link connects 2 Objects.
Structural Link connects 2 Processes.

The only exception to this is the exhibition-characterization relation defined below.

7.8.2 Procedural Links

*A **procedural link** is a link that specifies the short-term, time-dependent relations between two things.*

Procedural links usually connect two things that have different persistence values, namely, an object and a process.

7.9 OPM Structure Modeling

As noted, structural links graphically express static, time-independent relations between pairs of entities, most often between two objects. Structural links, shown as the middle group of six symbols in Fig. 7.4, are of two types: fundamental and tagged. Fundamental structural links are a set of four structural links that are used to denote frequently occurring relations between two entities in a system. Due to their prevalence and usefulness, and in order to prevent too much text from cluttering the diagram, these relations are designated by the four distinct triangular symbols shown in Fig. 7.4. The four fundamental structural relations are as follows:

1. **Aggregation–participation**, a solid triangle, ▲, which denotes the relation between a whole thing and its parts;
2. **Generalization–specialization**, a blank triangle, △, which denotes the relation between a general thing and its specializations, giving rise to inheritance;
3. **Exhibition–characterization**, a solid interior blank triangle, ▲, which denotes the relation between an exhibitor – a thing exhibiting one or more features (attributes or operations) – and the things that characterize the exhibitor; and
4. **Classification–instantiation**, a solid circle inside a blank triangle, ▲, which denotes the relation between a class of things and an instance of that class.

Table 7.2 lists the four fundamental structural links and their respective OPDs and OPL sentences. The name of each such relation consists of a pair of dash-separated words, e.g., *aggregation–participation*. The first word in each pair is the *forward relation* name, i.e., the name of the relation as seen from the viewpoint of the refinee – the thing up in the hierarchy that is being refined – down to its refineables. The second word is the *backward relation* name, i.e., the name of the relation as seen from the viewpoint of the refineables – the things down in the hierarchy of that relation looking up to the refinee.

Each fundamental structural link has a default, preferred direction, determined by how natural the OPL sentence that expresses its semantics sounds. In Table 7.2, the preferred shorthand name for each relation is underlined. The forward direction is the preferred one in all the links except the classification–instantiation.

Table 7.2 Fundamental structural relation names, OPD symbols, and OPL sentences

Structural Relation Name		Refinee- Refineables	OPD with 3 refineables	OPL Sentences with 1, 2, and 3 refineables
Forward	Backward			
Aggregation	Participation	Whole- Parts		A consists of **B**. A consists of **B** and **C**. A consists of **B**, **C**, and **D**.
Exhibition	Characterization	Exhibitor- Features		A exhibits **B**. A exhibits **B** and **C**. A exhibits **B**, **C**, and **D**.
Generalization	Specialization	General- Specializations		**B** is an **A**. **B** and **C** are **A**s. **B**, **C**, and **D** are **A**s.
Classification	Instantiation	Class- Instances		**B** is an instance of **A**. **B** and **C** are instances of **A**. **B**, **C**, and **D** are instances of **A**.

As Table 7.2 shows, each one of the four fundamental structural relations is characterized by the hierarchy it induces between the refinee – the thing attached to the tip of the triangle – and the refineables – the thing(s) attached to the base of the triangle, as follows.

1. In aggregation–participation, the tip of the solid triangle, ▲, is attached to the whole thing, while the base is attached to the parts.
2. In generalization–specialization, the tip of the blank triangle, △, is attached to the general thing, while the base is attached to the specializations.
3. In exhibition–characterization, the tip of the solid interior blank triangle, ▲, is attached to the exhibitor (the thing which exhibits the features), while the base is attached to the features (attributes and operations).
4. In classification–instantiation, the tip of the solid circle inside a blank triangle, ▲, is attached to the thing class, while the base is attached to the thing instances.

Table 7.3 presents the structural relation names, OPD symbols, OPL sentences, and semantics. It shows that there is almost symmetry between objects and processes in that for all the structural relations, whatever applies to objects also applies to processes.

Having presented the common features of the four fundamental structural relations, in the next four subsections we provide a small example of each one separately.

Table 7.3 Structural relation names, OPD symbols, OPL sentences, and semantics

STRUCTURAL LINKS			▲ ▲ △ ▲ → ↩
Name	**Symbol**	**OPL**	**Semantics**

<table>
<tr><td rowspan="10">Fundamental Structural Relations</td><td rowspan="2">Aggregation-
Participation

▲</td><td></td><td>A consists of B and C.</td><td rowspan="2">A is the whole, B and C are parts.</td></tr>
<tr><td></td><td>A consists of B and C.</td></tr>
<tr><td rowspan="2">Exhibition-
Characterization

▲</td><td></td><td>A exhibits B, as well as C.</td><td>Object B is an attribute of A and process C is its operation (method).</td></tr>
<tr><td></td><td>A exhibits B, as well as C.</td><td>A can be an object or a process.</td></tr>
<tr><td rowspan="2">Generalization-
Specialization

△</td><td></td><td>B is an A.
C is an A.</td><td>A specializes into B and C.</td></tr>
<tr><td></td><td>B is A.
C is A.</td><td>A, B, and C can be either all objects or all processes.</td></tr>
<tr><td>Classification-
Instantiation

▲</td><td></td><td>B is an instance of A.
C is an instance of A.</td><td>Object A is the class, for which B and C are instances. Applicable to processes too.</td></tr>
</table>

Unidirectional & bidirectional tagged structural links → ↩		A relates to B. (for unidirectional) A and C are related. (for bidirectional)	A user-defined textual tag describes any structural relation between two objects or between two processes.

7.9.1 Aggregation–Participation

Aggregation–participation denotes the relation between a whole and its comprising parts or components. Consider, for example, the excerpt taken from Sect. 2.2 of the RDF Primer [28]:

> *… each statement consists of a subject, a predicate, and an object.*

This is a clear case of a whole–part, or aggregation–participation, relation. The OPM model of this statement is shown in Fig. 7.7. The OPL sentence, "**RDF Statement consists of Subject, Predicate**, and **Object**" was generated by OPCAT auto-

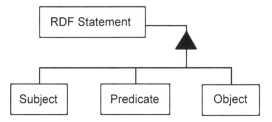

Fig. 7.7 OPD of the sentence "**RDF Statement consists of Subject, Predicate, and Object**"

matically from the graphic input and is almost identical to the one cited from the RDF Primer. The same OPD (disregarding the graphical layout) can be produced exactly by inputting the text of the OPL sentence above. This is a manifestation of the OPM graphics–text equivalence principle.

7.9.2 Generalization–Specialization

Generalization–specialization is a fundamental structural relationship between a general thing and one or more of its specializations. Continuing our example from the RDF Primer [28], consider the very first sentence from the abstract:

> *The Resource Description Framework (RDF) is a language for representing information about resources in the World Wide Web.*

Let us take the main message of this sentence, which is that *RDF is a language*. This is exactly in line with the OPL syntax, so we can input the OPL sentence "**RDF is a Language**" into OPCAT and see what we get.

The result, without any diagram editing, is shown in Fig. 7.8, along with the conversation window titled "Add new OPL sentence," in which this sentence was typed prior to the OPD creation. In fact one can justifiably argue that RDF is not a specialization of a language but rather an *instance* of a language. Indeed, instances are the leaves of the specialization hierarchy [11]. In this case we would use the classification–instantiation link, which is exemplified below.

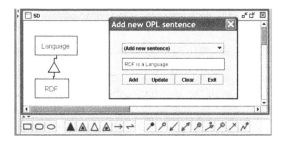

Fig. 7.8 OPD obtained by inputting into OPCAT the OPL sentence "**RDF** is a **Language**"

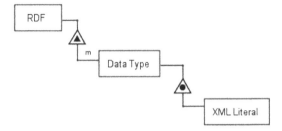

Fig. 7.9 The OPD representing the sentence *"RDF has a simple data model"*

7.9.3 Exhibition–Characterization

We continue to scan the RDF Primer [28], where in Sect. 2.2.1 we find the sentence *RDF has a simple data model.*

To model this statement, we need to rephrase this sentence into the following three sentences:

1. RDF is characterized by a data model.
2. The data model of RDF is characterized by a complexity attribute.
3. The value of this complexity attribute is "simple."

These three sentences are further rephrased to conform to the OPL syntax as follows:

1. **RDF** exhibits **Data Model**.
2. **Data Model** exhibits **Complexity**.
3. **Complexity** is **simple**.

Figure 7.9 shows the OPD representing the sentence *"RDF has a simple data model."*

7.9.4 Classification–Instantiation

Reading through the RDF Primer, we find in Sect. 3.3 on data types the following sentence:

> 1. *Data types are used by RDF in the representation of values, such as integers, floating point numbers, and dates.*
> ...
> 2. *RDF predefines just one data type, rdf:XMLLiteral, used for embedding XML in RDF.*

An OPL interpretation of the structural aspect of these two sentences, respectively, is as follows:

1. **RDF exhibits** many **Data Types**.
2. **XML Literal** is an instance of **Data Type**.

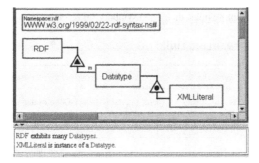

Fig. 7.10 The OPM model of **XML Literal**, an instance of a **Data Type** of **RDF**

Figure 7.10 is the OPM model of **XML Literal**, an instance of a **Data Type** of **RDF**.

7.10 OPM Behavior Modeling

Procedural links connect entities (objects, processes, and states) to express the dynamic, time-dependent behavior of the system. Behavior, the dynamic aspect of a system, can be manifested in OPM in three ways, giving rise to three types of procedural links:

1. An object can *enable* a process without being transformed by it, giving rise to *enabling links*.
2. A process can *transform* (generate, consume, or change the state of) one or more objects, giving rise to *transforming links*.
3. A thing can *control* the behavior of a system, giving rise to *control links*.

The control is done via a condition link, an event link, or an exception link. An object or a process can *trigger* an event that might, in turn, invoke a process if, as explained earlier, the process precondition is met, i.e., all the objects in the preprocess object set exist, each in its required state.

7.10.1 Enabling Links

The first group of procedural links in Table 7.4 presents the group of the three enabling links.

*An **enabler** of a process is an object that must be present, possibly at some specified state, for that process to occur.*

Table 7.4 The OPM enabling links, their OPD symbols, OPL sentences, and semantics

OPM ENABLING LINKS			
Name	Symbol	OPL	Semantics
Agent Link	A — B	A handles B.	Denotes that object A is a human operator who triggers process B.
Instrument Link	A — B	B requires A.	"Wait until" semantics: Process B cannot happen if object A does not exist.
State-Specified Instrument Link	A s1 — B	B requires s1 A.	"Wait until" semantics: Process B cannot happen if object A is not at state s1.

*An **enabling link** is a procedural link that links an enabler to the process it enables.*

Enablers are of two types: *agents* and *instruments*.

*An **agent** is a human enabler. An **instrument** is a nonhuman enabler.*

The distinction between these two types of enablers is made primarily since humans and other objects need to be addressed differently. Humans are capable of intelligent decision making and need good interface with the system. Table 7.4 specifies the OPM enabling links, their OPD symbols, OPL sentences, and semantics. **Agent link**, the first line in Table 7.4, is a "black lollipop" – a line ending with a solid, filled-in circle.

The agent link has the semantics of a trigger – an event that attempts to launch the process to which it is attached. Indeed, humans are triggers to many high-level processes in complex systems, following which nonhuman instruments take over control of lower-level subprocesses.

An agent is just an enabler and is not supposed to be affected by the process it enables. If the human triggering a process is affected by that process, then he is no longer just an enabler but, more importantly, an affectee. For example, a person taking a medication is affected by the process of medication taking. In this case, the effect link, described below, shall be used instead of the agent link.

The agent link helps system designers to quickly locate all the places in the system where humans interact with the system, as these are places where more than just adequate human–machine interfaces will have to be designed.

Instrument link, the second line in Table 7.4, is a "white lollipop" – a line ending with a blank, white circle. An easy way to remember this difference is to think of a human as being worth more than an instrument, so the former is filled, while the latter is empty.

The semantics of an instrument link is that of a wait-until, in the sense that when triggered, the process in question cannot start unless the instrument exists. In other words, the process is enabled if and only if the instrument exists.

The **state-specified instrument link**, shown in the bottom line of Table 7.4, is an instrument link from a specific state, s1, of object A to process B. The semantics of this link is also that of a wait-until, in the sense that when triggered, the process in question cannot start unless the instrument exists in the specified state. In other words, process B is enabled if and only if A is in state s1.

As we shall see next when discussing the transforming links, the set of two links – instrument link and its refined state-specified instrument link – is a repeating pattern of two related links: a procedural link and its state-specified refinement. At the metamodel level, we can think of the state-specified link as a specialization of the corresponding link that does not involve a state.

> A *stateless–stateful links pair* is a pair of procedural links with almost identical semantics, in which one link connects an object to a process while the other link connects an object state to a process.

One can justifiably ask, then, what about a state-specified agent link? There is no state-specified agent link since we can always use an instrument link from a specific value or state of an attribute of the agent. For example, a voter can elect a US president if and only if she or he is a US citizen, so while the agent link will be from **Voter** to the **President Electing** process, the instrument link will be from the state **US citizen** of the attribute **Citizenship** of **Voter** to the **President Electing** process. The OPL paragraph of this system follows.

Voter exhibits Citizenship.
Citizenship can be US citizen, resident alien, or nonresident alien.
Voter handles **President Electing.**
President Electing requires **US citizen Citizenship.**
President Electing yields **President.**

7.10.2 Transforming Links

By the definition of process, a process must transform at least one object. State change is the least drastic transformation that an object can undergo. The transformation of an object can be done in one of three ways: (1) consumption of an object, (2) generation of an object, or (3) change of an object's state. Accordingly, and similar to the stateless–stateful instrument link pair discussed above, there are three pairs

Table 7.5 The OPM transforming links, their OPD symbols, OPL sentences, and semantics

OPM TRANSFORMING LINKS			
Name	Symbol	OPL	Semantics
Consumption Link	A → B	B consumes A.	Process B consumes Object A.
State-Specified Consumption Link	A s1 → B	B consumes s1 A.	Process B consumes Object A when it is at State s1.
Result Link	A ← B	B yields A.	Process B creates Object A.
State-Specified Result Link	A s1 ← B	B yields s1 A.	Process B creates Object A at State s1.
Effect Link	A ↔ B	B affects A.	Process B changes the state of Object A; the details of the effect may be added at a lower level.
State-Specified Effect Link (*Input-Output Links Pair*)	A [s1] [s2] ↕ B	B changes A from s1 to s2.	Process B changes the state of Object A from State s1 to State s2.

of stateless–stateful transforming links, giving rise to the six transforming links in Table 7.5.

1. The pair consisting of a consumption link and its refined state-specified consumption link has the semantics of consumption. Referring to the first two lines in Table 7.5, the consumption link denotes that occurrence of process B eliminates object A. The state-specified consumption link denotes that the occurrence of process B eliminates object A, provided that object A is at state s1.

2. The pair consisting of a result link and its refined state-specified result link has the semantics of generation or creation. Referring to the two middle lines in Table 7.5, the result link denotes that the occurrence of process B yields object A. The state-specified result link denotes that the occurrence of process B yields object A at state s1.

3. The pair consisting of an effect link and its refined state-specified effect link has the semantics of state change. Referring to the two bottom lines in Table 7.5, the effect link denotes that the occurrence of process B changes the state of object A. The state-specified effect link, also called an *input–output links pair*, is a pair of two links in opposite directions, denoting that the occurrence of process B changes the state of object A from its input state s1 to its output state s2.

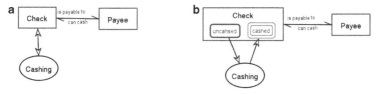

Fig. 7.11 Effect link (**a**) and state-specified effect link (**b**). The effect link denotes that **Cashing** changes the state of **Check**. The state-specified effect link denotes that **Cashing** changes **Check** from **uncashed** to **cashed**

Figure 7.11 exemplifies the effect link in Fig. 7.11a and the state-specified effect link in Figure 7.11b. We can think of the effect link as an abstraction of its refined version. Sometimes we may not be interested in specifying the states of an object but still show that a process does affect an object by changing its state from some unspecified input state to another unspecified output state. To express this, we suppress (hide) the input and output states of the object, so the edges of the input and output links "migrate" to the contour of the object and coincide, yielding the bidirectional effect link as a superposition of two opposite-pointing arrows.

An effect is object transformation in which a process changes the state of an object from some input state to another output state. When these two states are expressed (i.e., shown explicitly), as in the OPD in Fig. 7.11b, then we can use the pair of input and output links to specify the source and destination states of the transformation. When the states are suppressed (hidden), we express the state change by the effect link, a more general and less informative transformation link.

The two more extreme transformations are generation and consumption, denoted respectively by the result and consumption links. Generation is a transformation that causes an object that had not existed prior to the process execution to become existent. In contrast to generation, consumption is a transformation that causes an object that had existed prior to the process execution to become nonexistent.

7.10.3 Control Links

The OPM control links (Table 7.6) control the dynamics of the system, expressed as the conditions and order of flow of processes and the associated object transformations that take place as the system becomes operational. Most OPM control links are combinations of a procedural link with an event or a condition.

The first stateless–stateful links pair is the instrument event link and its refined *state-specified instrument event link*. The **instrument event link** combines the semantics of the instrument link with the semantics of event. Referring to the first line in Table 7.6, the creation of object A is an event that triggers process B. B will start executing if its precondition (i.e., all the objects in the preprocess object set exist, and are in their required states, if so specified) is met. Since A is an instrument, it will not be affected by B.

Table 7.6 OPM control links, their OPD symbols, OPL sentences, and semantics

OPM CONTROL LINKS			
Name	**Symbol**	**OPL**	**Semantics**
Instrument Event Link	A — B	A triggers B. B triggers A.	Generation of object A is an event that triggers process B. B will start executing if its precondition is met. Since A is instrument it will not be affected by B.
State-Specified Instrument Event Link	A [s1] — B	A triggers B. when it enters s1. B requires s1 A.	Entering state s1 of object A is an event that triggers process B. B will start executing if its precondition is met. Since A is instrument it will not be affected by B.
Consumption Event Link	A — B	A triggers B. B consumes A.	Generation of object A is an event that triggers process B. B will start executing if its precondition is met, and if so it will consume A.
State-Specified Consumption Event Link	A [s1][s2] — B	A triggers B when it enters s2. B consumes s2 A.	Entering state s2 of A is an event that triggers process B. If B is triggered, it will consume A. B will start executing if its precondition is met, and if so it will consume A.
Condition Link	A — B	B occurs if A exists.	Existence of object A is a condition for the execution of B. If A does not exist, then B is skipped and regular system flow continues.
State-Specified Condition Link	A [s1][s2] — B	B occurs if A is s1.	Existence of object A at state s2 is a condition for the execution of B. If A is not in s2, then B is skipped and regular system flow continues.
Invocation Link	B → C	B invokes C.	Execution termination of process B is an event that triggers process C. B yields a temporary object that is immediately consumed by C and therefore not shown explicitly in the model.
Exception Link	A (3s 4s) — B	A triggers B when it lasts more than 4 seconds.	Process A has to be assigned with maximal acceptable time duration, which, if exceeded, triggers process B.

The **state-specified instrument event link** combines the semantics of the state-specified instrument link with the semantics of event. Referring to the second line in Table 7.6, entering state s1 of object A is an event that triggers process B. B will start executing if its precondition is met, again without affecting B since A is an instrument.

The second stateless–stateful links pair is the *consumption event link* and its refined *state-specified consumption event link*.

The **consumption event link** combines the semantics of the consumption link with the semantics of event. Referring to the third line in Table 7.6, the creation of object A is an event that triggers process B. B will start executing if its precondition is met, in which case it will consume B.

The **state-specified consumption event link** combines the semantics of the state-specified consumption link with the semantics of event. Referring to the fourth line in Table 7.6, entering state s2 of object A is an event that triggers process B. B will start executing if its precondition is met, in which case it will consume B.

The third stateless–stateful links pair is the *condition link* and its refined *state-specified condition link*. Referring to the fifth line in Table 7.6, the semantics of the **condition link** is that the existence of object A is a condition for the execution of B. If A does not exist, then B is skipped and regular system flow continues.

Referring to the sixth line in Table 7.6, the semantics of the **state-specified condition link** is that the existence of object A in state s2 is a condition for the execution of B. If A does not exist in s2, then B is skipped and regular system flow continues.

A fourth stateless–stateful links pair is the *consumption condition link* and its refined *state-specified consumption condition link*. This pair, which does not appear in Table 7.6, is graphically similar to the consumption event link and its refined *state-specified consumption event link*, except that the letter c appears instead of the letter e. The semantics of this pair is similar to the condition link and its refined state-specified condition link, except that *if B occurs, it consumes A*.

The last two control links, shown in the two bottom lines in Table 7.6, are the invocation link and the exception link. They are exceptional among the procedural links, as unlike the other procedural links, which connect an object with a process, they connect two processes. The **invocation link** semantics is that execution termination of process B is an event that triggers process C. B yields a temporary object that is immediately consumed by C and therefore not shown explicitly in the model. The **exception link** semantics requires that process A be assigned with maximal acceptable time duration, which, if exceeded, triggers process B. This is a way to avoid indefinite waiting for a process that, for some reason, got stuck and delays further execution of the system. C is an exception handling process, which has to be designed to take care of the failure of B to terminate within the time allotted for its execution by taking a remedial action or notifying a human.

7.11 Complexity Management

Complexity is inherent in real-life systems. An integral part of a system development methodology must therefore include control and management of this complexity. Like most classical engineering problems, complexity management entails a trade-off that must be balanced between two conflicting requirements: completeness and clarity. On one hand, *completeness* requires that the system details be stipulated in the model to the fullest extent possible. On the other hand, the need for *clarity* implies that no diagram of the model be too cluttered or overloaded. This can be achieved by imposing an upper limit on the level of complexity of each individual diagram. OO development methods, notably the UML standard [30] and its SysML derivative, address the problem of managing systems complexity by dividing the system model into different views for the various aspects of the system – structure, dynamics, event sequence, physical architecture, state transitions, etc.

The approach OPM takes is orthogonal, advocating the integration of the various system aspects into a single model. Rather than applying a separate model for each system aspect, OPM handles the inherent system complexity by introducing a number of abstraction–refinement mechanisms. These enable presenting and viewing the things that comprise the system at various detail levels. The entire system is completely specified through its OPD set – a hierarchical set of interconnected OPDs that together provide a full picture of the system being investigated or developed. Along with the OPD set goes the automatically generated OPL system specification. This section elaborates on these complexity management issues and specifies the various abstracting–refining mechanisms.

Complexity is managed in OPM via three refinement–abstraction mechanisms: in-zooming and out-zooming, unfolding and folding, and state expression and suppression. These mechanisms allow for looking at any complex system at any desired level of granularity without losing the context and the "big picture." We elaborate on complexity management in this section.

7.11.1 The Need for Complexity Management

The very need for systems analysis and design strategies stems from complexity. If systems or problems were simple enough for humans to grasp by merely glancing at them, no methodology would be required. Due to the need for tackling sizeable, complex problems, a system development methodology must be equipped with a comprehensive approach, backed by a set of reliable and useful tools, for controlling and managing this complexity. This challenge entails balancing two forces that pull in opposite directions and need to be traded off: completeness and clarity. *Completeness* means that the system must be specified to the last relevant detail. *Clarity* means that to communicate the analysis and design outcomes, the documentation, be it textual or diagrammatic, must be legible and comprehensible. To tackle complex systems, a methodology must be equipped with adequate tools for complexity management that address and solve this problem of completeness–clarity tradeoff by striking the right balance between these two contradicting demands.

OPM achieves clarity through abstracting and completeness through refining. Abstracting, the inverse of refining, saves space and reduces complexity, but it comes at the price of completeness. Conversely, refining, which contributes to completeness, comes at the price of loss of clarity. There are "no free meals"; as is typically the case with engineering problems, there is a clear tradeoff between completeness of details and clarity of their presentation. The solution OPM proposes is to keep each OPD simple enough and to distribute the system specification over a set of consistently interrelated OPDs that contain things at various detail levels. Abstracting and refining are the analytical tools that provide for striking the right balance between clarity and completeness.

Analysis and design are the first steps in the lifecycle of a new system, product, or project. Creating (sometimes unconscious) resistance on the side of the prospective audience to accept the analysis and design results, because they look too complex and intimidating, may have an adverse effect of jeopardizing the success of subsequent phases of the product development. The severity and frequency of this detail explosion problem calls for an adequate solution to meet the needs of the systems analysis community. A major test of any analysis methodology is therefore the quality of tools for managing the ever-growing complexity of analysis outcomes in a coherent, clear, and useful manner. Such complexity management tools are extremely important for organizing the knowledge the architect accumulates and generates during the system architecting process. Equally important is the role of complexity management mechanisms in facilitating the communication of the analysis and design results to stakeholder, including customers, peers, superiors, and system developers down the development cycle road – implementers, testers, and users.

7.11.2 *Middle-Out as the De Facto Architecting Practice*

Analyzing is the process of gradually increasing the human analyzer's knowledge about a system's structure and behavior. Designing is the process of gradually increasing the amount of details about the system's architecture, i.e., the structure and behavior combination that enables the system to attain its function. For both analysis and design, managing the system's complexity therefore entails being able to present and view the system at various levels of detail that are consistent with each other. Ideally, analysis and design start at the top and make their way gradually to the bottom – from the general to the detailed. In real life, however, analysis typically starts at some arbitrary detail level and is rarely linear. The design is not linear either. Almost invariably, these are iterative processes, during which knowledge, followed by understanding, is gradually accumulated and refined in the conceptual model.

The system architect often cannot know in advance the precise structure and behavior of the very top of the system – this requires analysis and becomes apparent at some point along the analysis process. Step by step, the analyst builds the system specification by accumulating and recording facts and observations about things in the system and relations among them. Using OPM, the accumulated knowledge is represented through a set of OPDs and their corresponding OPL paragraphs. The sheer amount of details contained in any real-world system of reasonable size overwhelms the system architect soon enough during the architecting process. Trying to incorporate the details into one diagram, the amount of drawn symbols gets very large, and their interconnections quickly become an entangled web. For all but the simplest systems, this information overload happens even if the method advocates using multiple diagram types for the various system aspects. Because the diagram has become so cluttered, it is increasingly difficult to comprehend it. System architects experience this detail-explosion phenomenon on a daily basis, and anyone who has tried to analyze a system will endorse this description. The problem calls for effective and efficient tools to manage this inherent complexity.

Due to the nonlinear nature of these processes, unidirectional "bottom-up" or "top-down" approaches are rarely applicable to real-world systems. Rather, it is frequently the case that the system under construction or investigation is so complex and unexplored that neither its top nor its bottom is known with certainty from the outset. More commonly, analysis and design of real-life systems start in an unknown place along the system's detail-level hierarchy. The analysis proceeds *"middle-out"* by combining top-down and bottom-up techniques to obtain a complete understanding and specification of the system at all the detail levels. It turns out that even though architects usually strive to work in an orderly top-down fashion, more often than not, the de facto practice is the middle-out mode of analysis and design. Rather than trying to fight it, we should build software tools that provide facilities to handle this middle-out architecting mode. Such facilities cater also to both top-down and bottom up approaches.

During the middle-out analysis and design process, facts and ideas about objects in the system and its environment, and processes that transform them, are being gathered and recorded. As the analysis and design proceed, the system architect tries to *concurrently* specify both the structure and the behavior of the system in order to enable it to fulfill its function. For an investigated (as opposed to an architected) system, the researcher tries to make sense of the long list of gathered observations and to understand their cause and effect relation. In both cases, the system's structure and behavior go hand in hand, and it is very difficult to understand one without the other. Almost as soon as a new object is introduced into the system, the process that transforms it or is enabled by it begs to be modeled as well. By supplying the single object–process model, OPM caters to this structure–behavior concurrency requirement. It enables modeling these two major system aspects at the same time within the same model without the need to constantly switch between different diagram types.

If the OPD that is being augmented becomes too crowded, busy, or unintelligible, a new OPD is created. This descendant OPD repeats one or more of the things in its ancestor OPD. These repeated things establish the link between the ancestor and descendant OPDs. The descendant OPD does not usually replicate all the details of its ancestor, as some of them are abstracted, while others are simply not included. This new OPD is therefore amenable to refinement of new things to be laid out in the space that was saved by not including things from the ancestor OPD. In other words, there is room in it to insert a certain amount of additional details before it gets too cluttered again. When this happens, a new cycle of refinement takes place, and this goes on until the entire system has been completely specified.

7.11.3 The Completeness-Comprehension Dilemma

We face a dilemma here, called the *completeness-comprehension dilemma*, which is typical in conceptual modeling. The dilemma is that on one hand we wish to continue adding facts to the system under study or design, but on the other hand we do not want to compromise the clarity of the graphics by overcluttering it. This dilemma pops up regardless of the conceptual modeling language used – it is simply an unavoidable outcome of details starting to pile up that require and compete for diagram "real estate."

A balance needs to be struck and a tradeoff has to be found between completeness of details on the one hand and keeping the model legible on the other. The solution OPM offers to solve this problem is dividing the model into a set of separate yet logically integrated and hierarchically organized OPDs via a couple of refinement mechanisms. The mechanism we have used is *in-zooming*. In-zooming creates a new, descendant OPD and provides for refining the blown-up process by modeling its subprocesses and their interactions with lower-level objects. Another OPM refinement mechanism is unfolding, in which refineables of a thing are linked using one of the fundamental structural links in a new OPD or in an existing one.

7.12 Applications and Standardization of OPM

OPM has been applied in a variety of domains, including real-time systems [32], Web-based systems [35, 43], Enterprise Resource Planning [15, 39], systems architecture [38], web service composition [51], Product Lifecycle Engineering [14], molecular biology [13], data warehouse construction [12], privacy management in medical records [4], software reuse and design patterns [36, 37], domain analysis [41], exceptions modeling [33], intelligent house [52], and multiagent systems [42].

The domain-independent nature of OPM makes it suitable as a general, comprehensive, and multidisciplinary framework for knowledge representation and reasoning that emerge from conceptual modeling, analysis, design, implementation, and lifecycle management. The ability of OPM to provide comprehensive lifecycle support for systems of all kinds and complexity levels is due to its foundational ontology that builds on a most minimal set of stateful objects and processes that transform them. Another significant trait of OPM is its unification of system knowledge from both the structural and behavioral aspects in a single model expressed diagrammatically via the OPD set and textually via the set of corresponding OPL paragraphs. OPM features dual knowledge representation in graphics and text, so users have the capability to automatically switch between these two modalities. It is hard to think of a significant domain of discourse and a system within it where structure and behavior are not interdependent and intertwined. Due to its single model, expressed in both graphics and text, OPM lends itself naturally to representing and managing knowledge, as it is uniquely positioned to cater to the tight interconnections between structure and behavior that are so hard to separate, making it a most suitable language for structure–behavior codesign. The ability to model physical and informatical things also makes OPM ideal for hardware–software codesign.

OPM is not just a language but also a system development and lifecycle-support methodology, for which a comprehensive reflective metamodel (which uses OPM) has been developed [34]. Indeed, in a 2008 survey by INCOSE – the International Council on Systems Engineering [18] – OPM was recognized as one of the six leading model-based systems engineering (MBSE) methodologies, which include also IBM Telelogic Harmony-SE, INCOSE Object-Oriented Systems Engineering Method, IBM Rational Unified Process for Systems Engineering for Model-Driven Systems Development, Vitech Model-Based System Engineering Methodology, and JPL State Analysis.

Several activities are being undertaken to leverage the potential benefits of OPM in international standardization bodies. Work is under way by ISO TC184/SC5 OPM Working Group to develop a Draft International Standard (DIS) for OPM that will be the basis for authoring model-based enterprise standards and other technical documents [20, 24, 25]. This DIS is expected to be presented in the ISO TC184/WG5 annual meeting in the USA in 2011.

References

1. American Heritage Dictionary of the English Language (1996) Houghton Mifflin, Boston, 4th edn
2. Baddeley A (1992) Working memory. Science 255:556–559
3. Beckhoff B, Kanngießer B, Langhoff N, Wedell R, Wolff H (2006) Handbook of practical x-ray fluorescence analysis. Springer, Berlin Heidelberg New York
4. Beimel D, Peleg M, Dori D, Denekamp Y (2008) Situation-based access control: privacy management via patient data disclosure modeling. J Biomed Inform 41(6):1028–1040
5. Bunge MA (1977) Treatise on basic philosophy, vol 3: Ontology I: the furniture of the world. Reidel, Boston
6. Bunge MA (1979) Treatise on basic philosophy, vol 4. Ontology II: a world of systems, Reidel, Boston
7. Chandler P, Sweller J (1991) Cognitive load theory and the format of instruction. Cogn Instr 8:293–332
8. Clark JM, Paivio A (1991) Dual coding theory and education. Educ Psychol Rev 3:149–210
9. Dodaf (2007) http://cio-nii.defense.gov/docs/DoDAF_Volume_I.pdf
10. Dori D (1995) Object-process analysis: maintaining the balance between system structure and behavior. J Log Comput 5(2):227–249
11. Dori D (2002) Object-Process Methodology: a holistic systems paradigm. Springer, Berlin Heidelberg New York
12. Dori D (2008) Words from pictures for dual channel processing. Commun ACM 51(5):47–52
13. Dori D, Choder M (2007) Conceptual modeling in systems biology fosters empirical findings: the mRNA lifecycle. In: Proceedings of the library of science ONE (PLoS ONE), September 2007.
   http://www.plosone.org/article/info
14. Dori D, Shpitalni M (2005) Mapping knowledge about product lifecycle engineering for ontology construction via object-process methodology. CIRP Ann Manuf Technol 54(1):117–122
15. Dori D, Golany B, Soffer P (2005) Aligning an ERP system with enterprise requirements: an object-process based approach. Comput Ind 56(6):639–662

16. Dori D, Feldman R, Sturm A (2008) From conceptual models to schemata: an object-process based data warehouse construction method. Inf Syst 33:567–593

17. Dori D, Reinhartz-Berger I, Sturm A (2003) Developing complex systems with object-process methodology using OPCAT. In: Proceedings of ER 2003. Lecture notes in computer science, vol 2813. Springer, Berlin, pp 570–572

18. Estefan J (2008) Survey of model-based systems engineering (MBSE) methodologies. http://www.incose.org/productspubs/pdf/techdata/MTTC/\discretionary-MBSE_\discretionary-Methodology_Survey_2008-0610_RevB-JAE2.pdf

19. Glenberg AM, Langston WE (1992) Comprehension of illustrated text: pictures help to build mental models. J Mem Lang 31:129–151

20. Howes DB, Blekhman A, Dori D (2010) Model based verification and validation of a manufacturing and control standard. In: Proceedings of Manufacturing and Service Operations Management Society (MSOM) annual conference, Maalot, Israel, June 2010

21. Hegarty M (1992) Mental animation: inferring motion from static displays of mechanical systems. J Exp Psychol Learn Mem Cogn 18:1084–1102

22. Hayes P, Menzel C (2001) A semantics for the knowledge interchange format. In: IJCAI 2001 workshop on the IEEE Standard Upper Ontology

23. IDEF (2001) A structured approach to enterprise modeling and analysis. www.idef.com. IDEF Family of Methods

24. ISO N1049 (2009) OPM study group, terms of reference. Plenary Meeting Resolutions 2009-04-23/24

25. ISO-N1078 ISO/TC 184/SC 5 (2010) Plenary Meeting Resolutions 2010-03-25/26

26. Mayer RE (2003) The promise of multimedia learning: Using the same instructional design methods across different media. Learn Instr 13:125–139

27. Mayer RE, Moreno R (2003) Nine ways to reduce cognitive load in multimedia learning. Educ Psychol 38(1):43–52

28. Manola F, Miller E (2004) RDF primer. http://www.w3.org/TR/rdf-primer

29. Miller GA (1956) The magical number seven, plus or minus two: Some limits on our capacity for processing information. Psychol Rev 63:81–97

30. OMG: Object Management Group (2010) http://www.omg.org

31. Ontology Markup Language Version 0.3. http://www.ontologos.org/OML/OML

32. Peleg M, Dori D (2000) The model multiplicity problem: Experimenting with real-time specification methods. IEEE Trans Softw Eng 26(8):742–759

33. Peleg M, Somekh J, Dori D (2009) A methodology for eliciting and modeling exceptions. J Biomed Inform 42(4):736–747

34. Reinhartz-Berger I, Dori D (2005) A reflective metamodel of object-process methodology: the system modeling building blocks. Idea Group, Hershey, PA, pp 130–173

35. Reinhartz-Berger I, Dori D, Katz S (2002) OPM/Web – object-process methodology for developing web applications. Ann Softw Eng 13:141–161

36. Reinhartz-Berger I, Dori D, Katz S (2009) Reusing semi-specified behavior models in systems analysis and design. J Softw Syst Model 8:221–234

37. Shlezinger G, Reinhartz-Berger I, Dori D (2010) Modeling design patterns for semi-automatic reuse in system design. J Database Manag 21(1):29–57

38. Soderborg N, Crawley E, Dori D (2003) OPM-based system function and architecture: definitions and operational templates. Commun ACM 46(10):67–72

39. Soffer P, Golany B, Dori D (2003) ERP modeling: a comprehensive approach. Inf Syst 28(6):673–690

40. Sowa JF (2000) Knowledge representation: logical, philosophical, and computational foundations. Brooks Cole, Pacific Grove, CA

41. Sturm A, Dori D, Shehory O (2009) Application-based domain analysis approach and its object-process methodology implementation. Int J Softw Eng Knowl Eng 19(1)

42. Sturm A, Dori D, Shehory O (2010) An object-process-based modeling language for multi-agent systems. IEEE Trans Syst Man Cybern C Appl Rev 40(2):227–241

43. Toch E, Gal A, Reinhartz-Berger I, Dori D (2007) A semantic approach to approximate service retrieval. ACM Trans Internet Technol 8(1):2:1–2:30

44. University of Arizona (2001) NATS-online. http://www.ic.arizona.edu/~nats101/n1.html
45. Von Glaserfeld E (1987) The construction of knowledge: contributions to conceptual semantics. Intersystems, Seaside, CA
46. Wand Y, Weber R (1989) An ontological evaluation of systems analysis and design methods. Elsevier, North Holland, pp 145–172
47. Wand Y, Weber R (1993) On the ontological expressiveness of information systems analysis and design grammars. J Inf Syst 3:217–237
48. Wand Y, Storey VC, Weber R (1999) An ontological analysis of the relationship construct in conceptual modeling. ACM Trans Database Syst 24(4):494–528
49. Webster's Encyclopedic Unabridged Dictionary of the English Language (1984) Portland House, New York
50. Webster's New Dictionary (1997) Promotional Sales Books
51. Yin L, Wenyin L, Changjun J (2004) Object-process diagrams as explicit graphic tool for web service composition. J Integr Des Process Sci Trans SDPS 8(1):113–127
52. Zoref L, Bregman D, Dori D (2009) Networking mobile devices and computers in an intelligent home. Int J Smart Home 3(4):15–22

Chapter 8
Business Process Modeling and Workflow Design

Horst Pichler and Johann Eder

Abstract Detailed knowledge about the structure and functionality of a business process within an enterprise is of utter importance for a thorough understanding of organizational sequences. This is a crucial requirement in business process management (BPM) and business process re-engineering (BPR), which cover the entire process lifecycle, from modeling and design, to execution, monitoring, and optimization. Throughout this lifecycle, process models are required to represent an enterprise's processes, so that they can be documented, communicated, verified, simulated, analyzed, automated, evaluated, or improved. This chapter provides an overview of business process modeling and workflow design, discusses their commonalities and differences, explains how different process perspectives are modeled, and gives an overview of several business process modeling related research topics.

8.1 Introduction

Detailed knowledge about the structure and functionality of a business process within an enterprise is of utter importance for a thorough understanding of organizational sequences. This is a crucial requirement in business process management (BPM) and business process re-engineering (BPR), which cover the entire process lifecycle, from modeling and design, to execution, monitoring, and optimization. Throughout this lifecycle, process models are required to represent an enterprise's processes, so that they can be documented, communicated, verified, simulated, analyzed, automated, evaluated, or improved.

Horst Pichler
Institute for Informatics-Systems, Alpen-Adria Universität Klagenfurt, Austria, e-mail: horst. pichler@uni-klu.ac.at

Johann Eder
Institute for Informatics-Systems, Alpen-Adria Universität Klagenfurt, Austria, e-mail: johann. eder@uni-klu.ac.at

D. W. Embley and B. Thalheim (eds), *Handbook of Conceptual Modeling.*
DOI 10.1007/978-3-642-15865-0, © Springer 2011

In this chapter, we provide an overview of process modeling and workflow design, which is organized as follows: Section 8.1 clarifies relevant terms and concepts. Section 8.2 explains which perspectives are typically part of a process model, distinguishes different modeling techniques, and discusses current standardization efforts. Section 8.3 goes into depth on three of the most extensively described process perspectives: the control flow perspective, the organizational perspective, and the data perspective.

The remainder of the chapter deals with selected research topics. Section 8.4 describes various problems that can arise in the control flow and explains how to detect and avoid them. Section 8.5 deals with the correctness and generation of process views. Section 8.6 shows how to model timed processes and describes a method that exploits temporal information in order to improve the performance and the quality of processes.

8.1.1 Business Process Modeling and Workflow Design

A *business process* is set of one or more activities (tasks) that collectively realize a business objective or policy goal, normally within the context of an organizational structure defining functional roles and relationships. A *workflow* is the automation of a business process, in whole or part, during which documents, information, or tasks are passed from one participant to another. A workflow requires a *workflow management system (WfMS)*, which is a system that defines, creates, and manages the execution of workflows, interacts with workflow participants, and – where required – invokes the use of IT tools, applications, and services [1].

Business process modeling is the activity of capturing and representing all required information about an enterprise's business process, whereas *workflow design* aims at creating an executable model of this process within the enterprise's technical environment. A *business process model* is the description of an operational sequence of a real world business process, whereas a *workflow model* (aka workflow process definition or workflow schema) is the mapping of a process model to a information system.

8.1.2 Business Process Modeling Versus Workflow Design

Naturally, business process models and workflow models have many things in common, as they are often just separate steps in the life cycle of one specific business process: from business process modeling for documentation, communication, and analysis purposes, to workflow design for automatization purposes. Correspondingly, the disciplines of process modeling and workflow design continuously grow together, e.g., business process modeling tools that export process definitions to workflow systems or the other way around in re-engineering scenarios.

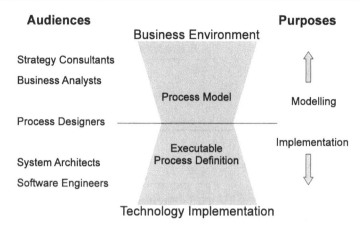

Fig. 8.1 The BPM hourglass [2]

Figure 8.1 shows the relationship between a business process model (in this case a BPMN model) and the corresponding executable process definition (in this case a BPEL process definition) [2]. The different audiences require information about diverse process perspectives on different levels of detail. For example, a business analyst may be interested in the organizational structure or in the communication sequences with external systems, but might not be interested in the technical details of selecting a specific participant from an organizational resource repository and assigning a task to him, or in the parameter types of called interfaces, which is an indispensable piece of information for software engineers. Therefore it is important to notice that although business process modeling and workflow design have many things in common, workflow models have a focus on technical issues, which are often not required in business process models.

8.1.3 Workflow Characteristics

When talking about workflows, one must in principle distinguish between the build time and the run time phase, as shown in Fig. 8.2 [3].

During the *build time phase* (design phase), a process designer analyzes and defines the process. The result is a formal *process definition*, which describes every required perspective of the process such that it can be interpreted and executed by the WfMS. This definition contains among other things the steps of the process, a description of the order of execution for these steps, the participants involved, data used, applications invoked, constraints, and exceptions.

During the *run time phase* (execution phase), the workflow process definition serves as description for process execution. Each time a process is started, the *workflow enactment service* (workflow engine) creates a new instance of the process and executes it according to the sequence of activities specified in the process definition. The workflow engine assigns tasks to participants (agents), which are presented as

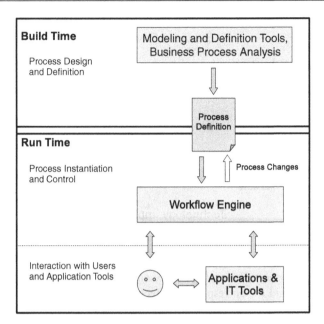

Fig. 8.2 Workflow system characteristics [3]

work items in their worklists. Apart from driving the process, the workflow engine is responsible for the interaction with workflow participants and external applications; it logs every step, and it monitors whether instances are still compliant to specified constraints.

8.2 An Overview of Process Modeling

As mentioned previously, process models are used for different purposes – like documentation, analysis or automatization – in different stages of the process life cycle. Correspondingly, the information required for each of these purposes will vary according to the goals to be achieved and the target environments. Therefore, there is no common agreement about the information that a process model should contain, nor is there a global consensus about how this information shall be represented. This section gives a brief overview of the information to be captured in a process model, the various representation techniques, and current standardization efforts.

8.2.1 Process Perspectives

A process model (or process definition) is composed of information on diverse process perspectives (also called process aspects). The following five perspectives are the most frequently mentioned (e.g. [4–6]):

1. The *control flow perspective* (behavior perspective) specifies the execution order of activities (steps) in a process.
2. The *organizational perspective* (resource perspective) specifies the organizational structure, process participants, roles, or resources, and their assignment to specific activities in the process.
3. The *data perspective* (information perspective) deals with data objects used and accessed in the process as well as with the flow of data between process activities.
4. The *functional perspective* (task perspective) describes the semantics and functionality of each activity in the process. Such a step is a logical unit of work with characteristics that may include a description, the set of operations to be performed, pre-conditions, priority, triggers, expected duration, and due date.
5. The *operational perspective* (application perspective) describes the implementation of operations within each activity, for example: the invocation of programs for the manual manipulation and the presentation of associated data, the invocation of applications, or the message exchanges with external services.

Which perspectives are part of a process model and how detailed they must be described depends on the business goals, the application area, and the target environment or system. For instance, the operational perspective will be required for process automation within a workflow environment; this is not necessarily the case if one wants to model a process for mere documentation purposes.

Note that this list is neither complete nor fixed; it may be arbitrarily modified or extended, depending on the needs of a specific application domain. Other perspectives might include a temporal perspective that comprises activity durations and temporal constraints like deadlines, which are required for the determination of critical paths in a process; a performance perspective that describes process arrival frequencies, activity duration estimations, and branching probabilities for simulation in a process analysis tool such as ADONIS[1]; a history perspective that comprises data in a workflow log; a causal perspective that describes the conditions under which a process can be executed; a integrity and failure perspective; a compensation perspective; a transactional perspective, and more (e.g., [5, 6]).

There is often no clear distinction between perspectives. For example, in BPMN, diverse perspectives such as failure, compensation, or transaction are integral parts of the control flow perspective[2]. Furthermore, complex perspectives cannot always be captured directly in the process model, but only through referral to an external resource repository. For instance, elements in the organizational model of an ERP system (users, organizational units, roles) are referred by activities in the control flow model to describe possible assignments of activities to resources – thus the organizational structure itself is not part of the process model [5].

---

[1] http://www.boc-group.com.

[2] BPMN meta model download available at http://www.bpmn.org.

8.2.2 Process Modeling Techniques

Many process modeling techniques have been proposed for the specification of business processes and workflows, either as graphical notations or text-based languages. Many of them are based on existing modeling techniques, such as flow charts, Gantt charts, or Petri nets, and others are proprietary techniques tailored to specific workflow systems. In 1998 the US National Institute for Standards and Technology provided a survey of techniques frequently applied for process modeling [7]. They identified several dozen different techniques and showed that most of them focus on the control flow perspective and that none is perfectly suited for process modeling, as often diverse techniques have to be combined to capture all required perspectives of a business process. Basically, process modeling techniques can be categorized as follows (e.g., [5–8]):

- *Specification types* – The most frequently applied specification type is *activity-based*, which focuses on modeling the tasks involved in a process and their precedence dependencies. Less often applied are *constraint-based methods* and *rule-based methods*, which describe a process by means of a set of constraints and rules on tasks, which are used to decide when a task is enabled and ready for execution. Rarely applied types are *communication-based* or speech-act approaches that model a process as an interaction between (at least) two participants that follow a structured cycle of conversation.
- *Supporting modeling concepts* are the modeling notations used for process modeling, for instance: example flow charts, precedence graphs, activity diagrams, role activity diagrams, sequence diagrams, state charts, Petri nets, and so on. The majority of these notations are representations for activity-based process specification.

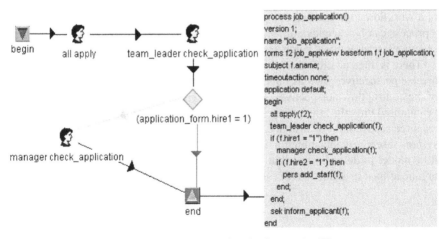

Fig. 8.3 Graphical and textual process representations in @enterprise [9]

• *Representation types* – Process models may have a *graphical representation* (a notation), usually based on one of the supporting modeling concepts and/or a *textual representation* (a language), which is usually defined in a programming language-style.

Figure 8.3 shows the graphical representation and the corresponding textual representation of a process in the WfMS @enterprise [9]. It offers an activity-based specification, with flow charts as supporting modeling concept, augmented with specific elements for the control flow perspective, the data perspective, and the organizational perspective. The textual representation of this process is a process definition written in @enterprise's proprietary Workflow Process Language WPL.

8.2.3 Standardization Efforts

Since the early 1990s, diverse endeavors have aimed at the development of standard business process modeling notations and languages. Among the most prominent representatives are: the process interchange format PIF, the ICAM definition languages IDEF, the Process Specification Language PSL, the Business Process Definition Language BPDL, or even the Unified Modeling Language UML 2.0, which features several concepts specifically introduced for business process modeling.

Standardization efforts in the workflow field are even more problematic, as nearly every workflow system provides its own proprietary process definition language. Concept and structure of these languages are based on inherent features and underlying process representation models, which are tailored to the specific needs of the particular field of application. Nevertheless, the WfMC[3] introduced a standard specification for process definitions – also known as a process definition interface [10] – as part of their workflow meta model, along with its XML-based successor, the XML Processing Description Language XPDL [11].

The most recent standardization effort is the graphical Business Process Modeling Notation BPMN [12]. It is already supported by many tool vendors and its acceptance increased dramatically with the WfMC's decision to use XPDL 2.0 as textual representation format to exchange BPMN process models between tools and systems of different vendors [11]. Additionally, BPMN can be used to visualize inter-organizational process models defined with the textual XML-based Web Service Business Process Execution Language WS-BPEL, specifically designed for executable inter-organizational workflows [12, 13]. These examples are further proof that business process modeling and workflow design continuously grow together.

---

[3] The Workflow Management Coalition (WfMC, www.wfmc.org) is a global organization that creates and contributes to process related standards.

8.3 Modeling Process Perspectives

8.3.1 Control Flow Perspective

The control flow or behavior perspective has a central position in the definition of a business process as it specifies the execution order of activities, such that tasks can be assigned to participants in this anticipated order. Information about other perspectives is often attached to elements of the control flow. Correspondingly, it is the most intensively researched and described perspective. For instance, in the BPMN meta model, the majority of several dozen classes describe the control flow, whereas the organizational perspective is only reflected by the classes Pool and Lane, or the data perspective which is reflected by MessageFlow, Data Object, and Association.

8.3.1.1 Control Flow Representation

Numerous modeling techniques are in use, but among all alternatives one class is favored: the activity-based directed graph representation, like flow charts augmented with special symbols, Petri net variants like WF-nets, precedence graphs with control nodes, and so on. Figure 8.4 shows a BPMN process model as an example of such a representation. Sequence flows (directed edges, transitions) specify the precedence between diverse types of nodes, where rectangles represent activities or tasks to be executed by agents and diamonds represent gateways (control nodes) with special execution semantics. Splits (forks) are control nodes where a single path of execution is split into several paths of execution, and joins (merges) are control nodes where multiple paths are merged into one path.

The popularity of this representation form has various reasons: clear and simple concepts make them intuitively comprehensible, as they follow the natural ordering of individual tasks; they are well suited for monitoring purposes, as it is easy to determine the current state of execution; and the flow-based model can be completed with additional information from other perspectives, like the data flow [15] or temporal constraints between tasks [14]. This is also of advantage when discussing business processes with non-experts or customers. Therefore, the majority of process modeling standards and workflow systems also rely on this modeling paradigm.

8.3.1.2 Control Flow Patterns

Although many control flow structures are used and interpreted alike in process and workflow models, there was for a long time no real common consensus about their execution semantics. In the mid-nineties the Workflow Management Coalition provided a definition of some basic control flow elements in their terminology [1]. Some years later the notion of control flow patterns was introduced [16]. A control flow pattern is a frequently applied flow structure with defined execution semantics.

Basic control flow patterns are supported by most process modeling notations and languages. The execution semantics of the basic patterns in Fig. 8.4 are to be interpreted as follows:

- *Sequence* – A node in a process is enabled after the completion of another node in the same process instance. Sequences are represented as a single directed edge between a predecessor and its successor node. Activity B will (can) be started when activity A is finished, and after B the succeeding parallel split will be performed.
- *Parallel split, And-split* – A point in the process where a single thread of control splits into multiple threads of control which can be executed in parallel, thus allowing activities to be executed simultaneously or in any order. Note that where a process includes parallel activities, a process instance may include multiple concurrent threads of execution, which also means that multiple activity instances are executed at the same time [1]. In BPMN the parallel split it is called and-gateway – a diamond with a plus-sign – with multiple outgoing transitions. Activity C and activity D will be started when activity B is finished.
- *Synchronization, And-join* – A point in the process where two or more parallel executing activities converge into a single common thread of control. At this point, an execution thread waits until all parallel execution threads are completed and the next activity can be initiated [1]. In BPMN, the and-join is also represented by an and-gateway (this time with multiple incoming transitions). The and-gateway will wait until the parallel paths via C and via D are completed in order to synchronize the two threads of execution.
- *Exclusive choice, Xor-split* – A point within the process where a single thread of execution decides which branch to take when encountered with multiple alternative workflow branches [1]. This structure is exclusive, as exactly one of several branches must be chosen, according to specified conditions. An undefined result of condition evaluation is usually not permitted [6], which is avoided by either adding an otherwise-transition [11] or marking one of the transitions as default transition to be selected if none of the other conditions evaluate to true [12]. In BPMN, the exclusive choice is represented by an xor-gateway – a diamond with

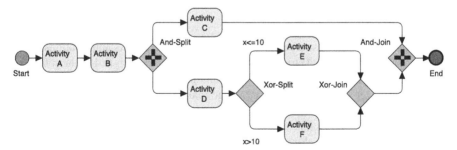

Fig. 8.4 BPMN Sample process – basic control flow patterns

an x. After the execution of activity D, activity E will be started when the condition $x \le 10$ holds; otherwise, activity F will be started.

* *Simple merge, Xor-join* – A point within the process where two or more alternative workflow branches re-converge to a single common activity as the next step within the workflow [1]. It will be triggered once any of the incoming transitions are triggered [16]. In BPMN, the xor-join is also represented by an xor-gateway (this time with multiple incoming arcs), where the process execution proceeds when any of the preceding activities – either E or F – finishes.

Advanced control flow patterns Most commercial workflow systems offer many more additional control flow elements with diverse semantics. To date, 41 different control flow patterns have been identified[4]. Besides (1) *basic patterns*, they can be categorized as follows: (2) *Iteration patterns* deal with repetitive behavior in processes, for instance the structured loop pattern or the recursion pattern. (3) *Advanced branching and synchronization patterns* add more complex branching and merging concepts which arise in business processes. This includes, for instance, the multi-choice pattern (m out of n paths may be executed in parallel, according to defined conditions) and the corresponding multi-merge pattern. (4) *Termination patterns* describe the circumstances under which a process is considered to be completed, for instance, explicit termination when the end node of the process has been reached. (5) *Cancellation and force completion patterns* deal with the cancellation of activities which may already be active. For instance, the cancel region pattern, which can be used to disable a set of tasks in a process instance when an exception is thrown in this region. (6) *Multiple instance patterns* describe situations where there are multiple threads of execution active in a process model that relate to the same activity (and hence share the same implementation definition). (7) *State-based patterns* reflect situations that require the notion of a process or system state. For instance, the milestone pattern, which allows execution of a certain activity only if the process has reached a defined state (for example, another activity in a parallel branch must already be finished). Finally, (8) *Trigger Patterns* deal with situations where external signals are required to start certain tasks.

8.3.2 *Organizational Perspective*

The organizational or resource perspective deals with elements and relations in an enterprise's organizational structure and how activities are assigned to them for execution. Most graphical process modeling notations provide a few concepts, which direct the viewer's attention to the organizational perspective. For instance, BPMN shows the organizational affiliation of activities by placing them into pools, which can be divided into swimlanes, which may again be divided into further swimlanes (which allows tree hierarchies of organizational units or roles). Figure 8.5 presents a simple example. The organizational model of BPMN is obviously very simplistic,

---

[4] http://www.workflowpatterns.com.

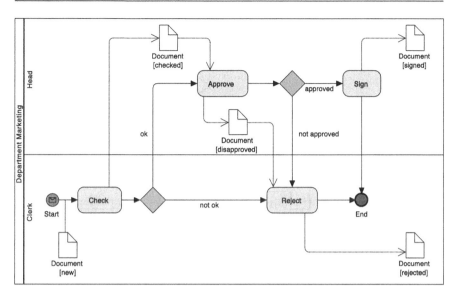

Fig. 8.5 BPMN process model with organizational and data perspective

which is mainly caused by the fact that the specification of BPMN 1.0 had a very strong focus on the Web Service-based Business Process Execution Language WS-BPEL, where such a model suffices.

8.3.2.1 Organizational Model

However, an organizational model like the one in BPMN is not sufficient for defining the organizational view of in-house processes or workflows, as enterprises often implement very complex organizational structures and task assignment mechanisms. An activity may for instance be assigned to a certain organizational unit (e.g., a department) for execution, where only certain users who inhabit a specific role within this unit may be allowed to execute this activity.

Although standardization approaches aimed to capture these structures in organizational meta models, they were bound to fail. For instance, the organizational meta model of the WfMC [3], as depicted in Fig. 8.6, assigns activities of a process to participants, like users, roles, resources, or organizational units, which may be related to each other and hierarchically structured. First of all, there is no global common consensus on the elements, their semantics, and how they are related to each other. Further, this model contains only part of the organizational concepts required and supported in real workflow systems like FlowMark or Workparty or even more complex models of ERP systems like SAP [21]. Especially, ERP systems feature complex human resource (HR) modules, to be used by not only the workflow component but also by other modules. In such an environment, the organizational structure is an external component to be referenced in process models for the as-

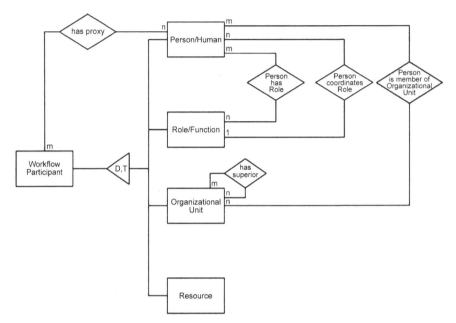

Fig. 8.6 WfMC Organizational meta model [3]

signment of activities to specific system resources (e.g., users) described by various organizational characteristics.

8.3.2.2 Basic Assignment Policies

Assignment policies describe how activities are assigned to resources. In [5] three different policies are distinguished, which are to be specified as part of the organizational perspective (usually attached to activities) in a process model or workflow definition:

- *Direct designation* – An activity is assigned to one or more resources (users) of the organizational model. At run time, a workflow engine can directly look up these resources and assign a corresponding task to one of them. Although this concept is very easy to handle for process designers and administrators, it is rather inflexible, as every modification of the organizational population or change of assignment rules results in the modification of the process definition.
- *Assignment by role* – This concept was introduced to decouple the resource model from the process model. A user may inhabit one or more roles, which describe a specific organizational role or function (e.g., head of department, engineer). These roles can be assigned to activities, which means that every user who inhabits the specified role may be selected to perform this activity. Pools and swimlanes in BPMN can be used to model this concept. Figure 8.3 shows

the realization of such a role concept in the workflow system @enterprise: all users are allowed to perform the activity 'apply', only team leaders are allowed to perform 'check_application', and so on.

- *Assignment by formal expression* – The most complex form of task assignment allows the specification of expressions on the resource model which are evaluated during run time. For instance, an expression like *superior(resource(process-Starter)) or role(boss)* may be used to select possible users for task assignment. Naturally these expressions require knowledge about the resource model, its entity types, and their relationships, as well as a set of operations to query the model (e.g., superior). Additionally, it must feature attributes that are dependent on the currently running process instance (e.g., processStarter).

8.3.2.3 Resource Patterns

Closely related to these three basic assignment policies are the resource patterns [22], which aim at the description of the various ways resources are represented, utilized, and assigned in workflow systems. At this point, 43 different resource patterns[5] have been identified, categorized, and described in detail. The most frequently applied categories are: (1) *Creation patterns* are specified at design time and come into effect at the time a task (or work item) – for an activity that is ready for execution – is created and must be assigned to a resource. The three basic assignment policies explained above are also creation patterns. (2) *Push patterns* describe situations where a new task is automatically distributed to resources for execution by the system, as opposed to (3) *pull patterns*, in which the resource takes the initiative and selects tasks offered by the system, either directly or through a shared worklist. (4) *Detour patterns* refer to situations where tasks are interrupted either by the system or by the assigned resource itself, in order to be delegated to another resource, cancelled, postponed to be finished later, and so on.

8.3.3 Data Perspective

The data or information perspective deals with all kinds of data used by a process and how the data is accessed by the process. The workflow community distinguishes between three different types of data related to a business process [1, 23]. (1) *Workflow relevant data*, also known as case data, is required by the process instance. For instance, data artifacts (like forms) passed from user to user or expressions in conditions to determine a path after an xor-split. Workflow relevant data is primarily of interest for process models. (2) *Application data* is specific to applications invoked by the process and not accessible by the workflow management system (for instance, an external database). (3) *Workflow control data* is only accessed by the workflow

---

[5] http://www.workflowpatterns.com.

engine and is not directly accessible by processes. Examples of this include the current state of process instances, information on recovery and restart points, and so on.

8.3.3.1 Modeling Workflow Relevant Data

The specification of data is required for a thorough understanding of a business process as well as for the execution of a workflow process. In graphical notations like BPMN, the possibilities of representing data usage are usually very limited. Although the BPMN standard describes diverse data-related properties, there is no graphical representation for most of them. A simple example is presented in Fig. 8.5, where an order form is passed from one activity to another activity. BPMN modeling tools usually also allow one to attach sample forms (documents) to the process model, which helps analysts to comprehend which data is used and and how it is accessed in the process.

However, in BPMN there is no possibility to define the structure of the order form with fields, data types, constraints, or to indicate that the variable 'approved' is related to a field of the same name in the order form, which are indispensable features for workflow process definitions. The process definition language XPDL, which can also be used to export BPMN models, features additional data-related concepts, for instance the specification of parameter sets for applications invoked in steps of the process. In the Business Process Execution Language WS-BPEL, the structures of data passed between process and Web services must be specified in XML Schema, which is usually supported by process modeling tools. Accordingly, vendors of BPMN modeling tools that feature XPDL or WS-BPEL export offer additional specification dialogs where data-specific details can be entered (e.g., ActiveBPEL[6], Oryx[7]).

An executable workflow definition requires a lot more information on data. The process definition in Fig. 8.3 shows how the usage of data is specified in the WfMS @enterprise. The field 'hire1' of an attached form 'application_form' is used in an xor-node to determine which path shall be chosen after the activity 'check_application'. In addition to this the process designer must specify the structure of the 'application_form' with the fields it contains and their data types, along with access permissions (read, write) for organizational roles in the different steps of the workflow [9].

---

[6] http://www.activevos.com.

[7] http://bpt.hpi.uni-potsdam.de.

8.3.3.2 Data Flow

Apart from the structure and usage of data in a process, it is also of interest how data is passed between activities of a process. Basically, three different types of data flow can be distinguished [23]:

- *Explicit data flow* – In this approach, the data flow is explicitly modeled between different activities. The data flow transitions are distinct from control flow transitions, but the data flow is not independent from the control flow. For instance, an activity with incoming data flow transitions cannot be executed until the required data arrives, even if it is ready for execution according to the control flow. The BPMN process in Fig. 8.5 contains an explicit data flow, where a document is passed from activity 'Review Order' to activity 'Approve Order'. Please note that as both control flow and data flow between these activities are modeled in the example, they describe the same flow behavior: 'Review Order' must be finished before 'Approve Order' can be started.
- *Implicit data flow integrated with control flow* – In this approach, the control flow is used to pass data from one activity to another. Data and control transitions are always identical. The main disadvantage of this approach is that data created in one activity and required by another activity must be transported over all activities on the path between them. Such an approach is also called 'case processing'. For instance, in administrative processes, a folder of documents is often passed from participant to participant [23].
- *Implicit data flow via shared elements* – This approach is similar to data handling used in many programming languages. Shared data elements (variables) are passed to activities as input or output parameters. This approach is used by the majority of workflow systems. For instance, SAP workflow uses so-called workflow containers to hold all variables accessed in a process[8]. For each step in the process, it is required to define the data flow from the container into each step (before the step is executed) and the data flow from each step into the container (after the step has been finished). The data flow with shared elements can be analyzed by deriving an explicit data flow from the specification of variable accesses in the process steps.

In addition to data flow, BPMN also features *message flow* between activities of different processes in inter-organizational scenarios. Message flows also indicate from where in the internal process external services and processes are accessed. This is also of interest when using BPMN as modeling notation for executable WS-BPEL processes.

8.3.3.3 Data Patterns

Workflow data patterns aim to capture the various ways in which data is represented and utilized in workflows [24]. Thus far, 40 different data patterns have been identi-

---

[8] http://help.sap.com.

fied[9], which were categorized as follows. (1) *Data visibility patterns* describe where workflow related data (including control data and application data) is visible and can be accessed, for example: task data, which is accessible within tasks of a process, or case data, which is accessible by all components of a process during execution. (2) *Data interaction patterns* deal with different variants of data flow within a process (e.g., from task to task, from case to task, etc.), whereas (3) *data transfer patterns* focus on the implementation details of the data flow (e.g., transfer by value or reference, input transformations), and (4) *data-based routing patterns* capture the various ways how data elements interact with information from other perspectives (e.g., pre- and post-conditions for task execution).

8.4 Detection and Avoidance of Control Flow Errors

Many modeling notations and languages allow arbitrary combinations of control flows elements. The reasons for this are very pragmatic: it offers a greater degree of modeling freedom and is easy to learn for non-experts. However, the problem is that arbitrary combinations of control flow patterns enable the specification of process structures which may cause problems during process execution (in a workflow system). As these errors result in very costly failures at run-time, they must be detected and avoided during the process design phase.

8.4.1 Control Flow Errors

Several run time problems may arise due to such control flow errors. The most frequently mentioned include incorrect usage (dangling or unconnected nodes or edges), deadlock or livelock (process is stuck and cannot be finished), unintended multiple execution (activities are executed multiple times), or active termination (process ends, although activities are still active) [17, 18]. Figure 8.7 presents two examples which show that problems are frequently caused by an inappropriate combination of splits and joins of different types. To represent the current state of execution, we added tokens (black dots) to the currently active tasks in the process.

- *Unintended multiple execution* – This example combines an and-split with an xor-join. The and-split produced two tokens, one for each of its successors A1 and B1, and the xor-join passes each received token to its successor C1, which therefore will be executed twice.
- *Deadlock* – This example combines an xor-split with an and-join, which produces a typical deadlock situation. After the execution of activity *A2*, the token is passed to the succeeding and-join, which has to wait for the second token from activity *B2*, which never arrives because the xor-split generated only one token.

---

[9] http://www.workflowpatterns.com.

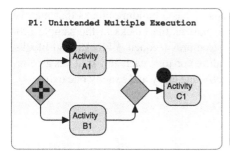
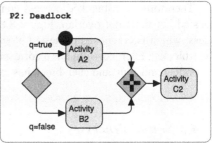

Fig. 8.7 Examples of control flow errors

8.4.2 Blocked Structures

The WfMC distinguishes three different conformance classes for control-flow models: non-blocked, loop-blocked, and full-blocked [10]. (1) *Non-blocked* means that there are no structural restrictions for processes of this class. Activities and control nodes may be connected in an arbitrary order. (2) The conformance class *loop-blocked* demands that for cycles, only a blocked representation may be used (cmp. to loop-statements in structured programming languages). Arbitrary cycles[10] are not allowed, which implies that the activities and transitions of the process definition must form an acyclic directed graph. (3) *Full-blocked* demands that for each split, there is exactly one corresponding join of the same kind.

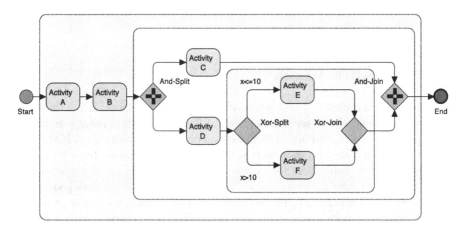

Fig. 8.8 BPMN Sample process – full-blocked control flow

---

[10] Arbitrary cycles are possible in languages with GOTO-statements; which allows jumps from any point to any other point in the process.

Therefore a full-blocked process consists of basic building blocks that may be nested but must not overlap. Figure 8.8 visualizes the blocks in the sample process, which is composed of nested block structures (sequence-blocks, and-blocks, xor-blocks). Each xor-split has a corresponding xor-join, each and-split has a corresponding and-join, and each block has exactly one entry and exactly one exit.

8.4.3 Sound Processes

It is important to note that because of the restrictions imposed on full-blocked models, they render the above mentioned control flow errors impossible [16]. One way of guaranteeing valid control flows, therefore, is to allow only full-blocked control flow models. Some languages and workflow systems, such as SAP workflow or the Business Process Execution Language WS-BPEL, force designers to define the control flow in a full-blocked fashion. Many modeling notations and workflow languages don't, for instance, the languages of Tibco Staffware or @enterprise. They use transition-based models or allow concepts like the goto-statement. Therefore, designers must be made aware of the problems that may occur, as well as of the existence of modeling concepts, patterns, anti-patterns, and verification tools that aim at error-free control flows. To examine process control flow structures and identify possible design errors, the concept of soundness has been introduced. Literally a workflow is sound *"if and only if, for any case, the process terminates properly, i.e., termination is guaranteed, there are no dangling references, and deadlock or livelock are absent"* [19]. To check the soundness and detect control flow errors at build time, verification tools like Woflan [20] may be used. In this section, we briefly describe the formal foundations of the soundness property – as introduced in [19] – which is based on Petri net theory.

8.4.3.1 Petri Nets and WF-Nets

A **Petri net** is a triple (P, T, F), where P is a finite set of places, T is a finite set of transitions, and F is a set of arcs (directed flow relations). A place p is called an input place of a transition t, if there exists a directed arc from t to p. Place p is called an output place of transition p, if there exists a directed arc from p to t. $\bullet t$ denotes the set of input places for a transition t, $t\bullet$ denotes the set of output places for a transition t, and the notations $\bullet p$, $p\bullet$ are to be interpreted analogously for a place p. A *path* is defined by two nodes (place or transition) that are connected by sequences of arcs. A Petri net is *strongly connected* if a directed path exists between any pair of nodes n_1 and n_2, where $n_1, n_2 \in P \cup T, n_1 \neq n_2$.

A workflow net or **WF-net** is a Petri net with two additional constraints. (1) A WF-net has exactly one source place i, where $\bullet i = \emptyset$, and exactly one sink place o, where $o\bullet = \emptyset$. (2) If we add a transition that connects place o with i, then the

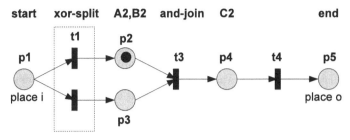

Fig. 8.9 Petri net of Process 2 in Fig. 8.7

resulting Petri net is strongly connected, which means that every node is on a path between the source and the sink (no dangling places or transitions). The example in Fig. 8.9 shows the WF-net representation of Process 2 in Fig. 8.8. As shown, the activities are represented as places, the xor-split as two separate transitions, and the and-join as transition that merges two incoming arcs.

8.4.3.2 Execution of Petri Nets

Petri nets are used to describe and analyze the execution semantics of business processes. Any place may contain an arbitrary number of tokens – drawn as black dots – to represent the current state of execution. The number of tokens in place changes during the execution of the net according to the following firing rules: (1) A transition is enabled if each of its input places contains at least one token. (2) Each enabled transition may fire. (3) If a transition fires, it consumes one token from each input place and produces one token in each output place.

A state – also called marking – is described by a distribution of tokens over places. For instance, $M = (0, 1, 0, 0, 0)$ represents the current state of the process in Fig. 8.9, where place 1 contains no token, place 2 contains 1 token, and so on. A state M_2 is *reachable* from a state M_1 if there exists a firing sequence that produces the state M_2 starting from the state M_1. Figure 8.10 shows the whole reachability graph of the WF-net introduced above, where the initial marking has exactly one token in the input place, followed by two markings that can be reached by either firing transition $t1$ or transition $t2$ (which describes the or-split semantics). After that, no other transition is enabled.

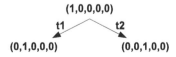

Fig. 8.10 Reachability graph for WF-net in Fig. 8.9

8.4.3.3 Soundness Property

The initial state M_i is described by a marking with exactly one token in the source place i, and the final state M_o is described by a marking where all tokens are in the sink place o and all other places are empty. A WF-net is sound if: (1) For every state M reachable from the initial state M_i, there exists a firing sequence leading from M to the final state M_o. (2) The final state M_o is the only state reachable from the initial state M_i with at least one token in place o. (3) There are no dead transitions, which means that for each transition t there exists a state M that is reachable from M_i, where t is enabled.

The soundness property ensures that for any case, the process can terminate, which means that it contains no infinite loops and is free of deadlocks. Furthermore, there are no activities in the process that cannot be reached, and at the moment the process terminates, there are no active activities. The example process in Fig. 8.9 is not sound, as it violates the condition that the output place o can never be reached, due to a deadlock caused by a wrong combination of xor-split and and-join.

8.5 Process Views

Business process models may contain hundreds of connected activities, augmented with information of diverse perspective, which are – corresponding to the application domain – required for the presentation of the process's universe of discourse. Accordingly, it is hard for various stakeholders in the process lifecycle to get a focus on the areas of interest. For instance, consider a business analyst who wants to examine the activities of certain user groups or roles, a process manager who wants to see the critical regions with error-prone activities or frequently overloaded resources, or a software engineer striving to find out which parts of the process are required to communicate with external processes. Furthermore, external stakeholders might only be allowed to see permitted parts of a process. This can be accomplished by means of *process views*. A process view is an extract of a process that contains only relevant (selected) activities or aggregations of them. Currently, most process view-related research publications are either focused on visualization of process views for different stakeholders (e.g., [25]) or the generation of views with correct control flows (e.g., [26, 27]). The latter either apply activity aggregation or activity elimination methods, assuming that a set of already selected view-relevant control flow elements is given, such that the resulting view fulfills certain correctness criteria. In this section, we outline the formal foundations of view correctness and view generation as described in [27].

8.5.1 Process Graph

A process graph $G = (N, E)$ consists of a set of nodes N and a set of edges E. The type of a node $n \in N$ can either be $n.t = activity$ or one of the control types $n.t = start \mid end \mid or\text{-}split \mid or\text{-}join \mid and\text{-}split \mid and\text{-}join$. An edge $(n_1, n_2) \in E$ determines the execution sequence of two nodes $n_1, n_2 \in N$, such that n_1 must be finished before n_2 can be started. Additionally $n\bullet$ determines a single successor of n and $n\circ$ depicts the set of multiple successors of n (for split nodes). Analogously, we define $\bullet n$ for a single predecessor and $\circ n$ for the set of predecessors (for join nodes).

8.5.2 Correctness of Process Views

In order to construct correct process views, it is necessary that activities in a view have the same ordering as in the original process. In other words, a process view must not change the ordering of the activities of the original workflow. Such a view is called an order-preserving view and is formally defined as follows: A process graph $G' = (N', E')$ is a correct view of a process graph $G = (N, E)$ if the following properties hold:

- G' is a valid full-blocked process graph.
- $N' \subset N$
- $\forall a, b \in N \cap N'$: $[a > b]_{G'} \Leftrightarrow [a > b]_G$, where $[a > b]_{G'}$ and $[a > b]_G$ denote the existence of a directed path between nodes a and b in G and G' respectively.

The second property defines that all nodes of G' must also be nodes of G. The last property defines the requirement that if a node b is a direct or transitive successor of node a in the original process graph, it must also be a direct or transitive successor in the process view.

8.5.3 Generation of Process Views by Activity Elimination

The input for the algorithm is $G = (N, E)$, which must be block-structured, and R, a set of view-relevant activities. The algorithm generates a process view G' by deleting all irrelevant activities $a \in N - R, a.type = activity$ from G while preserving still required control flow structures.

1. **Remove irrelevant activities**: Remove every irrelevant activity $a \in N - R$ from N, and every corresponding edge (a, s) and (p, a) from E, and connect a's predecessor with its successor, which means add (p, s) to E.
2. **Treat and-pairs**: An empty path is a direct connection (s, j) between and-split s and and-join j. If only empty paths between s and j are left, remove both nodes

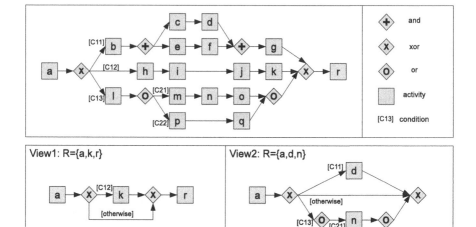

Fig. 8.11 Generation of process views

and corresponding edges, and connect the predecessor of *s* with the successor of *j*. If only a single non-empty path between *s* and *j* is left, remove both nodes and corresponding edges and connect the predecessor of *s* to the successor of *s*, and the predecessor of *j* with the successor of *j*.

3. **Treat (x)or-pairs**: If only empty paths between the (x)or-split *s* and the (x)or-join *j* are left, proceed as in step 2. If at least one empty path and at least one non-empty path are left, then remove the direct edges (*s*, *j*) of all empty paths and add an 'otherwise' edge between *s* and *j*.

The output of the algorithm is again a block-structured valid process graph. Step 3 describes the insertion of an 'otherwise' edge, which is necessary if one or more complete conditional paths between an xor-split and an xor-join are eliminated. This edge expresses the fact that an activity in the view will only be executed under certain conditions defined on the corresponding still existing conditional edge, and otherwise not. Figure 8.11 presents an example of an original process graph along with two views with different sets of relevant activities.

8.6 Timed Processes

Temporal information about business processes, like expected execution durations of activities or process deadlines, is essential for process designers and for process execution. Apart from documentation and simulation purposes, this information can be used to generate timed process graphs, which allow temporal analysis and temporal verification of the process. Examples of this include: the calculation of the

expected remaining time between an activity and the end of the process to be communicated to impatient customers or the prediction of future deadline violations in
already late processes [29]; the identification of activities on the critical path (with
the longest execution duration) to be monitored carefully, as delays on this path will
delay the whole process; or checking the satisfiability of time constraints during design time, which means identifying constraints that are specified too tight and can
therefore never be fulfilled [28]. In this section, we describe how temporal information is modeled in BPMN and show a method which helps to improve the quality
and performance of processes.

8.6.1 Modeling the Temporal Perspective

The temporal perspective of a process comprises different types of temporal information [6]. For instance, activity durations are often used for process analysis
and simulation purposes. Activity durations may stem from empirical knowledge
(extracted from the workflow history, where past process executions are logged),
derived from expert estimations, or even defined by third parties in case an activity communicates with an external process or service. Furthermore, processes may
inhibit different types of time constraints: maximum activity durations and process
deadlines that must not be exceeded, fixed-date constraints to bind the execution
of tasks to certain dates and times, lower bound constraints to specify minimum
time spans between two tasks, or upper bound constraints to specify maximum time
spans between two tasks [14, 28]. Such time constraints usually stem from laws,
organizational rules, or contracts placed with customers (which may also include
penalty payments if a deadline is exceeded).

We have already mentioned that perspectives are sometimes integrated into other
perspectives, which is often the case for temporal information. For instance, the
process definition language XPDL offers task attributes to specify the estimated duration of tasks. Additionally, this duration can be divided into waiting time (queuing
time) and working time (execution time) of a task. Furthermore, XPDL features
timer elements to model deadlines, maximum durations, timed triggers, and even
forced process pauses (e.g., 'wait for one hour'). They can be specified on single
tasks, groups of tasks, a whole process, and on transitions between tasks (to model
pauses). In BPMN, these timers are represented by a specific timer symbol (a clock)

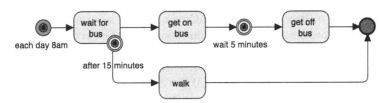

Fig. 8.12 Temporal concepts in BPMN

to be inserted into the control flow of the process. Figure 8.12 shows a simple example of how timer elements are used in a BPMN process model that contains the following temporal concepts: a new process instance will be started each day at 8 a.m.; if activity 'wait for bus' is not finished within 15 minutes, then 'walk', otherwise 'get on bus' then ride the bus for 5 minutes and finally get of the bus.

8.6.2 Timed Graph

Structural control flow information and temporal information about activity durations and process deadlines can be exploited to calculate a timed graph which can be applied for various predictive and proactive time management applications [28, 29].

8.6.2.1 Temporal Information

Explicit temporal information is described by means of [min,max]-intervals. For instance, the expected duration of a node $n \in N$ is denoted by an interval $n.d = [d_{min}, d_{max}]$, which implies that the duration of n will presumably not fall below d_{min} and presumably not exceed d_{max}. Furthermore, a process may be constrained by a maximum duration δ, which must not be exceeded by any process instance. We assume that these values are specified in a predefined basic time unit like seconds, minutes, or hours. The following interval operations are required for the subsequent calculations:

- *Interval addition*: $[a_1, b_1] + [a_2, b_2] = [a_1 + a_2, b_1 + b_2]$
- *Interval subtraction*: $[a_1, b_1] + [a_2, b_2] = [a_1 - a_2, b_1 - b_2]$
- *Interval disjunction*: $[a_1, b_1] \vee [a_2, b_2] = [min(a_1, a_2), max(b_1, b_2)]$
- *Interval conjunction*: $[a_1, b_1] \wedge [a_2, b_2] = [max(a_1, a_2), max(b_1, b_2)]$

As the disjunction and conjunction are commutative and associative, they can be extended to j time intervals t_i denoted as $\bigvee_{i=1}^{j} t_i$ and $\bigwedge_{i=1}^{j} t_i$.

8.6.2.2 Timed Graph Calculation

Now we can calculate three time properties for each node: (1)The *earliest possible start n.eps* of a node n determines the duration between the start of the process and the start of n. It is calculated by adding up durations of nodes in a forward topological sort order, starting from the first node. (2) The *expected remaining time n.rt* of a node n determines the duration between the end of the process and the end of node n. It is calculated by adding up durations of nodes in a backward topological sort order, starting from the end node. (3) If a deadline δ is available, we can also determine the *latest allowed end n.lae* by subtracting the expected remaining time of a node n from the deadline. Table 8.1 gives an overview of the forward and

Table 8.1 Calculation rules per node type

$n.type$	Forward calculation of $n.eps$	Backward calculation of $n.rt$	Calculation of $n.lae$
Start	$[0,0]$	$n\bullet.rt + n\bullet.d$	$\delta - n.rt_{max}$
End	$\bullet n.eps + \bullet n.d$	$[0,0]$	$\delta - n.rt_{max}$
Activity	$\bullet n.eps + \bullet n.d$	$n\bullet.rt + n\bullet.d$	$\delta - n.rt_{max}$
And-split	$\bullet n.eps + \bullet n.d$	$\bigwedge_{\forall s\in no}(s.rt + s.d)$	$\delta - n.rt_{max}$
And-join	$\bigwedge_{\forall p\in on}(p.eps + p.d)$	$n\bullet.rt + n\bullet.d$	$\delta - n.rt_{max}$
Or-split	$\bullet n.eps + \bullet n.d$	$\bigvee_{\forall s\in no}(s.rt + s.d)$	$\delta - n.rt_{max}$
Or-join	$\bigvee_{\forall p\in on}(p.eps + p.d)$	$n\bullet.rt + n\bullet.d$	$\delta - n.rt_{max}$

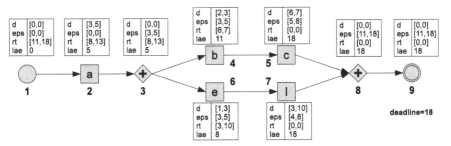

Fig. 8.13 Timed Process Graph

backward calculation operations for each node type. Figure 8.13 shows an example of a timed graph along with timed properties for each node. The numbers below the nodes indicate the forward topological sort order required for the calculation of eps-intervals, which are to be reversed for the backward calculation of rt-intervals. The lae-values are determined by means of the given maximum duration $\delta = 18$ (deadline).

8.6.2.3 Timed Graph Application

The timed graph can be used to achieve several objectives:

- Checking constraint satisfiability – If any $n.lae, n \in N$ is negative, the deadline is defined too tight. To guarantee a violation-free execution, the deadline must be relaxed or the process has to be redesigned. Alternatively, it is also an option to optimize single activities in order to speed them up (decrease their duration $n.d$).
- Determination of buffer times and critical activities – The buffer time (slack) of an activity is extra time that may be consumed without endangering the overall process deadline. It is determined as $n.slack = n.lae - (n.eps_{max} + n.d_{max})$. Buffer time is produced by relaxed deadlines, parallel control flow structures, and during run time by activities that finished faster than expected. Negative buffer times indicate that a future deadline violation is very likely. Critical activities

are activities with zero buffer time – a delay immediately endangers the process deadline, therefore they should be monitored during process execution,

- Scheduling – The earliest possible start time $n.eps$ and latest allowed end time $n.lae$ determine the valid execution interval of an activity n, as it cannot start earlier than $n.eps$ and must not end later than $n.lae$. This knowledge can be exploited for task scheduling and task predispatching when a new process is instantiated.
- Forecasts – At process instantiation and during process run time, the remaining time $n.rt$ enables us to predict the expected remaining duration (or alternatively the finishing date) of a process. Furthermore, the earliest possible start time $n.eps$ can be used to forecast the expected arrival of tasks in order to inform participants about upcoming future tasks.
- Early deadline violation detection and avoidance – The latest allowed end time $n.lae$ defines when an activity n must be finished in order to meet the overall deadline of the process. If this threshold is exceeded during process execution, a future deadline violation is very likely. When the system detects this, diverse (evasive) actions may be invoked, such as adding extra resources to speed up the process, skipping tasks that are not essential (e.g., a second review), calling for administrators' help, early escalation which may save time and money, and so on.

8.7 Conclusions

Business process models and workflow models contain information about different process perspectives. Depending on goals to be achieved and the current stage in the business process life cycle, the information required will vary and therefore also the perspectives that need to be modeled. Correspondingly, it is hard to define common standards for process modeling notations and process definition languages that are suitable for all possible purposes. Nevertheless, great standardization efforts in research and industry are currently under way to close the gap between the disciplines of process modeling and workflow design, for example, business process modeling tools that export executable process definitions to workflow systems or the other way around in re-engineering scenarios. In addition to these standardization efforts, research in the area of process modeling frequently identifies and tackles a great variety of different problems. We have introduced a few selected topics: the detection of control flow problems, the generation of process views, and the calculation and validation of temporal information in timed processes.

References

1. Workflow Management Coalition (1999) Terminology & Glossary. http://www.WfMC.org, document number WFMC-TC-1001
2. White S (2004) Introduction to BPMN. http://www.BPMN.org
3. Workflow Management Coalition (1995) The Workflow Reference Model. http://www.WfMC.org, document number TC00-1003
4. Bussler C, Jablonski S (1996) Workflow Management: Modeling Concepts, Architecture and Implementation. International Thomson Computer Press, London
5. Zur Muehlen M (2002) Workflow-based Process Controlling. Logos, Berlin
6. Gruber W (2004) Modeling and Transformation of Workflows with Temporal Constraints. Akademische Verlagsgesellschaft, Mannheim
7. Knutilla A et al. (1998) Process Specification Language: An Analysis of Existing Representations. US National Institute for Standards and Technology, Gaithersburg
8. Mentzas G, Halaris C, Kavadias S (2001) Modelling business processes with workflow systems: an evaluation of alternative approaches. Int J Inf Manag 21(2):123–135
9. Groiss H (2001) Business Process Management with @enterprise. @enterprise course material. http://www.groiss.com
10. Workflow Management Coalition (1999) Interface 1: Process Definition Interchange – Process Model. http://www.Wfmc.org, document number TC00-1016-P
11. Workflow Management Coalition (2005) Workflow Process Definition Interface – XML Process Definition Language (XPDL). http://www.Wfmc.org, document number WFMC-TC-1025
12. Object Management Group (2009) Business Process Model and Notation (BPMN). Document number: formal/2009-01-03, http://www.OMG.org
13. Barreto C et al. (2009) OASIS Web Services Business Process Execution Language (WS-BPEL). http://www.aasis.org
14. Marjanovic O (2001) Methodological considerations for time Modeling in workflows. In: Proceedings of the twelfth Australasian conference on information systems, Coffs Harbour, December 2001
15. Kiepuszewski B (2002) Expressiveness and suitability of languages for control flow modelling in workflows. PhD thesis, Queensland University of Technology
16. Van der Aalst WMP et al. (2003) Workflow patterns. Distributed and Parallel Databases, 14(3):5–51
17. Sadiq W, Orlowska ME (1999) Applying graph reduction techniques for identifying structural conflicts in process models. In: Proceedings of the 11th international conference on advanced information systems engineering CAiSE June 1999, Heidelberg
18. Kiepuszewski B et al. (2003) Fundamentals of control flow in workflows. Acta Inform 39(3):143–209
19. Van der Aalst, WMP (1997) Verification of workflow nets. In: Proceedings of the 18th international conference on application and theory of Petri nets. Lect Notes Comput Sci 1248:407–426
20. Verbeek H et al. (1999) Diagnosing workflow processes using Woflan. Comput J 44(4)
21. Muehlen MZ (2004) Organizational management in workflow applications–issues and perspectives. Inform Technol Manag 5(3-4)
22. Russell N et al. (2005) Workflow resource patterns: identification, representation and tool support. Lect Notes Comput Sci 3520:216–232
23. Lehmann M (2006) Data Access in Workflow Management Systems. Akademische Verlagsgesellschaft, Mannheim
24. Russell N et al. (2005) Workflow data patterns: identification, representation and tool support. Proceedings of 24th international conference on conceptual modeling ER 2005. Lect Notes Comput Sci 3716:353–368
25. Jablonski S, Goetz M (2008) Perspective oriented business process visualization. Business process management workshops. Lect Notes Comput Sci 4928:144-155

26. Chebbia I, Dustdar S, Tataa S (2006) The view-based approach to dynamic inter-organizational workflow cooperation. Data Knowl Engineer 56(2)56:139–173
27. Tahamtan NA (2009) Modeling and verification of web service composition based interorganizational workflows. PhD thesis, University of Vienna
28. Eder J, Panagos E (2001) Managing time in workflow systems. In: Workflow Handbook 2001, Future Strategies Inc. Workflow Management Coalition (WfMC): 109–132
29. Eder J, Pichler H (2002) Duration Histograms for Workflow Systems. In: IFIP conference proceedings, Kanazawa

Chapter 9
BPMN Core Modeling Concepts: Inheritance-Based Execution Semantics

Egon Börger and Ove Sörensen

Abstract We define an abstract model for the dynamic semantics of the core process modeling concepts in the OMG standard for BPMN 2.0. The UML class diagrams associated therein with each flow element are extended with a rigorous behavior definition, which reflects the inheritance hierarchy structure by refinement steps. The correctness of the resulting precise algorithmic model for an execution semantics for BPMN can be checked by comparing the model directly with the verbal explanations in [8]. Thus, the model can be used to test reference implementations and to verify properties of interest for (classes of) BPMN diagrams. Based on the model the second author has implemented a native BPMN 2.0 Process Engine.[1]

9.1 Introduction

The Business Process Modeling Notation (BPMN) is standardized by the Object Management Group (OMG). We explain here its main modeling concepts with a focus on the behavioral meaning of processes, based upon the currently (March 2010) available OMG document [8]. As a distinctive feature we adapt a stepwise refinement technique to follow the successive detailing of the BPMN execution semantics along the inheritance hierarchy in [8].

Egon Börger
Visiting ETH Zürich, hosted by the Chair for Information Security, on sabbatical leave from Computer Science Department, University of Pisa, Italy, e-mail: boerger@di.unipi.it

Ove Sörensen
Institut für Informatik, Christian-Albrechts-Universität zu Kiel, Olshausenstraße 40, D-24098 Kiel, Germany, e-mail: ove@is.informatik.uni-kiel.de

[1] The work of the first author has been partially supported by a Research Award from the Alexander von Humboldt Foundation (*Humboldt Forschungspreis*) and partially supported by the Italian Government under the project PRIN 2007 D-ASAP (2007XKEHFA).

D. W. Embley and B. Thalheim (eds), *Handbook of Conceptual Modeling.*
DOI 10.1007/978-3-642-15865-0, © Springer 2011

We associate with each UML class diagram defined in [8] for the syntax of behavioral BPMN elements a description of their behavior. These descriptions make the natural language formulations in the standard document precise at the minimal level of rigor needed to faithfully capture a common understanding of business processes by business analysts and operators, information technology specialists and users (suppliers and customers). Such a common understanding, which must not be obfuscated by mere formalization features, is crucial to faithfully link the three different views of business processes by designers, implementors, and users.

To obtain such a *precise, inheritance-hierarchy-based high-level description of the execution semantics of BPMN*, we use the semantic framework developed in [6] for business process modeling notations and applied there to BPMN 1.0 [7]. Since it is based only on standard document terms, it allows one to check by direct inspection the faithfulness of the description with respect to the verbal explanations in [8]. On the other hand, the rigorous operational character of the description offers the possibility to use it as the reference model for two purposes: (a) for testing and for comparing different implementations among them and with the refinement of the model to an implementation of a native BPMN 2.0 Process Engine in [9], where processes can be linked with graphical models; (b) for a mathematical analysis of properties of interest for classes of BPMN process diagrams, comparable to the Event-B-based work done in 2010 by W. Wei (pers. comm.). Since the standardization process is still ongoing, our BPMN model leaves all those issues open that are not (yet?) sufficiently clarified in [8]. However, our work shows that it would have been possible to provide a succinct and complete, rigorous, and thereby objectively checkable BPMN execution semantics, although the OMG standardization committee seems to have voted against such an endeavor ([8], Chap. 14) in favor of an informal description with various loose ends that later implementations will have to clarify.

Technically speaking, we assume the reader has an understanding of what it means to execute simultaneously finitely many transition rules of the form

if *Condition* **then** *Actions*

prescribing a set of actions to be undertaken if some events happen; the occurrence of events is expressed by conditions becoming true. For a simple foundation of the semantics of such rule systems, which constitute abstract state machines (ASMs) and can be viewed as a rigorous form of pseudocode, we refer the interested reader to [5]. Such rules are inserted as behavioral elements at appropriate places in the BPMN class hierarchy. The ASM refinement concept supports strictly following the inheritance steps in the BPMN class hierarchy. In Sect. 9.2 we describe the class hierarchy of BPMN elements, focusing on message flow and the behaviorally relevant diagram structure, which is represented by the so-called sequence flow of flow nodes. In Sects. 9.3–9.5 we describe the three main subclasses of the BPMN *FlowNode* class, namely, for gateways, activities, and events. To avoid repetitions, we frequently rely upon the explanations or illustrating diagrams in the standard document and assume the reader will have a copy of it at hand.

9.2 Structure of the Class Hierarchy of BPMN 2.0

We restrict our attention to those features of the BPMN class hierarchy that are relevant for the behavioral description of single processes, namely, diagram structure, flow elements, and message flow. The class *FlowElement* in [8], Fig. 8.23, contains, besides *SequenceFlows* and *FlowNodes*, also *Data objects*, which we represent by ASM locations. Their read/write operations represent what is called a "data association execution" ([8], Fig. 10.63). Due to space limitations we investigate the single process view (called orchestration) and treat process interaction features – the collaboration of and communication between processes, called choreography – in terms of abstract interface conditions.

9.2.1 Message Flow

The interaction between multiple processes happens in BPMN via communication (messages between pools, activities, and events) or shared data. The concept of monitored locations in the ASM framework provides an exact interface of process instances to message handling, which abstracts in particular from the BPMN choreography diagrams in [8, Sect. 12], and in particular from correlation issues for the delivery of messages. Consider an abstract operation SEND($payload(m)$, $receiver(m)$) that is refined for all related elements of the BPMN *MessageFlow* class diagram [8, Fig. 8.38]; we write *sender* for *sourceRef* and *receiver* for *targetRef*. The operation is restricted by the stipulation that the receiver of a message is a participant (here appearing as a pool), an activity, or an event. Thus message arrival is reflected as an update by $payload(m)$ of a location that is monitored by $receiver(m)$; reading a message means to read such a monitored location.

9.2.2 Diagram Structure (Sequence Flow)

The BPMN diagram structure is used to pictorially represent a business process and is defined by the *SequenceFlow* class diagram [8, Fig. 8.48]. The sequence ("control") flow shows the order of flow elements in a process. Such a diagram is a graph of flow nodes (gateways, activities, events) connected by arcs (Fig. 9.1).

Therefore we use standard graph-theoretic concepts like *source*(*arc*) and *target* (*arc*) for the source and target nodes of an *arc* (denoted *sourceRef* resp. *targetRef* and restricted by [8, Table 8.60], to certain flow nodes), *pred*(*node*) for the (possibly ordered) set of source nodes of arcs with target *node*, *inArc*(*node*) for the set of arcs ingoing the target *node*, *succ*(*node*) for the (possibly ordered) set of target nodes of arcs with source *node*, *outArc*(*node*) for the set of arcs outgoing the source *node*, etc. If in a diagram a node has only one incoming or one outgoing arc, and if from the context the node in question is clear, we write *in*/*out* instead of *inArc*(*node*) = {*in*}*outArc*(*node*) = {*out*}.

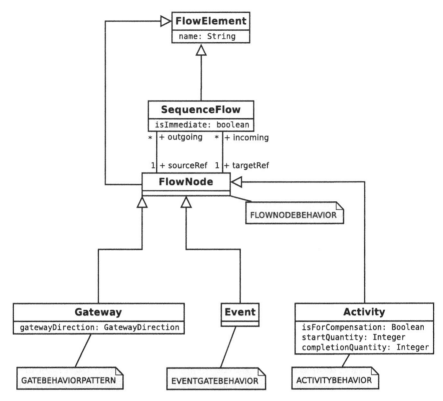

Fig. 9.1 Basic class hierarchy of diagram contents

We model the token-based BPMN interpretation of control flow by associating tokens – elements of an abstract set *Token* – to arcs, using a dynamic function *token(arc)*. Since a token is characterized by the process ID of the process instance *pi* to which it belongs (via its creation at the start of the process instance), we distinguish tokens belonging to different instances of one process *p*, writing *token$_{pi}$* to represent the current token marking in the process diagram instance of the process instance *pi* a token belongs to. Thus *token$_{pi}$(arc)* denotes the multiset of tokens belonging to process instance *pi* and currently residing on *arc*. We can suppress the parameter *pi* due to the single process view where *pi* is clear from the context.

For a *rule* at a target node of incoming arcs to become fireable some arcs must be *Enabled* by tokens being available at the arcs. This condition is usually required to be an atomic quantity formula stating that the number of tokens (belonging to a process instance *pi*) and currently associated to *in* (read: the cardinality of *token$_{pi}$(in)*, denoted | *token$_{pi}$(in)* |, used in particular in connection with complex gateways and called there *ActivationCount*, but also for readying activities where it is called *StartQuantity*) is at least the quantity *inQty(in)* required for incoming tokens at this arc. Unless otherwise stated the assumption is made that *inQty(in)* = 1, as suggested by the warning in Table 10.3, Sect. 14.2.2. [8].

$Enabled(in) = (\mid token(in) \mid \geq inQty(in))$

Correspondingly the control operation CTLOP of a workflow usually consists of two parts, one describing which (how many) tokens are CONSUMEd on which incoming arcs and one describing which (how many) tokens are PRODUCEd on which outgoing arcs, indicated by using an analogous abstract function *outQty* (for activities called *CompletionQuantity*). We use macros to encapsulate the details.

$CONSUME(t, in) = DELETE(t, inQty(in), token(in))$
$PRODUCE(t, out) = INSERT(t, outQty(out), token(out))$
$CONSUMEALL(X) = \textbf{forall } x \in X \ CONSUME(x)$
$PRODUCEALL(Y) = \textbf{forall } y \in Y \ PRODUCE(y)$

The use of abstract DELETE and INSERT operations instead of directly updating $token(a, t)$ serves to make the macros usable in a concurrent context, where multiple agents may want to simultaneously operate on the tokens on an arc. It is also consistent with the special case that in a transition with both DELETE(in, t) and INSERT(out, t) one may have $in = out$, so that the two operations are not considered as inconsistent, but with a cumulative effect.

Structural relations between the consumed incoming and the produced outgoing tokens can be expressed by using an abstract function *firingToken*(A), which is assumed to select for each element a of an ordered set A of incoming arc tokens from $token_{pi}(a)$ that enable a and can be CONSUMEd. *firingToken*$([a_1, \ldots, a_n])$ $= [t_1, \ldots, t_n]$ denotes that for each i, t_i is the (set of) token occurrence(s) selected to be fired on arc a_i. We write *firingToken*$(in) = t$ instead of *firingToken* $(\{in\}) = [t]$. Apparently the idea of a hierarchical token structure, which appeared in [8] and was modeled in [6], has been abandoned for BPMN 2.0 [10] so that we write CONSUME(in) and PRODUCE(out), where the type of underlying tokens (assumed to belong to one process instance) is irrelevant or clear from the context.

9.2.3 Flow Nodes

The behaviorally central class is *FlowNode*, a subclass of *FlowElement* and coming with subclasses *Gateway*, *Activity*, *Event* (as explained above, we disregard the fourth subclass *ChoreographyActivity*). Each instance *node* of this subclass represents a workflow construct whose behavioral meaning is expressed by a transition rule FLOWNODEBEHAVIOR$(node)$ stating upon which events and under which further conditions – typically on the control flow, the underlying data, and the availability of resources – the rule can fire to execute the following actions:

- Perform specific operations on the underlying data ("how to change the internal state") and control flow ("where to proceed").
- Possibly trigger new events (besides consuming the triggering ones) and releasing some resources.

FLOWNODEBEHAVIOR($node$) =
   if $EventCond(node)$ **and** $CtlCond(node)$ **and** $DataCond(node)$
      and $ResourceCond(node)$ **then**
         DATAOP($node$)
         CTLOP($node$)
         EVENTOP($node$)
         RESOURCEOP($node$)

FLOWNODEBEHAVIOR, associated with the class *FlowNode*, is a rule scheme, technically an ASM with well-defined semantics (see [5]). Its abstractions are refined by further detailing in the next three sections the guards (conditions) resp. the operations (submachines) for workflow transitions to describe the behavioral meaning for instances of each of the three subclasses of *FlowNode*. When we need to consider to which process instance a flow *node* instance belongs, we write *procInst(node)*, to be distinguished from *process(node)* (the BPMN diagram) *node* belongs to.

9.3 Gateways

Gateway is a subclass of *FlowNode* used to describe the divergence (splitting) or convergence (merging) of control flow [8, p. 263] in two forms:

- To create parallel actions or to synchronize multiple actions,
- To select (one or more) among some alternative actions.

Gateway has five concrete subclasses for exclusive, inclusive, parallel, event-based, and complex gateways (Fig. 9.2), which come with specific constraints (formulated in [8, Table 8.47]) in terms of an attribute *gatewayDirection* on the number of their incoming and outgoing arcs.

Each gateway behavior is an instance of a scheme GATEBEHAVIORPATTERN associated with the abstract class *Gateway* and is defined as follows, refining the FLOWNODEBEHAVIOR: two (possibly ordered) sets of incoming resp. of outgoing arcs are selected where tokens are consumed resp. produced. To describe these sets we use functions the $select_{Consume}(node)$ and $select_{Produce}(node)$, which will be constrained in various ways for specific gateways. The general control condition[2] is that all arcs in the selected (usually required or assumed to be nonempty) set of incoming arcs are enabled and that the process instance the gateway *node* belongs to is *Active* (see Sect. 9.4 for the concept of activity lifecycle). The control operation consists in (a) consuming the firing tokens on each selected incoming arc and (b) producing the required tokens on each selected outgoing arc (in the normal case that no exception occurs). DATAOP($node$) consists of multiple *assignments(o)* associated to the outgoing arcs o.

The THROW($exc, node$) macro is used to indicate when an *exception* is thrown from a *node* to its possible catcher, triggering an event that is attached to the inner-

---

[2] Except the special case analyzed in Sect. 9.3.4.1 of an event-based gateway used to start a process.

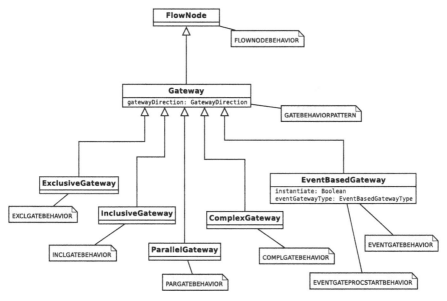

Fig. 9.2 Basic class hierarchy of gateways

most enclosing scope instance (if any) and may be able to catch the *ex*ception. We assume a detailed definition of this macro to include the performance of the data association for throw events. This has the effect that when a throw event is triggered, it happens with the corresponding data in its scope assigned to what [8] calls the "event data," from where the related catch event assigns them (Sect. 9.5) to the so-called data elements in the scope of the catch event [8, Sect.10.4.1].

GATEBEHAVIORPATTERN(*node*) =
   let I = *select*$_{\text{Consume}}$(*node*)
   let O = *select*$_{\text{Produce}}$(*node*)
      FLOWNODEBEHAVIOR(*node, I, O*) **where**
  CtlCond(*node, I*) = **forall** *in* $\in$ *I Enabled*(*in*)
        and *Active*(*procInst*(*node*))
CTLOP(*node, I, O*) =
   CONSUMEALL($\{(t_j, in_j) \mid 1 \leq j \leq n\}$)
      where $[t_1, \ldots, t_n]$ = *firingToken*(*I*), $[in_1, \ldots, i\,n_n]$ = *I*
   if *NormalCase*(*node*) **then** PRODUCEALL(*O*)
     else THROW(*GateExc, node*)
DATAOP(*node, O*) = **forall** $o \in O$
   forall $i \in assignments(o)$ ASSIGN($to_i, from_i$)

Active(p) = (lifeCycle(p) = active)
We now refine this rule to the behavior of the five gateway subclasses.

9.3.1 Parallel Gateway (Fork and Join)

PARGATEBEHAVIOR is associated with the class *ParallelGateway*. Its behavior is to synchronize multiple concurrent branches (called AND-Join) by consuming one token on each incoming arc, and to spawn new concurrent threads (called AND-Split or Fork) by producing one token on each outgoing arc. A parallel gateway is not allowed to throw an exception. Thus it refines GATEBEHAVIORPATTERN.

$\text{PARGATEBEHAVIOR}(node) = \text{GATEBEHAVIORPATTERN}(node)$ **where**
$select_{\text{Consume}}(node) = inArc(node)$ // AND-JOIN merging behavior
$select_{\text{Produce}}(node) = outArc(node)$ // AND-SPLIT (branching behavior
$NormalCase(node) = true$ // gate throws no exception
forall $in \in inArc(node)$ $inQty(in) = 1$
forall $out \in outArc(node)$ $outQty(out) = 1^3$

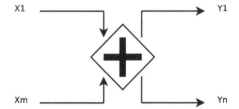

Fig. 9.3 Parallel gateway – unconditionally spawn and synchronize threads of execution

9.3.2 Exclusive Gateway (Data-Based Exclusive Decision)

EXCLGATEBEHAVIOR is associated with the class *ExclusiveGateway*.

Its behavior is to react to the enabledness of just one incoming arc (no matter which one, a feature named *pass-through semantics*), namely, by consuming an enabling token, and to enable exactly one outgoing arc, namely, the first one (in the diagram order) whose associated *DataCond*ition evaluates to true (so-called exclusive data-based decision). Usually a default case is specified to cover the situation where

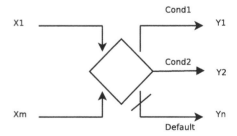

Fig. 9.4 Exclusive gateway – choose exactly one thread of execution for synchronization and spawning

---

[3] The two constraints on *inQty* and *outQty* seem to be intended for all flow node instances, except where stated differently, so that from now on we assume them to be added implicitly.

none of these *DataCond*itions is true; otherwise in this case an exception is thrown. Thus EXCLGATEBEHAVIOR is an instantiation of GATEBEHAVIORPATTERN.

EXCLGATEBEHAVIOR(*node*) $=$ GATEBEHAVIORPATTERN(*node*) **where**
  | *select*$_{\text{Consume}}$(*node*) |$= 1$ // exclusive merge
  select$_{\text{Produce}}$(*node*) $= fst(\{a \in outArc(node) \mid DataCond(a)\})$
  NormalCase(*node*) if and only if
    $\{a \in outArc(node) \mid DataCond(a)\} \neq \emptyset$ **or**
      some default sequence flow is specified at *node*

9.3.3 Inclusive Gateway

INCLGATEBEHAVIOR is associated with the class *InclusiveGateway*.

It enables every outgoing arc whose associated *DataCond*ition is true (branching [8, 10.5.3]), with the same convention on exceptions as for exclusive gateways, and to synchronize the (required-to-be-nonempty) set of incoming arcs that are enabled or have an "upstream token" (*UpstreamToken* $\neq \emptyset$) in the graph, not waiting for tokens on those unenabled arcs that "have no token upstream."

INCLGATEBEHAVIOR(*node*) $=$ GATEBEHAVIORPATTERN(*node*) **where**
  select$_{\text{Consume}}$(*node*) $=$ // NB. all to be enabled to fire
    $\{in \in inArc(node) \mid Enabled(in)$ **or** $UpstreamToken(in) \neq \emptyset\}$
  select$_{\text{Produce}}$(*node*) $= \{a \in outArc(node) \mid DataCond(a)\}$
  CtlCond(*node*, *I*, *O*) $=$
    CtlCond$_{\text{GATEBEHAVIORPATTERN}}$(*node*, *I*, *O*) **and** $I \neq \emptyset$
  NormalCase(*node*) $= NormalCase_{\text{EXCLGATEBEHAVIOR}}(node)$

An incoming arc "without token anywhere upstream" is defined in [8, Table 14.3], as an unenabled arc to which there is no directed sequence flow *path* from any (arc with a) token unless

- *path* visits the inclusive gateway or
- *path* visits a node that has a directed path to a nonempty incoming sequence flow of the inclusive gateway and does not visit the gateway.[4]

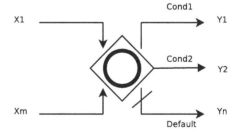

Fig. 9.5 Inclusive gateway – synchronize and spawn some threads of execution

---

[4] The last conjunct has been added in [10], correcting the definition which originally appeared in [8]. Upstream tokens are called there tokens that have an inhibiting path but no anti-inhibiting path to the gateway.

$t \in UpstreamToken(in)$ if and only if $InhibitingPath(t, in) \neq \emptyset$ **and**
thereIsNo $j \in inArc(node)$ $AntiInhibitingPath(t, j) \neq \emptyset$
where
   $p \in InhibitingPath(t, in) =$
      $p \in Path(t, in)$ **and** $token(in) = \emptyset$ **and** $target(in) \notin VisitedBy(p)$
   $p \in AntiInhibitingPath(t, in) =$
      $p \in Path(t, in)$ **and** $token(in) \neq \emptyset$ **and** $target(in) \notin VisitedBy(p)$
   $VisitedBy(p) = \{n \mid n \in Node$ **and** n occurs as source or target on $p\}$
   $Path(t, in) = Path(arc, in)$ **if** $t \in token(arc)$

9.3.4 Event-Based Gateway (Event-Based Exclusive Decision)

For event-based gateways the standard describes two behaviors, depending on whether the gateway is used to start a process or not, resulting in two ASM rules associated to the class *EventBasedGateway*. The EVENTGATEBEHAVIOR for the second case, in which the gateway is required to have some incoming sequence flow, is pictorially represented by Fig. 9.6. In the first case the event-based gateway may have no (or only some special) incoming sequence flow; its EVENTGATEPROCSTARTBEHAVIOR is described in Sect. 9.3.4.1.

EVENTGATEBEHAVIOR does not throw any exception. It has pass-through semantics for incoming sequence flow and the activated outgoing arc is defined to be the first one at which an associated *gateEvent Occurs* and can be CONSUMEd. Thus EVENTGATEBEHAVIOR refines GATEBEHAVIORPATTERN as follows:

- $select_{Consume}(node)$ chooses for each activation one incoming sequence flow.
- $select_{Produce}(node)$ yields one (dynamically determined[5]) outgoing sequence flow, namely, the one whose associated *gateEvent Occurs* first (so-called exclusive event-based decision).
- $NormalCase(node) = true$: event-based gateways "cannot throw any exception."
- The selected *gateEvent* is CONSUMEd.

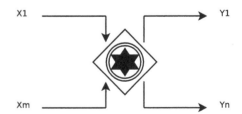

Fig. 9.6 Event-based gateway
– choose exactly one thread of
execution, depending on the
first triggered gate event

---

[5] The standard document interprets this choice as "deferred until one of the subsequent Tasks or Events completes" [8, Sect. 14.3.3]. This creates an ambiguity for two successive enablings of the gate with deferred choice of an outgoing branch. We avoid this ambiguity by letting EVENTGATEBEHAVIOR fire only when the choice is possible due to at least one gate event occurring.

We use a dynamic function *fst* to select an outgoing arc among those whose associated *gateEvent* (required to be either an *event* that has to be *Triggered* or a *receiveTask* that has to be *Completed*) *Occurs* "first"; *fst* resolves the conflict for concurrently occurring events. Receive tasks are tasks that wait for a message to arrive and are *Completed* by receiving the message [8, p. 139 and Sect. 9.4.1].

EVENTGATEBEHAVIOR($node$) = // case with incoming arcs
   GATEBEHAVIORPATTERN($node$) **where**
| $select_{\mathrm{Consume}}(node)$ |= 1
$EventCond(node) =$
               forsome $a \in outArc(node)$ $Occurs(gateEvent(a))$
$select_{\mathrm{Produce}}(node) = fst(\{a \in outArc(node) \mid Occurs(gateEvent(a))\})$
EVENTOP($node$) = CONSUME($gateEvent(select_{\mathrm{Produce}}(node))$)
$NormalCase(node) = true$ // event gate throws no exception
$Occurs(gateEvent(a)) =$
  $\begin{cases} Triggered(event(a)) & \textbf{if } gateEvent(a) = event(a) \\ Completed(receiveTask(a)) & \textbf{if } gateEvent(a) = receiveTask(a) \end{cases}$

9.3.4.1 Event-Based Gateways for Process Start

If event-based gateways are used to start a process P, to be declared by setting their *instantiate* attribute to true, it is required that (except for the case described in the next footnote) they have no incoming sequence flow – the only case of gateways with no ingoing arc [8, Sect. 14.4.1].[6] The standard document considers two cases depending on whether there is only one event-based gateway (called *exclusive event-based gateway*) or a group of multiple event-based gateways that are used to start P. Such group elements are required to participate in the same conversation, and at each gateway one event "needs to arrive; the first one creates a new process instance, while the subsequent ones are routed to the existing instance" [8, Sect. 14.4.1] "rather than creating new process instances" [8, p. 402]. In both cases EVENTGATEPROCSTARTBEHAVIOR is obtained by analogous refinement conditions as for event-based gateways with incoming sequence flow; however, the incoming arc selection and related control condition are empty and the control operation essentially creates a new instance of P.

To precisely reflect what is intended to happen when some expected gate events happen concurrently at multiple event-based gateways belonging to the same *group* (and to avoid a repetition of the first part of the behavior, which is almost the same for singleton and multiple-element groups), we use a virtual node *group* to which EVENTGATEPROCSTARTBEHAVIOR is attached.[7] The formulation uses two *modes*

---

[6] The allowed case of incoming sequence flow whose source is an untyped start event [8, p. 276] is covered by the description explained below, including the usual conditions and operations for pass-through semantics.

[7] The standard document makes the distinction in terms of an *eventGatewayType* attribute set to *parallel* for the case of multiple *group* elements.

with corresponding subbehaviors, the second one being performed only if the group has more than one element. This reflects the requirement that for *group*s with multiple elements upon a "first" event a new process instance is created "while the subsequent ones are routed to the existing instance" [8, p. 252].

$$\text{EVENTGATEPROCSTARTBEHAVIOR}(group) =$$
$$\text{EVENTGATEPROCSTARTBEHAVIOR}_{\text{Start}}(group)$$
$$\text{EVENTGATEPROCSTARTBEHAVIOR}_{\text{Progress}}(group)$$

In *mode* = *Start*, upon the "first" arrival of an event EVENTGATEPROCSTART BEHAVIOR$_{\text{Start}}$ performs the following three actions:

- Create a new instance of the to-be-started process and make it *Active*.[8]
- Mimic the EVENTGATEBEHAVIOR(g) for a node $g \in$ *group* where a *gate Event Occurs* "first."
- In case there are other group members, switch to *mode* = *Progress*, whereby the EVENTGATEPROCSTARTBEHAVIOR$_{\text{Progress}}$ becomes firable if some *gate Event Occurs* at some other group member.

We use the dynamic abstract function *fst* here to select both a *group* member and an outgoing arc where a "first" *gateEvent Occurs*.

$$\text{EVENTGATEPROCSTARTBEHAVIOR}_{\text{Start}}(group) =$$
$$\text{GATEBEHAVIORPATTERN}(group) \quad \textbf{where}$$
$$select_{\text{Consume}}(group) = \emptyset$$
$$CtlCond(group) = (mode(group) = Start)$$
$$EventCond(group) = \textbf{forsome } g \in group \; Occurs(gateEvent(g))$$
$$\textbf{let } g = fst(\{ g \in group \mid Occurs(gateEvent(g)) \})$$
$$\quad select_{\text{Produce}}(group) = fst(\{ a \in outArc(g) \mid$$
$$\qquad Occurs(gateEvent(g, a)) \})$$
$$\quad \text{CTLOP}(group, O) =$$
$$\qquad \textbf{let } P = \textbf{new } Instance(process(group))$$
$$\qquad\quad \text{PRODUCE}(select_{\text{Produce}}(group)_{\text{P}})$$
$$\qquad\quad lastCreatedProcInst(group) := P$$
$$\qquad\quad lifeCycle(P) := active$$
$$\qquad Seen(g) := true$$
$$\qquad \textbf{if } \mid group \mid > 1 \textbf{ then } mode := Progress$$
$$\qquad \text{EVENTOP}(group) = \text{CONSUME}(gateEvent(select_{\text{Produce}}(g)))$$
$$\quad NormalCase(group) = true \; // \text{ no event gate throws an exception}$$
$$\quad Occurs(gateEvent(g)) = \textbf{forsome } a \in$$
$$\qquad outArc(g) Occurs(gateEvent(g, a))$$

---

[8] In general upon being enabled a process first becomes *Ready* and can GETACTIVE only after some input became available, see Sect. 9.4. But since at an event-based gateway the only allowed triggers are catch events or receive tasks that have no input data assignment, the newly created process becomes immediately *Active*.

EVENTGATEPROCSTARTBEHAVIOR$_{\text{Progress}}$ is executed in *mode* $=$ *Progress* each time a *gateEvent* for a remaining *group* member *Occurs* – until each *group* member has been *Seen*, in which case *mode*(*group*) switches back to *Start* and resets *Seen*.[9] The standard document leaves this case underspecified. For definiteness we formulate here the following interpretation: (a) once a *group* element has been *Seen* (because one of its *gateEvent*s *Occurs*), it is not reconsidered for another *gateEvent* to *Occur* before each group element has been *Seen*; (b) no subsequent *gateEvent* PRODUCES additional tokens (on the arc where the *gateEvent Occurs*) before each group element has been *Seen*.

EVENTGATEPROCSTARTBEHAVIOR$_{\text{Progress}}$(*group*) $=$
 GATEBEHAVIORPATTERN(*group*) **where**
select$_{\text{Consume}}$(*group*) $= \emptyset$
CtlCond(*group*) $= (mode(group) = Progress)$
EventCond(*group*) $=$
 forsome $g \in \{g \in group \mid$ **not** $Seen(g)\}$ $Occurs(gateEvent(g))$
let $g = fst(\{g' \in group \mid Occurs(gateEvent(g'))$ **and** **not** $Seen(g')\})$
 select$_{\text{Produce}}$(*group*) $= fst(\{a \in outArc(g) \mid$
    $Occurs(gateEvent(g, a))\})$
  EVENTOP(*group*) $=$ CONSUME(*gateEvent*(*select*$_{\text{Produce}}$(*group*)))
  CTLOP(*group*, O) $=$
   if $LastSeen(g, group)$ **then** // reset *group* state
    $mode(group) := Start$
     forall $g' \in group$ $Seen(g') := false$
   else $Seen(g) := true$
    PRODUCE(*select*$_{\text{Produce}}$(*group*)$_{\text{lastCreatedProcInst(group)}}$)
NormalCase(*group*) $= true$
LastSeen(g, *group*) $= (group = \{g' \mid Seen(g')\} \cup \{g\})$

9.3.5 Complex Gateway

COMPLGATEBEHAVIOR is associated with the class *ComplexGateway*. It has two rules [8, Table 14.5]: COMPLGATEBEHAVIOR$_{\text{start}}$ describing the behavior in mode *waitingForStart* and COMPLGATEBEHAVIOR$_{\text{reset}}$ for *reset* mode.

$$\text{COMPLGATEBEHAVIOR} = \frac{\text{COMPLGATEBEHAVIOR}_{\text{start}}}{\text{COMPLGATEBEHAVIOR}_{\text{reset}}}$$

If *waitingForStart*, a complex gateway waits for its *activationCondition* to become true. This attribute expresses a (somehow restricted) condition on data and the number of tokens on incoming arcs (called *activationCount*) so that we represent it as *DataCond*. When the rule fires, it consumes a token from each enabled

---

[9] This reflects the standard document requirement that "one event out of each group" has to arrive to complete the process instance created upon the "first" arrival of an event.

Fig. 9.7 Complex gateway – user-defined split-
ting/synchronizing behavior

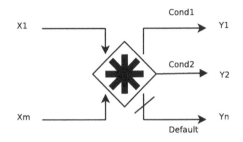

incoming arc and produces a token on each outgoing arc whose associated condition is true. The evaluated expressions may depend on the value of *waitingForStart*.
If none of these conditions is true and no default flow has been specified, an exception is thrown. In addition, when no exception occurs, (a) the mode switches by
setting *waitingForStart* to false and (b) the set of in *waitingForStart* mode enabled
incoming arcs (where therefore a token has been consumed) is recorded for use in
reset mode. Thus COMPLGATEBEHAVIOR$_{start}$ refines GATEBEHAVIORPATTERN as
follows:

COMPLGATEBEHAVIOR$_{start}$(*node*) = GATEBEHAVIORPATTERN(*node*)
where
DataCond(*node*) = *activationCondition*(*node*) **and**
        waitingForStart(*node*)
select$_{Consume}$(*node*) = {*in* ∈ *inArc*(*node*) | *Enabled*(*in*)}
select$_{Produce}$(*node*) = {*o* ∈ *outArc*(*node*) | *DataCond*(*a*) = *true*}
CTLOP(*node*, *I*, *O*) =
    CTLOP$_{GATEBEHAVIORPATTERN}$(*node*, *I*, *O*)
    if *NormalCase*(*node*) **then**
        atStartEnabledArc(*node*) := *select*$_{Consume}$(*node*)
        waitingForStart := *false*
NormalCase(*node*) = *NormalCase*$_{EXCLGATEBEHAVIOR}$(*node*)

In the *reset* case (i.e., if *waitingForStart* = *false*), a complex gateway awaits a token on each incoming arc that has not been enabled when *waitingFor*
Start, except on unenabled arcs that have no token upstream (as defined above
for inclusive gateways). It consumes tokens from each of these arcs, produces
a token on each outgoing arc whose associated condition is true, and resets its
mode to *waitingForStart* = *true*. No exception is thrown in *reset* mode. Thus
COMPLGATEBEHAVIOR$_{reset}$ is an instantiation of GATEBEHAVIORPATTERN, refined as follows:

COMPLGATEBEHAVIOR$_{reset}$(*node*) = GATEBEHAVIORPATTERN(*node*)
where
    DataCond(*node*) = **not** *waitingForStart*(*node*)
    select$_{Consume}$(*node*) = {*in* ∈ *inArc*(*node*) \ *atStartEnabledArc*(*node*) |
    Enabled(*in*) **or** *UpstreamToken*(*in*) ≠ ∅}
        // NB. all to be enabled to fire

$select_{Produce}(node) = \{o \in outArc(node) \mid DataCond(a) = true\}$
$\text{CTLOP}(node, I, O) =$
$\quad \text{CTLOP}_{\text{GATEBEHAVIORPATTERN}}(node, I, O)$
$\quad waitingForStart := true$
$NormalCase(node) = true \mathbin{/\!/} \text{no exception thrown in mode } reset$

9.4 Activities

The *Activity* subclass of *FlowNode* is associated with an ACTIVITYBEHAVIOR that describes the general form of the behavior of an *Activity* node, whether atomic or compound and whether performed once or repeatedly. It is refined for each of the three subclasses *Task*, *SubProcess*, and *CallActivity* of *Activity* (Fig. 9.8).

Activities have associated *InputSets* and *OutputSets* that define the data requirements for input/output to/from the activity (via an *InputOutputSpecification*; [8, Fig. 10.54]. At least one InputSet must be *Available* for the activity to become *Active* with data input from the first *Available* set; at the *completion* of the activity, some data output may be produced from the first *Available* OutputSet if it satisfies the activity's IORule expressing a relationship between that OutputSet and the InputSet used to start the activity. An exception is thrown if there is no *Available* OutputSet at all or if the IORule is not satisfied for the first *Available* OutputSet [8, Sect. 14.2.2].

Activities can be without incoming sequence flow. Examples are compensation activities, (event) subprocesses, and a Receive task in a process without start event

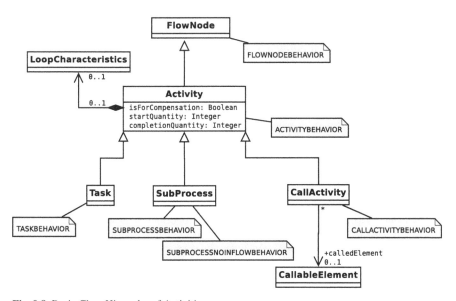

Fig. 9.8 Basic Class Hierarchy of Activities

that is used to start this process. We treat such specialized activities separately and describe first the behavior of activities that do have some incoming sequence flow.

When at least one among possibly multiple incoming arcs is *Enabled*[10] (so-called uncontrolled flow), a new activity instance is created, is linked by a *parent* function to the process that triggered it, and becomes *Ready* waiting to GET ACTIVE.[11] The two parameters for the corresponding set *InstSet* of process instances and the trigger process *TriggerProc* will be instantiated below to describe variations of this ACTIVITYENTRY behavior. If the activity is not *Interrupted*, its lifecycle switches to *Active*, to STARTEXECution, after an input set from *Inputsets* becomes *Available* (in which case this set is recorded for use when the activity is completed) [8, pp. 130, 393]. *select*$_{\text{InputSets}}$ expresses which input set is chosen, specified by the standard document as the first available input set (with respect to a given order). INTERRUPT, among others, switches the *lifeCycle* to *Withdrawn, Failed,* or *Terminated*; we abstain from completing here the loose declaration of intents for the activity lifecylce in [8, Sect. 14.2.2].

ACTIVITYENTRY(*node, InstSet, TriggerProc*) =
        FLOWNODEBEHAVIOR(*node*)
where
CtlCond(*node*) = **forsome** *in* ∈ *inArc*(*node*) *Enabled*(*in*)
CTLOP(*node*) =
  let *arc* = *select*$_{\text{Consume}}$({*in* ∈ *inArc*(*node*) | *Enabled*(*in*)})
    CONSUME(*firingToken*(*arc*), *arc*)
  let *a* = **new** *InstSet*
    lifeCycle(*a*) := *ready*
    parent(*a*) := *TriggerProc*
  step GETACTIVE(*a, node*)[12]
GETACTIVE(*a, node*) =
  if *Ready*(*a*) **and** **forsome** *i* ∈ *inputSets*(*node*) *Available*(*i*) **then**
    let *i* = *select*$_{\text{InputSets}}$({*i* ∈ *inputSets*(*node*) | *Available*(*i*)})
      STARTEXEC(*a, node*)
      lifeCycle(*a*) := *active*
      currInputSet(*node*) := *i*
  if *Interrupted*(*a*) **then** INTERRUPT(*a*)
  Ready(*a*) = (*lifeCycle*(*a*) = *ready*)

---

[10] Enabledness is defined here to mean that "the required number of *Tokens* ...*StartQuantity* ... is available," as reflected by our macro definition in Sect. 9.2.2.

[11] The 1.0 standard version required in addition that the activity must have no currently active instances, in accordance with the suggested transformation to BPEL. Such an additional guard guarantees that all instances of an activity are ultimately triggered by one enabling token, which reflects the intended termination behavior of all activity instances in case of a failure. Probably also for 2.0 this guard should be added.

[12] **step** denotes the interruptable FSM-like variant of sequential execution of ASMs (see [4] for an explicit definition).

ACTIVITYBEHAVIOR is an instance of ACTIVITYENTRY, where the instance *node* of the activity is added to the set of instances of this activity in the process instance that *node* belongs to, and the *parent* process is this process instance.

ACTIVITYBEHAVIOR(*node*) = ACTIVITYENTRY(*node*,
  Instance(*node*, *procInst*(*node*)), *procInst*(*node*))

In the following subsections this rule is instantiated for the three *Activity* subtypes by refining the abstract STARTEXEC machine. See Sect. 9.4.4 for the instantiation for iterated activities (standard loops and multi-instance loops).

9.4.1 Tasks

A task is an atomic activity describing work in the given process that "cannnot be broken down to a finer level of detail" [8, Sect. 10.2.3], although it may take its (in the process not traceable) execution time. This atomicity is expressed by the sequentiality operator **seq** for structuring ASMs (see [5]), which turns a low-level sequential execution view of two machines M followed by N into a high-level atomic view of one machine $M\,\mathbf{seq}\,N$.

Therefore STARTEXEC(*task*, *t*) means (a) to EXECute the *task* (instance to which the triggering token *t* belongs) whose exact definition depends on the type of the *task* and (b) when the execution is *Completed* without failure to produce an outgoing sequence flow [*CompletionQuantity*(*task*) many tokens on each arc are emitted by the *task* [8, pp. 130, 393], possibly together with some output.[13] *select*~OutputSets~ is defined as yielding the first available output set in a given order [8, p. 393]. Thus TASKBEHAVIOR refines ACTIVITYBEHAVIOR as follows:

TASKBEHAVIOR(*node*) = ACTIVITYBEHAVIOR(*node*) **where**
  STARTEXEC(*a*, *node*) = EXEC(*a*) **seq**
    if *Completed*(*a*) **then** EXIT(*a*, *node*)
    if *Interrupted*(*a*) **then** INTERRUPT(*a*)
    if *CompensationOccurs*(*a*) **then**
      TRIGGERCOMPENSATION(*a*)
      lifeCycle(*a*) := *compensating*
  EXIT(*a*, *node*) =
    forall *o* ∈ *outArc*(*node*)PRODUCE(*o*)[14]
    DELETE(*a*, *Instance*(*node*, *procInst*(*node*)))
    PUSHOUTPUT(*a*, *node*)

---

[13] We skip the cases where a task may fail or terminate due to a fault in the environment. We also skip the *Completing* activity mode, which is foreseen for the final 2.0 version of the standard but not yet further specified in [8, p. 393].

[14] Here again our macro definition of PRODUCE captures that the "number of tokens indicated by ... *CompletionQuantity* is placed" on the outgoing arcs [8, p. 393].

PUSHOUTPUT(*a*, *node*) =
  if forall *o* ∈ *outputSets*(*node*)   **not** *Available*(*o*)
  then THROW(*noAvailOutputExc*, *node*)
  else   let *o* = *select*₍OutputSets₎
      ({*o* ∈ *outputSets*(*node*) | *Available*(*o*)})
      if *IORules*(*node*)(*o*, *currInputSet*(*a*)) = *false*
        then THROW(*noIORulesExc*, *node*)
        else PUSH(*output*(*o*))

Remark. In the case of an activity without an outgoing sequence flow, **forall***o* ∈ *outArc*(*task*) PRODUCE(*o*) is an empty rule, so that if there are no end events in the containing (sub)process, the activity terminates here.

There are seven types (subclasses) of *Task*, each coming with characteristic attributes, constraints, and meaning of EXECution [8, Fig. 10.10]; no further specified tasks are considered as abstract tasks.

TaskType = {*Send, Receive, Service, User, Manual, Script,*
  BusinessRule}

Each of these subclasses is associated with a refinement of TASKBEHAVIOR defined by refining EXEC(*task*[, *i*]) and *Completed*(*task*) as follows. A further specification of the abstractions we use in these definitions appears either in the standard document or comes with the task instantiation. For example, RECEIVE(*m*) is described as "waiting for *m* until it arrives" [8], Sect. 14.2.3), *job*(*t*) for *type*(*t*) ∈ {*Service, Script, User, Manual*} as the associated service or script or user task or manual task [also denoted *operationRef*(*t*) for service tasks]. Since abstract tasks (read: with undefined type) are considered as "never actually executed by an IT system," we treat them here as empty actions.

EXEC(*t*) =   **let** *i* = *currInputSet*(*a*) **in**
$\begin{cases}
\text{SEND}(payload(mssg(t)), receiver(mssg(t))) \\
\quad \textbf{if } type(t) = Send \\
\text{RECEIVE}(mssg(t)) \\
\quad \textbf{if } type(t) = Receive \\
\text{INVOKE}(job(t), i) \\
\quad \textbf{if } type(t) \in \{Service, Script\} \\
\text{ASSIGN}(job(t), i, performer(job(t), i)) \\
\quad \textbf{if } type(t) \in \{User, Manual\} \\
\text{CALL}(businessRule(t), i) \\
\quad \textbf{if } type(t) = BusinessRule \\
\textbf{skip} \\
\quad \textbf{if } Abstract(t)
\end{cases}$

Sent(*mssg*(*t*)) is described for *t* of type *Send* as true "upon instantiation" of *t*, *Received*(*mssg*(*t*)) for *t* of type *Receive* as true "when the message arrives."

$$
Completed(t) =
\begin{cases}
Sent(mssg(t)) & \text{if } type(t) = Send \\
Received(mssg(t)) & \text{if } type(t) = Receive \\
Completed(job(t)) & \text{if } type(t) \in \{Service, Script\} \\
Completed(businessRule(t)) & \text{if } type(t) = BusinessRule \\
Done(job(t)) & \text{if } type(t) \in \{User, Manual\} \\
true & \text{if } Abstract(t)
\end{cases}
$$

There is a special case that requires an additional rule. A Receive *task* that is "used to start a Process," a fact indicated by an *Instantiate(task)* flag, is required to either have no *in*coming arc in its associated process without a start event or to have an *in*coming arc with *source(in)* being a start event of the associated process [8, p. 139]. For the first case a special instance of FLOWNODEBEHAVIOR(*task*) is added that has no control condition and no control operation and where *Event Cond(task)* is defined as *Received(mssg(task))*.

There are also further refinement constraints for some tasks. For example service tasks are required to have exactly one input set and at most one output set.

9.4.2 Subprocesses

Subprocesses are activities that encapsulate a process [8, p. 394]. They define a contextual *scope* that can be used for attribute visibility or for the handling of transactions, events, exceptions, and compensations [8, p. 152]. Their behavior concerning exception handling and compensation is described below when explaining the behavior of intermediate events that are placed on the boundary of an activity. Their normal behavior along their inner sequence flow is described by the behavior of tasks, events, and gateways, which constitute their internal details. What remains to be described for arbitrary subprocesses is (a) the activation of subprocesses, which involves an activity instantiation and passing data from caller to callee, and (b) how to EXIT subprocesses upon their completion. For the special internal control and exit behavior of elements of the *AdHocProcess* subclass of class *SubProcess*, see Sect. 9.4.2.2, for elements of the subclass *Transaction* of *SubProcess*, Sect. 9.4.2.3.

9.4.2.1 Subprocess Activation

There are two cases of subprocess activation, depending on whether the subprocess *node* has an incoming sequence flow or not. In the first case the associated SUBPROCESSBEHAVIOR refines ACTIVITYBEHAVIOR; in the second case SUBPROCESSNOINFLOWBEHAVIOR refines FLOWNODEBEHAVIOR.

For a subprocess with some incoming sequence flow its activation is triggered through tokens produced by the *caller* process on the (unique) incoming arc. It consists in (a) creating a new instance of the subprocess as child process of the caller

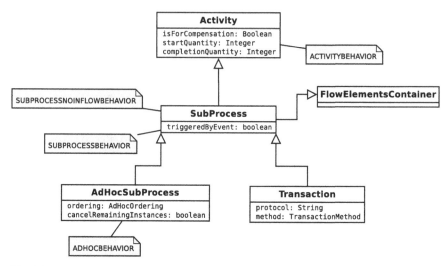

Fig. 9.9 Basic class hierarchy of subprocesses

process (which we retrieve, for the sake of example, from the token produced by the latter on the arc *in*coming the subprocess) and (b) triggering its start.

Triggering the new process instance has in [8, 14.2.4] two versions, depending on whether the subprocess either has a (and then unique) *startEvent* or otherwise a nonempty set *StartNode* of "activities and gateways without incoming sequence flow." In the first subcase, simply the *startEvent* is triggered.

In the second subcase we interpret the stipulation that "all such activities and gateways get a *token*" by associating in the graph with each $n \in StartNode$ a (virtual) entry arc $in(n)$ that can be enabled by producing a new token on it (in the new process instance, thus triggering n there; using a process subscript distinguishes elements in the current process from their analogs in the new instance).

SUBPROCESSBEHAVIOR($node$) = ACTIVITYBEHAVIOR($node$) **where**
STARTEXEC($a, node$) =
  if $startEvent(node) \neq$ **undef then**
    let $\{t\} = trigger(startEvent(a))$
    $TriggerOccurs_p(t, startEvent(a)) := true$
  else
    forall $n \in StartNode(node)$ PRODUCE($startToken(a, node), in(n)$)

For a subprocess without an incoming sequence flow, there must be a nonempty set *StartEvent* of "start events that are the target of sequence flow from outside the subprocess" [8, 14.2.4]. It is stipulated that each such start event "that is reached by a *token*"[15] generates a new subprocess instance, similar to the pass-through semantics for incoming sequence flow. In other words a triggered start event with a trigger

---

[15] This sounds ambiguous: where should the token arrive if there is no incoming sequence flow? We interpret it as meaning that some *caller* process triggers a start event in the callee, the *targetyRef* subprocess node [8, p. 215].

is chosen, it is consumed, a new process instance is created, and the trigger of the chosen start event is set in the new subprocess instance.

For the special case of a so-called *event subprocess* (denoted by setting the *triggeredByEvent* flag), it is required that it have no incoming or outgoing sequence flow and exactly one *startEvent*, so that *StartEvent* = {*startEvent*}. In this case a new instance is started each time this *startEvent* is triggered while the *parent* process is active.[16] The *parent* process can be interrupted or not, depending on whether the start event *isInterrupting* or not.

We incorporate both behaviors into one refinement EVENTSUB PROCESSBEHAVIOR of FLOWNODEBEHAVIOR, defined for event subprocess *nodes* as follows. The corresponding start event rule defined in Sect. 9.5 describes how the new subprocess instance starts its execution once (one of) its start events is triggered.

EVENTSUBPROCESSBEHAVIOR(*node*) = FLOWNODEBEHAVIOR(*node*)
where
   EventCond(*node*) =
     forsome $e \in$ *StartEvent*(*node*) *Happened*(*e*)
       and **if** *triggeredByEvent*(*node*)
            then *Active*(*parent*(*procInst*(*node*)))
   let $e = select_{\text{StartEvent}}(\{n \in StartEvent(node) \mid Happened(e)\}$
   let $\{t\} = select_{\text{Trigger}}\{t \in trigger(e) \mid TriggerOccurs(t, e)\}$
     EVENTOP(*node*) = CONSUME(*t*, *e*)
     CTLOP(*node*) =
       let $P =$ **new** *Instance*(*process*(*node*))

$$caller(P) := \begin{cases} parent(procInst(node)) \\ \qquad \textbf{if } triggeredByEvent(node) \\ caller(node) \\ \qquad \textbf{else} \end{cases}$$

       $TriggerOccurs_{\text{P}}(t, e) := true$
     if *isInterrupting*(*node*) **then** CANCEL(*parent*(*procInst*(*node*)))
   Happened(*e*) = **forsome** $t \in trigger(e)$ *TriggerOccurs*(*t*, *e*)

9.4.2.2 Ad hoc Processes

Ad hoc processes are called nonoperational elements for which "only a conceptual model is provided which does not specify details needed to execute them on an engine" [8, p. 389]. This means that the standard document intends to specify ad hoc processes only loosely so that we leave their treatment here at the same degree of underspecification. Each subprocess marked as ad hoc has a static set of

---

[16] Op. cit., p. 156., Sect. 14.4.4 says "Running," a term which is not defined in Fig. 14.2 and seems to request an active parent process only for initiating a non-interrupting event subprocess. We disregard here the baroque looking additional feature mentioned on p. 405 that "An Event Sub-Process can optionally retrigger the Event through which it was triggered, to cause its continuation outside the boundary of the associated Sub-Process."

InnerActivities intended to be executed (if *Enabled*) in an order that is mainly "determined by the performers of the activities" [8, Sect. 10.2.5, p. 161]. We denote by *EnabledInnerAct(node)* the runtime set of *Enabled* elements of *InnerActivities*, which is required to be initially the set of inner activities without an incoming sequence flow [8, Sect. 14.2.5]. We reflect the performers' choice by a function *select*EnabledInnerAct(*node*) together with a monitored predicate *ActivationTime* to express the moment where a new selection takes place. Nevertheless an *adHocOrdering* function is provided to specify either a parallel execution (the default case that the dynamic and initially empty set *RunningInnerAct* of concurrently running inner activities is finite) or a sequential execution [where "only one activity can be performed at a time" [8, Table 10.22] so that *RunningInnerAct* is empty or a singleton set]. An *AdHocCompletionCond*ition is evaluated each time an inner activity completes and defines whether the subprocess completes by EXITing (possibly producing some output). In the parallel case this depends on whether the attribute *CancelRemainingInstances* is true: if it is, all elements of *RunningInnerAct* are CANCELed, otherwise the ad hoc subprocess is required to wait for completion until each element of *RunningInnerAct* has completed or terminated. We use the **await** *Cond M* construct to describe such waiting for the execution of *M* until the *Cond*ition becomes true, as defined for ASMs in [3].

Therefore the behavior ADHOCBEHAVIOR of class *AdHocProcess* elements is the following refinement of ACTIVITYBEHAVIOR. For simplicity of exposition and without loss of generality we assume that each launched inner activity upon completion enables a (virtual) link that enters the evaluation of the *AdHocCompletion Condition* of its ad hoc subprocess.

ADHOCBEHAVIOR(*node*) = ACTIVITYBEHAVIOR(*node*) **where**
STARTEXEC(*a, node*) =
  while **not** *AdHocCompletionCond(node)*
    if *adHocOrdering(node)* = *Sequential*
      then LAUNCHINNERACT(*node*)
    if *adHocOrdering(node)* = *Parallel* **then**
      if *ActivationTime(node)* **then** LAUNCHINNERACT(*node*)
  seq
    if *CancelRemainingInstances(node)* **then**
      forall *a* ∈ *RunningInnerAct(node)*
        CANCEL(*a*)
        EXIT(*a, node*)
    else **awaitforall** *a* ∈ *RunningInnerAct(node)*
      Completed(a) **or** *Terminated(a)*
      EXIT(*node*)
LAUNCHINNERACT(*node*) =
  if *enabledInnerAct(node)* ≠ ∅ **then**
    let *e* = *select*EnabledInnerAct(*node*)(*EnabledInnerAct(node)*)
      ACTIVITYBEHAVIOR(*e*)
      INSERT(*e, RunningInnerAct(node)*)
      DELETE(*e, EnabledInnerAct(node)*)

9.4.2.3 Transaction

Transactions are subprocesses whose behavior is also controlled by a transaction protocol, which is assumed to be given. They come with a special method to undo a transaction when it is cancelled. The behavioral instantiation of a transaction comes up to add in the specification of the entry and exit actions the details for creating the transactional scope and for what should happen when a transaction fails (rollback and possibly compensation of the involved processes). We do not specify this behavior here because it is only loosely hinted at in the BPMN standard document.

9.4.3 Call Activity

Any *CallActivity* (also called a reusable subprocess) "calls a pre-defined process" and "results in the transfer of control" to the "CallableElement being invoked," using the data inputs and outputs as well as InputSets and OutputSets of the *reference*d callable element [8, 10.2.5/6]. We denote the called activity by *activity*(*reference*(*node*)), of which a new instance is created and added to the set of active instances of the activity, having triggered one of its start events (possibly provided with some available input).

$$\text{CALLACTIVITYBEHAVIOR}(node) =$$
$$\quad \text{ACTIVITYENTRY}(node, Instance(activity(reference(node))), node)$$
where $\text{STARTEXEC}(a, node) =$
  choose $n \in \{n \in StartEvent(a) \mid trigger(n) = None\}$
  $TriggerOccurs_a(None, n) := true$
  $\text{INSERT}(a, ActiveProcInst(activity(reference(node)))))$

9.4.4 Iterated (Loop) Activities

Loop and Multiple Instances activities act as wrappers for an activity that can be iterated resp. spawn multiple instances in parallel or sequentially. We interpret the wrapper as providing the input, but probably other interpretations are allowed by the standard. An activity with *LoopCharacteristics* has an iterative behavior either of a *StandardLoopCharacteristics* or of a *MultiInstanceLoopCharacteristics* type [8, Fig. 10.6].

The standard loop characteristics define a *LoopCond*ition that is checked, as indicated by a *testBefore* attribute, either before or after an execution of the loop *body* to decide whether the loop completes at this moment or not:

- If *testBefore* is true, then *LoopCond* is evaluated before the first iteration of the activity to be iterated is started (and then again after each iteration), in which case the loop activity corresponds to the **while** construct.

- If *testBefore* is false, then *LoopCond* is evaluated *after* the first iteration has finished (and then again after each iteration), in which case the loop activity corresponds to the **until** construct.

A *loopMaximum* can be used in the *loopCond*. We use a function *inputs* to describe the data flushed to the selected input set *currInputSet(node)* in the following refinement STANDARDLOOPBEHAVIOR of ACTIVITYBEHAVIOR. To ACTIVATE the loop body means to trigger the execution of the BPMN process defined by the body; ACTIVATE is defined depending on the type of its argument process. For simplicity of exposition and without loss of generality we make a similar assumption as for the ADHOCBEHAVIOR rule, namely, that each body process upon its completion enables a (virtual) link that enters the evaluation of the *loopCondition*.

$$
\begin{aligned}
&\text{STANDARDLOOPBEHAVIOR}(node) = \text{ACTIVITYBEHAVIOR}(node) \textbf{ where} \\
&\quad \text{STARTEXEC}(a, node) = \\
&\quad\quad \textbf{let } i = inputs(currInputSet(node)) \\
&\quad\quad\quad \textbf{if } testBefore(node) = true \textbf{ then} \\
&\quad\quad\quad\quad \textbf{while } loopCond(a, node) \text{ ACTIVATE}(body(a, node), i) \\
&\quad\quad\quad \textbf{if } testBefore(node) = false \textbf{ then} \\
&\quad\quad\quad\quad \textbf{until } loopCond(node) \text{ ACTIVATE}(body(a, node), i) \\
&\quad\quad \textbf{seq } \textbf{if } Completed(a, node) \textbf{ then } \text{EXIT}(a, node) \\
&\quad\quad Completed(a, node) = \\
&\quad\quad\quad \begin{cases} \textbf{not } loopCond(a, node) & \textbf{if } testBefore(node) = true \\ loopCond(a, node) & \textbf{if } testBefore(node) = false \end{cases}
\end{aligned}
$$

The multi-instance loop characteristic determines how many instances of an activity are spawned to be executed sequentially or in parallel. A *loopCardinality* expression defines the number of activity instances to be created, and an *isSequential* attribute determines whether the instances are executed sequentially ("a new instance is generated only after the previous one has been completed") or in parallel. As for ad hoc activities, a *MiCompletionCondition* is evaluated each time an instance completes, and when it becomes true, the remaining instances are cancelled and the multi-instance loop completes. There are four types of instance completion *behavior* determining "when events shall be thrown from an activity instance that is about to complete" [8, Table 10.26]:

- Case *behavior* = *All*: "no event is ever thrown; a token is produced after completion of all instances."
- Case *behavior* = *None*: An event *noneBehaviorEventRef* is thrown each time an instance completes.
- Case *behavior* = *One*: An event *oneBehaviorEventRef* is thrown "upon the first instance completing."
- Case *behavior* = *Complex*: A *complexBehaviorDefinition* determines "when and which events are thrown."

MULTINSTLOOPBEHAVIOR refines ACTIVITYBEHAVIOR in two respects:

- Refining the input selection and output production to data collections whose elements are associated to the activity instances; this is a signature refinement defined in [8, Sect. 14.2.7], as is the corresponding refinement of the PUSHOUTPUT(p) component of EXIT(p) for multiple instance activities p.
- Refining the definition of STARTEXEC.

For simplicity of exposition and without loss of generality we make a similar assumption as for the STANDARDLOOPBEHAVIOR rule, namely, that each inner activity instance upon completion enables a (virtual) link entering the *MiCompletion-Condition* evaluation. The events thrown by EMITEVENT each time an inner activity completes are instances of the class *ImplicitThrowEvent*, read: events that are automatically thrown to be caught by a boundary event on the multi-instance activity [8, Table 10.28]. The standard document does not explain the data input/output behavior of multiple instances, so we do not enter its formalization here.

MULTINSTLOOPBEHAVIOR = ACTIVITYBEHAVIOR(*node*) **where**
STARTEXEC(a, *node*) =
  while *MiCompletionCond*(a, *node*) = *false*
    if *isSequential*(*node*) **then**
      LAUNCHINSTANCE(*node*) // run first instance until completion
      step // creation of further instances
        while *loopCardinality*(*node*) >| *ActiveInnerAct*(a, *node*) |
          LAUNCHINSTANCE(a, *node*) // run next instance until completion
    else // parallel case: new instances created at activation time
      while *loopCardinality*(*node*) >| *ActiveInnerAct*(a, *node*) |
        if *ActivationTime*(*node*) **then** // run one more instance
          LAUNCHINSTANCE(a, *node*)
  step
    forall $b \in$ *ActiveInnerAct*(a, *node*) CANCEL(b)
    EXIT(a, *node*) // NB with refined PUSHOUTPUT
LAUNCHINSTANCE(a, n) =
  let *act* = **new** *Instance*(*innerAct*(n))
    $\begin{cases} \text{ACTIVATE}(act) \\ \text{INSERT}(act, ActiveInnerAct(a, n)) \end{cases}$
    step   await *Completed*(*act*) EMITEVENT(n)
EMITEVENT(n) =
  $\begin{cases} \text{THROW}(noneBehaviorEventRef(n), n) \text{ if } behavior(n) = None \\ \text{THROW}(oneBehaviorEventRef(n), n) \quad \text{if } behavior(n) = One \\ \quad \textbf{and} | \ Instance(innerAct(n)) \ | = 1 \\ \textbf{forall } e \in ComplexBehaviorDefinition \\ \quad \text{THROW}(e, n) \qquad\qquad\qquad \text{if } behavior(n) = Complex \end{cases}$

9.5 Events

Events are used in BPMN to control the execution order or timing of process activities [8, Sect. 8.3.6]. *Event* splits into two subclasses, *ThrowEvent* and *CatchEvent*, both of which can contain intermediate events, which may throw or catch triggers, the causes of events. *EndEvents* are *ThrowEvents* because they typically "throw" a result when a process ends, whereas *StartEvents* "catch" a trigger to start a process and thus form a subclass of *CatchEvent*, as do the elements of *BoundaryEvent* which are typically attached as intermediate events to an activity. When an event is thrown, its trigger is propagated to the innermost enclosing scope instance where an attached event can catch the trigger. For some cases (e.g. for errors or escalations) it is intentionally left underspecified what should happen when no catching event can be found.

We indicate by *trigger(node)* the set of types of event *triggers* that may be associated to *node* as defined in [8, Table 10.77]: a message (arriving from another participant), a timer, a condition, a signal (broadcasted from another process) or none (and in event subprocesses also escalation, error, or compensation).

In the following subsections we explain the behavior of these *Event* subclasses, mostly abstracting from the data events may carry. The (throw) behavior of so-called implicit throw events, which are used in connection with multi-instance activities, has already been described when defining the EMITEVENT macro in Sect. 9.4.4.

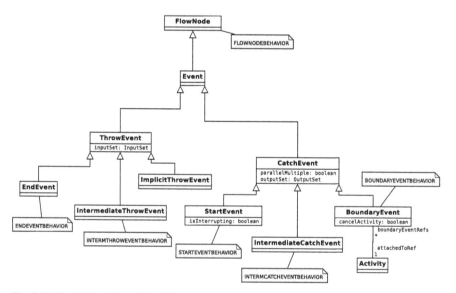

Fig. 9.10 Basic Class Hierarchy of Events

9.5.1 Start Events

A start event has no incoming arc (except when attached to the boundary of a sub-process to which a higher-level process may connect), and every process containing some (possibly more than one) start event is required to have no other flow elements without incoming sequence flow (except intermediate events attached to an activity boundary, event subprocesses or compensation activities, see below) [8, Chap. 10.4.2]. When at a start event a *TriggerOccurs* – a predicate representing that an event "happens" during the course of a business process, see definition in Sect. 9.5.3.2 – a new process instance is created and started by producing a (unique) *startToken* on every outgoing arc.

If there are multiple ways to trigger a process, only one trigger is required to occur except in the special case where all elements of *trigger(node)* must be triggered to instantiate the process. This is expressed by the following two refinements of FLOWNODEBEHAVIOR(*node*) for start event *node*s without incoming arc.[17]

STARTEVENTBEHAVIOR(*node*) = FLOWNODEBEHAVIOR(*node*)
   where // normal case without parallel multiple trigger
     EventCond(node) = *ParallelMultiple* $\notin$ *trigger(node)* **and**
       forsome $e \in$ *trigger(node)* *TriggerOccurs(e, node)*
     EVENTOP(*node*) =
       choose $e \in \{e \in$ *trigger(node)* | *TriggerOccurs(e, node)*$\}$
         CONSUME(*triggerOccurrence(e)*)

     CTLOP(*node*) =
       let P = **new** *Instance(process(node))*
       forall $o \in$ *outArc$_P$(node$_P$)* PRODUCE(*startToken$_P$(node$_P$), o*)

STARTEVENTPARMULTBEHAVIOR(*node*) = FLOWNODEBEHAVIOR(*node*)
   where // case with parallel multiple triggers
     EventCond(node) = *ParallelMultiple* $\in$ *trigger(node)* **and**
       forall $e \in$ *trigger(node)* \ {*ParallelMultiple*}
         TriggerOccurs(e, node)
     EVENTOP(*node*) =
       forall $e \in$ *trigger(node)* \ {*ParallelMultiple*}
         CONSUME(*triggerOccurrence(e)*)

Fig. 9.11 Start Events – None, Message, Timer, Escalation, Error, Compensation, Signal, Multiple, Parallel Multiple

---

[17] Since in this chapter we do not investigate BPMN choreography features, we disregard the case of start events that participate in a conversation including other start events where only one new process instance is created for the specific conversation.

$\text{CTLOP}(node) =$
    let $P = $ **new** $Instance(process(node))$
    forall $o \in outArc_\text{P}(node_\text{P})$ $\text{PRODUCE}(startToken_\text{P}(node), o)$

In the special case of a start event *node* with an incoming arc *in*, the event must be attached to the boundary of a subprocess to which a higher-level process may connect. This situation can be modeled by treating *in* as a virtual incoming arc that can be *Enabled* by a token produced by the higher-level process, so that *Triggered(node)* is instantiated to *Enabled(in(node))* and CONSUMEVENT *(node)* to CONSUME*(firingToken(in(node)), in(node))*.

Remark on processes without a start event. Constructs without an incoming arc and belonging to a process without a start event must be activated when the process is instantiated. For simplicity of exposition we model such processes by equipping them with a virtual start event from which a virtual arc leads to each construct without incoming sequence flow. Then these constructs are all triggered when by the instantiation of the process the start event is triggered.

Table 10.77 in [8] explains how *TriggerOccurs* is defined. For a conditional trigger *e* CONSUME*(triggerOccurrence(e))* is required to let the corresponding condition become false between two occurrences of that trigger.

9.5.2 End Events

An end event is used to indicate where a process will end and thus has incoming arcs (where each arriving token will be consumed) and no outgoing sequence flow (except when the end event is attached to the boundary of a subprocess from where a higher-level process may proceed); furthermore every process containing some (possibly more than one) end event is required to have no other flow elements without an outgoing sequence flow (except compensation activities, see below) [8, Sect. 10.4.3]. An end event may emit (possibly multiple) results belonging to its *resultType* set containing elements of the following types: message, signal, terminate, error, escalation, cancel, compensation, or none [8, Table 10.81].

Thus ENDEVENTBEHAVIOR refines FLOWNODEBEHAVIOR as follows:

ENDEVENTBEHAVIOR*(node)* = FLOWNODEBEHAVIOR*(node)* **where**
$CtlCond(node) = $ **forsome** $in \in inArc(node)$ $Enabled(in)$
$\text{CTLOP}(node) = $ **choose** $in \in \{in \in inArc(node) \mid Enabled(in)\}$
    CONSUME$(firingToken(in), in)$

Fig. 9.12 End Events – None, Message, Escalation, Error, Cancel, Compensation, Signal, Multiple, Termination

if *Multiple* $\notin$ *resultType(node)* // normal case without multiple results
then   **let** $\{res\}$ = *resultType(node)* **in** EMITRESULT(*res, node*)
else   **forall** *res* $\in$ *resultType(node)* \ {*Multiple*}
  EMITRESULT(*res, node*)

EMITRESULT is detailed in [8, Table 10.81]. For a message result type the *MessageFlow* determines the message(s) to be sent from the *sender* to the *receiver*. For a signal result type the corresponding *signalRef* is BROADCAST from *node* to "any process that can receive it" (we write *receivers(signalRef(node), node)*). An error result type yields THROWing an error – to be caught by an enclosing intermediate event if there is any; otherwise it is intentionally left unspecified as to what should happen – and terminating all the activities that are currently active in the subprocess (assumed to include all instances of multi-instances). Similarly THROWing an *Escalation* or *Cancel* type from *node* has the effect of triggering an enclosing *targetIntermEv(escalation, node)* in an attempt to catch the escalation and, in case it is not caught there, to propagate it further up; the cancel case is required to be used only within a transaction subprocess, with *targetIntermEv(resType, node)* attached to the boundary of the transaction, and in addition a transaction protocol cancel message has to be sent to any entities involved in the transaction; we represent this behavior as a CALLBACK to each participant in the set *listener(Cancel, node)*. A compensation result type yields THROWing a compensation event, which is required to activate the compensation handler of the corresponding activity (or set of activities) *actRef(node)* after their completion. If *resType* = *Terminate* "all activities in the process should be immediately ended," including multiple instances; this can be achieved by deleting all tokens on any arc in the given *process(node)* and in any active inner activity, deleting the latter from the set of active inner activities. For *resType* = *None* in the special case of an end *node* of a subprocess that has completed, when the subprocess is *Completed* the flow has to go back to the caller process, to which effect a token is PRODUCEd on the arc which *out*goes the caller of the process instance to which the end *node* belongs, and the process instance is deleted from the set of active instances of the called *activity(reference(node))*.

EMITRESULT(*resType, node*) =
  if *resType* = *Message* **then**   **forall** $m \in$ *MessageFlow*
    if *sender(m)* = *node* **then** SEND(*payload(m), receiver(m)*))
  if *resType* = *Signal* **then**
    BROADCAST(*signalRef(node), receivers(signalRef(node), node)*))
  if *resType* = *Error* **then**
    THROW(*error, node*)
    forall $a \in$ *ActiveActivity(process(node))* TERMINATE(*a*)
  if *resType* $\in$ {*Cancel, Escalation*} **then**
    THROW(*resType, node*)
    if *resType* = *Cancel* **then**
      CALLBACK(*mssg(Cancel, node), listener(Cancel, node)*))
  if *resType* = *Compensation* **then**
    THROW((*compensation, actRef(node)*), *node*)

if *resType* = *Terminate* **then** INTERRUPT(*process*(*node*))
if *resType* = *None* **and** *IsSubprocessEnd*(*node*)
  and *Completed*(*process*(*node*)) **then**
    PRODUCE(*returnToken*(*node*), *out*(*caller*(*process*(*node*))))
    DELETE(*process*(*node*),
                ActiveProcInst(*activity*(*reference*(*node*)))))
where
  CALLBACK(*m*, *L*) = **forall** *l* ∈ *L* SEND(*payload*(*m*), *l*)
  INTERRUPT(*p*) =
    DELETEALLTOKENS(*p*)
    forall *q* ∈ *ActiveInnerAct*(*p*)
      DELETEALLTOKENS(*q*)
      DELETE(*q*, *ActiveInnerAct*(*p*))

9.5.3 Intermediate Events

Intermediate events occur between start and end events and may either throw or catch triggers, namely, to send or receive messages or to establish a condition or to react to its satisfaction, where the conditions may concern timing features or exceptions or compensations. If an intermediate event is enabled during normal process flow, it will either ("throw use") immediately set off the event trigger and perform its normal sequence flow CTLOP (CONSUME its enabling token and PRODUCE tokens on its outgoing sequence flow) or ("catch use") wait to perform its normal CTLOP until its trigger occurs. When intermediate events are used in an *activity* to describe exception or compensation handling that is outside the normal flow of the *activity*, they are attached to the boundary of that *activity* (represented by *attachedTo* = *activity*), formally as elements of *boundaryEventRefs*(*activity*). Such events can only catch their triggers during an execution of the activity they are attached to, thereby starting an exception or compensation flow that may interrupt the activity (as error or cancel intermediate events always do).

The intermediate events that can be used in normal flow or as attached to an activity boundary are listed in [8, Tables 10.82 and 10.83]. In the following two sections we describe the associated normal flow behavior; for the boundary event behavior see Sect. 9.5.4.

9.5.3.1 Intermediate Throw Events in Normal Flow

An intermediate throw event is required to have some ("uncontrolled" if multiple) incoming and (except intermediate link events) some (simultaneously activated if multiple) outgoing sequence flow [8, Sect. 10.4.4]. The details of its event operation SETEVENTTRIGGER depend on the trigger type associated to the event.

Fig. 9.13 Intermediate Throw Events – Message, Escalation, Compensation, Signal, Multiple

SETEVENTTRIGGER yields message SENDing in the case of a *Message* trigger type, a BROADCAST for a *Signal* trigger type, triggering (the unique) *targetLink* for trigger type *Link* and THROWing an escalation or compensation[18] for an *Escalation* or *Compensation* trigger type. If *trigger(node)* contains multiple trigger elements, then SETEVENTTRIGGER(*node*, *t*) is performed for each trigger element $t \in$ *trigger(node)*.

Thus INTERMEDIATETHROWEVENTBEHAVIOR refines FLOWNODEBEHAVIOR as follows and is associated to the class INTERMEDIATETHROWEVENT:

INTERMEDIATETHROWEVENTBEHAVIOR(*node*) =
 FLOWNODEBEHAVIOR(*node*) **where**
CtlCond(node) = **forsome** *in* $\in$ *inArc(node)* *Enabled(in)*
CTLOP(*node*) = **choose** *in* $\in$ {*in* $\in$ *inArc(node)* | *Enabled(in)*}
 CONSUME(*firingToken(in)*, *in*)
 PRODUCEALL(*outArc(node)*)[19]
EVENTOP(*node*) =
 if *Multiple* $\notin$ *trigger(node)* // case with only one trigger
  then **let** {*t*} = *trigger(node)* **in** SETEVENTTRIGGER(*t*, *node*)
  else **forall** *t* $\in$ *trigger(node)* \ {*Multiple*}
      SETEVENTTRIGGER(*t*, *node*)
SETEVENTTRIGGER(*t*, *n*) =
$\left\{ \begin{array}{l} \textbf{forall } m \in MessageFlow \textbf{ with } sender(m) = node \\ \quad \text{SEND}(payload(m), receiver(m)) \\ \qquad \textbf{if } t = Message \\ \text{BROADCAST}(signalRef(n), receivers(signalRef(n), n)) \\ \qquad \textbf{if } t = Signal \\ Triggered(targetLink(n)) := true \\ \qquad \textbf{if } t = Link \\ \text{THROW}(escalation, n) \\ \qquad \textbf{if } t = Escalation \\ \text{THROW}((compensation, actRef(node)), node) \\ \qquad \textbf{if } t = Compensation \end{array} \right.$

---

[18] We do not provide further details about compensation because this concept is only unsatisfactorily sketched in the standard document, in particular when it comes to speak about compensation of multiple activities.

[19] If for a source intermediate link event *outArc(node)* = $\emptyset$, then PRODUCEALL($\emptyset$) = $SKIP$.

9.5.3.2 Intermediate Catch Events in Normal Flow

An intermediate catch event, when token *Enabled*, will wait to perform its normal CTLOP until its *EventCond*ition is satisfied expressing that the triggers to be caught occur. When it becomes true, the normal CTLOPeration is performed and the occurring event triggers are consumed (where relevant, e.g., for link types where the *Triggered* predicate at *sourceLink(node)* has to be reset to false; [8, Sect. 10.4.6]).

Thus INTERMEDIATECATCHEVENTBEHAVIOR refines FLOWNODEBEHAVIOR as follows and is associated to the class INTERMEDIATECATCHEVENT. The predicate *TriggerOccurs(t, node)* is defined in [8, Table 10.82].

INTERMEDIATECATCHEVENTBEHAVIOR(*node*) =
    FLOWNODEBEHAVIOR(*node*) **where**
CtlCond(node) =   **forsome** *in* ∈ *inArc(node) Enabled(in)*
EventCond(node) =
        (*ParallelMultiple* ∉ *trigger(node)*
                // only one trigger required to occur
        and   forsome *t* ∈ *trigger(node) TriggerOccurs(t, node)*)
    or
        (*ParallelMultiple* ∈ *trigger(node)* // all triggers required to occur
            and   forall *t* ∈ *trigger(node) TriggerOccurs(t, node)*)
EVENTOP(*node*) =
    let *TriggOcc* = {*t* ∈ *trigger(node)* | *TriggerOccurs(t, node)*)}
        if *ParallelMultiple* ∉ *trigger(node)* **then**
            choose *t* ∈ *TriggOcc* CONSUME(*triggerOccurrence(t)*)
        else   forall *t* ∈ *TriggOcc* CONSUME(*triggerOccurrence(t)*)
CTLOP(*node*) =   **choose** *in* ∈ {*in* ∈ *inArc(node)* | *Enabled(in)*}
    CONSUME(*firingToken(in), in*)
    PRODUCEALL(*outArc(node)*)
TriggerOccurs(t, node) =
$$\begin{cases} \textbf{forsome } m \in \textit{Message Received}(m, \textit{node}) & \textbf{if } t = \textit{Message} \\ \textit{TimerCondition}(\textit{node}) = \textit{true} & \textbf{if } t = \textit{Timer} \\ \textit{EventExpression}(\textit{node}) = \textit{true} & \textbf{if } t = \textit{Conditional} \\ \textit{Triggered}(\textit{sourceLink}(\textit{node})) = \textit{true} & \textbf{if } t = \textit{Link} \end{cases}$$

As shown in Table 10.94 in [8], the *TimerCondition(node)* typically involves *timeData(node)* or *cycleData(node)*. Timer as well as conditional triggers are implicitly thrown, meaning that when activated they wait until *TriggerOccurs*, namely, when their time-based or state-based condition becomes true.

Fig. 9.14 Intermediate Catch Events – Message, Timer, Escalation, Error, Cancel, Compensation, Signal, Multiple, Parallel Multiple

9.5.4 Boundary Events

An intermediate event that is *attachedTo* the boundary of an *activity* has no incoming but has (possibly multiple) outgoing sequence flows – except intermediate events with a *Compensation* trigger that are required not to have any outgoing sequence flows, although they may have an outgoing association. When a boundary intermediate event is triggered, three things happen: (a) the event trigger occurrence is consumed; (b) if the *cancelActivity(act)* attribute is true,[20] the *activity* is INTERRUPTed (including all its inner activity instances in case of a multi-instance *activity*; see the definition in Sect. 9.5.2); (c) the CTLOP enables the outgoing sequence flow activating an event handler [8, pp. 234, 253, Sect. 14.4.3]. For a compensation event trigger to occur means that the *toBeCompensatedActivity* has *Completed*, so that the compensation handler for that activity is activated (for which reason a compensation event must be noninterrupting).

Thus BOUNDARYEVENTBEHAVIOR refines FLOWNODEBEHAVIOR. The definition of *TriggerOccurs(t, node)* from Sect. 9.5.3.2 is extended by [8, Table 10.83]

BOUNDARYEVENTBEHAVIOR(*node*) = FLOWNODEBEHAVIOR(*node*)
      where
EventCond(node) =
    (*ParallelMultiple* ∉ *trigger(node)*
             // only one trigger required to occur
    and **forsome** $t \in$ *trigger(node)* *TriggerOccurs(t, node)*)
  or
    (*ParallelMultiple* ∈ *trigger(node)* // all triggers required to occur
      and **forall** $t \in$ *trigger(node)* *TriggerOccurs(t, node)*)
EventOp(node) =
    let *TriggOcc* = {$t \in$ *trigger(node)* | *TriggerOccurs(t, node)*)}
    if *ParallelMultiple* ∉ *trigger(node)* **then** **choose** $t \in$ *TriggOcc*
      CONSUME(*triggerOccurrence(t)*)
      if t = *Compensate* **then**
        ACTIVATE(*compensation(attachedTo(node))*)
    else **forall** $t \in$ *TriggOcc*
      CONSUME(*triggerOccurrence(t)*)

Fig. 9.15 A task activity with an intermediate catching error event attached to its boundary

---

[20] It is required to always hold for Error and to never hold for Compensate type.

$$\textbf{if } Compensate \in TriggOcc \textbf{ then}$$
$$\text{ACTIVATE}(compensation(attachedTo(node)))$$

$\text{CTLOP}(node) =$
$\quad \text{PRODUCEALL}(outArc(node))$
$\quad \textbf{if } cancelActivity(attachedTo(node))$
$\qquad\qquad \textbf{then } \text{INTERRUPT}(attachedTo(node))$

$TriggerOccurs(t, node) =$

$$\begin{cases}
\textbf{forsome } m \in Message\ Received(m, node) & \textbf{if } t = Message \\
TimerCondition(node) = true & \textbf{if } t = Timer \\
EventExpression(node) = true & \textbf{if } t = Conditional \\
\textbf{forsome } n\ node \in receivers(signalRef(n), n) & \\
\quad \textbf{and } Arrived(signalRef(n), node) & \textbf{if } t = Signal \\
triggerOccurrence(t) = (Completed, a) & \\
\quad \textbf{and } Completed(a) & \textbf{if } t = Compensate \\
Caught(t, node) & \\
\quad \textbf{if } t \in \{Escalation, Error, Cancel\}
\end{cases}$$

9.6 An Example

We illustrate the preceding definitions by the workflow in Fig. 9.16. It has two pools: One is used as an abstract blackbox for an external participant and is left empty, the other one is assumed to contain all the other elements and is drawn with an invisible outline.

The workflow execution begins with the start event in the upper left corner. Since there is no specific trigger type associated with this event, it has to be triggered *manually*. When such a manual *TriggerOccurs*, *EventCond* is true and the underlying BPMN scheduler can choose to fire this start event. This process consumes through the EVENTOP the event trigger and produces through CTLOP a token on the outgoing edge, thus enabling the following subprocess to start. The subprocess is instantiated by SUBPROCESSBEHAVIOR through triggering its start event.

Within the subprocess, the exclusive gateway is used as a join. It can fire upon the arrival of the produced single incoming token because EXCLGATEBEHAVIOR restricts its consumption function by $|select_{\text{Consume}}(node)| = 1$. The next workflow element is a collapsed subprocess, Process Input, which loops over some input that is not further specified, using multiple instances, as indicated by the vertical bars. After consuming the firing token through an application of ACTIVITYBEHAVIOR, the refined version of STARTEXEC for multi-instance looping activities invokes its inner activity with simultaneous multiple instances because the loop is marked as nonsequential. The exact mechanism involves mapping a collection of input data to those instances by means of some input association and is carried out by the interpreter. The inner process activities are instantiated via the ACTIVATE macro.

In case none of the created instances raises an error, the loop activity will eventually be finalized via EXIT, which places a token on the ougoing edge of the loop

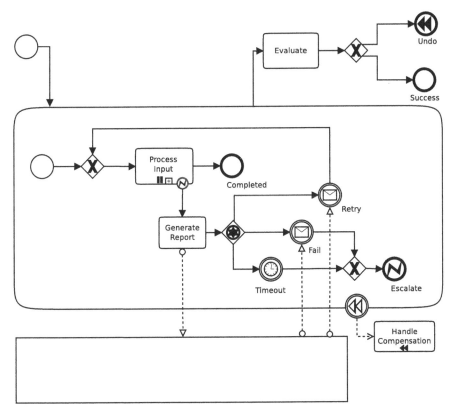

Fig. 9.16 Example – a compensatable process with a remote arbiter

activity. In case at least one instance of the loop subprocess raises an error that is not caught within its scope, all instances of the subprocess are terminated by EMITRESULT. The interpreter searches now for a suitable boundary event matching this error, rethrowing it on every level in the process hierarchy. In the example there is a catching intermediate event of type error directly on the boundary of the Process Input subprocess. Assuming that its definition matches the error that was thrown, the interpreter will signal its associated trigger, thereby fulfilling its *EventCond*.

The only flow node that can be fired at this stage is the Generate Report task. Apart from collecting and processing information about the caught error, it dispatches a message to the external participant represented by the empty pool. From the local point of view of the single example process no details about what happens in the empty pool are known except that its participant adheres to the message exchange indicated in the diagram. The following event-based gateway due to its *EventCond* can only be enabled after one of its associated events is triggered. This can be an external message requesting to repeat the Process Input activity, a message informing that the process failed, or a failure to receive at least one of these messages within a certain time frame. The latter case is also regarded as a failure.

Choosing the appropriate outgoing edge on which to place a token relies on an ordering among the triggers, as expressed by the *fst* function that is used in *select*_{Produce} within EVENTGATEBEHAVIOUR.

In the *Retry* case, a token is placed on the edge leading back to the exclusive join, resulting in another iteration. In the failure and timeout cases, the token is produced on a path that ends with the error end event Escalate. The intermediate event on whose incoming edge the token is placed initially has in all possible cases a true *EventCondition* and thus can fire without delay. This is guaranteed by the *select*_{Produce} function of the event-based gateway and the fact that the triggers are only cleared by the following events.

The subprocess can be exited via one of the two end events or via some uncaught terminating trigger further down in the process hierarchy. The Escalate end event signals a terminal failure of the process and throws an error that can possibly be caught in an enclosing context to handle the exception. Because the outermost process that is modeled in this diagram has no designated event handlers, it would automatically be terminated as well when this end event is triggered. The other end event only throws the none trigger, so if the subprocess token arrives, it is *Completed* there and thus via EMITRESULT returns to the caller process.

Finally, the top-level process exits via either the Success or the Undo end event. In the first case, control is returned to the calling instance higher in the hierarchy, or to the interpereter if there was no such instance. The Undo end event has an attached trigger of type compensation. The trigger that it throws contains a reference to the activity that is to be compensated, as expressed by the $actRef$ function in EMITRESULT. Compensations are different from errors in that they are usually directed from an outer toward an inner context. As described in the text, we assume that the interpreter will catch the trigger and find the associated compensation activity of the enclosed reference. In our case, the Undo end event references the inner subprocess, so the Handle Compensation activity would be invoked to undo the effects of the Process Input subprocess.

9.7 Conclusion

One could simplify considerably the BPMN execution semantics by restricting it to a core of BPMN constructs in terms of which all the other constructs could be defined, to streamline the standard as suggested already in already in [6]. Up to now missing or ambiguous issues one would like to see clarified by the standard document can be integrated into the model once they are decided. We believe that the standard document leaves too many relevant issues underspecified, e.g., the lifecycle concept for activities and its relation with exception handling and compensation. As a consequence, it remains doubtful whether this standard will provide a practical basis for truly interoperable (platform independent) business process specifications; reference implementations are no remedy. The underspecification also limits serious verification efforts for challenging real-life process properties, in particular if machine-supported verification is at stake. The fact that the invariants needed in [11] to reflect details that are missing in the OMG document seem to grow even for simple properties at an extradinary rate with the complexity of the analyzed diagrams points in this direction. Comparable Event-B-based verification efforts for properties of BPEL processes in [1, 2] seem not to suffer from such a deficiency.

Appendix: BPMN in a Nutshell

We list here the behavioral rules associated with the subclasses of the BPMN *FlowNode* class.

FLOWNODEBEHAVIOR($node$) =
   if *EventCond*($node$) **and** *CtlCond*($node$) **and** *DataCond*($node$)
     and *ResourceCond*($node$) **then**
       DATAOP($node$)
       CTLOP($node$)
       EVENTOP($node$)
       RESOURCEOP($node$)

9.7.1 Gateway Behavior

GATEBEHAVIORPATTERN($node$) =
   let $I = select_{Consume}(node)$
   let $O = select_{Produce}(node)$
    FLOWNODEBEHAVIOR($node, I, O$)
where
   CtlCond($node, I$) =   **forall** $in \in I$ *Enabled*(in)
        and *Active*($procInst(node)$)
   CTLOP($node, I, O$) =
     CONSUMEALL($\{(t_j, in_j) \mid 1 \leq j \leq n\}$) **where**
      $[t_1, \ldots, t_n] = firingToken(I), [in_1, \ldots, in_n] = I$
     if *NormalCase*($node$) **then** PRODUCEALL(O)
      else THROW($GateExc, node$)
   DATAOP($node, O$) =   **forall** $o \in O$ **forall** $i \in assignments(o)$
        ASSIGN($to_i, from_i$)
   Active(p) = ($lifeCycle(p) = active$)

PARGATEBEHAVIOR($node$) = GATEBEHAVIORPATTERN($node$) **where**
  $select_{Consume}(node) = inArc(node)$ // AND-JOIN merging behavior
  $select_{Produce}(node) = outArc(node)$ // AND-SPLIT (branching behavior
  NormalCase($node$) = *true* // gate throws no exception

$\text{ExclGateBehavior}(node) = \text{GateBehaviorPattern}(node)$ **where**
| $select_{\text{Consume}}(node)$ |$= 1$ // exclusive merge
$select_{\text{Produce}}(node) = fst(\{a \in outArc(node) \mid DataCond(a)\})$
$NormalCase(node) = NormalCase_{\text{ExclGateBehavior}}(node)$

$\text{InclGateBehavior}(node) = \text{GateBehaviorPattern}(node)$ **where**
$select_{\text{Consume}}(node) =$ // NB. all to be enabled to fire
   $\{in \in inArc(node) \mid Enabled(in) \text{ or } UpstreamToken(in) \neq \emptyset\}$
$select_{\text{Produce}}(node) = \{a \in outArc(node) \mid DataCond(a)\}$
$CtlCond(node, I, O) =$
   $CtlCond_{\text{GateBehaviorPattern}}(node, I, O) \text{ and } I \neq \emptyset$
$NormalCase(node)$ if and only if // as for the exclusive case
   $\{a \in outArc(node) \mid DataCond(a)\} \neq \emptyset$ **or**
      some default sequence flow is specified at $node$

$\text{EventGateBehavior}(node) =$ // case with incoming arcs
   $\text{GateBehaviorPattern}(node)$ **where**
| $select_{\text{Consume}}(node)$ |$= 1$
$EventCond(node) =$
                     forsome $a \in outArc(node) \; Occurs(gateEvent(a))$
$select_{\text{Produce}}(node) = fst(\{a \in outArc(node) \mid Occurs(gateEvent(a))\})$
$\text{EventOp}(node) = \text{Consume}(gateEvent(select_{\text{Produce}}(node)))$
$NormalCase(node) = true$ // event gate throws no exception
$Occurs(gateEvent(a)) =$
   $\begin{cases} Triggered(event(a)) & \text{if } gateEvent(a) = event(a) \\ Completed(receiveTask(a)) & \text{if } gateEvent(a) = receiveTask(a) \end{cases}$

$\text{EventGateProcStartBehavior}(group) =$
   $\text{EventGateProcStartBehavior}_{\text{Start}}(group)$
   $\text{EventGateProcStartBehavior}_{\text{Progress}}(group)$

$\text{EventGateProcStartBehavior}_{\text{Start}}(group) =$
   $\text{GateBehaviorPattern}(group)$ **where**
$select_{\text{Consume}}(group) = \emptyset$
$CtlCond(group) = (mode(group) = Start)$
$EventCond(group) =$ **forsome** $g \in group \; Occurs(gateEvent(g))$
let $g = fst(\{g \in group \mid Occurs(gateEvent(g))\})$
   $select_{\text{Produce}}(group) =$
           $fst(\{a \in outArc(g) \mid Occurs(gateEvent(g, a))\})$
      $\text{CtlOp}(group, O) =$
        let $P = $ **new** $Instance(process(group))$
           $\text{Produce}(select_{\text{Produce}}(group)_P)$
           $lastCreatedProcInst(group) := P$
           $lifeCycle(P) := active$
        $Seen(g) := true$
        if | $group$ |> 1 **then** $mode := Progress$
      $\text{EventOp}(group) = \text{Consume}(gateEvent(select_{\text{Produce}}(g)))$

$NormalCase(group) = true$ // no event gate throws an exception
$Occurs(gateEvent(g)) =$
      forsome $a \in outArc(g)$ $Occurs(gateEvent(g, a))$

$\textsc{EventGateProcStartBehavior}_{Progress}(group) =$
  $\textsc{GateBehaviorPattern}(group)$ **where**
$select_{Consume}(group) = \emptyset$
$CtlCond(group) = (mode(group) = Progress)$
$EventCond(group) =$
  forsome $g \in \{g \in group \mid$ **not** $Seen(g)\}$ $Occurs(gateEvent(g))$
let $g = fst(\{g' \in group \mid Occurs(gateEvent(g'))$ **and** **not** $Seen(g')\})$
  $select_{Produce}(group) =$
          $fst(\{a \in outArc(g) \mid Occurs(gateEvent(g, a))\})$
    $\textsc{EventOp}(group) = \textsc{Consume}(gateEvent(select_{Produce}(group)))$
    $\textsc{CtlOp}(group, O) =$
        if $LastSeen(g, group)$ **then** // reset $group$ state
          $mode(group) := Start$
          forall $g' \in group$ $Seen(g') := false$
        else $Seen(g) := true$
        $\textsc{Produce}(select_{Produce}(group)_{lastCreatedProcInst(group)})$
$NormalCase(group) = true$
$LastSeen(g, group) = (group = \{g' \mid Seen(g')\} \cup \{g\})$

$$\textsc{ComplGateBehavior} = \frac{\textsc{ComplGateBehavior}_{start}}{\textsc{ComplGateBehavior}_{reset}}$$

$\textsc{ComplGateBehavior}_{start}(node) = \textsc{GateBehaviorPattern}(node)$
where
$DataCond(node) = activationCondition(node)$
          and $waitingForStart(node)$
$select_{Consume}(node) = \{in \in inArc(node) \mid Enabled(in)\}$
$select_{Produce}(node) = \{o \in outArc(node) \mid DataCond(a) = true\}$
$\textsc{CtlOp}(node, I, O) =$
  $\textsc{CtlOp}_{\textsc{GateBehaviorPattern}}node, I, O)$
    if $NormalCase(node)$ **then**
      $atStartEnabledArc(node) := select_{Consume}(node)$
      $waitingForStart := false$
$NormalCase(node) = NormalCase_{\textsc{ExclGateBehavior}}(node)$

$\textsc{ComplGateBehavior}_{reset}(node) = \textsc{GateBehaviorPattern}(node)$
where
  $DataCond(node) =$ **not** $waitingForStart(node)$
  $select_{Consume}(node) = \{in \in inArc(node) \setminus atStartEnabledArc(node) \mid$
  $Enabled(in)$ **or** $UpstreamToken(in) \neq \emptyset\}$
                // NB. all to be enabled to fire
$select_{Produce}(node) = \{o \in outArc(node) \mid DataCond(a) = true\}$

$\text{C\scriptsize TL}\text{O\scriptsize P}(node, I, O) =$
$\quad \text{C\scriptsize TL}\text{O\scriptsize P}_{\text{G\scriptsize ATE}\text{B\scriptsize EHAVIOR}\text{P\scriptsize ATTERN}}(node, I, O)$
$\quad waitingForStart := true$
$\quad NormalCase(node) = true$ // no exception thrown in mode $reset$

9.7.2 Activity Behavior

$\text{A\scriptsize CTIVITY}\text{E\scriptsize NTRY}(node, InstSet, TriggerProc) =$
$\qquad \text{F\scriptsize LOW}\text{N\scriptsize ODE}\text{B\scriptsize EHAVIOR}(node)$
where
$CtlCond(node) = \textbf{forsome } in \in inArc(node) \ Enabled(in)$
$\text{C\scriptsize TL}\text{O\scriptsize P}(node) =$
$\quad \textbf{let } arc = select_{\text{Consume}}(\{in \in inArc(node) \mid Enabled(in)\})$
$\qquad \text{C\scriptsize ONSUME}(firingToken(arc), arc)$
$\quad \textbf{let } a = \textbf{new } InstSet$
$\qquad lifeCycle(a) := ready$
$\qquad parent(a) := TriggerProc$
$\quad \textbf{step } \text{G\scriptsize ET}\text{A\scriptsize CTIVE}(a, node)$
$\text{G\scriptsize ET}\text{A\scriptsize CTIVE}(a, node) =$
$\quad \textbf{if } Ready(a) \textbf{ and } \textbf{forsome } i \in inputSets(node) \ Available(i) \textbf{ then}$
$\qquad \textbf{let } i = select_{\text{InputSets}}(\{i \in inputSets(node) \mid Available(i)\})$
$\qquad\quad \text{S\scriptsize TART}\text{E\scriptsize XEC}(a, node)$
$\qquad\quad lifeCycle(a) := active$
$\qquad\quad currInputSet(node) := i$
$\quad \textbf{if } Interrupted(a) \textbf{ then } \text{I\scriptsize NTERRUPT}(a)$
$Ready(a) = (lifeCycle(a) = ready)$

$\text{A\scriptsize CTIVITY}\text{B\scriptsize EHAVIOR}(node) = \text{A\scriptsize CTIVITY}\text{E\scriptsize NTRY}(node,$
$\qquad Instance(node, procInst(node)), procInst(node))$

$\text{T\scriptsize ASK}\text{B\scriptsize EHAVIOR}(node) = \text{A\scriptsize CTIVITY}\text{B\scriptsize EHAVIOR}(node) \textbf{ where}$
$\text{S\scriptsize TART}\text{E\scriptsize XEC}(a, node) = \text{E\scriptsize XEC}(a) \textbf{ seq}$
$\quad \textbf{if } Completed(a) \textbf{ then } \text{E\scriptsize XIT}(a, node)$
$\quad \textbf{if } Interrupted(a) \textbf{ then } \text{I\scriptsize NTERRUPT}(a)$
$\quad \textbf{if } CompensationOccurs(a) \textbf{ then}$
$\qquad \text{T\scriptsize RIGGER}\text{C\scriptsize OMPENSATION}(a)$
$\qquad lifeCycle(a) := compensating$
$\text{E\scriptsize XIT}(a, node) =$
$\quad \textbf{forall } o \in outArc(node) \ \text{P\scriptsize RODUCE}(o)$
$\quad \text{D\scriptsize ELETE}(a, Instance(node, procInst(node)))$
$\quad \text{P\scriptsize USH}\text{O\scriptsize UTPUT}(a, node)$
$\text{P\scriptsize USH}\text{O\scriptsize UTPUT}(a, node) =$
$\quad \textbf{if } \textbf{forall } o \in outputSets(node) \ \textbf{not } Available(o)$
$\quad\quad \textbf{then } \text{T\scriptsize HROW}(noAvailOutputExc, node)$
$\quad\quad \textbf{else } \textbf{let } o = select_{\text{OutputSets}}(\{o \in outputSets(node) \mid Available(o)\})$

if $IORules(node)(o, currInputSet(a)) = false$
 then THROW$(noIORulesExc, node)$
 else PUSH$(output(o))$

EXEC$(t, i) =$ **let** $i = currInputSet(a)$ **in**

$$\begin{cases} \text{SEND}(payload(mssg(t)), receiver(mssg(t))) \\ \qquad\qquad \textbf{if } type(t) = Send \\ \text{RECEIVE}(mssg(t)) \\ \qquad\qquad \textbf{if } type(t) = Receive \\ \text{INVOKE}(job(t), i) \\ \qquad\qquad \textbf{if } type(t) \in \{Service, Script\} \\ \text{ASSIGN}(job(t), i, performer(job(t), i)) \\ \qquad\qquad \textbf{if } type(t) \in \{User, Manual\} \\ \text{CALL}(businessRule(t), i) \\ \qquad\qquad \textbf{if } type(t) = BusinessRule \\ \textbf{skip} \\ \qquad\qquad \textbf{if } Abstract(t) \end{cases}$$

SUBPROCESSBEHAVIOR$(node) =$ ACTIVITYBEHAVIOR$(node)$ **where**
STARTEXEC$(a, node) =$
 if $startEvent(node) \neq$ **undef** **then**
  let $\{t\} = trigger(startEvent(a))$
  $TriggerOccurs_\text{p}(t, startEvent(a)) := true$
 else
  forall $n \in StartNode(node)$ PRODUCE$(startToken(a, node), in(n))$

EVENTSUBPROCESSBEHAVIOR$(node) =$ FLOWNODEBEHAVIOR$(node)$
where
 $EventCond(node) =$
  forsome $e \in StartEvent(node)$ $Happened(e)$
   and **if** $triggeredByEvent(node)$
      then $Active(parent(procInst(node)))$
 let $e = select_\text{StartEvent}(\{n \in StartEvent(node) \mid Happened(e)\}$
 let $\{t\} = select_\text{Trigger}\{t \in trigger(e) \mid TriggerOccurs(t, e)\}$
  EVENTOP$(node) =$ CONSUME(t, e)
  CTLOP$(node) =$
   let $P =$ **new** $Instance(process(node))$
    $caller(P) :=$
     $\begin{cases} parent(procInst(node)) \text{ if } triggeredByEvent(node) \\ caller(node) \qquad\qquad \textbf{else} \end{cases}$
    $TriggerOccurs_\text{p}(t, e) := true$
   if $isInterrupting(node)$ **then** CANCEL$(parent(procInst(node)))$
 $Happened(e) =$ **forsome** $t \in trigger(e)$ $TriggerOccurs(t, e)$

ADHOCBEHAVIOR$(node) =$ ACTIVITYBEHAVIOR$(node)$ **where**
STARTEXEC$(a, node) =$
 while **not** $AdHocCompletionCond(node)$

if $adHocOrdering(node) = Sequential$ **then**
$\qquad$ LAUNCHINNERACT$(node)$
if $adHocOrdering(node) = Parallel$ **then**
$\quad$ **if** $ActivationTime(node)$ **then** LAUNCHINNERACT$(node)$
seq
$\quad$ **if** $CancelRemainingInstances(node)$ **then**
$\qquad$ **forall** $a \in RunningInnerAct(node)$
$\qquad\quad$ CANCEL(a)
$\qquad\quad$ EXIT$(a, node)$
$\quad$ **else** **await** **forall** $a \in RunningInnerAct(node)$
$\qquad$ $Completed(a)$ **or** $Terminated(a)$
$\qquad$ EXIT$(node)$
LAUNCHINNERACT$(node) =$
$\quad$ **if** $enabledInnerAct(node) \neq \emptyset$ **then**
$\qquad$ **let** $e = select_{\text{EnabledInnerAct}(node)}(EnabledInnerAct(node))$
$\qquad$ ACTIVITYBEHAVIOR(e)
$\qquad$ INSERT$(e, RunningInnerAct(node))$
$\qquad$ DELETE$(e, EnabledInnerAct(node))$

CALLACTIVITYBEHAVIOR$(node) =$
ACTIVITYENTRY$(node, Instance(activity(reference(node))), node)$
where STARTEXEC$(a, node) =$
$\quad$ **choose** $n \in \{n \in StartEvent(a) \mid trigger(n) = None\}$
$\quad$ $TriggerOccurs_a(None, n) := true$
$\quad$ INSERT$(a, ActiveProcInst(activity(reference(node)))))$

STANDARDLOOPBEHAVIOR$(node) =$ ACTIVITYBEHAVIOR$(node)$ **where**
STARTEXEC$(a, node) =$
$\quad$ **let** $i = inputs(currInputSet(node))$
$\qquad$ **if** $testBefore(node) = true$ **then**
$\qquad\quad$ **while** $loopCond(a, node)$ ACTIVATE$(body(a, node), i)$
$\qquad$ **if** $testBefore(node) = false$ **then**
$\qquad\quad$ **until** $loopCond(node)$ ACTIVATE$(body(a, node), i)$
$\quad$ **seq** **if** $Completed(a, node)$ **then** EXIT$(a, node)$
$\quad$ $Completed(a, node) =$
$\qquad \begin{cases} \textbf{not } loopCond(a, node) & \textbf{if } testBefore(node) = true \\ loopCond(a, node) & \textbf{if } testBefore(node) = false \end{cases}$

MULTINSTLOOPBEHAVIOR $=$ ACTIVITYBEHAVIOR$(node)$ **where**
STARTEXEC$(a, node) =$
$\quad$ **while** $MiCompletionCond(a, node) = false$
$\qquad$ **if** $isSequential(node)$ **then**
$\qquad\quad$ LAUNCHINSTANCE$(node)$ // run first instance until completion
$\qquad\quad$ **step** // creation of further instances
$\qquad\qquad$ **while** $loopCardinality(node) > \mid ActiveInnerAct(a, node) \mid$
$\qquad\qquad\quad$ LAUNCHINSTANCE$(a, node)$ // run next instance until completion

else // parallel case: new instances created at activation time
    while $loopCardinality(node) > | ActiveInnerAct(a, node) |$
      if $ActivationTime(node)$ **then** // run one more instance
        LAUNCHINSTANCE$(a, node)$
step
  forall $a \in ActiveInnerAct(a, node)$ CANCEL(a)
  EXIT$(a, node)$ // NB with refined PUSHOUTPUT
LAUNCHINSTANCE$(a, n) =$
  let $act =$ **new** $Instance(innerAct(n))$
  $\begin{cases} \text{ACTIVATE}(act) \\ \text{INSERT}(act, ActiveInnerAct(a, n)) \end{cases}$
  step **await** $Completed(act)$ EMITEVENT(n)
EMITEVENT$(n) =$
$\begin{cases} \text{THROW}(noneBehaviorEventRef(n), n) & \textbf{if } behavior(n) = None \\ \text{THROW}(oneBehaviorEventRef(n), n) & \textbf{if } behavior(n) = One \\ \textbf{and} \quad | Instance(innerAct(n)) | = 1 \\ \textbf{forall } e \in ComplexBehaviorDefinition \\ \quad \text{THROW}(e, n) & \textbf{if } behavior(n) = Complex \end{cases}$

9.7.3 Event Behavior

STARTEVENTBEHAVIOR$(node) =$ FLOWNODEBEHAVIOR$(node)$
  where // normal case without parallel multiple trigger
    $EventCond(node) = ParallelMultiple \notin trigger(node)$ **and**
      forsome $e \in trigger(node)$ $TriggerOccurs(e, node)$
    EVENTOP$(node) =$
      choose $e \in \{e \in trigger(node) \mid TriggerOccurs(e, node)\}$
        CONSUME$(triggerOccurrence(e))$
    CTLOP$(node) =$
      let $P =$ **new** $Instance(process(node))$
      forall $o \in outArc_P(node_P)$ PRODUCE$(startToken_P(node, o), o)$

STARTEVENTPARMULTBEHAVIOR$(node) =$ FLOWNODEBEHAVIOR$(node)$
  where // case with parallel multiple triggers
    $EventCond(node) = ParallelMultiple \in trigger(node)$ **and**
      forall $e \in trigger(node) \setminus \{ParallelMultiple\}$
      $TriggerOccurs(e, node)$
    EVENTOP$(node) =$
      forall $e \in trigger(node) \setminus \{ParallelMultiple\}$
        CONSUME$(triggerOccurrence(e))$
    CTLOP$(node) =$
      let $P =$ **new** $Instance(process(node))$
      forall $o \in outArc_P(node_P)$ PRODUCE$(startToken_P(node, o), o)$

ENDEVENTBEHAVIOR(*node*) = FLOWNODEBEHAVIOR(*node*) **where**
CtlCond(*node*) =   **forsome** *in* ∈ *inArc*(*node*) *Enabled*(*in*)
CTLOP(*node*) =   **choose** *in* ∈ {*in* ∈ *inArc*(*node*) | *Enabled*(*in*)}
   CONSUME(*firingToken*(*in*), *in*)
   if *Multiple* ∉ *resultType*(*node*) // normal case without multiple results
   then   **let** {*res*} = *resultType*(*node*) **in** EMITRESULT(*res*, *node*)
   else   **forall** *res* ∈ *resultType*(*node*) \ {*Multiple*}
      EMITRESULT(*res*, *node*)

INTERMEDIATETHROWEVENTBEHAVIOR(*node*) =
   FLOWNODEBEHAVIOR(*node*) **where**
CtlCond(*node*) =   **forsome** *in* ∈ *inArc*(*node*) *Enabled*(*in*)
CTLOP(*node*) =   **choose** *in* ∈ {*in* ∈ *inArc*(*node*) | *Enabled*(*in*)}
   CONSUME(*firingToken*(*in*), *in*)
   PRODUCEALL(*outArc*(*node*))
EVENTOP(*node*) =
   if *Multiple* ∉ *trigger*(*node*) // case with only one trigger
      then   **let** {*t*} = *trigger*(*node*) **in** SETEVENTTRIGGER(*t*, *node*)
      else   **forall** *t* ∈ *trigger*(*node*) \ {*Multiple*}
               SETEVENTTRIGGER(*t*, *node*)
SETEVENTTRIGGER(*t*, *n*) =
   ⎧ **forall** *m* ∈ *MessageFlow* **with** *sender*(*m*) = *node*
   ⎪   SEND(*payload*(*m*), *receiver*(*m*))
   ⎪   **if** *t* = *Message*
   ⎪ BROADCAST(*signalRef*(*n*), *receivers*(*signalRef*(*n*), *n*))
   ⎪   **if** *t* = *Signal*
   ⎨ *Triggered*(*targetLink*(*n*)) := *true*
   ⎪   **if** *t* = *Link*
   ⎪ THROW(*escalation*, *n*)
   ⎪   **if** *t* = *Escalation*
   ⎪ THROW((*compensation*, *actRef*(*node*)), *node*)
   ⎩   **if** *t* = *Compensation*

INTERMEDIATECATCHEVENTBEHAVIOR(*node*) =
   FLOWNODEBEHAVIOR(*node*) **where**
CtlCond(*node*) =   **forsome** *in* ∈ *inArc*(*node*) *Enabled*(*in*)
EventCond(*node*) =
   (*ParallelMultiple* ∉ *trigger*(*node*)
            // only one trigger required to occur
      and   **forsome** *t* ∈ *trigger*(*node*) *TriggerOccurs*(*t*, *node*))
   or
      (*ParallelMultiple* ∈ *trigger*(*node*) // all triggers required to occur
         and   **forall** *t* ∈ *trigger*(*node*) *TriggerOccurs*(*t*, *node*))
EVENTOP(*node*) =
   let *TriggOcc* = {*t* ∈ *trigger*(*node*) | *TriggerOccurs*(*t*, *node*))}
      if *ParallelMultiple* ∉ *trigger*(*node*) **then**

$$\mathbf{choose}\ t \in TriggOcc\ \textsc{Consume}(triggerOccurrence(t))$$
$$\mathbf{else}\quad \mathbf{forall}\ t \in TriggOcc\ \textsc{Consume}(triggerOccurrence(t))$$
$$\textsc{CtlOp}(node) = \quad \mathbf{choose}\ in \in \{in \in inArc(node) \mid Enabled(in)\}$$
$$\textsc{Consume}(firingToken(in), in)$$
$$\textsc{ProduceAll}(outArc(node))$$
$$TriggerOccurs(t, node) =$$
$$\left\{ \begin{array}{ll} \mathbf{forsome}\ m \in Message\ Received(m, node)\ \mathbf{if}\ t = Message \\ TimerCondition(node) = true & \mathbf{if}\ t = Timer \\ EventExpression(node) = true & \mathbf{if}\ t = Conditional \\ Triggered(sourceLink(node)) = true & \mathbf{if}\ t = Link \end{array} \right.$$

$\textsc{BoundaryEventBehavior}(node) = \textsc{FlowNodeBehavior}(node)$
where
$EventCond(node) =$
$\quad (ParallelMultiple \notin trigger(node)$
$\qquad\qquad$ // only one trigger required to occur
$\quad\quad \mathbf{and}\quad \mathbf{forsome}\ t \in trigger(node)\ TriggerOccurs(t, node))$
$\quad \mathbf{or}$
$\quad (ParallelMultiple \in trigger(node)$ // all triggers required to occur
$\quad\quad \mathbf{and}\quad \mathbf{forall}\ t \in trigger(node)\ TriggerOccurs(t, node))$
$\textsc{EventOp}(node) =$
$\quad \mathbf{let}\ TriggOcc = \{t \in trigger(node) \mid TriggerOccurs(t, node))\}$
$\quad\quad \mathbf{if}\ ParallelMultiple \notin trigger(node)\ \mathbf{then}\quad \mathbf{choose}\ t \in TriggOcc$
$\quad\quad\quad \textsc{Consume}(triggerOccurrence(t))$
$\quad\quad\quad \mathbf{if}\ t = Compensate\ \mathbf{then}$
$\quad\quad\quad\quad \textsc{Activate}(compensation(attachedTo(node)))$
$\quad\quad \mathbf{else}\quad \mathbf{forall}\ t \in TriggOcc$
$\quad\quad\quad \textsc{Consume}(triggerOccurrence(t))$
$\quad\quad\quad \mathbf{if}\ Compensate \in TriggOcc\ \mathbf{then}$
$\quad\quad\quad\quad \textsc{Activate}(compensation(attachedTo(node)))$
$\textsc{CtlOp}(node) =$
$\quad \textsc{ProduceAll}(outArc(node))$
$\quad \mathbf{if}\ cancelActivity(attachedTo(node))$
$\quad\quad\quad \mathbf{then}\ \textsc{Interrupt}(attachedTo(node))$

$TriggerOccurs(t, node) =$
$$\left\{ \begin{array}{ll} \mathbf{forsome}\ m \in Message\ Received(m, node) & \mathbf{if}\ t = Message \\ TimerCondition(node) = true & \mathbf{if}\ t = Timer \\ EventExpression(node) = true & \mathbf{if}\ t = Conditional \\ \mathbf{forsome}\ n\ node \in receivers(signalRef(n), n) \\ \quad \mathbf{and}\ Arrived(signalRef(n), node) & \mathbf{if}\ t = Signal \\ triggerOccurrence(t) = (Completed, a) \\ \quad \mathbf{and}\ Completed(a) & \mathbf{if}\ t = Compensate \\ Caught(t, node) \\ \quad\quad \mathbf{if}\ t \in \{Escalation, Error, Cancel\} \end{array} \right.$$

Acknowledgements We thank Wei Wei and Son Thai for helpful comments on the first draft of this chapter and Hagen Völzer for information on the current status of the work on the OMG BPMN standardization committee.

References

1. Aït-Sadoune I, Ameur YA (2009) A proof based approach for modelling and verifying Web services compositions. In: 14th IEEE international conference on engineering of complex computer systems (ICECCS'09), pp 1–10
2. Aït-Sadoune I, Ameur YA (2010) A proof based approach for formal verification of transactional BPEL Web services. In: Frappier M, Glässer U, Khurshid S, Laleau R, Reeves S (eds) Abstract state machines, alloy, B and Z. Lecture notes in computer science, vol 5977. Springer, Berlin, pp 405–406
3. Altenhofen M, Börger E (2009) Concurrent abstract state machines and ^{+}CAL programs. In: Corradini A, Montanari U (eds) WADT 2008. Lecture notes in computer science, vol 5486. Springer, Berlin, pp 1–17
4. Börger E, Craig I (2009) Modeling an operating system kernel. In: Diekert V, Weicker K, Weicker N (eds) Informatik als Dialog zwischen Theorie und Anwendung. Vieweg+Teubner, Wiesbaden, pp 199–216
5. Börger E, Stärk RF (2003) Abstract state machines: a method for high-level system design and analysis. Springer, Berlin
6. Börger E, Thalheim B (2008) A method for verifiable and validatable business process modeling. In: Börger E, Cisternino A (eds) Advances in software engineering. Lecture notes in computer science, vol 5316. Springer, Berlin, pp 59–115
7. OmgBpmn (2006) Business Process Modeling Notation Specification v.1.0. dtc/2006-02-01 at http://www.omg.org/technology/documents/spec_catalog.htm
8. OmgBpmn (2009) Business Process Modeling Notation (BPMN). FTF beta 1 for version 2.0. http://www.omg.org/spec/BPMN/2.0, dtc/2009-08-14
9. Sörensen O (2010) Meek – a native BPMN 2.0 process engine based on an ASM model of the standard. Code documentation requests to be sent to ove@is.informatik.uni-kiel.de
10. Voelzer H (2010) A new semantics for the inclusive converging gateway in safe processes. Business Process Management 1:294–309. http://www.springerlink.com/index/171751MQ8084521H.pdf
11. Bryans JW and Wei W (2010) Formal Analysis of BPMN Models Using Event-B. In: Kowalewski S and Roveri M (eds) Formal Methods for Industrial Critical Systems – 15th International Workshop, Lecture notes in computer science, vol 6371. Springer, Berlin Heidelberg, pp 33–49. http://dx.doi.org/10.1007/978-3-642-15898-8_3

Part IV
User Interface Modelling

Chapter 10
Conceptual Modelling of Interaction

Nathalie Aquino, Jean Vanderdonckt, José Ignacio Panach, and Óscar Pastor

Abstract The conceptual model of an information system cannot be considered to be complete after just specifying the structure and behaviour of the system. It is also necessary to specify how end users will interact with the system. Even though there are several proposals for modelling interaction, none of them have become widely known or widely used in academia and industry. After illustrating the state of the art in this field, this chapter briefly presents a practical approach with the aim of showing how interaction modelling can be faced. The presented approach is called OO-Method, a Model-Driven Engineering method that allows full functional systems to be generated from a conceptual model. The chapter explains how OO-Method supports the interaction modelling by means of its Presentation Model. Apart from this description, the chapter comments on some limitations of the presentation model to satisfy end user interaction requirements related to preferences and different contexts of use. This problem is faced by distinguishing an abstract and a concrete level for interaction modelling. The abstract perspective focuses on what must be presented to end users in order to allow their interaction with an information system, and the concrete perspective focuses on how those elements are presented.

Nathalie Aquino
Centro de Investigación en Métodos de Producción de Software, Universidad Politécnica de Valencia, Camino de Vera s/n, 46022 Valencia, Spain, e-mail: naquino@pros.upv.es

Jean Vanderdonckt
Université catholique de Louvain, Louvain School of Management (LSM), Place des Doyens, 1-B-1348, Louvain-la-Neuve, Belgium
Centro de Investigación en Métodos de Producción de Software, Universidad Politécnica de Valencia, Camino de Vera s/n, 46022 Valencia, Spain, e-mail: jean.vanderdonckt@uclouvain.be

José Ignacio Panach
Centro de Investigación en Métodos de Producción de Software, Universidad Politécnica de Valencia, Camino de Vera s/n, 46022 Valencia, Spain, e-mail: jpanach@dsic.upv.es

Óscar Pastor
Centro de Investigación en Métodos de Producción de Software, Universidad Politécnica de Valencia, Camino de Vera s/n, 46022 Valencia, Spain, e-mail: opastor@dsic.upv.es

D. W. Embley and B. Thalheim (eds), *Handbook of Conceptual Modeling.*
DOI 10.1007/978-3-642-15865-0, © Springer 2011

335

Upon the basis of a whole interaction model, abstract and concrete perspectives are separated. On the one hand, the OO-Method presentation model is shown to be an example of abstract interaction modelling. On the other hand, an extension based on transformation templates is proposed to cover the concrete interaction modelling perspective. To illustrate how both interaction modelling levels can be used, this chapter models the interaction of a photography agency system.

10.1 Introduction

The idea that the conceptual model is the code is becoming more and more a reality in software engineering and information systems design. Some explicit statements for this perspective can be found in the conceptual schema-centric development (CSCD) challenge [24], the Extreme Non-Programming initiative [21, 25], and the set of both academic and industrial approaches and tools proposed within the frame of model-driven engineering (MDE), with the intention of providing operative solutions. Conceptually aligned with these ideas and specifically represented in this book under the term Conceptual Modelling Programming (see Chap. 1), we strongly believe that conceptual modelling is programming. As stated in the manifesto of Chap. 1, *the conceptual model, with which modellers program, must be complete and holistic*. In practice, this statement requires every necessary aspect of data (structure), behaviour (function), and interaction (both component interaction and user interaction) to be adequately included.

User interaction modelling is the issue in this chapter. We are especially concerned with the answer to an apparently simple question: What are the most relevant conceptual primitives or modelling elements that should guide the construction of a conceptual interaction model? This question arises since the conceptual model community provides widely accepted and widely used data models with strong standards such as the entity-relationship model (ERM) [10] or UML Class Diagrams, as well as widely accepted and widely used behaviour models (from the "old" data flow diagrams [34] to the more recent collaboration, sequence, or activity UML Diagrams). However, it is surprising that clear and concrete conceptual models to represent interaction have not yet been provided. There are still questions about which interaction models will allow us to address conceptual modelling of user interfaces and how these models can be properly embedded into the whole conceptual model, which includes data, behaviour, and interaction. This is particularly surprising since the answer to these questions are so evident for the data and behaviour perspectives of conceptual modelling, especially when considering the great importance of user interface design in the whole process of building an information system. Everyone accepts that a final software application is much more than a well-defined database and a set of programs that incorporate the needed functionality. If a conceptual model is to be viewed as the code of the system, every essential aspect of software must be considered, and, of course, user interface plays a basic role in this context. Going back to the Conceptual Modelling Programming manifesto in Chap. 1, to make the goal of having a conceptual model complete and holistic a reality, the proper specification of user interface conceptual models (not only user interface sketches of the system) is strictly required. Therefore, the conceptual modelling elements behind user interface specification must be defined precisely, and must be based on a corresponding ontological agreement that fixes the concepts and their associated representation and notation.

To achieve these goals, this chapter explores two aspects. First, a particular example of what user interface modelling means in terms of modelling primitives and model specification is introduced. The selected approach is the presentation model of OO-Method [27]. This approach constitutes a practical case of how interaction modelling from the user interface perspective is joined to data and behaviour modelling in a unified way, and how this conceptual model includes all the relevant information that is needed to face the subsequent conceptual model compilation process to obtain the corresponding software system. Conceptual primitives are introduced to show how user interface modelling can be specifically put in practice, bridging the gap between "conventional" (data- and behaviour-oriented) conceptual modelling and user interface modelling.

Second, this chapter deals with an important feature that is associated with user interface modelling. An interaction model can fix the presentation style, but this presentation style normally needs to be adapted to the end user's tastes and wishes. Talking about the user interface is not the same as talking about the final data and program structure. In general, end users want to participate in defining the way in which the human-software interaction is going to be accomplished, and this cannot be done if the user interface model does not allow the conceptual model to be adapted to their particular interaction requirements. Some authors use the term "beautification" to refer to this situation [31].

A common solution for solving this problem consists in explicitly distinguishing between two levels in the interaction conceptual model: an abstract level and a concrete level. This approach has been presented in several works ([9, 16, 18, 22, 30, 39], among others), and it is currently being applied in the context of user interface development according to MDE. While the abstract level focuses on the high-level perspective of the interaction, the concrete level identifies several possible representations of the abstract modelling primitives and gives modelers the chance to adapt them according to the target platform and the end user's preferences.

This distinction between abstract and concrete provides a two-level approach that makes it possible to differentiate concerns that are very important within the scope of interaction modelling. On the one hand, there are higher-level abstractions that fix the main relevant user interface properties (e.g., the set of interaction units that should make up the main menu of an application). These abstractions represent which elements are going to be shown in each interface. On the other hand, there is a more concrete level where interfaces are specified for particular software environments. This concrete model represents how the elements of the interface will be presented (e.g., the particular, concrete presentation style chosen for presenting those main menu options to the end users).

In accordance with these ideas, this chapter is structured in the following way: in Sect. 10.2, a related work analysis is presented to understand what other authors have proposed and how the interaction modelling issue is confronted from a conceptual model perspective in current MDE approaches. In Sect. 10.3, the presentation model of OO-Method is introduced as an example of how interaction modelling is properly embedded in an MDE-based software production process where conceptual models are the only key software artefacts. In Sect. 10.4, we propose an extension to explicitly distinguish between the abstract level and the concrete level, indicating how to accomplish this distinction in practice. The chapter ends with concluding remarks and the list of references used.

10.2 Related Work

Since its inception in the 1980s, the domain of human-computer interaction (HCI) has experienced a dramatic increase in research and development, to the point where it is recognized that interaction should also be modeled just like any other aspect of an interactive system. For more than a decade, several model-based approaches have evolved in parallel in order to cope with the different challenges raised by the design and development of user interfaces in continuously evolving technological settings. We can identify various generations of works in this area [36].

The first generation of model-based approaches focused basically on deriving abstractions for graphical user interfaces (for example, UIDE [13]). At that time, user interface designers focused mainly on identifying relevant aspects for this kind of interaction modality. A second generation of approaches focused on expressing the high-level semantics of the interaction. This was mainly supported through the use of task models and associated tools, which were aimed at expressing the activities that users intend to accomplish while interacting with the application (for example, Adept [15], GTA [42], ConcurTaskTrees (CTT) [29], Trident [5], Humanoid [35]). Since then, a consensus has been reached in the community to structure interaction modelling according to different levels of abstraction in almost the same way as in other areas (i.e. database engineering and information systems).

In this context, one of the most recent works is the Cameleon Reference Framework [9]. Cameleon structures the development life cycle into four levels of abstraction, starting from task specification to a running interface (see Fig. 10.1):

- Task and concepts: This level considers (a) the logical activities (tasks) that need to be performed in order to reach the end users' goals; and (b) the domain objects manipulated by these tasks.
- Abstract User Interface (AUI): This level represents the user interface in terms of interaction spaces (or presentation units), independently of which interactors are available and even independently of the modality of interaction (e.g., graphical, vocal, haptic).
- Concrete User Interface (CUI): This level represents the user interface in terms of "concrete interactors", which depend on the type of platform and media available

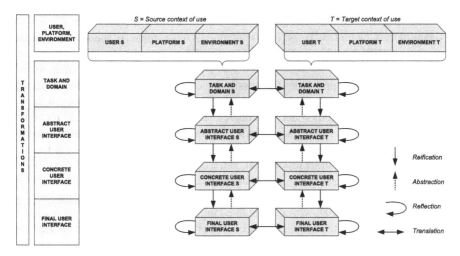

Fig. 10.1 Relationships between components in the Cameleon reference framework

and which have a number of attributes that more concretely define how the user interface should be perceived by the end user.

- Final User Interface (FUI): This level consists of source code, in any programming or markup language (e.g., Java, HTML5, VoiceXML, X+V). It can then be interpreted or compiled.

These levels are structured with both a relationship of reification, going from a more abstract level to a more concrete one, and a relationship of abstraction, going from a more concrete level to a more abstract one. There can also be a relationship of translation between models at the same level of abstraction, but conceived for different contexts of use. These relationships are depicted in Fig. 10.1.

There are other approaches for representing the interaction based on UML models (http://www.uml.org/). Wisdom [23] is a UML-based software engineering method that proposes an evolving use-case-based method in which the software system is iteratively developed by incremental prototypes until the final product is obtained. The UML notation has been enriched with the necessary stereotypes, labeled values, and icons to allow user-centered development and a detailed user interface design. Three of its models are concerned with interaction modelling at different stages: the interaction model, at the analysis stage, and the dialog and presentation models during the design stage, as refinements of the interaction model.

Another important proposal is UMLi [12], which is a set of user interface models that extends UML to provide greater support for user interface design. UMLi introduces a new diagram: the user interface diagram, which can be considered to be the first reliable proposal of UML to formally capture the user interface. However, the models are so detailed that the modelling turns out to be very difficult. Middle-sized models are very hard to specify, which may be the reason why UMLi has not been adopted in industrial environments.

In addition, there are several proposals that model the interaction abstractly by means of the ConcurTaskTrees (CTT) notation [29]. Examples of these types of proposals are TERESA [22] and SUIDT [4]. TERESA (Transformation Environment for inteRactivE Systems representAtions) is a tool that supports transformations in a top-down manner, providing the possibility of obtaining interfaces for different types of devices from logical descriptions. This tool starts with an overall envisioned task model and then derives concrete and effective user interfaces for multiple devices. SUIDT (Safe User Interface Design Tool) is a tool that automatically generates interfaces using several models that are related to each other: a formal functional core, an abstract task model, and a concrete task model. CTT notation is used in the abstract task model and in the concrete task model.

We have mentioned different types of approaches for representing the interaction in an abstract manner. However, a suitable language that enables integration within the development environment is still needed. For this purpose, the notion of User Interface Description Language (UIDL) has emerged to express any of the aforementioned models. A UIDL is a formal language used in HCI to describe a particular user interface independently of any implementation technology. As such, the user interface might involve different interaction modalities (e.g., graphical, vocal, tactile, haptic, multimodal), interaction techniques (e.g., drag and drop), or interaction styles (e.g., direct manipulation, form fillings, virtual reality). A common fundamental assumption of most UIDLs is that user interfaces are modeled as algebraic or model-theoretic structures that include a collection of sets of interaction objects together with behaviours over those sets.

The design process for a UIDL encompasses the definition of the following artefacts:

- Semantics: This expresses the context, meaning, and intention of each abstraction captured by the underlying meta-models on which the UIDL is based.
- Abstract syntax: This is a syntax that makes it possible to define user interface models (in accordance with the UIDL semantics) independently of any representation formalism.
- Concrete syntax/es: These are (one or more) concrete representation formalisms intended to syntactically express user interface models.
- Stylistics: These are graphical and textual representations of the UIDL abstractions that maximize their representativity and meaningfulness in order to facilitate understanding and communication among different people.

As we have seen in this section, there are a lot of proposals to represent the interaction. Each proposal is based on a specific notation, like UML or CTT. However, as far as we know, these proposals support interaction modelling but do not support the modelling of the persistence and functionality of a system. Moreover, the works mentioned in this section have seldom been used in industrial environments.

In the next section, we present an approach that has solved both of these limitations: the modelling of interaction in a holistic conceptual modelling approach and the practical applicability of interaction modelling in an industrial context. Furthermore, we show how the interaction can be represented by means of conceptual primitives.

10.3 The Presentation Model of OO-Method

OO-Method [27] is an object-oriented method that allows the automatic generation of software applications from conceptual models. These conceptual models are structured in four system views. (1) The Object Model specifies the static properties of the interactive application by defining the classes and their relationships. (2) The Dynamic Model controls the application objects by defining their life cycle and interactions. (3) The Functional Model describes the semantics of object state changes. (4) The Presentation Model specifies the user interface.

OO-Method is supported by a commercial software suite named OlivaNOVA that was developed by CARE Technologies (http://www.care-t.com). OlivaNOVA edits the various models involved and applies subsequent transformations until the final code of a fully functional application (persistence, logic, and presentation) is generated for different computing platforms: C# or ASP running on .NET or .NET 2.0; and EJB, JSP, or JavaServer Faces running on Java. Thus, OO-Method defines a holistic conceptual model that includes the interaction perspective as well as the structural and behavioural ones. Furthermore, it is currently being used successfully in an industrial environment.

This section presents the conceptual primitives of the OO-Method presentation model. These primitives allow a user interface to be modeled in a convenient way, and offer enough expressiveness to represent any management information system interface. In this section and the following, we present an illustrative example related to a photography agency system. The agency manages illustrated reports for distribution to newspaper editorials, and operates with photographers who work as independent professionals.

The OO-Method presentation model is structured with a set of interaction patterns that were defined in [20]. These interaction patterns are ordered in three levels (see Fig. 10.2):

- Level 1 – Hierarchical Action Tree (HAT) organizes the access to the system functionality through a tree-shaped abstraction.
- Level 2 – Interaction Units (IUs) represent the main interactive operations that can be performed on the domain objects (executing a service, querying the population of a class, and visualizing the details of a specific object).
- Level 3 – Elementary Patterns (EPs) constitute the building blocks from which IUs are constructed.

In the next three subsections, we provide more details about the interaction patterns from these three levels, going from the most specific to the most general ones.

10.3.1 Elementary Patterns

Elementary patterns (EPs) constitute the primitive building blocks to build IUs. They represent specific aspects of the interaction between a human and a system and cannot be combined in an arbitrary way. On the contrary, each of them is applicable in specific IUs.

In the current OO-Method presentation model, there are 11 EPs that can be related to their corresponding relevant IUs (see Fig. 10.2):

- Introduction captures the relevant aspects of data to be entered by the end user. Interaction aspects that can be specified include edit masks and valid value ranges.
- Defined selection enables the definition (by enumeration) of a set of valid values for an associated model element.
- Argument grouping defines the way in which input arguments for a given service are presented to the end user allowing these input arguments to be arranged in groups and subgroups.

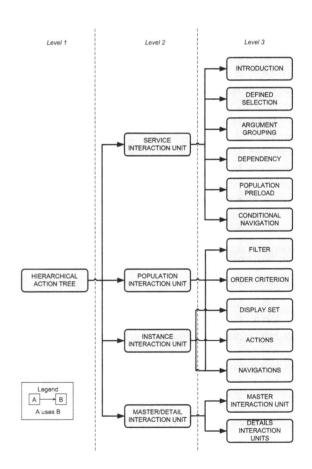

Fig. 10.2 OO-Method presentation model

- Dependency enables dependency relationships to be defined between the value or state of an input argument of a service and the value or state of other input argument of the same service. The definition is based on ECA-type rules (event, condition, action).
- Population preload allows the designer to specify that the selection of an object as an input argument of a service will be carried out with or without changing the interaction context.
- Conditional navigation allows navigation to different IUs after the successful or failed execution of a service. In order to specify which IU to navigate to, it is also necessary to establish a condition that must hold after the execution of the service.
- Filter defines a selection condition over the population of a class, which can be used to restrict the object population of the class, thereby facilitating further object search and selection operations.
- Order criterion defines how the population of a class is to be ordered. Ordering is done on the values of one or more properties of the objects, taking into account ascending/descending options.
- Display set determines which properties of a class are to be presented to the user and in what order.
- Actions define the set of available services that can be performed on the objects of a given class.
- Navigations determine the information set that can be accessed via navigation of the structural relationships found in an initial class.

10.3.2 Interaction Units

An Interaction Unit (IU) describes a particular scenario of the user interface through which users are able to carry out specific tasks. In the OO-Method approach, there are three different basic kinds of interaction scenarios: execution of a service, manipulation of one object, and manipulation of a collection of objects. For each of these basic interaction scenarios, the OO-Method approach proposes a specific IU that is appropriate for handling it. A fourth IU is proposed to combine the other IUs. As shown in Fig. 10.2, the OO-Method presentation model defines these four IUs:

- Service IU: enables a scenario to be defined in which the user interacts with the system in order to execute a service. The user must provide the arguments and launch the service.

  As shown in Fig. 10.2, six of the EPs can be used to complete the specification of a Service IU: introduction, defined selection, argument grouping, dependency, population preload, and conditional navigation. Figure 10.3 shows the final user interface generated from a Service IU.

  The user interface for this Service IU allows a photographer to fill in an application form for working in a photography agency. The photographer must provide personal and contact data as well as data related to its professional equipment.

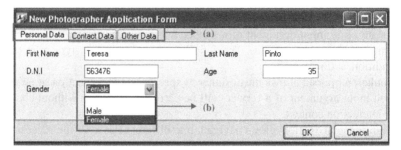

Fig. 10.3 User interface generated from a Service IU with argument groupings (a) and defined selection (b)

- Instance IU: represents a scenario in which information about a single object is displayed, including the list of services that can be executed on it, as well as the scenarios of related information to which the user can navigate. All this information is structured by means of three EPs: display set, actions, and navigations (see Fig. 10.2).

  Figure 10.4 shows the final user interface generated from an Instance IU. The user interface for this Instance IU shows data related to a photographer of the agency.

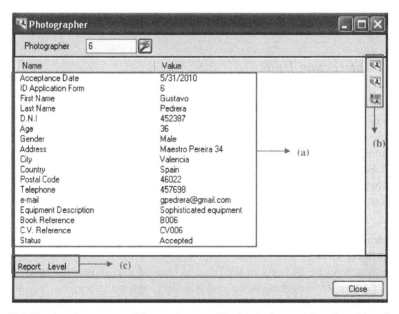

Fig. 10.4 User interface generated from an Instance IU with display set (a), actions (b), and navigations (c)

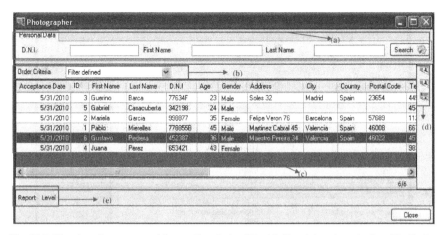

Fig. 10.5 User interface generated from a Population IU with filter (a), order criterion (b), display set (c), actions (d), and navigations (e)

- Population IU: represents an interaction scenario where multiple objects are presented. This scenario includes the appropriate mechanisms to do the following: select and sort objects, choose the information and available services to be shown, and list other scenarios that can be reached. All this information is structured by means of five EPs: filter, order criteria, display set, actions, and navigations (see Fig. 10.2).

   Figure 10.5 shows the final user interface generated from a Population IU. The user interface for this Population IU shows data related to multiple photographers of the agency at the same time.

- Master/Detail IU: presents the user with a scenario for the interaction with multiple collections of objects that belong to different interrelated classes. This forms a composite scenario in which two kinds of roles can be defined: a master role, which represents the main interaction scenario, and detail roles, which represent secondary, subordinated interaction scenarios that are kept synchronized with the master role (see Fig. 10.2).

   Figure 10.6 shows the final user interface generated from a Master/Detail IU in which the master role corresponds to an Instance IU, which shows data related to a photographer of the agency, and the detail role corresponds to a Population IU, which shows the list of reports related to the photographer.

The user interfaces depicted in Figs. 10.3–10.6 have been generated by OlivaNOVA for the desktop .NET platform.

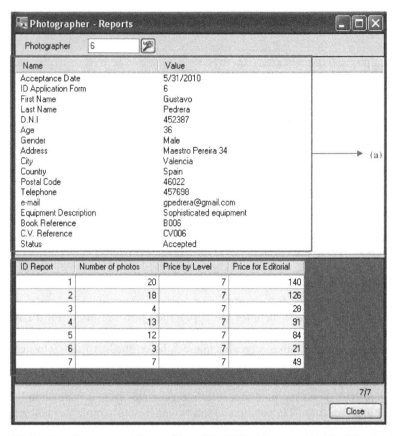

Fig. 10.6 User interface generated from an Master/Detail IU with master role (a) and detail role (b)

10.3.3 Hierarchical Action Tree

Once the interaction scenarios have been described through the corresponding IUs, it is necessary to determine how these IUs are to be structured, organized, and presented to the user. This structure will characterize the top level of the user interface, establishing what could be described as the main menu of the application. The Hierarchical Action Tree (HAT) serves this purpose.

The HAT defines an access tree that follows the principle of gradual approximation to specify the manner in which the interactive user can access system functionality. This is achieved by arranging actions into groups and subgroups by using a tree abstraction, from the most general to the most detailed. Intermediate (i.e., non-leaf) nodes in the tree are simply grouping labels, whereas tree leaves reference pre-existing IUs (see Fig. 10.2).

10.4 Explicitly Distinguishing Abstract
and Concrete Interaction Modeling in OO-Method

The OO-Method presentation model constitutes a unified interaction model in which there is no explicit distinction between an abstract level and a concrete level. This model can be considered a good starting point for adequately modelling interaction, since it provides a good basis to include user interface generation in the conceptual model compilation process. However, it still presents an important problem: the interaction style of the resultant software application is fixed by the model compiler, and there is no way to adapt the presentation style to the particular needs and individual tastes of end users. In this section, we show how to make this distinction feasible. We also extend the above approach in this direction, and add a concrete level that incorporates decisions related to platforms and users. In particular, the transformation templates approach is presented as a means for concrete interaction modelling.

10.4.1 Abstract Interaction Modeling

As explained in Sect. 10.3, the OO-Method presentation model provides primitives that allow the designer to define user interfaces in a homogeneous and platform-independent way. All of its interaction patterns, from the three levels, capture the necessary aspects of the user interface without delving into implementation issues. In other words, the OO-Method presentation model focuses on what type of user interaction is desired, and not on how this interaction will be implemented in the resulting software product. Therefore, the OO-Method presentation model can be considered an abstract model from which the model compiler can automatically generate a user interface for different interaction modalities and platforms.

10.4.2 Concrete Interaction Modeling: Transformation Templates

At the abstract level, the OO-Method presentation model does not provide primitives that allow the structure, layout, and style of user interfaces to be expressed. These decisions are delegated to the model compiler and are hard-coded in it. Thus, design knowledge and presentation guidelines are implicit and fixed in the tool that performs the model-to-code transformation and cannot be edited or customized. Thus, even though different final user interface implementations are potentially valid when moving from the abstract to the final user interface, it is not possible to adapt the user interface generation according to end user requirements and preferences. This results in the generation of predetermined user interfaces, all of which look alike, and which may not always satisfy the end user.

Fig. 10.7 An OO-Method
presentation model and
a transformation template
are inputs for the model compiler

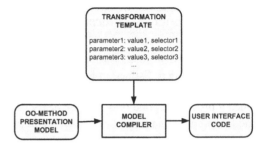

Because of these issues, it has been necessary to extend the OO-Method presentation model with a new concrete level that provides the required expressiveness in order to enable the customization of user interfaces before their generation. An approach based on transformation templates has been defined for this purpose.

A transformation template [2, 3] aims to specify the structure, layout and style of a user interface according to preferences and requirements of end users, as well as according to the different hardware and software computing platforms and environments in which the user interface will be used.

A transformation template is composed of parameters with associated values that parameterize the transformations from the OO-Method presentation model to code. Figure 10.7 illustrates the use of a transformation template with OO-Method. The model compiler takes a presentation model and a transformation template as input. The transformation template provides specifications that determine how to transform the presentation model to code. The specifications are expressed by means of parameters with values and selectors. Selectors define the set of elements of the OO-Method presentation model that are affected by the value of the parameter. The transformation engine follows the specifications to generate the code.

In this way, transformation templates externalize the design knowledge and presentation guidelines and make them customizable according to the characteristics of the project that is being carried out. Transformation templates can then be reused in other projects with similar characteristics.

Even though the idea behind transformation templates is based on cascading style sheets [6], there are significant differences between the two approaches, with the main one being that transformation templates are applied to user interface models and not directly to the code. Another difference is that transformation templates are supposed to be used in an MDE process for user interface generation for different contexts of use, not only for web environments.

Figure 10.8 depicts the main concepts or primitives that characterize the transformation templates approach. The concepts in this figure are related to context, to user interface models, and to the transformation templates themselves. These concepts are explained in the following paragraphs.

10.4.2.1 Context

- Context (see Fig. 10.8): refers to the context of use of an interactive system. We have defined context according to the Cameleon reference framework [9], which is widely accepted in the HCI community. According to this framework, a context of use is composed of the stereotype of a user who carries out an interactive task with a specific computing platform in a given surrounding environment. The purpose of conceptualizing context is that we want it to be possible to define different transformation templates for different contexts of use.

10.4.2.2 User Interface Models

The transformation templates approach makes use of two concepts related to user interface models (see Fig. 10.8):

- User interface meta-element: represents, in a generic way, any of the OO-Method interaction patterns presented in Sect. 10.3.
- User interface element: represents an element of the OO-Method presentation model, that is, a specific instance of any of the above mentioned interaction patterns.

Note that even though in this chapter we are presenting the transformation templates approach as an extension of OO-Method, it can also be used with other MDE approaches related to user interface development. In fact, the user interface meta-element is a generic representation of any meta-element of a user interface meta-model. Similarly, the user interface element is a generic representation of any element of a user interface model.

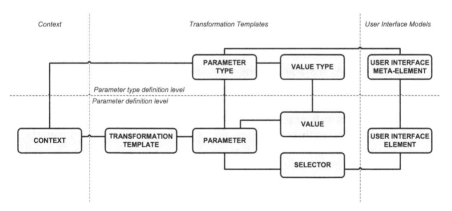

Fig. 10.8 Main concepts of the transformation templates approach

10.4.2.3 Transformation Templates

With regard to concepts specifically related to the transformation templates approach, we distinguish between two levels: one in which parameter types are defined, and another one in which the previously defined parameter types are instantiated as parameters in a transformation template.

In the parameter type definition level, there are two concepts (see Fig. 10.8):

- Value type: refers to a specific data type (e.g., integer, URI, colour, etc.) or to an enumeration of the possible values that a parameter type can assume.
- Parameter type: represents a design or presentation option related to the structure, layout, or style of the user interface. We can distinguish between low-level and high-level parameter types. Low-level ones operate at the attribute level of user interfaces; for instance, colour or font type are low-level parameter types related to style. High-level parameter types operate at the concept level of user interfaces and can be used to specify the structure of the user interface, the type of components (containers, widgets) that will be used, or the alignment of the components.

Defining a parameter type subsumes specifying the list of user interface metaelements that are affected by it, as well as its value type. A parameter type, with all or a set of its possible values, can be implemented in different contexts of use. In order to decide about these implementations, we propose that each possible value receive an estimation of its importance level and its development cost for different relevant contexts of use. In this way, possible values with a high level of importance and a low development cost can be implemented first in a given context, followed by those with a high level of importance and a high development cost, and so on. Possible values with a low level of importance and a high development cost would not have to be implemented in the corresponding context. For each relevant context of use, usability guidelines can be assigned to each possible value of a parameter type. These guidelines will help user interface designers in choosing one of the possible values by explaining the conditions under which the values should be used.

Table 10.1 shows an example of the definition of a parameter type named *grouping layout for input arguments*. This parameter type is useful for deciding how to present the input arguments of a service that have been grouped using the argument grouping interaction pattern presented in Sect. 10.3.1.

Table 10.1 (a) shows that this parameter type affects two interaction patterns of the OO-Method presentation model. It also shows that four different possible values have been defined.

Table 10.1 (b) shows that the parameter type has been associated to two contexts of use: a desktop platform and a mobile one. For each context of use and each possible value, the importance level and development cost have been estimated.

Table 10.1 (c) presents a list of usability guidelines for the desktop context and each possible value of the parameter type. These usability guidelines have been proposed from an extraction from [14].

Table 10.1 Parameter type: grouping layout for input arguments

Parameter Type Name	Affects	Possible values enumeration	
		Value	Graphical description
Grouping layout for input arguments	Two patterns of the OO-Method presentation model: Service IU and argument grouping	Group box	Personal Data Contact Data
		Tabbed dialog box	Personal Data Contact Data
		Wizard	Personal Data / Next Cancel — Contact Data / Ok Cancel
		Accordion	Personal Data / Contact Data

(a)

Possible value	Contexts SW: C# on .NET - HW: laptop or PC		SW: iPhone OS - HW: iPhone	
	Importance level	Development cost	Importance level	Development cost
Group box	High	Low	High	Low
Tabbed dialog box	High	Low	Medium	Medium
Wizard	Medium	Medium	Low	High
Accordion	Low	Medium	Medium	Medium

(b)

Possible value	Usability guidelines (for desktop context)
Group box	Visual distinctiveness is important. The total number of groups will be small
Tabbed dialog box	Visual distinctiveness is important. The total number of groups is not greater than 10
Wizard	The total number of groups is between 3 and 10. The complexity of the task is significant. The task implies several critical decisions. The cost of errors is high. The task must be done infrequently. The user lacks the experience it takes to complete the task efficiently
Accordion	Visual distinctiveness is important. The total number of groups is not greater than 10

(c)

In the parameter definition level, there are four concepts (see Fig. 10.8):

- Transformation template gathers a set of parameters for a specific context of use.
- Parameter: each parameter of a transformation template corresponds to a parameter type and has both a value and a selector.
- Value is an instance of a value type. The value of a parameter corresponds to a possible value of the corresponding parameter type.

- Selector delimits the set of user interface elements that are affected by the value of a parameter. We have defined different types of selectors that allow the designer to choose a specific user interface element; all the user interface elements of a certain type; the first or last element contained in a specific type of user interface element; or other options.

Figure 10.9 represents the user interface that could be obtained for the Service IU that was presented in Fig. 10.3, if the parameter *grouping layout for input arguments* is applied with value *wizard* (see Table 10.1) and if the following two parameters are also applied: a parameter for specifying the widget to be used to display defined selections with value *radio button*; and a parameter for specifying the alignment of labels with value *vertical*.

10.5 Conclusion

This chapter emphasizes the importance of interaction modelling on the same level of expressiveness as any other model involved in the development life cycle of an interactive application. In the same way that a conceptual model of the domain could be used to derive a database for a future application, a conceptual model of the interaction could be used to derive a user interface for this same application [37]. A system with a suitable functionality and persistence may be rejected by end users if the interface does not satisfy their expectations. Therefore, the designer must be provided with the suitable conceptual primitives to represent every relevant characteristic of the final interface; otherwise, a complete code generation from a conceptual model cannot become a reality.

Today, the community has reached a level of progress in which this has now become a reality that goes beyond mere prototypes. In the past, *model-based approaches* were exploited to capture the essence of a user interface into a conceptual model of the user interface to be subsequently used for design, specification, generation, and verification. More recently, *model-driven engineering* (MDE) approaches have been introduced in order to make the user interface development life cycle more precise, rigorous, and systematic.

The main difference between model-based approaches and model-driven engineering approaches [40, 41] is that in the former, only models are used, while in the latter all models comply with a meta-model that is itself defined according to a meta-meta-model. Similarly, all operations are captured through transformations that are themselves compliant with the same meta-model, as opposed to earlier approaches in which no meta-model was present. Not all model-based approaches for user interface development could be considered as compliant with Model-Driven Architecture (MDA) [40].

Indeed, the following MDE/MDA definition was approved unanimously by 17 participants of the ORMSC – Object and Reference Model Subcommittee of the Architecture Board of the Object Management Group (OMG) – plenary session

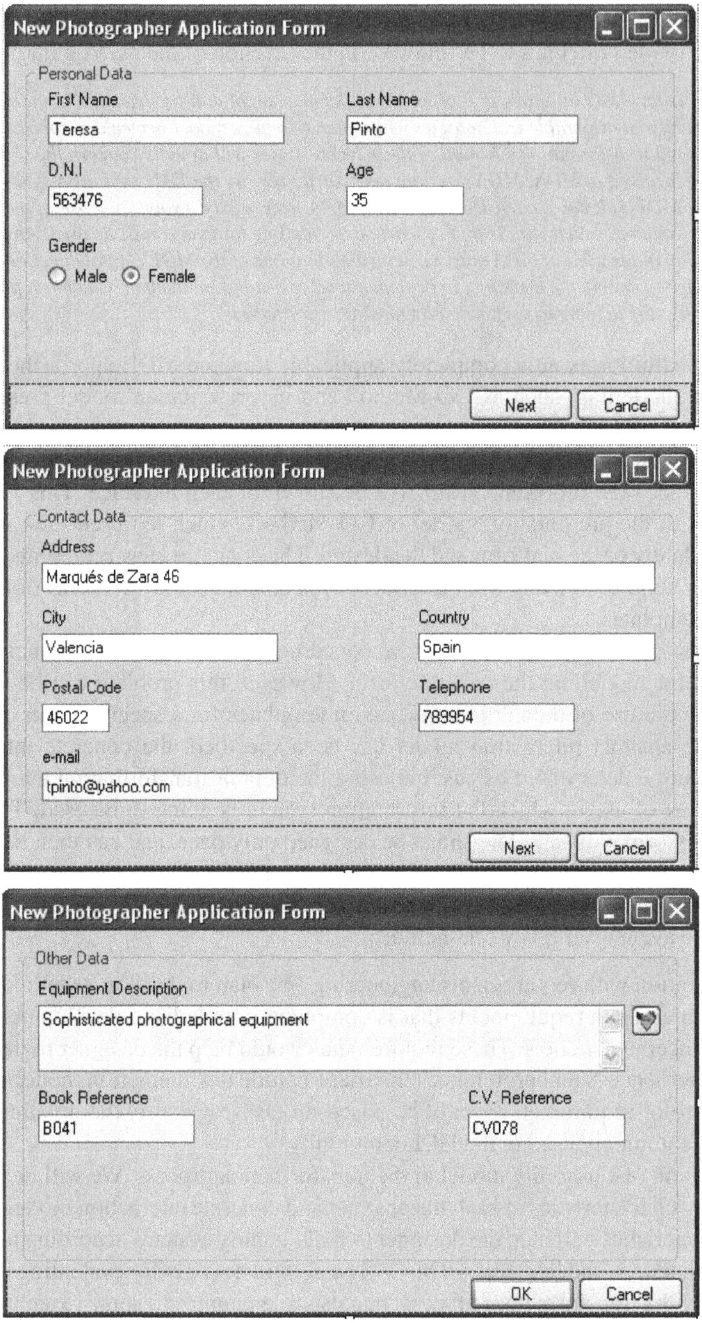

Fig. 10.9 User interface that could be generated from a Service IU after applying different parameters

meeting in Montreal on 23–26 August 2004. The stated purpose of the paragraph was to provide principles to be followed in the revision of the MDA guide:

> *"MDA is an OMG initiative that proposes to define a set of non-proprietary standards that will specify interoperable technologies with which to realize model-driven development with automated transformations. Not all of these technologies will directly concern the transformation involved in MDA. MDA does not necessarily rely on the UML, but, as a specialized kind of MDD (Model-Driven Development), MDA necessarily involves the use of model(s) in development, which entails that at least one modelling language must be used. Any modelling language used in MDA must be described in terms of the MOF (MetaObject Facility) language to enable the metadata to be understood in a standard manner, which is a precondition for any activity to perform automated transformation".*

This definition is now completely applicable to some MDE approaches for interaction modelling, such as OO-Method and its presentation model presented in this chapter. Taking this presentation model as input, we state that the interaction modelling must be divided into two views: abstract [27, 38, 39] and concrete [2, 3]. The abstract view represents *what* will be shown in each interface. This view corresponds to the presentation model of OO-Method, which represents the interface independently of the platform and the design. The concrete view represents *how* the elements will be shown in each interface. This model is built by means of transformation templates.

At first glance, designers might be concerned that more effort on their part is required for modelling the concrete level. However, this problem can be resolved thanks to the use of default transformation templates for a specific context of use. Once the abstract interaction model has been specified, the concrete interaction model can be determined by just choosing the default transformation template for the context of use in which the information system is going to be used. These default transformation templates must be designed only once, and can then be reused. Designers might only have to change the value and/or scope of some parameters in order to adequate the concrete modelling to end user requirements.

Future avenues of this work include:

- Integration with requirements engineering. We plan to develop a method to capture interaction requirements that is compliant with holistic development based on conceptual models. These requirements would help the designer to determine the user's needs and preferences in order to guide the interaction modelling. The capture of requirements would be based on tasks, which is the notation that is most commonly used in the HCI community.
- Inclusion of a usability model in the transformation process. We will include usability characteristics in both the abstract and concrete interaction models. These characteristics will help the designer to build quality systems according to usability guidelines and heuristics. This will be helpful not only for evaluating usability during the transformation process, but also to guarantee to some extent that user interfaces issued by this approach are somewhat usable by construction [1] so as to provide a general computational framework for user interfaces [32].
- Building various transformation sets for various development paths. We will build new transformation sets that would support other development paths [17]

than merely forward engineering. For instance, ReversiXML [7, 8] performs reverse engineering of web pages into a concrete interface model expressed in UsiXML [18] by using derivation rules, but not transformation rules. Similarly, MultimodaliXML [33] generates multimodal user interfaces based on the same conceptual models, but involves other sets of transformation rules.

- Building multi-fidelity editors for each model. We plan to develop model editors that enable modelers to rely on different levels of fidelity, not just high fidelity [19], for instance by sketching the model [11], ranging from low fidelity to high fidelity.

As for any MDA approach, it is crucial to develop any work that contributes to obtain a low threshold, a high ceiling, and wide walls as much as possible to expand the capabilities of expressiveness and their transformation into a larger gamma of user interfaces. This is reflected in Fig. 10.10: the first generation of MDA software usually suffered from a high threshold (they required a high amount of resources to get some results), a low ceiling (the capabilities of the user interface generated were limited), and narrow walls (there was only one user interface generated for one computing platform). The second generation improved this situation by lowering the threshold, increasing the ceiling, and enlarging the walls. Right now, we are in the third generation, where user interface capabilities have been expanded for multiple computing platforms and contexts of use.

This race is to be continued.

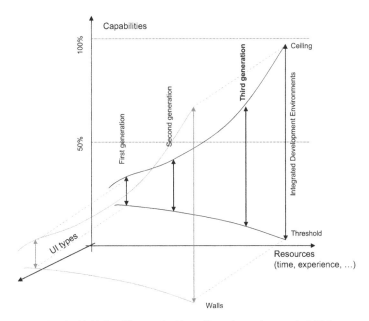

Fig. 10.10 Low threshold, high ceiling, and wide walls as determinants of a MDA approach

Acknowledgements We gratefully acknowledge the support of the ITEA2 Call 3 UsiXML project under reference 20080026; the MITYC under the project MyMobileWeb, TSI-020301-2009-014; the MICINN under the project SESAMO, TIN2007-62894, co-financed with ERDF; the Generalitat Valenciana under the project ORCA, PROMETEO/2009/015, and the grant BFPI/2008/209. Jean Vanderdonckt also thanks the FP7 Serenoa project supported by the European Commission.

References

1. Abrahão S, Iborra E, Vanderdonckt J (2008) Usability evaluation of user interfaces generated with a model-driven architecture tool. In: Law E, Hvannberg E, Cockton G (eds) Maturing usability: quality in software, interaction and value, HCI Series, vol. 10. Springer, London, pp 3–32
2. Aquino N, Vanderdonckt J, Pastor O (2010) Transformation templates: adding flexibility to model-driven engineering of user interfaces. In: Shin SY, Ossowski S, Schumacher M, Palakal MJ, Hung CC (eds) Proceedings of the 25th ACM symposium on applied computing, SAC 2010, Sierre, March 2010. ACM Press, New York, pp 1195–1202
3. Aquino N, Vanderdonckt J, Valverde F, Pastor O (2009) Using profiles to support model transformations in the model-driven development of user interfaces. In: López Jaquero V, Montero Simarro F, Molina Masso JP, Vanderdonckt J (eds) Computer-aided design of user interfaces VI, Proceedings of 7th international conference on computer-aided design of user interfaces, CADUI 2008, Albacete, June 2008. Springer, Berlin, pp 35–46
4. Baron M, Girard P (2002) SUIDT A task model based GUI-builder. In: Pribeanu C, Vanderdonckt J (eds) Task models and diagrams for user interface design: Proceedings of the first international workshop on task models and diagrams for user interface design, TAMODIA 2002, Bucharest, July 2002. INFOREC Publishing House, Bucharest, pp 64–71
5. Bodart F, Hennebert AM, Provot I, Leheureux JM, Vanderdonckt J (1994) A model-based approach to presentation: a continuum from task analysis to prototype. In: Paternò F design, specification and verification of interactives systems'94, Proceedings of the first international Eurographics workshop, Bocca di Magra, June 1994. Springer, Berlin, pp 77–94
6. Bos B, Çelik T, Lie HW, Hickson I (2007) Cascading style sheets level 2 revision 1 (CSS 2.1) specification. Technical report. World Wide Web Consortium (W3C), http://www.w3.org. Accessed 6 December 2010
7. Bouillon L, Limbourg Q, Vanderdonckt J, Michotte B (2005) Reverse engineering of web pages based on derivations and transformations. In: Proceedings of 3rd Latin American Web congress LA-Web 2005 Aires, 31 October 2005. IEEE Computer Society Press, Los Alamitos, pp 3–13
8. Bouillon L, Vanderdonckt J, Chow KC (2004) Flexible re-engineering of Web sites. In: Proceedings of 8th ACM international conference on intelligent user interfaces IUI 2004, Funchal, 13–16 January 2004. ACM Press, New York, pp 132–139
9. Calvary G, Coutaz J, Thevenin D, Limbourg Q, Bouillon L, Vanderdonckt J (2003) A unifying reference framework for multi-target user interfaces. Interact Comput 15(3):289–308
10. Chen PP (1976) The entity-relationship model – toward a unified view of data. ACM Trans Database Syst 1(1):9–36
11. Coyette A, Vanderdonckt J (2005) A sketching tool for designing anyuser, anyplatform, anywhere user interfaces. In: Costabile MF, Paternò F (eds) Proceedings of 10th IFIP TC 13 international conference on human–computer interaction, INTERACT 2005, Rome, 12–16 September 2005, Lecture Notes in Computer Science, vol 3585. Springer, Berlin, pp 550–564
12. da Silva PP, Paton NW (2003) User interface modeling in UMLi. IEEE Softw 20(4):62–69
13. Foley JD, Sukaviriya PN (1994) History, results, and bibliography of the user interface design environment (UIDE), an early model-based system for user interface design and implementation. In: Paternò F design, specification and verification of interactives systems'94. Proceed-

ings of the first international Eurographics workshop, Bocca di Magra, June 1994. Springer, Berlin, pp 3–14.
14. Galitz, WO (2002) The essential guide to user interface design: an introduction to GUI design principles and techniques. Wiley, New York
15. Johnson P, Wilson S, Markopoulos P, Pycock J (1993) ADEPT: advanced design environment for prototyping with task models. In: Ashlund S, Mullet K, Henderson A, Hollnagel E, White TN (eds) Human–computer interaction. Proceedings of INTERACT '93, IFIP TC13 international conference on human–computer interaction, Amsterdam, 24–29 April 1993. ACM Press, New York, p 56
16. Limbourg Q, Vanderdonckt J (2004) USIXML: a user interface description language supporting multiple levels of independence. In: Matera M, Comai C (eds) Engineering advanced web applications: Proceedings of workshops in connection with the 4th international conference on web engineering, ICWE 2004, Munich, 28–30 July 2004. Rinton Press, Paramus, pp 325–338
17. Limbourg Q, Vanderdonckt J (2009) Multi-path transformational development of user interfaces with graph transformations. In: Seffah, A, Vanderdonckt J, Desmarais M (eds) Human-centered software engineering, HCI Series. Springer, London, pp 109–140
18. Limbourg Q, Vanderdonckt J, Michotte B, Bouillon L, López-Jaquero V (2005) USIXML: A language supporting multi-path development of user interfaces. In: Bastide R, Palanque PA, Roth J (eds) Proceedings of 9th IFIP working conference on engineering for human-computer interaction jointly with 11th international workshop on design, specification, and verification of interactive systems, EHCI-DSVIS 2004, Hamburg, 11–13 July 2004. Lecture Notes in Computer Science, vol 3425. Springer, Berlin, pp 200–220
19. Michotte B, Vanderdonckt J (2008) GrafiXML, a multi-target user interface builder based on UsiXML. In: Greenwood D, Grottke M, Lutfiyya H, Popescu M (eds) Proceedings of 4th international conference on autonomic and autonomous systems, ICAS 2008 Gosier, 16–21 March 2008. IEEE Computer Society Press, Los Alamitos, pp 15–22
20. Molina PJ, Meliá S, Pastor O (2002) Just-UI: a user interface specification model. In: Kolski C, Vanderdonckt J (eds) Computer-aided design of user interfaces III, Proceedings of the 4th international conference on computer-aided design of user interfaces, CADUI 2002, Valenciennes, 15–17 May 2002. Kluwer, Alphen aan den Rijn, pp 63–74
21. Morgan T (2004) Doing IT better. Keynote address at the 3rd conference on information systems technology and its applications, ISTA 2004. Salt Lake City, 15–17 July 2004
22. Mori G, Paternò F, Santoro C (2004) Design and sevelopment of multidevice user interfaces through multiple logical descriptions. IEEE Trans Softw Eng 30(8):507–520
23. Nunes NJ, e Cunha JF (2000) Wisdom: A software engineering method for small software development companies. IEEE Software 17(5):113–119
24. Olivé A (2005) Conceptual schema-centric development: a grand challenge for information systems research. In: Pastor O, e Cunha JF (eds) Advanced information systems engineering, Proceedings of 17th international conference, CAiSE 2005, Porto, 13–17 June 2005, Lecture Notes in Computer Science, vol 3520. Springer, Berlin, pp 1–15
25. Pastor O (2006) From extreme programming to extreme non-programming: is it the right time for model transformation technologies? In: Bressan S, Küng J, Wagner R (eds) Proceedings of 17th international conference on database and expert systems applications, DEXA 2006, Krakow 4–8 September 2006, Lecture Notes in Computer Science, vol 4080. Springer, Berlin, pp 64–72
26. Pastor O, e Cunha JF (eds) Advanced information systems engineering, Proceedings of 17th international conference, CAiSE 2005, Porto, 13–17 June 2005, Lecture Notes in Computer Science, vol 3520. Springer, Berlin
27. Pastor O, Molina JC (2007) Model-driven architecture in practice: a software production environment based on conceptual modeling. Springer, Secaucus
28. Paternò F (ed) (1994) Design, specification and verification of interactive systems'94, Proceedings of the first international Eurographics workshop, 8–10 June 1994, Bocca di Magra. Springer, Berlin
29. Paternò F. (1999) Model-based design and evaluation of interactive applications. Springer, London

30. Paternò F, Santoro C, Spano LD (2009) MARIA: a universal, declarative, multiple abstraction-level language for service-oriented applications in ubiquitous environments. ACM Trans Comput-Hum Interact, 16(4)
31. Pederiva I, Vanderdonckt J, España S, Panach JI, and Pastor O (2007) The beautification process model-driven engineering of user interfaces. In: Baranauskas MCC, Palanque PA, Abascal J, Barbosa SDJ (eds) Proceedings of 11th IFIP TC 13th international conference on human–computer interaction, INTERACT 2007, Río de Janeiro, 10–14 September 2007, Lecture Notes in Computer Science, vol 4662. Springer, Berlin, pp 411–425
32. Puerta AR, Eisenstein J (1999) Towards a general computational framework for model-based interface development systems, Knowl-Based Syst 12(8):433–442
33. Stanciulescu A, Limbourg Q, Vanderdonckt J, Michotte B, Montero F (2005) A transformational approach for multimodal web user interfaces based on UsiXML. In: Lazzari G, Pianesi F, Crowley JL, Mase K, Oviatt SL (eds) Proceedings of the 7th international conference on multimodal interfaces, ICMI 2005, Trento, 4–6 October 2005. ACM Press, New York, pp 259–266
34. Stevens WP, Myers GJ, Constantine LL (1974) Structured Design. IBM Syst J 13(2):115–139
35. Szekely PA (1990) Template-based mapping of application data interactive displays. In: Hudson SE (ed) Proceedings of the 3rd annual ACM symposium on user interface software and technology, UIST 1990, Snowbird, 3–5 October 1990. ACM Press, New York, pp 1–9
36. Szekely PA (1996) Retrospective and challenges for model-based interface development In: Bodart F, Vanderdonckt J (eds) Design, specification and verification of interactive systems'96, Proceedings of the 3rd International Eurographics workshop, Namur, 5–7 June 1996. Springer, Berlin, pp 1–27
37. Torres I, Pastor O, Limbourg Q, Vanderdonckt J (2005) Una experiencia práctica de generación de interfaces de usuario a partir de esquemas conceptuales. In: Puerta AR and Gea M (eds) Proceedings of VI congreso interacción persona ordenador, Interacción 2005 – CEDI 2005, Granada, 13–16 September 2005. Thomson Paraninfo, Madrid, pp 401–404
38. Valverde F, Panach JI, Aquino N, Pastor O (2009) New trends on human–computer interaction. Research, development, new tools and methods. Dealing with abstract interaction modelling in an MDE development process: a pattern-based approach. Springer, London, pp 119–128
39. Valverde F, Panach JI, Pastor O (2007) An abstract interaction model for a MDA software production method. In: Grundy JC, Hartmann S, Laender AHF, Maciaszek LA, Roddick. JF (eds) Challenges in conceptual modelling. Proceedings of tutorials, posters, panels and industrial contributions at the 26th international conference on conceptual modeling, ER 2007, Auckland, 5–9 November 2007, CRPIT, vol 83. Australian Computer Society, pp 109–114
40. Vanderdonckt J (2005) A MDA-compliant environment for developing user interfaces of information systems. In: Pastor O, e Cunha JF (eds) Advanced information systems engineering, Proceedings of 17th international conference, CAiSE 2005, Porto, 13–17 June 2005, Lecture Notes in Computer Science, vol 3520. Springer, Berlin, pp 16–31
41. Vanderdonckt J (2008) Model-driven engineering of user interfaces: promises, successes, and failures. In: Buraga S, Juvina I (eds) Proceedings of 5th annual Romanian conference on human–computer interaction ROCHI'2008, Iasi, 18–19 September 2008. Matrix ROM, Bucarest, pp 1–10
42. Van Der Veer GC, Lenting BF, Bergevoet BAJ (1996) GTA: groupware task analysis – modeling complexity. Acta Psychol 1:297–322

Chapter 11
Conceptual Modelling of Application Stories

Antje Düsterhöft and Klaus-Dieter Schewe

Abstract The development of complex systems requires an understanding of how the system is supposed to be used. This corresponds to describing how actors are supposed to navigate through the system and which actions they are to execute in order to perform certain tasks. As descriptions of navigation paths correspond to "telling stories" about the system usage, a conceptual model for application stories is needed. This chapter highlights the key concepts of storyboarding such as actors, scenarios and tasks, and the composed action scheme called "plot". Furthermore, the pragmatics of storyboards is addressed, i.e. what the model means to users. The chapter is rounded out by discussing inferences to analyse storyboards.

11.1 Introduction

Since its very beginnings conceptual modelling has aimed at describing complex systems – existing ones as well as those still to be built – on a high level of abstraction, such that the model could be used to mediate between the technically-oriented system developers and the users, who understand the system from an application point of view. Thus, conceptual models have to be grounded in the application and at the same time be precise to serve as a blueprint for further system development.

Application stories describe how a system is supposed to be used. Naturally, a conceptual model for application stories must be centred around users: what they do and why. The conceptual model of storyboarding (see e.g. [26]) takes this up by providing an integrated model comprising the story space capturing the stories and the plot, actors and tasks. Inspired by approaches in theatre and film, the story space

Antje Düsterhöft
Hochschule Wismar, Department of Electrical Engineering and Computer Science, Wismar, Germany, e-mail: antje.duesterhoeft@hs-wismar.de

Klaus-Dieter Schewe
Software Competence Center Hagenberg, Hagenberg, Austria, e-mail: kd.schewe@scch.at

D. W. Embley and B. Thalheim (eds), *Handbook of Conceptual Modeling.*
DOI 10.1007/978-3-642-15865-0, © Springer 2011

comprises scenes and actions on these scenes, and the plot describes the details of the action scheme. Furthermore, the model describes actors in these scenes, i.e. groups of users, which leads to roles, profiles, goals, preferences, obligations and rights. The actors are linked to the story space by means of tasks.

The link to system requirements (see e.g. [21]) is achieved via pragmatics, which analyses the meaning of storyboards for users, and provides guidelines to derive the complex storyboards from informal ideas without any technical bias. Based on a fundamental understanding of facets of intentions, the key concepts for storyboard pragmatics are life cases, user models and contexts. Life cases capture observations of user behaviour in reality. Life cases can be used in a pragmatic way to specify the story space. User models comprise user and actor profiles, and actor portfolios, which can be used to get a better understanding of the tasks.

As storyboards are centred around the users, it becomes desirable to customise them to user preferences. Storyboarding provides an inferential approach to personalisation on the basis of an algebraic formalisation of plots (see e.g. [27]). Furthermore, storyboards are also governed by obligations and rights that correspond to roles. Storyboarding permits formal reasoning about these.

Chapter Overview In Sect. 11.2 we first present the syntax and semantics of storyboards. We emphasise the key concepts such as scenes, actions, actors, tasks and plots, and illustrate them by a detailed example. We also highlight various supplementary details. Section 11.3 complements the picture by a discussion of storyboard pragmatics, i.e. the question of what the storyboard means to its users. We emphasise the modelling of system usage by means of life cases, user models and contexts, and continue with our illustrative example. Section 11.4 is devoted to formal aspects of storyboards such as consistency with respect to deontic constraints, which govern the rights and obligations of actors, and customisation to user preferences through inferences. We conclude the chapter by bibliographic remarks in Sect. 11.5 about the historic development of storyboarding and its relation to other published work.

11.2 The Conceptual Model of Storyboarding

On a high level of abstraction the usage of an information system can be described by a storyboard [26], which in an abstract way specifies *who* will be using the system, *in what way* and *for what goals*. In a nutshell, a *storyboard* consists of three parts:

- A *story space*, which itself consists of a hierarchy of labelled directed graphs called *scenarios*, one of which is the main scenario, whereas the others define the details of *scenes*, i.e. nodes in a higher scenario, and a *plot* which is specified by an assignment-free process, in which the basic actions correspond to the labels of edges in the scenarios;

- A set of *actors*, i.e. abstractions of user groups that are defined by *roles*, which determine obligations and rights, and *user profiles*, which determine user preferences; and
- A set of *tasks* that are associated with *goals* the users may have.

In addition, there are many constraints comprising pre- and postconditions, triggering and enabling the events, rights and obligations of roles, preference rules for user types, and other dependencies on the plot. Details of storyboarding have been described in [26]. An overview of our method for the design of WISs was presented in [25].

11.2.1 The Storyboard

For modelling application stories we may think of a set of abstract locations through which users navigate, and on their navigation paths they execute a number of actions. We regard a location together with local actions, i.e. actions which do not change the location, as a unit called a *scene*. Then the *story space* can be described by an edge-labelled directed multi-graph, in which the vertices represent the scenes and the edges represent transitions between scenes. Each such transition may be labelled by an action.

A *story* is a path in the story space. It tells what a user of a particular type might do with the system. The combination of different stories to a subgraph of the story space can be used to describe a "typical" system usage. Therefore, we call such a subgraph a *scenario*. Usually storyboarding starts with modelling scenarios instead of stories, coupled by the integration of scenarios to the story space. Furthermore, we may add a triggering *event*, a *precondition* and a *postcondition* to each action, i.e. we specify exactly, under which conditions, an action can be executed and what effects it will have. In the same way we may further add entry conditions and completion conditions to scenes. Scenarios can be organised in a hierarchical way, i.e. the details in a scene can be described by a scenario.

Example 11.1. Let us consider a tourism service, where users have a choice between three different kinds of tours:

Fly&Sleep: A user interacts with the system to book a flight, one or more hotels, and optionally also some events.
All-Inclusive: A user interacts with the system to book a flight, accommodation and events.
Bicycle: A user interacts with the system to book accommodation and optionally some events.

Each package is coupled with specific expectations. In our case, Fly&Sleep tours are characterised by the aim of finding hotels close to the airport, where users can choose between several hotels and events. For All-Inclusive tours a user can book a bundle consisting of a flight, hotel and optional events. Bicycle tours are characterised by the need to find hotels not too far away from each other.

We use abbreviations α_i for the actions:

$\alpha_1 = $ get_intention $\alpha_2 = $ book_flight $\alpha_3 = $ book_hotel

$\alpha_4 = $ book_event $\alpha_5 = $ confirm $\alpha_6 = $ proceed_payment

$\alpha_7 = $ cc_details $\alpha_8 = $ bank_details

The story space is illustrated by the labelled graph in Fig. 11.1, which results from integrating three scenarios for the different kinds of tours. Actually, only the scenario for the Bicycle tour differs from the complete story space, as it does not contain the scene 'Flight Booking'. The dashed arrows in the figure highlight a story for a Bicycle tour.

We also use the following abbreviations for conditions:

$\varphi_1 \equiv $ fly&sleep $\varphi_2 \equiv $ all-inclusive $\varphi_3 = $ bicycle

$\varphi_4 \equiv $ flight_selected $\varphi_5 \equiv $ hotel_selected $\varphi_6 \equiv $ events_selected

$\varphi_7 \equiv $ pay_by_cheque $\varphi_8 \equiv $ pay_by_credit $\varphi_9 \equiv $ pay_by_direct-debit

Then, $\varphi_1 \vee \varphi_2 \vee \varphi_3$ is the postcondition of α_1, and $\varphi_1 \vee \varphi_2$ is a precondition for α_2. For the scene 'Hotel Booking' the information production consists of travel_period and number_travellers, while the information consumption comprises hotel_list. The leave condition for the scene is φ_5.

Users can be classified according to their roles, intentions and behaviour. We use the term *actor* for such a group of users. The *role* of an actor indicates a particular purpose of the system. As such, it is usually associated with obligations and rights,

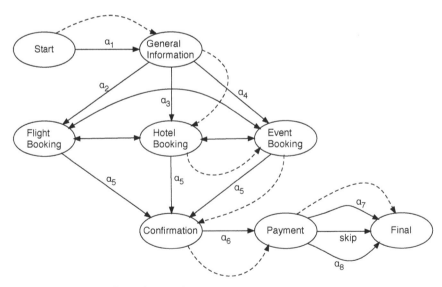

Fig. 11.1 Story space of a tourism service

which lead to deontic integrity constraints. The *intention* of an actor can be modelled by goals, i.e. postconditions to the story space, which are also connected with the *tasks*. Modelling the behaviour of an actor leads to *user profiles*, which can be modelled by giving values for various properties that characterise a user. Furthermore, each profile leads to rules that can again be expressed by constraints on the story space.

In addition, each actor has an *information portfolio*, which specifies the information needs as well as the information entered into the system. We do not model the information portfolio as part of an actor, but instead we will model the information 'consumed' and 'produced' with each more-detailed specification of a scene.

The presence of roles indicates a particular purpose of the system. A *role* is defined by the set of actions that an actor with this role may execute. Thus, a role is associated with obligations and rights, i.e. which actions have to be executed or which scenes are disclosed. An *obligation* specifies what an actor in a particular role has to do. A *right* specifies what an actor in a particular role is permitted to do. Both obligations and rights together lead to complex deontic integrity constraints. We use the following logical language $\mathcal{L}$ for this purpose:

- All propositional atoms are also atoms of $\mathcal{L}$.
- If α is an action on scene s and r is a role associated with s, then $\mathbf{O}\ do(r, \alpha)$, $\mathbf{P}\ do(r, \alpha)$, $\mathbf{F}\ do(r, \alpha)$, and $do(r, \alpha)$ are atoms of $\mathcal{L}$.
- For $\varphi, \psi \in \mathcal{L}$ we also have that $\neg\varphi$, $\varphi \wedge \psi$, $\varphi \vee \psi$, $\varphi \Rightarrow \psi$ and $\varphi \Leftrightarrow \psi$ are also formulae in $\mathcal{L}$.

The interpretation is standard. In particular, $\mathbf{O}\ do(r, \alpha)$ means that an actor with role r is obliged to perform action α, $\mathbf{P}\ do(r, \alpha)$ means that an actor with role r is permitted to perform action α, $\mathbf{F}\ do(r, \alpha)$ means that an actor with role r is forbidden to perform action α, and $do(r, \alpha)$ means that an actor with role r actually performs action α.

Example 11.2. In the tourism service Example 11.1 we have only a single role 'customer', but three different tasks. Therefore, for deontic constraints we simple write $do(\alpha)$ instead of $do(\text{customer}, \alpha)$. We then have the following (selected) deontic constraints expressing the rights and obligations of customers:

$$\varphi_1 \Rightarrow \mathbf{O}\ do(\alpha_2) \wedge \mathbf{O}\ do(\alpha_3) \wedge \mathbf{P}\ do(\alpha_4)$$
$$\varphi_2 \Rightarrow \mathbf{O}\ do(\alpha_2) \wedge \mathbf{O}\ do(\alpha_3) \wedge \mathbf{O}\ do(\alpha_4)$$
$$\varphi_3 \Rightarrow \mathbf{F}\ do(\alpha_2) \wedge \mathbf{O}\ do(\alpha_3) \wedge \mathbf{P}\ do(\alpha_4)$$
$$do(\alpha_5) \Rightarrow \mathbf{O}\ do(\alpha_6) \qquad \varphi_8 \Rightarrow \mathbf{O}\ do(\alpha_7)$$

Modelling the behaviour of an actor leads to *user profiles*. We may ask which properties characterise a user and provide values for each of these properties. Each combination of such values defines a profile, but usually the behaviour for some of these profiles is the same. Furthermore, each profile leads to rules that can again be expressed by constraints on the story space.

The dimensions used in user profiles depend on the application, e.g. the ability to search for solutions, solve problems, detect and resolve conflicts, and schedule work tasks, the communication skills and computer literacy, the knowledge and education level regarding the task domain, the frequency and intensity of system usage, the way information is handled, i.e. the direction of the information flow, the necessary and optional input, the intended information usage, the amount and size of information and the complexity of information, and the experience in working with the system and with associated tasks.

Formally, in order to describe such user profiles, we take a finite set Δ of *user dimensions*, and for each dimension $\delta \in \Delta$ we assume to be given a set $sc(\delta)$ of possible values called the *scale* of δ. For $\Delta = \{\delta_1, \dots, \delta_n\}$ the *set of user profiles* is $gr(\Delta) = sc(\delta_1) \times \cdots \times sc(\delta_n)$. A *user type* over Δ is a subset $U \subseteq gr(\Delta)$.

We then add user types to the story space by assigning a set of user types to each scene. This indicates which stories will be supported for which user profiles.

Example 11.3. Without going into too much detail, we may have the following user types in our tourism service example. The type 'Leary' is only interested in getting the tour done, i.e. will always book a Flight&Sleep tour, but never books events. The type 'Saver' is interested in cheap offers, and therefore will always look for accommodation first. The type 'Culty' is culturally interested and will first look for events to book. We will use these types in Sect. 11.4 for personalisation.

The actions performed by a user usually correspond to a certain task. Such tasks can be the effort of a single user or the cooperative effort of several users. Tasks describe the general purposes of the system. They combine roles that are involved in the task, actions executed by actors in these roles, and consequently scenes to which these actions belong, information consumed by the actions, and data flowing between the actions. In addition, there is an event that triggers the task. Actions can be grouped together into subtasks to provide a more concise form of task specification.

Formally, a *task* τ consists of a set $act(\tau) = \{\tau_1, \dots, \tau_n\}$ of subtasks, which may be actions in the story space, and a triggering event $ev(\tau)$, which is the combination of a Boolean condition φ on the story space and the fact that a particular action α was executed by some role r, i.e. $ev(\tau) = (\varphi, do(r, \alpha))$. Furthermore, with each subtask τ_i we associate a set of scenes and a set of roles. If τ_i is atomic, i.e. an action α, then it will be associated with exactly one scene s and exactly one role r.

Example 11.4. We already mentioned in Example 11.2 that there are three different tasks, i.e. book a Fly&Sleep tour, an All-Inclusive tour, or a Bicycle tour. These three tasks define three different goals:

$$\varphi_{10} \equiv \text{book\_fly\&sleep} \qquad \varphi_{11} \equiv \text{book\_all-inclusive} \qquad \varphi_{12} \equiv \text{book\_bicycle}$$

For these we get the additional constraints:

$$\varphi_{10} \Rightarrow \varphi_1 \qquad \varphi_{11} \Rightarrow \varphi_2 \qquad \varphi_{12} \Rightarrow \varphi_3$$

11.2.2 Plots

Looking at scenarios or the whole story space from a different angle, we may concentrate on the flow of actions:

- For the purpose of storyboarding actions can be treated as atomic, i.e. we are not yet interested in how an underlying database might be updated. Then each action also belongs to a uniquely determined scene.
- Actions have pre- and postconditions, so we can use annotations to express conditions that must hold before or after an action is executed.
- Actions can be executed sequentially or in parallel, and we must allow (demonic) choice between actions.
- Actions can be iterated.
- By adding an action `skip` we can then also express optionality and iteration with at least one execution.

These possibilities to combine actions lead to operators of an algebra, which we will call a *story algebra*. Thus, we can describe the *plot* of a storyboard by an element of a suitable story algebra.

Let us now take a closer look at the storyboarding language `SiteLang` [32], which in fact defines a story algebra. So, let $Sc = \{s_1, \ldots, s_n\}$ be a set of scenes, and let $\mathcal{A} = \{\alpha_1, \ldots, \alpha_k\}$ be a set of (atomic) actions. Furthermore, assume a mapping $\sigma : \mathcal{A} \to Sc$, i.e. with each action $\alpha \in \mathcal{A}$ we associate a scene $\sigma(\alpha)$.

This can be used to define inductively the set of *processes* $\mathcal{P} = \mathcal{P}(\mathcal{A}, Sc)$ determined by $\mathcal{A}$ and S. Furthermore, we can extend σ to a partial mapping $\mathcal{P} \to Sc$ as follows:

- Each action $\alpha \in \mathcal{A}$ is also a process, i.e. $\alpha \in \mathcal{P}$, and the associated scene $\sigma(\alpha)$ is already given.
- `skip` is a process, for which $\sigma(\texttt{skip})$ is undefined.
- If p_1 and p_2 are processes, then also the *sequence* $p_1; p_2$ is a process. Furthermore, if $\sigma(p_1) = \sigma(p_2) = s$ or one of the p_i is `skip`, then $\sigma(p_1; p_2)$ is also defined and equals s, otherwise it is undefined.
- If p_1 and p_2 are processes, then also the *parallel process* $p_1 \| p_2$ is a process. Furthermore, if $\sigma(p_1) = \sigma(p_2) = s$ or one of the p_i is `skip`, then $\sigma(p_1 \| p_2)$ is also defined and equals s, otherwise it is undefined.
- If p_1 and p_2 are processes, then also the *choice* $p_1 \square p_2$ is a process. Furthermore, if $\sigma(p_1) = \sigma(p_2) = s$ or one of the p_i is `skip`, then $\sigma(p_1 \square p_2)$ is also defined and equals s, otherwise it is undefined.
- If p is a process, then also the *iteration* p^* is a process with $\sigma(p^*) = \sigma(p)$, if $\sigma(p)$ is defined.
- If p is a process and φ is a Boolean condition, then the *guarded process* $\{\varphi\}p$ and the *post-guarded process* $p\{\varphi\}$ are processes with $\sigma(\{\varphi\}p) = \sigma(p\{\varphi\}) = \sigma(p)$, if $\sigma(p)$ is defined.

Doing this we have to assume tacitly that navigation between scenes is also represented by an activity in $\mathcal{A}$, and the assigned scene is the origin of the navigation.

SiteLang provides a few more constructs, which we have omitted here, because they can be represented by the constructs above, e.g. non-empty iteration p^+ and optionality $[p]$ can be expressed by $p^+ = p; p^*$ and $[p] = p\square\text{skip}$ respectively.

Mathematically, a story algebra carries the structure of a Kleene algebra with tests (see e.g. [26]). A *Kleene algebra* (KA) $\mathcal{K}$ consists of a carrier-set K containing at least two different elements 0 and 1 and a unary operation * and two binary operations $+$ and $\cdot$ on K such that the following axioms are satisfied (adopt the convention to write pq for $p \cdot q$, and assume that $\cdot$ binds stronger than $+$):

- $+$ and $\cdot$ are associative, i.e. for all $p, q, r \in K$ we have $p + (q + r) = (p + q) + r$ and $p(qr) = (pq)r$;
- $+$ is commutative and idempotent with 0 as neutral element, i.e. for all $p, q \in K$ we have $p + q = q + p$, $p + p = p$ and $p + 0 = p$;
- 1 is a neutral element for $\cdot$, i.e. for all $p \in K$ we have $p1 = 1p = p$;
- for all $p \in K$ we have $p0 = 0p = 0$;
- $\cdot$ is distributive over $+$, i.e. for all $p, q, r \in K$ we have $p(q + r) = pq + pr$ and $(p + q)r = pr + qr$;
- p^*q is the least solution x of $q + px \leq x$ and qp^* is the least solution of $q + xp \leq x$, using the partial order $x \leq y \equiv x + y = y$.

A *Kleene algebra with tests* (KAT) $\mathcal{K}$ consists of a Kleene algebra $(K, +, \cdot, ^*, 0, 1)$, a subset $B \subseteq K$ containing 0 and 1 and closed under $+$ and $\cdot$, and a unary operation $^-$ on B, such that $(B, +, \cdot, ^-, 0, 1)$ forms a Boolean algebra.

Example 11.5. Let us continue Example 11.1 using the abbreviations α_i and φ_j for actions and Boolean conditions (tests) respectively. Then the following KAT expression defines the plot of the story space:

$$\alpha_1(\varphi_1 + \varphi_2 + \varphi_3)((\varphi_1 + \varphi_2)(\alpha_2 \| \alpha_3 \| (\alpha_4 + \varphi_1)) + \varphi_3(\alpha_3 \| (\alpha_4 + 1)))$$
$$\varphi_4\varphi_5(\varphi_6 + \varphi_2\varphi_3)\alpha_5\alpha_6(\varphi_7 + \varphi_8\alpha_7 + \varphi_9\alpha_8)$$

With this formalisation preference rules associated with user types can be expressed by equations, e.g.:

- An equation $p_1 + p_2 = p_1$ expresses an unconditional preference of activity (or process) p_1 over p_2.
- An equation $\varphi(p_1 + p_2) = \varphi p_1$ expresses a conditional preference of activity (or process) p_1 over p_2 in case the condition φ is satisfied.
- Similarly, an equation $p(p_1 + p_2) = pp_1$ expresses another conditional preference of activity (or process) p_1 over p_2 after the activity (or process) p.
- An equation $p_1 p_2 + p_2 p_1 = p_1 p_2$ expresses a preference of order.

In the same way, constraints on the story space can also be captured by equations as follows:

- If an action p has a precondition φ, then we obtain the equation $\bar{\varphi} p = 0$.
- If an action p has a postcondition ψ, we obtain the equation $p = p\psi$.

- If an action p is triggered by a condition φ, we obtain the equation $\varphi = \varphi p$.
- In addition, we obtain exclusion conditions $\varphi\psi = 0$ and tautologies $\varphi + \psi = 1$.

Example 11.6. The preferences of the user types in Example 11.3 lead to the following KAT equations (here p refers to the complete plot as in Example 11.5):

$$\text{for Leary:} \quad \alpha_4 = 0 \quad\quad p = p\varphi_{10}$$
$$\text{for Saver:} \quad \alpha_2 + \alpha_3 = \alpha_3\alpha_2$$
$$\text{for Culty:} \quad \alpha_2 + \alpha_3 + \alpha_4 = \alpha_4(\alpha_2 + \alpha_3) \quad\quad p = p\varphi_6$$

11.3 Pragmatics of Storyboarding

In the previous section we looked at the syntax and semantics of storyboarding. Both syntax and semantics are part of semiotics, which in general is concerned with the relationship between signs, concepts and things of reality. With respect to modelling languages, syntax is concerned with the construction of the language, while semantics is concerned with the interpretation of the words of the language. The third main branch of semiotics is pragmatics, which is concerned with the use of the language and the context of words for the user.

So the storyboarding model would be incomplete without pragmatics. Due to the central importance of users for application stories, the key to understanding storyboard pragmatics is usage analysis (see e.g. [28]). For this we look at typical application scenarios, which lead to life cases, the classification of users, and contexts.

11.3.1 Life Cases

Life cases are characterised by observations, processes, assessment, individual profiles, inter-personal coherence, significance of time and place, user characteristics, and experiences and skills. We are interested in the collection and assessment of behaviour relating to a specific application. This would typically involve an observation of behaviour of users in real environments, including a background check that relates usage to intentions, goals or tasks.

This involves arranging all the actions observed in an application into a main logical and coherent pattern. In some case, deviations of the main pattern must be modelled through exceptions. In most cases, we can use parallel execution of independent actions. This further involves the reconstruction of the sequence of actions and specific behaviour of users, which will aid in understanding the role each individual has within the story, and it assists in developing the user profile. A list of background characteristics, including physical and behavioural characteristics, of individuals is conducted. This list can also be used for deriving the most appropriate interview technique, discussed below.

A variation in activity will relate to variations in other life cases. The choices made also depend on mobility, surroundings, and schedules of events of interest.

Individuals using a service may be grouped by characteristics. Based on this grouping a similar behaviour is observed. Individuals may have their own experience with services provided in real life and thus use different behavioural patterns of service employment.

In general, life case studies are designed to produce a picture of service employment that is as accurate as possible. Determining *why, how, where, when* and *why* a service is called using *which* data provides a better picture for a utilisation scenario. As life cases are used for quality control, we must carefully record our observations. We can either use a natural language specification or a semi-formal one.

Life cases may be developed and interpreted step by step:

1. The first step during life case collection is the survey of possible application cases we might consider. The observations could have more than one meaning and may follow a variety of user-related goals. In this case we consider the most likely meaning.
2. The second step involves a deep assessment of the life cases. We extract the different execution orders, the relationships among actions, and the roles individuals play in these actions.
3. The third step extracts those life case characteristics that are distinguishing features and are relevant for time and location. At the same time we search for similarities within these life cases.
4. The final step is concerned with the characterisation of potential users, their behavioural patterns, and their roles in various stages of the life case.

Collectively, this information will produce a picture of the life case intended to be supported. This may produce further life cases, or it may aid in reducing the amount of development. It may result in a prioritisation of life cases under consideration, assist in the linkage of potentially related life cases, provide the developers with relevant leads and strategies, and keep system development on track and undistracted. Life cases are mapped to scenarios in the sequel. The integration of scenarios can also be based on life cases.

Example 11.7. Let us look at the life case 'prepare_holiday_trip'. The general characterisation of the outcome is given by a trip schedule comprising decisions on dates and time, locations to visit, means of transportation, accommodations, and other activities. Tasks are to book transport if needed, book accommodations, and book other activities if desired. Main problems are to check the consistency and feasibility of the trip.

The life case flow comprises a coarse plan with milestones for confirmed bookings and feasibility and consistency checks. Content consumed comprises information about hotels, flights if needed, events if considered and costs. The produced content is defined by the schedule and the bookings made.

Actors associated with the life case are the scheduler and travel partner, e.g. family, club or company. Expected profiles can be all-inclusive tourists, eco-tourists or individuals. Collaboration is required for tour planning and feasibility checking.

11.3.2 User Modelling

While life case analysis supports the design of the story space, user models address the actors. In particular, user models support defining user profiles, which lead to preference rules that are decisive for personalisation. User modelling has changed the development to human–computer interfaces and allows for tailoring systems to users, their needs, abilities and preferences. User modelling is based on the specification of the *user profile*, which addresses a user's characterisation, and on the specification of the *user portfolio*, which describes a user's tasks, involvement and collaboration.

In general, user profiles can be specified through the *education profile* based on an insight into the knowledge, skills and abilities of potential users, the *work profile* with a specification of the specific work approaches of users, and the *personality profile* representing the specific properties of users. These three profiles cover the most important properties of users which influence the storyboard by means of preference rules associate with them.

- The *education profile* is characterised by properties obtained during education, training and other educational activities, i.e. education, capabilities and application knowledge. The *education* is characterised by the technical and professional training a user has received. Technical training emphasises the understanding and practical application of basic principles of science and mathematics. Professional training places major emphasis upon the theories, understanding and principles in such fields as science and engineering. It results in erudition, knowledge and literacy.
- The *work profile* is mainly characterised by task-solving knowledge and skills in the application area, i.e. task expertise and experience, system experience, and information and interaction profiles. For instance, task expertise describes the exact and partial knowledge of data, procedures, algorithms, functions, etc., while task experience identifies both positive experience, e.g. applicable knowledge, strategies, models and theories, and negative experience, e.g. development, support or knowledge deficits, etc. The information profile is based on the information needs of a user, discussed below, i.e. the intentions in approaching the system, the amount of information a user can cope with and the complexity of information a user can handle. The interaction profile of a user is determined by his frequency, intensity and style of system utilisation.
- The *personality profile* of a user characterises his/her general properties, his/her preferences in dealing with the WIS and his/her polarity profile, which addresses a user's psychological properties.

We group users by their information demand and requested content, their utilisation patterns and their specific utilisation and context. The abstraction of a group of users is called an *actor*. Actors are characterised by profiles and portfolios. As with users, actor profiles consist of the *education*, *work* and *personality* profiles. Profiles are used for the derivation of preferences. These preferences are used to adapt scenes to specific actors.

A portfolio in general is determined by the responsibilities one has and is based on a number of targets. Thus, the *actor portfolio* within an application is based on a set of tasks an actor has or intends to complete and for which solution the actor has the authority and control. The portfolio is additionally based on a description of involvement within the task solution.

Task modelling means understanding what a user wants to accomplish, and at the same may lead to a reorganisation of the work processes to be supported. Task analysis leads to a description of things users do and things they need to know. It does not specify how a task is accomplished. The supported tasks need to be representative of the application, relevant within the application, and completely supported. Task support can be customised depending on the profile and the context of the actors.

A *task* is a usually assigned piece of work which often has to be finished within a certain time by a user or a set of users whose duty is its completion. It implies work imposed by a user in authority and an obligation or responsibility to perform. A task may consist of subtasks, so we assume that tasks can be constructed on the basis of elementary tasks. Thus, a task is characterised by a problem statement, target states, initial states, profiles and instruments for task completion, and auxiliary conditions.

- Tasks are associated to problems, for which often a class of solution strategies is provided. Additionally, problems often require collaboration with the local and global systems and with other actors.
- After successfully completing a task we may observe a change in the state of the application system. Target states are specified by means of target conditions. Some of the target conditions can be optional. If no optional conditions are given, then all conditions are obligatory. Target states correspond to intentions.
- The necessity for task enactment is based on the insufficiency of the current state of affairs. Additionally, task enactment conditions may specify the circumstances under which task execution can be started.
- The completion of a task requires skills, experience and knowledge that must be presupposed by the user whenever the task is going to be activated. Tasks may be embedded into a certain organisational context. The profile also presupposes a certain technical environment, e.g. communication, information and workspace systems.
- Task enactment is supported by instruments such as actions and data. Problems are solved on the basis of an information demand and within a class of functions that might be used for task solution. Later on the information demand is mapped to database views or media objects. The function utilisation is organised on the basis of workflows.
- The settling of tasks may be restricted. Typical auxiliary conditions are based on rights for direct handling and retrieval, roles of the antagonist and the protagonist, and obligations required for settling a task.

Example 11.8. Let us look at the profile of an 'eco-tourist'. As part of the work profile we identify the task expertise, i.e. where the user wants to go and when. Task experience can be assumed to be general. General properties in the personality profile will characterise such a user as an individual who prefers using a bicycle and thus is not interested in booking flights. The profile is based on the goal φ_{12}, i.e. to book a Bicycle tour.

11.3.3 Contexts

Taking the commonly accepted meaning, a context characterises the situation in which a user finds him-/herself at a certain time in a particular location. More generally, a context captures everything that surrounds a utilisation situation of a user and can throw light on its meaning. Therefore, context is characterised by interrelated conditions for the existence and occurrence of the utilisation situation such as the external environment, the internal state, location, time, history, etc. This comprises the mental context which is based on the profile of the actor or user, the storyboard context which is based on the story leading to a situation, the data context which is based on the available data, the stakeholder context, and the collaboration context.

When determining context we already know the major life cases we would like to support, the user and actor characterisation on the basis of profiles and portfolios, and the technical environment we are going to use. These restrictions enable a more refined understanding of contexts. The user model, the specified set of life cases and the intentions can be used for a disambiguation of the meaning and an injection of context. In this way we distinguish between actor, storyboard, system and temporal contexts.

- The system is used by actors for a number of tasks in a variety of involvements and well-understood collaboration. These actors impose their quality requirements on the usage as described by their profiles. They need additional auxiliary data and auxiliary functions. The variability of use is restricted by the actor's context, which covers the actor's specific tasks and specific data and function demand, and by chosen involvement, while the profile of actors imposes exceptions. The involvement and collaboration of actors is based on assumptions of social behaviour and restrictions due to organisational decisions. These assumptions and restrictions are components of the actor's context.
- The meaning of content and functionality to users depends on the stories, which are based on scenarios which reflect life cases and the portfolios of users or actors. According to the profile of these users, a number of quality requirements such as privacy, security and availability must be satisfied. The actor's scenario context describes what the actor needs to understand in order to efficiently and effectively solve his/her tasks in the actual portfolio. The actors determine the policy for following particular stories.
- The purposes and intentions lead to a number of decisions about the system architecture, the technical environment and the implementation. The architecture has an impact on its utilisation, which often is only implicit and thus leads to puzzling system behaviour. The technical environment restricts the user due to restrictions imposed by server, channel and client properties. Adaptation to the

current environment is defined as context adaptation to the current channel, to the client infrastructure and to the server load. At the same time a number of legal decisions based on regulations, laws and business rules have been incorporated into the system.

• The utilisation of a scene by an actor depends on his/her utilisation history. Actors may interrupt and resume their activities at any given moment. As they may not be interested in repeating all previous actions they have already successfully completed, the temporal context must be taken into account. Depending on the availability of content and functionality, the current utilisation may lead to a different story within the same scenario.

Example 11.9. Let us look at the storyboard context for a Bicycle tour. In this case the intent 'Bicycle Tour' defines the pre-scene context for the 'Start' scene. Similarly, the post-scene context is defined by the possible continuation through the scene 'Hotel Booking', which would imply the action α_3, with the additional constraint that the hotel should be supportive of bikers. The super-imposed metadata for the scene context are defined by security data associated with the additional intent to prevent theft.

11.4 Analysis of Storyboards

The formal aspects of storyboards such as constraints and preference rules give rise to problems which have to be analysed. Let us concentrate on only two of these problems: personalisation and deontic consistency. For the former, the starting point is a plot and a set of preference rules. We want to obtain a simplified plot in which the choices corresponding to the preferences have already been incorporated. Following [27, 29] this problem can be addressed by term rewriting on KATs. For the latter problem we have to ensure that the deontic constraints, which express rights and obligations, make tasks executable. Following [29] this can also be addressed by term rewriting, which permits us to reduce the plot to one that is compatible with the deontic constraints. Combining both approaches, priority has to be given to rights and obligations, as these are binding.

11.4.1 Customisation with Respect to Preferences

The high-level specification by means of a storyboard is an open invitation for personalisation with respect to functionality. Assume a plot p to be given by an expression on the KAT $\mathcal{K}$, and let Σ denote a set of equations on $\mathcal{K}$ corresponding to preference rules. Then we look for a simplified KAT expression p' such that p and p' represent the same element in $\mathcal{K}/\Sigma$. In [27] it was suggested to use term rewriting for this. As is standard in order-sorted algebraic specifications, we take two *sorts* B and K ordered by $B \leq K$, and the following (nullary, unary, binary) *operators*:

$$0, 1 :\to B \quad +, \cdot : K\, K \to K \quad {}^* : K \to K \quad {}^- : B \to B$$

Using these sorts and operators we can define *terms* in the usual way. A *rewrite rule* is an expression of the form $\lambda \rightsquigarrow \varrho$, with terms λ and ϱ of the same sort, such that the variables on the right-hand side ϱ are a subset of those on the left-hand side λ. A *conditional rewrite rule* is an expression of the form $t_1 = t_2 \to \lambda \rightsquigarrow \varrho$, in which in addition the terms t_1 and t_2 contain the same variables and these form a superset of the set of variables in the left-hand-side term λ.

The application of a rewrite rule $\lambda \rightsquigarrow \varrho$ to a term t is standard: if t contains a subterm t' that can be matched with λ, i.e. there is a substitution θ such that the application of θ to λ results in t' (denoted $\theta.\lambda = t'$), then replace t' in t by $\theta.\varrho$.

The application of a conditional rewrite rule $t_1 = t_2 \to \lambda \rightsquigarrow \varrho$ to a term t is defined analogously. That is, if t contains a subterm t' that can be matched with λ, i.e. there is a substitution θ such that the application of θ to λ results in t' (denoted $\theta.\lambda = t'$), then replace t' in t by $\theta.\varrho$. However, in this case we have to show that $\theta.t_1 = \theta.t_2$ holds for the substitution θ. For this we start a separate term-rewriting process that aims at showing $\theta.t_1 \rightsquigarrow \cdots \rightsquigarrow \theta.t_2$. We call this separate rewriting process a *co-routine*, because we can run it in parallel to the main rewriting process. The risk is of course that if we fail to verify $\theta.t_1 = \theta.t_2$, then we will have to backtrack to t for the main rewriting process.

In order to exploit term-rewriting for the personalisation problem, we formulate the axioms of KATs and the personalisation equations as (conditional) rewrite rules, then start with $p\psi$ and apply the rules until we finally obtain a term of the form $p'\psi$ to which no more rules can be applied. Note that $p\psi$ is closed, i.e. it does not contain variables, so during the whole rewriting process we will only have to deal with closed terms.

We use $p, q, r, \ldots$ (if needed with additional indices) as *variables* of sort K, and $a, b, c, \ldots$ (also with indices) as *variables* of sort B. Then we use the following general (conditional) rewrite rules:

$$p + (q + r) \rightsquigarrow (p + q) + r \qquad\qquad p(qr) \rightsquigarrow (pq)r$$
$$p + p \rightsquigarrow p \qquad\qquad p + 0 \rightsquigarrow p$$
$$p1 \rightsquigarrow p \qquad\qquad 1p \rightsquigarrow p$$
$$p0 \rightsquigarrow 0 \qquad\qquad 0p \rightsquigarrow 0$$
$$p(q + r) \rightsquigarrow pq + pr \qquad\qquad (p + q)r \rightsquigarrow pr + qr$$
$$1 + pp^* \rightsquigarrow p^* \qquad\qquad 1 + p^*p \rightsquigarrow p^*$$
$$pq + q = q \to p^*q + q \rightsquigarrow q \qquad qp + q = q \to qp^* + q \rightsquigarrow q$$
$$p + q \rightsquigarrow q + p \qquad\qquad a\,b \rightsquigarrow ba$$
$$a\bar{a} \rightsquigarrow 0 \qquad\qquad \bar{a}a \rightsquigarrow 0$$
$$a + \bar{a} \rightsquigarrow 1 \qquad\qquad \bar{a} + a \rightsquigarrow 1$$

In addition, the personalisation equations from above give rise to further rewrite rules:

- A conditional preference equation gives rise to a rule of the form $a(p+q) \rightsquigarrow ap$.
- A precondition gives rise to a rule of the form $\bar{a}p \rightsquigarrow 0$.
- A postcondition gives rise to a rule of the form $p\bar{a} \rightsquigarrow 0$.
- An invariance condition gives rise to a rule of the form $a\ p\bar{a} + \bar{a}pa \rightsquigarrow 0$.
- An exclusion condition gives rise to a rule of the form $a\ b \rightsquigarrow 0$.

As is usual with term-rewriting approaches, we must solve two related problems: ensure termination and produce a unique final result (the Church-Rosser property). Both problems were handled in [29]. For termination a condition based on formal power series was developed exploiting a well-founded order on terms [7]. For the Church-Rosser property an approach based on critical pair completion [14] was adopted.

Example 11.10. Let us consider the plot from Example 11.5 together with the preferences for the user type 'Leary' in Example 11.6. In this case the plot can be simplified, i.e. personalised, as follows:

$$\alpha_1\varphi_1(\alpha_2\|\alpha_3)\varphi_4\varphi_5\alpha_5\alpha_6(\varphi_7 + \varphi_8\alpha_7 + \varphi_9\alpha_8)\varphi_{10}$$

11.4.2 Deontic Consistency

For deontic consistency we first need a formal semantics for the deontic logic. For this, a *status set* of $\mathcal{L}$ is a set $\mathcal{S}$ of atoms satisfying $\mathbf{P}\ do(r,\alpha) \in \mathcal{S}$ iff $\mathbf{F}\ do(r,\alpha) \notin \mathcal{S}$.

If Σ is a set of formulae in $\mathcal{L}$, then a status set $\mathcal{S}$ is *feasible* iff it satisfies Σ in the usual propositional sense, i.e. $\mathcal{S}$ determines the truth values of the atoms, and the usual interpretation of negation, conjunction and disjunction applies. $\mathcal{S}$ is *closed* iff we have $\mathbf{O}\ do(r,\alpha) \in \mathcal{S} \Rightarrow do(r,\alpha) \in \mathcal{S}$ and $do(r,\alpha) \in \mathcal{S} \Rightarrow \mathbf{P}\ do(r,\alpha) \in \mathcal{S}$. Obviously, we can use the rules defining closed status sets to build the closure of any status set.

Now consider a sequence $\mathcal{S}_0 \rightarrow \mathcal{S}_1 \rightarrow \cdots \rightarrow \mathcal{S}_n$ to be *enabled* iff all $\mathcal{S}_i$ are closed and feasible with respect to Σ, and for each $i = 0, \ldots, n-1$ there is some action α_i and some role r with $do(r,\alpha_i) \in \mathcal{S}_i$ such that the execution of α_i will produce the status set $\mathcal{S}_{i+1}$ and the sequence of actions $\alpha_0, \alpha_1, \ldots, \alpha_n$ is permitted by the plot.

As not all sequences of actions which are permitted by the plot are compatible with deontic constraints, the question arises whether the plot can be rewritten in a way that all stories it defines correspond to an enabled sequence of status sets.

For this we consider only deontic constraints associated with a single role. If Σ is such a set of deontic constraints, we can assume that each formula $\varphi \in \Sigma$ is written as a disjunction of literals, i.e. atoms or negated atoms. If this were not the case, we could transform φ into a conjunctive normal form, say $\varphi \equiv \varphi_1 \wedge \cdots \wedge \varphi_n$, and replace φ by $\varphi_1, \ldots, \varphi_n$. This does not change the semantics, as satisfaction of a conjunction of constraints is equivalent to satisfaction of all conjuncts.

For $\varphi \in \Sigma$ define $\mathcal{P}_\varphi$ as the set of Boolean atoms ψ with $\neg\psi$ occurring in φ, negated Boolean atoms $\bar{\psi}$ with ψ occurring in φ, and actions α such that one of $\mathbf{F}\, do(r, \alpha)$, $\neg\mathbf{P}\, do(r, \alpha)$, $\neg\mathbf{O}\, do(r, \alpha)$ or $\neg do(r, \alpha)$ occurs in φ. Let $\mathcal{C}_\varphi$ be the set of actions β such that $\mathbf{O}\, do(r, \alpha)$ or $do(r, \alpha)$ occurs in φ. Let $\mathcal{P}_\varphi = \{p_1, \ldots, p_k\}$ and $\mathcal{C}_\varphi = \{q_1, \ldots, q_m\}$. Then each permutation σ of $\{1, \ldots, k\}$ gives rise to an equation

$$p_{\sigma(1)} \cdots p_{\sigma(k)} = \sum_{j=1}^{m} p_{\sigma(1)} \cdots p_{\sigma(k)} q_j$$

which degenerates to $p_{\sigma(1)} \cdots p_{\sigma(k)} = 0$ in case $\mathcal{C}_\varphi = \emptyset$.

Thus, each set Σ of deontic constraints defines a set E of equations on the plot. In contrast to the preference rules, however, the equations in E do not just express preferences, but strict restrictions. Technically speaking, if we can rewrite the plot p to a plot p' using the equations in E, then each story enabled by p', i.e. a sequence of actions, corresponds to a sequence of status sets that is enabled by Σ. We can then apply term rewriting with respect to preference rules to the plot p'.

11.5 Bibliographic Remarks

The conceptual model of storyboarding originates from the field of Web information systems (WISs), i.e. database-backed information systems which are accessible via the World Wide Web. Here several conceptual models have been developed such as ARANEUS [2], WebML [4], WSDM [6], HERA [13], HDM [11], OOHDM [30], UML-based methods [5, 19], and the co-design approach [26]. These models share the view that content, navigation and presentation are key problems in WIS design, but storyboarding is one of the key features of the co-design approach. This was motivated by the basic consideration that WISs are open systems in the sense that they can be accessed by almost anyone, and thus an anticipation of user behaviour would be necessary.

The concrete shape of storyboards has undergone various changes, from its beginnings in the Cottbus*net* project [10] over the first formalisation of the algebraic language *SiteLang* [32] to the consolidated version in [26]. Linking storyboarding to strategic modelling as the initial step in WIS design was handled in [21]. It builds on and extends models of actors and goals [23]. Personalisation by term rewriting on Kleene algebras with tests [16–18] was intensively studied in [27, 29]. Consistency with respect to deontic constraints is based on the semantics of deontic action programs [9] with connections to more general studies of deontic constraints [3, 8, 34].

The study of storyboarding pragmatics started with work on metaphorical structures in [31]. Usage analysis, i.e. life cases, user models and contexts as decisive components of storyboarding pragmatics, was systematically handled in [28]. It builds on the immense work on user modelling, e.g. [12, 15, 20, 24], and abstracts from contextual information bases [1, 22, 33].

References

1. Akaishi M, Spyratos N, Tanaka Y (2002) A component-based application framework for context-driven information access. In: Kangassalo H et al (eds) Information modelling and knowledge bases XIII. IOS Press, Amsterdam, pp 254–265
2. Atzeni P, Gupta A, Sarawagi S (1998) Design and maintenance of data-intensive web sites. In: Proceedings of EDBT'98. Lecture notes in computer science, vol 1377. Springer, Berlin, pp 436–450
3. Broersen J, Wieringa R, Meyer JJC (2002) A fixed-point characterization of a deontic logic of regular action. Fundam Inform 49(4):107–128
4. Ceri S, Fraternali P, Bongio A, Brambilla M, Comai S, Matera M (2003) Designing data-intensive Web applications. Morgan Kaufmann, San Francisco
5. Conallen J (2003) Building Web applications with UML. Addison-Wesley, Boston
6. De Troyer O, Leune C (1998) WSDM: a user-centered design method for web sites. In: Proceedings of the 7th international WWW conference on computer networks and ISDN systems. Elsevier, Amsterdam, pp 85–94
7. Dershowitz N (1987) Termination of rewriting. J Symbol Comput 3(1/2):69–116
8. Dignum F, Meyer JJC, Wieringa R, Kuiper R (1996) A modal approach to intentions, commitments and obligations: intention plus commitment yields obligation. In: Brown MA, Carmo J (eds) DEON 1996, workshops in computing. Springer, Berlin, pp 80–97
9. Eiter T, Subrahmanian VS (1999) Deontic action programs. In: Polle T, Ripke T, Schewe KD (eds) Fundamentals of information systems. Kluwer Academic Publishers, pp 37–54
10. Feyer T, Schewe KD, Thalheim B (1998) Conceptual modelling and development of information services. In: Ling T, Ram S (eds) Conceptual modeling – ER'98. Lecture notes in computer science, vol 1507. Springer, Berlin, pp 7–20
11. Garzotto F, Paolini P, Schwabe D (1993) HDM – a model-based approach to hypertext application design. ACM Trans Inf Syst 11(1):1–26
12. Heckmann D, Schwartz T, Brandherm B, Schmitz M, von Wilamowitz–Möllendorff M (2005) Gumo – the general user model ontology. In: User modeling. Lecture notes in computer science, vol 3538. Springer, Berlin, pp 428–432
13. Houben GJ, Barna P, Frasincar F, Vdovjak R (2003) HERA: development of semantic web information systems. In: 3rd international conference on Web engineering – ICWE 2003. Lecture notes in computer science, vol 2722. Springer, Berlin, pp 529–538
14. Knuth DE, Bendix PB (1970) Simple word problems in universal algebras. In: Computational problems in abstract algebra. Pergamon, Oxford, pp 263–297
15. Kobsa A (2005) User modeling and user-adapted interaction. User Model User-Adapt Interact 15(1–2):185–190
16. Kozen D (1997) Kleene algebra with tests. ACM Trans Programm Lang Syst 19(3):427–443
17. Kozen D (2002) On the complexity of reasoning in Kleene algebra. Inf Comput 179(2):152–162
18. Kozen D, Smith F (1996) Kleene algebra with tests: completeness and decidability. In: van Dalen D, Bezem M (eds) Computer science logic. Lecture notes in computer science, vol 1258. Springer, Berlin, Heidelberg, pp 244–259
19. Lowe D, Henderson-Sellers B, Gu A (2002) Web extensions to UML: using the MVC triad. In: Spaccapietra S, March ST, Kambayashi Y (eds) Conceptual modeling – ER 2002. Lecture notes in computer science, vol 2503. Springer, Berlin, pp 105–119
20. Magnini B, Strapparava C (2004) User modelling for news web sites with word sense based techniques. User Model User-Adapt Interact 14(2–3):239–257

21. Moritz T, Schewe KD, Thalheim B (2005) Strategic modelling of web information systems. Int J Web Inf Syst 1(4):77–94
22. Mylopoulos J, Motschnig-Pitrik R (1995) Partioning information bases with contexts. In: Proceedings of CoopIS '95. Springer, Berlin, pp 44–55
23. Mylopoulos J, Fuxman A, Giorgini P (2000) From entities and relationships to social actors and dependencies. In: Conceptual modeling – ER 2000. Springer, Berlin, pp 27–36
24. Razmerita L, Angehrn AA, Maedche A (2003) Ontology-based user modeling for knowledge management systems. In: Brusilowsky P, Corbett AT, de Rosis F (eds) User modeling, Lecture notes in computer science, vol 2702. Springer, Berlin. , Heidelberg, pp 213–217
25. Schewe KD, Thalheim B (2005) The co-design approach to web information systems development. Int J Web Inf Syst 1(1):5–14
26. Schewe KD, Thalheim B (2005) Conceptual modelling of web information systems. Data Knowl Eng 54(2):147–188
27. Schewe KD, Thalheim B (2007) Personalisation of web information systems – a term rewriting approach. Data Knowl Eng 62(1):101–117
28. Schewe KD, Thalheim B (2007) Pragmatics of storyboarding for web information systems: Usage analysis. Int J Web Grid Serv 3(2):128–169
29. Schewe KD, Thalheim B, Wang Q (2009) Customising web information systems according to user preferences. World Wide Web 12(1):27–50
30. Schwabe D, Rossi G (1998) An object oriented approach to web-based application design. Theory Pract Object Syst 4(4):207–225
31. Thalheim B, Düsterhöft A (2000) The use of metaphorical structures for internet sites. Data Knowl Eng 35:161–180
32. Thalheim B, Düsterhöft A (2001) SiteLang: conceptual modeling of internet sites. In: Kunii HS, Jajodia S, Sølvberg A (eds) Conceptual modeling – ER 2001. Lecture notes in computer science, vol 2224. Springer, Berlin, pp 179–192
33. Theodorakis M, Analyti A, Constantopoulos P, Spyratos N (2002) A theory of contexts in information bases. Inf Syst 27(3):151–191
34. Wieringa R, Meyer JJC (1993) Actors, actions, and initiative in normative system specification. Ann Math Artif Intell 7(1–4):289–346

Part V
Special Challenge Area

Chapter 12
Evolution and Migration of Information Systems

Meike Klettke and Bernhard Thalheim

Abstract Modernisation of information systems is a fundamental but sometimes neglected aspect of conceptual modelling. The management of evolution, migration and refinement and the ability for information systems to deal with modernisation is an essential component in developing and maintaining truly useful systems that minimise service disruption and down time and maximise availability of data and applications. Many approaches to handling evolution and migration have been proposed in various areas of data management. Most of them are rather informal descriptions of the project management of either evolution management or migration management. Typical problems that have been considered are modelling and management of evolution and migration; handling of changes and versioning; managing information system upgrades and schema changes; semantics of modernisation in time and space; handling changes in metadata, schema evolution, migration and versioning; change detection, monitoring and mining.

This chapter provides a systematic inside look at the first two problems. We show that migration and evolution are interwoven aspects. Three migration strategies (big bang, chicken little, butterfly) can be based on systematic evolution steps. Evolution steps use the theory of model suites. An information system is specified by models such as the database structure model, the view model, the functionality model and the interaction model. Model suites thus support the co-evolution of models during system evolution and migration. We restrict migration and evolution to model aspects. The theory, technics and methodology can, however, be extended to database or information base evolution and migration by the derivation of corresponding support functions based on mappings among the models.

Meike Klettke
Computer Science Institute, Rostock University, Albert-Einstein-Str. 21, 18051 Rostock, Germany,
e-mail: meike@informatik.uni-rostock.de

Bernhard Thalheim
Department of Computer Science, Christian-Albrechts University Kiel, 24098 Kiel, Germany,
e-mail: thalheim@is.informatik.uni-kiel.de

D. W. Embley and B. Thalheim (eds), *Handbook of Conceptual Modeling.*
DOI 10.1007/978-3-642-15865-0, © Springer 2011

12.1 Introduction

12.1.1 Information System Modernisation

Information system *modernisation*, e.g. by evolution and migration, is clearly among the most challenging engineering tasks to date. The problem of database evolution and migration arises in the context of long-lived database applications, where data have become valuable in their own right and are worthy of being preserved even following any changes made to database specifications and database technology. Database modernisation includes a wide range of operations such as explicit architecture changes, versioning of databases, restructuring of databases or parts of them, adaptation to new technology or languages, application redevelopment, interface modernisation, change of platforms or DBMS, wrapping and componentisation of databases, or redevelopment of a database. Typically, modernisation should not result in loss of (legacy or, better, heritage) data. It needs to be conservative in the sense that it allows for querying of all data through user-definable version interfaces.

We may distinguish a number of targets for system modernisation. Modernisation of an information system may be oriented towards a modernisation of the database, the interfaces, the DBMS or the paradigms.

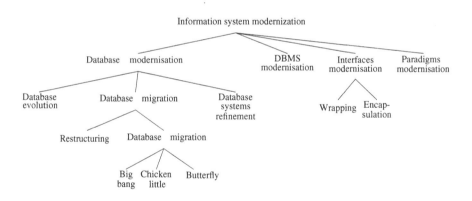

This chapter mainly discusses the main database modernisation techniques: evolution and migration.

12.1.2 Models for Information Systems

Theories for evolution and migration of information systems should be independent of whatever modelling technique or language has been used. The intention is, however, to be able to handle all kinds of modifications of all components of the information system model.[1] We therefore intend to develop an approach that handles changes in database structuring, database functionality, and database support models. Several approaches can be taken to the modelling of information system model evolution. We can explicitly add an orthogonal component to models that handle the validity of models through macro states for birth, transformation, death, etc. Another approach is based on the explicit representation of the version history of the application model in its entirety. A third approach is to keep the version history per element of the application model. Since database structuring and functionality are based on the principle of compositionality, we consider the third approach the most appropriate one.

An information system is typically specified by an application model that consists of a database model for specification of the database schema, of a functionality model for specification of information system operation, and of support models such as views or interaction schemata.

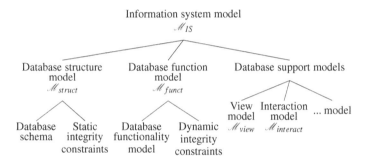

Therefore, the modernisation of an information system may involve a large variety of improvement steps. We concentrate in this chapter on the following modification operations in the following tree.

---

[1] This chapter considers mainly changes in information system models. We do not consider changes in databases themselves.

12.2 Overview of System Modernisations

Successful database systems have been used for decades, and the amount of data stored in databases is enormous. Long-living databases are called *legacy databases*. They have some significant characteristics:

- Data are stored over very long periods of time without or only with minor database changes. Therefore, data in a databases become very comprehensive.
- Usually, data in databases are very important or even essential for a company or organisation to run its business.

Database structures and functions of these systems were developed many years ago. Often, the original developers are no longer available. Code that is uncommented, hard to understand, and hard or impossible to maintain is rather common.

Nevertheless, sometimes changes in a legacy system are necessary. There are several reasons for changes:

1. Errors in the database structure or incompleteness of the structure may require extensions or modifications of databases.
2. The whole environment changes, for instance new interfaces, new applications, or new laws require adaptations of the legacy systems.
3. New kinds of information need to be added or new functions need to be provided.
4. More efficient solutions are necessary.
5. Technology changes bring about the need for migration processes.

Databases usually exist much longer than other software products. This results in necessary modernisation operations from time to time. System modernisation (introduced by Comella-Dorda et al. in [8]) ensures that a system will be adapted to new requirements and that errors in a system will be corrected. Small changes are called maintenance or the *evolution* of a system.

12.2.1 Fundamental Terms

Evolution

According to Roddick [26], 'Schema evolution deals with the need to retain current data when database schema changes are performed. Formally, schema evolution is accommodated when a database system facilitates database schema modification without the loss of existing data.'

We extend this definition. Not only may the database structure change and the data have to be preserved. Changes include also *user-defined functions, stored procedures, defined views, integrity constraints, check constraints,* and the *interfaces of a database.* All these kinds of information are influenced by changes in database structures and have to be retained or adapted.

Data Migration

Data migration implies that the platform used for data storage is replaced. A new version of a database management system, another database management system or new hardware requires such data migration. During the migration, it has to be guaranteed that a version of the database (as an operational database system) will always be available. The data migration process is often embedded into a system migration.

System Migration

System migration means that a complete application is moved onto a new platform. In this way, data consistency and the functionalities of the system have to be preserved. System migration is a project on its own. It is a complicated process consisting of several subtasks. Different existing migration strategies (big bang, chicken little, and butterfly) exist and will be explained in Sect. 12.4. A system migration project usually requires several attempts; an operational system has to be available during the entire migration process.

Legacy System

A legacy system is a system that is established, contains valuable data or important functionalities and is in use for some time. A legacy system represents a proven and successful solution. It is difficult to maintain, change or evolve a legacy system, which is why it is preserved and encapsulated.

12.2.2 Interrelationships Between Migration, Evolution, and Legacy Systems

Figure 12.1 shows the typical life cycle of a software product. Business requirements determine the design process. A system becomes operational and is in use over a long period of time. Changes in business requirements cause *a step-by-step evolution* of the application. These are minor changes which are executed from time to time and adapt the functions, interfaces, data storage and so forth.

System migrations are larger changes which replace the complete system and which are necessary if the application no longer meets the business requirements.

Within a system migration, all components are redesigned and evolved. That means that the *evolution* of an existing application is a part of the *migration process*.

During a system migration some components can be preserved. These components are called *legacy systems*; they are not changed or adapted, and access takes

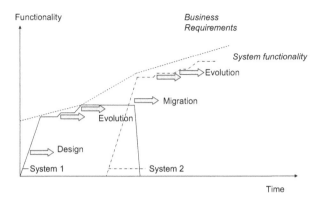

Fig. 12.1 Evolution and migration in the application life cycle; figure similar to that of [8]

place using interfaces. The reasons for keeping legacy systems unchanged are multi-faceted. It is possible that:

- Developers who completely understand the legacy source code are no longer available.
- An application consists of uncommented source code or monolithic blocks of code. The risk from changing such code is considerable.
- Costs for redevelopment are too high.
- The legacy system is very efficient, efficient enough for current and future requirements.

If one or more of these conditions is met, we preserve the legacy system instead of migrating it and use it as a component in a complex application, e.g. black-box evolution in Sect. 12.2.3.

12.2.3 Evolving Information Systems

An evolving information system model is given

- by an information system model $\mathcal{M}_{IS}$ defined in some language $\mathcal{L}$ and
- a set of model changes $\mathfrak{M}$ that can be applied to a model.

Model modifications are typically built on a sequence of elementary model changes.

Model modifications typically have a *scope* within a model. For instance, if an attribute is changed, then the corresponding functions, triggers, stored procedures, views and interactions must be changed as well. Therefore, a *model change* is given by a rule:

if *cond* **then** *Apply(ChangeOperation(Model))* **by** *Bindings*

This specification frame is similar to the specification frame used in Chap. 9. The bindings are not random; they are induced by the changes within the model and those model elements that are not changed but interrelated to the changed elements. We develop a contracting approach for explicit binding.

An *evolution trace* consists of an initial application model $\mathcal{M}_I$ and a finite set of model modifications $O_{i,j}$ where i, j denote a pair of versions that induce a tree partial order $\rightsquigarrow$ over model versions, i.e. $O_{i_k}(O_{i_{k-1}}(\ldots(O_{i_2}(O_{i_1}(cal\,M_I)))))$ is the model derived from $\mathcal{M}_I$ by application of operations $O_{i_1}, O_{i_2}, \ldots, O_{i_k}$ for a sequence of indexes $i_1, \ldots, i_k$ with $i_j \rightsquigarrow i_{j+1}$ for $1 \leq j < k$. This sequence is called the *evolution path* for $\mathcal{M}_I$.

We thus introduce model changes in an incremental form. The semantics of changes is obvious and is thus omitted. Operations may change model semantics.

Evolution involves more extensive changes than maintenance. It aims at the conservation of a significant portion of an existing system. These changes typically include system restructuring, important function enhancements, or new software artefacts. Typically, the information system undergoing modernisation still has a business value that must be preserved. We may distinguish evolution frameworks by the level of system changes and the evolution effort.

White-Box Evolution Frameworks

White-box evolution requires an initial reverse engineering to gain an understanding of the information system. Components of the system are identified, and a representation of the system at a higher level of abstraction is produced. The understanding of the application system involves modelling of all system components and includes database structuring, database functionality and database support systems. It creates an abstraction that allows one to understand the system architecture. This abstraction can be used for analysing the system.

After the information system is analysed and understood, white-box evolution includes system restructuring, mutation and component selection. *Restructuring* can be understood as the transformation from one representation form to another at the same relative abstraction level, while preserving those components that are harder to maintain, e.g., components responsible for external systems behaviour. *Mutation* changes the relationship between constructs in the database model and the view model. *Selection* removes elements from a database model and from a view model. Selections are typically forgetful and do not allow one to re-establish the previous information system. Database slicing is a particularly popular technique of selection. It is based on the notion of cohesion among system components.

White-box evolution is typically based on a *quality improvement plan*. Evolution is typically used to augment some of the quality characteristics of the information system.

Black-Box Evolution Frameworks

Black-box evolution is based on a description of the behaviour of the information system. Typically, the inputs and the outputs of a system under modernisation is examined in order to gain an understanding of the system's external behaviour.

Black-box evolution is often based on wrapping and encapsulation techniques. *Wrapping* consists of surrounding the system under modernisation with a software layer that hides the unwanted complexity of the old system and exports a modern interface. It allows one to remove mismatches between the interface exported by the old system and interfaces required by current integration practices. Ideally, information systems' internals are ignored.

Encapsulation is a stronger architecture evolution technique. The system or some of its components are enclosed within or as if within walls. Any structure or function that is not visible in the black-box input–output behaviour is captured by the old system. These system components define the interoperability interface. The old system is kept as a local system within a distributed system. Nothing is changed within the old system.

Differences between these approaches from an outside perspective can be given by the following table:

	$\mathcal{M}_{struct}$	$\mathcal{M}_{funct}$	$\mathcal{M}_{view}$	$\mathcal{M}_{interact}$
White-box	Visible/ changeable	Visible/ changeable	Visible/ changeable	Visible/ changeable
Black-box: wrapping	Invisible	Invisible	Visible	Visible/ changeable
Black-box: encapsulation	Invisible	Invisible	Invisible	Visible

Note that migration frameworks also apply *replacement* (chicken little) approaches to those system components that cannot keep pace with business needs and for which evolution is not possible or cost-effective.

12.3 Foundations of Evolution and Migration Transformations

12.3.1 Specification of Information System Models

Typically, a model is defined in a certain language. A model language $\mathcal{L} = \mathcal{L}_{\mathbb{SC}}$ for a model uses some signature $\mathbb{S}$ and a set of constructors $\mathbb{C}$ that allows one to build a set of all possible expressions in this language. Typically constructors are defined by structural recursion [31]. The set of constructors may allow one to build expressions that do not fulfill certain quality or, more generally, integrity conditions. Therefore we introduce a set $\Sigma_{\mathbb{SC}}$ of well-formedness conditions.

Example 12.1. The enhanced entity-relationship (ER) model HERM is based on a number of well-formedness conditions. Each entity type has at least one attribute, and each attribute must be used at least once. Attribute types are compositionally built through the application of constructors. Basis attribute types are associated to a domain type. Entity types have at least one identification through keys. The type structure is strictly hierarchical, and each cluster and relationship type has at least one component type. A key has at least one component. Keys use components of the same type. Classes of types are defined through set semantics. Each structure in the higher-order ER model is also based on a set of *implicit model-inherent integrity constraints*:

Component-construction constraints   are based on the existence, cardinality and inclusion of components. These constraints must be considered in the translation and implication process.

Identification constraints   are implicitly used for the set constructor. Each object either does not belong to a set or belongs only once to the set.

Acyclicity and finiteness   of structuring supports the axiomatisation and definition of the algebra. It must, however, be explicitly specified. Constraints such as cardinality constraints may be based on potential infinite cycles.

Some model languages allow several equivalent expressions for the same model. Some of them might be inadequate. For instance, *superficial structuring* leads to the representation of constraints through structures. In this case, the implication of constraints is difficult to characterise. Superficial structuring also results in performance and maintenance traps.

The *unique name assumption* requires that elements with different names be different. If we need to use the same name for different purposes, then we use *name spaces* if a unique identification is needed. The *closed world assumption* presumes that the only possible elements are those which are specified. The *domain closure assumption* limits the elements in the language to those which can be named through the vocabulary, the states of the vocabulary or the rules. The *unique meaning assumption* postulates that any function or rule has the same meaning despite modularisation. Due to the variety of choices we might use additional assumptions for development. The most general *architectural assumption* is the possibility of *layering* a system into subsystems. $\square^{\text{EoE}}$

A model kind $\mathcal{K}_{\mathcal{L}_{\text{SC}}} = (\mathcal{L}_{\text{SC}}, \Sigma_{\mathcal{L}_{\text{SC}}})$ is defined by a pair consisting of the language of the model $\mathcal{L}_{\text{SC}}$ of signature $\mathbb{SC}$ and by constraints $\Sigma_{\mathcal{L}_{\text{SC}}} \in \mathcal{L}(\Sigma_{\text{SC}}^{\text{WellFormed}})$ applicable to all models defined in the given language.

Model kinds allow one to restrict models to a specific form. The extended entity-relationship (EER) model uses, for instance, a strict separation of structural model elements into attribute, entity, relationship and cluster types. This separation is a variant of the 'Salami slice' form of XML documents which require that each element represent an object and use an ensemble of XML elements which are interrelated by references. XML models may be based on the so-called Venetian blind or Russian doll representation. The latter specific form requires that elements be closed in the sense that they contain all essential definitions of type, element and attribute declarations.

Model languages $\mathcal{L}_{\mathbb{S}_1 \mathbb{C}_1}, \ldots \mathcal{L}_{\mathbb{S}_1 \mathbb{C}_n}$ may be bound to each other by *partial* mappings $\mathbb{R}_{i,j} : \mathcal{L}_{\mathbb{S}_i \mathbb{C}_i} \to \mathcal{L}_{\mathbb{S}_j \mathbb{C}_j}$ based on their signatures. These mappings typically define the association of elements among the languages.

A model is based on an expression in a given language. Typically, it has a structure definition, a semantic definition and a pragmatics definition. Semantics restricts the models we are interested in, whereas pragmatics restricts the scope of model users. We explicitly define a model $\mathcal{M}$ by an expression $struct_{\mathcal{M}}$ in a language $\mathcal{L}_{\mathbb{SC}}$ which obeys $\Sigma_{\mathcal{L}_{\mathbb{SC}}}$ and by a set of constraints $\Sigma_{\mathcal{M}}$ defined in the logics of this language. Therefore, each model has its model kind. We denote by $\mathcal{M}_{\mathcal{K}}$ or $\mathcal{M}_i$ for some i the set of all models of this type.

Example 12.2. The language of the EER model allows one to define an EER schema $\mathcal{M}_{EER}$ through its structure and a set of static integrity constraints, i.e. $(\mathcal{S}, \Sigma)$ for a finite set $\mathcal{S}$ of types. A typical requirement for an EER schema is that it be *closed*, i.e. any non-basic element used is defined within the schema. Attribute types in an EER schema are defined by the type equation $t = b \mid (A_1 : t_1, \ldots, A_n : t_n) \mid \{t\} \mid [t] \mid \ell : t$ where b denotes a base type and ℓ a label. Similarly, we may define entity, relationship and cluster types, e.g. for cluster types $C \overset{\circ}{=} (\ell_1 : t_1) + \ldots + (\ell_n : t_n)$ for entity, relationship or cluster types t_i. $\square^{\text{EoE}}$

An expression $\mathcal{M}$ in a language is incrementally built. Therefore we can define a subexpression $\mathcal{M}'$ of $\mathcal{M}$ and denote this relation by $\mathcal{M}' \preceq \mathcal{M}$. We typically assume that $\mathcal{M}'$ is a model as well. Any model $\mathcal{M}$ introduces a set of new names. This *name set* is denoted by $N(\mathcal{M})$.

The information system model is defined by a number of interrelated languages:

- The *database structure language* $\mathcal{L}_{\text{struct}}$ is based on a notion of a (ground) database schema $\mathcal{M}_{\text{struct}}$ that reflects the structure of the database and its (static) integrity constraints.
- The *database functionality language* $\mathcal{L}_{\text{funct}}$ is defined on top of $\mathcal{L}_{\text{struct}}$ through application of algebraic operations. The application of these operations may be bound by dynamic integrity constraints. Operations use parameters which are related to schema or view notions. Instead we may use any other functional language.
- The *database support language* $\mathcal{L}_{support}$ contains at least a view-specification language $\mathcal{L}_{\text{view}}$ and a language for interaction specification $\mathcal{L}_{\text{interact}}$. Views can recursively be defined as algebraic expressions of the language $\mathcal{L}_{\text{funct}}$ on top of $\mathcal{L}_{\text{struct}}$.
- The *database management system language* is outside the scope of this chapter.

An information system model consists of at least four submodels

$$\mathcal{M}_{\text{IS}} = (\mathcal{M}_{\text{struct}}, \mathcal{M}_{\text{funct}}, \mathcal{M}_{\text{view}}, \mathcal{M}_{\text{interact}})$$

which define the information system:

- The database *structure model* is given by a database schema $\mathcal{M}_{\text{struct}}$ from $\mathcal{L}_{\text{struct}}$.
- The database *view model* is given by a view schema $\mathcal{M}_{\text{view}}$ from $\mathcal{L}_{\text{view}}$.
- The database *functionality model* is given by an operation model $\mathcal{M}_{\text{funct}}$ from $\mathcal{L}_{\text{funct}}$ whose parameters are restricted to $\mathcal{M}_{\text{struct}}$ and $\mathcal{M}_{\text{view}}$.
- The database *interaction model* $\mathcal{M}_{\text{interact}}$ is given by an interaction schema, by a storyboard and interface expressions from $\mathcal{L}_{\text{interact}}$.

We omit the subscript IS if we consider the entire information system model. We assume that the model is *closed*, i.e. all types $t \in \mathcal{M}_{\text{IS}}$ are defined within $\mathcal{M}_{\text{IS}}$ or are base types.

This general definition allows one to consider a variety of application models such as ER-based models, object-oriented models, object-relational models and XML models.

12.3.2 Model Construction and Combination

The *model construction and association algebra* $(\mathcal{M}, \mathcal{O}, \mathcal{P})$ consists of

- A manifold of models $\mathcal{M}$ of model kinds $\mathcal{K}_{\mathcal{L}_{S_1 C_1}}, \ldots \mathcal{K}_{\mathcal{L}_{S_m C_m}}$ under consideration;
- Algebraic operations $\mathcal{O}$ for computing complex models such as a combination $\bowtie$ of models, abstraction π, σ of models by projections or selections, quotient $\div$ of models, renaming ρ of models, union $\uplus$ of models, intersection $\cap$ of models, and recombination $\curvearrowright$ of a model;
- Predicates $\mathcal{P}$ stating associations among models such as the submodel relation $\preccurlyeq$, a statement $\overset{\exists}{\cap}$ about whether models can be potentially associated with each other, a statement $\overset{\nexists}{\cap}$ about whether models cannot be potentially associated with each other, a statement $\overset{\exists}{\uplus}$ about whether models are potentially compatible with each other, and a statement $\overset{\nexists}{\uplus}$ about whether models are incompatible with each other.

We will not define these operations in detail and will only sketch their definitions in the sequel. We abstract from integrity constraints.

The *combination* $\mathcal{M}_1 \bowtie \mathcal{M}_2$ of two models results in a model which has all components of the two models.

The *abstraction* is used for a reduction of the components of a model either by restricting $\pi(\mathcal{M}, X)$ the model to components in X and their definitions or by restricting $\sigma(\mathcal{M}, \alpha)$ to those components which satisfy α.

The *quotient* $\mathcal{M}_1 \div \mathcal{M}_2$ allows one to concentrate on those components of the first model which do not appear in the second model. It is the largest submodel $\mathcal{M}_1'$ of $\mathcal{M}_1$ with $N(\mathcal{M}_1') \cap N(\mathcal{M}_2) = \emptyset$.

Renaming $\rho_\eta(\mathcal{M})$ is based an a bijective mapping η of the name space of a model $N(\mathcal{M})$ to $\eta(N(\mathcal{M}))$.

The *union* $\mathcal{M}_1 \uplus \mathcal{M}_2$ takes all components of the two models but does not combine common components into one component. We additionally assume that $N(\mathcal{M}_1) \cap N(\mathcal{M}_2) = \emptyset$. The *intersection* $\mathcal{M}_1 \cap \mathcal{M}_2$ of models is the largest submodel $\mathcal{M}'$ of both $\mathcal{M}_1$ and $\mathcal{M}_2$.

These operations can be used for to define derived operations. The *insertion* of a model $\mathcal{M}_1$ into a model $\mathcal{M}$ can be defined by the union $\mathcal{M} \uplus \mathcal{M}_1$. The *deletion* of a model $\mathcal{M}_1$ from a model $\mathcal{M}$ can be defined by the quotient $\mathcal{M} \div \mathcal{M}_1$. An *update* of a model is defined by a deletion followed by an insertion. *Recombination* $\looparrowright$ consists of a sequence of insertion, deletion and update operations.

Operations can also be defined by λ-expressions. For instance, union is definable by the property $\lambda \mathcal{M}_3 (\forall \mathcal{M}_4 ((\mathcal{M}_4 \succcurlyeq \mathcal{M}_3) \leftrightarrow (\mathcal{M}_4 \succcurlyeq \mathcal{M}_1 \wedge \mathcal{M}_4 \succcurlyeq \mathcal{M}_1)))$.

The predicates should not span all possible associations among the models but only those which are meaningful in a given application area. We may assume that two models are either potentially associated or cannot be associated with each other. The same restriction can be made for compatibility.

This model world is very general and allows one to derive more advanced operations and predicates. If we assume completeness of compatibility and association predicates, we may use expressions defined by the operations and derived predicates:

The predicate $Y := \overset{\exists}{\cap} \wedge \overset{\nexists}{\uplus}$ is used for diverging models.

The predicate $\lozenge := \overset{\nexists}{\cap} \wedge \overset{\nexists}{\uplus}$ is used for models which are isolated from one another.

The predicate $\curlywedge := \overset{\exists}{\cap} \wedge \overset{\exists}{\uplus} \wedge \not\succ \wedge \not\prec$ is used for homogenisable models.

The predicate $\curlyvee := \overset{\nexists}{\cap} \wedge \overset{\exists}{\uplus}$ is used for heterogeneous models.

These operations and predicates are very general. We aim to introduce a general setting for evolution and migration. This general setting can be defined for more specific model languages with direct specialisation of operations and predicates to the model language.

Example 12.3. The higher-order ER model in Chap. 6 uses a number of primitive operations for direct changes in ER schemata. The property of being a model is based on the enforcement of changes. A type has an environment, i.e. types that use the type. Therefore, the environment must be taken into consideration. Since HERM is built incrementally, we can use a definition frame for each of the operations and the required enforcement. Given two models $\mathcal{M}_1$ and $\mathcal{M}_2$, where $\mathcal{M}_1 \preceq \mathcal{M}$ for the model $\mathcal{M}$ that is going to be changed. Additionally we use a context $\mathcal{M}_C$ and its binding to $\mathcal{M}_1$ and $\mathcal{M}_2$. The binding associates each component in $\mathcal{M}_C$ to one component in $\mathcal{M}_1$ and to one component in $\mathcal{M}_2$. Any change operation O in a HERM structured model $\mathcal{M}_{\text{struct}}$ is represented by the frame

$$O (\mathcal{M}_C, \mathcal{M}_1, \mathcal{M}_2, \varXi) .$$

The change operation can be represented by a *graph production rule*

$$O_G : \mathcal{M}_1 \uplus \mathcal{M}_C \Rightarrow \mathcal{M}_2 \uplus \mathcal{M}_C$$

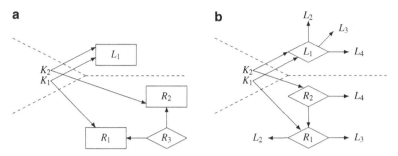

Fig. 12.2 Model change operations `decompose` (**a**) and `pivot` (**b**) with split of context

that is applied to a given model $\mathcal{M}$ with $\mathcal{M}_1 \uplus \mathcal{M}_C \preceq \mathcal{M}$ that uses

a *left side* $\mathcal{M}_1 \uplus \mathcal{M}_C$,

a *context graph*   that binds each component in $\mathcal{M}_C$ to one component in $\mathcal{M}_1$ and
to one component in $\mathcal{M}_2$, and

a *right side* $\mathcal{M}_2 \uplus \mathcal{M}_C$.

The resulting model $\mathcal{M}'$ glues $\mathcal{M}_2 \uplus \mathcal{M}_C$ into $\mathcal{M}$ along the context graph instead
of $\mathcal{M}_1 \uplus \mathcal{M}_C$.

The *decomposition* operation can be applied to any type that is used in $\mathcal{M}_{\text{struct}}$. It
must also consider the components of $\mathcal{M}_{\text{struct}}$ which refer to the type under decomposition. The context can either also be split to the new types or remain with one of
the types. The *pivot* operation decomposes a relationship type into two relationship
types where the first of these is based on the second one.

For illustration let us consider the model $\mathcal{M}_{\text{struct}}$, its types L_1, L_2, L_3, L_4, K_1,
K_2, and the model change operations

$$\texttt{decompose}\,(\{K_1, K_2\}, \{L_1\}, \{R_1, R_2, R_3\}, \varXi_{\text{d}})$$

$$\texttt{pivot}\,\big(\{K_1, K_2\}, \{L_1, L_2, L_3, L_4\}, \{R_1, R_2, L_2, L_3, L_4\}, \varXi_{\text{p}}\big)$$

in Fig. 12.2. The given model $\mathcal{M}$ has a context K_1, K_2 for the type L_1. This environment is associated to the types R_1 and R_2 in the resulting schema. The result is
a schema that splits the environment together with the decomposition or the pivoting.

12.3.3 Evolving Information Systems

Model Mappings

Evolution and migration of information systems and of application systems can be
based on mappings between these models. These mappings must be faithful in the
sense that the corresponding databases are synchronised. To introduce this synchro-

nisation we first develop a general notion of model embedding and database model transformation.

Heterogeneous models $\mathcal{M}_1, \mathcal{M}_2$ which should be synchronised consist of converging submodels, i.e. $\mathcal{M}_1 = \mathcal{M}_{1,0} \uplus \mathcal{M}_{1,2}$ and $\mathcal{M}_2 = \mathcal{M}_{2,0} \uplus \mathcal{M}_{1,2}$ with $\mathcal{M}_{1,0} \curlyvee \mathcal{M}_{1,2}$ and $\mathcal{M}_{2,0} \curlyvee \mathcal{M}_{1,2}$.[2] Moreover, this model is limited by the assumption that the submodel $\mathcal{M}_{1,2}$ is common for both models. For heterogeneous models we assume that $\mathcal{M}_i = \mathcal{M}_{i,0} \uplus \mathcal{M}_{i,1}$ from $\mathfrak{L}_i$ and $\mathcal{M}_j = \mathcal{M}_{j,0} \uplus \mathcal{M}_{j,1}$ from $\mathfrak{L}_j$ for models $\mathcal{M}_i, \mathcal{M}_j$ that are going to be synchronised where the submodels $\mathcal{M}_{i,0}, \mathcal{M}_{i,1}$ and $\mathcal{M}_{j,0}, \mathcal{M}_{j,1}$ are disjoint. Given, furthermore, a mapping $t_{i,j} : \mathcal{M}_{i,1} \longmapsto \mathcal{M}_{j,1}$ $t_{j,i} : \mathcal{M}_{j,1} \longmapsto \mathcal{M}_{i,1}$ for which extensions of $\mathbb{R}_{i,j}, \mathbb{R}_{j,i}$ exist in $\mathfrak{L}_i$ and $\mathfrak{L}_j$, respectively.

$$\mathcal{M}_i \xrightarrow{\text{extract } e_{i,j}} \mathcal{M}_{i,1} \xrightarrow{\text{transform } t_{i,j}} \mathcal{M}_{j,1} \xrightarrow{\text{load } l_{i,j}} \mathcal{M}_j$$

The product $e_{i,j} \circ t_{i,j} \circ l_{i,j}$ of the mappings is denoted by $put_{i,j}$. This product is neither left-inverse to $put_{j,i}$ nor must have a right-inverse $put_{j,i}$. This phenomenon is well known for updates of views in databases [1, 15]. Since models must obey integrity constraints of their types, we might have models for which $put_{i,j}$ is not defined. Two models $\mathcal{M}_i$ and $\mathcal{M}_j$ are called *coexisting* if $put_{i,j}(\mathcal{M}_i) \preccurlyeq \mathcal{M}_j$ and $put_{j,i}(\mathcal{M}_j) \preccurlyeq \mathcal{M}_i$. We observe that a model $\mathcal{M}_i$ may have many coexisting models $\mathcal{M}_j$.

The mappings $put_{i,j}$, $e_{i,j}$, $t_{i,j}$, and $l_{i,j}$ may be generally given for the set of all models defined on the model types $\mathcal{K}_{\mathcal{L}_{S_i} C_i}$ and $\mathcal{K}_{\mathcal{L}_{S_j} C_j}$. In this case the submodel embedding must be canonical.

Co-Evolution and Coexistence of Models

We observe that a model $\mathcal{M}_i$ may have many coexisting models $\mathcal{M}_j$. If we use a canonical embedding, then the mappings $put_{i,j}$ can be defined on the basis of the constant complement [1, 15], i.e. $h(\mathcal{M}_j, i) = \mathcal{M}_j \boxminus e_{j,i}(\mathcal{M}_j)$. We may now extend the mapping $put_{i,j}$ by the constant complement of the range model and define an integration condition by $\mathcal{M}_j = put^*_{i,j}(\mathcal{M}_i, h(\mathcal{M}_j, i))$. If the integration condition is valid for coexisting models, then we may also support changes in one model and propagate the changes to the other model.

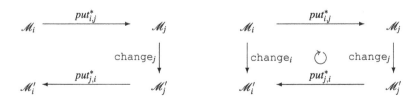

---

[2] $\uplus$ denotes the generalised union of models, $\curlyvee$ denotes the separatability or divergency of models, and $\bowtie$ denotes the generalised join.

We require that the put^* mappings be well behaved, i.e.

$put^*_{j,i}(put^*_{i,j}(\mathcal{M}_i, \hbar(\mathcal{M}_j, i)), \hbar(\mathcal{M}_i, j))$ must be defined and
$put^*_{j,i}(put^*_{i,j}(\mathcal{M}_i, \hbar(\mathcal{M}_j, i)), \hbar(\mathcal{M}_i, j)) = \mathcal{M}_i$.

The coexistence of models is not sufficient for change propagation. If $\mathcal{M}_j$ is changed to $\mathcal{M}'_j$ by the change operation change_j, then the change diagram should commute, i.e. this change operation has a related change operation change_i that allows one to change $\mathcal{M}_i$ directly to $\mathcal{M}'_i$. The change operation is defined on two arguments: the original model $\mathcal{M}_j$ and an auxiliary model $\mathcal{M}_{\mathrm{aux}}$. Model suite change is called *synchronised* for i, j and a set $\mathcal{O}^{\mathrm{change}}_j$ of change operations defined on $\mathcal{M}_j$ if for each change operation $o_j(\mathcal{M}_j, \mathcal{M}_{\mathrm{aux}})$ from $\mathcal{O}^{\mathrm{change}}_j$ a change operation $o_i(\mathcal{M}_i, \mathcal{M}_{\mathrm{aux}})$ in the set $\mathcal{O}_i$ of operations on $\mathcal{M}_i$ exists so that the change diagram commutes for the same auxiliary model $\mathcal{M}_{\mathrm{aux}}$, i.e. $o_i(\mathcal{M}_i, \mathcal{M}_{\mathrm{aux}}) = put^*_{j,i}(\mathcal{M}'_j, \hbar(\mathcal{M}_i, j))$ for $\mathcal{M}'_j = o_j(put^*_{i,j}(\mathcal{M}_i, \hbar(\mathcal{M}_j, i)), \mathcal{M}_{\mathrm{aux}})$. The complement should be constant. Therefore, we may use $\hbar(\mathcal{M}_i, j)$ instead of $\hbar(o_i(\mathcal{M}_i, \mathcal{M}_{\mathrm{aux}}), j)$.

Change operations are used for model evolution. The order of changes is important. We call two change operations o_i, o_j *liberal* with respect to the models $\mathcal{M}_i, \mathcal{M}_j$ if $\mathcal{M}'_i = put^*_{j,i}(\mathcal{M}'_j, \hbar(\mathcal{M}_i, j))$ and $\mathcal{M}'_j = put^*_{i,j}(\mathcal{M}'_i, \hbar(\mathcal{M}_j, i))$ for $\mathcal{M}'_i = o_i(\mathcal{M}_i, \mathcal{M}_{\mathrm{aux}})$ and $\mathcal{M}'_j = o_j(\mathcal{M}_j, \mathcal{M}_{\mathrm{aux}})$. Liberality can be extended to confluence and Church–Rosser properties [31]. Liberal change operations allow one to change a model and then to apply all the changes to coherent model suites.

This liberal change condition is necessary since the application model consists of at least four interdependent submodels. Therefore, we easily get into a change situation like the following one.

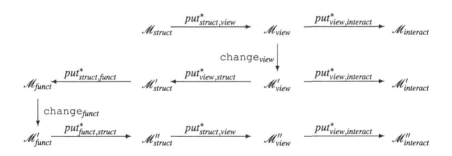

12.3.4 Properties of Evolving Information Systems

Model Coherence Through Contracts

Coherence within an information system model can be specified through a set of logical formulas that are specified in an appropriate language. Information system models typically use layered models. The function model $\mathcal{M}_{funct}$ uses the structure model $\mathcal{M}_{struct}$. Both models are used to describe the view model $\mathcal{M}_{view}$. The three models are used to describe the interaction model $\mathcal{M}_{interact}$. Therefore, we can use *model inclusion constraints* for change propagation throughout the information system model. These constraints allow us to track which construct C is defined in which submodel $\mathcal{M}_1$ and which model $\mathcal{M}_2$ uses the construct C. Therefore, we can formally express this property by the constraint $\mathcal{M}_1[C] \subseteq \mathcal{M}_2[C]$. This form of model inclusion constraints can be axiomatised in a form similar to the classical relational inclusion constraints [31].

We may, however, also use an information system model which is not entirely layered. For instance, the view model may introduce constructs which are used in the structure model. An information system model is called *coherent* if it obeys all model inclusion constraints. Let us denote the model inclusion constraints by

$$\Sigma_{\mathcal{M}_{IS}}^{Coherence} = \bigcup_{\substack{i,j \in \{\mathcal{M}_{funct}, \mathcal{M}_{struct}, \mathcal{M}_{view}, \mathcal{M}_{interact}\} \\ i \neq j}} \Sigma_{i,j}^{Coherence} .$$

We base our approach on a four-layer treatment in contracted development:

1. Declaration of constraints which are applied to a singleton model or to sets of collaborating models;
2. Description of enforcement mechanisms (when the constraint must be checked, how the constraint is checked, what to do if the constraint is violated, what mechanism can be used to trigger the constraint) which support constraint validity during development, change, and evolution of model suites;
3. Description of change and evolution steps which can be applied for refinement or modification of sets of model suites based on scopes of constraints and operational use of constraints;
4. Support by tools or workbenches that maintain the validity of constraints.

The third layer may also consider the development of model suites within development teams. In this case, team members are supported by approaches to collaboration, e.g. explicit services and exchange frames [30].

An information system model *contract* $\mathfrak{C}$ consists of a declaration of constraints, a description of the enforcement mechanism and a prescription of modification steps which change a coherent information system model into a coherent one. A contract may include obligations, permissions and sanctions.

Therefore:

• Contracts declare the correctness of an information system model, separate exceptional states from normal states for these models, and forbid meaningless models.
• Contracts enable the direct change of the model as transparently as possible and offer the required feedback in the case of invalidation of constraints based on echo back, visualisation of implications, deferred validation, instant projection and hypothetical compilation.

- Contracts consider mechanisms which address the long-term coherence of a model by forecasting confirmation, by anticipating changes made in a team, by providing a mechanism for adjusting and confirming correctness and by specifying diagnostic queries for inspection of models.

The contract $\mathfrak{C}$ on $\mathcal{M}_{IS}$ consists of the constraints $\Sigma_{\mathcal{M}_{IS}}^{\text{Coherence}}$, a description of the enforcement mechanisms for any operation which can be used for a change of one model, and a set of consistent evolution transformations.

Contract management becomes in this case rather simple. Enforcement may directly be applied to all coexisting models. We also may restrict a change operation by `no action`, `cascade`, and `oblige` enforcements. `No action` means that if a change operation cannot be propagated to another model, then this change operation is rolled back. `Cascade` enforcement requires that the other model be changed as well. `Oblige` enforcement allows one to delay the change operation on the other model to a later stage.

Evolution and Migration Changes

Migration and evolution are lossless changes of an information system. We are interested in maintaining the legacy database after application of change operations. The mappings between models have been so far only partial. We also need to establish a database equivalence between information system models. This equivalence is defined through two mappings between two models $\mathcal{M}_1$ and $\mathcal{M}_2$ on the basis of $\mathcal{M}_{1,\text{struct}} \uplus \mathcal{M}_{1,\text{view}}$ and $\mathcal{M}_{2,\text{struct}} \uplus \mathcal{M}_{2,\text{view}}$. Let us assume that there are mappings $put_{1,2}$ and $put_{2,1}$ between $\mathcal{M}_{1,\text{struct}} \uplus \mathcal{M}_{1,\text{view}}$ and $\mathcal{M}_{2,\text{struct}} \uplus \mathcal{M}_{2,\text{view}}$. These mappings can also be extended to the databases and the views for these models, i.e. $\widehat{put}_{1,2}$ and $\widehat{put}_{2,1}$. We use the database as well as the views since views may be materialised. Also, view object sets may be equivalent to database object sets and thus be used instead of the latter.

These mappings are based on an extraction mapping $e_{i,j}$, a transformation mapping $t_{i,j}$ and a load mapping $l_{i,j}$. We also may extend these mappings to instance mappings. The mapping $\widehat{put}_{1,2}$ is called *conservative* if for each database DB_1 and its views V_1 on $\mathcal{M}_1$ there exist a database DB_2 and its views V_2 on $\mathcal{M}_2$ such that $\widehat{put}_{1,2}(DB_1 \uplus V_1) = \widehat{e}_{2,1}(DB_2 \uplus V_2)$. Conservative mappings provide an embedding of databases on $\mathcal{M}_1$ into databases on $\mathcal{M}_2$.

Example 12.4. The mapping $put_{1,2}$ may decompose a type T into types $T_1, \ldots, T_k$. In this case, the mapping $\widehat{put}_{1,2}$ translates objects from T^C into objects from $T_1^C, \ldots, T_k^C$. At the same time, migration must be faithful in the sense that it does not introduce new objects in DB_2 if there are no corresponding objects in DB_1.
$\square^{EoE}$

Consistency of Models Through Infomorphisms

The mappings $\widehat{put}_{1,2}$ and $\widehat{put}_{2,1}$ form an *infomorphism* of $\mathcal{M}_1$ and $\mathcal{M}_2$ if for i, j with $\{i, j\} = \{1, 2\}$ and for each database DB_i and its views V_i on $\mathcal{M}_i$ there exist a database DB_j and its views V_j on $\mathcal{M}_j$ such that $\widehat{put}_{i,j}(DB_i \uplus V_i) = DB_j \uplus V_j$.

Infomorphisms allow that one of the databases and its views are redundant and have a lower granularity and a different structuring. We may extend this notion also by an introduction of OIDs. In this case $\mathcal{M}_{\text{funct}}$ must also provide an explicit mechanism for the creation of identifiers.

An evolving information system model is called *lossless* if an infomorphism exists for each change operation from $\mathfrak{M}$.

A *conservative migration* of one information system IS_1 to another IS_2 structured by models $\mathcal{M}_{1,IS}$ and $\mathcal{M}_{2,IS}$, respectively, is defined

- by mappings of database structuring models $put_{1,2}, put_{2,1}$ that relate models to each other, i.e. $put_{1,2}(\mathcal{M}_1) \preceq \mathcal{M}_2$ and $\mathcal{M}_1 \preceq put_{2,1}(\mathcal{M}_2)$, and
- by mappings $map_{1,2}$ and $map_{1,2}$ of databases DB_1, DB_2 induced by $put_{1,2}$ and $put_{2,1}$
- such that $map_{1,2}(o_1) \unlhd DB_2$ iff $map_{2,1}(o_2) \unlhd DB_1$ for each object $o_1 \in DB_1$ and $o_2 \in DB_2$.

A *forgetful mapping* is a mapping $\widehat{put}_{1,2}$ from $\mathcal{M}_{1,\text{struct}} \uplus \mathcal{M}_{1,\text{view}}$ to $\mathcal{M}_{2,\text{struct}} \uplus \mathcal{M}_{2,\text{view}}$ for which no corresponding mapping $\widehat{put}_{2,1}$ exists that could form an infomorphism with $\widehat{put}_{1,2}$. It thus removes types from the database model and the view model in such a way that the original database and views cannot be reestablished.

An *evolutionary selection* uses additionally a selection function σ_α from $\mathcal{M}_{i,\text{funct}}$ for $\widehat{put}_{i,j}(\sigma_\alpha(DB_i \uplus V_i))$. Archiving is based on evolutionary selection. Also, aging is based on evolutionary selection. An *evolutionary mutation* is based on exchanges of types between the database model and the view model which defines an infomorphism. An *evolutionary recombination* is based on changes through recombination operations which define an infomorphism. An *evolutionary Baldwin[3] change* is based on a change in the database model due to changes in the view model. This kind of change is typically observed during performance tuning of a database schema due to quality and performance requirements which stem from the application itself.

12.4 Strategies for Migration

From time to time, a legacy system containing voluminous databases has to be modernised. That means this legacy system (with its legacy databases usually with very valuable data) has to be redesigned on a new platform, on a new database management system, or for a new version of the database management system. Otherwise the application becomes old and cannot fulfill its task.

---

[3] The Baldwin effect is observed for the genotype after the phenotype is changed through a learning process.

During the migration step database structures as well as functions will be:

- extended,
- reduced, or
- changed.

Only in some cases is exactly the same functionality redeveloped.

Concerning the migration, different strategies can be applied known as *big bang* (in the literature sometimes also called cold turkey), *chicken little*, and *butterfly*. The strategies are distinguished by the following characteristics:

- When are the redeveloped components available for end users?
- How long do parallel versions of the legacy system and the evolved system exist?
- Which kinds of data are used for testing the redesigned system?
- How long is the system unavailable during the take-over of the data?

All migration strategies have their advantages and disadvantages. In the following sections, we describe the three different migration strategies in detail. The decision on which strategy is best suited for a concrete application depends on:

- System complexity,
- Modularisation of the legacy system,
- Frequency of data changes,
- Amount of data in the database, and
- Acceptable delay time of the system.

In the following sections, we also want to show which migration strategy is suitable for which kinds of applications.

12.4.1 Big Bang

Big bang entails the following migration strategy. A legacy application is the starting point. All user accesses are realised on the legacy application. During the whole redevelopment process of the system, the legacy application is the operational system (Fig. 12.3a).

Using a big bang migration strategy, the complete legacy system is redeveloped at once (Fig. 12.3b). All tasks occurring in the software life cycle (requirements analysis, design, implementation, test and so on) are made for the target system that will replace the legacy system. Redevelopment means that all available functions, programs, data and interfaces are newly developed from the ground up. The aim is to design a system on new hardware using a modern architecture. Ideally, the target system is modularised to be prepared for future changes.

The target database design cannot be completed prior to the target system's implementation is finished and tested. All data from the legacy database are transformed into the structure of the target database and inserted into the target database (Fig. 12.3c).

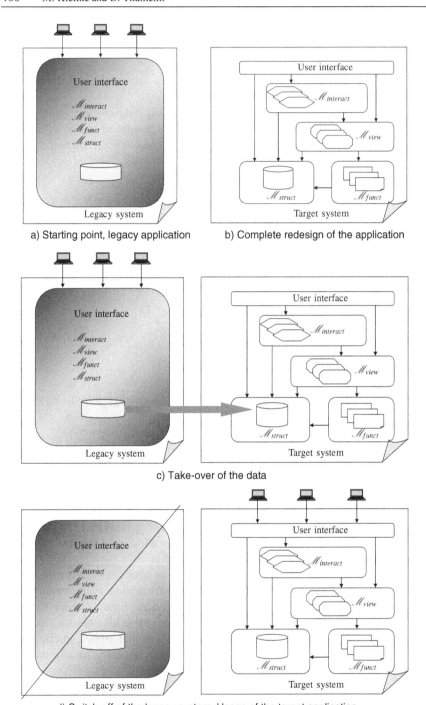

a) Starting point, legacy application   b) Complete redesign of the application

c) Take-over of the data

d) Switch-off of the legacy system, Usage of the target application

Fig. 12.3 Phases of big bang migration strategy

The migration process is finished when the target system is fully implemented and tested and also the data are transferred from the legacy database to the target database. From this point on, the new system replaces the legacy application (Fig. 12.3d). The target system becomes operational and the legacy system is deactivated. These steps happen at once.

The advantage of this method is that the migration process is quite easy to manage. The migration process is a completely new development, all parts of the new system are tested with test data only (selected from the legacy database) and the results are compared with the results of the legacy system. The new functions or programs have to produce the same results and have to have the same behaviour as the legacy system.

However, this strategy contains several disadvantages as well.

- This method has the risk that the take-over of a system may cause errors. In this case it might happen that the complete system is not available.
- A complete redevelopment of existing applications can take a long time (several months or, for real applications, even several years). During that time end users cannot see the modified system. Thus, it is not possible to consider end-user feedback.
- Because system development takes a very long time, legacy system changes and adaptations to new requirements during that time cannot be prevented. All changes in the legacy system must also be taken into account in the new system.
- The redevelopment of a system usually takes several years. During that time, technology advances and the new system becomes obsolete before it becomes operational.
- There is a risk that the new (redeveloped) system will only be tested as a standalone and not in interaction with other systems. This can lead to errors when the evolved system becomes operational.
- The take-over of the active data from a legacy system to a redeveloped system may take a long time, especially if another database system is used and if the database schema has been changed. During that time of the take-over, neither the legacy application nor the target application will be available for end-users.

12.4.1.1 Evaluation of the Big Bang Migration Strategy

The following table enumerates the strengths, weaknesses and risks of the big bang migration strategy.

Because of these disadvantages, this strategy can only be applied in some cases. If the time that is necessary for redevelopment is acceptably short, a big bang strategy seems promising.

Strengths:	• The migration process is easily managed.
	• Application redesign is clean.
	• Testing may be done with selected data from the legacy application.
Weaknesses:	• Requires a long development time (for the whole application); during that time:
	– Requirement changes must be considered.
	– There is no feedback from users for developers.
	– Technology improves; the new system may become obsolete before it becomes operational.
Risks:	• All operating data are taken over at one time.
	• The system is not available during data take-over.

12.4.2 Chicken Little

Another approach, called chicken little, is based on the complete modularisation of a legacy system. By applying a *divide-and-conquer strategy* for the migration process, all components are migrated separately. Thus, a complex migration task is separated into several small and easy-to-handle migration tasks. All the components (including data, applications, programs, and functions) are adapted step by step.

In this section, we give an overview of this migration strategy, the subtasks that developers have to fulfil and the advantages and disadvantages of the strategy.

Figure 12.4 represents the main phases of the chicken little approach. The starting point is a legacy application (Fig. 12.4a) consisting of a legacy database with a defined database structure M_{struct}, views M_{view}, stored procedures, triggers, functions M_{funct}, integrity constraints and check constraints. The legacy application consists of a legacy program, user interfaces and interfaces to access the data.

The first task is to divide the application into modules or components. The aim is to separate the different functions and processes of an application with as few dependencies as possible remaining between the modules (Fig. 12.4a). Even if we decompose a complex application into separate components, there will be some interactions between the components that will have to be taken into account in the migration process.

The chicken little migration strategy redevelops the components step by step. If a component is completely redeveloped, then end users can use this component immediately. Thus, the redevelopment of the whole application is divided into the redevelopment of smaller components. Each of these takes only a short time to develop (Fig. 12.4b,c).

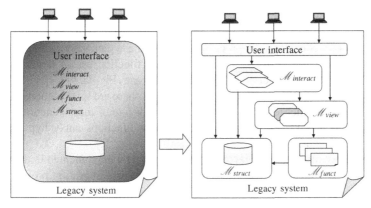

a) Starting point: modularisation of the existing legacy application

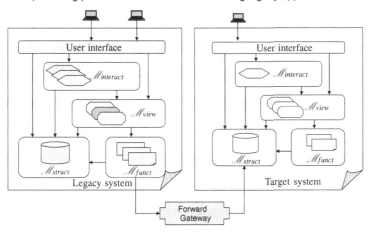

b) Redevelopement of the target application, usage of foreward gateways

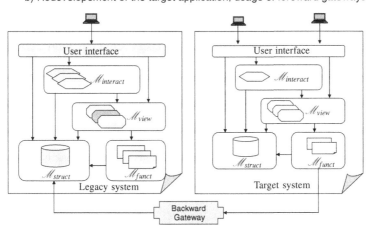

c) Redevelopement of the target application, usage of backward gateways

Fig. 12.4 Chicken little migration, use of backward and forward gateways

We first mentioned that during the migration process there are still interactions or connections between the components. Therefore, database gateways are necessary during the redevelopment process. These database gateways enable functions to access the databases, in cases where a legacy function uses a target database (Fig. 12.4b) or a target function uses a legacy database (Fig. 12.4c).

Furthermore, *function gateways* are necessary if there are interrelations between two functions and the evolution process starts with one of these functions. These function gateways ensure that interrelations between functions can be bypassed during the redevelopment process.

These different kinds of necessary gateways must be implemented in the migration process and make the management of chicken little migration projects more complex.

Database-First Approach (Forward Migration Method)

A chicken little migration strategy may start with the migration of the database. The first step here is redesigning the database within a new database system. The data are migrated to the target database and all applications must access the data in the new database. To do this, *forward gateways* are used which translate the queries from the existing database to the target database (Fig. 12.4c).

Database-Last Approach (Reverse Migration Method)

Another possibility is to start the migration process by programming the target functions (Fig. 12.4c). Functions and programs are renewed. During redevelopment, the new functions use the data of the legacy database. *Backward gateways* are applied to access these data.

The second step entails redesigning and migrating of the database. When the database redesign is completed, then the data of this component are copied from the legacy database to the target database. The take-over of the information system is realised incrementally. After finishing the migration, all target components are operational and the gateways are no longer necessary.

12.4.2.1 Evaluation of the Chicken Little Migration Strategy

Following a divide-and-conquer strategy, a complex migration task is divided into several subtasks. The migration strategy has the following characteristics:

Strenght:	• The divide-and-conquer approach divides the migration task into several easy-to-handle small migration projects. • The necessary development time for the redesign of each component is short; several advantages arise: • Requirement changes are uncommon during the migration process. • Feedback from end users can be used for the redesign of the next components immediately. • Short migration processes increase the motivation of developers.
Weaknesses:	• The interactions between legacy and target applications and data have to be realised during the entire migration process. • Database and function gateways are necessary; hence the migration project is more costly in terms of labour and time. • The development of gateways requires additional effort.
Risks:	• Unstable states during the migration: components of legacy and target applications have to interact via gateways during the migration process.

The main advantage of this migration strategy is that the risk of this approach is reduced because the migration process is done incrementally. The development time is short for the redevelopment of each single component.

12.4.3 Butterfly

This strategy combines elements from the big bang and the chicken little migration approaches. The main focus is on the migration of the database because of the assumption that data in the database are the most important part of the legacy system.

The butterfly strategy includes the following steps:

1. An available legacy application is the starting point. As the first step, *the database is frozen* and used in the following procedure as a *read-only storage solution* for the legacy application. All changes in the data (comprising updates as well as schema evolution) are logged in temporary data stores (TDS_x) (Fig. 12.5b).

2. A legacy system needs an interface to access the data because the data are available either in the read-only database or in a temporary data store (TDS_x) if it has already been changed during the migration process.[4]
   This interface is called the *Data Access Allocator* (DAA) and uses the database as well as all temporary data stores $TDS_1, \ldots, TDS_n$. During the entire evolution process end users are able to use the legacy application.

3. A data transformation process starts with the database. First, we transform the data of the read-only database. During the migration process, we successfully transfer all temporary data stores (TDS_x) to the new database. A crystalliser component is responsible for this task (Fig. 12.5c). The crystalliser transfers the

---

[4] Data access in the butterfly migration approach is similar to computer caches: data can be available in the cache (here: *TDS*) or on the storage device (here: read-only database).

Fig. 12.5 Butterfly: stepwise data transformation, redevelopment of system. **a** Starting point, ▶
legacy application. **b** Freezing the database, adding temporary data stores. **c** Take-over of read-
only database and data in temporary data stores. **d** Take-over, transformation of last temporal data
store

data from the legacy database format and the temporary data stores TDS to the
target database structure and inserts the data into the target database.

4. In the temporary data stores TDS_x, all data that have been changed are collected.
   If the data store TDS_x attains a given size, then the crystalliser transforms the
   data of TDS_x. The legacy application stores all further data changes in TDS_{x+1}.
5. After the introduction of the DAA interface, the legacy system is evolved, and
   new functions are implemented and tested against the available data. The butterfly migration approach demands a complete redesign of the entire application.
   Similar to the big bang approach, end users use only the legacy system during
   the entire migration process.
6. At the end of the migration process, all programs, functions, interfaces and so
   forth are redeveloped. The take-over of the data is easy because only the data in
   the last TDS_n (containing the last updates) have to be transformed into the new
   data format (Fig. 12.5c).

The user is now able to use the new target system; the old system is no longer
necessary and can be deactivated.

12.4.3.1 Advantages

- One advantage of the butterfly approach is that the take-over is easy to realise.
  During the take-over, only the last temporary data store has to be transferred to
  the target database.
  The butterfly migration approach means that the data are transferred successively,
  each TDS_x separately. The risk of this iterative data transferral is much lower than
  in the big bang methodology.
- Furthermore, the butterfly method does not need gateways during the migration
  process because end users use one system at a time. During the migration process the legacy system and after the cut-off the redesigned system are used. The
  administration of butterfly migrations therefore is easier than chicken little migrations.

12.4.3.2 Disadvantages

- This approach starts with a new database design prior to functions being redeveloped. Therefore, the legacy database influences the target database solution
  heavily; it makes it difficult to consider changes and new requirements because
  they cause schema evolution steps of the target database.

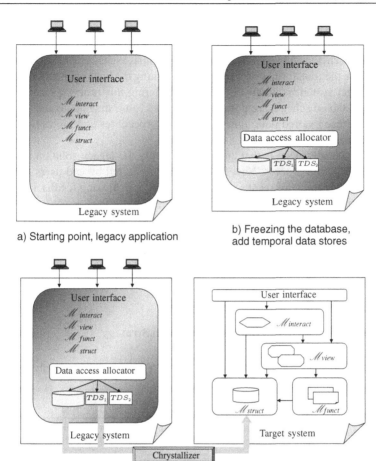

a) Starting point, legacy application

b) Freezing the database,
add temporal data stores

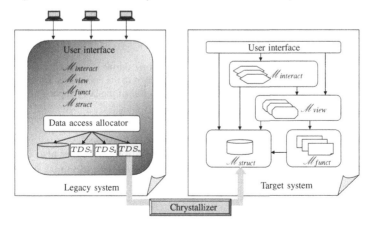

c) Take-over of the read-only database and the data in temp data stores

d) take-over, transformation of the last temporal data store

- The temporary data stores can easily deal with updates of values. They store all data in the structure of the legacy database. Most likely, the structure of the target database schema will differ from the legacy database schema. The crystalliser has to realise the transformation steps for overcoming the heterogeneous schemas.
- The target system is iteratively developed; during this process, changes in the target database schema are possible. They also cause the update and adaptation of the already stored data, functions, stored procedures and views which must take place.
- Another disadvantage is that end users use only the legacy solution during the entire migration process. New functions are not tested by end users during the evolution process; this results in missing interaction, missing feedback and missing motivation for the developers.
- Efficiency of query realisation decreases because of the overhead of the DAA which has to query the read-only database and all temporary data stores (TDS_1, ..., TDS_n). The amount of data in the temporary data stores increases constantly and leads to a decrease in efficiency of querying data in the legacy system.

12.4.3.3 Evaluation of the Butterfly Migration Strategy

The following overview summarises the characteristics of the butterfly migration strategy.

Strenght:	• An entire application is redesigned, and tests can be conducted with real data from the legacy application which is already available during the migration process.
	• The migration process is quite easy to manage.
Weaknesses:	• There is a long development time for the whole application (requirement changes during that time which have to be considered, no feedback for the developers, technology improves, the new system may become obsolete before it is operational).
	• The database design of the target system is influenced heavily by the legacy database.
	• Schema evolution on the target database during the migration process is complicated; database evolution and changes to the crystalliser are necessary.
Risks:	• The risk is very low; only the take-over of the last temporary data store has to be carried out.

Besides redesign on a new platform, all migration strategies also contain the system evolution. The next section introduces this modernisation task in detail.

12.5 Evolution

12.5.1 Evolution on a Small Scale

Small-step structuring evolution – also called database model change – is a small change to a database schema which improves database structuring without changing the semantics of the database. Refactoring has been introduced as a programming technique which supports a disciplined restructuring of code in small steps. It thus merely improves the design of the code – nothing more and nothing less. A database model change is a simple change to a database schema that improves its design while retaining its semantics.

There are two fundamental reasons why one would want to adopt small-step evolution:

- To repair existing legacy databases: Small-step evolution supports local changes to an information system without changing the system outside the scope of the change. This is clearly much less risky than a "big bang" approach where you rewrite the information system model.
- To support evolving information system development: Most information system development processes are evolutionary in nature. Modern co-design processes are based on both information system structuring and database functionality.

Methodologies for Evolution of Information System Models

The conceptual model for evolving information system models is based on a formal *evolution methodology* consisting of

- an extended information system model $\mathcal{M}_{IS}$ which supports a standard notion of evolving models (equipped with all the usual model change operators) for which a semantics is provided;
- a collection of interesting reasoning tasks to support the design and management of an evolving model;
- a set of tasks that are combined into a transformation portfolio, a testing portfolio and a data migration portfolio for transformation.

This methodology allows one to define specific evolution steps. For instance, the *change methodology* (generalised from [2]) consists of two evolution steps:

- The *intermediate evolution step* transforms the *initial model* to an *intermediate model* that is tested in application situations and has a validity deadline. If the validity deadline is reached without transformation success, then the initial model and the initial database are enabled and the intermediate model and databases are disabled.
- The *finalisation evolution step* transforms the intermediate model to the finalised model and applies this transformation to the application system as well in the case where the validity deadline has successfully been reached.

A methodology typically provides a comprehensive set of constructs and rules for their application that serve as the background for constructing applications. We may systematically separate a number of concerns according to the classical project management frame: 'what' (level 1) provides a specification; 'how' (level 2) defines the way the framework is going to work; 'do' (level 3) prescribes the application of the operations and their effect; 'plan' (level 4) provides the methodology for the application; 'manage' (level 5) allows the governance of the change framework; 'coordinate' (level 6) integrates the framework into the entire development process; and 'optimize' (level 7) revises the change management.

We will elaborate only levels 1, 2 and 3 of the methodology. The *specification level* consists of a specification of model changes. It can be extended by specific policies for various development methods such as agile development. The *control* or *technical level* provides guidance for the control procedures such as setting the control management, deriving the scope of control and defining the control tasks and their actors. The *application* or *technology level* handles the management of changes.

Structural Elementary Model Changes

Simple structural elementary schema change operations that can be applied to schemata in the EER model are as follows: add a type, drop a type, change type name and change attribute domain type. The types under consideration can be attribute types, entity types, relationship types and cluster types. The change operation taxonomy is thus built by combining model language elements, which are subject to change, with the elementary modifications, add, drop, and change, which they undergo.

Elementary change steps evolve an existing application model and the corresponding database in small steps at a time to improve the quality of the model and the application without changing the static and dynamic semantics and interaction.

Any modification of an application model must be verified by a full regression test on the system. We must ensure that the application model and the database actually work.

We shall illustrate now structural elementary model changes. We use *control functions* for the control of the intermediate evolution. Control functions are attached to type structures or their components or to functions. For instance, the controls *[event = on update\insert of invoice]*, *[modification kind = slave]*, *[policy = materialise]* and *[drop date = 1-1-2011]* denote the automatic enforcement of evaluation of a value of a function or value, the master–slave change of a dependent value or function, the explicit storage of results of function applications and the maintenance deadline of the intermediate schema.

Example 12.5. Let us consider a simplified example used for managing transportation data in Fig. 12.6. We assume that cars which are owned by owners are used to transport goods from one store belonging to a supplier to another store belonging to a market. The first choice could be a complex relationship type on entity types

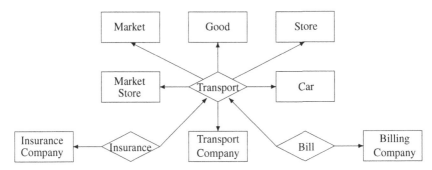

Fig. 12.6 Decomposable independent concepts

Owner, Car, Market, Supplier and *Store*, where store type is used recursively. We abstract from attributes such as *Time* for *Transport*.

This schema can be restructured if we take into account a number of observations:

- Insurance is issued for cars and companies. The transport application is restricted to this kind of insurance.
- Billing is typically applied to the entire transportation event.
- Cars and owners from the first side, markets and their stores from the second side, and good and their location from the third side are relatively independent from each other. This relative independence is not complete.

This schema is now going to be restructured based on the application of the pivoting graph grammar rule and on application of the decomposition graph grammar rule.

- We may separate by pivoting rules cars with their owners and insurance from the transport request and transport events.
- Markets have their stores (MLocation). Goods are stored at a store (GLocation). We thus separate these direct associations by pivoting.
- A transport request relates goods with their location to markets with their stores. We thus reduce transports to transport requests.
- A transport event relates a transport request with a car used for transport. We thus pivot transport events from transport requests.
- Billing applies to the transport event and thus relates to the transporting car and the transport request. It inherits thus the transport request. The transformation to a relational schema that does not use identifier attributes for separate types results in a relational schema with markets, their stores, goods and their stores, cars and additional attributes such as time of the transport event. Billing is issued to the market that requested a transport. We do not assume other kinds of billing.

The resulting schema is displayed in Fig. 12.7. This schema is the result of a sequence of operations:

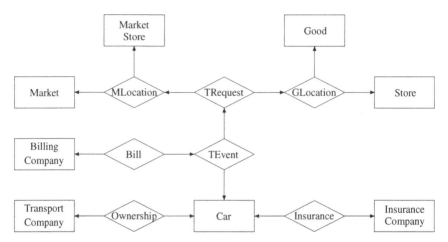

Fig. 12.7 Representation of independent concepts by relationship types

1. *Projection:* Cars and transport companies are associated to each other. We may introduce a new type ownership.
2. *Shifting:* Transports are carried by cars. The ownership for cars is independent.
3. *Pivoting:* Transports are completed events based on an issuing event such as requests.
4. *Multiple shifting:* Insurances are issued for cars and are independent of transport events and transport requests. They are assumed to be independent of ownership.
5. *Decomposition:* Transport requests are considered to relate markets with their stores to goods with their location. Therefore, we introduce the new types MLocation and GLocation. These new types form the basis for storing data about transport requests.

12.5.2 Wrapper-Based Evolution

Black-box evolution frameworks are based on wrapping [32] or encapsulation of the existing system. Both approaches extend the lifetime of existing components by facilitating an integration of existing subsystems into modern distributed systems. The subsystems are typically not altered. At the same time, heterogeneity is provided due to the extensive use of interfaces that are added to the subsystems. New capabilities are going to be added on the basis of interfaces. These subsystems can be used either through both their interfaces and the subsystem itself or only through their interfaces. The first approach is based on the development of wrappers. The second approach results in the introduction of system components.

A *wrapper* is defined by a *wrapper schema* and a *common query language* for the data as viewed through the wrapper schema. In this case, we use the models of an

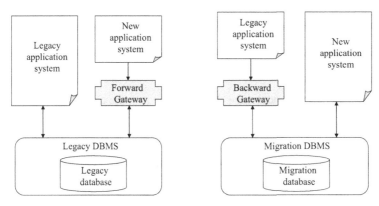

Fig. 12.8 Forward and backward wrappers supporting the coexistence of new and legacy applications

information system model $\mathcal{M}_{IS} = (\mathcal{M}_{struct}, \mathcal{M}_{funct}, \mathcal{M}_{view}, \mathcal{M}_{interact})$ in a specific form. The database function model $\mathcal{M}_{funct}$ allows one to define the database view model $\mathcal{M}_{view}$. The database view model is used for associating the new application or legacy application systems with the database. It is thus a *'washer'* between the database and the applications. The query language allows one to directly access the wrapped data to modify these data. Wrappers may either be used as *forward wrappers* which connect the existing system to new applications or as *backward wrappers* which connect the old application with the migration database.

Backward wrappers are used for incomplete migration of applications. Forward wrappers are typically applied during system evolution.

Wrapper models $(\mathcal{M}_{struct}, \mathcal{M}_{funct}, \mathcal{M}_{view}, \mathcal{M}_{funct}^{view})$ are introduced as a special kind of media type [23]. At the core of a wrapper model we have a view which is extended by operations. First recall that a view is nothing but a stored query. For this we assume familiarity with the higher-order ER model (HERM) in Chap. 6. A *view* V on a HERM schema $\mathcal{M}_{struct} = (\mathcal{S}, \Sigma)$ consists of a schema $\mathcal{S}_V$ and a query q_V with a query mapping $inst(\mathcal{S}, \Sigma) \rightarrow inst(\mathcal{S}_V)$. A view model $\mathcal{M}_{view}$ for wrappers consists of a set of views.

The addition of operations leads first to the notion of wrapper type as defined (in a simplified form) next. A *wrapper type* W over an extended ER schema $\mathcal{M}_{struct} = (\mathcal{S}, \Sigma)$ primarily consists of a view $V_W = (\mathcal{S}_W, q_W)$ and a set $\mathcal{O}$ of *interaction operations*. Each wrapper operation in $\mathcal{O}$ from $\mathcal{M}_{funct}^{view}$ consists of an operation name op, a list of input parameters $i_1 : D_1, \ldots, i_k : D_k$ with domain names D_i, an (optional) output domain D_{out}, a subattribute sel of X_E, and a wrapper operation body, which is built from the usual programming constructs operating on instances over $\mathcal{M}_{struct} = (\mathcal{S}, \Sigma)$ and constructs for creating and deleting wrapper objects.

Apart from this, wrapper types extend types by *cohesion* in order to enable adaptivity. *Cohesion* introduces a controlled form of information loss exploiting the partial order $\geq$ on nested attributes. If X_M is the representing attribute of a type M and $sub(X_M)$ is the set of all nested attributes Y with $X_M \geq Y$, then a preorder $\preceq_M$ on $sub(X_M)$ extending the order $\geq$ is called a *cohesion preorder*.

Large elements in $sub(X_M)$ with respect to $\preceq_M$ define information to be kept together, if possible. Clearly, X_M is maximal with respect to $\preceq_M$. This enables a controlled form of information decomposition [29]. Thus we obtain the following (simplified) definition of a wrapper type. A *wrapper type* is a type M together with a cohesion preorder $\preceq_M$.

As the core of a wrapper type is defined by a view, the core problem of wrapper type integration is that of view integration. So we start with two views V_1 and V_2 on an EER schema $\mathcal{M}_{struct} = (\mathcal{S}, \Sigma)$. The result should be a new integrated view V such that $\mathcal{S}_V$ results from the integration of the schemata $\mathcal{S}_{V_1}$ and $\mathcal{S}_{V_2}$, and for each instance db over $(\mathcal{S}, \Sigma)$ the two query results $q_{V_1}(db)$ and $q_{V_2}(db)$ together are equivalent to $q_V(db)$.

In particular, view integration requires precise notions for schema dominance and equivalence, which we will introduce now. A HERM schema $\mathcal{M}'_{struct} = (\mathcal{S}', \Sigma')$ *dominates* another HERM schema $\mathcal{M}_{struct} = (\mathcal{S}, \Sigma)$ by means of the language $\mathcal{L}$ (notation: $(\mathcal{S}, \Sigma) \sqsubseteq_{\mathcal{L}} (\mathcal{S}', \Sigma')$) iff there are mappings $f : inst(\mathcal{S}, \Sigma) \to inst(\mathcal{S}', \Sigma')$ and $g : inst(\mathcal{S}', \Sigma') \to inst(\mathcal{S}, \Sigma)$, both expressed in $\mathcal{L}$ such that the composition $g \circ f$ is the identity. If we have $(\mathcal{S}, \Sigma) \sqsubseteq_{\mathcal{L}} (\mathcal{S}', \Sigma')$ as well as $(\mathcal{S}', \Sigma') \sqsubseteq_{\mathcal{L}} (\mathcal{S}, \Sigma)$, we say that the two schemata are *equivalent* with respect to $\mathcal{L}$ [notation: $(\mathcal{S}, \Sigma) \cong_{\mathcal{L}} (\mathcal{S}', \Sigma')$].

We may obtain different notions of dominance and equivalence. $\sqsubseteq_{\mathcal{H}}$ and $\cong_{\mathcal{H}}$ refer to the use of the HERM algebra or, equivalently, the HERM calculus [31] as the language in which transformations f and g are to be expressed. Analogously, $\sqsubseteq_{\mathcal{H}_{ext}}$ and $\cong_{\mathcal{H}_{ext}}$ refer to the use of the extended HERM algebra or the extended HERM calculus [31]. In what follows we will always refer to $\sqsubseteq_{comp}$ and $\cong_{comp}$ and therefore drop the index and simply write $\sqsubseteq$ for dominance and $\cong$ for equivalence.

Now, if schemata $\mathcal{S}_{V_1}$ and $\mathcal{S}_{V_2}$ are 'cleaned', we may combine queries q_{V_1} and q_{V_2} into one, yielding a query mapping $inst(\mathcal{S}, \Sigma) \to inst(\mathcal{S}_{V_1} \cup \mathcal{S}_{V_2})$ defined by the query $q_{V_1} \cup q_{V_2}$. If we simply integrate schemata $\mathcal{S}_{V_1}$ and $\mathcal{S}_{V_2}$ into $\mathcal{S}_V$ according to the method described above, we obtain an induced mapping $f : inst(\mathcal{S}_{V_1} \cup \mathcal{S}_{V_2}) \to inst(\mathcal{S}_V)$. As we deal with computable queries, f is the query mapping of some computable query q_f. Taking $q_V = q_f \circ (q_{V_1} \cup q_{V_2})$, V becomes a view over $\mathcal{M}_{struct} = (\mathcal{S}, \Sigma)$ with schema $\mathcal{M}_{view} = \mathcal{S}_V$ and defining query q_V. Finally, we must adapt wrapper operations and the cohesion preorder. *View cooperation* [31] provides an alternative to view integration in which the integrated view is only virtual. That is, the constituting views are kept and exchange functions are designed to provide the same functionality as if the views were integrated. Let $V_i = (\mathcal{S}_{V_i}, q_{V_i})$ $(i = 1, 2)$ be views (on the same or different HERM schemata). V_1 *cooperates* with V_2 iff there are subschemata $\mathcal{S}'_{V_i}$ of $\mathcal{S}_{V_i}$ and functions $f_1 : inst(\mathcal{S}'_{V_1}) \to inst(\mathcal{S}'_{V_2})$ and $f_2 : inst(\mathcal{S}'_{V_2}) \to inst(\mathcal{S}'_{V_1})$, such that both $f_1 \circ f_2$ and $f_2 \circ f_1$ are the identity function.

Basically, view cooperation expresses that part of view V_1; precisely that one corresponding to subschema $\mathcal{S}'_{V_1}$ can be expressed by the part of view V_2 corresponding to subschema $\mathcal{S}'_{V_2}$. Now, if we want to obtain a cooperation between given views V_1 and V_2, we may simply apply view integration to them using the same transformation rules. This will result in an integrated view $V = (\mathcal{S}_V, q_V)$. With respect to this integrated view both $\mathcal{S}'_{V_1}$ and $\mathcal{S}'_{V_2}$ will be identified with a subschema $\mathcal{S}'_V$. In particular, we obtain functions $f_i' : inst(\mathcal{S}_{V_i}') \to inst(\mathcal{S}_V')$ and $g_i' : inst(\mathcal{S}_V') \to inst(\mathcal{S}_{V_i}'))$ ($i = 1, 2$), with $g_i' \circ f_i' = id$ and $f_i' \circ g_i' = id$. Thus, $f_1 = g_2' \circ f_1'$ and $f_2 = g_1' \circ f_2'$ define the view cooperation functions. Consequently, if the view integration method takes care of operations and cohesion, we also obtain cooperating wrapper types.

12.5.3 Refinement of the Information System Model

The theory of conceptual modelling may also be used for a selection and development of an assembly of modelling styles. Typical well-known styles [31] are inside-out refinement, top-down refinement, bottom-up refinement, modular refinement and mixed skeleton-driven refinement.

The perspectives and styles of modelling rule the kind of refinement styles. As an example we consider structure-oriented strategies of development:

Inside-out refinement uses the given specification for extending it by an additional part. These parts are hocked onto the current specification without changing it.

Top-down refinement uses the decomposition of functions in the vocabulary and refinement of rules. Additionally, the specification may be extended by functions and rules that have not yet been considered.

Bottom-up refinement applies the composition and generalisation of functions and of rules to more general or complex ones. Bottom-up refinement also uses the generation of new functions and rules that have not yet been considered.

Modular refinement is based on parqueting of applications and on the separation of concern. Refinement is only applied to one module and does not affect others. Modules may also be decomposed. Modules are typically associated through a skeleton that reflects the application architecture or the technical architecture.

Mixed skeleton-driven refinement is a combination of refinement techniques. It uses a skeleton of the application or a draft of the architecture. This draft is used for deriving plans for refinement. Each component or module is developed on its own based on top-down or bottom-up refinement.

These different kinds of refinement styles allow one to derive *plans* and *primitives* for refinement.

Börger and Schellhorn [6, 27] have developed a general theory of refinement. Control of correctness of refinement takes into account (a) a notion of refined structure and refined vocabulary, (b) a restriction to information system structures of interest, (c) abstract information system computation segments, (d) a description of database segments of interest, and (e) an equivalence relation among those data of interest. The theory developed in [6, 27] allows one to check whether a given refinement is correct or not.

Given two information system models $\mathcal{M}_{IS}$ and $\mathcal{M}_{IS}^*$, a *refinement* of information systems is based on

a refinement of the information systems' structure by a mapping $\mathcal{F}$ from $\mathcal{M}_{struct}$ to $\mathcal{M}_{struct}^*$,

Fig. 12.9 Information system
application models and information system refinement
scheme

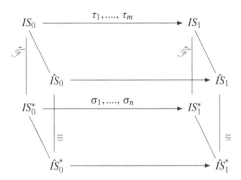

a correspondence relation $\simeq$ between the information systems' application mod-
  els of interest $(\hat{\mathcal{M}}_{\text{struct}}, \hat{\mathcal{M}}_{\text{view}}, \hat{\mathcal{M}}_{\text{interact}})$ and $(\hat{\mathcal{M}}^*_{\text{struct}}, \hat{\mathcal{M}}^*_{\text{view}}, \hat{\mathcal{M}}^*_{\text{interact}})$, whereby
  these models of interest are submodels of $\mathcal{M}_{\text{IS}}$ and $\mathcal{M}^*_{\text{IS}}$, respectively,
information systems' transaction computations $\tau_1, \ldots, \tau_m$ on $\mathcal{M}_{\text{IS}}$ and $\sigma_1, \ldots, \sigma_n$
  on $\mathcal{M}^*_{\text{IS}}$,
information systems' segments of interest IS and IS^* defined on $(\hat{\mathcal{M}}_{\text{struct}}, \hat{\mathcal{M}}_{\text{view}},$
  $\hat{\mathcal{M}}_{\text{interact}})$ and on $(\hat{\mathcal{M}}^*_{\text{struct}}, \hat{\mathcal{M}}^*_{\text{view}}, \hat{\mathcal{M}}^*_{\text{interact}})$, respectively, and
an equivalence relation $\approxeq$ on information systems' segments of interest.

We use a partial correspondence relation $\simeq$ between the structures since modernisation of information systems is partial in the sense that some structures are not refined
but remain within the old models (e.g. wrapper architectures such as in Fig. 12.8).
Figure 12.9 displays a refinement scheme with the refinement mapping $\tilde{\mathcal{F}}$ extended
to IS and IS^* and the correspondence relation $\simeq$ and with abstract information
systems' computation segments that transfer IS' and IS' and IS^* and IS'^*, respectively. The transaction computations $\tau_1, \ldots, \tau_m$ and $\sigma_1, \ldots, \sigma_n$ can differ in
length and in behaviour. Their final result matches, however, for $\tilde{\mathcal{F}}$ and $\approxeq$. The front
part consisting of $\hat{IS}^*_0, \hat{IS}^*_1, \hat{IS}_0$ and $\hat{IS}_1$ can be considered the observable part of
the information systems.

$\mathcal{M}^*_{\text{IS}}$ is called a *correct refinement* of $\mathcal{M}_{\text{IS}}$ if

- for each $\mathcal{M}^*_{\text{IS}}$ transaction computation $IS^*_0, \ldots, IS^*_k, \ldots$
- there is an $\mathcal{M}_{\text{IS}}$ transaction computation $IS_0, \ldots, IS_s, \ldots$ and
- sequences $i_0 < i_1 < \ldots$ and $j_0 < j_1 < \ldots$ such that
- $i_0 = j_0 = 0$ and $\hat{IS}_{i_k} \approxeq \hat{IS}^*_{j_k}$ for each k and
- both computations terminate and their final states are the last pair of equivalent
  states.

A *complete refinement* is given if $\mathcal{M}_{\text{IS}}$ is a correct refinement of $\mathcal{M}^*_{\text{IS}}$ and $\mathcal{M}^*_{\text{IS}}$
is a correct refinement of $\mathcal{M}_{\text{IS}}$.

12.6 Related Work

Parnas enumerates the reasons why software ages and why software evolution is necessary [24]. He also illustrates why software modernisation is such a complicated task. We used the chicken little and big bang methods introduced in [7] and aimed at defining these approaches in a precise way. This definitions could also be used for a definition of the butterfly approach to migration. This chapter has concentrated on model-based evolution and migration. Database evolution follows model-based evolution and is based on a transaction approach [21].

Comella-Dorda et al. represent in [8] an overview on the subtasks of system modernisation. They establish the term modernisation, in contrast to maintenance of existing systems and replacement (migration). The notion of system modernisation was introduced in [25]. The notion of evolving database systems is sketched in [12].

Some publications [3, 4] introduce different migration strategies, enumerating migration issues and subtasks of each migration strategy. The most detailed article [3] introduces big bang, chicken little, and butterfly migrations, enumerating the advantages and disadvantages of each migration strategy. Small-step evolution or chicken little strategies can be based on refactoring techniques [2, 33]. This chapter extended refactoring and wrapping [32] by graph grammar rules for transformation. Our approach to evolution and migration got its practical experimentation in [19] and in [28].

Some publications develop schema evolution approaches which propagate evolution steps on a conceptual model to database or XML schema evolution steps [10, 16–18].

Evolution and migration are based on model mapping techniques, e.g. [5, 13, 14, 20, 22]. These techniques target model compilation, transformation or interpretation within another target model. We extended these techniques to the integration of models. [11] bases co-evolution of information system models on model suites. Model suites extend the versioning approach in [12] and the category approach used in [9]. The view injection used in this chapter is based on view updates [15] and on system collaboration [30]. Model suites can be based on the EER model [31] as well as on other incrementally definable model languages.

Refinement and data refinement techniques are often defined in a rather fuzzy way. The calculus of model suites extends the approach introduced by [25] and the redefined model suite refinement using abstract state machine refinement [6].

References

1. Abiteboul S, Hull R, Vianu V (1995) Foundations of databases. Addison-Wesley, Reading
2. Ambler SW, Sadalage PJ (2006) Refactoring databases – Evolutionary database design. Addison-Wesley, Reading
3. Bisbal J, Lawless D, Wu B, Grimson J, Wade V, Richardson R, O'Sullivan D (1997) An overview of legacy system migration. APSEC, pp 529–531

4. Bisbal J, Lawless D, Wu B, Grimson J (1999) Legacy information systems: issues and directions. IEEE Softw 16:103–111
5. Bernstein PA, Melnik S (2007) Model management 2.0: manipulating richer mappings. In: ACM SIGMOD conference, pp 1–12
6. Börger E (2003) The ASM refinement method. Formal Aspects Comput 15:237–257
7. Brodie ML, Stonebraker M (1995) Migrating legacy systems: gateways, interfaces, and the incremental approach. Morgan Kaufmann, San Francisco
8. Comella-Dorda S, Wallnau K, Seacord R, Robert J (2000) A survey of black-box modernization approaches for information systems. In: ICSM '00: Proceedings of the international conference on software maintenance (ICSM'00), Washington, DC. IEEE Computer Society, p 173
9. Diskin Z (2008) Algebraic models for bidirectional model synchronization. In: MoDELS. Lecture notes in computer science, vol 5301. Springer, Berlin, pp 21–36
10. Domínguez E, Lloret J, Rubio AL, Zapata MA (2005) Evolving XML schemas and documents using UML class diagrams. In: Andersen KV, Debenham JK, Wagner R (eds) Proceedings of the 16th international conference on database and expert systems applications. DEXA 2005, Copenhagen. Lecture notes in computer science, vol 3588. Springer, Berlin, pp 343–352
11. Dahanayake A, Thalheim B (2010) Co-evolution of (information) system models. In: Enterprise, business-process and information systems modeling. LNBIB, vol 50. Springer, Berlin, pp 314–326
12. Franconi E, Grandi F, Mandreoli F (2000) A semantic approach for schema evolution and versioning in object-oriented databases. In: Computational logic. Lecture notes in computer science, vol 1861. Springer, Berlin, pp 1048–1062
13. Fagin R, Haas LM, Hernández MA, Miller RJ, Popa L, Velegrakis Y (2009) Clio: schema mapping creation and data exchange. In: Conceptual modeling: foundations and applications, Lecture notes in computer science, vol 5600. Springer, Berlin, pp 198–236
14. Fagin R, Kolaitis PG, Popa L, Tan WC (2004) Composing schema mappings: Second-order dependencies to the rescue. In: PODS. ACM, New York, pp 83–94
15. Hegner SJ (2008) Information-optimal reflections of view updates on relational database schemata. In: FoIKS 2008. Lecture notes in computer science, vol 4932. Springer, Berlin, pp 112–131
16. Hick J-M, Hainaut J-L (2003) Strategy for database application evolution: the DB-MAIN approach. In: Conceptual modeling – ER. Lecture notes in computer science, vol 2813. Springer, Berlin, pp 291–306
17. Klettke M (2007) Conceptual XML schema evolution – the CoDEX approach for design and redesign. In: Jarke M, Seidl T, Quix C, Kensche D, Conrad S, Rahm E, Klamma R, Kosch H, Granitzer M, Apel S, Rosenmüller M, Saake G, Spinczyk O (eds) BTW workshops, Datenbanksysteme in Business, Technologie und Web (BTW 2007), Aachen, Germany. Verlagshaus Mainz, pp 53–63
18. Klettke M (2007) Modellierung, Bewertung und Evolution von XML-Dokumentkollektionen. Postdoctoral lecture qualification, University of Rostock, Computer Science Institute. Logos, Berlin.
19. Koch S (2006) Funktionale Migration von Informationssystemen. Master's thesis, CAU Kiel, Institut für Informatik
20. Melnik S, Bernstein PA, Halevy AY, Rahm E (2005) Supporting executable mappings in model management. In: SIGMOD conference. ACM, New York, pp 167–178
21. Moon HJ, Curino C, Deutsch A, Hou C-Y, Zaniolo C (2008) Managing and querying transaction-time databases under schema evolution. PVLDB 1(1):882–895
22. Melnik S (2005) Model management: First steps and beyond. In: BTW, LNI, vol 65, pp 455–464
23. Ma H, Schewe K-D, Thalheim B (2005) Integration and cooperation of media types. In: ISTA'05
24. Parnas DL (1994) Software aging. In: ICSE: Proceedings of the 16th international conference on software engineering, Los Alamitos, CA. IEEE Press, New York, pp 279–287

25. Pons C, García D (2006) Practical verification strategy for refinement conditions in uml models. In: IFIP workshop on advanced software engineering. IFIP, vol 219. Springer, Berlin, pp 47–61
26. Roddick JF (2009) Schema evolution. In: Liu L, Özsu MT (eds) Encyclopedia of database systems. Springer, New York, pp 2479–2481
27. Schellhorn G (2005) ASM refinement and generalizations of forward simulation in data refinement: a comparison. Theor Comput Sci 336(2–3):403–435
28. Schulz S (2008) Einsatz von Replikationsverfahren für die Softwareevolution. Thesis, University of Rostock, Germany
29. Schewe K-D, Thalheim B (2005) Conceptual modelling of web information systems. Data Knowl Eng 54:147–188
30. Schewe K-D, Thalheim B (2007) Development of collaboration frameworks for web information systems. In: 20th international joint conference on artificial intelligence (IJCAI'07), section EMC'07 (Evolutionary models of collaboration). Hyderabad, India, pp 27–32
31. Thalheim B (2000) Entity-relationship modeling – foundations of database technology. Springer, Berlin
32. Thiran P, Hainaut J-L, Houben G-J, Benslimane D (2006) Wrapper-based evolution of legacy information systems. ACM Trans Softw Eng Methodol 15(4):329–359
33. Velegrakis Y, Miller RJ, Popa L (2003) Mapping adaptation under evolving schemas. In: VLDB, pp 584–595

Chapter 13
Conceptual Geometric Modelling

Hui Ma and Klaus-Dieter Schewe

Abstract This chapter starts with a review of existing spatial data models in the literature to show some key problems that need to be addressed by conceptual models to include spatial data and more generally geometric data. Motivated among other things by the need to support spatial modelling for the sustainable land use initiative we present a geometrically enhanced ER model (GERM), which preserves the key principles of ER modelling and at the same time introduces bulk constructions and types that support geometric objects. The model distinguishes between a syntactic level of types and an explicit internal level, in which types give rise to polyhedra that are defined by algebraic varieties. It further emphasises the stability of algebraic operations by means of a natural modelling algebra that extends the usual Boolean operations on point sets.

13.1 Introduction

In recent years there have been increasing demands from applications to store, process and manage spatial data. Applications that use spatial data include geographical information systems (GISs), environmental management, urban planning, transportation, land use management, CAD-CAM, architecture, visual perception and autonomous navigation, tracking and medical imaging, etc. [24, 33].

Therefore, conceptual models need to be extended to model spatial information. In general, conceptual data models abstract from details of data storage and therefore serve as communication tools between users and application developers. Conceptual modelling of spatial data concerns geometry of spatial objects, the geometric

H. Ma
School of Engineering and Computer Science, Victoria University of Wellington, New Zealand,
e-mail: hui.ma@ecs.vuw.ac.nz

K.-D. Schewe
Software Competence Center Hagenberg, Hagenberg, Austria, e-mail: kd.schewe@scch.at

D. W. Embley and B. Thalheim (eds), *Handbook of Conceptual Modeling*.
DOI 10.1007/978-3-642-15865-0, © Springer 2011

relationship between the objects, their representation at multiple resolutions, their geometric evolution over time, and their spatial integrity constraints [33].

The goal of our research is to provide a conceptual model supporting geometric modelling. One motivation is the need for spatial data modelling in the context of the sustainable land use initiative (SLUI), which addresses erosion problems in the hill country. At the core of the SLUI whole farm plans (WFPs) are required, which capture farm boundaries, paddocks, etc. and provide information about land use capability (LUC) such as rock, soil, slope, erosion, vegetation, plants, poles, etc. This should then be used to get an overview of erosion and vegetation levels and water quality, and to use this information for sustainable land use change.

As spatial data are a special case of geometric data, we consider it appropriate to look more generally at conceptual geometric models. For instance, technical constructions such as rotary piston engines can be supported by trochoids, which are plan algebraic curves that were already known by the Greeks [2]. Bézier curves and patches [26] are also commonly applied in these applications. Together with hull operators [12] they can also be used for 3-D models of hill shapes in WFPs.

There is a lot of sophisticated mathematics around to address geometric modelling in landcare, and this has a very long tradition, as shown in [2]. Nonetheless, spatial and geometric modelling within conceptual modelling has mainly followed two lines of research; for an overview see [32]. The first one is based on modelling spatial relationships such as disjointness, touching, overlap, inside, boundary overlap, etc. and functions such as intersection, union, etc. that are used for spatial primitives such as points, lines, polygons, regions, etc. In [33] pictograms are added to the common ER model to highlight spatial objects and relationships. Price et al. deal in particular with part–whole relationships [25], Ishikawa et al. apply constraint logic programming to deal with these predicates [15], McKenny et al. handle problems with collections [21], and Chen et al. use the predicates in an extension of SQL [8]. Point is defined as an entity type in [18].

The work in [5, 8] links to the second line of research expressing the spatial relationships by formulae defined on point sets applying basic Euclidean geometry or standard linear algebra respectively. Likewise, point sets are used in [30] to express predicates on meshes of polygons in order to capture motion. Frank classifies spatial algebra operation into local, focal and zonal ones based on whether only values of the same location, of a location and its immediate neighbourhood, or all of all locations in a zone, respectively, are combined [9].

In Sect. 13.2 we will review spatial data models which focus on how to store data and how to effectively and efficiently realise operations on such data. This is hardly what is needed in conceptual modelling, which aims at capturing application domain knowledge. The spatial relationships and functions discussed in the literature are in fact derived from underlying representations of point sets, so we need representations on multiple levels, as also proposed in [4]. Furthermore, when dealing with point sets it is not sufficient to define spatial relationships and functions in a logical way. We also have to ensure "good nature" in the numerical sense, i.e. the operations must be as accurate as possible when realised using floating-point arithmetics. For instance, Liu et al. [17] discuss spatial conflicts such as determining the accurate spatial relationship for a winding road along a winding river as opposed to a road crossing a river several times, leading to a classification of line–line relationships. The accuracy problem has motivated a series of modifications to algebras on point sets that go way beyond the standard Boolean operators [12].

Therefore, in Sect. 13.3 we introduce the geometrically enhanced ER model (GERM) as an approach to dealing with the problems discussed. As the name suggests, the intent is to preserve the aggregation-based approach of the ER model [13] by means of (higher-order) relationship types [34], but we enhance roles in relationship types by supporting choice and bulk constructors (sets, lists, multisets). However, unlike [14], neither the bulk constructors nor the choice constructor is used to create first-class objects (defining so-called clusters in [34]).

Furthermore, GERM retains the fundamental distinction between data types such as points, polygons, Bézier curves, etc. and concepts. The former are used to define the domains of (nested) attributes, while the latter are represented by entity and relationship types, e.g. a concept such as a paddock is distinguished from the curve defining its boundary. In this way we also guarantee a smooth integration with non-geometric data such as farm ownership, processing and legal information, etc., which is also relevant for WFPs but does not present any novel modelling challenges.

As already stated, GERM supports modelling on multiple levels. On a syntactic level we provide an extendible collection of data types such as line sequences, polygons, sequences of Bézier curves, Bézier patches, etc. with easy surface representations. For instance, a polygon can be represented by a list of points, and a Bézier curve of order n can be represented by $n + 1$ points – the case $n = 2$ captures the most commonly known quadratic Bézier curves that are also supported in LaTeX. On an explicit internal level we use a representation by polyhedra [12] that are defined by algebraic varieties, i.e. sets of zeros of polynomials in n variables. All curves that have a rational parametric representation such as Bézier curves [26] can be brought into this 'implicit' form, e.g. Gao and Chou describe a method for implicitisation based on Gröbner bases [10], and many classical curves that have proven their values in landcare for centuries can be represented in this way [2]. This kind of explicit representation is in fact equivalent to the polynomial model of spatial data introduced by Paredaens and Kuijpers [24], except that the ploynomial model permits quantifiers, which due to an old result by Tarski can be eliminated. The internal level of GERM is discussed in Sect. 13.4.

The use of a good natured algebra on point sets defines in fact a third derived level, which we present in Sect. 13.4.1. For the algebra we build on the research in [12] to guarantee stability by using a generalised natural modelling algebra, which supports much more than just Boolean operations. The leveling of GERM determines the outline of the paper. In Sect. 13.3 we introduce the basic GERM model emphasising the syntactic level. This remains more or less within the framework of the ER model in the general form defined in [34] with the differences discussed above.

13.2 Spatial Data Models

There are many spatial data models discussed in the literature. In [11] spatial data models are classified into two types, object-based models and the field-based models, with the latter ones also being referred to as tessellation models. Taking a similar architectural approach as for databases, spatial data types can be studied at three levels: user model, conceptual model, and implementation [27].

The focus of the study in [27] is on describing the structure of spatial objects (e.g. points, lines and regions) and spatial operations representing geometric functions and can be applied to these objects. Paredaens et al. [23, 24] compare five spatial data models: the raster model and the Peano model, which represent spatial data by finite point sets that are either uniformly or non-uniformly distributed over the plane, respectively, the spaghetti model based on contours defined as polylines, the polynomial model based on formulae that involve equality and inequality of polynomials, and the PLA model, which uses some kind of topological information without dealing with exact position and shape.

Paredaens et al. use the term 'geomatic data models' to distinguish them from the classical data models by four characteristics [23].

- Geomatic data models can be used to model information about the n-dimensional space $\mathbb{R}^n$, i.e. an infinite and non-enumerable set of points. To represent infinite information, different intentional techniques are used in a geomatic data model. For a particular geomatic database, the choice of data model depends on the operations to be defined and on the efficiency requirement of the implementation.
- Operations are either defined within the model or user-defined and as such influenced by the intentional aspect of the geomatic data model. The models must be closed under all the operations. This property is hard to have satisfied because of a rich set of operations required by geomatic applications.
- Some particular algorithms, are needed to implement the vast information, which do not have the elegant geometric properties of a human-created structure, but mostly use visualisation of symmetryless phenomena abstracted from nature. The algorithms are based on algebraic, geometric and topological properties.
- The genericity property that normally applies to classical data models does not hold for geomatic data models. That is, the result of some operations in geomatic data models is intrinsically influenced by the content.

In what follows we briefly review some common spatial data models – the survey in [24] is much more detailed – and show one of their key problems, the lack of conceptual abstraction. The conclusion drawn in [23, 24] is that while some models lack theoretical foundations, those that are grounded in theory do not bother much about efficient implementations. On the other hand, there are several attempts to use the ER model for spatial information systems; however, they hardly permit any of the needed spatial operations. In particular, the complexity of spatial problems leads to the request for significant extensions [18].

The Raster Model. The raster model represents geomatic information by a finite number of raster points using the semantics whereby points in the environment of a raster point p have the same properties as p [23]. To represent lines that contain no raster points, many applications approximate them with representable lines. Due to the approximation, translation-generic queries are not supported by the raster model. The raster model is a field-based model.

The Vector Model. The vector model first uses points and their coordinates to represent spatial features such as points, lines and areas and then organises geometric objects and their spatial relationships into digital data files so that a computer can access, interpret and process them [6]. The vector model is an object-oriented approach built on two common concepts: decomposing spatial objects into points, lines and polygons (or areas) and using topology to represent spatial objects [19].

The Spaghetti Model. The spaghetti model represents space as a series of discrete point lines of polygon units which are geographically referenced by cartesian coordinates. When vector data are collected but not structured, it is said to be in a spaghetti data model. For example, vector data obtained by map digitising is in this model. This is demonstrated in [18] with some examples to show how the spaghetti model can be used for conceptual modelling of line-oriented objects, e.g. polylines, polygons and polyhedra. For example, a conceptual model for a set of polygons can be delimited by polylines which are defined by end points and inner points.

The Peano Model. The Peano model represents information with a finite number of points which are not uniformally distributed. It makes use of quadtrees, in which a node is either a leaf or has four children. The Peano model is used to represent areas and volumes that are not based on contours. Spatial data is stored in relations with each tuple representing subsquares. The relation takes the form $PR(OID, PID, S, A_1, \ldots, A_n)$, where PR is the name of the Peano relation, OID is an object identifier, PID is the Peano key, which is the label of the bottom-left unit subsquare of the square it represents, S is the edge length of the subsquare, and $A_1, \ldots, A_n$ are attributes. For example, $(background, 0, 2, white)$ is a tuple over relation schema $FACE(OID, PID, S, Colour)$. For the Peano model some algebra is proposed to perform joins. However, as mentioned in [23], it has not been proven that the operation is complete.

The Polynomial Model. Similar to the Peano model, the polynomial model also stores information in relations whose schema contains at most one spatial attribute and some non-spatial attributes. The spatial attribute is in the form $\{(x_1, \ldots, x_n) \mid x_1, \ldots, x_n \in \mathbb{R} \wedge P\}$. For example, for a given relation schema PATTERN($From$, $Name$, $Colour$), $(\{(x, y) \mid x = 8 \wedge y = 3\}, A, black)$ is a query over the schema. Queries in the polynomial model can be expressed in polynomial calculus, but not all the queries can be [23].

The PLA Model. The PLA model handles topological information on points, lines and areas without dealing with the exact position and form of the spatial objects [7]. The two-dimensional plane is described by a set of cells with the information about the interrelation of the position of the lines, the areas and the points. For this model a suitable query language needs to be defined so that queries and their results can be expressed in the model [23].

13.3 Geometrically Enhanced ER Model (GERM)

In this section we start with the presentation of GERM focussing on the syntactic (or surface) level, which is what will be needed first for modelling geometrically enhanced applications. We will concentrate on the definition of entity and relationship types and their semantics, but we will dispense with discussing keys or other constraints. For attributes we will permit structuring.

13.3.1 Data Types and Nested Attributes

Definition 13.1. A *universe* is a countable set $\mathcal{U}$ of simple attributes together with a type assignment tp that assigns to each attribute $A \in \mathcal{U}$ a data type $tp(A)$.

In most cases the associated type $tp(A)$ for $A \in \mathcal{U}$ will be a base type, but we do not enforce such a restriction. We do not further specify the collection of base types. These can be *INT, FLOAT, STRING, DATE, TIME*, etc. A base data type t is associated with a countable set of values $dom(t)$ called the domain of t. For the types listed the domain is the standard one. For an attribute $A \in \mathcal{U}$ we let $dom(A) = dom(tp(A))$, and also call $dom(A)$ the domain of A.

We use constructors to define complex data types. In particular, we use $(\cdot)$ for record types, $\{\cdot\}$, $[\cdot]$ and $\langle\cdot\rangle$ for finite-set, list and multiset types, respectively, $\oplus$ for (disjoint) union types, and $\rightarrow$ for map types. Together with a trivial type $\mathbb{1}$ – its domain is a singleton set: $dom(\mathbb{1}) = \{\perp\}$ – we can define (complex types) t by abstract syntax (here b represents base types):

$$t = \mathbb{1} \mid b \mid (a_1 : t_1, \ldots, a_n : t_n) \mid (a_1 : t_1)$$
$$\oplus \cdots \oplus (a_n : t_n) \mid \{t\} \mid [t] \mid \langle t \rangle \mid t_1 \rightarrow t_2$$

with pairwise different labels a_i in record and union types. Furthermore, we allow complex types to be named and used in type definitions in the same way as base types with the restriction that cycles are forbidden. Domains are then defined in the usual way.

Example 13.1. We can define named complex types that can be used for geometric modelling such as *Point* $= (x : FLOAT, y : FLOAT)$ for points in the two-dimensional plane, *Polygon* $=$ [*Point*], *PolyLine* $=$ [*Point*], *Bezier* $=$ [*Point*], and *PolyBezier* $=$ [*Bezier*]. In particular, these constitute examples of types with equal surface representations but different geometric semantics (as we will discuss in Sect. 13.4). A polyline is a curve that is defined piecewise linearly, while a polygon is a region that is defined by a polyline border. A sequence of n points defines a Bézier curve of order $n - 1$, and a curve that is defined piecewise by Bézier curves is a PolyBézier curve.

The trivial type $\mathbb{1}$ can be used in combination with the union constructor to define enumerated types, i.e. types with finite domains such as $Bool = (\mathbf{T} : \mathbb{1}) \oplus (\mathbf{F} : \mathbb{1})$, $Gender = (\text{male} : \mathbb{1}) \oplus (\text{female} : \mathbb{1})$ or $(n) = (1 : \mathbb{1}) \oplus \cdots \oplus (n : \mathbb{1})$ for any positive integer n, which gives a domain representing $\{1, \ldots, n\}$. The map constructor can be used to define arrays such as $Patch = (i : (n), j : (m)) \to Point$ representing Bézier patches, and vectorfields of different dimensions such as $Vectorfield1 = \{Point\} \to FLOAT$, which could be used for sensor data such as water levels, and $Vectorfield2 = \{Point\} \to Point$, which could be used for modelling other measurements such as wind capturing force and direction by a two-dimensional vector. Finally, $TimeSeries = (d : DATE, t : TIME) \to Vectorfield1$ could be used to model a series of observed data over time.

Complex types are used in connection with nested attributes extending the definitions in [34].

Definition 13.2. The set $\mathcal{A}$ of *nested attributes* (over universe $\mathcal{U}$) is the smallest set with $\mathcal{U} \subseteq \mathcal{A}$ satisfying $X(A_1, \ldots, A_n)$, $X\{A\}$, $X[A]$, $X(A_1 \to A_2)$, $X\langle A \rangle$, $X_1(A_1) \oplus \cdots \oplus X_n(A_n) \in \mathcal{A}$ with labels $X, X_1, \ldots, X_n$ and $A, A_1, \ldots, A_n \in \mathcal{A}$.

The type assignment tp extends naturally from $\mathcal{U}$ to $\mathcal{A}$ as follows:

- $tp(X(A_1, \ldots, A_n)) = (a_1 : tp(A_1), \ldots, a_n : tp(A_n))$ with labels $a_1, \ldots, a_n$,
- $tp(X_1(A_1) \oplus \cdots \oplus X_n(A_n)) = (X_1 : tp(A_1)) \oplus \cdots \oplus (X_n : tp(A_n))$,
- $tp(X\{A\}) = \{tp(A)\}, tp(X[A]) = [tp(A)], tp(X\langle A \rangle) = \langle tp(A) \rangle$, and
- $tp(X(A_1 \to A_2)) = tp(A_1) \to tp(A_2)$.

13.3.2 Entity and Relationship Types

Following [34] the major difference between entity and relationship types is the presence of components $r : R$ (with a role name r and a name R of an entity or relationship type) for the latter ones. We will therefore unify the definition and simply talk of database types as opposed to the data types in the previous subsection. We will, however, permit structured components.

Definition 13.3. The set $\mathcal{C}$ of *component expressions* is the smallest set containing all database type names E, all set and multiset expressions $\{E\}$ and $\langle E \rangle$, respectively, all union expressions $E_1 \oplus \cdots \oplus E_n$ with component expressions E, E_i that are not union expressions, and all list expressions $[E]$ with component expressions E. A *structured component* is a pair $r : E$ with a role name r and a component expression $E \in \mathcal{C}$.

Note that this definition permits neither record and map constructors in component expressions nor full orthogonality for union, set, list and multiset constructors. The reason for the absence of the record constructor is that it corresponds to aggregation, i.e. whenever a component of a relationship type has the structure of a record, it can be replaced by a separate relationship type. The reason for the absence of the map constructor is that functions on entities and relationships that depend on instances seem to make very little sense and are not needed at all. The reason for allowing only restricted combinations of the other constructors are the intrinsic equivalences observed in [31]. If in $\{E\}$ we had a union component expression $E = E_1 \oplus \cdots \oplus E_n$, this would be equivalent to a record expression $(\{E_1\},\ldots,\{E_n\})$, to which the argument regarding records can be applied. The same holds for multiset expressions, while nested union constructors can be flattened. In this way we guarantee that we will deal only with normalised, and thus simplified, structured components that contain no hidden aggregations.

Definition 13.4. A *database type* R of level $k \geq 0$ consists of a finite set $comp(R) = \{r_1 : E_1,\ldots,r_n : E_n\}$ of structured components with pairwise different role names $r_1,\ldots,r_n$, and a finite set $attr(R) = \{A_1,\ldots,A_k\} \subseteq \mathcal{A}$ of nested attributes. Each E_i is a database type of level at most $k-1$, and unless $comp(R) = \emptyset$, at least one of the E_i must have exactly the level $k-1$.

Note that this definition enforces $comp(R) = \emptyset$ iff R is a type of level 0. So we call types of level 0 *entity types* and types of level $k > 0$ relationship types. In what follows we use the notation $R = (comp(R), attr(R))$ for a type.

Note that while we discarded full orthogonality for component constructors, we did not do this for the nested attributes, leaving a lot of latitude to modellers. The rationale behind this flexibility is that the attributes should reflect pieces of information that are meaningful within the application context. For instance, using an attribute shape with $tp(shape) = Polygon$ (thus, shape $\in \mathcal{U}$) indicates that the structure of polygons as lists of pairs of floating-point numbers is not relevant for the conceptual model of the application, whereas the alternative, having a nested attribute shape([point(x-coord, y-coord)]) with $tp(\text{x-coord}) = tp(\text{y-coord}) = FLOAT$, would indicate that points and their coordinates are conceptually relevant beyond representing a data type. Nested attributes also give rise to generalised keys, whereas we do not delve into the structure of complex types for this discussion.

Furthermore, the way we define structured components permits alternatives and bulk constructions in database types which can be used to model a farm with a set of paddocks and a time series of measured water levels, but neither disjoint unions nor sets, lists and multisets can be used to model first-class database types, i.e. a set of paddocks will never appear outside a component. This differs from [34], where disjoint union *clusters* are used independently of relationship types, and from [14], where this has been extended to sets, lists and multisets. The reason is that such stand-alone constructors are hardly needed in the model, unless they appear within a component of a database type.

13.3.3 Schemata and Instances

Finally, we put the definitions of the previous subsections together to define schemata and their instances in the usual way.

Definition 13.5. A *GERM schema* S is a finite set of database types such that whenever $r_i : E_i$ is a component of $R \in S$ and the database type name E appears in E_i, then also $E \in S$ holds.

The definition of a structural schema, which is normally just called a schema, covers the syntactic side of our conceptual model. For the semantics we need instances of schemata, which we will define next starting with 'entities'. For this, if $\mathcal{I}(E)$ is a set of values for a database type name E, then this defines a unique set of values $\mathcal{I}(E_i)$ for each $E_i \in \mathcal{C}$. This extension is defined in the same way as the extension of *dom* from base types to complex types.

Definition 13.6. An *entity* e of type R is a mapping defined on $comp(R) \cup attr(R)$ that assigns to each $r_i : E_i \in comp(R)$ a value $e_i \in \mathcal{I}(E_i)$, and to each attribute $A_j \in attr(R)$ a value $v_j \in dom(A_j)$. Here $\mathcal{I}(E_i)$ is built from sets of entities $\mathcal{I}(E)$ for all E appearing in E_i.

We use the notation $e = (r_1 : e_1, \ldots, r_n : e_n, A_1 : v_1, \ldots, A_k : v_k)$ for an entity e of type $R = (\{r_1 : E_1, \ldots, r_n : E_n\}, \{A_1, \ldots, A_k\})$. Strictly speaking, if R is of level $k > 0$, e should be called a *relationship*.

Definition 13.7. An *instance* $\mathcal{I}$ of a GERM schema S is an S-indexed family $\{\mathcal{I}(R)\}_{R \in S}$, such that $\mathcal{I}(R)$ is a finite set of entities of type R, and only these sets are used in the definition of entities.

13.4 Geometric Types and Algebraic Varieties

Usually, the domain of a type defines the set of values that are used for operations. This is no longer the case with geometric types. For instance, a value of type *Bezier* as defined in the previous section is simply a list of $n + 1$ points $\vec{p}_0, \ldots, \vec{p}_n \in \mathbb{R}^2$. However, it defines a Bézier curve of order n in the two-dimensional Euclidean plane, i.e. a set of points.

Thus, we need a different association *gdom*, which associates with a geometric type t a set of point sets in n-dimensional Euclidean space $\mathbb{R}^n$ together with a mapping $dom(t) \to gdom(t)$. In what follows we will concentrate on the case $n = 2$, i.e. we focus on points, curves and regions in the plane, but most definitions are not bound to this restriction. We will use algebraic varieties and polyhedra to define point sets of interest.

Definition 13.8. An *(algebraic) variety* V of dimension n is the set of zeros of a polynomial P in n variables, i.e. $V = \{(x_1, \ldots, x_n) \in \mathbb{R}^n \mid P(x_1, \ldots, x_n) = 0\}$.

A *base polyhedron* H is the intersection of half planes, i.e. $H = \{(x_1, \ldots, x_n) \mid P_i(x_1, \ldots, x_n) \geq 0$ for $i = 1, \ldots, k\}$ with polynomials $P_1, \ldots, P_k$. A *polyhedron* H is the finite union of base polyhedra $H_1, \ldots, H_\ell$.

Algebraic varieties in the plane cover all classical curves [2]. As $P(x_1, \ldots, x_n) = 0 \Leftrightarrow P(x_1, \ldots, x_n) \geq 0 \wedge -P(x_1, \ldots, x_n) \geq 0$ holds, base polyhedra are simple generalisations.

A representation as in Definition 13.8 by means of zeros of polynomials is called an *implicit* representation, as opposed to an explicit parametric representation $\gamma(u)$ for real u [10]. Each parametric representation can always be turned into an implicit one, but the converse is not necessarily true. For most curves of interest, however, we also find rational parametric representations.

Example 13.2. A Bézier curve of degree n is defined by $n + 1$ points $\vec{p}_0, \ldots, \vec{p}_n$. A parametric representation is $B(u) = \sum_{i=0}^{n} B_{in}(u) \cdot \vec{p}_i$ $(0 \leq u \leq 1)$ with the ith Bernstein polynomial $B_{in}(u)$ of degree n defined as $B_{in}(u) = (n\ i)\, u^i (1 - u)^{n-i}$.

A Bézier curve of order 1 is simply a straight line between the two points defining it. For $n = 2$ and $B(u) = (x, y)$ we obtain quadratic equations $x = au^2 + bu + c$ and $y = du^2 + eu + f$. Dividing these by a and d, respectively, and subtracting them from each other eliminates the quadratic term u^2. This can then be solved to give u, plugged back in to give x and y, leading to a polynomial in x and y of degree 2 that defines the implicitisation of the Bézier curve.

Similarly, an $(n \times m)$ array of points $\vec{p}_{ij}$ defines a Bézier patch with a parametric representation $P(u, v) = \sum_{i=0}^{n} \sum_{j=0}^{m} B_{in}(u) \cdot B_{jm}(v) \cdot \vec{p}_{ij}$. In this case $u = 0$ and $v = 0$ define Bézier curves $P(0, v)$ and $P(u, 0)$, respectively.

Definition 13.9. The *geometric domain gdom(t)* of a geometric data type t is a set of point sets. Each element of *gdom(t)* has an implicit representation by a polyhedron $H = H_1 \cup \cdots \cup H_\ell$ with base polyhedra H_i $(i = 1, \ldots, \ell)$ defined by polynomials $P_{i1}, \ldots, P_{in_i}$. In addition, the variety defined by P_{ij} has an explicit parametric representation $\gamma_{ij}(\vec{u})$, unless this is impossible.

The definition of polyhedra for polygons or, more generally, lists of Bézier curves that define a region may require some triangulisation.

Note that in general polyhedra are closed under union and intersection, but not under set difference. Polyhedra are always closed with respect to the standard topology on $\mathbb{R}^n$, but the difference of closed sets is not necessarily closed. We may, however, regain a polyhedron by building the closure. Thus, it may be useful to have the *interior* $\overset{\circ}{X}$, *boundary* ∂X, and the *closure* $\bar{X}$ available for any point set X. These are defined in the usual way by $\overset{\circ}{X} = \{x \in X \mid \exists U(x).U(x) \subseteq X\}$, $\partial X = \{x \mid \forall U(x).U(x) \cap X \neq \emptyset \neq U(x) - X\}$, and $\bar{X} = X \cup \partial X$. Here $U(x)$ denotes an open environment of point x.

13.4.1 Natural Modelling Algebra

The two layers of GERM support the storage and retrieval of geometric objects within a conceptual model. The challenge is, however, the manipulation of such objects by queries and transactions. For this we now present an algebra on geometric objects. As we always have an internal representation by point sets, we first focus on these.

Standard operations on point sets are of course the Boolean ones, i.e. union, intersection and difference (or complement). In combination with interior, closure and boundary these operations are in principle sufficient to express a lot of relationships between the geometric objects as discussed widely in the conceptual GIS literature (see e.g. [5, 32]). For instance, $A - B = \emptyset$ is equivalent to $A \subseteq B$, so we only need difference and an emptyness test. Similarly, $\overset{\circ}{A} \cap B = \emptyset \wedge \partial A \cap \partial B \neq \emptyset$ express that A and B touch each other but do not intersect.

However, relying on the Boolean set operations is insufficient. We have to address at least two problems. (1) The set of point sets of interest must be closed under the operations. We already remarked at the end of the previous section that this is not true for the set difference (and likewise for the complement). (2) The operations must be numerically stable in the sense that they do not produce larger errors than those that are unavoidable due to the rounding that is necessary when dealing with floating-point representations of real numbers.

We may circumvent the closure problem, as we are merely interested in point sets 'up to their boundary', i.e. we could deal with an equivalence relation $\sim$ with $A \sim B$ iff $\bar{A} = \bar{B}$. Then each equivalence class has exactly one closed representative, a polyhedron. The problem is then that the Boolean operations do not preserve this equivalence, and we lose some of the properties of a Boolean algebra. However, these properties are lost anyway by the necessary modifications that we propose to deal with the stability problem.

As for the stability problem, some conceptual modellers will argue that this concerns only an implementation. We do not share this opinion, as any result obtained by operations of point sets, i.e. the polyhedra on the internal level, must be reinterpreted by a value of some data type on the surface level. For instance, the union and intersection of polygons must again be represented as a polygon with a surface representation by a sequence of points. Similarly, we must take into account that the intersection of two curves may be more than just a discrete set of points, if stability is addressed. Thus, stability considerations have a non-negligible impact on the surface level of GERM.

It is known that Boolean operations on point sets may be unstable. For instance, for the intersection point of two straight lines may be only obtainable with an intolerable error. This problem occurs when the angle between the two lines is very small. Our solution will replace the intersection operation by a modified operation, which in this case will enlarge the result – so we actually obtain a point set instead of a single point. The enlargement will depend on the operands, so that for the uncritical cases we almost preserve the Boolean operations.

In general, we use the following new operations on point sets: $A \uplus B = A \cup B \cup q(A, B)$ and $A \cap\!\!\!\cap B = (A \cap B) \cup q(A, B)$ with a *natural modelling function q* that assigns a point set to a pair of point sets. We do not modify the complement X' of a set X. With $A \uplus\!\!\!\!\cdot B = (A' \cap\!\!\!\cap B')'$ and $A \cap\!\!\!\!\cdot B = (A' \uplus B')'$ we obtain two more modified operations.

The simple idea behind these operations is to slightly enlarge (or reduce) unions and intersections in order to cope with the stability problem. The enlargement (or reduction) depends on the arguments; critical operands require larger modifications than uncritical ones. The name 'natural modelling' is adopted from [12], as it should reflect properties associated with stability and the original union and intersection operations in a natural way.

Definition 13.10. A function q from pairs of point sets to point sets is called a *natural modelling function* iff it satisfies the following properties for all A, B:

$$q(A, B) = q(B, A) \qquad q(A', B) = q(A, B) \qquad q(A, \emptyset) = \emptyset \, .$$

We require q to be symmetric as the stability problem for building intersections and unions does not depend on the order. Analogously, the potential instability caused by A and B is the same as that caused by A' and B.

Definition 13.11. The *natural modelling algebra* consists of the set of equivalence classes of polyhedra with respect to $\sim$ and the operations $\uplus$, $\cap\!\!\!\cap$, $\cap\!\!\!\!\cdot$ and $\uplus\!\!\!\!\cdot$ with a natural modelling function q.

Hartwig has studied the algebraic properties of the *direct* modelling algebra $(\mathcal{P}(E), \uplus, \cap\!\!\!\cap)$ and the *small* modelling algebra $(\mathcal{P}(E), \uplus, \cap\!\!\!\cap)$ [12]. In both cases we obtain a *weak Boolean algebra*, i.e. the existence of neutral and inverse elements is preserved, and the de Morgan laws still hold, but other properties of Boolean algebras have been abandoned.

13.4.2 Computing with Polyhedra and Surface Representations

The key question is of course how to choose a good natural modelling function q. Before addressing this let us first look at the modified operations on polyhedra. As

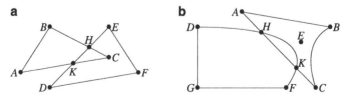

Fig. 13.1 a: intersection of two polygons; **b**: intersection of two regions with a boundary defined by Bézier curves

these are defined by algebraic varieties, it will be decisive (and sufficient) to understand the operations on two half-planes $A = \{(x_1, \ldots, x_n) \mid P(x_1, \ldots, x_n) \geq 0\}$
and $B = \{(x_1, \ldots, x_n) \mid Q(x_1, \ldots, x_n) \geq 0\}$. If A and B are plane curves, we have
to compute their intersection point(s) in order to determine a surface representation
of their union and intersection respectively. Let us discuss this further for polygons
and regions defined by a sequence of Bézier curves.

Example 13.3. Let us look at the union/intersection of two polygons depicted in
Fig. 13.1a, one defined by the points A, B, C, the other by D, E, F. With $A =
(1, 1)$, $B = (3, 4)$, $C = (7, 2)$, $D = (3, 0)$, $E = (7, 4)$ and $F = (9, 1)$ the line
through D and E is defined by $P(x, y) = x - y - 3 = 0$, and the line through
B and C is defined by $Q(x, y) = x + 2y - 11 = 0$. They intersect at the point
$H = (5.66, 2.66)$. This intersection divides the plane into four parts depending on
whether $P(x, y)$ and $Q(x, y)$ take positive or negative values.

   If we can compute the intersection points H and K, then A, B, H, E, F, D, K
defines the surface representation of the union, while K, H, C defines that of the
intersection.

   However, the angle between lines DE and AC at intersection point K is rather
small, which may cause a different result defined by the operations ⊎ and ⩀instead
of $\cup$ and $\cap$ respectively. The resulting polygon for the modified union may become
$A, B, H, E, F, D, K_1, K_2$, while the resulting polygon for the modified intersection
may become K_1', H, C, K_2', with points K_1, K_2, K_1', K_2' in a small neighbourhood
of K.

   At H the angle between the two intersecting lines is nearly a right angle, so the
modified intersection may coincide with the normal one.

Example 13.4. Look at the two regions defined in Fig. 13.1b, both defined by values of type *PolyBezier*, the first one by $[(A, B), (B, E, C), (C, A)]$, the second one
by $[(D, B, F), (F, G), (G, D)]$. As in the previous example, the two intersection
points H and K of line (A, C) with Bézier curve (D, E, F) are decisive for the
computation of the union and intersection.

   With $A = (16, 5)$, $B = (22, 4)$, $E = (20, 3)$, $C = (21, 0)$, $D = (13, 4)$, $F =
(19, 0)$ and $G = (13, 0)$ the parametric representation of the Bézier curve can be
easily obtained as $B(u) = (-12u^2 + 18u + 13, -4u^2 + 4)$, and the straight line gives
rise to $x + y - 21 = 0$. Substituting $B(u) = (x, y)$ in this gives rise to a quadratic
equation with the roots $u_{1/2} = \frac{9 \pm \sqrt{17}}{16}$, i.e. $u_1 = 0.304$ and $u_2 = 0.82$, which define $H = (17.32, 3.64)$ and $K = (19.69, 1.31)$. Then the union can be represented
by $[(A, B), (B, E, C), (C, K), (K, F', F), (F, G), (G, D), (D, D', H), (H, A)]$ of
type *PolyBezier*, while the intersection is represented by $[(H, H', K), (K, H)]$.
Once H and K are known, it is no problem to obtain the necessary points D' and
H', as sections of Bézier curves are again Bézier curves.

   As in Example 13.3 the computation of point K can be expected to be relatively stable, whereas H is not. Using ⊎ instead of the usual union, we end
up with a modified union represented by $[(A, B), (B, E, C), (C, K), (K, F', F),
(F, G), (G, D), (D, D', H_1), (H_1, H_2), (H_2, A)]$ of type *PolyBezier*, where H_1 and
H_2 are points in the vicinity of H on the Bézier curve and the straight line

(H, A) respectively. Analogously, using $\cap$ instead of $\cap$, we obtain a representation $[(H_2', H_1')(H_1', H', K), (K, H_2')]$ with points H_1', H_2' in the vicinity of H on the Bézier curve and the straight line (H, K) respectively.

13.4.3 The Choice of the Natural Modelling Function

In view of the discussion in the previous subsection, it is sufficient to consider base polyhedra, i.e. if $H = H_1 \cup \cdots \cup H_n$ and H' are polyhedra, we define $q(H, H') = \bigcup\limits_{i=1}^{n} q(H_i, H')$. Furthermore, for base polyhedra it is sufficient to consider the boundary, i.e. if H and H' are base polyhedra, we define $q(H, H') = q(\partial H, \partial H')$. In the two-dimensional plane $E = \mathbb{R}^2$ we can therefore concentrate on plan curves. If such a curve γ is defined by a union of (sections of) algebraic varieties, say $V_1 \cup \cdots \cup V_n$, then we define again $q(\gamma, \gamma') = \bigcup\limits_{i=1}^{n} q(V_i, \gamma')$. If q is symmetric, the naturalness conditions in Definition 13.10 are obviously satisfied.

In order to obtain a good choice for the natural modelling function q, it is therefore sufficient to look at two curves γ_1 and γ_2 defined by polynomials $P(x, y) = 0$ and $Q(x, y) = 0$ respectively. Let $\vec{p}_1, \ldots, \vec{p}_n$ be the intersection points of these curves – unless $\gamma_1 = \gamma_2$, we can assume that there are only finitely many. Then we define $q(\gamma_1, \gamma_2) = \bigcup_{i=1}^{n} U_i$ with environments $U_i = U_{\gamma_1, \gamma_2}(\vec{p}_i)$, as defined next.

Definition 13.12. For $\varepsilon > 0$ the ε-*band* of a variety $V = \{(x, y) \mid P(x, y) = 0\}$ is the point set $B_\varepsilon(V) = \{(x', y') \mid \exists (x, y) \in V.|x - x'| < \varepsilon \wedge |y - y'| < \varepsilon\}$.

13.5 Key Application Area GIS

Spatial data models which contain spatial data types, operations and predicates are used universally to represent geometric information in all kinds of spatial applications. Application areas include geosciences, e.g. geography, hydrology, soil sciences, and government and administration. It is predicted that geoinformation technology will be one of the most important and promising technologies in the future [29].

As we mentioned, this study is motivated by the need for spatial data modelling in the context of the sustainable land use initiative (SLUI). Now let us look in more detail at the information that should be kept for the SLUI program. To manage land in the hill country sustainably, the aim of the SLUI and whole farm plans (WFPs) is to propagate land use change. For the long term the SLUI programme has an objective of having 75,000 ha of land improved in the next 10 years. To demonstrate that the considerable funds being spent are achieving worthwhile outcomes, WFPs should be monitored to measure the progress toward the objective. For example, WFP data, including spatial and non-spatial data, need to be kept to create WFPs

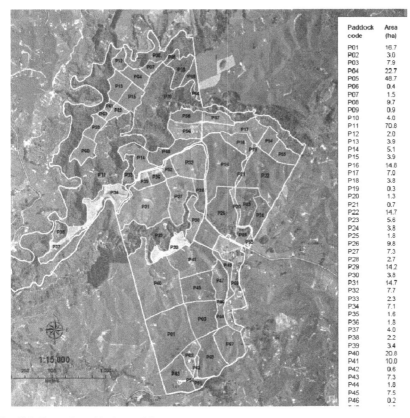

Paddock code	Area (ha)
P01	16.7
P02	3.0
P03	7.9
P04	22.7
P05	48.7
P06	0.4
P07	1.5
P08	9.7
P09	0.9
P10	4.0
P11	70.8
P12	2.0
P13	3.9
P14	5.1
P15	3.9
P16	14.8
P17	7.0
P18	3.8
P19	0.3
P20	1.3
P21	0.7
P22	14.7
P23	5.6
P24	3.8
P25	1.8
P26	9.8
P27	7.3
P28	2.7
P29	14.2
P30	3.8
P31	14.7
P32	7.7
P33	2.3
P34	7.1
P35	1.6
P36	1.8
P37	4.0
P38	2.2
P39	3.4
P40	20.8
P41	10.0
P42	0.6
P43	7.3
P44	1.8
P45	7.5
P46	0.2

Fig. 13.2 Example paddock map [1]

and to analyse the effectiveness of the programme, e.g. area of land being improved. During the environmental assessment of farms a bunch of artefacts is generated, including legal titles and parcels maps, paddock maps, Land Resource Inventory and Land Use Capability maps, soil fertility and nutrient maps, pasture production maps, summary of resource issues and recommendations for sustainable management of land resources. Figure 13.2 contains an example paddock map which shows the boundary of paddocks within a farm. To model the maps, we need to consider spatial data, e.g. paddock boundaries, as well as non-spatial data, e.g. paddock codes.

Land resources have been described and evaluated according to the Land Resource Inventory (LRI) and Land Use Capability (LUC) classification. The area under study is divided into landscape units by drawing boundaries around areas with similar soil characteristics. A unit polygon represents an area of similar soil characteristics. The LRI system involves delineating landscape units according to five inventory factors. LRI is then classified as LUC, which further groups similar units according to their capacity for sustainable production under arable, pastoral, forestry or conservation uses. The LUC code indicates general capability (1 to 8 classes), the major limitations and the capability unit to link with regional classifi-

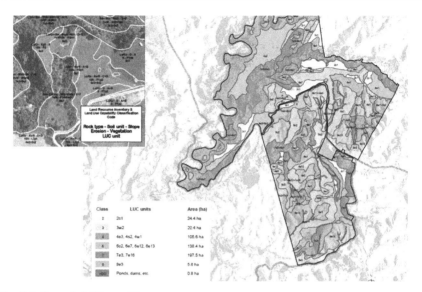

Fig. 13.3 Example LUC map [1]

cations and known best management practices. Figure 13.3 shows a LUC and a LRI map. Again to model the information on LRI and LUC maps, we need to consider spatial data, e.g. LRI and LUC boundaries, and non-spatial data, e.g. LUC code, class and subclass of each LUC unit.

Detailed assessment of land strengths and weaknesses are given by LUC unit. Based on this assessment, a catalogue of environmental works is recommended. Recommendations for either land use change or management change are based primarily on the degree, severity and location of the soil erosion and the resultant effects. A set of maps is created to show the locations of planned work. For example, as shown in Fig. 13.4, the location of tree planting or a fence to be built is shown on the maps. To model the data on WFP maps, we need to model the location information of the planned work, presented as polygons, points or arcs, as well as additional information of the planned work, which includes the financial support information provided by the regional council.

As we see, WFP data include classic relational or non-spatial data (attribute data), such as owner information, investment information and land usability data, and spatial data (locational data), such as paddock boundaries, LUC unit boundaries, buildings, land and water resources, bridges, tracks, track crossings, enhancement plantings, fences and stone pickings. There is a need to integrate the spatial and non-spatial data in the SLUI application so that users can analyse the effectiveness of the SLUI program, e.g. by calculating the areas of land units that have some LUC properties improved. Our goal is to support conceptual modelling of WFPs for integration into the SLUI information system by providing representations of the spatial relationships and functions on multiple levels, by providing relationships

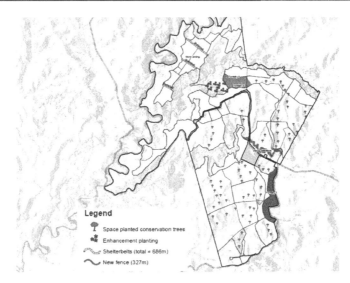

Fig. 13.4 Example WFP map [1]

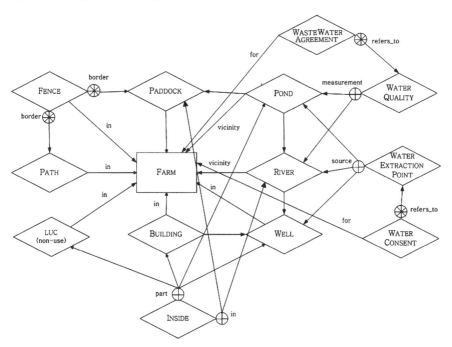

Fig. 13.5 Sketch of a GERM schema for a WFP (attributes omitted) including types for water consent, quality and waste water agreement

and functions in a logical way when dealing with point sets, and by providing suitable operations when realised using floating-point arithmetic.

Example 13.5. Let us look at a sketch of a GERM schema for a WFP as illustrated in Fig. 13.5. At its core we have a schema capturing the geographic information related to a farm. The central entity type FARM will have the attributes owner, boundary and address with tp(boundary) = *PolyBezier*, and tp(owner) = tp(address) = *STRING*. The type PADDOCK is used to capture the major (farming) units with the attributes boundary and usage of types tp(boundary) = *PolyBezier* and tp(usage) = (cattle : $\mathbb{1}$) ⊕ (dairy : $\mathbb{1}$) ⊕ (hort : $\mathbb{1}$) ⊕ (sheep : $\mathbb{1}$) ⊕ ⋯ ⊕ (other : $\mathbb{1}$) respectively. For BUILDING we have the attributes kind and area with another enumeration type associated with kind, and tp(area) = *Polygon*. Other landcare units with non-agricultural usage are captured by the type LUC with an attribute luc with tp(luc) = (bush : $\mathbb{1}$) ⊕ (rock : $\mathbb{1}$) ⊕ (slope : $\mathbb{1}$). The relationship type FENCE has a set of PADDOCK components, a set of PATH components referring to the paddocks and paths it borders and attribute shape with tp(shape) = {*PolyLine*}. The type PATH has the attribute location with tp(location) = POLYBEZIER indicating the course of the path by a curve, and an attribute width with tp(width) = *FLOAT*.

The types RIVER, POND and WELL model the water resources of farms. RIVER has the attributes left and right, both of type *PolyBezier*, which are used to model the course of the left and right border of a river. For WELL we have the attributes depth and boundary of types *FLOAT* and *Circle*, respectively, and POND has a type boundary of type *PolyBezier*. The relationship type INSIDE is needed to model that some units may lie inside others, e.g. a rock LUC may be inside a paddock, a river may have islands, a well may be inside a paddock, a path may cross a paddock, etc. This relationship makes it easier to model 'holes' rather than permitting them to be considered as part of the data types.

A water consent for a farm refers to several water extraction points, each referring to a source, which is a river, well or pond. Therefore, WATEREXTRACTION-POINT has the attributes location, minimum, and capacity of types *Point*, *Month* → *FLOAT*, and *FLOAT* respectively. The latter two model the (season-dependent) water level below which it cannot fall and the amount of water that could be taken out. WATERCONSENT has an the attribute allowance of type *Month* → *FLOAT* modelling the total amount of water the farm is permitted to use.

Similarly, WATERQUALITY models the measurement of oxygen, nitrate and other levels, and WASTEWATERAGREEMENT models the contracted minimum and maximum values governing water quality. We omit further details.

13.6 Conclusion

In this chapter we analysed approaches to conceptual geometric modelling, an area comprising in particular spatial models and geographic models. We discovered first that many published models either remain on the surface not linking concepts to underlying geometric objects or are exclusively devoted to lower-level spatial data types and operations on them.

We then presented the geometrically enhanced ER model (GERM) as an approach to conceptual geometric modelling. GERM preserves aggregation as the primary abstraction mechanism of the ER model, but loosens the definition of relationship types permitting bulk and choice constructors to be used for components without first-class status of bulk objects. Geometric objects are dealt with within attributes, which can be associated with types for geometric modelling. This defines a syntactic level of GERM that largely remains within the ER framework and thus enables a smooth integration with non-geometric modelling. It also allows users to deal with modelling tasks that involve geometry in a familiar, non-challenging way, thereby preserving all the positive experience gained with conceptual ER modelling.

The syntactic level is complemented by an internal level which employs algebraic varieties, i.e. sets of zeros of polynomials, to represent geometric objects as point sets. The use of such varieties leads to a significant increase in expressiveness way beyond standard approaches which mostly support points, lines and polygons. In particular, common shapes as defined by circles, ellipses, Bézier curves and patches, etc. are captured in a natural way. However, for polynomials of high degrees we face computational problems.

The highly expressive internal level of GERM makes geometric modelling not only very flexible, but it is the only basis for an extended algebra that generalises and extends the standard Boolean operators on point sets. By using this algebra, GERM enables a higher degree of accuracy for derived geometric relationships.

GERM is still under development with planned investigations of further back-and-forth translations between the syntactic and the internal level of GERM and special cases of the natural modelling algebra for specific applications [22].

References

1. AgResearch (2005) Farm plan prototype for SLUI. Retrieved online from the New Zealand Association of Resource Management: http://www.nzarm.org.nz/KinrossWholeFarmPlan_A4_200dpi_secure.pdf
2. Brieskorn E, Knörrer H (1981) Plane algebraic curves. Birkhäuser, Basel
3. Balley S, Parent C, Spaccapietra S (2004) Modelling geographic data with multiple representations. Int J Geogr Inf Sci 18(4):327–352
4. Balley S, Parent C, Spaccapietra S (2004) Modelling geographic data with multiple representations. Int J Geogr Inf Sci 18(4):327–352
5. Behr T, Schneider M (2001) Topological relationships of complex points and complex regions. In: Kunii HS et al (eds) Conceptual modeling – ER 2001. Lecture notes in computer science, vol 2224. Springer, Berlin, pp 56–69
6. Chang K-T (2008) Introduction to geographic information systems. McGraw-Hill, New York
7. Corbett JP (1979) Topological principles in cartography. Technical paper 48, US Bureau of Census, Washington, DC
8. Chen CX, Zaniolo C (2000) SQLST: a spatio-temporal data model and query language. In: Laender AHF, Liddle SW, Storey VC (eds) Conceptual modeling – ER 2000. Lecture notes in computer science, vol 1920. Springer, Berlin, pp 96–111
9. Frank AU (2005) Map algebra extended with functors for temporal data. In: Akoka J et al (eds) Perspectives in conceptual modeling – ER 2005 workshops. Lecture notes in computer science, vol 3770. Springer, Berlin, 194–207

10. Gao XS, Chou SC (1992) Implicitization of rational parametric equations. J Symbol Comput 14:459–470
11. Goodchild MF (1992) Geographical data modeling. Comput Geosci 18(4):401–408
12. Hartwig A (1996) Algebraic 3-D modeling. Peters, Wellesley
13. Hull R, King R Semantic database modeling: survey, applications, and research issues. ACM Comput Surv 19(3):201–260
14. Hartmann S, Link S Collection type constructors in entity-relationship modeling. In: Parent C et al. (eds) Conceptual modeling – ER 2007. Lecture notes in computer science, vol 4801. Springer, Berlin, pp 307–322
15. Ishikawa Y, Kitagawa H (2001) Source description-based approach for the modeling of spatial information integration. In: Kunii HS et al (eds) Conceptual modeling – ER 2001. Lecture notes in computer science, vol 2224. Springer, Berlin, pp 41–55
16. Kösters G, Pagel B-U, Six H-W (1997) Gis-application development with geoooa. Int J Geogr Inf Sci 11(4):307–335
17. Liu W, Chen J, Zhao R, Cheng T (2005) A refined line-line spatial relationship model for spatial conflict detection. In: Akoka J et al (eds) Perspectives in conceptual modeling – ER 2005 workshops. Lecture notes in computer science, vol 3770. Springer, Berlin, pp 239–248
18. Laurini R, Thompson D (1992) Fundamentals of spatial information systems. Academic, London
19. Lo CP, Yeung AKW (2006) Concepts and techniques of geographic information systems, 2nd edn. Ph series in geographic information science. Prentice-Hall, Upper Saddle River
20. Mackay A (2007) Specifications of whole farm plans as a tool for affecting land use change to reduce risk to extreme climatic events. AgResearch
21. McKenny M, Schneider M (2007) PLR partitions: a conceptual model of maps. In: Hainaut J-L et al (eds) Advances in conceptual modeling – foundations and applications, ER 2007 workshops. Lecture notes in computer science, vol 4802. Springer, Berlin, 368–377
22. Ma H, Schewe K-D, Thalheim B (2009) Geometrically enhanced conceptual modelling. In: Laender A et al (eds) Conceptual modeling – ER 2009. Lecture notes in computer science, vol 5829. Springer, Berlin, pp 219–233
23. Paredaens J (1995) Spatial databases, the final frontier. In: Gottlob G, Vardi MY (eds) Database theory – ICDT'95. Lecture notes in computer science, vol 893. Springer, Berlin, pp 14–32
24. Paredaens J, Kuijpers B (1998) Data models and query languages for spatial databases. Data Knowl Eng 25(1–2):29–53
25. Price R, Tryfona N, Jensen CS (2001) Modeling topological constraints in spatial part-whole relationships. In: Kunii HS et al (eds) Conceptual modeling – ER 2001. Lecture notes in computer science, vol 2224. Springer, Berlin, pp 96–111, 27–40
26. Salomon D (2005) Curves and surfaces for computer graphics. Springer, Berlin
27. Schneider M (1997) Spatial data types for database systems, finite resolution geometry for geographic information systems. Lecture notes in computer science, vol 1288. Springer, Berlin
28. Schneider M (2009) Spatial and spatio-temporal data models and languages. In: Encyclopedia of database systems, pp 2681–2685
29. Schneider M (2009) Spatial data types. In: Encyclopedia of database systems, pp 2698–2702
30. Stoffel E-P, Lorenz B, Ohlbach H-J (2007) Towards a semantic spatial model for pedestrian indoor navigation. In: Hainaut J-L et al (eds) Advances in conceptual modeling – foundations and applications, ER 2007 workshops. Lecture notes in computer science, vol 4802. Springer, Berlin, pp 328–337
31. Sali A, Schewe K-D (2009) A characterisation of coincidence ideals for complex values. J Univers Comput Sci 15(1):304–354
32. Shekhar S, Xiong H (eds) (2008) Encyclopedia of GIS. Springer, Berlin
33. Shekhar S, Vatsavai RR, Chawla S, Burk TE (1999) Spatial pictogram enhanced conceptual data models and their translation to logical data models. In: Agouris P, Stefanidis A (eds) Integrated spatial databases, digital images and GIS. Lecture notes in computer science, vol 1737. Springer, Berlin, pp 77–104
34. Thalheim B (2000) Entity relationship modeling – foundations of database technology. Springer, Berlin

Chapter 14
Data Integration

Sonia Bergamaschi, Domenico Beneventano, Francesco Guerra, and Mirko Orsini

Abstract Given the many data integration approaches, a complete and exhaustive comparison of all the research activities is not possible. In this chapter we will present an overview of the most relevant research activities and ideas in the field investigated in the last 20 years. We will also introduce the MOMIS system, a framework to perform information extraction and integration from both structured and semistructured data sources, that is one of the most interesting results of our research activity. An open source version of the MOMIS system was delivered by the academic startup DataRiver (www.datariver.it).

14.1 Outcomes and Challenges in Data Integration

Modern enterprises are often organized as "virtual networks," where the nodes, i.e., enterprises, operate through inter-enterprise cooperative processes. The enterprises hold proprietary information systems, i.e., legacy systems, thus the problem of *data exchange* among autonomous, possibly heterogeneous, data sources must be faced.

Sonia Bergamaschi
University of Modena and Reggio Emilia, Via Vignolese 905, 41125, Modena, Italy, e-mail: sonia.bergamaschi@unimore.it

Domenico Beneventano
University of Modena and Reggio Emilia, Via Vignolese 905, 41125, Modena, Italy, e-mail: domenico.beneventano@unimore.it

Francesco Guerra
University of Modena and Reggio Emilia, V.le Berengario 51, 41100, Modena, Italy, e-mail: francesco.guerra@unimore.it

Mirko Orsini
DataRiver Srl, Via Vignolese 905, 41125, Modena, Italy, e-mail: mirko.orsini@datariver.it

D. W. Embley and B. Thalheim (eds), *Handbook of Conceptual Modeling.*   441
DOI 10.1007/978-3-642-15865-0, © Springer 2011

A key issue, in managing inter-enterprise processes and data exchange systems, is *mediating* among the many heterogeneous information systems. *Data integration* is the best technological solution to perform *mediation*.

One of the key challenges in data integration is dealing with the problems arising from the heterogeneity of data sources (both structural and semantic):

- *Structural heterogeneity* arises when the data sources use different data models or when the same data model is used but a different *conceptualization* is chosen to represent the same data in different sources.

- *Semantic heterogeneity* derives from different meanings and interpretations: schemata might use the same term to denote different concepts (homonyms) or different terms to denote the same concept (synonyms). A seminal work addressing these problems for E/R schemata integration in 1986 is [5]. Data sources are *structurally heterogeneous* when different data models are adopted to represent real-world objects (e.g., relational databases, XML files, object-oriented databases and linked open data sources, etc.). Structural heterogeneity may also arise in the presence of the same data model if the same concept is represented in different ways in different sources. The same real object is represented as a (set of) class(es), (set of) property(ies), or a combination of both, thus generating the need for a structural reconciliation.

  Another important issue concerns *semantic heterogeneity*, i.e., detecting homonyms and synonyms. Different techniques for identifying the fragments of the databases related to the same concept use rule-based and learning-based techniques [65] and *annotations* of the source terms with respect to external knowledge bases and ontologies [64].

On the side of available commercial solutions for integrating data coming from different databases, we cannot ignore data warehouse platforms [44]. Data warehouse is defined as a "subject-oriented, integrated, time-variant (temporal), non-volatile collection of summary and detailed data, used to support strategic decision-making processes for the enterprise." We can refer to the data warehouse approach as *materialized data integration*: the information from the source databases is extracted, transformed, and then loaded into the data warehouse (the ETL process) (Fig. 14.1).

The aim of this chapter is to describe the different approaches to performing data integration, i.e., *virtual data integration*, emerging from the research community and facing the problem of integrating heterogeneous and distributed data sources (Fig. 14.2). An integration designer builds a *mediated schema* (often called a *global schema*) over which a user poses queries. Data reside at the data sources, which are interfaced with wrappers, if needed (wrappers are format translators). A generally agreed definition of virtual data integration or data integration is the following: "Data integration is the problem of combining data residing at different sources, and providing the user with a unified view of these data" [virtual global schema (GS)] [48].

The research community has been investigating *data integration* for about 20 years: several research communities (Database, Artificial Intelligence, Semantic

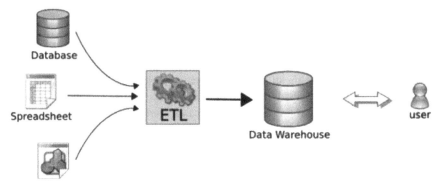

Fig. 14.1 Data warehouse: materialized data integration

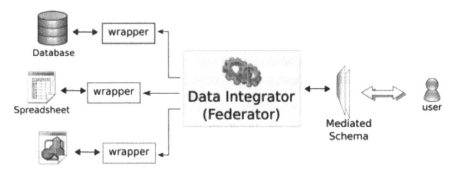

Fig. 14.2 Virtual data integration

Web) have been developing and addressing issues related to data integration from different perspectives. Many different theoretical approaches and a large number of prototypes have been proposed, making it difficult to provide a complete overview. In what follows we will try to provide the basic concepts, approaches, and systems proposed.

Data integration assumes over time different shades, with respect to the particular contexts where integration has been applied, the different technologies supporting the process and the evaluation of related technologies.

We observe that the majority of the research effort has been devoted to investigating issues related to providing techniques for the integration of the schemata of the different sources. The assumption of the systems based on these techniques is that data integration passes through the integration of a set of database schemas, thus providing a common container, i.e., a *global schema*, for heterogeneous data sources. This implies the development of techniques for many difficult tasks: *data cleaning, reconciliation, and fusion* [22], to manage inconsistent or overlapping databases. Moreover, the creation of a uniform view of the data sources, i.e., the global schema, does not cover all the issues to be solved. The capability of quering the global scheme receiving a unique and complete answer is another relevant issue for a data integration system.

Given the many data integration approaches, we will propose in the following an overview of the most relevant research outcomes and challenges. This overview does not provide an exhaustive and detailed analysis of the state of the art, but a point of view of researchers (the authors) working on the area since 1998.

In one of the first classifications proposed in the literature [43], the data integration approaches were grouped into (1) *integrated read-only views*, where a schema of the integrated data sources (usually called a *mediated schema*) is available and queries can be made against that schema; (2) *federated systems*, i.e., systems able to interconnect databases with a minimized central authority yet support partial sharing and coordination among database systems [42]; (3) *integrated read-write views*, where the integrated view is materialized thereby increasing the system performance; and (4) *workflow systems* providing a uniform interface for specifying the multitude of interactions that take place between the databases of an enterprise.

The advantage of this classification is to envisage three possible perspectives: *virtual integration*, *materialized integration*, and *integration achieved through coordination tasks*.

The last perspective may be considered only "improperly" as an integration approach, actually being an "integrated use" of multiple databases. Therefore, workflow solutions are no longer considered as facets of the data integration area but as autonomous research directions.

Virtual integration builds and integrates the database schemas, keeping the database instances on the original data sources (Fig. 14.2). On the other hand, *materialized integration* integrates a copy of the original databases (both schemas and instances).

The advantages of a virtual approach are related to the management of the changes in the sources. Since in database applications schemas do not frequently change, virtual approaches do not require strong updating policies as data are retrieved at run time. In contrast, in materialized approaches, the need to keep the integrated database aligned leads to restart in prefixed intervals the integration process (as in the case of data warehouses). The performance achieved with a materialized approach makes possible its use in commercial environments as a part of the ETL system populating the data warehouse.[1]

The number of sources involved in a data integration process is a critical factor for determining the success of the integration.

A few data sources may allow the user supervising the process to manually build the global schema, whereas a large number of data sources makes it impossible, requiring semiautomatic techniques (as will be shown in what follows). In the case of peer-to-peer architectures, the number and the independence of the data sources require the adoption of automatic techniques. This is the motivation of the development of peer data management systems (PDMSs) that aim to replace the single logical schema with an interlinked collection of semantic mappings between peers individual schemas [40].

---

[1] See for example Talend, http://www.talend.com, an open source ETL and data integration system.

Moreover, the advent and growth of the Semantic Web has determined the development of a large amount of ontology-based applications and, consequently, the need to apply integration techniques to perform ontology matching. In this context, integration is typically in the form of *alignments that express correspondences between concepts belonging to different ontologies* (see [31, 77] for a complete survey of the approach).

Finally, most recent data integration approaches propose a pay-as-you-go approach, i.e., the integration system needs to be able to incrementally evolve its understanding of the data it encompasses as it runs [54]. The idea behind these systems is to implement as much as possible automatic techniques, able to model uncertainty at all levels: queries, mappings, and underlying data. The result is a "shallow" integrated schema in the form of clusters of schema elements, where the mappings between them are approximate. In PAYGO [54], structured queries are replaced by keyword-based search queries providing a ranked set of results.

This chapter is organized as follows. In Sect. 14.1.1, we introduce *mediator-based systems*, which definitely represent the most studied architecture for data integration systems, and we reference the most famous research systems developed. Moreover, we describe the matching and mapping techniques proposed in the Database and Semantic Web research area. In Sect. 14.2, an open source system, MOMIS, based on this architecture, is described. MOMIS has been developed by the DBGROUP of the University of Modena and Reggio Emilia (www.dbgroup. unimore.it). A startup company, DATARIVER, was founded in 2009 by some members of the DBGROUP to deploy MOMIS, and the first release of the open source MOMIS system was delivered on April 2010 (www.datariver.it).

14.1.1 Mediator-Based Systems

Mediators definitely represent the main component of the architectures of data integration systems. Several systems were developed by research centers between the years 1995 and 2002 (e.g., some of the pioneer systems are TSIMMIS [50], Information Manifold [49], GARLIC [71], SIMS [3], COIN [23], MOMIS, and OB-SERVER [57]). Later on, the research community moved on addressing specific aspects of the data integration such as the development of techniques and architectures improving the automation of the data integration process, the management of uncertainty and the development of techniques for *entity recognition and record linkage (object fusion)* [22].

In the most general definition, a mediator is "a software module that exploits encoded knowledge about certain sets or subsets of data to create information for a higher layer of applications" [84]. To achieve this goal, the mediator builds a unified schema, a.k.a. a global schema, of several (heterogeneous) information sources, a.k.a. local sources, and allows users to formulate queries on it. By managing all the collected data in a common way, the GS allows the user to pose a query according

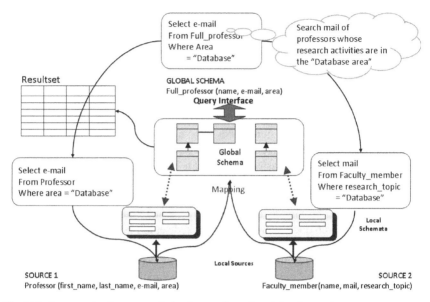

Fig. 14.3 An example of query resolution in a mediator-based data integration system

to a global perception of the handled information. A query over the GS is translated and executed on the local sources.

Figure 14.3 shows a simple example of how such systems work. The user formulate a query over the GS (in most cases in SQL). The mediator provides a translation of the user's query for each source involved in the integration process. Such a translation takes into account the schema and the language adopted by the source. In the example case, both the global and local schemas are relational. Consequently, the mediator formulates a new SQL query for each source on the basis of its local schema. The query is executed by any local source and the results are *fused* by the mediator and the answer returned to the user.

The typical architecture of mediator-based systems is composed of three layers: the layer of the data sources (data layer), which represents the sources to be integrated, the mediator layer containing the modules enabling the integration process, and the user layer, which manage the user's interaction with the system. A mediator performs two main tasks: the creation of the unified representation (publishing task) and the formulation and execution of a query in the unified representation (querying task). For each task and for each layer, there are several issues that a mediator-based system must deal with, as shown in Fig. 14.4 [85].

In what follows, we will analyze each layer for the publishing task, elaborating on the main outcomes achieved by the research community and the open challenges where more research is still needed. Elaborating on the main outcomes and challenges of the querying task is beyond the scope of this chapter.

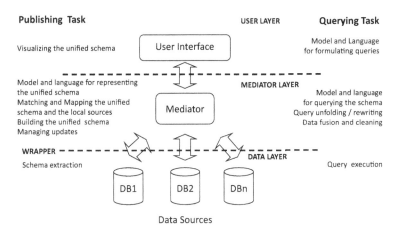

Fig. 14.4 The architecture of mediator-based data integration systems

14.1.1.1 The Data Layer

Wrappers are specific software modules in charge of managing the interaction between the mediator layer and the data sources [72]. Wrappers logically guarantee two main operations: (1) in the publishing task, translate the schema from the local source model into the common data model adopted by the mediator, dealing with the necessary conversions, and (2) in the querying task, execute the query on the local source and return its result to the mediator.

For conventionally structured information sources (e.g., relational databases, object-oriented databases, flat files), the local schema is available for authorized users and can be directly translated into the selected common data model by wrappers. Available wrappers for these kinds of sources usually perform syntactic and semantic transformations. For semistructured and unstructured information sources, schema description is in general not directly available, since the schema is specified directly within data. In these more complex cases, the application of information extraction techniques allows the extraction of structured information such as entities, relationships between entities, and attributes describing entities [74].

Concerning the querying task, wrappers typically perform only the role of interface between the mediator, which provides the queries in the language adopted by the source, and the data source, where the query is executed.

The development of wrappers has been addressed by a substantial amount of work (see, e.g., TSIMMIS [50], FLORID [52], DEByE [47], W4F [73], Lixto [36], and MOMIS [17], for research systems).

14.1.1.2 The Mediator Layer

This layer is the core of the integration system since it is in charge of building the integrated schema GS (publishing task) and performing the querying task.

The building of a GS implies addressing the following issues:

- Selection/development of a model and a language for representing the GS;
- Selection/development of techniques for supporting the creation of the GS;
- Selection/development of techniques for *matching and mapping* the GS and the local sources;
- Selection/development of techniques for managing updates on the local sources.

The querying task requires addressing the following issues:

- Selection/development of a model and language for querying the GS;
- Selection/development of techniques for query unfolding/rewriting w.r.t. the local sources;
- Selection/development of techniques for data fusion and cleaning, i.e., to perform the process of fusing multiple records representing the same real-world object into a single, consistent, and clean representation [22].

Models and languages for representing the integrated schema. The GS is a schema, thus the requirements on it its data model/language is that its expressiveness be greater than/equal to the ones of the data sources to be integrated.

Different models have been proposed in the literature. The relational data model (e.g., the Information Manifold, extends it with a Description Logics layer), object-oriented models (e.g., MOMIS and GARLIC extended in different ways the ODMG standard model, SIMS and COIN proposed an object-oriented model enriched with logics capability), and semistructured models (e.g., OEM in TSIMMIS). Finally, some more recent systems support XML, RDF/RDF-S.

Modeling the mapping among sources and the GS is a crucial aspect. Two basic approaches for specifying this mapping have been proposed in the literature: local-as-view (LAV), and global-as-view (GAV) [39, 48, 81] (Fig. 14.5).

The LAV approach is based on the assumption that the classes[2] of each source are modeled as *views* over the GS. This assumption is effective when the data integration system is based on a GS that is stable and well established in the organization (not

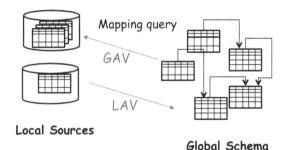

Mapping query

GAV

LAV

Local Sources

Fig. 14.5 GAV vs. LAV

Global Schema

---

always true). Another negative aspect of LAV is the complexity of query processing to be performed [39]. On the other hand, as a positive aspect, the LAV approach favours the dynamics of the integration process: adding a new source simply means enriching the mapping with a new assertion, without other changes.

The GAV approach is based on the assumption that the classes of the GS are modeled as *views* over the local sources. GAV favors the system in carrying out query processing, because the knowledge of "how to use the local sources to retrieve data" is coded into the views and by *query unfolding* the queries to be executed by the local sources are more easily obtained. This is the reason for which most systems are based on the GAV approach. However, extending a system with a new source is now more difficult: the new source may indeed have an impact on the definition of various classes of the GS whose associated views need to be redefined.

Let us show a simple example of the two approaches.

LAV approach: example

- Global schema with all the professors:
  `Prof_DB (name, email, area, country)`
- Local source S1 contains professors from the database area:
  `S1 (name, email, country)`
  Thus, the view over the GS that has to be created for S1 is as follows:

```
CREATE VIEW S1 AS
    SELECT name, email, country
    FROM Prof_DB
    WHERE area = 'database'
```

Since in LAV sources are modeled as views over the GS, we have to answer queries on the basis of the available data in the views, rather than on the raw data in the database; then query processing needs reasoning (query reformulation complex) [48].

- Local source S2 contains Italian professors:
  `S2 (name, email, area)`
  Thus, the view over the GS that must be created for S2 is as follows:

```
CREATE VIEW S2 AS
    SELECT name, email, area
    FROM Prof_DB
    WHERE country = 'Italy'
```

GAV approach: example

- Source S1 contains professors from the database area:
  `S1 (name, email, country)`
- Source S2 contains Italian professors:
  `S2 (name, email, area)`

- The GS will contain a global class `Prof_DB` whose attributes are the union of the attributes of the two local classes (`name, email, area, country`), and the view will be defined by a view over S1 and S2; for example, a *full outer join* on the `name` attribute, i.e., (S1 JOIN S2) UNION {tuples of S1 and not in S2 with null values for the area attribute and tuples of S2 and not in S1 with null values in the country attribute}.

Matching and Mapping Techniques. Matching and mapping techniques are exploited for data management mainly in two contexts. In data integration, mappings are exploited for connecting the GS with the local source schemata (as shown above). Mappings may also be used for data translations, when they connect source and target preexisting schemata potentially describing different data semantics [33]. Techniques for matching and mapping the GS and local source schemata are exploited in both the GAV and LAV approaches. In Fig. 14.6 the difference beteween schema mapping and schema integration is shown. Both schema mapping systems (CLIO, SF, S-MATCH, LSD) and the schema integration system (MOMIS) are in general considered data integration systems.

A simple example of matching is shown in Fig. 14.7.

Matching may be applied to the schema elements, i.e., *schema matching*, and in this case it takes two schemata as input and produces a mapping between elements of the two schemata that semantically correspond to each other [70].

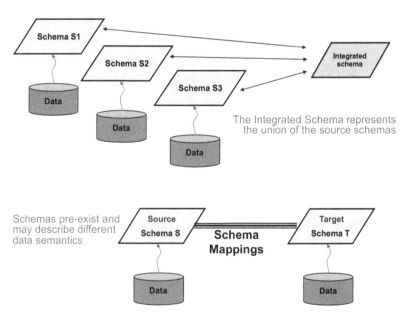

Fig. 14.6 Schema integration and schema mapping (thanks to Yannis Velegrakis, University of Trento)

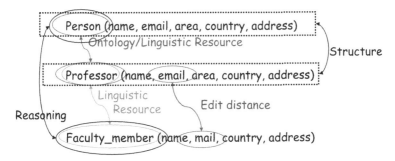

Fig. 14.7 Schema matching: a simple example

Instance matching, a.k.a. record linkage, is the task of quickly and accurately identifying records corresponding to the same entity from one or more data sources [27, 46].

Schema and instance matching have been extensively investigated by the research community since they represent the core of data integration systems. Schema matching typically relies on the analysis of the schema labels and of the schema structures.

Instance matching is generally based on techniques for *entity resolution* providing each object with an identifier. Instance analysis is computationally a heavy task since it involves a great number of elements.

Schema matching techniques have been classified under several perspectives. In [70], the authors show that matchers may be based on one (i.e., individual matcher) or several techniques (i.e., combining matchers, as the Schemr prototype [29] and COMA++ [4]). Such techniques may analyze the data source elements or the structures applying linguistic-based, constraint-based approaches or techniques based on external knowledge sources (Fig. 14.8).

In [35], the previous classification is further elaborated on. The authors observe that matching techniques can be based on string, language, linguistic resources, constraint, graph analysis, taxonomy analysis, repository of structures, and model analysis. These techniques may be applied with different granularities, i.e., to the data source elements and to the structures (Fig. 14.9).

The CLIO project, similarity flooding, and the corpus-based technique represent interesting examples of matching techniques. The Clio project [32], a joint project between the IBM Almaden Research Center and the University of Toronto begun in 1998 [59], pioneered the use of schema mappings, developing a tool for semi-automatically creating mappings between two data sources. In the Clio framework a *source* schema is mapped onto a different, but fixed, *target* schema. Moreover, the semiautomatic tool for creating schema mappings, developed in Clio, employs a mapping-by-example paradigm that relies on the use of value mappings, describing how a value of a target attribute can be created from a set of values of source attributes. In the first idea, mappings in CLIO were in the form of 1:1 correspondences [67]. Recently, a more general form of mapping connecting a number of source attributes with a target attribute via transformation functions has been proposed [55].

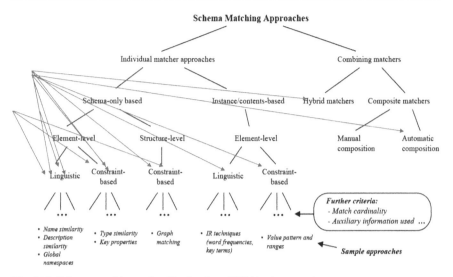

Fig. 14.8 Schema matching – classification from [70] (database area)

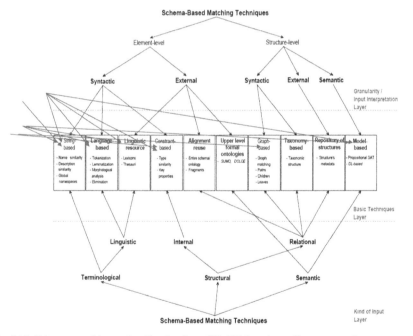

Fig. 14.9 Schema matching – classification from [31, 77] (ontology alignment area)

Similarity flooding [56] is a fixpoint computation-based matching technique that is usable in different scenarios. For computing the matches, the algorithm intuition is that elements of two distinct models are similar when their adjacent elements are similar. The approach is iterative: a set of mappings, eventually surpervised by the user, is selected. These mappings are used to increase the strength of other mappings until a fixpoint is achieved (Figs. 14.10 and 14.11). Depending on the particular matching goal, we then choose a subset of the resulting mapping using adequate filters after the algorithm is run; a human is expected to check and, if necessary, adjust the results. The protoplasm matcher [19] is based on this algorithm.

In [53] a corpus of schemas and mappings to augment the evidence about the schemas being matched (so they can be matched better) is exploited. The corpus is used in two ways: first, to increase the evidence about each element being matched by examining similar elements in the corpus. Second, statistics about elements and their relationships provide hints about the semantics of the elements in the schemas.

Building the GS schema. In the majority of approaches, the unified schema is manually provided by the user. In these cases, the data integration process is really similar to a "data transformation" process.

The automatic building of an integrated view from a set of sources is a complex issue since the heterogeneity of the data sources generates some conflicts between the global and the local representations. In [68], such conflicts are classified as representation, metamodel, and fundamental conflicts. Representation conflicts arise when two source schemas describe the same concept in different ways. Metamodel conflicts occur when the merge result violates schema constraints specific to a given metamodel, e.g., we have to map an XML source onto a relational source. Finally, fundamental conflicts arise when the merge result is not a well-formed schema according to the rules of the meta-meta-model, e.g., two attributes in two different sources represent the same real-world features through two different data types. An algorithm for automatically reconciling these kinds of conflicts is proposed.

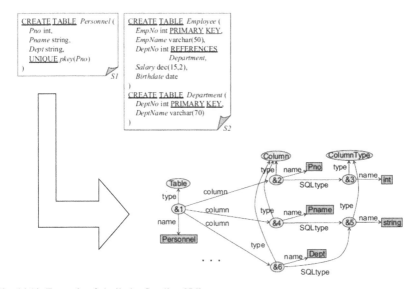

Fig. 14.10 Example of similarity flooding [56]

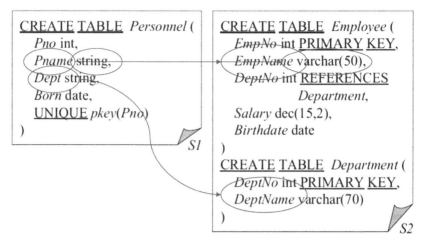

Pname is Similar to EmpName → Personnel.Pname is similar to Employee.EmpName

Personnel.Pname is similar to Employee.EmpName → string is similar to varchar

string is similar to varchar → Personnel.Dept is similar to Department.DeptName

Fig. 14.11 Example of similarity flooding [56]

In [69], some requirements that a mediated schema should satisfy are proposed. In particular, the authors propose completeness (all information in the source schema should be exposed in the global schema), overlap/extended overlap preservation (each overlapping element and instances specified in the input mapping is exposed in the global schema), normalization (independent entities and relationships in the source schemata should not be grouped together in the same relation of the global schema), and minimality as features that an integrated view has to satisfy. An algorithm that generates mediated schema according to the above features is introduced.

Managing the updates. In an integration system, changes occur when the data sources change or when the users/applications using the integrated data source need a different conceptualization. For data integration systems following the LAV approach, managing dynamics means adding/modifying/removing at the local source level. In this case, a change in a local data source does not affect the other sources. For systems following the GAV approach, a change in a local data source may affect the unified view. Consequently, all the mappings between the global view and the local sources may in principle be affected by a source change.

Two main approaches have been developed for managing source dynamics: the evolution approach [9], which aims at facing the dynamics problem in all its complexity and managing all the consequences that changes require, and the versioning approach, which tries to cope with the complexity of the problem of computing multiple versions of the same integration [45].

14.1.1.3 The User Layer

Data integration systems are typically queried by means of requests expressed in the native query languages (in general structured and typed query languages such as SQL, OQL, SPARQL, etc.). This is definitely a limit for a large exploitation of these systems: it requires skilled users and also imposes on data integration systems some of the limitations intrinsic to the query languages. A complete knowledge of the underlying data structures and their semantics is needed to formulate queries in a structured query language. Unfortunately, the former require the user to deeply explore the structure of the source, which is an error-prone and time-consuming process when a source is composed of hundreds of unknown tables and attributes. The latter may be too large and too complex to be communicated to the user. Understanding the semantics conveyed by the unified view means to know both the semantics conveyed by the data sources involved in the integration process and how the semantics of the local views are mapped to the integrated view. Therefore, it is clear that such a requirement may nullify the whole motivation for integrating sources.

Keyword-based searching has been introduced as a viable alternative to the highly structured query languages. Nevertheless, the current approaches to keyword searching over databases are based on information retrieval indices that allow the discovery of the structures that are related to one or more keywords. This kind of approach is not applicable to mediator systems since there is no data materialization and consequently it is not possible to build indices on the database contents. Only a few approaches propose keyword searching interfaces for mediators: in [75] an extension of the XQuery language called CQuery is proposed, and in [34] some indices on the concepts represented in the mediator system are exploited for solving user keyword queries. Keymantic is a project[3], currently under development, that aims to develop a keyword-based search engine based only on the data source structural knowledge [38].

14.1.1.4 The Querying Task

Issues related to the querying task in a GAV approach (see below) will be described in Sect. 14.2.4, with reference to the MOMIS system. For data integration systems, the interested reader may refer to [48] for a survey about query unfolding/rewriting issues and to [22] for a complete introduction to data fusion. Nevertheless, we need to introduce here some definitions to present the issues. Whether the system is GAV or LAV, partial answers are returned by the local sources including objects not overlapping/overlapping. To have a unified answer, we need to retrieve and fuse partial answers to identify different instantiations of the same object in different sources and to solve inconsistencies arising from inconsistent data on the same real-world object.

---

[3] See http://www.dbgroup.unimo.it/keymantic/.

The first step in a data fusion process is *object identification*, i.e., the identification of instantiations of the same object in different sources (also known as record linkage, duplicate detection, reference reconciliation, and many other names).

The topic of object identification is a very active research area with significant contributions both from the artificial intelligence [80] and database [2, 28] communities. The *full outer join* is the operator one needs when the local data sources are relational to keep all tuples in both the left and the right relations when no matching tuples are found, padding attributes present in only one relation with *null* values [82].

The second step in a data fusion process is *data reconciliation*, i.e., to solve conflicts among instantiations of the same object in different sources.

Taking into account the problem of inconsistent information among sources is a hot research topic [20, 37, 51, 63]. The querying task in a GAV data integration system will be described in Sect. 14.2.

14.2 The MOMIS Integration Framework

The MOMIS (Mediator envirOnment for Multiple Information Sources) [17] is a framework for performing information extraction and integration from both structured and semistructured data sources. An object-oriented language, called ODL_{I^3}, derived from the standard ODMG with an underlying Description Logics, is introduced for information extraction. Information integration is then performed in a semiautomatic way by exploiting the knowledge in a common thesaurus (defined by the framework) and ODL_{I^3} descriptions of source schemata with a combination of clustering techniques and Description Logics. This integration process gives rise to a virtual integrated view of the underlying sources (the GS – *GS*) for which mapping rules and integrity constraints are specified to handle heterogeneity.

An open source version of the MOMIS system is delivered by the academic startup DataRiver (www.datariver.it).

14.2.1 The MOMIS Integration System

MOMIS follows a GAV approach for the definition of mappings between a GS (*GS*) and local schemata: the GS is expressed in terms of the local schemata. This means that for each global class G a *view* over the local classes of G must be defined.

An Integration System $IS = \langle GS, \mathcal{N}, \mathcal{M} \rangle$ is constituted by:

- A GS, which is a schema expressed in ODL_{I^3} [17], a modified version of the Object Definition Language[4]; In particular, in the *GS* we have *is-a* relationships and both *key* and *foreign key* constraints.

---

[4] www.service-architecture.com/database/articles/odmg_3_0.html.

- A set $\mathcal{N}$ of *local sources*; each local source has a *schema* also expressed in ODL_{I3};
- A set $\mathcal{M}$ of GAV mapping assertions between GS and $\mathcal{N}$, expressed as follows. For each global class $G \in GS$ we define:

  1. A nonempty set of local classes, denoted by $\mathcal{L}(G)$, belonging to the local sources in $\mathcal{N}$;
  2. A query Q_G over $\mathcal{L}(G)$.

Intuitively, the GS is the intentional representation of the information provided by the Integration System, whereas the mapping specifies how such an intensional representation relates to the local sources managed by the Integration System. The semantics of an Integration System is defined in [15, 24].

The GS and the mapping assertions (mappings for short) have to be defined at design time by the integration designer. This is done by using the integration builder graphical interface, built upon the MOMIS framework. One of the main innovations of the MOMIS system is that information integration is performed in a semiautomatic way: an integration process gives rise to a GS of the underlying sources and, for each global class of the GS, the associated view may be automatically composed by the system. The integration process has the integration designer as actor and is composed of the following main steps:

1. **Global schema generation:** The system automatically extracts the schemata of the local sources and, on the basis of a semiautomatic annotation activity of the local sources, detects semantic similarities among the involved source schemas, automatically generates a bootstrap GS and the semantic relationships among the GS and the local schemata (Sect. 14.2.2);
2. **Global schema refinement:** The integration designer interactively refines and completes the integration process as follows (Sect. 14.2.3):

   a. The semantic relationships that have been automatically created by the system are fine-tuned;
   b. The query associated to each global class is refined/defined;
   c. The global schema can be enriched by adding *is-a* relationships and *key* and *foreign key* constraints.

14.2.2 Global Schema Generation

The MOMIS process for GS generation (Fig. 14.12), has five phases (for a more detailed description of this process, please refer to [17]; for an example of the process please see the manual of the MOMIS system available at www.datariver.it):

1. *Extraction of Local Source Schemata*:
   Wrappers acquire schemas of the involved local sources and convert them into into the common language ODL_{I3}. Schema description of structured sources

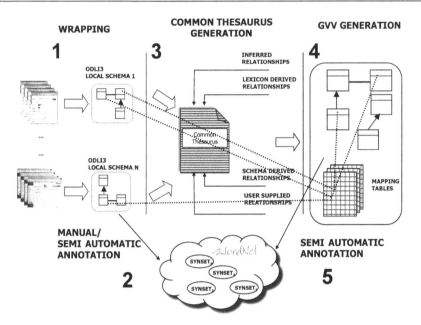

Fig. 14.12 Functional representation of the process for building the GS

(e.g., relational database and object-oriented database) can be directly translated, while the extraction of schemata from semistructured sources requires
suitable techniques as described in [1]. To perform information extraction and
integration from HTML pages, research, and commercial Web data, extraction
tools such as ANDES [60], Lixto [6], and RoadRunner [30] have been tested
and adopted in some research projects.

2. *Local Source Annotation*:
   In this step, we want to render explicit the meaning of terms, that may come
   from different sources and possibly expressed in different languages in the local
   ontologies, with respect to a common multilingual lexicon ontology. Therefore,
   we perform an *annotation*, which is a mapping of a given term (class and attribute names) into a well-defined set of concepts of a lexical ontology. In the
   current version of MOMIS we adopt as lexical ontology Wordnet [58]; we also
   use a multilingual lexical ontology such as EuroWordNet [83].
   The integration designer can manually choose the appropriate Wordnet mean-
   ing(s) for each term or perform an automatic annotation that associates to each
   term the first meaning of Wordnet. The manual annotation is a two-step process:

   a. **Word form choice:** In this step, the WordNet morphologic processor aids
      the designer by deriving the correct word form corresponding to the given
      term. More precisely, the morphologic processor stems (i.e., converts to
      a common root form) the term and checks if it exists as a word form. If the
      stemmed term is not available as a word form, if there is an ambiguity [e.g.,

axes has three word forms: *ax* (1 sense), *axis* (5 senses), *axe* (2 senses)], or the selected word form is not satisfactory, the designer can choose another word form from the list available in WordNet.

b. **Meaning choice:** The designer can choose to map an element on zero, one, or more senses. For example, WordNet has 14 meanings for the word form *address*, from which the most appropriate ones to the particular context are chosen.

If the reference lexical ontology does not contain a satisfactory meaning for a concept expressed in a given data source, the integration designer may annotate it with a similar one, generating a *partial* loss of knowledge. On the other hand, the integration designer might not annotate the concept at all, with a *total* loss of semantics. In [7], we proposed *WNEditor*, a tool that aims at guiding the integration designer during the creation of a domain lexicon ontology, extending the preexisting WordNet ontology. New terms, meanings, and relations between terms are virtually added and managed by preserving the WordNet internal organization.

3. *Common Thesaurus Generation*:
   Starting from the annotated local schemata, MOMIS builds a common thesaurus that describes intra- and interschema knowledge in the form of the following semantic relationships: synonyms (*SYN*), broader terms/narrower terms (*BT/NT*), meronymy/holonymy (*RT*), equivalence (SYN_{ext}), and generalization (BT_{ext}) relationships. The common thesaurus is incrementally built by adding *schema-derived* relationships (automatic extraction of intraschema relationships from each schema separately), *lexicon-derived* relationships (interschema lexical relationships derived by the annotated sources and Wordnet interaction), *designer-supplied* relationships (specific domain knowledge capture), and *inferred* relationships (via Description Logics equivalence and subsumption computation).

4. *GS Generation*:
   Starting from the common thesaurus and the local source schemata, MOMIS generates a GS consisting of a set of global classes, plus mappings to connect the global attributes of each global class with the local sources' attributes. MOre precisely, GS generation is a process whereby ODL_{I^3} classes describing the same or semantically related concepts in different sources are identified and clusterized into the same global class. Then the system automatically generates a *mapping table* (MT) for each global class G of the GS whose columns represent the local classes $\mathcal{L}(G)$ belonging to G and whose rows represent the global attributes of G. An element $MT[GA][L]$ represents the set of local attributes of the local class L that are mapped onto the global attribute GA. The integration designer may interactively refine and complete the proposed integration results; in particular, the mappings that have been automatically created by the system can be fine-tuned, as will be discussed in the next section.

5. *GS annotation and OWL exportation*:
   The GS is semiautomatically annotated, i.e., each of its element is associated to the meanings extracted from the annotated sources; the GS annotation can be

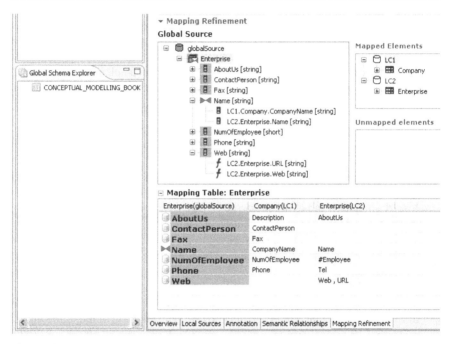

Fig. 14.13 Mapping table of *Enterprise*

useful for making the GS available, as a domain ontology, to external users and applications, as discussed in [9]. Moreover, the GS may be exported in OWL format.

In [8] we showed our methodology applied to the integration of five Web sites, three Italian and two American, that describe enterprises and products in the textile domain. The result of the GS generation phase was five global classes with the corresponding mapping tables: *Enterprise, Business_Organization, Category, ProductClassification*, and *Goods* (Fig. 14.14). Figure 14.13 shows a screenshot taken from the open source version of the MOMIS system at www.datariver.it; in particular, the mapping table of the global class *Enterprise* that groups the local classes *Company* and *Enterprise* is shown.

14.2.3 Global Schema Refinement

In this phase of the integration process, the integration designer interactively refines and completes the integration result obtained in the GS generation.

First of all, for a global class, its mapping table, which representes the semantic relationships automatically created by the system among global and local attributes, may be fine-tuned by changing its elements or by adding some new global attributes.

Then, the integration designer defines, for each global class, the associated mapping query Q_G; this is the main task of global schema refinement, and it is performed in the following two steps:

1. *Data Transformation:* To transform local attribute values into a global attribute value by means of the *data transformation functions.*
2. *Data Fusion:* A global class performs *data fusion* among its local class instances when multiple records coming from local classes and representing the same real-world object are fused into a single and consistent record of the global class [22]. The integration designer must decide if he or she wants the system to perform data fusion on a global class or not. If so, the query Q_G associated to the global class is automatically composed by the system on the basis of the process described in the **Data Fusion** section below. If not, the integration designer may update the query automatically associated to the global class or compose the mapping query.

Data Transformation. The integration designer defines how local attribute values are to be transformed into corresponding global attribute values by means of *data transformation functions.* For each local class L and for each non-null element $MT[GA][L]$ of the mapping table a *data transformation function* $DTF[GA][L]$ must be specified. $DTF[GA][L]$ is a function that must be *executable/supported* by the local source of class L; for example, for relational sources, $DTF[GA][L]$ is an SQL value expression. The following defaults hold: if $MT[GA][L] = \{LA\}$, then $DTF[GA][L] = LA$, i.e., no transformation is applied (*identity transformation*); if $MT[GA][L]$ contains more than one string attribute, then $DTF[GA][L]$ is the *string concatenation.*

In [12] we proposed the *data transformation system* of MOMIS and we demonstrated its capability by responding to all challenges provided by the THALIA benchmark. THALIA (Test Harness for the Assessment of Legacy information Integration Approaches) [41] provides researchers with a collection of downloadable data sources representing university course catalogs, a set of 12 benchmark queries, and a scoring function for ranking the performance of an integration system. The THALIA benchmark focuses on syntactic and semantic heterogeneities in order to pose the greatest technical challenges to the research community.

As an example of the data transformation function, let us consider $L2 = Enterprise$ and the global attribute Web (Fig. 14.13); for the element $MT[Web][L2] = \{URL, Web\}$, we define $DTF[Web][L2] = \texttt{coalesce}(web, URL)$, where $\texttt{coalesce}$ returns the first non-null value from the list of its arguments. In this way, the WEB value at the global level is the WEB value at the local level, if non-null; otherwise the URL value is considered.

Data Fusion. In the MOMIS system, *data fusion* is performed at the level of global classes, by the mapping query Q_G associated to a global class. The first step of the data fusion process is *object identification*, which is a problem beyond the scope of the MOMIS framework. In what follows we introduce the concept of *join conditions* as a convenient way to perform object identification when it is possible to assume that error-free and shared object identifiers exist among different sources (see the example below). Moreover, this is a situation where the step of object identification has already been performed and its result is the assignment of an object identifier to each record: two records with the same object identifier indicate the same object in different sources.

Join Conditions. Given a global class G, to identify instances coming from its local classes and representing the same real-world object, we introduce *join conditions* among pairs of local classes defined as follows. We specify a set of global attributes **JA** of G, called *join attributes*, such that for each join attribute $JA \in \mathbf{JA}$ and for each local class $L \in \mathcal{L}(G)$ belonging to G, the element $MT[JA][L]$ is not null. Given $\mathbf{JA} = \{JA_1, JA_2, \ldots, JA_k\}$, for each pair of local classes $L_1, L_2 \in \mathcal{L}(G)$, the *join condition* between L_1 and L_1, denoted by $JC(L_1, L_2)$, is defined as follows:

$$DTF[JA_1][L_1] = DTF[JA_1][L_2]$$
$$\textbf{and} \ldots \textbf{and} \quad DTF[JA_k][L_1] = DTF[JA_k][L_2] \,.$$

As an example, if the global attribute $Name$ is chosen as a join attribute for the global class $Enterprise$ (Fig. 14.13), we have that $JC(L_1, L_2)$ is equal to $L_1.CompanyName = L_2.Name$. If $Name$ and $Phone$ are chosen as join attributes, i.e., $JA1 = Name$ and $JA2 = Phone$, then $JC(L_1, L_2)$ is equal to

$$L_1.CompanyName = L_2.Name \quad \textbf{and} \quad L_1.Phone = L_2.Tel \,.$$

On the basis of these join conditions, multiple records (coming from different local classes and representing the same real-world object) are combined into a single record by means of a *full outer join* operator.

Resolution Functions. In a global class, conflicts may arise for global attributes mapped onto more than one local class; data reconciliation is then performed by *resolution functions*, as proposed in [22, 63]. In other words, for each global attribute GA such that there is more than one nonempty element $MT[GA][L]$, we must define a resolution function to obtain, starting from the values computed by the transformation functions $DTF[GA][L]$, the corresponding value for GA. The MOMIS system provides some standard kinds of resolution functions:

- *Random function*: results in having the value of one of the local attributes randomly chosen;
- *Aggregation functions*: for numerical attributes: SUM, AVG, MIN, MAX, etc.;
- *Precedence function*: the highest informational quality value on the basis of an information quality model;
- *Coalesce function*: the first non-null value among the local attributes values.

As an example, in the global class *Enterprise* we can use for *AboutUs* as resolution function a *precedence function* to say that *LC1.Description* has a higher precedence than *LC2.AboutUs*.

If the integration designer knows that there are no data conflicts for a global attribute mapped onto more than one source (that is, the instances of the same real object in different local classes have the same value for this common attribute), he can define this attribute as a *homogeneous attribute*. Of course, for homogeneous attributes resolution functions are not necessary.[5]

To sum up, in the MOMIS system, data fusion is performed by combining the SQL operator of a full outer join with resolution functions; this operation is called a *full outer join merge* [62]. This data fusion operation is automatically defined by the MOMIS system; the integration designer must only define data transformation and resolution functions and the join attributes.

On the other hand, the integration designer may change the query automatically created for a global class, i.e., Q_G, by explicitly composing it.

Finally, the integration designer can enrich the GS by adding *is-a* relationships and *key* and *foreign key* constraints. In our example, the GS contains five global classes, *Enterprise*, *Business_Organization*, *Category*, *ProductClassification*, and *Goods* (Fig. 14.14); the integration designer defines the following is-a relationships (represented by a green arrow in the figure): *Business_Organization is-a Enterprise* and *ProductClassification is-a Category*; moreover, the integration designer defines the following foreign key constraints (represented by a blue arrow in the figure): in *Business_Organization*, the attribute *HasCategory* refers to *Category* and in *ProductClassification* the attribute *HasGoods* refers to *Goods*.

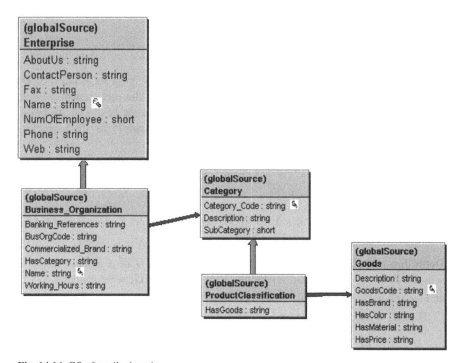

Fig. 14.14 GS of textile domain

---

[5] A global attribute mapped onto only one source is a particular case of a homogeneous attribute.

14.2.3.1 Full Outerjoin-Merge Operator

In this section we first introduce the definition of the *full outerjoin-merge* operator (as given in [62]) and use it to define the mapping query for a global class. Then we will show an SQL implementation of this operator.

The join-merge operator returns tuples for G that are joined from tuples in L_i and L_j using the join condition defined by join attributes. Without loss of generality we consider a single join attribute denoted by ID. For all the attributes provided only by L_i the values of L_i are used, and for all attributes provided only by L_j the values of L_j are used. For the common attributes, the join-merge operator applies the resolution function f to determine the final value. The values of all other attributes of G are padded with null values.

Definition 14.1 (Resolution function). Let D be an attribute domain and $D^+ := D \cup \perp$, where $\perp$ represents the null value. A resolution function f is an associative function $f : D^+ \times D^+ \to D^+$ with

$$
f(x, y) := \begin{cases} \perp & \text{if } x = \perp \text{ and } y = \perp, \\ x & \text{if } y = \perp \text{ and } x \neq \perp, \\ y & \text{if } x = \perp \text{ and } y \neq \perp, \\ g(x, y) & \text{else}, \end{cases}
$$

where $g : D \times D \to D$. Function g is an internal associative resolution function.

Let G be a global class with schema $S(G)$ and let L be a local class of G; we denote by L^T the transformation of L by means of the *data transformation function DTF*; the schema of L^T, denoted by $S(L^T)$, is a set of global attributes, i.e., $S(L^T) \subseteq S(G)$; in particular, $ID \in S(L^T)$. As an example, for the local class $LC2=Enterprise$, we have (Fig. 14.13):

$$(S(LC2^T) = \{AboutUs, ID, NumOfEmployee, Phone, Web\}),$$
$$with(ID = Name).$$

Given a set of global attributes $X \subseteq S(G)$, the *null tuple* on X, denoted by $t_\perp[X]$, has a null value assigned for all attributes in X.

Definition 14.2 (Full outerjoin-merge operator $\sqcup$). Let G be a global class with schema $S(G)$, and let L_i and L_j be two local classes of G; we consider L_i^T, L_j^T and the related schemas $S(L_i^T)$ and $S(L_j^T)$.

The *full outerjoin-merge* of L_i^T and L_j^T, denoted by $L_i^T \sqcup L_j^T$, is defined as

$$L_i^T \sqcup L_j^T = JoinMerge \cup LeftPart \cup RightPart$$

where

$$JoinMerge = \{r[ID]r[XL_i]s[XL_j]res[XL_iL_j]t_\perp[X] \mid \exists r \in L_i^T, \exists s \in L_j^T$$

$$\text{with } r[ID] = s[ID],$$

where

$XL_i = S\left(L_i^T\right) \setminus S\left(L_j^T\right)$, i.e., the global attributes provided only by L_i,

$XL_j = S\left(L_j^T\right) \setminus S\left(L_i^T\right)$, i.e., the global attributes provided only by L_j,

$XL_iL_j = S\left(L_j^T\right) \cap S\left(L_i^T\right)$, and $\forall A \in XL_iL_j, A \neq ID$,

$$res[A] = f(r[A], s[A]),$$

where f is a resolution function as defined above,

$$X = S(G) \setminus (S\left(L_j^T\right) \cup S\left(L_i^T\right)).\}$$

$$LeftPart = \{r[S\left(L_i^T\right)]t_\perp[X] \mid \exists r \in L_i^T, \nexists s \in L_j^T$$

$$\text{with } r[ID] = s[ID], X = S(G) \setminus S\left(L_i^T\right)\}$$

$$RightPart = \{s[S\left(L_j^T\right)]t_\perp[X] \mid \exists s \in L_j^T, \nexists r \in L_i^T$$

$$\text{with } s[ID] = r[ID], X = S(G) \setminus S\left(L_j^T\right)\}$$

On the basis of the above definitions, resolution functions and full outerjoin-merge is defined on transformed local classes, L^T. As an example, Fig. 14.15 shows $LC_1^T \sqcup LC_2^T$ (where $LC_1 = Company$ and $LC_2 = Enterprise$ are the local classes of $Enterprise$ introduced in Fig. 14.13) (some attributes are omitted); we use the following resolution functions:

- *precedence* for *AboutUs*: $precedence(LC_1^T.AboutUs, LC_2^T.AboutUs)$
- *coalesce* for *Phone*: $coalesce(LC_1^T.Phone, LC_2^T.Phone)$
- *AVG* for *NumOfEmployee*: $AVG(LC_1^T.NumOfEmployee, LC_2^T.NumOf\text{-}Employee)$

Given a global class G with local classes $\mathcal{L}G$, the mapping query Q_G associated to G is defined on the basis of the *full outerjoin-merge* operator, using ID as join attribute.

When the global class has more than two local classes, the evaluation order is not relevant, since the $\sqcup$ operator is an associative operator.

Proposition (associativity of $\sqcup$). Let G be a global class. Then:

$$\left(L_1^T \sqcup L_2^T\right) \sqcup L_3^T = L_1^T \sqcup \left(L_2^T \sqcup L_3^T\right)$$

for each L_1, L_2, and L_3 belonging to G.

Definition 14.3 (Mapping query Q_G). Let G be a global class and let $\mathcal{L}(G)$ be the set of its local classes. The mapping query Q_G associated to G is defined as follows:

$$Q_G = \bigsqcup \{L_i^T \mid L_i \in \mathcal{L}(G)\}.$$

$$LC_1^T$$

AboutUs	ContactPerson	Fax	Name	NumOfEmployee	Phone
Champions	Moratti	3-3-3	Inter	11	4231
D. Alberto	Milito	3-3-3	Il principe	30	1234
Special One	Mourinho	NULL	Triplete	3	NULL

$$LC_2^T$$

AboutUs	Name	NumOfEmployee	Phone
Campioni	Inter	13	NULL
Bernal	Il principe	34	1234
Zeru Tituli	Milan	-12	6-0

$$LC_1^T \sqcup LC_2^T$$

AboutUs	ContactPerson	Fax	Name	NumOfEmployee	Phone
Champions	Moratti	3-3-3	Inter	12	4231
D. Alberto	Milito	3-3-3	Il principe	32	1234
Special One	Mourinho	NULL	Triplete	3	NULL
Zeru Tituli	NULL	NULL	Milan	-12	6-0

Fig. 14.15 Example of full outerjoin-merge

In [21, 62] an implementation of the full outerjoin-merge operator is proposed; the underlying engine of the entire process is the *XXL* framework, an extensible library for building database management systems [16]. In the MOMIS system, an SQL implementation of the *full outerjoin-merge* operator is adopted: first, the full outer-join expression is computed with an SQL engine and then resolution functions are applied. To get an intuition of this implementation, the computation of $Q_G = \bigsqcup \{L_1^T, L_2^T, L_3^T\}$ is performed in the following two steps:

1. The SQL query, denoted by $FOJ(L_1^T, L_2^T, L_3^T)$, is executed:

   ```
   (T_L1 full join T_L2 on JC(L1,L2))
           full join T_L3 on (JC(L1,L3) OR JC(L2,L3))
   ```

2. Q_G is obtained by applying the resolution functions to the attributes resulting from *FOJ*: for each global attribute *GA* the related resolution function is applied.

As we will show in the next section, at query time, this computation of Q_G is executed over the partial results coming from the local classes on the basis of the query unfolding process described in Sect. 14.2.4.2.

14.2.4 Querying the MOMIS System

A query is intended to provide the specification of which data to extract from the *virtual database* represented by the integration system. Queries are posed in terms of the GS and are expressed in a query language over the alphabet GS; we will restrict our attention to *conjunctive queries*.

For example, given the GS of the textile domain of Fig. 14.14, suppose we want to find the name, address, and Web address of the enterprises having a category, a contact person, and a Web address that ends with ".com." For the sake of simplicity, we consider the query in an SQL-like format:

```
Q = SELECT Name, Address, Web
    FROM Enterprise, BusinessOrganization, Category
    WHERE Enterprise.Name=BusinessOrganization.Name
    AND BusinessOrganization.HasCategory=
                Category.Category_Code
    AND ContactPerson = 'yes'
    AND NumOfEmployee < 100
    AND Web LIKE '*.com'
```

Query processing is carried out in two steps:

1. **Query expansion:** The query posed in terms of the GS is expanded to take into account the integrity constraints (in our case, *is-a* relationships, key constraints, and foreign key constraints): all constraints in the GS are compiled in the expansion, so that the expanded query can be processed by ignoring constraints. Then, the atoms (i.e., subqueries referring to a single global class) are extracted from the expanded query.

2. **Query unfolding:** The atoms in the expanded query are unfolded by taking into account the mappings between the GS and its local sources.

In what follows, we show an example of query expansion (the algorithm for query expansion was introduced in [25, 26]; then it was adapted in the context of the MOMIS system in [15]), and we discuss the unfolding process of an atom by taking into account the mapping query Q_G introduced in Sect. 14.2.3.

14.2.4.1 Query Expansion Example

The output of the query expansion process is an expanded query (called *EXPQuery*) and its atoms (called *EXPAtoms*); *EXPQuery* is a union of conjunctive queries on the GS; an *EXPAtom* is a single class query on a global class of the GS.

As an example, the query expansion process for the previous query Q produces:

- *EXPQuery* = Q1 UNION Q2, where Q1 = Q and Q2 is obtained from Q by substituting Category with ProductClassification, i.e., Q2 takes into account the constraint *ProductClassification is-a Category*:

```
Q = SELECT Name, Address, Web
    FROM Enterprise, BusinessOrganization,
       ProductClassification
    WHERE Enterprise.Name=BusinessOrganization.Name
```

```
AND BusinessOrganization.HasCategory=
    ProductClassification.Category_Code
AND ContactPerson = 'yes'
AND NumOfEmployee < 100
AND Web LIKE '*.com'
```

- A set of EXPAtoms:

```
ExpAtom1 = SELECT Name, Address, Web
        FROM Enterprise,
        WHERE ContactPerson = 'yes'
        AND NumOfEmployee < 100
        AND Web LIKE '*.com'

ExpAtom2 = SELECT HasCategory
        FROM BusinessOrganization

ExpAtom3 = SELECT Category_Code
        FROM ProductClassification
```

14.2.4.2 Query Unfolding

The query unfolding process is performed for each *EXPAtom* which is a *single global query* Q over a global class G of the GS:

```
Q = SELECT <Q_SELECT-list>
    FROM G
    WHERE <Q_condition>
```

where `<Q_condition>` is a Boolean expression of positive atomic constraints: (GA1 op value) or (GA1 op GA2), with GA1 and GA2 attributes of G. Let $L, L2, \ldots Ln$ be the local classes related to the G, i.e., which are integrated into G.

To answer a query over a global class G, the query must be rewritten as an equivalent set of queries expressed on the local schemata (local queries); this query translation is performed by considering the mapping between the global class and the local schemata. MOMIS follows a GAV approach and for each global class G a mapping query Q_G over the schemas of its local classes $L(G)$. Then the query translation is performed by means of query unfolding, i.e., by expanding a global query on a global class G of the PVV according to the definition of this mapping query Q_G.

The query unfolding of a global query Q produces, for each local class L belonging to G, a local query Q_L:

```
Q_L = SELECT <Q_L_SELECT-list>
    FROM L
    WHERE <Q_L_condition>
```

where the select list is a list of local attributes of L and the local query condition on L. These local queries are executed on the local sources, and local query answers are then fused by means of the mapping query Q_G to obtain the answer of the global query.

In what follows we will give an intuitive and informal description of the query unfolding process by considering some examples; for more details see [15].

Let us consider the SQL version of EXPAtom1:

```
SELECT Name,Address,Web
FROM Enterprise
WHERE Web like '*.com'
AND ContactPerson = 'yes'
AND NumOfEmployee < 100
```

The mapping table of the class Enterprise involved in the query is in Fig. 14.13. The steps to compute a local query Q_L are as follows:

(1) Local Query Condition:
In this step, the constraint is rewritten into one that can be supported by the local class L. The atomic constraint mapping is performed on the basis of the mapping functions defined in the mapping table. Moreover, the atomic constraint mapping depends on the presence of nonhomogeneous attributes and of the related resolution function. For example, if the numerical global attribute GA is mapped onto L1 and L2, and we define the AVG function as a resolution function, the constraint (GA = value) cannot be pushed at the local sources because the AVG function must be calculated at a global level, so the constraint may be globally true but locally false. In this case, the constraint is mapped as true in both the local sources.

On the other hand, if GA is a homogeneous attribute, the constraint can be pushed at the local sources; recall that a global attribute GA mapped on only one local class is a particular case of a homogeneous attribute.

We can summarize as follows. An atomic constraint (*GA op* value) is mapped onto the local class L as follows:

$$(DTF[GA][L] \ op \ \text{value}) \text{ if } GA \text{ is a homogeneous attribute and}$$
$$DTF[GA][L] \text{ is not null and}$$
$$\text{the } op \text{ operator is supported in } L$$
$$true \text{ otherwise}$$

In our example, we have the following local query conditions:

- for Company: `coalesce(Web,URL) LIKE '*.com'`
- for Enterprise: `ContactPerson='yes'`

(2) Residual Condition:
Intuitively, as explained before, conditions expressed over notnomogeneus attributes are *residual*, i.e., must be solved at the global level. More precisely, an atomic constraint (*GA op* value) is a residual if there exists a local class L such that $DTF[GA][L]$ is not null and (*GA op* value) is mapped onto L as true.

In the example, the residual condition is equal to: `NumOfEmployee < 100`.

(3) Local Select List:

The select list of query LQ for the local class L is obtained by the union of the attributes of the global select list, the join condition, and the residual condition; these attributes are transformed on the basis of the mapping table. With the local select list the local query is complete.

In the example, we have the following local queries:

```
Q_Company = SELECT CompanyName,Address,Web,
   Employee_avg
        FROM Company
        WHERE coalesce(Web,URL) LIKE '*.com'

Q_Enterprise = SELECT Name,Address,Web, mean_Employee
        FROM Enterprise
        WHERE ContactPerson='yes'
```

(4) Full Outer Join Computation:

Generation of $FOJ(LQ1, LQ2, \ldots, LQn)$, which computes the full outerjoin-merge of the LQs (Sect. 14.2.3.1). The SQL implementation of FOJ (Sect. 14.2.3.1) in our example is:

```
\textit{FOJ} = Q_Company full join Q_Enterprise on
   (Q_Company.CompanyName=Q_Enterprise.Name)
```

(5) Application of the Resolution Functions:

For the GA of the global query the related resolution function $f(LQ_1.GA,$ $LQ_2.GA, \ldots, LQ_n.GA)$ is applied; in our example the result is the relation R_FOJ(Name,Address,Web,NumOfEmployee).

(6) Application of the Residual Condition:

The result of the global query is obtained by applying the residual condition to R_FOJ:

```
SELECT Name,Address,Web
FROM R_FOJ
WHERE NumOfEmployee < 100
```

Such a query unfolding process is fully implemented in the MOMIS system, which uses a "relational engine" to perform steps 4 (FOJ Computation) and 6 (Application of the Residual Condition).

Let us conclude this section with some open issues related to query optimization. First, the full join operation in the FOJ computation can be optimized by re-ducing it to a left, right join or to an inner join; some preliminary ideas are discussed in [10]. Moreover, to support algebraic query optimization, [61] analyzes different properties of the resolution functions, e.g., commutativity, order depen-dance, decomposability, etc; these play an important role when deciding whether a condition can be pushed down below a join. Rules for decomposable, order-, and duplicate-insensitive functions, such as max and min, can be taken from the litera-ture on the optimization of grouping and aggregation. In [61] some rules are introduced to perform this kind of optimization, for some specific resolution functions; however, it is an open issue for general and more complex functions.

14.2.5 New Trends in the MOMIS System

In this section we briefly discuss some extensions to the MOMIS system that we are studying and developing (not included in the software release at www.datariver. com).

Automatic Annotation by PWSD.   Instead of forcing the determination of a unique best meaning of a term, in [66] we proposed the *Probabilistic Word Sense Disambiguation* (PWSD) method that automatically annotates source elements and associates to any annotation a probability value that indicates the reliability level of the annotation. The PWSD method is based on a probabilistic combination of different WSD algorithms. The use of different WSD algorithms leads to an epistemic uncertainty, i.e., the type of uncertainty that results from a lack of knowledge about a system; for this reason, we explored the Dempster–Shafer theory, which best deals with this kind of uncertainty [76]. After this task of probabilistic lexical annotation, it is possible to automatically extract probabilistic lexical relationships across elements of different schemata/ontologies, on the basis of relationships defined among meanings in the lexical database (WordNet in our case). PWSD has been implemented in the *Automatic Lexical Annotation* tool [78].

Schema Label Normalization.   The accuracy of semiautomatic lexical annotation methods on real-world schemata suffers from an abundance of nondictionary words such as compound nouns and word abbreviations. In [79], we addressed this problem by proposing a method of performing schema label normalization that increases the number of comparable labels. Unlike other solutions, this method semiautomatically expands abbreviations and annotates compound terms (a minimal manual effort is required if the user wants to set configuration parameters). We empirically proved that our normalization method helps in the identification of similarities among schema elements of different data sources, thus improving schema matching accuracy by reducing the number of false positive/false negative lexical relationships. Moreover, in [11] we proposed a new method for the annotation of nondictionary compound nouns, which draws its inspiration from works in the natural language disambiguation area.

Toward a Unified View of Data and Services.   The increasing availability of data and eServices on the Web allows users to search for relevant information and to perform operations through eServices. Current technologies do not support users in the execution of such activities as a unique task; thus users have first to find interesting information and then, as a separate activity, to find and use eServices. In [14, 18] we presented a framework capable of building and querying a semantically unified view of data and semantically described eServices.

Data and Multimedia Sources.   In [13] the capabilities of the MOMIS integration system and the MILOS multimedia content management system were coupled, thus providing a methodology and a tool for building and querying a populated ontology representing data and multimedia sources.

14.3 Conclusions

Given the many data integration approaches, a complete and exhaustive comparison of all the research activities is not possible. In this chapter, we presented an overview of what we think are the most relevant research activities and ideas in the field in the last 20 years.

We also introduced the MOMIS system, a framework to perform information extraction and integration from both structured and semistructured data sources, that is one of the most interesting results of our research activity. An open source version of the MOMIS system is delivered by the academic startup DataRiver (www.datariver.it).

Acknowledgements The work presented in this paper is an extension of the tutorial on data and service integration delivered at WISE 2009 (Poznan, Poland). The work has been partially supported by the Italian FIRB project RBNE05XYPW NeP4B – Networked Peers for Business.

References

1. Abiteboul S, Buneman P, Suciu D (1999) Data on the Web: from relations to semistructured data and XML. Morgan Kaufmann, San Francisco
2. Ananthakrishna R, Chaudhuri S, Ganti V (2002) Eliminating fuzzy duplicates in data warehouses. In Proceedings of the 28th international conference on Very Large Bases, Hong Kong, China, VLDB Endowment, p 586–597
3. Arens Y, Knoblock CA (1993) Sims: retrieving and integrating information from multiple sources. In: Buneman P, Jajodia S (eds) Proceedings of the 1993 ACM SIGMOD international conference on management of data, Washington, DC, 26–28 May 1993. ACM, New York, pp 562–563
4. Aumueller D, Do HH, Massmann S, Rahm E (2005) Schema and ontology matching with coma++. In: Özcan F (ed) SIGMOD conference. ACM, New York, pp 906–908
5. Batini C, Lenzerini M, Navathe SB (1986) A comparative analysis of methodologies for database schema integration. ACM Comput Surv 18(4):323–364
6. Baumgartner R, Flesca S, Gottlob G (2001) Declarative information extraction, web crawling, and recursive wrapping with lixto. In: Eiter T, Faber W, Truszczynski M (eds) LPNMR. Lecture notes in computer science, vol 2173. Springer, Berlin, pp 21–41
7. Benassi R, Bergamaschi S, Fergnani A, Miselli D (2004) Extending a lexicon ontology for intelligent information integration. In: Proceedings of the 16th Eureopean conference on artificial intelligence (ECAI'2004), pp 278–282
8. Beneventano D, Bergamaschi S (2007) Semantic search engines based on data integration systems. In: Cardoso J (ed) Semantic Web services: theory, tools and applications. IGI Global, Hershey, pp 317–341

9. Beneventano D, Bergamaschi S, Guerra F, Vincini M (2003) Synthesizing an integrated ontology. IEEE Internet Comput 7(5):42–51
10. Beneventano D, Bergamaschi S, Mbinkeu CRN (2006) Full outer join optimization techniques in integration information systems. Technical report, Dipartimento di Ingegneria dell'Informazione. http://www.dbgroup.unimo.it/prototipo/paper/cleandb.pdf
11. Beneventano D, Bergamaschi S, Sorrentino S (2009) Extending wordnet with compound nouns for semi-automatic annotation in data integration systems. In: Proceedings of the international conference on natural language processing and knowledge engineering (NLP–KE), 24–27 September 2009, Dalian, China, pp 1–8
12. Beneventano D, Bergamaschi S, Vincini M, Orsini M, Nana RC (2007) Query translation on heterogeneous sources in momis data transformation systems. In: VLDB 3rd international workshop on database interoperability (InterDB 2007)
13. Beneventano D, Gennaro C, Guerra F (2008) A methodology for building and querying an ontology representing data and multimedia sources. In: ODBIS, pp 37–40
14. Beneventano D, Guerra F, Maurino A, Palmonari M, Pasi G, Sala A (2009) Unified semantic search of data and services. In: Proceedings of the 3rd international conference on metadata and semantic research (MTSR 2009), Milan, Italy, 1–2 October 2009. Communications in computer and information science, vol 46. Springer, Berlin, pp 95–107
15. Beneventano D, Lenzerini M (2005) Final release of the system prototype for query management. Sewasie, deliverable D3.5, Dipartimento di Ingegneria dell'Informazione. http://dbgroup.unimo.it/TechnicalReport/D3.5Final.pdf
16. den Bercken JV, Blohsfeld B, Dittrich JP, Krämer J, Schäfer T, Schneider M, Seeger B (2001) Xxl – a library approach to supporting efficient implementations of advanced database queries. In: Apers PMG, Atzeni P, Ceri S, Paraboschi S, Ramamohanarao K, Snodgrass RT (eds) VLDB, pp 39–48. Morgan Kaufmann, San Francisco
17. Bergamaschi S, Castano S, Vincini M, Beneventano D (2001) Semantic integration of heterogeneous information sources. Data Knowl Eng 36(3):215–249
18. Bergamaschi S, Maurino A (2009) Toward a unified view of data and services. In: Vossen G, Long DDE, Yu JX (eds) Proceedings of the 10th international conference on Web information systems engineering (WISE 2009), Poznan, Poland, 5–7 October 2009. Lecture notes in computer science, vol 5802. Springer, Berlin, pp 11–12
19. Bernstein PA, Melnik S, Petropoulos M, Quix C (2004) Industrial-strength schema matching. SIGMOD Rec 33(4):38–43
20. Bertossi LE, Chomicki J (2003) Query answering in inconsistent databases. In: Chomicki J, van der Meyden R, Saake G (eds) Logics for emerging applications of databases. Springer, Berlin, pp 43–83
21. Bleiholder J, Draba K, Naumann F (2007) Fusem – exploring different semantics of data fusion. In: Koch C, Gehrke J, Garofalakis MN, Srivastava D, Aberer K, Deshpande A, Florescu D, Chan CY, Ganti V, Kanne CC, Klas W, Neuhold EJ (eds) VLDB. ACM, New York, pp 1350–1353
22. Bleiholder J, Naumann F (2008) Data fusion. ACM Comput Surv 41(1):1–41
23. Bressan S, Goh CH, Levina N, Madnick SE, Shah A, Siegel M (2000) Context knowledge representation and reasoning in the context interchange system. Appl Intell 13(2):165–180
24. Calì A, Calvanese D, Giacomo GD, Lenzerini M (2002) Data integration under integrity constraints. In: Proceedings of the 14th international conference on advanced information systems engineering (CAiSE '02). Springer, London, pp 262–279
25. Calì A, Lembo D, Rosati R (2003) Query rewriting and answering under constraints in data integration systems. In: Gottlob G, Walsh T (eds) Proceedings of the international joint conference on artificial intelligence. Morgan Kaufmann, pp 16–21
26. Calvanese D, Giacomo GD, Lembo D, Lenzerini M, Rosati R (2004) What to ask to a peer: ontology-based query reformulation. In: Dubois D, Welty CA, Williams MA (eds) Principles of Knowledge Representation and Reasoning. Proceedings of the Nineth International Conference (KR2004), Whistler, Canada, June 2–4 2004, AAAi Press, Menlo Park, pp 469–478
27. Castano S, Ferrara A, Lorusso D, Montanelli S (2008) On the ontology instance matching problem. In: DEXA workshops. IEEE Computer Society, Washington, DC, pp 180–184

28. Chaudhuri S, Ganjam K, Ganti V, Motwani R (2003) Robust and efficient fuzzy match for online data cleaning. In: SIGMOD conference, pp 313–324
29. Chen K, Madhavan J, Halevy AY (2009) Exploring schema repositories with schemr. In: Proceedings of the ACM SIGMOD international conference on management of data (SIGMOD 2009), Providence, RI, 29 June–2 July 2009. ACM, New York, pp 1095–1098
30. Crescenzi V, Mecca G, Merialdo P (2001) Automatic web information extraction in the roadrunner system. In: Arisawa H, Kambayashi Y, Kumar V, Mayr HC, Hunt I (eds) ER (workshops). Lecture notes in computer science, vol 2465. Springer, Berlin, pp 264–277
31. Euzenat J, Shvaiko P (2007) Ontology matching. Springer, Heidelberg
32. Fagin R, Haas LM, Hernández MA, Miller RJ, Popa L, Velegrakis Y (2009) Clio: schema mapping creation and data exchange. In: Borgida A, Chaudhri VK, Giorgini P, Yu ESK (eds) Conceptual modeling: foundations and applications. Lecture notes in computer science, vol 5600. Springer, Berlin, pp 198–236
33. Fagin R, Kolaitis PG, Miller RJ, Popa L (2005) Data exchange: semantics and query answering. Theor Comput Sci 336(1):89–124
34. Geist I (2004) Index-based keyword search in mediator systems. In: Lindner W, Mesiti M, Türker C, Tzitzikas Y, Vakali A (eds) EDBT workshops. Lecture notes in computer science, vol 3268. Springer, Berlin, pp 24–33
35. Giunchiglia F, Yatskevich M, Shvaiko P (2007) Semantic matching: algorithms and implementation. J Data Semant 9:1–38
36. Gottlob G, Koch C, Baumgartner R, Herzog M, Flesca S (2004) The lixto data extraction project – back and forth between theory and practice. In: Deutsch A (ed) PODS. ACM, New York, pp 1–12
37. Greco G, Greco S, Zumpano E (2003) A logical framework for querying and repairing inconsistent databases. IEEE Trans Knowl Data Eng 15(6):1389–1408
38. Guerra F, Bergamaschi S, Orsini M, Sala A, Sartori C (2009) Keymantic: a keyword-based search engine using structural knowledge. In: Cordeiro J, Filipe J (eds) ICEIS, vol 1, pp 241–246
39. Halevy AY (2001) Answering queries using views: a survey. VLDB J 10(4):270–294
40. Halevy AY, Ives ZG, Madhavan J, Mork P, Suciu D, Tatarinov I (2004) The piazza peer data management system. IEEE Trans Knowl Data Eng 16(7):787–798
41. Hammer J, Stonebraker M, Topsakal O (2005) Thalia: test harness for the assessment of legacy information integration approaches. In: ICDE, pp 485–486
42. Heimbigner D, McLeod D (1985) A federated architecture for information management. ACM Trans Inf Syst 3(3):253–278
43. Hull R (1997) Managing semantic heterogeneity in databases: a theoretical perspective. In: PODS, pp 51–61
44. Inmon WH (1992) Building the data warehouse. QED Information Sciences, Wellesley
45. Klein MCA, Fensel D, Kiryakov A, Ognyanov D (2002) Ontology versioning and change detection on the web. In: Gómez-Pérez A, Benjamins VR (eds) EKAW. Lecture notes in computer science, vol 2473. Springer, Berlin, pp 197–212
46. Köpcke H, Rahm E (2010) Frameworks for entity matching: a comparison. Data Knowl Eng 69(2):197–210
47. Laender AHF, Ribeiro-Neto BA, da Silva AS (2002) Debye – data extraction by example. Data Knowl Eng 40(2):121–154
48. Lenzerini M (2002) Data integration: a theoretical perspective. In: Popa L (ed) PODS. ACM, New York, pp 233–246
49. Levy AY, Rajaraman A, Ordille JJ (1996) Querying heterogeneous information sources using source descriptions. In: Vijayaraman Tm, Buchmann AP, Mohan C, Sarda NL (eds) VLDB. Morgan Kaufmann, San Francisco, pp 251–262
50. Li C, Yerneni R, Vassalos V, Garcia-Molina H, Papakonstantinou Y, Ullman JD, Valiveti M (1998) Capability based mediation in tsimmis. In: Proceedings of the ACM SIGMOD international conference on management of data (SIGMOD 1998), 2–4 June 1998, Seattle. ACM Press, New York, pp 564–566

51. Lin J, Mendelzon AO (1998) Merging databases under constraints. Int J Cooperative Inf Syst 7(1):55–76
52. Ludäscher B, Himmeröder R, Lausen G, May W, Schlepphorst C (1998) Managing semistructured data with florid: a deductive object-oriented perspective. Inf Syst 23(8):589–613
53. Madhavan J, Bernstein PA, Doan A, Halevy AY (2005) Corpus-based schema matching. In: ICDE, pp 57–68
54. Madhavan J, Cohen S, Dong XL, Halevy AY, Jeffery SR, Ko D, Yu C (2007) Web-scale data integration: you can afford to pay as you go. In: CIDR, pp 342–350. www.crdrdb.org
55. Mecca G, Papotti P, Raunich S (2009) Core schema mappings. In: Proceedings of the ACM SIGMOD international conference on management of data (SIGMOD 2009), Providence, RI, 29 June–2 July 2009. ACM, New York, pp 655–668
56. Melnik S, Garcia-Molina H, Rahm E (2002) Similarity flooding: A versatile graph matching algorithm and its application to schema matching. In: ICDE, pp 117–128. IEEE Computer Society, Washington, DC
57. Mena E, Illarramendi A, Kashyap V, Sheth AP (2000) Observer: an approach for query processing in global information systems based on interoperation across pre-existing ontologies. Distrib Parallel Databases 8(2):223–271
58. Miller GA (1995) Wordnet: a lexical database for english. Commun ACM 38(11):39–41. http://doi.acm.org/10.1145/219717.219748
59. Miller RJ (1998) Using schematically heterogeneous structures. In: Proceedings of the ACM SIGMOD international conference on management of data (SIGMOD 1998), 2–4 June 1998, Seattle. ACM Press, New York, pp 189–200
60. Myllymaki J (2002) Effective web data extraction with standard xml technologies. Comput Netw 39(5):635–644
61. Naumann F, Bilke A, Bleiholder J, Weis M (2006) Data fusion in three steps: resolving schema, tuple, and value inconsistencies. IEEE Data Eng Bull 29(2):21–31
62. Naumann F, Freytag JC, Leser U (2004) Completeness of integrated information sources. Inf Syst 29(7):583–615
63. Naumann F, Häussler M (2002) Declarative data merging with conflict resolution. In: Fisher C, Davidson BN (eds) IQ, pp 212–224. MIT, Cambridge
64. Noy NF (2004) Semantic integration: a survey of ontology-based approaches. SIGMOD Rec 33(4):65–70
65. Noy NF, Doan A, Halevy AY (2005) Semantic integration. AI Mag 26(1):7–10
66. Po L, Sorrentino S, Bergamaschi S, Beneventano D (2009) Lexical knowledge extraction: an effective approach to schema and ontology matching. In: European conference on knowledge management (ECKM 2009), 3–4 September 2009, Vicenza, Italy
67. Popa L, Velegrakis Y, Miller RJ, Hernández MA, Fagin R (2002) Translating web data. In: VLDB. Morgan Kaufmann, San Francisco, pp 598–609
68. Pottinger R, Bernstein PA (2002) Creating a mediated schema based on initial correspondences. IEEE Data Eng Bull 25(3):26–31
69. Pottinger R, Bernstein PA (2008) Schema merging and mapping creation for relational sources. In: Kemper A, Valduriez P, Mouaddib N, Teubner J, Bouzeghoub M, Markl V, Amsaleg L, Manolescu I (eds) EDBT. ACM international conference proceeding series, vol 261. ACM, New York, pp 73–84
70. Rahm E, Bernstein PA (2001) A survey of approaches to automatic schema matching. VLDB J 10(4):334–350
71. Roth MT, Arya M, Haas LM, Carey MJ, Cody WF, Fagin R, Schwarz PM, II JT, Wimmers EL (eds) The garlic project. In: Jagadish HV, Mumick IS (eds) SIGMOD conference. ACM Press, New York, p 557
72. Roth MT, Schwarz PM (1997) Don't scrap it, wrap it! a wrapper architecture for legacy data sources. In: Jarke M, Carey MJ, Dittrich KR, Lochovsky FH, Loucopoulos P, Jeusfeld MA (eds) VLDB. Morgan Kaufmann, San Francisco, pp 266–275
73. Sahuguet A, Azavant F (2001) Building intelligent web applications using lightweight wrappers. Data Knowl Eng 36(3):283–316

74. Sarawagi S (2008) Information extraction. Found Trends Databases 1(3):261–377
75. Sattler KU, Geist I, Schallehn E (2005) Concept-based querying in mediator systems. VLDB J 14(1):97–111
76. Shafer G (1976) A mathematical theory of evidence. Princeton University Press, Princeton
77. Shvaiko P, Euzenat J (2008) Ten challenges for ontology matching. In: Meersman R, Tari Z (eds) OTM conferences (2). Lecture notes in computer science, vol 5332. Springer, Berlin, pp 1164–1182
78. Sorrentino S, Bergamaschi S, Alberto C (2009) Dealing with uncertainty in lexical annotation. In: Poster ER, Demo session 2009, in Special issue of Journal of Theoretical and Applied Informatics (Revista de Informatica Terica e Aplicada RITA) 2009. (An extended version of this paper has been submitted to the "Semantic Integration of Data, Multimedia, and Services" special issue of Information Systems Journal)
79. Sorrentino S, Bergamaschi S, Gawinecki M, Po L (2009) Schema normalization for improving schema matching. In: ER '09: Proceedings of the 28th international conference on conceptual modeling. Springer, Berlin, pp 280–293. [An extended version of this paper has been submitted to the ER special issue of Data and Knowledge Engineering (DKE) Journal]
80. Tejada S, Knoblock CA, Minton S (2001) Learning object identification rules for information integration. Inf Syst 26(8):607–633
81. Ullman JD (1997) Information integration using logical views. In: Afrati FN, Kolaitis PG (eds) ICDT. Lecture notes in computer science, vol 1186. Springer, Berlin, pp 19–40
82. Ullman JD, Garcia-Molina H, Widom J (2001) Database systems: the complete book. Prentice-Hall, Upper Saddle River
83. Vossen P (ed) (1998) EuroWordNet: a multilingual database with lexical semantic networks. Kluwer, Norwell
84. Wiederhold G (1992) Mediators in the architecture of future information systems. IEEE Comput 25(3):38–49
85. Wiederhold G (1993) Intelligent integration of information. In: Proceedings of the 1993 ACM SIGMOD international conference on management of data, Washington, DC, 26–28 May 1993. ACM Press, New York, pp 434–437

Chapter 15
Conceptual Modeling Foundations for a Web of Knowledge

David W. Embley, Stephen W. Liddle, and Deryle W. Lonsdale

Abstract The semantic web purports to be a web of knowledge that can answer our questions, help us reason about everyday problems as well as scientific endeavors, and service many of our wants and needs. Researchers and others expound various views about exactly what this means. Here we propose an answer with conceptual modeling as its foundation. We define a web of knowledge as a collection of interconnected knowledge bundles superimposed over a web of documents. Knowledge bundles are conceptual model instances augmented with facilities that provide for both extensional and intensional facts, for linking between knowledge bundles yielding a web of data, and for linking to an underlying document collection providing a means of authentication. We formally define both the component parts of these augmented conceptual models and their synergistic interconnections. As for practicalities, we discuss problems regarding the potentially high cost of constructing a web of knowledge and explain how they may be mitigated. We also discuss usage issues and show how untrained users can interact with and gain benefit from a web of knowledge.

15.1 Introduction

Ideas about the semantic web have been with us ever since Tim Berners-Lee published his book *Weaving the Web* [9], and his *Scientific American* article *The Semantic Web* [10] with Hendler and Lassila. They and others have continued to discuss these ideas in an effort to more fully explain the Semantic Web vision – its practicalities, successes, and challenges [1, 57]. The W3C Web site introduces the semantic web simply as "a web of data" [64].

David W. Embley, Stephen W. Liddle, Deryle W. Lonsdale
Brigham Young University, Provo, Utah 84602, USA, e-mail: embley@cs.byu.edu, e-mail: liddle@byu.edu, e-mail: lonz@byu.edu

D. W. Embley and B. Thalheim (eds), *Handbook of Conceptual Modeling.*
DOI 10.1007/978-3-642-15865-0, © Springer 2011

Many of these ideas hark back even to the days of Plato [48] and Aristotle [5] and the beginnings of philosophical discussions about ontology, epistemology, and logic. Here, we begin with this ancient view of semantics and show how it leads to a view of the semantic web rooted in conceptual modeling. In particular, we show how conceptual modeling can unify a view of these fundamental concepts and provide a practical way to realize them. Our intent is not to resolve questions about what the semantic web is, but rather to provide a practical view of one possible path toward realizing some of the benefits claimed by semantic web visionaries. We call our conceptual-modeling view of the semantic web a "web of knowledge" (a "WoK").

To motivate our vision of a WoK, consider the current web of pages, which contains a wealth of knowledge. Unfortunately, most of the knowledge is not encoded in a way that enables direct user query. We cannot, for example, directly google for a car that is a 2003 or newer selling for under 15 grand; or for the names of the parents of great-grandpa Schnitker; or for countries whose population will likely decrease by more than 10% in 50 years. A way to enable direct query for facts embedded in Web pages and facts implied by these stated facts is to annotate facts with respect to ontologies. Annotating facts implicitly populates these ontologies, turning them into a database over which structured queries can be executed. Annotation links also provide a form of provenance and authentication, allowing users to verify query results by checking original sources. Furthermore, facts and ontological concepts may appear in more than one populated ontology. Linking facts and ontological concepts across ontologies can provide navigation paths to explore additional, related knowledge. The web, with a superimposed layer of interlinked ontologies each annotating a myriad of facts from the underlying web, becomes a *web of knowledge*, a *WoK*.

Although this vision of a WoK is appealing, there are significant barriers preventing both its creation and its use. Ontology languages exist, with OWL being the de facto standard. RDF files can provide data for these ontologies and can also store annotation information linking data to facts in Web pages and linking equivalent information in RDF files to one another. The SPARQL query language is a standard for querying RDF data. SWRL rules can provide for reasoning. Thus, all constituent components for a WoK are W3C standards in common use, and they even all work together allowing for immediate WoK development and usage. Nevertheless, the barriers to creation and usage remain high and effectively prevent WoK deployment. The creation barrier is high because of the cost involved in developing OWL ontologies and annotating Web pages by linking RDF-encoded facts in Web pages to these OWL ontologies. The usage barrier is high because untrained users cannot write SPARQL queries and SWRL rules.

In this exposition, we show how conceptual modeling can enable a WoK – can provide a firm foundation for a WoK and ways to break through the barriers to WoK creation and usage. We begin in Sect. 15.2 by discussing a computational view of ontology, epistemology, and logic. We argue that conceptual models, augmented in a particular way, build nicely upon these philosophical ideas so as to enable a WoK. In Sect. 15.3 we formalize this foundation. The formalization leads to a clear understanding of what must be done to create a WoK and make it usable. We then discuss initiatives we have investigated to address these challenges and opportunities – for construction in Sect. 15.4 and for usage in Sect. 15.5. We conclude in Sect. 15.6.

15.2 WoK Conceptualization

To think about constructing and using a WoK, we first ask some fundamental questions: What are data? What are facts? What is knowledge? How does one reason and know? Philosophers have pursued answers to these questions for millennia; and although we do not pretend to be able to contribute to philosophy, we can use philosophers' ideas about ontology, epistemology, and logic to guide us in building and using a WoK.

- *Ontology* is the study of existence. It asks: "What exists?" In our quest to build a WoK, we must find computational solutions to the question: "What concepts, relationships, and constraints exist?" We answer computationally, saying that we can declare a formal conceptual model for some domain of knowledge that captures the relevant concepts along with the relationships among these concepts and the constraints over these concepts and relationships.[1]
- *Epistemology* is the study of the nature of knowledge. It asks: "What is knowledge?" and "How is knowledge acquired?" To build a WoK, we provide computational answers to "What is digitally stored knowledge?" and "How do raw data become algorithmically accessible knowledge?" Our answer is to turn raw data into knowledge by populating conceptual models – by embedding facts in the concepts and relationships in accord with constraints. We further follow Plato's lead in wanting our knowledge to be justified [48], and thus we provide (1) annotation links that connect facts embedded in ontologies to sources from which they are extracted and (2) data and concept "same-as" connections that link objects and concepts across populated ontologies.
- *Logic* comprises principles and criteria of valid inference. It asks: "What is known?" and "What can be inferred?" In the computational context of a WoK, it can answer the question "What are the known facts, both given and implied?" We ground our conceptual model in a description logic – a decidable fragment of first-order logic [12]. To make this logic practical for nonlogicians, we must and do add a query generator whose input consists of ordinary free-form textual expressions or ordinary fill-in-the-blank query forms. Both query modes fundamentally depend on conceptual-model-based ontologies to convert free-form and form-based queries to structured queries. Justification of query results relies on tracing annotation links back to source data and on following reasoning chains.

---

[1] Purists argue that conceptual models are not ontologies [39, 40, 58]. We agree that when conceptual models play their traditional role in aiding in database schema design, they typically are not ontologies. But when they are used to answer "What exists?" and thus when they formally capture the concepts, relationships, and constraints that exist in a domain, they are ontologies.

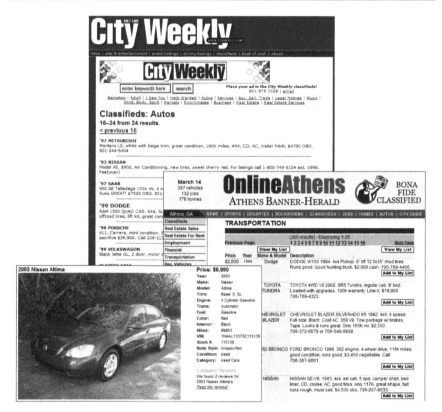

Fig. 15.1 Sample car ad Web pages

To illustrate these ideas, we give some examples. Suppose we wish to find a used car to purchase. We might pose this query: "Find me a red Nissan for under $5000, a 1990 or newer with less than 100 K miles on it," or this query: "I'd like a Japanese-made car for under 15 grand." Figure 15.1 shows some Web pages with cars for sale that satisfy these queries. Two of the three Nissans satisfy the first query, and all the Nissans and the Mitsubishi, but not the Toyota, satisfy the second query. Unfortunately, however, search engines do not access the facts within these ads in the way we would wish to find these cars. Our approach of superimposing a WoK over a web of pages makes these facts visible from outside the page and directly accessible to query engines (as opposed to search engines).

To make this work, we need an ontology for car ads. Figure 15.2 shows an example. The ontology is a conceptual model. It consists of object sets that are either lexical (dashed boxes in Fig. 15.2) or nonlexical (solid boxes). Instances in lexical object sets are strings of characters such as "Nissan" or "1990," whereas instances in nonlexical object sets are object identifiers that stand for real-world objects – Car_{73} and Car_{1194}, for example, identify specific cars. Relationship sets in the conceptual model are lines connecting object sets. Min–max participation constraints impose

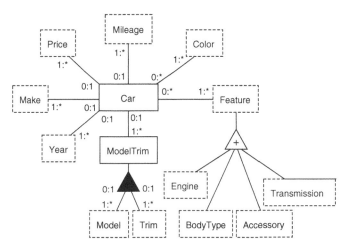

Fig. 15.2 Car ad ontology

restrictions on the relationship sets: a car described in a car ad can have zero or more features (*0:**), but at most one make (*0:1*). Ontologies for our WoK vision also support hypernym–hyponym is-a hierarchies and holonym–meronym part-of hierarchies. A white triangle denotes an is-a hierarchy, so that, for example, a *BodyType* is-a *Feature* in Fig. 15.2. The plus symbol (+) in the triangle specifies a disjointness constraint among the specializations; it is also possible to declare union constraints (∪) specifying that a generalization object set is a union of its specialization object sets and partition constraints (⊎) specifying that specialization object sets partition their generalization. A black triangle denotes a part-of hierarchy. In Fig. 15.2, for example, a model such as "Accord" aggregated with a trim specification such as "LX" constitutes the concept "Accord LX," which has some *ModelTrim* object identifier (e.g., $ModelTrim_{39}$).

Whereas an ontology tells us what kind of knowledge exists in our domain of interest, epistemological specifications tell us what the knowledge is and how it is acquired. For our WoK vision, populating an ontology yields knowledge. We can populate the car-ad ontology in Fig. 15.2 with facts derived from car ads. Assuming Car_{73} denotes the Nissan Altima pictured in Fig. 15.1, some of the object-set facts are *Car(Car₇₃)*, *Year(2003)*, and *Transmission("Automatic")*, and some of the relationship facts are *CarYear(Car₇₃, 2003)* and *CarFeature(Car₇₃, "Automatic")*.

The way we intend to acquire knowledge in our WoK vision is particularly interesting. Although possible to simply encode by hand, this is far too labor intensive and does not scale. We must find ways to automatically identify facts and associate them with ontologies. Sometimes information is structured in such a way that it is possible to reverse engineer it into an ontology; sometimes it is possible to resort to available outside knowledge sources to align semistructured information with an ontology; but sometimes the information yields to neither of these techniques. For this latter case, we augment the ontologies themselves so that they are capable of recognizing, annotating, and extracting relevant facts with respect to their ontologi-

Price
internal representation: Integer
external representation: \\$[1-9]\d{0,2},?\d{3} | \d?\d [Gg]rand | ...
context keywords: price|asking|obo|neg(\.|otiable)| ...

...

LessThan(p1: Price, p2: Price) **returns** (Boolean)
context keywords: (less than | < | under | ...)\s*{p2} | ...

...

Make

...

external representation: CarMake.lexicon

...

Fig. 15.3 Data frames

cal descriptions. We call these augmented ontologies *extraction ontologies* because they are capable of locating and extracting facts from any kind of document, unstructured as well as semistructured and structured.

The augmentation that turns an ontology into an extraction ontology is a data frame [30]. Data frames are linguistically grounded abstract data types – they encapsulate everything we wish to know about categorized data instances including their internal and external representations and their applicable operations. Linguistic grounding consists of providing recognizers for instances of object and relationship sets. Figure 15.3 shows examples of the kind of recognizers we currently use in our WoK vision, but any kind of information extractor [54] is possible, e.g., machine-learned wrappers (e.g., [66]), NLP-based recognition techniques (e.g., [35]), and elaborate handcrafted rules (e.g., [38, 41]). The recognizers in Fig. 15.3 are of two types – regular expressions and lexicons – which operate independently or together. The regular expression for the external representation of *Price* in Fig. 15.3 recognizes price instances such as "$23,900" and "15 grand." The external-representation recognizer for *Make*, on the other hand, is a lexicon that lists all the makes of cars, including their alternate spellings and abbreviations. Context keywords such as *price* and *asking* in Fig. 15.3 help disambiguate instances that may be recognized for more than one concept (e.g., MSRP price vs. asking price). Operators also have recognizers. Keywords such as "less than," "<," and "under" in Fig. 15.3 indicate the applicability of the *LessThan* operator. A price instance following these keywords becomes the second parameter p_2 in the operation, the car price being assumed as the first.

Justification of captured knowledge is a natural consequence of acquiring and semantically annotating knowledge. When we reverse engineer structured knowledge into a fact-filled ontology, align facts in a knowledge source with an ontology, or extract facts from data-rich documents, the WoK system keeps track of the source of each fact. Later, when someone queries for these facts, the WoK system provides, in addition to the standard query results, a cached page with the fact instances highlighted. For example, if we query for a red Nissan Altima for under 15 grand, as part of the answer the WoK system can retrieve the cached page of the Altima in Fig. 15.1 and display it with the strings *Red*, *Nissan*, *Altima*, and *$6,990* highlighted.

Besides enabling fact recognition in source documents, extraction ontologies also enable free-form query processing. For example, a WoK system with the ontology in Fig. 15.1 augmented with the data-frame recognizers in Fig. 15.3 can interpret and process the query: "Find me a red Nissan Altima for under 15 grand." The system associates the recognized instances "red," "Nissan," "Altima," and "15 grand," respectively, with the object sets *Color*, *Make*, *Model*, and *Price*, and it associates "under" with the *LessThan* operator in the *Price* data frame and the price "15 grand" with the operator's parameter *p2*. Generating a formal select-project-join query from these recognized associations is straightforward: do outer join over the ontology's structure, select based on the identified constants and Boolean operations, and project on the mentioned object sets.

Retrieving inferred facts is more complex. To illustrate, consider processing the query "I'd like a Japanese-made car for under 15 grand." For this query the WoK system needs a way to determine which cars are Japanese. Suppose we have a second ontology about car manufacturers such as the one in Fig. 15.4. Observe that the concept *Make* in Fig. 15.1 is semantically the same as the concept *Make* in Fig. 15.4. Connecting these concepts with a between-ontologies *same-as* link is an example of the interconnecting links in the weblike structure constituting a WoK. With these two ontologies and the interconnecting link, we now have the information we need to declare inference rules that can reason about a car being Japanese-made. A car in a car ad that has a make produced by a manufacturer whose headquarters is in Japan is a Japanese-made car.

Next observe that populated ontologies are in reality first-order-language theories of predicate calculus. Each object set S is a one-place predicate $S(x)$. Each n-ary relationship set R is an n-place predicate, $R(x_1, \ldots, x_n)$. The constraints of our conceptual-modeling language are all expressible as closed well-formed formulas of predicate calculus. Populating an ontology provides the ground facts for a first-order theory. When all the constraints hold for a populated ontology, we have a model of the first-order theory, and we can reason over the model with logic languages, appropriately restricted to make them decidable and tractable.

For our query about Japanese-made cars, suppose we have the following logic rule (expressed in Datalog-like syntax) for the car manufacturer ontology:

```
JapaneseMake(x) :- Make(x), CarManufacturerMake(y, x),
    CarManufacturerHeadquarters(y, z),
    CountryHeadquarters('Japan', z).
```

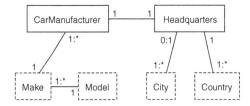

Fig. 15.4 Car manufacturer ontology

Similar to linguistically grounding operators in our ontologies, we can linguistically ground logic rules. Thus, the phrase "Japanese-made car" should indicate that this rule applies. Now, when a user poses a query for Japanese-made cars for under 15 grand, the WoK system recognizes that the two ontologies apply and generates the following formal query over the two theories *CarAd* and *CarManuf*:

```
CarAd.Car(x) :- CarAd.CarPrice(x, y),
    CarAd.LessThan(y, 15000), CarAd.CarMake(x, z),
    CarManuf.JapaneseMake(z).
```

Here, the *same-as* link lets us seamlessly navigate among populated ontologies in a WoK. As an aside, note the conversion of "15 grand" to the integer 15000. As indicated in the *Price* data frame in Fig. 15.3, the type for the internal representation is *integer*. As the WoK system extracts data for an ontology, it also converts the data to declared internal representations.

By way of summary for this informal introduction to our WoK vision, we see a WoK consisting of logic theories, interconnected and superimposed over web documents. Logic theories are populated ontologies. From an epistemological point of view, populated ontologies are extensional knowledge. And with the addition of inference rules, populated ontologies also embody intensional knowledge.

15.3 WoK Formalization

We base our foundational conceptualization for a WoK on the conceptual modeling language OSM (Object-oriented Systems Modeling) [27]. OSM, however, simply provides a graphical representation of a first-order-logic language. Here we restrict OSM to be decidable, yet powerful enough to represent desired ontological concepts and constraints. We call our restriction *OSM-O*, short for *OSM-Ontology*. We thus base our foundational conceptualization directly on an appropriate restriction of first-order logic. This WoK foundation should be no surprise since it is the basis for modern information systems and has been the basis for formalizing information since the days of Aristotle [5].

Definition 15.1. *OSM-O* is a triple (O, R, C):

- O is a set of object sets; each is a one-place predicate; and each predicate has a *lexical* or a *nonlexical* designation.
- R is a set of n-ary relationship sets ($n \geq 2$); each is an n-place predicate.
- C is a set of constraints:

  - Referential integrity: $\forall x_1 \ldots \forall x_n (R(x_1, \ldots, x_n) \Rightarrow S_1(x_1) \wedge \ldots \wedge S_n(x_n)$ for each n-ary relationship set R connecting object sets $S_1, \ldots, S_n$.
  - Participation constraint *min:max* cardinality: for every connection of an object set S to an n-ary relationship set R, $\forall x_i (S(x_i) \Rightarrow \exists^{\geq min} < x_1, \ldots, x_{i-1}, x_{i+1}, \ldots, x_n > (R(x_1, \ldots, x_n)))$ if $min > 0$, and $\forall x_i (S(x_i) \Rightarrow \exists^{\leq max} < x_1,$

$\ldots, x_{i-1}, x_{i+1}, \ldots, x_n > (R(x_1, \ldots, x_n)))$ if *max* is not * (the symbol denoting an unbounded maximum).

- Generalization/specialization: $\forall x(S_1(x) \vee \ldots \vee S_n(x) \Rightarrow G(x))$ for each generalization object set G of specialization object sets $S_1, \ldots, S_n$ in a hypernym–hyponym is-a hierarchy. In addition, $\forall x(S_i(x) \Rightarrow \neg S_j(x))$ for $1 \leq i, j \leq n$ and $i \neq j$ if the specialization object sets are disjoint and $\forall x(G(x) \Rightarrow S_1(x) \vee \ldots \vee S_n(x))$ if the generalization object set is complete is a union of the specialization object sets.
- Aggregation: holonym–meronym relationship sets grouped as an aggregation in an is-part-of hierarchy. □

Example 15.1. Figure 15.2 shows an OSM-O model instance. *Car(x)* and *Model-Trim(x)* are the one-place predicates for the two nonlexical object sets. *Mileage(x)* and *Engine(x)* are two of the one-place predicates for the lexical object sets. *CarYear(x, y)* is a two-place predicate for the relationship set connecting *Car* and *Year*. For readability, we may provide a more descriptive name for a relationship set so long as the naming phrase for the relationship set includes the names of its object sets. We then typically use infix notation and write, for example, *Car(x)hasYear(y)* for the *CarYear(x, y)* relationship set or *Car(x)costsPrice(y)* for the *CarPrice(x, y)* relationship set. One of the referential integrity constraints is $\forall x \forall y(CarYear(x, y) \Rightarrow Car(x) \wedge Year(y))$. One of the participation constraints is $\forall x(Car(x) \Rightarrow \exists^{\leq 1} y(CarYear(x, y)))$, where we drop the tuple-grouping angle brackets for the common case of only one variable being existentially quantified. The formula $\forall x(Engine(x) \vee BodyType(x) \vee Accessory(x) \vee Transmission(x) \Rightarrow Feature(x))$ defines the generalization/specialization; its disjointness constraint includes $\forall x(Engine(x) \Rightarrow \neg BodyType(x))$ as one of its terms. An aggregation groups several relationship sets denoting subparts of superparts: *Model(x)isSubpartOfModelTrim(y)* and *Trim(x)isSubpartOfModelTrim(y)* are the two relationship sets of the aggregation in Fig. 15.2; their inverses are, respectively, *ModelTrim(x)isSuperpartOfTrim(y)* and *ModelTrim(x)isSuperpartOfModel(y)*. Although graphical in appearance, an OSM-O diagram is merely a two-dimensional rendition of predicates and closed formulas as defined in Definition 15.1. □

Definition 15.2. Let $M = (O, R, C)$ be an OSM-O model instance. Let I be an interpretation for M that has a domain $D = L_{\text{ID}} \cup O_{\text{ID}}$, where $L_{\text{ID}} \cap O_{\text{ID}} = \emptyset$, and a declaration of **True** or **False** for each valid instantiation of each predicate in $O \cup R$. For predicates in O, valid instantiations require lexical predicates to be instantiated with values in L_{ID} and nonlexical predicates to be instantiated with values in O_{ID}. For predicates in R, valid instantiations require each value v to be lexical or nonlexical according to whether the connected object set for v is lexical or nonlexical, respectively. If all the constraints of C hold, I is a *model* of M, which we call a *valid interpretation* of M (to avoid an ambiguous use of the word "model" when also discussing conceptual models). An instantiated **True** predicate for a valid interpretation is a *fact*. □

Example 15.2. A valid interpretation of the OSM-O model instance in Fig. 15.2 contains facts about cars. A valid interpretation might include the facts *Car*(*Car*$_3$), *Year*(2003), *CarYear*(*Car*$_3$, 2003), *Model*("Accord"), *Trim*("LX"), *ModelTrim*(*ModelTrim*$_{17}$), *CarModelTrim*(*Car*$_3$, *ModelTrim*$_{17}$), and *Trim*("*LX*")*isPartOfModelTrim*(*ModelTrim*$_{17}$). The object sets *Car* and *Model-Trim*, being nonlexical, have object identifiers for their domain-value substitutions (which we denote by object-set names with a subscript). The constraint $\forall x\,(Car(x) \Rightarrow \exists^{\leq 1} y(CarYear(x, y)))$ holds for *Car*(*Car*$_3$) if *CarYear*(*Car*$_3$, 2003) is the only car-year pair that exists with *Car*$_3$ as its first element. $\square$

Similar to the work by Buitelaar et al. [7], we now show how to linguistically ground OSM-O. Linguistically grounding OSM-O turns OSM-O model instances into *OSM-Extraction-Ontology* model instances (*OSM-EO* model instances). We begin by defining an ordinary abstract data type for each object set and relationship set. We then add linguistic recognizers for instance values, operators, operator parameters, and relationships.

Definition 15.3. An *abstract data type* is a pair (V, O), where V is a set of values and O is a set of operations. $\square$

Definition 15.4. A *data frame* is an abstract data type augmented as follows:

1. The data frame has a name N designating the set of values V, and it may have a list of synonyms for N.
2. The value set V has instance recognizers that identify lexical patterns denoting values in V.
3. For a lexical object set, the operator set O includes input operators to convert identified instances to an internal representation and output operators to convert the internal representation of instances to displayable strings.
4. An operation o in O may have a recognizer that identifies lexical patterns in text that indicate that o applies. Further, the recognizer identifies lexical patterns that, along with instance recognizers, identify parameters for o. $\square$

Example 15.3. In Fig. 15.3 the value set V for the *Price* data frame is of the type *Integer*. Its recognizer is a potentially lengthy list of regular expressions augmented by keywords. Its operation set O includes the *LessThan* operator and potentially has many more operations. The *LessThan* operator has keyword phrases that indicate its applicability as well as how to identify its parameters. $\square$

For relationship sets, the definition of a data frame does not change, but a typical view of the definition shifts as we allow value sets to be n-tuples of values rather than scalar values. Further, like recognizers for operators, they rely on instance recognizers from the data frames of their connected object sets.

Example 15.4. Suppose the *Car* object set in Fig. 15.2 has a relationship set to a *Person* object set. The relationship-set data frame may have recognizers for any one of several possible relationships such as {*Person*} *is selling* {*Car*}, {*Person*} *posted* {*Car*} *ad*, or {*Person*} *is inquiring about* {*Car*}. Here, the braces enclose references to data frames for the nonlexical object sets *Car* and *Person*. $\square$

As is standard, implementations of abstract data types are hidden, and we hide implementations for data frames as well. Similar to data independence in database systems, this approach accommodates any implementation. In particular, it allows for new and better recognizers, which we can draw from the large body of work devoted to information extraction [54].

Definition 15.5. If M is an OSM-O model instance with a data frame for each object set and relationship set, M is an *OSM-EO* model instance. □

An OSM-EO model instance is linguistically grounded in the sense that it can both "read" and "write" in some natural language. To "read" means to be able to recognize facts in natural language text and to extract fact instances with respect to the ontology in the OSM-EO model instance. To "write" means to display fact instances so that they are human-readable.

How well a particular OSM-EO model instance can "read" and "write" makes a difference in how well it performs. Our experience is that OSM-EO model instances can "read" some documents well (over 95% precision and recall [22]), but it is clear that opportunities abound for further research and development. Writing human-understandable descriptions is less difficult to achieve – just select any one of the phrases for each object set and relationship set [e.g., *Person(Person$_{17}$) is selling Car(Car$_{734}$)*, *Car(Car$_{734}$) has Make(Honda)*]. Making written descriptions more pleasing, of course, is more difficult.

Continuing in our quest to define the components of our WoK vision, we now define its "knowledge," and we explain how we see its knowledge being justified and how we envision its knowledge components being interconnected.

Definition 15.6. The collection of facts in an OSM-O model instance constitutes its *extensional knowledge*. The collection of implied facts derived from the extensional knowledge by inference rules[2] constitutes its *intensional knowledge*. The extensional and intensional knowledge together constitute the *knowledge* of the OSM-O model instance. □

Although this view of knowledge is common in computing, Plato, and those who follow his line of thought, also demand of knowledge that it be a "justified true belief" [48]. "Knowledge" without some sort of truth authentication can be unsupported and even misleading. For our vision of a WoK, we attempt to establish truth via provenance and authentication. When an extraction ontology extracts a fact from a source document, it retains a link to the fact; and when a query answer requires reasoning over rules, the system records the reasoning chain. Users can ask to see fact sources and rule chains, and in this way they can authenticate facts and reasoning the way we usually do – by checking sources and fact-derivation rules.

Definition 15.7. A *knowledge bundle* (*KB*) is a 5-tuple (O, E, S, I, R), where O is an OSM-O model instance, E is an OSM-EO instance whose OSM-O instance is

---

[2] As the work on logic and particularly on description logics [12] continues to expand, we can take advantage of the work of this community (e.g., [16, 17, 53]) to employ better and more powerful reasoning engines.

O, S is a set of source documents from which facts for E are extracted, I is a valid interpretation for O whose facts are extracted from the documents in S, and R is a set of inference rules. $\square$

Finally, to make the envisioned WoK truly a *web* of knowledge, we interconnect knowledge bundles (KBs). Facts about the same object may appear in more than one KB. We can directly connect these objects so that users may navigate among KBs and obtain additional information about an object. Concepts in more than one KB may also be essentially the same as the concept *Make*, and also the concept *Model*, in their respective ontologies in Figs. 15.2 and 15.4. We also connect concepts across ontologies to provide additional navigation paths.

Definition 15.8. A *Web of Knowledge* (*WoK*) is a collection of knowledge bundles interconnected with binary links, $< x, y >$, of two types: (1) *object identity:* nonlexical object identifier x in knowledge bundle B_1 refers to the same real-world object as nonlexical object identifier y in knowledge bundle B_2. (2) *Object-set identity:* object set x in knowledge bundle B_1 designates the same kind of real-world objects as object set y in knowledge bundle B_2. $\square$

15.4 WoK Construction

To construct a WoK, we must be able to construct a knowledge bundle (KB), and we must be able to establish links among KBs. We can construct KBs and establish links among them by hand (and this should always be an option). However, scaling WoK construction demands semiautomatic procedures, with much of the construction burden placed on the system – all of it when possible. Our KB construction tools transform, or aid in transforming, source information into KB components. For links among KBs we apply record-linkage and schema-mapping tools.

Definition 15.9. A *transformation* is a 4-tuple (R, S, T, Σ), where R is a set of resources, S is the source conceptualization, T is the target conceptualization for an S-to-T transformation, and Σ is a set of source-to-target transformation statements. $\square$

Definition 15.9 leaves several of its components open – to take on specific meanings in a variety of KB building tools. The "set of resources" is undefined, but we intend this to mean semantic resources such as WordNet and a data-frame library. "Target conceptualizations" are KBs or KB components. "Source conceptualizations" depend on sources whose fact conceptualizations can be formal, semiformal, or informal. "Source-to-target transformation statements" can be declarative or procedural and can be written in a variety of formal languages.

To the extent possible, we want our transformations to preserve the information and constraints in source documents and repositories. When sources are formalized as predicate calculus or in a formalization equivalent to predicate calculus, we can guarantee the preservation information and constraints. We identify the predicates and the facts for the predicates (thus preserving information) and formulate a closed well-formed formula for each constraint (thus preserving constraints). If the source interpretation is valid, the target interpretation will be valid as well. When sources are informal with respect to predicate calculus, the predicates, facts for the predicates, and constraints are implicit. The challenge is nevertheless to discover and extract them.

Definition 15.10. Let S be a predicate calculus theory with a valid interpretation, and let T be a populated OSM-O model instance constructed from S by a transformation t. Transformation t *preserves information* if there exists a procedure to compute S from T. Let C_S be the closed, well-formed formulas of S, and let C_T be the closed, well-formed formulas of T. Transformation t *preserves constraints* if $C_T \Rightarrow C_S$. $\square$

Our goal has been and is to successfully develop automatic and good semiautomatic transformations over a broad spectrum of documents for a variety of ontological contexts. For sources whose facts and constraints over these facts have formal declarations, transformations should preserve all facts and constraints. For sources whose facts and constraints are implicit, we seek to identify the facts and constraints that are applicable to a given ontology, or, in the absence of a given ontology, we seek to determine and populate the implicit ontology based on the documents' data and on applicable external knowledge resources.

Longstanding research endeavors can all contribute to various parts of WoK construction. These include reverse engineering [2], table and form understanding [20, 23], ontology learning [18], ontology alignment [31], data integration [13, 42, 50], and record linkage [24]. In Sects. 15.4.1–15.4.4 we explain how we have taken advantage of some of this work for WoK construction. In Sect. 15.4.1 we show how to reverse engineer XML data repositories into KBs. In Sect. 15.4.2 we describe how we can interpret collections of nested tables in hidden Web pages and thus turn the collection into a KB. In Sect. 15.4.3 we explain how we integrate a group of semantically overlapping tables to create a KB. And in Sect. 15.4.4 we give a way via form creation and information harvesting to generate KBs. Finding and implementing other ways to construct WoK components are interesting and worthwhile research endeavors.

15.4.1 Construction via XML Reverse Engineering

We have designed a conceptual model for XML, called C-XML (Conceptual XML). C-XML adds a few XML-specific concepts to OSM-O, including, in particular, a sequencing construct and a choice construct. Being formally defined as templates over OSM-O constructs, however, these additions remain within the purview of OSM-O.

Reverse engineering an XML schema to C-XML effectively defines a mapping to OSM-O for all XML documents complying with the XML schema [3]. The basic translation strategies for mapping XML Schema to C-XML are straightforward, although some parts of the translation require some sophisticated manipulation. In the translation, elements and attributes become object sets. Elements that have simple types become lexical object sets, while elements that have complex types become nonlexical object sets. Attributes become lexical object sets since they always have a simple type. Built-in data types and simple data types for an element or an attribute in XML Schema are specified in the data frame associated with the object set representing the element or the attribute. XML parent–child connections among elements and XML element–attribute connections both become binary relationship sets in C-XML. The constraints *minOccurs* and *maxOccurs* translate directly to participation constraints in C-XML.

Unfortunately, not everything is straightforward. Translations for keys, extension, restriction, substitution groups, and mixed content are all quite interesting. The translation also involves a myriad of detail extending to over 40 pages in [3]. Although extensive, the translation details provide a constructive proof that the transformation from XML Schema to C-XML preserves both information and constraints.

The result of doing information- and constraint-preserving transformations of XML documents complying to an XML schema is a KB. Further, to the extent that we can automatically infer an XML schema specification directly from an XML document, we can also reverse engineer raw XML documents into populated C-XML model instances and thus into KBs.

15.4.2 Construction via Nested Table Interpretation

Table Interpretation with Sibling Tables (TISP) is a tool of ours that interprets tables in sibling pages [59]. To interpret a table is to properly associate table category labels with table data values. Using Fig. 15.5 as an example, we see that *Identification*, *Location*, and *Function* are labels for the large rectangular table. Inside the cell labeled *Identification* is another table with headers *IDs*, *NCBI KOGs*, *Species*, etc. Nested inside of this table are two more tables, the first starting with the label *CGC name* and the second starting with the label *Gene Model*. We associate labels with data values by observing the table structure. A cell in a table associates with its header label (or labels in the case of multidimensional tables). For nested tables, we trace the sequence of labels from the outermost label to the data cell. Thus, for example, the label for the value *F47G6.1* under *Sequence name* is *Identification.IDs.Sequence_name*.

Although automatic table interpretation can be complex, if we have another page, such as the one in Fig. 15.6, that has essentially the same structure, the system can usually obtain enough information to make automatic interpretation possible. We call pages that are from the same Web site and have similar structures *sibling pages*. The two pages in Figs. 15.5 and 15.6 are sibling pages. They have the same basic structure, with the same top banners that appear in all the pages from this Web site, with the same table title (*Gene Summary for* some particular gene), and

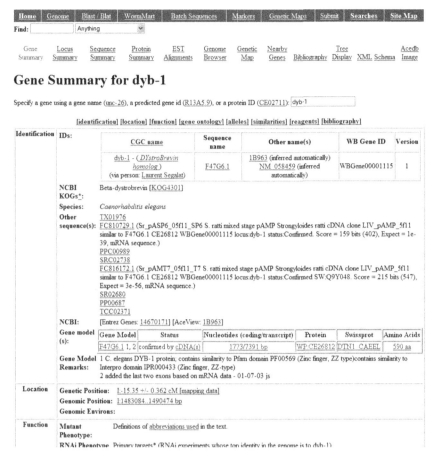

Fig. 15.5 Nested table from a molecular-biology Web page

a table that contains information about the gene. Corresponding tables in sibling pages are called *sibling tables*. If we compare the two large tables in the main part of the sibling pages, we can see that the first columns of each table are exactly the same. If we look at the cells under the *Identification* label in the two tables, both contain another table with two columns. In both cases, the first column contains the identical labels *IDs*, ..., *Remarks*, although the table in Fig. 15.6 has one additional label, *Notes*. Further, the tables under *Identification.IDs* also have identical header rows, and the tables under *Identification.Gene model(s)* have nearly identical header rows. The data values, however, vary considerably. Generally speaking, we can look for commonalities in sibling tables to find labels and look for variations to find data values.

Given that we can interpret a table – find labels and values and properly associate them – we can create a conceptualization of the table linking labels as metadata with values as instance data. This simple conceptualization may not always be best, but

| Home | Genome | Blast / Blat | WormMart | Batch Sequences | Markers | Genetic Maps | Submit | **Searches** | **Site Map** |

Find: [   ] [Anything ▼]

Gene Summary for cdk-4

Specify a gene using a gene name (unc-26), a predicted gene id (R13A5.9), or a protein ID (CE02711): |cdk-4

[identification] [location] [function] [gene ontology] [alleles] [similarities] [reagents] [bibliography]

Identification	IDs:					
		CGC name	**Sequence name**	**Other name(s)**	**WB Gene ID**	**Version**
		cdk-4 - (Cyclin-Dependent Kinase family) (via person: Michael Krause)	F18H3.5	XO136 (inferred automatically) NM_077855 (inferred automatically)	WBGene00000406	1

	NCBI KOGs *:	Protein kinase PCTAIRE and related kinases [KOG0594]
	Species:	Caenorhabditis elegans
	Other sequence(s):	AF083878 (Caenorhabditis elegans cyclin-dependent kinase CDK-4 (cdk-4) mRNA, complete cds.)
	NCBI:	[Entrez Genes: 15718266] [AceView: XO136]

	Gene model(s):	**Gene Model**	**Status**	**Nucleotides (coding/transcript)**	**Protein**	**Amino Acids**
		F18H3.5a 1, 2	confirmed by cDNA(s)	1029/3051 bp	WP:CE18608	342 aa
		F18H3.5b 1, 2, 3	partially confirmed by cDNA(s)	1221/1704 bp	WP:CE28918	406 aa

	Gene Model Remarks:	1 C. elegans CDK-4 protein; contains similarity to Pfam domain PF00069 (Protein kinase domain)contains similarity to Interpro domains IPR002290 (Serine/threonine protein kinase), IPR011009 (Protein kinase-like), IPR001245 (Tyrosine protein kinase), IPR008271 (Serine/threonine protein kinase, active site), IPR000719 (Protein kinase) 2 Annotated using Pfam 3 [010828 kj] Modified second exon according to EST yk76f3.5 using gaze prediction. But: This EST matches a lot of other clones and creates a massive CeRep overlap here so maybe it should be ignored...
	Notes:	The deletion allele was isolated in a PCR-based screen following the method of Barstead and Moulder. The deletion break points have been identified by sequence. We have rescued the cdk-4(gv3) mutant using a wild type copy of the cdk-4 cDNA expressed under the control of cdk-4 ~3 kb of 5' flanking sequences.Map position created from combination of previous interpolated map position (based on known location of sequence) and allele information. Therefore this is not a genetic map position based on recombination frequencies or genetic experiments. This was done on advice of the CGC. (via CGC data submission).

Location	Genetic Position:	X:12.68 +/- 0.009 cM [mapping data]
	Genomic Position:	X:13518824..13515774 bp
	Genomic Environs:	

Function	Mutant Phenotype:	[Krause MW] cdk-4 is a cyclin dependent kinase related to cdk-4 and cdk-6 from other organisms. Homozygous cdk-4(gv3) animals usually arrest in L2 due to no, or limited, proliferation of the post-embryonic blast cells. About 3% of animals make it to a late stage of development. Definitions of abbreviations used in the text.

Fig. 15.6 Sibling page of the page in Fig. 15.5

for some tables it works well. In particular, it works well for nested tables like those in Figs. 15.5 and 15.6.

Observe that for these nested tables, the conceptual, nested, label-value structure is isomorphic to a simple XML schema. There exists a single, nested, label path to every data value. For the sequence name *F47G6.1* in the top row of the table in Fig. 15.5, the label path is *Identification.IDs.Sequence_name*. This nested-label property lets us conceptualize these tables in an XML-like conceptual tree with labels as tags and instance values as leaf strings in a nested tag structure, as Fig. 15.7 illustrates. Note that the tree structure in Fig. 15.7 precisely captures the nesting of the tables in Figs. 15.5 and 15.6. Note also that the conceptualization can account for the variation among tables. In Fig. 15.7, for example, *Gene Models* relates optionally to *Swissprot* because the ontology-generation process observes that one table (Fig. 15.5) has an entry for *Swissprot* whereas the other (Fig. 15.6) does not. The end result is an automatically generated KB containing all the data from the given set of sibling tables.

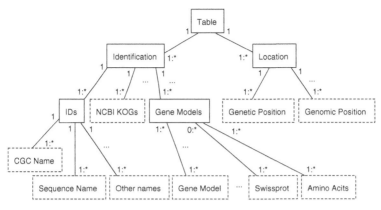

Fig. 15.7 Generated conceptual model instance

15.4.3 Construction via Semantic Integration

Table ANalysis for Generating Ontologies (TANGO) provides another way to create KBs. Given a collection of tables all in the same application domain, we reverse engineer each table into a conceptual-model instance and then integrate the conceptual-model instances into an ontology that represents the domain. During the process we analyze each table individually, inferring concepts, relationships among concepts, and data values for concepts and relationships. The result of this process is a conceptual-model instance for the table, which we call a "mini-ontology" – "mini" because the number of concepts in a table is usually small. We then exploit schema-mapping techniques to discover interrelationships among the mini-ontologies, enabling us to merge the generated conceptual-model instances into an ontological structure for the domain.

TANGO operates in three steps:

1. Recognize and canonicalize table information.
2. Construct mini-ontologies from canonicalized tables.
3. Discover interontology mappings and merge mini-ontologies into a growing application ontology.

We illustrate with an example.

15.4.3.1 Table Recognition and Canonicalization

Tables appear in many shapes and sizes; most, but not all, have rectangular grid layouts. Figure 15.8 is an example of a table without a clearly delineated grid layout.

In our first step, we canonicalize tables by converting them to "Wang notation," a layout-independent formalization for tables [65]. Wang notation has two parts: (1) label structure and (2) data-value/label-structure association. The label structure

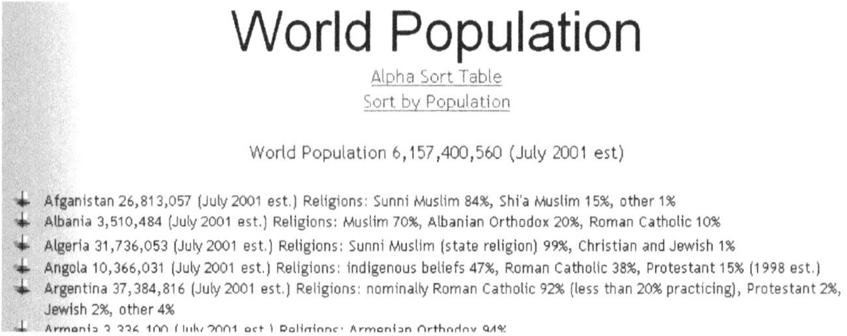

World Population

Alpha Sort Table
Sort by Population

World Population 6,157,400,560 (July 2001 est)

- Afganistan 26,813,057 (July 2001 est.) Religions: Sunni Muslim 84%, Shi'a Muslim 15%, other 1%
- Albania 3,510,484 (July 2001 est.) Religions: Muslim 70%, Albanian Orthodox 20%, Roman Catholic 10%
- Algeria 31,736,053 (July 2001 est.) Religions: Sunni Muslim (state religion) 99%, Christian and Jewish 1%
- Angola 10,366,031 (July 2001 est.) Religions: indigenous beliefs 47%, Roman Catholic 38%, Protestant 15% (1998 est.)
- Argentina 37,384,816 (July 2001 est.) Religions: nominally Roman Catholic 92% (less than 20% practicing), Protestant 2%, Jewish 2%, other 4%
- Armenia 3,336,100 (July 2001 est.) Religions: Armenian Orthodox 94%

Fig. 15.8 World populations and religions

consists of a collection of dimension trees, one for each coordinate that indexes a data cell. A dimension tree organizes labels in a tree structure: each path from root to leaf provides an index coordinate for a data value. In our example, the table in Fig. 15.8 has two dimensions. In Wang notation, these two dimension trees are:
(DT1Root, {

                (Population (July 2001 est.), $\emptyset$),

                (Religion, {

                        (Albanian Orthodox, $\emptyset$),

                        (Muslim, $\emptyset$),

                        (Roman Catholic, $\emptyset$),

                        (Shi'a Muslim, $\emptyset$),

                        (Sunni Muslim, $\emptyset$),

                        . . .

                        (other, $\emptyset$)

                      }))

(Country, {

                (Afghanistan, $\emptyset$),

                (Albania, $\emptyset$),

                . . .

                })

Wang associates data with dimension trees in δ-statements. Each combination of paths through dimension trees can have a value:

    δ(DT1Root.Population (July 2001 est.), Country.Afghanistan) = 26,813,057
    δ(DT1Root.Religion.Albanian Orthodox, Country.Afghanistan) = $\bot$
    . . .
    δ(DT1Root.Religion.other, Country.Afghanistan) = 1%
    δ(DT1Root.Population (July 2001 est.), Country.Albania) = 3,510,484
    . . .

Here, the first statement is for the data cell containing 26,813,057, the population of Afghanistan. The other three index an empty cell, the 1% for "other" religions

Table 15.1 Canonicalized table for world religious populations

Country	Population (July 2001 est.)	Religion							
		Albanian Orthodox	Muslim	Roman Catholic	Shi'a Muslim	Sunni Muslim	...	Other
Afghanistan	26,813,057				15%	84%		1%
Albania	3,510,484	20%	70%	10%				
...								

Table 15.2 Canonicalized table for people

Country	Population (July 2003 est.)	Median Age (2002)			Population Growth Rate (2003 est.)
		Total	Male	Female	
Afghanistan	28,717,213	18.9 years	19.1 years	18.7 years	3.38%*
Albania	3,582,205	26.5 years	24.8 years	28.1 years	1.03%
...					

* Note: this rate does not take into consideration the recent war and its continuing impact

Table 15.3 Canonicalized table for geography

Country	Location Description	Geographic Coordinates
Afghanistan	Southern Asia, north and west of Pakistan, east of Iran	33 00 N, 65 00 E
Albania	Southeastern Europe, bordering on the Adriatic Sea and Ionian Sea, between Greece and Serbia and Montenegro	41 00 N, 20 00 E
...		

in Afghanistan, and the 3,510,484 for the population of Albania. Similarly, we can index all values for all countries in Fig. 15.8.

We consider any collection of data that we can represent in Wang notation to be a table. Further, given a table in Wang notation, we can display the table in a standard grid form. We place the first dimension above the data, the second to the left of the data, the third to the left of the second with the second replicated for every leaf of the third, ... We omit implicit roots, such as the root *DT1Root* for Dimension Tree 1. Table 15.1 displays the table in Fig. 15.8 in this standard way. Tables 15.2–15.6 show several additional examples, which together with Fig. 15.8 constitute, for our example here, the tables to be merged into a KB.

We [23, 44, 60], and others (e.g., [20, 37, 49, 52, 69]), are working toward fully automatic table-interpretation tools. These tools take as input a table such as the one in Fig. 15.8 and produce as output Wang notation, which we can display in a standard way. In our tools, we augment Wang notation so that it can capture more than just labels and values. We also capture a table's title, its footnotes, and its units of measure. In the absence of fully automated tools, we have developed tools that let a user efficiently mark a table's label areas, data areas, title, and other augmentations [43, 47]. As a principle, it should always be possible for a knowledge worker to manually specify any output to be generated by the system, even though we aim to automate as much as possible. Manual specification ensures that we can always

Table 15.4 Canonicalized table for largest populations

	Population
Asia	3,674,000,000
Africa	778,000,000
...	
New York City, New York	8,040,000
Los Angeles, California	3,700,000
...	
Mumbai, India	12,150,000
Buenos Aires, Argentina	11,960,000
...	
China	1,256,167,701*
India	1,017,645,163*
...	

*January 15, 2000

Table 15.5 Canonicalized table for US topographical maps

Place	Type	Elevation*	USGS Quad	Lat	Lon
Bonnie Lake	Reservoir	Unknown	Seivern	33 72 N	81 42 W
Bonnie Lake	Lake	Unknown	Mirror Lake	40 71 N	110 88 W
...					
New York	Town/city	Unknown	Jersey City	40 71 N	74 01 W
New York	Town/city	149 meters	Leagueville	32 17 N	95 67 W
New York	Mine	Unknown	Heber City	40 62 N	111 49 W
...					

*Elevation values in this table are approximate, and often subject to a large degree of error. If in doubt, check the actual value on the map.

Table 15.6 Canonicalized table for most-spoken languages

Pos	Language	Speakers	Where Spoken (Major)
1	Mandarin	885,000,000	China, Malaysia, Taiwan
2	Spanish	332,000,000	South America, Central America, Spain
3	English	322,000,000	USA, UK, Australia, Canada, New Zealand
...			

complete a task and that we can correct any errors our automated procedures may introduce.

15.4.3.2 Construction of Mini-Ontologies

Figure 15.9 gives a graphical representation of each of the mini-ontologies for our six sample canonicalized tables in Tables 15.1–15.6. The notation differs slightly from our earlier notation for OSM-O. In this notation, we represent graphically the four common participation constraints: *0:**, *0:1*, *1:**, and *1:1*. A zero minimum makes participation optional, which we denote with an "o" on the relationship-set line near the object set whose objects participate optionally. The absence of an "o" makes the participation mandatory – equivalent to a *1-minumum* in a participation

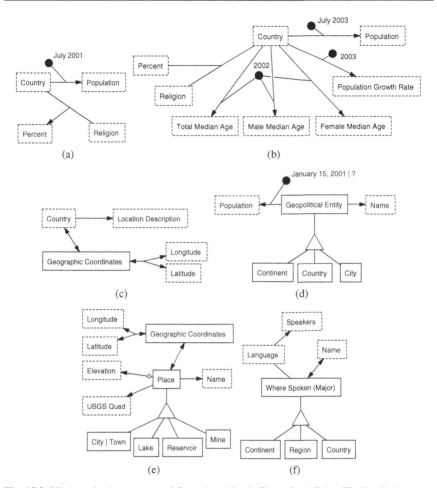

Fig. 15.9 Mini-ontologies constructed from the tables in Figs. 15.1–15.6. **a** World religious populations. **b** People. **c** Geography. **d** Largest populations. **e** US topographical maps. **f** Most-spoken languages

constraint. Thus, for example, the mini-ontology in Fig. 15.9e declares that a *Place* must have a *Name* and may, but need not, have an *Elevation*. A *1-maximum* in a participation constraint makes the relationship set functional, which we denote with an arrowhead on the opposite side of a relationship-set line. Thus, for example, in Fig. 15.9, a *Place* has one *Name*, at most one *Elevation*, one *USGS Quad* (the map in which the center of the place appears), and one pair of *Geographic Coordinates*. The functional (arrowhead) notation also allows us to express functional dependencies whose left-hand side is composite. Thus, for example, in Fig. 15.9 we have the functional dependency *Country Religion → Percent*. The notation also provides explicitly for object values with large black dots, which are object sets (one-place predicates) limited to having a single value.

To construct mini-ontologies from canonicalized tables, we must discover what concepts (object sets) are involved and how they are related (relationship sets). We must also determine the constraints that hold over the relationship sets (functional, mandatory/optional participation, aggregations) and among the object sets (generalization/specialization). We do so by appealing to the structural constraints of canonicalized tables and to outside resources such as WordNet and a data-frame library [45]. Aligning model instances with outside resources also makes them easier to integrate.

As an example, we obtain the mini-ontology in Fig. 15.9a from the table in Fig. 15.1 as follows. *Country* is a key and appears in the leftmost column, strongly suggesting that it should be the tail side of functional dependencies. *Population* depends on *Country* but also on *July 2001*. Knowledge from the data-frame library recognizes that the values in the *Religion* columns are *Percent* values. The religions, which could either be object sets or values, are values since there are many (our current threshold is five). Given that religions are values, we therefore have a ternary relationship among *Country*, *Religion*, and *Percent*. Based on constraint mining, we can determine that *Country* and *Religion* together functionally determine *Percent*. Creation of the remaining five mini-ontologies is similar.

15.4.3.3 Mapping Discovery and Ontology Merge

Our approach to discovering interontology mappings is multifaceted [25, 26], which means that we use all evidence at our disposal to determine how to match concepts. These facets include label matching [25], value similarity [25], expected values via matching values with data frames [25, 33], constraints [8], and structure [26, 32]. In using this evidence we look not only for direct matches, as is common in most schema-matching techniques [11, 36, 50], but also for indirect matches [68]. Thus, for example, we are able to split or join columns to match the single *Geographic coordinates* column in Fig. 15.3 with the pair of columns *Lat* and *Lon* in Fig. 15.5, and we are able to divide the values in the *Place* column in Fig. 15.5 into several different object sets.

Once we have discovered mappings between mini-ontologies or between a mini-ontology and the ontology we are building, we can begin the merge process. Sometimes the match is such that we can directly fuse two ontologies by simply keeping all the nodes and edges of both and merging nodes and edges that directly correspond. Often, however, merging induces conflicts that must be resolved. We resolve conflicts synergistically based on Issue/Default/Suggestion (IDS) statements [8, 46]. When a conflict arises, the system brings the issue to the attention of a knowledge worker. It provides a default resolution – the one it will take if the user does not intervene – and it makes some suggestions about alternate possibilities. In the tool we have created [46], a user can specify mappings that the automated matching algorithms may miss, can remove mappings that the matching algorithms may have incorrectly suggested, can run the merge automatically (allowing the system to take all the default resolutions for any conflict), can run merge interactively (re-solving each IDS statement manually), and can manually adjust the results after merge.

Given a collection of mini-ontologies, such as those in Fig. 15.9, we look initially for mini-ontologies that exhibit as large of an overlap as possible (as measured by the number of interontology mappings); thereafter we select mini-ontologies with the largest overlap with our growing ontology. In our example we begin by merging the mini-ontologies in Figs. 15.9a and 15.9b.

1st Merge   *Country* matches *Country* and *Population* matches *Population*. Both *July 2001* and *July 2003* are date components associated with *Population*, and we merge them as *Date*.

2nd Merge   Building on the 1st Merge, we add the mini-ontology in Fig. 15.9d and obtain the emerging ontology in Fig. 15.10. Here, we encounter IDS statements that help us reconcile the lexical/nonlexical *Country* object sets so that *Country* becomes nonlexical with an associated name and also that *Population* becomes an inherited property and is thus omitted from the *Country* specialization.

3rd Merge   Continuing, we merge the mini-ontology in Fig. 15.9f with the grow-ing ontology in Fig. 15.10. Here, the data in the object sets *Geopolitical Entity* and *Where Spoken* largely overlap, but it is not 100% clear whether one set should be a subset of the other, whether they are overlapping siblings in an is-a hierarchy, or whether they should be the same set. An IDS statement is therefore appropri-ate, and we assume the issue is resolved by declaring that the sets are the same and should be called *Geopolitical Entity*. This merge thus adds *Region* as a spe-cialization of *Geopolitical Entity* and adds *Language* and *Speakers* connected to *Geopolitical Entity* in the same way they are connected to *Where Spoken (Major)* in Fig. 15.9f.

4th Merge   Continuing, we next add the mini-ontology in Fig. 15.9c. Here, the constraints on the *Location Description* in Fig. 15.9c declare that the relation-ship is mandatory for both *Country* and *Location Description* and functional from *Country* to *Location Description*. Because of the lack of location descriptions for most countries in our growing collection, however, we have enough evidence to override the mandatory declaration and make the relationship for *Country* op-tional.

5th Merge   Continuing, we next add the mini-ontology in Fig. 15.9e and obtain the growing ontology in Fig. 15.11. Here, with the help of IDS statements, we must recognize that *Geopolitical Entity* is a specialization of *Place*. Other adjustments come readily, including inheriting *Name* from *Place* and making the existence of *USGS Quad* optional for *Place* based on a lack of map locations for most places.

As we transform tables into mini-ontologies and merge them, we also retain the data. The end result is a populated ontology and thus a KB that represents the do-main described by the given collection of tables.

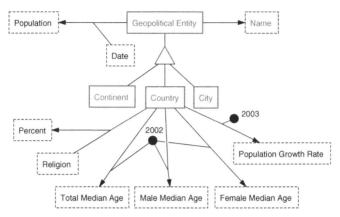

Fig. 15.10 Growing ontology after merging the mini-ontologies in Figs. 15.9a, 15.9b, and 15.9d. (The object sets with *lighter-shaded, "red," borders* are those most recently added)

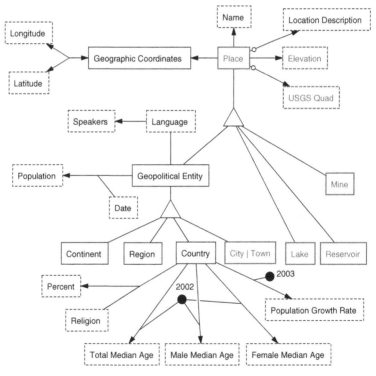

Fig. 15.11 Growing ontology after merging all mini-ontologies. (The object sets with *lighter-shaded, "red," borders* are those most recently added)

15.4.4 Construction via Form Filling

Although the KB construction methods discussed in Subsects. 15.4.1–15.4.3 are largely automatic, they have the disadvantage that users have little or no control over the ontological structure created and the data that populate the ontological structure. Users could take the final generated result and edit it by hand – a reasonable possibility if the desired ontological structure and the data are almost the same as the generated structure and data. In this subsection, we discuss an alternative that gives users a way to create a custom-designed ontological structure for a KB and to populate it with values harvested from a diverse collection of Web pages. This method works particularly well when the information to be collected for the KB comes from machine-generated collections of semistructured Web pages such as those commonly found in most hidden-Web/deep-Web sites.

Forms-based Ontology Creation and Information Harvesting (FOCIH) [62] is a tool that lets users specify ontologies without having to know any conceptual-modeling language or any ontology language. We observe that forms are a natural way for humans to collect information. As an everyday activity, people create forms and ask others to fill in the blanks. FOCIH lets users create their own forms to describe information they wish to harvest. Once defined, users can fill in forms from Web pages by copy and paste. From the form specification and user cut-and-paste actions, FOCIH generates an ontology, extracts data, and annotates the Web page with respect to the ontology. Further, if the Web page is machine-generated and has sibling pages, FOCIH is able to harvest the specified information from all the sibling pages, often without further user intervention.

FOCIH's form-creation mode provides users with an intuitive method for defining different kinds of form features. FOCIH has five types of form fields: *single-label/single-value*, *single-label/multiple-value*, *multiple-label/multiple-value*, *mutually exclusive choice*, and *nonexclusive choice*. Users create standard forms by stringing these form elements together in any order and nesting them within one another to any depth. The form in the left panel of Fig. 15.12 shows an example. The form is for collecting country information. It starts with three single-label/single-value fields for *Name*, *Capital*, and *Geographic Coordinates*, followed by a single-label/multiple-value field for *Religion*, and a multiple-label/multiple-value field for *Population-Year* estimates. The *Life Expectancy* field is a nonexclusive choice field for either *Male* or *Female Life Expectancy* or both. The final field shows the nesting of three form fields for *Water*, *Land*, and *Total* under a single-label/single-value field for *Area*.

FOCIH's form-fill-in mode lets users browse to a Web page they wish to annotate and copy and paste values into form fields. A user highlights values in the page and then clicks on the form field to fill in a value. Figure 15.12 shows a Web page for the Czech Republic in the right panel. Copied values from the Web page appear in the form in the left panel. The pencil icon lets a user drop a highlighted value into a form field, and the x icon lets a user remove a value. The plus icon lets a user concatenate a second part of the value to a partial value already in the form field. Thus, for example, if the latitude and longitude values are disjoint, perhaps labeled

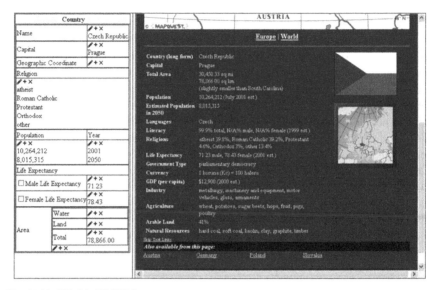

Fig. 15.12 Filled-in FOCIH form

Latitude: and *Longitude:* and appearing on separate lines in a web page, a user can concatenate the two as a single value in the *Geographic Coordinates* field.

From the filled-in form FOCIH can generate a conceptual model and populate it with values. Note that filled-in nested forms are identical in structure to the nested tables discussed in Sect. 15.4.2. Thus, the generated ontologies are similar and are like the OSM-O model instance in Fig. 15.7. In addition to generating a conceptual model and populating it, FOCIH also records the following information: (1) paths to leaf nodes in the DOM tree of an HTML page containing each value and, for concatenated values, each value component; (2) for each value the most specific instance recognizer from the data-frame library (e.g., string, number, percentage, year, geographic coordinate); and (3) enough left, right, and delimiter context within each leaf node to identify the value or values within the DOM-tree node. This enables FOCIH to harvest the same information from other machine-generated sibling pages from the same Web site.

The result of running FOCIH over a collection of sibling pages is a custom-built KB containing the information in the collection. Further, FOCIH can harvest information from other sibling-page collections with respect to the same custom-built ontology, which can further augment the KB.

15.5 WoK Usage

The construction of extraction ontologies leads to "understanding" within a WoK. This "understanding" leads to the ability to answer a free-form query because, as we explain in this section, a WoK system can identify an extraction ontology that applies to a query and match the query to the ontology. Hence, a WoK system can reformulate the free-form query as a formal query, so that it can be executed over a KB. In addition, "understanding" leads to establishing a context of discourse, allowing the system to expose its conceptualization of the subject and thus allowing users to more effectively communicate their information needs to the system. In both cases results returned for a query include not only answers to queries but also answer justification. Users can obtain a reasoning chain justifying each answer as well as provenance links identifying each ground fact supporting the answer.

Definition 15.11. Let S be a source conceptualization and let T be a target conceptualization formalized as an OSM-EO model instance. We say that T *understands* S if there exists an S-to-T transformation that maps each one-place predicate of S to an object set of T, each n-place predicate of S to an n-place relationship set of T ($n \geq 2$), each fact of S to a fact of T with respect to the predicate mappings, and each operator of S to an operator in a data frame of T, such that the constraints of T all hold over the transformed predicates and facts. □

Observe that although Definition 15.11 states how T is formalized, it does not state how S is formalized. Thus, the predicates and operators of S may or may not be directly specified. This is the hard part of "understanding" – to recognize the applicable predicates and operators. But this is exactly what extraction ontologies are meant to do. If an OSM-EO model instance is linguistically well grounded, then it can "understand" so long as what is stated in S is within the context of T – that is, if there is an object set or relationship set in T for every predicate in S and if there is an operator in a data frame of T for every operator in S.

Applications of understanding include free-form query processing, grounded reasoning chains, and KB building for research studies. We explain and illustrate each in turn. In doing so, we also illustrate our WoK prototype system, which we are building as a way to experiment with our vision of a WoK [28].

15.5.1 Free-Form Query Processing

Figure 15.13 illustrates free-form query processing within our WoK prototype. To "understand" a user query, our WoK prototype first determines which extraction ontology applies to the query by seeing which one recognizes the most instances, predicates, and operators in the query request. For the query in Fig. 15.13, we assume that the WoK prototype chooses the *Car* extraction ontology illustrated in Figs. 15.2 and 15.3. The WoK prototype then applies the S-to-T transformation highlighting what it "understands" ("Find me a honda, 2003 or newer for under 15 grand"). Figure 15.14 shows the result of this transformation – each predicate and each operation is mapped correctly and the constraints of the OSM-EO model instance all hold. Given this "understanding," it is straightforward to generate a SPARQL query. Before executing the query, our WoK prototype augments it so that it also obtains

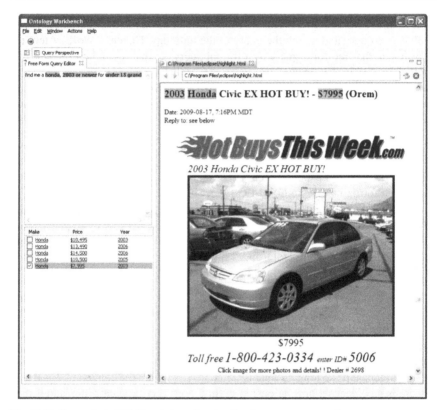

Fig. 15.13 Screenshot of WoK prototype showing free-form query processing

the stored annotation links. Then, when our WoK prototype displays the results of the query (e.g., in the lower-left box in Fig. 15.13), it makes returned values clickable. Clicking on a value causes our WoK prototype to find the page from which the value was extracted, highlight it, and display the page appropriately scrolled to the location that includes the value. The right panel of Fig. 15.13 shows several highlighted values, which happens when a user checks one or more checkboxes before clicking. □

The form in Fig. 15.14 is for an alerter system that we have implemented for craigslist.org. We use the form in two ways: (1) for comprehensive feedback to indicate its "understanding" of the query and (2) for giving users advanced options for query specification. As feedback, it lets users know the context in which the system "understands" the query being asked (i.e., the system displays the name of the extraction ontology and its details as form elements) and (2) it lets users know exactly what has been "understood" (i.e., the system displays constant values in fields for object sets or for operations applicable to object sets). With respect to advanced options, it lets users know what else can be asked in the context of the query. A user then has the opportunity to adjust the query or add ad-

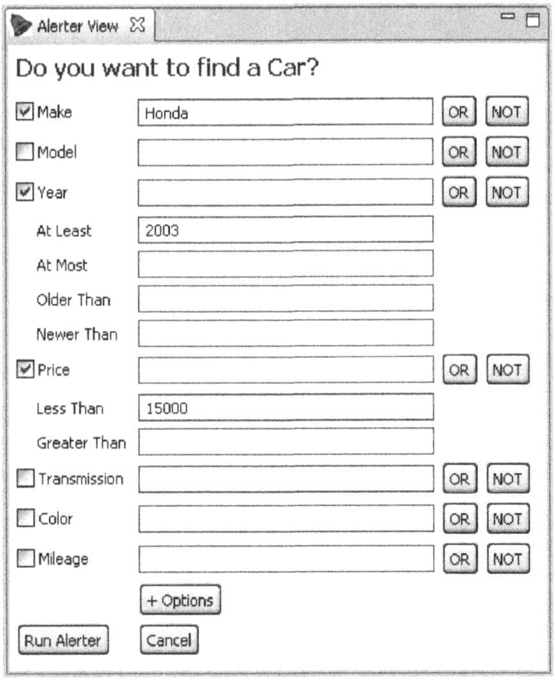

Fig. 15.14 Generated form showing the system's "Understanding" – its "Understood" instances within its "Understood" ontological context

```
Alerter View  ⊠                                    ▭ ☐

Do you want to find a Car?

☑ Make      │ Honda                      │   [OR] [NOT]

☐ Model     │                            │   [OR] [NOT]

☑ Year      │                            │   [OR] [NOT]

   At Least │ 2003                       │

   At Most  │                            │

   Older Than │                          │

   Newer Than │                          │

☑ Price     │                            │   [OR] [NOT]

   Less Than │ 15000                     │

   Greater Than │                        │

☐ Transmission │                         │   [OR] [NOT]

☐ Color     │                            │   [OR] [NOT]

☐ Mileage   │                            │   [OR] [NOT]

              [ + Options ]

 [Run Alerter]  [Cancel]
```

ditional constraints. For example, besides Hondas, a user may wish to also know if Toyotas are for sale but only if they are not Camrys. Clicking on *OR* for *Make* and adding *Toyota* and then clicking on *NOT* for *Model* and adding *Camry* makes this possible. The plus icons show that more operators are available; clicking on the plus displays them. For example, a user may wish to limit the search to cars whose odometer reading is less than 100 K miles; clicking on the "+ Options" button shows the Boolean operators for *Mileage* and lets a user enter this limitation.

15.5.2 Grounded Reasoning Chains

To illustrate grounded reasoning chains, we give an example from family-history research. Many millions of handwritten records such as those in the census record in Fig. 15.15 have been transcribed by human indexers [34]. Using extraction ontologies, we can extract from the transcription to associate names, dates, places, and other information with a genealogical ontology. Bounding boxes for names and other information in the image are also available, so we know where in the image information appears.

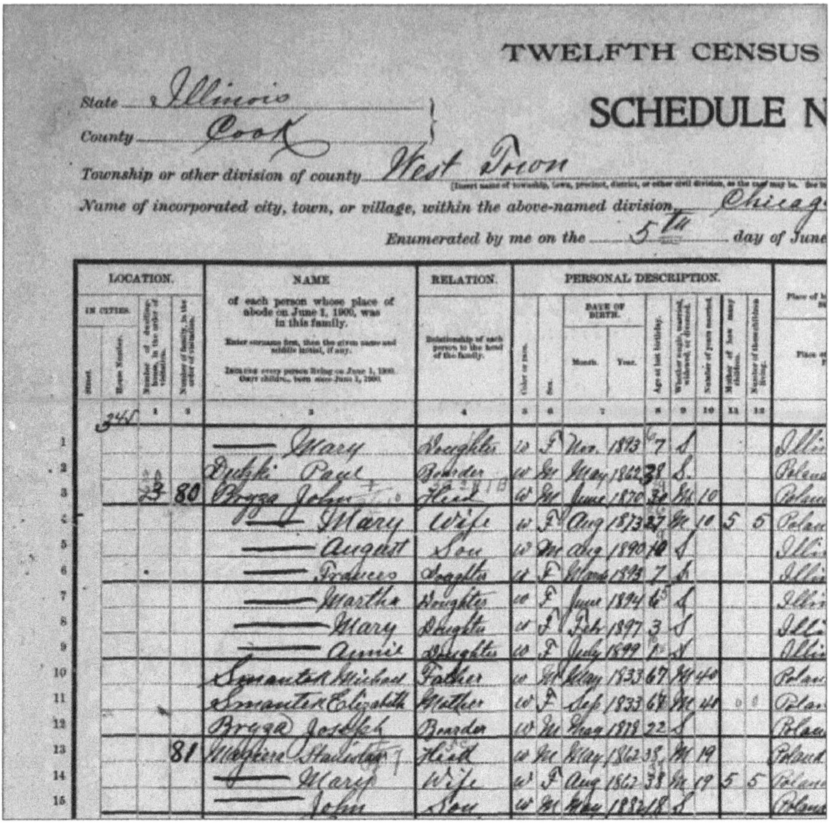

Fig. 15.15 Census record

It is not hard to see that, among others, the following rules hold and are useful for establishing family relationships implied by the information in the census record in Fig. 15.15:

```
Person(x)isHusbandOfPerson(y) :- Person(x), Person(y),
    Person(x)hasGender('Male'),
    Person(x)hasRelationToHead('Head'),
    Person(y)hasRelationToHead('Wife'),
    Person(x)isInSameFamilyAsPerson(y).
Person(x)isInSameFamilyAsPerson(y) :-
    Person(x)hasFamilyNumber(z)inCensusRecord(w),
    Person(y)hasFamilyNumber(z)inCensusRecord(w).
Person(x)named(y)isHusbandOfPerson(z)named(w) :-
    Person(x)isHusbandOfPerson(z),
    Person(x)hasName(y),
    Person(z)hasName(w).
```

The first rule states that a person x is the husband of person y if x is a male head of the family, y is the wife, and x and y are in the same family. The second rule assures that they are in the same family by checking to see that their family number is the same, and the last rule associates the husband and wife with their names.

When we associate a rule with an ontology, we must ensure that it is grounded in the base predicates of the ontology. The set of rules forms a graph over a "head predicate depends-on body predicate" relation, and this graph must lead to predicates declared in the ontology as object-set predicates, relationship-set predicates, or Boolean operations declared for the ontology. Recursive rules such as the following rules to compute ancestors are possible but must also be grounded.

```
Person(x)isAncestorOfPerson(y) :-
    Person(x)isParentOfPerson(y).
Person(x)isAncestorOfPerson(y) :-
    Person(x)isParentOfPerson(z),
    Person(z)isAncestorOfPerson(y).
```

Here, the predicate *Person(x)isParentOfPerson(y)* must be a rule head that eventually resolves down to ground predicates such as *Person(x)hasRelationToHead('Son')* or *Person(x)hasRelationToHead('Daughter')*.

Linguistically we ground a rule r by declaring a data frame for r in the same way we declare a data frame for an object set (if the head of r is a one-place predicate) or for a relationship set (if the head of r is an n-place predicate, $n \geq 2$). Thus, for example, $\{Person\}\backslash s*is\backslash.*husband\backslash s*of\backslash s*\{Person\}$ may be one of the regular expressions for the rule head *Person(x)isHusbandOfPerson(y)*.

Now when we pose the query "Who is the husband of Mary Bryza?," we can match the query to our genealogy ontology and specifically to the rule and thus also the chain of rules needed to answer the query. The returned result would yield "John Bryza" and perhaps others if other Mary Bryzas are known within the KB. Clicking on "John Bryza" yields both the reasoning chain in Fig. 15.16 and the highlighted

Person(p1) named('John Bryza') is husband of Person(p2) named('Mary Bryza')
because:
   Person(p1) is husband of Person(p2) and Person(p1) has Name('John Bryza')
     and Person(p2) has Name('Mary Bryza');
and Person(p1) is husband of Person(p2)
because:
   Person(p1) has gender('Male') and Person(p1) has relation to Head('Head'),
     and Person(p2) has relation to Head('Wife')
     and Person(p1) is in same family as Person(p2).
and Person(p1) is in same family as Person(p2)
because:
   Person(p1) has family number(80) in Census Record(r1)
     and Person(p2) has family number(80) in Census Record(r1).

Fig. 15.16 Reasoning chain for query

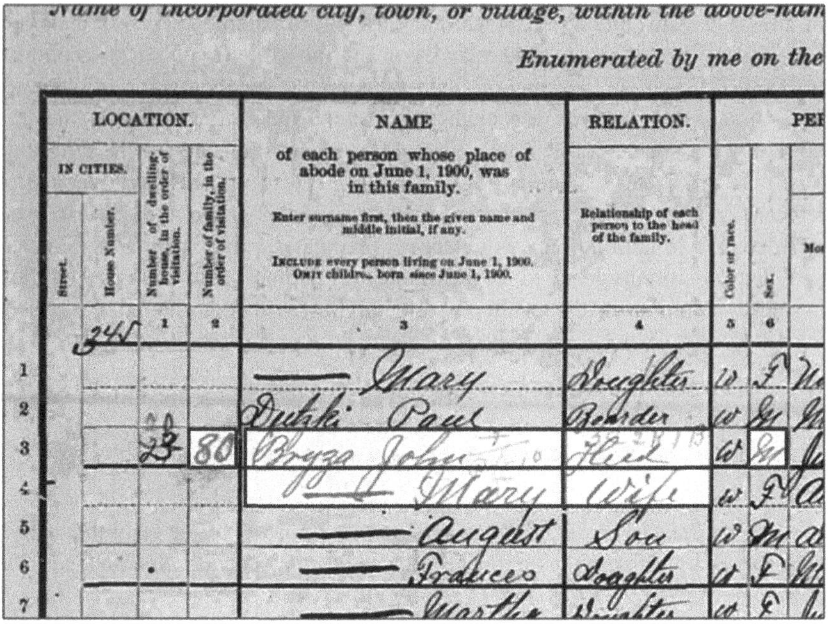

Fig. 15.17 Census record with ground facts highlighted

census record in Fig. 15.17. The reasoning chain is simply a list of rules invoked with instance data filled in for the variables and reformatted to be more readable. The highlighted census record shows the source of all the extracted ground fact values used to yield the answer.

15.5.3 Knowledge Bundles for Research Studies

In addition to "understanding" queries, it should be clear that "understanding" is also about fact finding. The fundamental intent of linguistically grounding extraction ontologies is to allow them to recognize facts in structured, semistructured, and unstructured text. As an example, we give a plausible scenario, based on the WoK components we have presented, for gathering facts for a bioresearch study and storing them as a KB for further analysis [29]. Gathering tasks for these research studies often take trained bioresearchers several man-months of work. Thus any significant speed-up extraction ontologies can provide would be of great benefit in biomedical research.

Suppose a bioresearcher B wishes to study the association of TP53 polymorphism and lung cancer. To do this study, B wants information from the NCBI db-

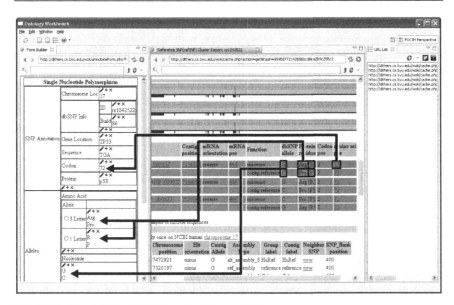

Fig. 15.18 Form filled in with information from an SNP page

SNP repository[3] about SNPs (chromosome location, SNP ID and build, gene location, codon, and protein), about alleles (amino acids and nucleotides), and about the nomenclature for amino-acid levels and nucleotide levels. *B* also needs data about human subjects with lung cancer and needs to relate the SNP information to human-subject information.

To gather information from dbSNP, *B* uses FOCIH to construct the form in the left panel in Fig. 15.18. Form construction consists of selecting types of form fields and organizing and nesting form fields so that they are a conceptualization of the information *B* wishes to harvest for the research study. *B* next finds a first SNP page in dbSNP from which to begin harvesting information. (The created form and located page need not have any special correspondence – no schema correspondence, no name correspondence, and no special structure requirements – but, of course, the page should have data of interest for the research study and thus for the created form.) *B* then fills in the form by cut-and-paste actions, copying data from the page in the center panel in Fig. 15.18 to the form in the left panel.

To harvest similar information from the numerous other dbSNP pages, *B* gives a list of URLs, as the right panel in Fig. 15.18 illustrates (although there would likely be hundreds rather than just the six in Fig. 15.18). The FOCIH system automatically harvests the desired information from the dbSNP pages referenced in the URL list. Since one of the challenges bioresearchers face is searching through the pages to determine which ones contain the desired information, FOCIH should

---

[3] The Single Nucleotide Polymorphism database (dbSNP) is a public-domain archive for a broad collection of simple genetic polymorphisms hosted by the National Center for Biotechnology Information (NCBI) at www.ncbi.nlm.nih.gov/projects/SNP/.

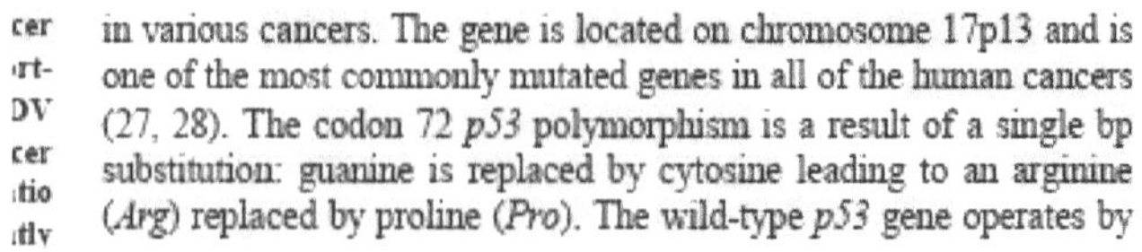

cer	in various cancers. The gene is located on chromosome 17p13 and is
'rt-	one of the most commonly mutated genes in all of the human cancers
⊃V	(27, 28). The codon 72 *p53* polymorphism is a result of a single bp
cer	substitution: guanine is replaced by cytosine leading to an arginine
tio	(*Arg*) replaced by proline (*Pro*). The wild-type *p53* gene operates by
tlv	

Fig. 15.19 Paper retrieved from PMID using an extraction ontology

provide a filtering mechanism. By adding constraints to form fields, bioresearchers can cause the FOCIH harvester to gather information only from pages that satisfy the constraints. B, for example, might only want coding SNP data with a significant heterogeneity (i.e., minor allele frequency > 1%).

For the research scenario, B may also wish to harvest information from other sites such as GeneCard. B can use FOCIH with the same form to harvest from as many sites as desired. Interestingly, however, once FOCIH harvests from one site, it can use the knowledge it has already gathered to do some of the initial cut-and-paste for B. In addition to just being a structured knowledge repository, the KB being produced also becomes an extraction ontology capable of recognizing data items it has already seen. It can also recognize data items it has not seen but are like the data it has seen, e.g., numeric values or DNA snippets.

Using KBs as extraction ontologies also lets bioresearchers search the literature. Suppose B wishes to find papers related to the information harvested from the db-SNP pages. B can point the extraction ontology to a repository of papers to search and cull out those that are relevant to the study. Using the KB as an extraction ontology provides a sophisticated query of the type used in information retrieval resulting in high-precision document filtering. For example, the extraction ontology recognizes the highlighted words and phrases in the portion of the paper in Fig. 15.19. With the high density of not only keywords but also data values and relationships all aligned with the ontological KB, the system can designate this paper as being relevant for B's study.

For collecting human-subject information, B may decide to obtain information from INDIVO, a database containing personally controlled health records. Based on reverse-engineering techniques, the system can automatically reverse engineer the INDIVO database to a KB and present B with a form representing the schema of the database. Figure 15.20 shows an example. B can then modify the form, deleting fields not of interest and rearranging fields to suit the needs of the study. Further, B can add constraints to the fields so that the system only gathers data of interest.

With all information harvested and organized into a KB, B can now issue queries and reason about the data to do some interesting analysis. Figure 15.21 shows a sample SPARQL query over the data harvested from the pages referenced by the six URLs listed in Fig. 15.18. The query finds three SNPs that satisfy the query's criteria and, for each, returns the dbSNP ID, the gene location, and the protein residue. As Fig. 15.21 shows, B wishes to see the source of the query result <*rs55819519, TP53, His Arg*>.

Medical Document			
Demographics	Sex		
	DateofBirth		
	Deceased		
	Race		
	Ethnicity		
	HighestEducationLevel		
Family History	Condition	Relationship	
Medication	Prescription	Dose	Duration

Fig. 15.20 Some human-subject information reverse engineered from INDIVO

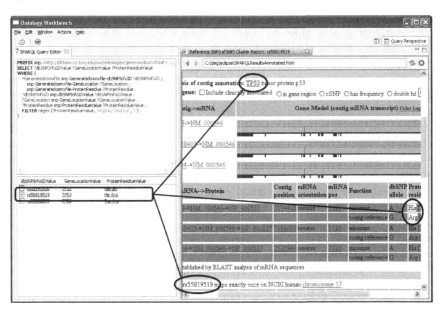

Fig. 15.21 Screenshot of our WoK prototype

15.6 Conclusion

We have described a web of knowledge (WoK) as a collection of interconnected KBs superimposed over a web of documents. Our WoK vision has conceptual modeling at its foundation. As described, a WoK consists of KBs, which are conceptual-model instances augmented with facilities that provide for (1) both extensional and intensional facts, (2) linking between KBs yielding a web of data, and (3) authentication by linking to source documents and explicating reasoning chains.

We have provided a formal foundation for WoK components – ontologies (OSM-O) in terms of decidable first-order logic and extraction ontologies (OSM-EO) linguistically grounded via data-frame recognizers. In addition, we have formalized a WoK as a collection of interconnected knowledge bundles (KBs) consisting of OSM-EO model instances with valid interpretations superimposed over source documents.

Further, we have addressed concerns about WoK construction. Transformations map source conceptualizations to target conceptualizations. Information- and constraint-preserving transformations guarantee that target conceptualizations completely and accurately capture source conceptualizations. We have explained how reverse engineering of some documents can yield source conceptualizations guaranteed to preserve information and constraints. We conclude, however, that many source conceptualizations (ranging from semistructured sources such as ordinary human-readable tables and forms to unstructured sources such as free-running text) likely require best-effort automation methods and may involve some user supervision. We have given, as examples, a way to transform a collection of ordinary tables with overlapping information from some domain into a KB and a way to construct KBs via form creation and form filling.

Finally, we have addressed concerns about WoK usage. When transformations exist that map source predicates and operations to an established ontology, the ontology is said to have "understood" the information in the source. "Understanding" applied to free-form queries allows untrained users to query the envisioned WoK. Users receive direct answers to queries, rather than pages that may contain answers. They may, however, ask for justification by clicking on displayed answers, which yields the pages from which the answers were taken and also yields an explanation of any reasoning used to generate inferred answers for the query. As another example of WoK usage, we have illustrated the process of creating a KB for biomedical research studies.

We have implemented a WoK prototype [28] including some prototypical extraction ontologies [22]. We have also done some work on automated extraction-ontology construction [45, 60–62] and some work on free-form query processing [4, 63]. We nevertheless still have much work to do, even on fundamental WoK components such as creating a sharable data-frame library, constructing data frames for relationship sets, finding ways to more easily produce instance recognizers, developing processes for reverse engineering additional genres of semistructured sources into KBs, investigating bootstrapping as a way to construct extraction ontologies, enhancing query processing, incorporating reasoning, and addressing performance scalability. We also see many opportunities for incorporating the vast amount of work done by others on information extraction, information integration, and record linkage. We cite the following as relevant examples: KnowItAll [21], OMNIVORE [15], best-effort information extraction [56], C-PANKOW [19], Q/A systems [51], bootstrapping pay-as-you-go data integration [55], large-scale deduplication [6], and OpenDMAP [41].

These collective efforts will eventually lead to a WoK – a realization of ideas of visionaries from Bush [14] to Berners-Lee [10] and Weikum [67]. Conceptual modeling can and should play a foundational role in these efforts.

Acknowledgements Many students and colleagues have contributed in various ways to the web-of-knowledge vision presented here – as colleagues: Douglas M. Campbell, George Nagy, Dennis Ng, Dallan Quass, Yuri Tijerino; as PhD students: Reema Al-Kamha, Muhammed Al-Muhammed, Yihong Ding, Aaron Stewart, Cui Tao, Li Xu; as MS students: Tim Chartrand, Wendy Chen, Xueqi Helen Chen, Kimball Hewett, David Jackman, Stephen Jiang, Zonghui Lian, Stephen Lynn, Rob Lyon, Lars Olson, Craig Parker, Clint Tustison, Randy Smith, Mark Vickers, Troy Walker, Alan Wessman, Charla Woodbury, Sai Ho Tony Yau, Yuanqiu Joe Zhou, Andrew Zitzelberger; and as undergraduate research assistants: Robert Clawson, Derek McDaniel, Jeff Peters, Robby Watts. We appreciate the support of the National Science Foundation, whose grants have assisted many of these students in their educational endeavors (Grant Numbers IIS0083127 and IIS0414644).

References

1. Allemang D, Hendler J (2008) Semantic Web for the working ontologist: effective modeling in RDFS and OWL. Morgan Kaufmann, Burlington
2. Aiken PH (1998) Reverse engineering of data. IBM Syst J 37(2):246–269
3. Al-Kamha R (2007) Conceptual XML for systems analysis. PhD dissertation, Department of Computer Science, Brigham Young University, Provo, UT
4. Al-Muhammed M, Embley DW (2007) Ontology-based constraint recognition for free-form service requests. In: Proceedings of the 23rd international conference on data engineering (ICDE'07), Istanbul, Turkey, April 2007, pp 366–375
5. Aristotle (1993) Metaphysics. Oxford University Press, New York (1993 translation)
6. Arasu A, Re C, Suciu D (2009) Large-scale deduplication with constraints using Dedupalog. In: Proceedings of the 25th international conference on data engineering (ICDE 2009), Shanghi, China, March/April 2009, pp 952–963
7. Buitelaar P, Cimiano P, Haase P, Sintek M (2009) Towards linguistically grounded ontologies. In: Proceedings of the 6th European Semantic Web conference (ESWC'09), Heraklion, Greece, May/June 2009, pp 111–125
8. Biskup J, Embley DW (2003) Extracting information from heterogeneous information sources using ontologically specified target views. Inf Syst 28(3):169–212
9. Berners-Lee T (1999) Weaving the Web. Harper SanFrancisco, San Francisco
10. Berners-Lee T, Hendler J, Lassila O (2001) The semantic web. Sci Am 36(25):34–43
11. Bernstein PA, Melnik S, Petropoulos M, Quix C (2004) Industrial-strength schema matching. SIGMOD Rec 33(4):38–43
12. Baader F, Nutt W (2003) Basic description logics. In: Baader F, Calvanese D, McGuinness D, Nardi D, Patel-Schneider P (eds) The Description Logic handbook, Chap 2. Cambridge University Press, Cambridge, UK, pp 43–95
13. Bleiholder J, Naumann F (2008) Data fusion. ACM Comput Surv 41(1):1–41
14. Bush V (1945) As we may think. Atlantic Monthly 176(1):101–108
15. Cafarella MJ (2009) Extracting and querying a comprehensive web database. In: Proceedings of the conference on innovative data systems research (CIDR'09), Monterey
16. Calì A, Gottlob G, Lukasiewicz T (2009) Tractable query answering over ontologies with Datalog$^{\pm}$. In: Proceedings of the DL Home 22nd international workshop on Description Logics (DL 2009), Oxford

17. Cali A, Gottlob G, Pieris A (2009) Tractable query answering over conceptual schemata. In: Proceedings of the 28th international conference on conceptual modeling (ER 2009), Gramado, Brazil, November 2009, pp 175–190
18. Cimiano P (2006) Ontology learning and population from text: algorithms, evaluation and applications. Springer, New York
19. Cimiano P, Ladwig G, Staab S (2005) Gimme' the context: context-driven automatic semantic annotation with C-PANKOW. In: Proceedings of the 14th international World Wide Web conference (WWW205), Chiba, Japan, May 2005, pp 332–341
20. de Silva AC, Jorge AM, Torgo L (2006) Design of an end-to-end method to extract information from tables. Int J Doc Anal Recognit 8(2):144–171
21. Etzioni O, Cafarella M, Downey D, Kok S, Popescu A, Shaked T, Soderland S, Weld D, Yates A (2005) Unsupervised named-entity extraction from the web: an experimental study. Artif Intell 165(1):91–134
22. Embley DW, Campbell DM, Jiang YS, Liddle SW, Lonsdale DW, Ng Y-K, Smith RD (1999) Conceptual-model-based data extraction from multiple-record web pages. Data Knowl Eng 31(3):227–251
23. Embley DW, Hurst M, Lopresti D, Nagy G (2006) Table-processing paradigms: a research survey. Int J Doc Anal 8(2):66–86
24. Elmagarmid AK, Ipeirotis PG, Verykios VS (2007) Duplicate record detection: a survey. IEEE Trans Knowl Data Eng 18(1):1–16
25. Embley DW, Jackman D, Xu L (Multifaceted exploitation of metadata for attribute match discovery in information integration. In: Proceedings of the international workshop on information integration on the Web (WIIW'01), Rio de Janeiro, Brazil, April 2001, pp 110–117
26. Embley DW, Jackman D, Xu L (2002) Attribute match discovery in information integration: Exploiting multiple facets of metadata. J Brazil Comput Soc 8(2):32–43
27. Embley DW, Kurtz BD, Woodfield SN (1992) Object-oriented systems analysis: a model-driven approach. Prentice Hall, Englewood Cliffs
28. Embley DW, Liddle SW, Lonsdale D, Nagy G, Tijerino Y, Clawson R, Crabtree J, Ding Y, Jha P, Lian Z, Lynn S, Padmanabhan RK, Peters J, Tao C, Watts R, Woodbury C, Zitzelberger A (2008) A conceptual-model-based computational alembic for a web of knowledge. In: Proceedings of the 27th international conference on conceptual modeling (ER08), Barcelona, October 2008, pp 532–533
29. Embley DW, Liddle SW, Lonsdale DW, Stewart A, Tao C (2009) KBB: a knowledge-bundle builder for research studies. In: Proceedings of 2nd international workshop on active conceptual modeling of learning (ACM-L 2009), Gramado, Brazil, November 2009 (in press)
30. Embley DW (1980) Programming with data frames for everyday data items. In: Proceedings of the 1980 national computer conference, Anaheim, May 1980, pp 301–305
31. Euzenat J, Shvaiko P (2007) Ontology matching. Springer, Heidelberg
32. Embley DW, Tao C, Liddle SW (2002) Automatically extracting ontologically specified data from HTML tables with unknown structure. In: Proceedings of the 21st international conference on conceptual modeling (ER2002), Tampere, Finland, October 2002, pp 322–327
33. Embley DW, Xu L, Ding Y (2004) Automatic direct and indirect schema mapping: Experiences and lessons learned. SIGMOD Rec 33(4):14–19
34. Family search. http://familysearch.org
35. Finkel JR, Manning CD (2009) Nested named entity recognition. In: Proceedings of the 2009 conference on empirical methods in natural language processing, Singapore, August 2009, pp 141–150
36. Falconer SM, Noy NF, Storey M-A (2007) Ontology mapping – a user survey. In: Proceedings of the 2nd international workshop on ontology mapping (OM-2007), Bexco, Busan, Korea, November 2007, pp 49–60
37. Gatterbauer W, Bohunsky P, Herzog M, Krüpl B, Pollak B (2007) Towards domain-independent information extraction from web tables. In: Proceedings of the 16th international World Wide Web conference (WWW2007), Banff, Alberta, Canada, May 2007, pp 71–80

38. Grover C, Givon S, Tobin R, Ball J (2008) Named entity recognition for digitised historical texts. In: Proceedings of the 6th international conference on language resources and evaluation (LREC 2008), Marrakech, Morocco, May 2008
39. Gruber TR (1993) A translation approach to portable ontology specifications. Knowl Acquis 5(2):199–220
40. Guarino N (1998) Formal ontologies and information systems. In: Guarino N (ed) Proceedings of the 1st international conference on formal ontology in information systems (FOIS98), Trento, Italy, June 1998, pp 3–15
41. Hunter L, Lu Z, Firby J, Baumgartner Jr WA, Johnson HL, Ogren PV, Cohen KB (2008) OpenDMAP: an open source, ontology-driven, concept analysis engine, with applications to capturing knowledge regarding protein transport, protein interactions and cell-type-specific gene expression. BMC Bioinformat 9(8)
42. Halevy A, Rajaraman A, Ordille J (2006) Data integration: the teenage years. In: Proceedings of the 32nd international conference on very large data bases (VLDB'06), Seoul, September 2006, pp 9–16
43. Jha P, Nagy G (2008) Wang notation tool: layout independent representation of tables. In: Proceedings of the 19th international conference on pattern recognition (ICPR08), Tampa, December 2008
44. Jandhyala RC, Nagy G, Seth S, Silversmith W, Krishnamoorthy M, Padmanabhan R (2009) From tessellations to table interpretation. In: Lecture notes in artificial intelligence, vol 5625. Springer, Berlin, pp 422–437
45. Lynn S, Embley DW (2009) Semantically conceptualizing and annotating tables. In: Proceedings of the 3rd Asian Semantic Web conference, Bangkok, February 2009, pp 345–359
46. Lian Z (2008) A tool to support ontology creation based on incremental mini-ontology merging. Master's thesis, Department of Computer Science, Brigham Young University, Provo, UT, March 2008
47. Padmanabhan R, Jandhyala RC, Krishnamoorthy M, Nagy G, Seth S, Silversmith W (2009) Interactive conversion of large web tables. In: Proceedings of the 8th international workshop on graphics recognition (GREC 2009), La Rochelle, France, July 2009, pp 32–43
48. Plato (about 360 BC) Theaetetus. BiblioBazaar, Charleston. (translated by Benjamin Jowett)
49. Pivk A, Sure Y, Cimiano P, Gams M, Rajkovič V, Studer R (2007) Transforming arbitrary tables into logical form with TARTAR. Data Knowl Eng 60:567–595
50. Rahm E, Bernstein PA (2001) A survey of approaches to automatic schema matching. VLDB J 10:334–350
51. Roussinov D, Fan W, Robles-Flores J (2008) Beyond keywords: automated question answering on the web. Commun ACM 51(9):60–65
52. Rahman F, Klein B (2006) Special issue on detection and understanding of tables and forms for document processing applications. Int J Doc Anal 8(2):65
53. Rosati R (2005) On the decidability and complexity of integrating ontologies and rules. J Web Semant 3(1):61–73
54. Sarawagi S (2008) Information extraction. Found Trends Databases 1(3):261–377
55. Sarma AD, Dong X, Halevy A (2008) Bootstrapping pay-as-you-go data integration systems. In Proceedings of SIGMOD'08, Vancouver, British Columbia, Canada, June 2008, pp 861–874
56. Shen W, DeRose P, McCann R, Doan A, Ramakrishnan R (2008) Toward best-effort information extraction. In: Proceedings of the ACM SIGMOD international conference on management of data, Vancouver, British Columbia, Canada, June 2008, pp 1031–1042
57. Shadbolt N, Hall W, Berners-Lee T (2006) The semantic web revisited. IEEE Intell Syst 21(3):96–101
58. Smith B (2003) Ontology. In: Floridi L (ed) Blackwell guide to the philosophy of computing and information. Blackwell, Oxford, pp 155–166
59. Tao C (2008) Ontology generation, information harvesting and semantic annotation for machine-generated Web pages. PhD dissertation, Department of Computer Science, Brigham Young University, Provo, UT, December 2008

60. Tao C, Embley DW (2009) Automatic hidden-web table interpretation, conceptualization, and semantic annotation. Data Knowl Eng 68(7):683–703
61. Tijerino YA, Embley DW, Lonsdale DW, Ding Y, Nagy G (2005) Toward ontology generation from tables. World Wide Web Internet Web Inf Syst 8(3):261–285
62. Tao C, Embley DW, Liddle SW (2009) FOCIH: form-based ontology creation and information harvesting. In: Proceedings of the 28th international conference on conceptual modeling (ER2009), Gramado, Brazil, November 2009, pp 346–359
63. Vickers M (2006) Ontology-based free-form query processing for the semantic web. Master's thesis, Brigham Young University, Provo, UT, June 2006
64. W3C (World Wide Web Consortium) Semantic Web Activity Page. http://www.w3.org/2001/sw/
65. Wang X (1996) Tabular abstraction, editing, and formatting. PhD thesis, University of Waterloo
66. Wang J, Chen C, Wang C, Pei J, Bu J, Guan Z, Zhang WV (2009) Can we learn a template-independent wrapper for news article extraction from a single training site? In: Proceedings of the 15th ACM SIGKDD international conference on knowledge discovery and data mining, Paris, June/July 2009, pp 1345–1354
67. Weikum G, Kasneci G, Ramanath M, Suchanek F (2009) Database and information-retrieval methods for knowledge discovery. Commun ACM 52(4):56–64
68. Xu L, Embley DW (2006) A composite approach to automating direct and indirect schema mappings. Inf Syst 31(8):697–732
69. Zanibbi R, Blostein D, Cordy JR (2004) A survey of table recognition: models, observations, transformations, and inferences. Int J Doc Anal Recognit 7(1):1–16

Chapter 16
A Conceptual Modeling Approach to Improve Human Genome Understanding

Óscar Pastor, Matthijs van der Kroon, Ana M. Levin, Juan Carlos Casamayor, and Matilde Celma

Abstract Information systems cannot be designed nor programmed without prior elicitation of the knowledge they need to know. Representing this knowledge in an explicit form is the main application of a conceptual model. By allowing for a minor paradigm shift, one can imagine the human body as an information system; highly complex and built of biological molecules, rather than man-made hardware, but an information system nonetheless. It is this paradigm shift that allows for exciting possibilities. Just as acquiring the source-code of a man-made system allows for post-production modifications and easy software maintenance, the same could very well apply to the human body: essentially, the act of debugging life itself. Acquiring the source-code to the human information system begins with the first step in any information system development: the creation of a comprehensive, correct conceptual model of the human genome.

16.1 Introduction

As stated in [1], conceptual modeling is the activity that elicits and describes the general knowledge a particular information system needs to know. The main objec-

Óscar Pastor
Centro de Investigación en Métodos de Producción de Software, e-mail: opastor@pros.upv.es

Matthijs van der Kroon
Centro de Investigación en Métodos de Producción de Software, e-mail: mkroon@pros.upv.es

Ana M. Levin
Centro de Investigación en Métodos de Producción de Software, e-mail: alevin@pros.upv.es

Juan Carlos Casamayor
Centro de Investigación en Métodos de Producción de Software, e-mail: jcarlos@dsic.upv.es

Matilde Celma
Centro de Investigación en Métodos de Producción de Software, e-mail: mcelma@dsic.upv.es

D. W. Embley and B. Thalheim (eds), *Handbook of Conceptual Modeling.*   517
DOI 10.1007/978-3-642-15865-0, © Springer 2011

tive of conceptual modeling is to obtain that description. Information systems cannot be designed or programmed without first eliciting the knowledge they need to know. The only option we have is whether or not to explicitly describe that knowledge. But when this knowledge is not explicitly described, the behavior of the system that is to be built can be considered to be just unpredictable. This is a well-known phenomenon strongly recognized within the conceptual modeling and Model-Driven Development communities: only by having a well-defined conceptual model can a sound information system be constructed. The disadvantages of having the general knowledge of a system only in the designers' heads are well known; this is why, for many researchers, the conceptual model is the only important description that needs to be created in the development of an information system.

If we want to find a domain where such a well-defined and precise conceptual model can be seen as a strong need, and where its absence generates all the problems related with poor quality of data – problems that are so well-known in the context of information systems analysis and design – the bioinformatics domain clearly arises. In particular, if we want to answer the old and challenging question of why we are the way we are, we face a really big problem. If we try to use and manage the huge amount of information that has been generated in the recent years, and continues to be generated, in what we will call the genomic domain – a term that we will use to refer to the study of the genomes of organisms – the conclusion is clear: no precise conceptual model means no sound strategy to guide the correct storage and interpretation of the tons of data that daily increase the complexity of the domain.

This chapter proposes a concrete contribution to the definition of a conceptual modeling-based strategy by introducing a conceptual model that could be used to fix, clarify, and appropriately manage the concepts that characterize the human genome. If there is a domain where conceptual modeling can show clearly its benefits, it is the genomic domain. Many people talk about databases, talk about ontologies, but always as a partial approach, with no holistic, unified perspective. The lack of conceptual models makes it very complicated – although not impossible – to talk about data commonalities, differences, consistency, conceptual redundancy. In short, it becomes very difficult to talk about data quality and how to exploit the subsequent knowledge.

In Sect. 16.2, we elaborate on the idea of why a conceptual model for the human genome is so desirable, extending the arguments introduced above and justifying the genomic domain as a really challenging domain for modern conceptual modeling. Section 16.3 introduces the problem domain in more detail, with the intention of clarifying the biological terms that need to be understood through the rest of the chapter, such as genotype, phenotype, SNPs, attempts to store human genome data as HapMap, and ENCODE. Section 16.4 presents more concrete, existing modeling and ontology-based approaches that in some way face the analyzed problem, with the goal of introducing as a final, concrete result a proposal of a conceptual model for the human genome in Sect. 16.5.

16.2 Why a Conceptual Model for the Human Genome?

Today's genomic domain evolves around insecurity: too many imprecise concepts, too much information to be properly managed. Considering that conceptualization is the most exclusive human characteristic, it makes full sense to try to conceptualize the principles that guide the essence of why humans are as we are. This question can, of course, be generalized to any species, but we are especially interested in showing how conceptual modeling is strictly required to understand the "execution model" that human beings "implement". The main issue is to defend the idea that only by having an in-depth knowledge of the conceptual model that is associated to the human genome, can this human genome properly be understood. This kind of model-driven perspective of the human genome opens challenging possibilities, by looking at individuals as implementations of that conceptual model, where different values associated to different modeling primitives will explain the diversity among individuals and the potential, unexpected variations together with their unwanted effects in terms of illnesses.

It is true that genomics is often not an exact science, due to the immense complexity of nature and its processes. It is true that basic concepts like genes, alleles, and mutations are frequently variable in their precise definition. Their exact denotation often depends on both context and position in time. A gene, for instance, can be defined as a locatable region of genomic sequence, corresponding to a unit of inheritance, which is associated with regulatory regions, transcribed regions, and or other functional sequence regions. However, the existence of splicing, in which gene expression changes at runtime, complicates this view as is very well described by [2]: "*in eukaryotes, the gene is, in most cases, not yet present at DNA-level. Rather, it is assembled by RNA processing*". [3] and [2] provide recent insights on the evolution of the gene concept, and the matter is discussed in more detail in Sect. 16.3.

But for efficient research to take place, it is obvious that clear definitions of concepts and a common vocabulary are crucial. This is especially the case in research where worldwide various separate research groups are collaborating and exchanging information on a regular basis. Formally describing concepts, ruling out ambiguity and relating concepts to each other and their context is the main objective of model-driven software development. Simply put, a conceptual model is a simplified representation of reality, devised for a certain purpose and seen from a certain point of view. The objective of a conceptual model is simulation of reality; it therefore needs to react to input in the same way as reality would. It is in this context that a precise connection between the genomics domain and the conceptual modeling approach makes full sense.

Describing a system by means of conceptual models means viewing the world as consisting of objects that belong to different classes, have distinct properties, and are related to each other in various ways. This way of viewing a system provides a powerful representation and reasoning tool. When modeling a domain in term of concepts, either the models serve by use as a reasoning tool to gain a deeper understanding of the domain at hand, usually as part of the design of an information system, or they guide the creation of a system which is ultimately directed at controlling or modifying that same domain. In the first application, the conceptual model serves as a visual representation of the domain, linking concepts and their respective behaviors while the latter resembles the blueprint used in traditional building. Not surprisingly, conceptual models and ontologies are closely intertwined, as is discussed in Sect. 16.4.

From an information systems point of view, present-day genomics is largely situated in the first phase of systems design, the analysis. Due to the youth of the genomics domain, many aspects of what is driving the mechanisms of life are still unknown, even though science never sits still and regularly updates knowledge. This work presents an interdisciplinary approach, in which experience in information systems development is put to practice by applying a conceptual modeling approach to genomics, fixing the present-day knowledge about the human genome in a visual form.

By allowing for a minor paradigm-shift, the human genome (or any genome, more specifically) can be considered an information system, a natural and highly complex form perhaps, but an information system nonetheless. Stated in a very simplified manner, data that is stored in DNA undergoes recombination, processing, and ultimately translation to proteins. It is the combination of these proteins and the influence from external factors (the environment) that define how an individual looks and behaves. These characteristics map neatly to the generic characteristics usually associated with information systems, only replacing man-made hardware (in the form of chips and circuits) with biological molecules and physics. As Chikofsky and Cross [4] state, reverse engineering is defined as the process of analyzing a subject system to (i) identify the systems components and their inter-relationships and (ii) create representations of the system in another form or at a higher level of abstraction. Just as software can be reverse-engineered in order to apply after-market changes or facilitate maintenance [5], it might very well be possible to reverse-engineer life itself and create a higher level of abstract representation in the form of a conceptual model. In this case, after-market changes and maintenance include treatments and/or prevention of previously untreatable disorders and disease – in the jargon of information systems, debugging life itself.

The value of a conceptual model of the human genome is thus two-fold. First, it allows for a visual and formal representation of the domain. Fixing a vocabulary and conceptual gamut from which scientists can draw, in order to ensure communication, takes place based on the same dictionary, using the same concepts. The conceptual model that we propose here is expected to evolve along with the advancing understanding of the domain in time. This evolution capability is an extra value in itself for a domain where knowledge is continuously being generated, and thus continuously subject to change. Only by having a well-defined, precise conceptual background – the conceptual model – can this new knowledge be properly incorporated, be understood, and be adequately managed.

Second, as part of a more abstract and ambitious objective, modeling the human genome serves as a tool for deeper understanding itself. As has been proven in many other domains, before a successful system can be created, a thorough understanding of its context is crucial. The tools devised for exactly this purpose, among others the

MDD-based (model-driven design) software production tools, often based on the UML notation, are now applied to the area of genomics.

Before introducing and explaining the basic components of the intended conceptual model of the human genome, we provide a short but necessary summary of the main properties of the genomic domain. These properties need to be understood in order to be adequately represented in the target conceptual model.

16.3 Models: Explaining the Domain

In a conceptual modeling-based approach, it is essential to distinguish between problem space and solution space. In conventional programming terms, problem space is associated with conceptual models, while the solution space is associated with programs. In the genomic domain that we consider here, the problem space represents in a conceptual model the concepts and their relationships that characterize the human genome. The solution space is composed of the set of real-life facts that conform and explain our human life. When developing a conceptual model for the human genome, we proceed in a bottom-up way: from the "implementation" (as we consider individuals here), we can build the conceptual model that captures the essential, relevant concepts. To do this, it is necessary to have a precise understanding of the notions that are found in "our" solution space – life itself. The goal of this section is to fix these main concepts, to understand the domain that we want to model in this case.

The history of this domain is very recent. We can start by going back to 1990, when the human genome project was initiated to identify all the genes contained in it and determine the sequence of the three billion base pairs that make up human DNA [6]. The genomic data was then stored in databases and analyzed to improve disease diagnosis and determine genetic susceptibility [7]. Many different approaches to extract useful information from the genomic sequence followed the publication of the first draft sequence of the human genome in 2001 [8]. These so-called post-genomic approaches included high-throughput groups of technologies in genomics, transcriptomics, proteomics, and metabolomics that measure and analyze thousands of DNA sequences, RNA transcripts, proteins, and metabolic fluxes in a single experiment. Thanks to these studies, it is now possible to understand specific aspects of the disease process and develop clinical applications. Some of the diseases that have already benefited from these types of data are cardiovascular disease [9, 10], obesity [11–13] and diabetes [14–16], among others.

After the appearance of these approaches and the high-throughput fever, the focus switched to knowledge-based studies that aim to decipher functional associations by combining several types of biological evidence. This is due to the fact that the integration of information from multiple data types is seen as a more robust and accurate approach to unravel functional associations. With the attention shifting from genes and proteins to biological systems, enormous amounts of high-throughput experimental data from diverse sources have become available, with the subsequent urgent need for integration. Evolution of tools for large-scale function annotations of genes, multi-member gene families and networks is crucial. [17] is an example of such tools.

Genotype

The distinction between phenotype and genotype is fundamental to the understanding of heredity and development of organisms. A genotype can be defined as an individual's collection of genes. When the information encoded in the genes is used to make proteins and RNA molecules, we say that the genotype is expressed; the expression of the genotype contributes to the individual's observable traits, called the phenotype. The phenotype of an organism is the collection of observable traits, such as height, eye color, and blood type. Some traits are largely determined by the genotype, while other traits are largely determined by environmental factors [18].

Organisms are characterized by great variation from one to another. On average, there are three million nucleotide differences between any two people taken at random. Even very closely related individuals have many genetic differences. Only twins have identical genomes, but still many mutations occur during the process of growth and development of the cells that form our body, which means that even the cells of the same individual do not contain identical genomes. Moreover, identical twins differ from each other due to environmental variations. This is why every human is different.

With this brief introduction to genotypes and genomes, we now consider some of the most interesting attempts of extracting useful information from the enormous amount of data provided by the human genome project.

Single Nucleotide Polymorphisms (SNPs)

Single-nucleotide polymorphisms (SNPs) are variations in the DNA sequence that occur when only one nucleotide changes. An illustrative example of a SNP is the change of a sequence from TAGGCTCA to TTGGCTCA. The concept is old; before the human genome was sequenced, it was known as nucleotide substitution and was used by yeast, worm and fly geneticists. SNPs, which are the most common form of human genetic variation, occur once every 1200 base pairs (bp) in the human genome [19] and at least in 1% of the population [20]; nucleotide substitutions at lower frequencies are not considered SNPs but mutations. This is due to the fact that SNP variations have no negative effect on the organism. When a variation has a negative effect on the organisms that carry it, the intensity with which the environment tends to eliminate it from the population is high; this is why mutations that produce disease are present at lower frequencies in populations. The harmless effect of SNPs lowers the selective pressure, thus raising the frequency in random populations. However, it is widely accepted that some SNPs could predispose people to disease or influence their response to a drug. This is why scientists have sought statistically significant associations between one or a few SNPs and a certain phenotype, like response to certain drugs or complex diseases such as hypertension, Alzheimer's, or schizophrenia. At the same time, clinical pharmacologists have sought statistically significant associations between one or a few SNPs and a certain phenotype, like effects of a new drug on asthma, diabetes or heart disease, or a new drug on treating a type of cancer. Such publications have often been followed by several reports refuting the original conclusion, as is stated in [21].

The HapMap

The International HapMap Project [22], completed between 2003 and 2006, is a joint effort to identify and catalog genetic similarities and differences in human beings. The information obtained from the HapMap is used by researchers around the world in experiments aiming to find genes that affect health, disease, or individual responses to medications and environmental factors. To make this information freely available to all scientists, all the data generated by the Project can be downloaded with minimal constraints through the HapMap webpage [23]. DNA samples studied in the first phase included samples from the six participating countries: Yoruba in Ibadan, Nigeria (YRI); Japanese in Tokyo, Japan (JPT); Han Chinese in Beijing, China (CHB); and Centre d'Etude du Polymorphisme Humain (CEPH) samples from Utah, having Caucasian ancestry from northern and western Europe (EU). When the International HapMap Project was completed, the researchers demonstrated that the ten million SNPs described variants, clustered into local neighborhoods called haplotypes [24], and that they can be accurately sampled by as few as 300,000 carefully chosen SNPs. New technological systems allow these SNPs to be systematically studied in high-throughput facilities that dramatically lower the cost [25].

ENCODE

Another example of research using the human genome data has been the Encyclopedia of DNA Elements (ENCODE) Pilot Project that ran from 2004 to 2007. In this project, about 1% of the human genome (30 Mb) was carefully selected and studied in great detail by a worldwide consortium made up of several research groups with diverse backgrounds and expertise [26]. The idea was to map a large variety of sequences, genes (protein-coding and non-coding exons), promoters, enhancers and repressor/silencer sequences amongst others. The consortium produced more than 200 data sets, representing more than 400 million data points, 200 Mb of comparative sequences (e.g., human genome versus chimpanzee), and guidelines for rapid release of all data [27]. Some highlights of their discoveries are: extensive overlap of gene transcripts and many non-protein coding regions; complex networks of transcripts; many new transcription start-sites, with an arrangement of far more complex regulatory sequences and binding of transcription factors, as is explained in detail in [28]. The extremely elaborate findings of the ENCODE Project produced significant confusion in the field, since they questioned previous concepts of what constitutes a gene [2]. Previously, a gene was defined as *"A segment of DNA, including all regulatory sequences for that DNA, which encodes a functional product whether it is a protein, small peptide, or one of the many classes of regulatory RNA."* The proposed definition post-ENCODE, aiming to avoid complexities of regulation and transcription, changed to: *"A union of genomic sequences encoding a coherent set of potentially overlapping functional products"*. The success of the pilot project was enough to collect new funding from NHGRI in September 2007 to scale the ENCODE Project to a production phase on the entire genome. In this phase of the project, the consortium continues with additional pilot-scale studies but also includes a data coordination center and a data analysis center to track, store and display ENCODE data and assist in integrated analyses of it.

Genome-Wide Association (GWA) Studies

A genome-wide association study (GWAS) is an approach used in genetics research to associate specific genetic variations with particular diseases. The method involves scanning genomes from many different people looking for genetic markers that can be used to predict the presence of a disease. Once genetic markers are identified, they can be used to understand how genes contribute to the disease and develop better prevention and treatment strategies.

The basis of genome-wide association studies are the comparisons between cases (patient with a disease) and controls (unaffected people), to identify the genetic differences that make a healthy person become sick. In common diseases, these individual differences may be subtle, but many slightly altered genes together with a risky environment may add up resulting in a higher chance to develop that disease. By identifying those risks, new clues for the development of preventive therapies will be identified [29].

Only after the HapMap Project catalogued millions of SNPs used to detect common disease and the development of high-throughput genotyping platforms, were GWA scans of whole genomes financially achievable. An early example of success was the discovery of a variant in the complement factor H gene (major risk factor for age-related macular degeneration). This finding, discovered by GWAS, provided a completely new perspective to prevent blindness in the elderly [30].

Phenotype and Metabolism

Although the genetic information of an individual is an important component of its uniqueness, it accounts for only a portion of this variation. An individual's phenotype is achieved and maintained by every different metabolic activity of the cell and the complex interactions among genotype, metabolic phenotype, and the environment. High-throughput technologies producing millions of data from a single experiment have transformed studies from a reductionist concept into a holistic practice where many metabolic phenotypes and the genes involved in that metabolism can be measured through functional genomics and metabolic profiling.

Metabolites are small molecule intermediates and products of metabolism. It is widely accepted that small changes in the activities of individual enzymes lead to small changes in metabolic fluxes, but can lead to large changes in metabolite concentrations [31]. Metabolomics is the discipline that studies metabolite composition and dynamics, as well as interactions among them or responses to changes in their environment; it is widely used in medical and nutritional systems biology [32–36], where the metabolome is useful to link the genotype and the environment. Changes in metabolic composition are likely to be subtle in the early stages of any disease. Many key metabolites from different pathways have a role in disease development, and the ability to simultaneously detect and measure all these metabolites allows for a more global analysis of the state of the disease. This discipline is more than forty years old, but in its early years, knowledge and technologies available were very limited. Insufficient information existed to link metabolite measurements to the human genome or physiology. The key milestone in this context was again the publication of the human genome sequence [8] and the subsequent appearance of different -omics approaches to extract useful information from it [37]. In addition, the invention of electrospray ionization (ESI) [38] finally allowed studies of intact molecules and facilitated coupling of liquid chromatography to mass spectrometry, which was a real revolution in the field.

Since GWAS became affordable, the most costly steps for the discovery of the genetic bases of disease have switched from genotyping to phenotyping. The discipline of phenomics, described by [39] as "the systematic study of phenotypes on a genome-wide scale," is still in an early phase of development. The data obtained in the analysis of human genomes reflects only one level of biological knowledge that may impose new constraints on the modeling of higher-level phenotypes. The redefinitions of phenotypes should be guided not only by gene expression findings, but also by data produced using models of cellular systems and signaling pathways. As is suggested by [40] the human phenome project will keep biomedical scientists busy for the next century. Understanding the true dimensionality of the human genome and reduction of its complexity are the main concerns at the moment. But this problem is minimum in comparison to defining the dimensions of the human phenome.

The scientific problem behind the mapping of the human phenome is large, and the solution is still unclear. It is obvious that, due to the amount of data that should be taken into account, only those strategies based in computational methods will be successful. This is already happening. Bioinformaticians around the world work on solutions that aim to cluster genes based on metabolism and signaling pathways data. By using the same collaborative approach to describe phenomes, the pathways that connect genomic variation to phenotypes will be revealed. An extra modeling effort should be made to develop high quality models that link the knowledge derived from human genome analysis with the knowledge obtained from the phenomic data. This is the key aspect in the context of this work. While major improvements in computational methods have been constant in bioinformatics research, there is a lack of application of sound information systems notions that would allow to structure the huge amount of information that is involved in this process of continuous generation of knowledge. A detailed, precise conceptual schema of the human genome would enable researchers to organize the relevant concepts correctly in order to guide the process of understanding the genomic information, and manage it effectively and efficiently.

Privacy and Personal Health Records

The early years of the 21st century have been characterized by a rapid advance in the biomedical field, thanks to the publication of the human genome sequence and the subsequent development of -omics approaches coupled with the emerging new discipline of bioinformatics. A real revolution in medicine is predicted when data from genomics, metabolomics and phenomics can be combined to not only diagnose existing diseases but also predict those that may come. For decades, personalized medicine has captured the imagination of physicians, politicians, and patients in general. Any human-related behavioral pattern could be seen as the expression of well-localized genomic information, which may soon provide answers to a question that humans have tried to resolve for centuries: why we are as we are, and what are the concepts that explain our essential characteristics as species.

Numerous relevant publications and projects have been released in recent years, especially in the clinical application domain: the first disease with a whole genome sequence, the acute myeloid leukemia genome [41], the initiation of the 1000 Genomes Project [42] aiming to obtain a detailed catalogue of human genetic variation, and the International Human Microbiome Consortium [43], to study and understand the role of the human microbiome in the maintenance of health and cause of disease and to use that knowledge to improve the ability to prevent and treat disease [39]. Other collaborations are still in progress, such as the Copy Number Variation Project [44] and the Cancer Genome Atlas [45]. Furthermore, plenty of genome-wide association studies associate specific loci to a variety of diseases.

The personalized medicine of the future will develop new treatments that combine data from the variations in the patient with the molecular bases of the disease itself. It will also help to identify sub-groups of patients for whom the different treatments will work best or groups of patients with higher risk of developing some diseases and, ideally, will help them to change their lifestyle or give them treatments to delay onset of a disease or reduce its impact. In the coming decades, a healthcare revolution will take place. At the biomedical level, new diagnostic and prognostic tools will increase our ability to predict the outcomes of drug therapy, and the use of biomarkers – biological molecules that indicate a particular disease state – could result in more focused and targeted drug development. Personalized medicine also offers attractive possibilities for politicians and decision-makers, since it has the potential to make health care more cost-effective.

But personalized medicine is an issue that is yet to come, even as there is much hope in the field. Many optimistic reviews continue to appear [46–48], but others are quite critical that it is not yet possible to assign a patient to an *unequivocal* phenotype and especially relate it to an *unequivocal* genotype mostly due to the amount of new findings and studies that appear almost monthly and that will increase in the future. We maintain that a conceptual model for the human genome is essential to make all these challenges feasible.

Although the advantages of genetics research are obvious and large, there is also a downside. To understand the difficulties, one needs to look beyond the technical aspects of the problem. Potential difficulties include technical security issues that may never guarantee a digital genetic data-set to be perfectly protected from intruders, or the considerably larger impact of digital data theft. While an old-fashioned paper file is as prone to theft or loss as its digital equivalent, it is the ease with which thousands of digital files can be stolen or damaged instantly that make the impact so much greater. However, it is the characteristics of the domain itself that make the discussion of ethics so intricate. Ethics, privacy awareness, and confidentiality are concepts closely related to identity. And the success with which they are practiced is strongly correlated to the separation of an individual's identifying features, and the studied object. It is here that storing an individual's genetic sequence makes matters difficult. In addition to being the object under study, that sequence is at the same time the very essence of biological identity, crystallized in four base molecules. Who we are, what sets us apart from each and every other individual, is largely defined by our genetic sequence. Even excluding certain parts of the sequence in order to avoid identification is very difficult, due to linkage disequilibrium [49], as has been shown by [50] in their attempt to uncover the unpublished ApoE gene of Dr. James Watson.

As we have discussed, biomolecular research has experienced enormous progress over the last decade, from the completion of the human genome project to functional genomics. The application of this knowledge has greatly improved our understanding of health and disease. It is now clear that disease states cannot be explained only by genomic information, since it involves the interaction between our genome and the environment. This interaction, reflected in the phenotype, is starting to be understood thanks to the different visions of the same problem captured by different post-genomic approaches. The logical step forward is to integrate all of these visions into a high-level model that can be at the same time informative and predictive.

16.4 Existing Modeling/Ontology-Based Approaches

Today's geneticists must negotiate a wide variety of genomic data repositories. Present-day genomics is closely tied to diversity. As the subject under investigation often relates to genetic diversity, the storage of current genetic knowledge is highly dispersed over a variety of resources. The National Center for Biotechnology Information (NCBI) [51] is a United States government-run initiative to create automated systems for storing and analyzing knowledge about molecular biology, biochemistry and genetics. The Human Gene Mutation Database at the Institute of Medical Genetics in Cardiff (HGMD) [52] represents an attempt to collate known (published) gene lesions responsible for human inherited disease. The goal of MutDB [53] is to annotate human variation data with protein structural information and other functionally relevant information, if available. And many more repositories exist, among which BIC [54], HGNC [55], HapMap [22–25, 56] and EMBL [57]. It is clear that this variety of data sources, although understandable from a biologist's point of view, leads to undesirable effects. Undesired data redundancy, as an effect of heterogeneity, leads to problems in keeping data updated. Curation often happens by human effort, which is prone to introducing errors and is costly in both time and money. Centralizing these data repositories, not in terms of physical storage but rather underlying conceptual vocabulary, or logical design, is thus of main concern for any future research and exploitation of genetic data. Fixing a conceptual gamut is best done through the use of a conceptual model.

An informational approach to this specific biological problem space is not entirely new. [58] describes the conceptual schema of a DNA database using an extended entity-relationship model. [59] has indicated how an extended object data model can be used to capture the properties of scientific experiments, and [60] includes models for representing genomic sequence data. [61] advanced on this work by presenting a first effort in conceptually modeling the *S. cerevisiae* genome, which is a type of yeast, by proposing a collection of conceptual data models for genomic data. Among these conceptual models are a basic schema diagram for genomic data, a protein-protein interaction model, a model for transcriptome data, and a schema for modeling alleles. Whereas [62] provides a broader view by presenting conceptual models for describing both genome sequences and related functional data sets, [63] further elaborated on the basic schema diagram for genomic data, thereby narrowing the focus and specializing it for the human genome.

Banning ambiguity in the genomics domain has been subject of many earlier attempts, including ontologies and formal descriptions in natural language. From the computer scientist perspective, ambiguity is always considered an undesirable and often avoidable feature. Indeed, in computer design, the behavior of the system is always intended to be known. In biology, and especially genomics, this is simply not the case. Complexity, derived from the randomness that created the conditions allowing life to emerge, today obscures the processes driving this very same system. Earlier attempts at solving this undesired ambiguity include the application of ontologies. [64] provides an overview of gene ontology (GO) and how it is used to solve ambiguity in the genomics domain in general. [65] describes the application of gene ontology to the SNP concept. [66] then provides an ontology-based converter that allows for solving the notational problems associated with heterogeneous SNP descriptions. But all of these approaches are far from what we could call a precise conceptual definition. Generally, while the application of an ontology is considered necessary, it only forms part of the solution.

From our review of literature on the subject, it is clear that most of the work that has been going on is ontology-based. It appears crucial to identify the essential differences between ontologies and conceptual schemas, or more specifically, how they are complementary. We feel that the extensive use of different ontologies in the genomic domain denotes the lack of an adequate conceptual modeling-based approach in the domain, under the assumption that a formal ontology should constitute the conceptual base over which a conceptual model is properly elaborated. A common vocabulary is necessary, but not sufficient to structure and manage adequately the huge amount of information generated in the genomic context.

In the remainder of this section, we focus on describing both methods, especially focusing on the properties that – apparently – make them different. For a proper understanding of any domain, both are vital. Ontologies and conceptual schemas belong to two different epistemic levels, they have different objects, and are created with different objectives. As [67] states: ontologies should deal with general assumptions concerning the explanatory invariants of a domain – those that provide a framework enabling understanding and explanation of data across all domains inviting explanation and understanding. Conceptual schemas, on the other hand, should address the relation between such general explanatory categories and the facts that exemplify them in a particular domain.

Assmann [68] describes models as having a causal connection to the modeled part of reality; they must form true or faithful representations so that queries of the model make reliable statements about reality; simulate reality. That is, a model is an external and explicit representation of a part of reality as seen by the people who wish to use that model to understand, change, manage, and control that part of reality. Also, while models represent reality faithfully, they may abstract from irrelevant details. [68] describes ontologies as formal explicit specifications of a shared conceptualization. Considering that according to [69], an ontology is an explicit specification of a conceptualization, this definition implies that an ontology is a specific type of model. To identify the exact difference between models and ontologies, some other qualities of models require introduction. Following the above definition, ontologies are models shared by a group of people. In general, models are not necessarily shared. An important property of ontologies is the open-world assumption, stating that anything not explicitly expressed by an ontology is unknown. In contrast, most systems models underlie the assumption that what has not been specified is either implicitly disallowed or implicitly allowed, the so-called closed-world assumption. Further, models are usually considered to be of prescriptive nature in that they form the templates from which the system is later implemented. Because of their open-world assumptions, ontologies should then be regarded as descriptive models. Summarizing the above discussion, ontologies focus on description and conceptualization (structural modeling) of things, while models focus on the specification, control, and generation of systems. It is conceivable that a conceptual model can be used as visualization layer on top of an ontology, thus further fading the distinction.

The main difference between ontologies and conceptual models thus seems to exist in the intention with which they are created. Ontologies are considered descriptive by nature and usually serve to ensure that concepts are indicated by the same terms, essentially disambiguating domain jargon. Models are prescriptive, commonly defined as part of a design process. Their function is to disambiguate, and at the same time simulate reality. [70] states that two ontologies can be different in the vocabulary used (using English or Italian words, for instance), while sharing the same conceptualization. The vocabulary used in this work to capture the ontological concepts of the genomic domain comes in the form of a conceptual model. The conceptual modeling approach discussed here thus serves to specify an ontological description. It shows that representing concepts in a descriptive manner, as is common in creation of ontologies, is very well facilitated by the application of a conceptual model.

It is interesting to remark that, although many databases and ontologies exist and they include a lot of diverse genomic information, it is hard to see their corresponding, precise conceptual models that would enable characterization, comparison and evaluation of the quality of their data. It is the main goal of the next section to introduce such a conceptual model as the main contribution of this chapter, to show that it is possible to provide the required formal structure for all the data that are considered relevant to understand and interpret this huge amount of genomic information.

16.5 Results of Conceptual Modeling

This section proposes a conceptual model of the human genome. Due to sheer size, the model is divided in three main views: gene-mutation, transcription, and genome. Each view is discussed in turn. The model is described using the widely-accepted UML standard [71], using a data projection centered on attributes that allows one to see the final model as an ER-like model. Since the complete schema is too large to be presented in A4 format, we refer the reader to a digital version: http://www.pros. upv.es/images/stories/imgc_cshg.jpg. [62] describes the evolution of the conceptual model of the human genome, while [63] describes the evolution of the model more in general and provides a descriptive overview of how the model was initially configured, and from where it evolved to what it is now.

Gene-Mutation View

As depicted in Fig. 16.1, the gene-mutation view, models the knowledge about genes, their structure and their allelic variants. It models current knowledge about the atomic entity of heredity, genes, and the various real-world instances of this rather abstract concept. These instances are the actual encountered genetic sequences, or alleles, in individuals among populations. The principal classes in this view are the *Gene* class and the *Allele* class. The *Gene* class models the concept of a generic gene, independent of their samples stored in public databases. The attributes of the *Gene* class are: id_Hugo (universal code for the gene in HGNC [55]); id_symbol (alphanumeric code for the gene in HGNC, i.e. NF1 for Neurofibromin 1, a neurofibromatosis-related protein); name (name of the gene), summary (summary extracted from NCBI [51]); chromosome (chromosome number where the gene is

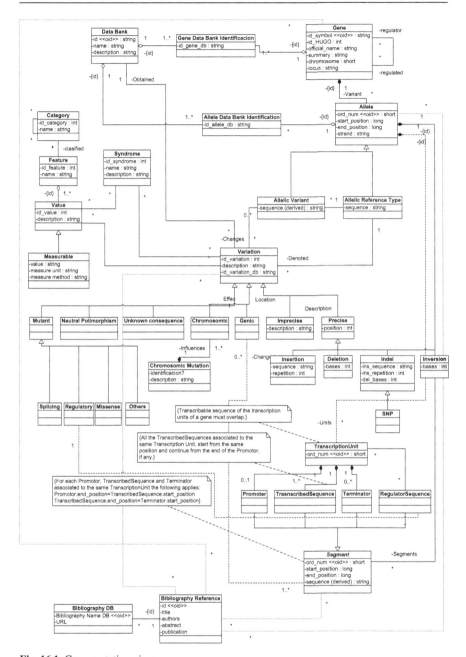

Fig. 16.1 Gene-mutation view

located), and locus (gene location within the chromosome). Genes have been historically characterized by their coding capacity; being able to synthesize protein through an everyday better-known transcription process. But this is not the only role of genes. Recent advances show, for instance, how important it is to identify DNA sequences that are able to activate/disactivate the coding behavior of genes. This important feature is easily incorporated into the model by introducing a self-referencing relation intended to represent which genes play the regulator function with respect to which genes.

The *Allele* class represents instances of a generic gene, as stored in public databases. The model represents relevant information about alleles: allele database source (through the class *DataBank*), type of allele (reference or variant), variants of an allele (mutations), *Allele* segmentation, and the corresponding transcription process. The attributes of the *Allele* class are: ord_num (internal identifier); start_position and end_position in the chromosomic sequence, and DNA sequence of the allele.

Alleles are classified as reference alleles or variant alleles (*Allelic Variant* and *Reference Type* classes as specializations of *Allele*). *Reference Type* represents the alleles used as references in public databases. The association between *Reference Type* and *Allelic Variant* represents the relationship between a reference allele and its variations. The specialization hierarchy from the *Allelic Variant* class classifies allelic variants by three criteria: (i) location, (ii) description, and (iii) effect.

Location represents the scope of the variation. In case the variation only affects one gene, it is said to be *Genic*. However, when the variation has an impact on various genes, and thus becomes a deviation at chromosomal level, it is considered *Chromosomic*.

Description represents the degree of completeness and accuracy to which the variation is described in the source, i.e. if the variation is precise (*Precise*) or imprecise (*Imprecise*). If the variation is imprecise, there is a description attribute that stores the information in the same format as in the source, generally natural language. If the variation is considered precise, the position of the variation within the corresponding allele is stored in the position attribute. The precise variations are classified in four specializing classes: (i) *Insertion*, (ii) *Deletion*, (iii) *Indel* and (iv) *Inversion*. Variations that qualify as *Insertions* introduce, at the specified position, a given sequence at a given amount of repetitions. *Deletions* qualify the event of mutations in which a number of bases are deleted from the sequence starting from the specified position. An *Indel* can be considered as the combination of an *Insertion* and a *Deletion*, in which, at the specified position, a deletion of del_bases nucleotides occurs, while inserting an ins_sequence of nucleotides, an ins_repetition amount of times at that very same position. *Inversion* indicates the event in which a mutation consists of an inversion of a number of nucleotides, as defined in the bases attribute.

Effect classifies the allelic variant by the effect(s) on phenotype, and determines if a variation is *Mutant* (i.e. has a pathologic effect), *Neutral Polymorphism* (has a neutral effect on phenotype), or *Unknown Consequence* (the effect is unknown). The *Mutant* class further classifies the mutation by its effect on the protein synthesis process. Its specialized classes are: (i) *Splicing*, in case the mutation affects the splicing process (frequently located at splice junctions); (ii) *Regulatory*, in case the mutation affects the regulation of the gene; (iii) *Missense*, in case a point mutation results in a codon change (usually resulting in a non-functional protein), and (iv) *Others*, including other types of point mutations like nonsense (in which the mutation results in a premature STOP-codon, and thus eventually a shortened protein) or mutations that provoke frame shift.

The *SNP* entity is one of the more recent additions to the model. It handles the Single Nucleotide Polymorphism concept discussed earlier in Sect. 16.2. The genomic domain has developed many uses, and accordingly various definitions to this specific term. A very practical, widely spread application of the SNP concept is as a predictive marker. Here, due to high costs of sequencing an entire genome, rather specific parts that contain so-called genetic markers (often SNPs) undergo sequencing. By using the property of linkage disequilibrium [49], it is then possible to predict certain alleles in other parts of the sequence. This application, born out of practical reasons and high costs, is not facilitated in the proposed conceptual model, as it does not contribute to a deeper understanding of the human genome itself. Rather, it is a clever solution to a problem risen from the relative youth of the field. An *SNP* itself is considered to be a single nucleotide polymorphism, thus a specific variation of the type *Indel*. Crucial to the SNP concept is that no causal relation exists with a negative phenotype, it can therefore only be a variation of the type *Neutral Polymorphism*.

The *Category*, *Feature*, *Value*, *Measurable* and *Syndrome* concepts associate a *Variation* with phenotype. A *Syndrome* is what corresponds most to the general concept of disease; neurofibromatosis and Huntington's disease are examples of instances of this class. A *Syndrome* can be provoked by a single or various variations, and a *Variation* can have multiple diseases associated to it. Syndromes are usually characterized by various features, instances of the class *Feature*; in the case of neurofibromatosis, this includes so-called cafe-au-lait spots. These *Features* are in turn classified by *Categories*, which have a recursive property indicated by the self-referencing relation. An example of a *Category* would be 'Cardiovascular', or 'Skeletal'. In the case of neurofibromatosis, the previously mentioned cafe-au-lait spots fall under the 'Skin' category. Adding to this, each *Feature* consists of a collection of *Values*, which represent the measurable effects on phenotype (*Measurable*). For instance, a *Feature* blood pressure that has *Value* 160/100 and has *Measurable* properties mm/Hg represents the *Syndrome* high blood pressure. In some cases, like cafe-au-lait spots, the *Feature* has no *Measurable*; rather, cafe-au-lait spots are present or not. It is important to note that *Variations* might have a *Value* associated directly to them, without provoking any *Syndrome*. This is the case for variations, typically SNPs, that provoke neutral phenotypes like eye-color.

This view also models the allele segmentation for the transcription process. (The part of the conceptual model associated to the transcription process itself is explained below.) The *Segment* class represents a segment of the allele. Its attributes are: ord_num (identifies a certain segment among all the allele segments), start_position and end_position (initial and end position of the segment in the chromosome), and sequence (DNA sequence between start_position and end_position). The *Segment* entity has four specialized entities classified by their function in the transcription process: *Promoter* (DNA sequence region that facilitates the initiation of the transcription process); *TranscribedSequence* (DNA sequence transcribed by the RNA polymerase II); *Terminator* (DNA sequence that signals the end of the transcription process); and *RegulatorSequence* (DNA sequence that regulates one or many transcription units). The *Transcription Unit* class models (as its name indicates) the biological concept of a transcription unit; the attribute ord_num identifies a specific transcription unit in the system. This class is defined as being a composite of a *Promoter* segment, many *TranscribedSequence* segments (many transcribed sequences may exist in the same transcription unit, all starting at the same position), many *Terminator* segments (a transcription unit may have more than one terminator segment), and many *RegulatorSequence* segments (a transcription unit may have many regulatory segments, shared by different transcription units belonging to several genes in the most general case). It is interesting to note here that regulator sequences do not necessarily have to reside within the gene they regulate, even more they can reside on entirely different chromosomes [72].

The model also includes some restrictions, expressed in natural language and mostly related to the allele segmentation for the transcription process. The restriction associated with the *Segment* entity regulates the order in which *TranscriptionUnits* can happen. The first *Segment* is always of the type *Promoter*, and the last is always a segment of the type *Terminator*; what comes between is a combination of *TranscribedSequences* and *RegulatorSequences*. Also, note that there cannot exist gaps between *Segments*; this means that every *Segment* needs to have a start_position equal to the end_position of the preceding *Segment*.

Transcription View

Transcription is the biological process in which the genetic sequence in DNA is transferred, or transcribed onto RNA, a molecule very similar to DNA. This allows the genetic sequence to leave the cell nucleus, in order to reach other biological systems that will eventually lead to the construction of complex proteins. A gene can be thought of as a set of separate blocks of nucleotides. The coding blocks, or exons, eventually form the transcript, although which exons are included in which version of the transcript may vary. The process that regulates which exons are included, and discards all of the introns, is called splicing; see [2] for more information. The transcription view in Fig. 16.2 models the basic steps in protein synthesis. The *Primary Transcript* class represents the transcribed copy from DNA to RNA of the *TranscribedSequence*. In the biological process of transcription, the primary transcript is an RNA molecule, containing a literal copy of the DNA sequence of a gene, including all coding (exons) and non-coding (introns) fragments. Its sequence attribute is a derived attribute from the *Segment* class. The *PrimaryTranscriptPath* class models the different splicing factor-driven partitions of the *Primary Transcript*; its attribute ord_num identifies a partition from the complete set of partitions of a *Primary Transcript*. In the *ElementTranscript* class, the ord_num attribute identifies a specific fragment within the partition. The *Exon* and *Intron* classes specialize the

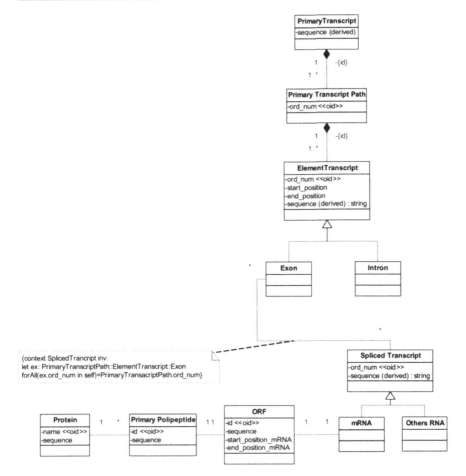

Fig. 16.2 Transcription view

type of partition fragments. The *Spliced Transcript* class represents different exon combinations (sequences) of a *Primary Transcript*; its ord_num attribute identifies it among all the allele spliced transcripts. The result of these combinations will be the *mRNA* and *others RNA* types (specialized classes from *Spliced Transcript*).

The *mRNA* contains a nucleotide sequence that could potentially encode a protein; this is known as *ORF* (Open Reading Frame). The id attribute of an *ORF* identifies it in the system, and the sequence attribute stores the codifying sequence. The *Primary Polypeptide* class describes the protein primary structure: the amino acid chain obtained as a result of the translation of an *ORF*. This amino acid chain undergoes chemical transformations, and the final result is a functional protein, represented in the model as the *Protein* class. A protein can consist of one or more *Primary Polypeptides*. In the *Protein*, its name attribute represents the name of the resulting protein, and its sequence attribute the amino acid sequence.

Genome View

The genome view in Fig. 16.3 models individual human genomes. This view is interesting for future applications, since massive parallel sequencing technologies will allow the complete sequencing of individual genomes at a very low price in the near future [10]. The class *Research Centre* represents the labs or research centers where an individual human genome is sequenced. A genome (*Genome*) is considered a set of chromosomes (*Chromosome*). The number attribute identifies a chromosome in a genome. The couple relation on the *Chromosome* class represents the concept of

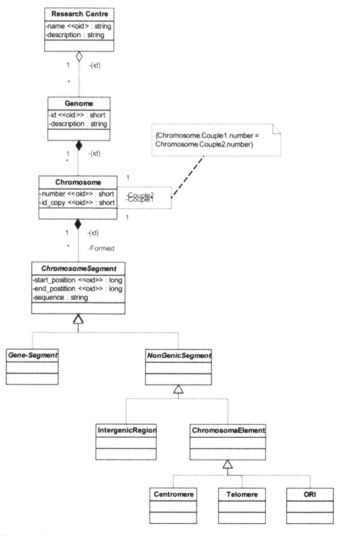

Fig. 16.3 Genome view

homologue pairing, i.e. every human cell will carry two equivalent chromosomes – one from the father and one from the mother – with the same genes but different alleles for each gene.

The *ChromosomeSegment* class represents the segments that constitute the chromosome. This class has a sequence attribute that stores the corresponding DNA sequence delimited by start_position and end_position attributes. A chromosome has two main types of segments: coding-related segments (*GenicSegment*) and non-coding-related segments (*NonGenicSegment*). Two classes specialize *NonGenicSegment*: the *IntergenicRegion* class (the regions between genes) and *ChromosomalElement* class, which in turn has three specializing classes that describe other elements of the chromosomes (*Centromere*, *Telomere* and *ORI*) whose function is to keep the chromosome functional and are not involved in protein production.

These three conceptual views are the components in which the entire conceptual model is structured. This conceptual model specification shows how conceptual modeling can improve the understanding of biological, genomic information. Taken together, these three views provide the desired, holistic conceptual model intended to enable the storage, management and subsequent adequate understanding of the information associated to the human genome.

16.6 Problem Statement and Conclusions

It has been our intention here to demonstrate that a conceptual model for the human genome is not only necessary but feasible. The precise interpretation of the human genome faces some of the most fascinating questions that humans have asked since the very beginning of civilization: Why are we as we are? What rules lead and explain our behavior? To answer these questions from a systemic perspective implies to specify the conceptual models that the genomic code of each individual implements. This systemic perspective would interpret an individual as a program whose instructions are executed according to that genetic code. To discover the basic instructions and their meaning directly from the final code seems to be a colossal task. We propose to face these questions from a pure conceptual modeling perspective, the main objective being to introduce a conceptual model intended to guide the design and implementation of a genomic database, where the link between genotype and phenotype is led by the conceptual model and not by the uncontrolled accumulation of information that is becoming more and more heterogeneous, inconsistent, redundant, and almost impossible to exploit adequately.

In this direction, we have introduced a conceptual model that covers the perspectives of genotype, phenotype, and variation/mutations. Concepts behind each perspective are determined and represented in the conceptual model, providing the basis for creating the required database where all relevant information associated with the human genome could be correctly represented and exploited.

We want to emphasize the potential of such a concept-centric database. Instead of having the current model of isolated islands of different types of genomic information, this logical central repository would be ready to represent all the relevant information in a way that would make possible to manage it, relating genotype with phenotype in a precise way.

More than that, the conceptual model-oriented characteristic of such a database would guarantee its evolution according to the incorporation of new knowledge to the domain, something that happens continuously in the genomic domain.

It is our intention to include all relevant information in such a formal data repository. Gene by gene, incorporating genotype and phenotype relationships already discovered from wherever they are stored, as well as incorporating new pieces of relevant information as they are discovered by the researchers, we can talk about building an information system for the human genome that adheres strictly to the good principles of conceptual modeling, assuring the quality of the stored data, and facilitating the mechanisms that should allow to exploit the information to enable – for instance – the objectives introduced in Sect. 16.3 when talking about personalized medicine.

We close with a challenging analogy to explore the possibilities that we have discussed here. We, humans, are able to create robots that in some years could reproduce particular human behavior. Let us imagine that these robots survive a climate disaster, unfortunately a fashionable topic nowadays, and that the silicon life resists where the organic life fails. These robots could evolve according to their programmed capabilities created by us, humans; at a given moment, they could wonder where they come from and why they are as they are. To answer this question, they would need to know and understand the conceptual models that their creators used to create them. We hope that this chapter could help them understand the path to follow in order that they might find their answers.

References

1. Olivé A (2007) Conceptual modeling of information systems. 1st edn. Springer, Berlin
2. Gerstein MB, Bruce C, Rozowsky JS, Zheng D, Du J, Korbel JO, Emanuelsson O, Zhang ZD, Weissman S, Snyder M (2007) What is a gene, post-ENCODE? History and updated definition. Genome Res, 17:669–681
3. Pearson H (2006) Genetics: What is a gene? Nature 441(7092):398–402
4. Chikofsky EJ, Cross II, JI (1990) Reverse engineering and design recovery: a taxonomy. IEEE Software 7(1):13–18
5. Canfora G, Di Penta M (2008) Frontiers of reverse engineering: a conceptual model. Proceedings of frontiers of software maintenance (FoSM 2008), pp 38–47 (2008)
6. Human Genome Project Information,   http://www.ornl.gov/sci/techresources/Human_ Genome/
7. Collins FS, Morgan M, Patrinos A (2003) The human genome project: lessons from large-scale biology. Science 300:286–290
8. Venter JC, Adams MD, Myers EW, Li PW, Mural RJ, Sutton GG, Smith HO, Yandell M, Evans CA, Holt RA, Gocayne JD, Amanatides P, Ballew RM, Huson DH, Wortman JR, Zhang Q, Kodira CD, Zheng XH, Chen L, Skupski M, Subramanian G, Thomas PD, Zhang J, Gabor Miklos GL, Nelson C, Broder S, Clark AG., Nadeau J, McKusick VA, Zinder N et al (2001) The sequence of the human genome. Science 291:1304–1351

9. Edwards AV, White MY, Cordwell SJ (2008) The role of proteomics in clinical cardiovascular biomarker discovery. Mol Cell Proteomics 7:1824–1837
10. Giovane A, Balestrieri A, Napoli C (2008) New insights into cardiovascular and lipid metabolomics. J Cell Biochem, 105:648–654
11. Blakemore AI, Froguel P (2008) Is obesity our genetic legacy? J Clin Endocrinol Metabol, 93(11-1):51–56
12. Chen X, Hess S (2008) Adipose proteome analysis: focus on mediators of insulin resistance. Expet Rev Proteomics 5:827–839
13. Pietilainen KH, Sysi-Aho M, Rissanen A, Seppanen-Laakso T, Yki-Jarvinen H, Kaprio J, Oresic M (2007) Acquired obesity is associated with changes in the serum lipidomic profile independent of genetic effects: a monozygotic twin study. PLoS ONE 2:18–32
14. Bougneres P, Valleron AJ (2008) Causes of early-onset type 1 diabetes: toward data-driven environmental approaches. J Exp Med 105:2953–2957
15. Frayling TM (2007) Genome-wide association studies provide new insights into type 2 diabetes aetiology. Nat Rev Genet 8:657–662
16. Orešic M, Simell S, Sysi-Aho M, NLnt-Salonen K, SeppLnen-Laakso T, Parikka V, Katajamaa M, Hekkala A, Mattila I, Keskinen P, Yetukuri L, Reinikainen A, Lehde J, Suortti T, Hakalax J, Simell T, Hyty H, Veijola R, Ilonen J, Lahesmaa R, Knip M, Simell O (2008) Dysregulation of lipid and amino acid metabolism precedes islet autoimmunity in children who later progress to type 1 diabetes. J Exp Med 205:2975–2984
17. Li J, Li X, Su H, Chen H, Galbraith DW (2006) A framework of integrating gene relations from heterogeneous data sources: an experiment on Arabidopsis thaliana. Bioinformatics 22:2037
18. Human Genome Research Institute, Glossary of genetic terms. http://www.genome.gov/glossary/
19. Vignal A, Milan D, SanCristobal M, Eggen A (2002) A review on SNP and other types of molecular markers and their use in animal genetics. Genetics 34:275
20. Zhao Z, Fu YX, Hewett-Emmett D, Boerwinkle E (2003) Investigating single nucleotide polymorphism (SNP) density in the human genome and its implications for molecular evolution. Gene 312:207–213
21. Nebert DW, Vesell, ES (2004) Advances in pharmacogenomics and individualized drug therapy: exciting challenges that lie ahead. Eur J Pharmacol 500:267–280
22. International HapMap Consortium (2003) The International HapMap Project. Nature 426:789–96
23. The HapMap project, http://www.hapmap.org
24. International HapMap Consortium (2005) A haplotype map of the human genome. Nature 437: 1229–1320
25. International HapMap Consortium (2007) A second generation human haplotype map of over 3.1 million SNPs. Nature 449: 851–862
26. The ENCODE Project Consortium (2004) The ENCODE (ENCyclopedia Of DNA Elements) Project. Science 306:636–640
27. The ENCODE (ENCyclopedia Of DNA Elements) Project, http://genome.ucsc.edu/ENCODE
28. The Encode Project Consortium (2007) Identification and analysis of functional elements in 1% of the human genome by the ENCODE pilot project. Nature 447:799–816
29. Hindorff LA, Sethupathy P, Junkins HA, Ramos EM, Mehta JP, Collins FS, Manolio TA (2009) Potential etiologic and functional implications of genome-wide association loci for human diseases and traits. Proceedings of the National Academy of Sciences, 106:9362–9369
30. Dewan A, Liu M, Hartman S, Zhang SS, Liu DT, Zhao C, Tam PO, Chan WM, Lam DS, Snyder M, Barnstable C, Pang CP, Hoh J (2006) HTRA1 promoter polymorphism in wet age-related macular degeneration. Science 314:989–992
31. Zhu J, Wiener MC, Zhang C, Fridman A, Minch E, Lum PY, Sachs JR, Schadt EE (2007) Increasing the power to detect causal associations by combining genotypic and expression data in segregating populations. PLoS Comput Biol 3:e69
32. Orešic M, Vidal-Puig A, Hanninen V (2006) Metabolomic approaches to phenotype characterization and applications to complex diseases. Expet Rev Mol Diagnos, 6:575e85

33. van Ommen B (2004) Nutrigenomics: exploiting systems biology in the nutrition and health arenas. Nutrition 20:48
34. Raamsdonk LM, Teusink B, Broadhurst D, Zhang N, Hayes A, Walsh MC, Berden JA, Brindle KM, Kell DB, Rowland JJ, Westerhoff HV, van Dam K, Oliver SG (2001) A functional genomics strategy that uses metabolome data to reveal the phenotype of silent mutations. Nat Biotechnol, 19: 45–50
35. Gieger C, Geistlinger L, Altmaier E, Hrab de Angelis M, Kronenberg F, Meitinger T, Mewes HW, Wichmann HE, Weinberger KM, Adamski J, Illig T, Suhre K (2008) Genetics meets metabolomics: a genomewide association study of metabolite profiles in human serum. PLoS Genet, 4:e1000282
36. Cascante M, Boros LG, Comin-Anduix B, de Atauri P, Centelles JJ, Lee PW-N (2002) Metabolic control analysis in drug discovery and disease. Nat Biotechnol, 20: 243e9
37. Collins F, Green E, Guttmacher A, Guyer M (2003) A vision for the future of genomics research. Nature 422:835e47
38. Fenn J, Mann M, Meng C, Wong S, Whitehouse C (1989) Electrospray ionization for mass spectrometry of large biomolecules. Science 246:64e71
39. Bilder RM, Sabb FW, Cannon TD, London ED, Jentsch JD, Stott Parker D, Poldrack RA, Evans C, Freimer NB (2009) Phenomics: the systematic study of phenotypes on a genome-wide scale. Neurosci 164:30–42
40. Freimer N, Sabatti C (2003) The human phenome project. Nat Genet 34:15–21
41. Ley TJ, Mardis ER, Ding L, Fulton B, McLellan MD, Chen K, Dooling D, Dunford-Shore BH, McGrath S, Hickenbotham M, Cook L, Abbott R, Larson DE, Koboldt DC, Pohl C, Smith S, Hawkins A, Abbott S, Locke D, Hillier LW, Miner T, Fulton L, Magrini V, Wylie T, Glasscock J, Conyers J, Sander N, Shi X, Osborne JR, Minx P et al (2008) DNA sequencing of a cytogenetically normal acute myeloid leukaemia genome. Nature 456:66–72
42. The 1000 Genomes Project, http://www.1000genomes.org/
43. The Human Microbiome, http://www.human-microbiome.org/
44. The Copy Number Variation Project, http://www.sanger.ac.uk/humgen/cnv/
45. The Cancer Genome Atlas, http://cancergenome.nih.gov/
46. Kroemer HK, Meyer zu Schwabedissen HE (2010) A piece in the puzzle of personalized medicine. Clin Pharmacol Therapeut 87:19–20
47. Mousses S, Kiefer J, von Hoff D, Trent J (2008) Using biointelligence to search the cancer genome: an epistemological perspective on knowledge recovery strategies to enable precision medical genomics. Oncogene 27(2):S58–66
48. Potti A, Dressman HK, Bild A, Riedel RF, Chan G, Sayer R, Cragun J, Cottrill H, Kelley MJ, Petersen R, Harpole D, Marks J, Berchuck A, Ginsburg GS, Febbo P, Lancaster J, Nevins JR: Genomic signatures to guide the use of chemotherapeutics. Nat Med 12:12941300
49. Devlin B, Risch N (1995) A comparison of linkage disequilibrium measures for fine-scale mapping. Genomics 29(2):311–322
50. Nyholt DR, Chang-En Y, Visscher PM (2009) On Jim Watsons APOE status: genetic information is hard to hide. Eur J Hum Genet 17(2):147–150
51. Maglott D, Ostell J, Pruitt KD, Tatusova T (2006) Entrez gene: gene-centered information at NCBI. Nucleic Acids Res 35:26–32
52. Stenson PD, Mort M, Ball EV, Howells K, Phillips AD, Thomas NST, Cooper DN (2009) The Human gene mutation database: 2008 update. Genome Med 1:13
53. Mooney SD, Altman RB (2003) MutDB: annotating human variation with functionally relevant data. Bioinformatics 19:1858–1860
54. Szabo C, Masiello A, Ryan JF, The BIC Consortium, Brody LC (2000) The breast cancer information core: database design, structure, and scope. Hum Mutat 16:123–131
55. Povey S, Lovering R, Bruford E, Wright M, Lush M, Wain H (2001) The HUGO gene nomenclature committee (HGNC). Hum Genet 109:678–680
56. Gibbs RA, Belmont JW, Hardenbol P, Willis TD, Yu F et al (2003) The international HapMap project. Nature 426:789–796
57. Stoesser G, Tuli MA, Lopez R, Sterk P (1999) The EMBL nucleotide sequence database. Nucleic Acids Res 27:18–24

58. Okayama T, Tamura T, Gojobori T, Tateno Y, Ikeo K, Miyazaki S, Fukami-Kobayashi K, Sugawara H (1998) Formal design and implementation of an improved DDBJ DNA database with a new schema and object-oriented library. Bioinformatics 14(6):472

59. Chen IMA, Markowitz V (1995) Modeling scientific experiments with an object data model. In: Proceedings of the SSDBM. IEEE Press, New York pp 391–400

60. Medigue C, Rechenmann F, Danchin A, Viari A (1999) Imagene, an integrated computer environment for sequence annotation and analysis. Bioinformatics 15(1):2

61. Paton NW, Khan SA, Hayes A, Moussouni F, Brass A, Eilbeck K, Goble CA, Hubbard SJ, Oliver SG (2000) Conceptual modeling of genomic information. Bioinformatics, 16 (6) 548–557

62. Pastor MA, Burriel V, Pastor O (2009) Conceptual modeling of human genome mutations: a dichotomy between what we have and what we should have. BIOSTEC Bioinformatics 2010, pp 160–166

63. Pastor O, Levin AM, Celma M, Casamayor JC, Eraso Schattka LE, Villanueva MJ, Perez-Alonso M (2010) Enforcing conceptual modeling to improve the understanding of the human genome. Proceedings of the IVth international conference on research challenges in information science RCIS 2010, Nice, France, IEEE Press, New York

64. Ashburner M, Ball CA, Blake JA (2000) Gene ontology: tool for the unification of biology. Nat Genet 25(1):25–30

65. Schwarz DF, Hädicke O, Erdmann J, Ziegler A, Bayer D, Möller S (2008) SNPtoGO: characterizing SNPs by enriched GO terms. Bioinformatics 24(1):146

66. Coulet A, Smal-Tabbone M, Benlian P, Napoli A, Devignes M-D (2006) SNP-converter: an ontology-based solution to reconcile heterogeneous SNP descriptions for pharmacogenomic studies. Lect Notes Bioinform 4075:82–93

67. Fonseca F, Martin J (2005) Learning the differences between ontologies and conceptual schemas through ontology-driven information systems. J Assoc Inform Syst, 8:129–142

68. Aßmann U, Zschaler S, Wagner G (2006) Ontologies, meta-models, and the model-driven paradigm. In: Calero C, Ruiz F, Piattini M (eds) Ontologies for software engineering and software technology. Springer, Berlin

69. Gruber TR (1993) A translation approach to portable ontology specification. Knowl Acquis 5:199–220

70. Guarino N (2006) Formal ontology in information systems (1998). In: Bennett B, Fellbaum C (eds) Proceedings of the fourth international conference (FOIS 2006), vol 150, IOS Press, Amsterdam

71. Booch, G, Rumbaugh, J, Jacobson, I (1999) The unified modelling language user guide. Addison-Wesley Professional. Pearson Education, Upper Saddle River

72. Spilianakis CG, Lalioti MD, Town T, Lee GR, Flavell RA (2005) Interchromosomal associations between alternatively expressed loci. Nature 435:637–645

Chapter 17
The Theory of Conceptual Models, the Theory of Conceptual Modelling and Foundations of Conceptual Modelling

Bernhard Thalheim

Abstract Conceptual modelling is a widely applied practice and has led to a large body of knowledge on constructs that might be used for modelling and on methods that might be useful for modelling. It is commonly accepted that database application development is based on conceptual modelling. It is, however, surprising that only very few publications have been published on a *theory of conceptual modelling*. *Modelling* is typically supported by languages that are well-founded and easy to apply for the description of the application domain, the requirements and the system solution. It is thus based on a *theory of modelling constructs*. Modelling is ruled by its purpose, e.g., construction of a system, simulation of real-world situations, theory construction, explanation of phenomena, or documentation of an existing system. Modelling is also an engineering activity with engineering steps and engineering results. It is thus *engineering*.

17.1 Towards a Theory of Conceptual Models and Conceptual Modelling

Models are different for different purposes. We may develop a model for analysis of an application domain, for construction of a system, for communicating about an application, for assessment, and for governance. These different purposes result in different goals and task portfolios.

Bernhard Thalheim
Department of Computer Science, Christian-Albrechts University Kiel, 24098 Kiel, Germany,
e-mail: thalheim@is.informatik.uni-kiel.de

D. W. Embley and B. Thalheim (eds), *Handbook of Conceptual Modeling.*   543
DOI 10.1007/978-3-642-15865-0, © Springer 2011

Models are an essential part of computer science. While preparing a survey on models, we realised that computer science uses more than 50 different models. In analysing these different models, we discover four commonalities:

Purpose: Models and conceptual models are governed by the purpose. The model preserves the purpose. Therefore the purpose is an invariant for the modelling process.

Mapping: The model is a mapping of an origin. It reflects some of the properties observed or envisioned for the origin.

Language as a carrier: Models use languages and are thus restricted by the expressive power of these languages. Candidates for languages are formal or graphical languages, media languages, illustration languages, or computer science constructions.

Value: Models provide a value or benefit based on their utility, capability and quality characteristics.

The purpose of a model covers a variety of different intentions and aims. Typical purposes are:

Perception support   for understanding the application domain.
Explanation and demonstration   for understanding an origin.
Preparation   to management and handling of the origin.
Optimisation   of the origin.
Hypothesis verification   through the model.
Construction   of an artifact or of a program.
Control   of parts of the application.
Simulation   of behaviour in certain situations.
Substitution   for a part of the application.

Depending on the purpose we shall use different models.

Models are author-driven and addressee-oriented. Figure 17.1 illustrates the association between an origin and the model.

A *model* is typically a schematic description of a system, theory, or phenomenon of an origin that accounts for known or inferred properties of the origin and may be used for further study of characteristics of the origin. *Conceptual modelling* aims to create an abstract representation of the situation under investigation, or more precisely, the way users think about it. Conceptual models enhance models with

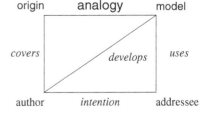

Fig. 17.1 The origin-model-author-addressee relationship for models

concepts that are commonly shared within a community or at least between the stakeholders involved in the modelling process.

This chapter extends the theory of conceptual models, conceptual modelling and modelling act proposed by [20] and systematises the four main dimensions of models: purpose, mapping, language, and value. It is based on an explicit application of concepts and constructs of languages.

The value of a model is given by the objective value and by the subjective value.

Models as enduring, justified and adequate artifacts.   The artifact can be qualified as an 'objective' model, if the artifact

1.   is adequate by certain notion of 'adequacy',
2.   is reusable in a rule system for new models and refinement of models, and
3.   is not equivalent to models, which can be generated with the aid of facts or preliminary models in the particular inventory of models by a rule system.

Models as the state of comprehension or knowledge of a user.   Models are used for comprehension of a user or stakeholder. Therefore, a model can be understood as the knowledge of a user. Different kinds of to know are:

1.   The state or fact of knowing.
2.   Familiarity, awareness, or understanding gained through experience or study.
3.   The sum or range of what has been perceived, discovered or learned.
4.   Learning; erudition: teachers of great knowledge.
5.   Specific information about something.
6.   Carnal knowledge.

We conclude that it is necessary to deliver models as enduring, justified and adequate artifacts to users depending on context, user demands, desiderata and intention, whereby these aspects are supported by the environment, the profile and tasks of the users. The tasks of users require a special model quality.

17.1.1 Artifacts, Concepts and Intentions

17.1.1.1 The Conceptual Model Space

At the same time, we may distinguish four different aspects of conceptual models. Conceptual models use concepts. Thus, the model space is characterised through (1) its origin, (2) its concepts, (3) its representation of model elements, and (4) its comprehension by users or stakeholders involved. Model elements cannot be considered in isolation. For this reason, we consider the use of *model chunks* as a suite of model elements consisting of images of pieces observed for the origin, concepts, representations and comprehension. These aspects are interdependent from each other. Figure 17.2 displays the conceptual model space.

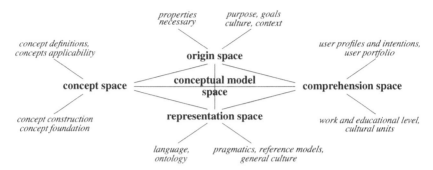

Fig. 17.2 The four aspects of the model space: origin aspect through properties, foundation aspect through concepts, representation aspect through language, user aspect through user comprehension

17.1.1.2 Intentions Driving Modelling

Modelling, and especially conceptual modelling, is not yet well understood and is misinterpreted in a variety of ways. The first goal of the chapter is to overcome some myths of conceptual modelling, such as:

1. Modelling equals documentation.
2. You can think everything through from the start.
3. Modelling implies a heavyweight software process.
4. You must "freeze" requirements and then you can start with modelling.
5. Your model is carved in stone and changes only from time to time.
6. You must use a CASE tool.
7. Modelling is a waste of time.
8. The world revolves around data modelling.
9. All developers know how to model.
10. Modelling is independent of the language.

The second goal of this chapter is the development of a framework for modelling. Modelling is based on an explicit choice of languages, on application of restrictions, on negotiation and on methodologies.

Restrictions depend on logics (deontic, epistemic, modal, belief, preferences) and use shortcuts, ambiguities, and ellipses.

Negotiation supports management or resolution of conflicts and the development of strategies to overcome these strategic, psychological, legal, and structural barriers.

Development methodologies are based on pragmatism and on paradigms. Since modelling is an activity that involves a number of actors, the choice of languages becomes essential.

Modelling is a process and is based on *modelling acts*. These modelling acts are dependent from the purpose of modelling itself. Therefore we can distinguish different modelling acts such as understand, define, conceptualise, communicate, abstract, construct, refine, and evaluate. Depending on the purpose of model development, we might use such acts as construct and evaluate as primary modelling acts.

The third goal of this chapter is to draw attention to explicit consideration of modelling properties both for the models themselves and for the modelling acts. This side of conceptual modelling is often only considered in an implicit form.

The modelling process is governed by goals and purposes. Therefore, we must use different models such as a construction model, a communication model or a discussion model. Modelling is restricted by the application context, the actor context, the system context and the theory and experience context. These contexts restrict the model and the modelling process.

17.1.2 Dimensions of Models and Modelling

17.1.2.1 Main Dimensions of Modelling

Building upon the commonalities observed above for computer science, we introduce four *main dimensions* of models and modelling:

Purpose ("wherefore")   of models and modelling, with the intentions, goals, aims, and tasks that are going to be solved by the model.

Mapping ("whereof"),   with a description of the solution provided by the model, the characterisation of the problem, phenomena, construction or application domain through the model.

Language ("wherewith"),   with a careful selection of the the carrier or cargo [10] that allows one to express the solution, the specification of the world or the construction.

Value ("worthiness")   of a model, by explicit statement of the internal and external qualities, and the quality of use, e.g. explicit statement of invariance properties relating the model to its associated worlds or by preservation properties that are satisfied by the model in dependence on the associated worlds.

These main dimensions of models and modelling govern the model and the modelling acts. There are extended by secondary dimensions that are used to shape and to adapt the model. We will discuss these dimensions after beginning with a discussion of the ruling dimension: the *purpose dimension*.

The task of model development is never completed (ta panta rhei ($\tau\alpha\ \pi\alpha\nu\tau\alpha\ \rho\epsilon\iota$), 'the rivers flow'). Models are changing artifacts due to changes imposed by:

Scope insight,   for conscious handling of restriction, capabilities, opportunities.

Guiding rules,   for convenience, for completion, refinement, and extension.

Development plans,   for partial delivery of models, partial usage and deployment.

Theories   supporting development of models.

Quality characteristics   for model completion, model evolution, model engineering.

Mapping styles   for mapping models among abstraction layers.

17.1.2.2 The Purposes Dimension

The purpose dimension rules the development of models and the application of models. The main reason for using a model is to provide a solution to a problem. We thus may describe the purpose by characterisation of the solution to the problem by the model. We can distinguish a number of concerns, such as:

The impact of the model ("whereto")   for a solution to a problem.

The insight into the origin's properties ("how")   by giving details how the world is structured or should be structured and how the functionality can be described.

Restrictions on applicability and validity ("when")   of a model for some specific solutions. for the validity interval, and the lifespan of a model.

Providing reasons for model value ("why")   such as correctness, generality, usefulness, comprehensibility, and novelty.

The description of how a model functions ("for which reason")   based on the model capacity.

This general characterisation of purposes of models can be specialised for database and information system models. The main purposes of information system models are given within Gregor's taxonomy [6]:

I. Analysis: Says what is.

The model does not extend beyond analysis and description. No causal relationships among phenomena are specified and no predictions are made. It thus provides a description of the phenomena of interest, analysis of relationships among those constructs, the degree of generalisability in constructs and relationships and the boundaries within which relationships, and observations hold.

II. Explanation: Says what is, how, why, when, and where.

The model provides explanations but does not aim to predict with any precision. There are no testable propositions. The model provides an explanation of how, why, and when things happened, relying on varying views of causality and methods for argumentation. This explanation will usually be intended to promote greater understanding or insights by others into the phenomena of interest.

III. Prediction: Says what is and what will be.

The model provides predictions and has testable propositions but does not have well-developed justificatory causal explanations. It states what will happen in the future if certain preconditions hold. The degree of certainty in the prediction is expected to be only approximate or probabilistic in IS.

IV. Explanation and prediction: Says what is, how, why, when, where, and what will be.

The model provides predictions and has both testable propositions and causal explanations. A special case of prediction exists where the model provides a description of the method or structure or both for the construction of an artifact (akin to a recipe). The provision of the recipe implies that the recipe, if acted upon, will cause an artifact of a certain type to come into being.

V. Design and action: Says how to do something.
The model gives explicit prescriptions (e.g., methods, techniques, principles of form and function) for constructing an artifact.

Based on this characterisation of the purpose, we infer a number of *requirements* for languages used for modelling and modelling methodologies:

Means of representation.   The model must be represented physically in some way: in words, mathematical terms, symbolic logic, diagrams, tables or graphically. Additional aids for representation could include pictures, models, or prototype systems.

Constructs.   These refer to the phenomena of interest in the model (Dubin's "units"). All of the primary constructs in the model should be well defined. Many different types of constructs are possible: for example, observational (real) terms, theoretical (nominal) terms and collective terms.

Statements of relationship.   These show relationships among the constructs. Again, these may be of many types: associative, compositional, unidirectional, bidirectional, conditional, or causal. The nature of the relationship specified depends on the purpose of the model. Very simple relationships can be specified.

Scope.   The scope is specified by the degree of generality of the statements of relationships (signified by modal qualifiers such as "some", "many", "all", and "never") and statements of boundaries showing the limits of generalizations.

Causal explanations.   The model gives statements of relationships among phenomena that show causal reasoning (not covering law or probabilistic reasoning alone).

Testable propositions (hypotheses).   Statements of relationships between constructs are stated in such a form that they can be tested empirically.

Prescriptive statements.   Statements in the model specify how people can accomplish something in practice (e.g., construct an artifact or develop a strategy).

17.1.2.3 The Artifact Dimension

The main product of modelling is the model, i.e. an artifact that is considered to be worthy for its purpose by the author. The model can, for instance, be used for the description of the world of origins or for the prescription of constructions. There are a number of explicit choices an author makes and that rule application of models. Modelling of information systems depends on the following choices:

The *abstraction layer*,   e.g., requirements, specification, realisation or implementation layer.

Chosen *granularity and precision*   of the work product itself.

Resources   used for development of a model such as the language.

Level of separation of concern   such as static/dynamic properties, local/global scope, facets.

Quality properties of the input,   e.g., requirements, completeness, conciseness, coherence, understandability.

Decomposition   of the work products into ensembles of sub-products.

In addition, modelling of information satisfies quality characteristics such as quality in use, internal quality, and external quality.

17.1.2.4 The User Dimension

A number of users are involved in the development of models. The user dimension thus reflects intentions, understanding, the comprehension and other characteristics of users in a variety of roles, for example:

Author ("by whom").   Results in reflections of the educational level, application of templates, pattern or reference models.
Addressee ("to whom").   Restricts the utilisation of the model or supports the extended application beyond the purpose originally intended.
The broad public ("whichever").   Develops a common understanding of the model depending on the group or the culture of the public.

Users are different and thus modelling has different results because of

attitudes of users   and their preferences;
the *ability*   to understand, to model, to reason, to survey, to communicate with others, to analyse, to construct systems, to validate, verify, or test models, to use or develop documentation;
mastering   of complexity, improvements, and realisation;
knowledge, skills, competency   of users for representing the world or for coping with representations;
restricted expressivity   due to restricted leads or due to human preference of local reasoning instead of global consideration of all properties of an artifact;
experience   to cope with varieties of problem solutions through generic problem solving; and
referential solutions   to be used for solution of similar problems together with refinement of the given approach.

One important relationship among the users is the form of partnership during the development or application of models. The partnership is characterised by:

Roles during activities   such as stakeholder, developer, consultant, supplier, contractor, documentation developers, or business user.
The practised collaboration partnership   based on communication acts, cooperation business processes, and coordination agreements.
Teamwork   during all activities with separation of different tasks.
Historical people   such as teachers, legacy (heritage) developers, or coders.
Builders   of earlier models.

Finally, the user dimension imposes an important restriction to the development, the application, the understanding of models: Models tend to be too large for a single person.

17.1.2.5 The Domain Dimension

The domain dimension clarifies:

- The *domain depending on the model's purpose ("for what")*, such as an application domain, properties reflected or neglected.
- The *scope to specific elements ("what")* that are considered to be typical and whose properties should be reflected.
- The *attention within the domain depending on the model's purpose ("where")* that limits the model to the 'normal' aspects.
- The *orientation of the domain ("wherefrom")* that restricts the attention and the directions for the current activities supported by the model.
- The *sources for origins or the infrastructure considered ("whence")* for the model.
- The *restrictions of the world ("wherein")* associated with the model.

A typical influence of the application domain can be illustrate by an example in [10]. Areas in Königsberg are connected through bridges. The question is whether there is a path that uses each bridge but only once. Such a path is called an Euler path.

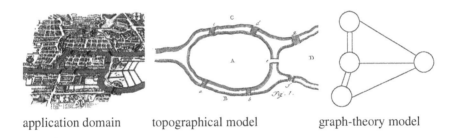

application domain   topographical model   graph-theory model

The two models display the same problem as in the original domain. We might also use a tree model that enumerates each starting point and associates a node with its predecessor and potential next point if there is an unused bridge. This model is inadequate for the general problem whether there is an Euler path within a topographical model. The main quality property for the models is the preservation of the Euler path problem.

17.1.2.6 The Context Dimension

The context dimension is typically used for restricting a model to a specific scope, and thus limits the general utilisation of models. It additionally requires an explicit consideration of these restrictions if the model is used outside its main application area. Context abstraction is a useful vehicle for restricting attention. Typical specific context restrictions to models include:

The *worlds ("whereat")*   considered for the model, such as the world that is currently accepted, the world that will be never considered, and the world that might be considered in future in dependence on the model value.

The *background knowledge ("whereabout")*   that forms the model and limits the model.

Envisioned *evolution paths ("whither")*   for the adaptation of the model to future requirements.

17.1.3 Postulates of Modelling

17.1.3.1 General Properties of Models

This discussion can be summarised in a number of postulates that are of importance for models, modelling, and modelling acts.

Mapping property: Each model has an origin and is based on a mapping from the origin to the artifact.

Truncation property: The model lacks some of the ascriptions made to the original and thus functions as an Aristotelian model by abstraction of irrelevant.

Pragmatic property: The model use is only justified for particular model users, tools of investigation, and period of time.

Amplification property: Models use specific extensions which are not observed for the original.

Distortion property: Models are developed for improving the physical world or for inclusion of visions of better reality, e.g. for construction via transformation or in Galilean models.

Idealisation property: Modelling abstracts from reality by scoping the model to the ideal state of affairs.

The first three properties are based on Stachowiak's theory of models [12, 16]. The fourth property has been formulated in [17]. The fifth property has been discussed in [9]. The sixth property has been developed within natural sciences (chemistry).

17.1.3.2 Prescription by Models and Description for Models

Figure 17.3 depicts the association between origin and artifacts.

Similarly, we may describe the application of models for construction of other artifacts such as software and hardware. Figure 17.4 gives the reflection of the postulate. We observe that the completion activities change compared with Fig. 17.3.

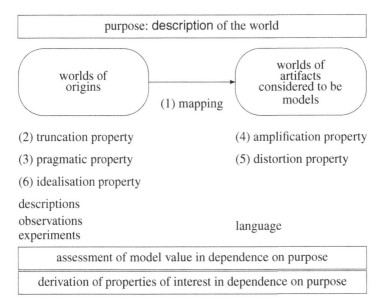

Fig. 17.3 The association of worlds and resulting postulates of models. The bottom rectangles describe the completion activities that should be completed according to the purpose

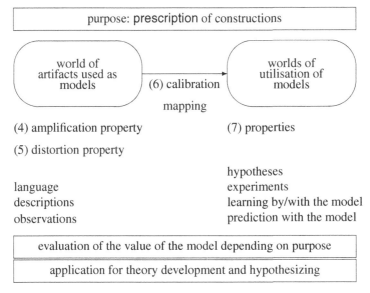

Fig. 17.4 The association of models with artifacts constructed with models as a blueprint

17.1.3.3 The Model Capacity

The model

*   is based on an *analogy* of structuring, functionality, or behaviour,
*   satisfies certain *model purposes*, and
*   provides a simple handling or *service* or consideration of the things under consideration.

    Any model is therefore characterised by a *model capacity* that describes

*   how the model provides some understanding of the origin or can be used depending on the purpose,
*   how the model provides an explanation of demonstration through auxiliary information and thus makes the origin or the associated elements easier or better to understand,
*   how the model provides an indication and facilities for making properties viewable,
*   how the model allows to provide variations and support optimisation,
*   how the model support verification of hypotheses within a limited scope,
*   how the model supports construction of technical artifacts,
*   how the model supports control of things in reality, or
*   how the model allows a replacement of things of reality and acts as a mediating means.

17.1.3.4 Resulting Restrictions To Be Accepted by Stakeholders

Models are governed by their purpose. They may support this purpose or not. They have a value and may thus be used depending on their capacity.

Prohibition of *estrangement*:   Models serve a purpose and cannot be used in general outside the scope of the purpose.

17.1.4 Artifacts and Models

The four aspects of the conceptual model space in Fig. 17.2 are interwoven. Models use artifacts. Models have their specific representation. Models are supported by conceptualisations.

The interrelationship between models, representations and concepts should be very flexible. We can assume that models may use different representations or artifacts. Artifacts may contain sub-artifacts. Conceptual models are based on concepts. Concepts may be typical for a model within a certain degree of typicality. Concepts may consist of sub-concepts. Therefore, we may associate a model with a concept that has its own sub-concepts.

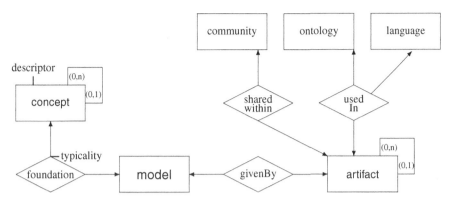

Fig. 17.5 The association between artifacts, representations, and concepts

We assume that concepts are independent of representations. Additionally, we may assume that representations are dependent on the language and some ontology to be used. They are typically commonly accepted or shared within a community or culture. This understanding leads to the structure displayed in Fig. 17.5.

17.2 The Theory of Conceptual Models

17.2.1 Conceptual Models and Languages

17.2.1.1 The Language Dimension

Models are represented by *artifacts* that satisfy the pragmatic purposes of users. We restrict this discussion to formal languages that are typically used for conceptual models. In this case, artifacts are linguistic expressions that describe the model. Linguistic expression are built within a language with some understanding. Therefore, artifacts use syntax, semantics and pragmatics built into the chosen language.

Semantic annotation in current content management systems is usually restricted to preselected ontologies and parameter sets. Rich conceptual data models are only available in more sophisticated systems. They are adapted to certain application domains that incorporate preselected and tailored ontologies.

The model-artifact association is agreed upon within a community. This community is based on a web of knowledge of their members (see Chap. 15).

17.2.1.2 Languages Used for Representation of Models

Languages are the carrier for models. We may accept a logics approach to semiotics and define the language similar to Chap. 12. Each constructive language is based on

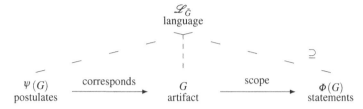

Fig. 17.6 Artifacts with a language, their properties and postulates

a signature, on a set of base items, and a set of constructors. The language consists of words that are allowed due to well-formedness constraints. Languages $\mathcal{L}$ are used for a number of reasons, e.g. reasoning, representation, illustration, etc. These reasons are driven by the model purposes in our case.

We may now use a subset of words and accept those as *postulates* for a model. To be considered faithful or useful, a model must satisfy these postulates.

We may develop different artifacts as a potential models. We are, however, interested in some properties that these models must satisfy. We therefore develop a general understanding of artifacts that are used for models within a language.

Postulates must be explicitly given. They might be changed whenever the purpose of modelling is changing. They do not restrict models to one artifact. Instead, we might also use a number of artifacts in parallel. Figure 17.6 displays the relationship between an artifact and its postulates and properties.

Constructive languages thus provide support for:

- prescribing postulates that restrict the judgement that an artifact can be accepted as a model,
- scoping our attention to those artifacts that can be considered for a model or for parts of a model, and
- orienting the user on certain properties that are of interest for the purpose of modelling.

This approach is very general. It can be applied in many areas. Consider, for instance, the following table:

$\mathcal{L}_{\tilde{G}}$	$\Psi(G)$	corresponds	G	scope	$\Phi(G)$
Logics	Axioms	Satisfy	Structure	Satisfy	Essential properties
$\mathbb{N}$	Peano axioms	Satisfy	Standard model	Derivable	Peano arithmetics
Empirism	Postulates	Accepted	Artifact	Supports	Observation
Technics	Construction requirements	Enforce	Product	Has	Properties

This approach also carries classical approaches used in mathematical logic:

$\mathcal{L}_{\tilde{G}}$	$\Psi(G)$	corresponds	G	scope	$\Phi(G)$
Logics	Axioms	Satisfy	Structure	Consider	Essential properties of G
Logics	Axioms	Satisfy	Structure	Satisfy	Relevant theorems of $(\mathcal{L}_{\tilde{G}}, \Psi(G))$

We, therefore, may define a theory by the pair $(\mathcal{L}_{\tilde{G}}, \Psi(G))$. The model class $\mathrm{MOD}^{\mathcal{L}_{\tilde{G}}}(\Psi(G))$ is defined to be the set of all structures that satisfy $\Psi(G)$. A structure G is a model of $\Psi(G)$ and thus $G \in \mathrm{MOD}^{\mathcal{L}_{\tilde{G}}}s(\Psi(G))$. A theory $Th(\mathcal{K}) \subseteq \mathcal{L}_{\tilde{G}}$ is given for a class $\mathcal{K}$ of structures and consists of all language expressions that are satisfied by each of the structures in $\mathcal{K}$.

The same approach can also be used for conceptual modelling:

$\mathcal{L}_{\tilde{G}}$	$\Psi(G)$	corresponds	G	scope	$\Phi(G)$
Database	Requirements	Realise	DB schema	Satisfy	Integrity constraints
Workflow	Requirements	Realise	WF schema	Satisfy	Integrity constraints

Thus, ingredients used for modelling of databases, information systems and workflow systems are languages, restrictions, negotiations for the property to be a model, and methodologies for artifact development. Languages are given with syntactics, semantics, and pragmatics. We typically use inductive expression formation based on alphabets. Inductive construction also supports the description of behaviour defined on expressions.

Restrictions depend on the logics to be used, e.g., first-order hierarchical predicate logics [18], deontic logics, epistemic logics, modal logics, logics for belief reasoning of for preference derivation. Negotiations provide a means to identify, define analyse barriers and manage or resolve conflicts. Methodologies of development are based on engineering approaches and are guided by certain pragmatism and a number of paradigms.

17.2.1.3 Principles of Language Use

Languages may, however, also restrict modelling. This restriction may either be compensated by over-development of language components or by multi-models. Over-development of language components has been observed within the theory of integrity constraints in the relational model of data. More than 95 different and necessary classes of integrity constraints have been developed. Multi-modelling is extensively used for UML. The Sapir-Whorf hypothesis [22] results in the following principle:

Principle of linguistic relativity: Actors skilled in a language may not have a (deep) understanding of some concepts of other languages. This restriction leads to problematic or inadequate models or limits the representation of things and is not well understood.

The principle of linguistic relativity is not well understood. Therefore, we illustrate this principle by a discussion that highlights the deficiencies we need to overcome.

17.2.1.4 The Matter of Language Choice

Let us consider a well-known example: *traffic light control*. Given a crossroad with two intersecting streets (north-south, east-west), and traffic lights that direct traffic, we assume at the first glance that traffic lights might switch from red to green and from green to red. We also might assume that both opposite cross lights show the same colour. Software engineering approaches, Petri net approaches, process algebra approaches etc. typically start with a model for each cross light. Next, the interdependence among the state changes is either modeled through integrity constraints or through implicit modelling constructs. The best solution we know so far is the Petri net solution depicted in Fig. 17.7. It uses an external timer and switches between the directions.

This model neither scales nor has a good development, internal, or dynamic quality. The extension to yellow colour is an intellectual challenge as well the extension to more flexible directing. This example is typically chosen due to everyday life experience of the students despite its complete inadequacy. This pitfall has already discussed in [8], who tried to find a better solution based on state change diagrams and failed due to complex integrity constraints. Implementations neglect this solution and implement a completely different solution.

The main reason for the poor quality and the conceptual and implementation inadequacy is its wrong attitude, wrong scope, wrong abstraction, and wrong granularity.

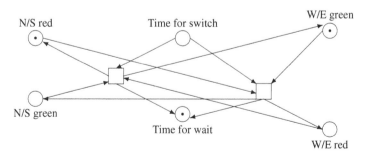

Fig. 17.7 Traffic control based on Petri nets

Explicit assumptions can also be derived for the traffic light control application. We first need to decide whether the analogy to real-life is based on the behaviour of the entire system or on the combined behaviour of the behaviour of components. This distinction directly implies a choice between a model that represents the entire application as one system and the components as its elements (*local-as-view model*) and a model that combines local models with a global one (*global-as-view model*). All conceptual solutions known in literature use the global-as-view model. In this case, state tables and (ASM) state transfer rules like the following ones are used:

Controller	location	state	clock	reset	switch
e	...	...	...	...	...

if Switch(e) then UPDATE(e,collocated(e)); CHANGESWITCH(e).

These states and rules may obey a number of rather complex integrity constraints.

We might prefer the local-as-view approach. States reflect the entire state of the crossroad, i.e. *NSredEWgreen, NSredEWred, NSgreenEWred*. The last state reflects that the north-south direction is open and the east-west direction is closed. We might add the state *NSredEWred* for representation of the exception state and the state *NSnothingEWnothing* for the start and the end state. The state *NSgreenEWgreen* is a conflict state and thus not used for the model.

The other decisions discussed in this section can now made in a similar manner. We choose a full controller for all lights. We might, however, choose a local controller for each cross light. In this case, the local controller is nothing else than a *view* on the global schema. The model we propose supports simulation as well as understanding, reasoning, variation and extension, optimisation and technical artifacts. The workmanship also includes a collection of extensions that seems to be probable, such as: people calling a state change, exceptional situations, yellow lights, specific directions, etc. The local schemata are based on views and on the master-slave principle. Update is central and display is local.

This model also allows one to explicitly specify which states are never under consideration, which states are a 'must' and which states are used for later extensions. We further assume that reality can be mapped to discrete variables, clocks are based on linear time logics, and control is restricted to vehicle and pedestrian direction gauge. This model also extends the real-life application by adding a global, combined state. Its main advantage is that the context conditions for correct traffic lights for all coexisting directions are directly coded into the model domain space and thus do not need any explicit support.

The local-as-view model is based on a *two-layer architecture* that uses a global schema and local view schemata. The extended ER model [25] provides a number of opportunities for the representation of hierarchies. A typical hierarchy in our traffic light application is the specialisation hierarchy for states. Since states can be multiply classified depending on the time of day and the day of the week, we might choose the bulk representation for the classification of types through a *StateKind* instead of

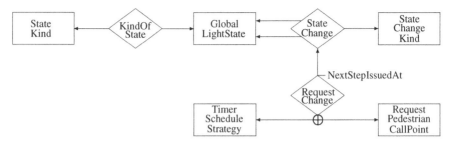

Fig. 17.8 The traffic light support database schema

explicit specialisation types. State changes may also be classified in a similar way. We might, however, prefer to separate calls for state change made by pedestrians from those state changes that are triggered by a clock.

Based on these choices, we derive modelling activities for the database schemata and workflow rules. We explicitly specify properties and binding among the global and local schemata, e.g. master-slave binding.

The given application can be specified through different modelling concepts. These modelling concepts provide a number of alternatives and a number of opportunities. The ER schema in Fig. 17.8 represents one of the possible schemata for the global schema. The state changes and the pedestrian calls are not recorded after they have been issued.

The scheduler is based on this schema and might use workflow diagrams, trigger rules or ASM rules [2] for specification of BPMN diagrams. We can use a generic pattern approach that supports extensions, e.g. for kinds of states and kinds of state changes. Typical examples are:

CHANGEACTION := getState; choosePossibleStateChange(state);
$\qquad\qquad\qquad\qquad$ apply(possibleStateChange(state)
ALARMACTION := on alarm changeStateToErrorState
CLOCK := on tick observeWhetherChangeRequired
NORMALACTION := if change = true then CHANGEACTION
PEDESTRIANCALL := on callAtPoint(cp) CHANGENEXTSTEPISSUEDAT(cp).

Similarly, we can specify views for local display.

17.2.1.5 Pragmatics that Cannot Be Neglected

While syntax and semantics of language expressions has been well explored, its pragmatics apart from the use of metaphors has not. Pragmatics is part of semiotics, which is concerned with the relationship between signs, semantic concepts and things of reality. This relationship may be pictured by the so-called semiotics triangle. The main branches of semiotics are *syntactics*, which is concerned with the syntax, i.e. the construction of the language; *semantics*, which is concerned with the interpretation of the words of the language; and *pragmatics*, which is concerned with the current use of utterances by the user and context of words for the user. Pragmatics permits the use of a variety of semantics depending on the user, the application and the technical environment. Most languages defined in computer science have a well-defined syntax. Some of them possess a well-defined semantics. Few of them use pragmatics through which the meaning might be different for different users.

Syntactics (often called syntax) is often based on a constructive or generative approach: Given an alphabet and an set of constructors, the language is defined as the set of expressions that can be generated by the constructors. Constructions may be defined on the basis of grammatical rules.

Semantics of generative languages can be either defined by meta-linguistic semantics, e.g. used for defining the semantics of predicate logics, by procedural or referential semantics, e.g. operational semantics used for defining the semantics of programming languages, or by convention-based semantics used in linguistics. Semantics is often defined on the basis of a set of relational structures that correspond to the signature of the language.

We must distinguish pragmatics from pragmatism. Pragmatism means a practical approach to problems or affairs, and is the "balance between principles and practical usage". Here, we are concerned with pragmatics, which is based on the behaviour and demands of users, and therefore depends on the understanding of users.

Let us consider an example for a well-known class of constraints in databases. A similar observation can be made for multivalued, join, inclusion, exclusion and key dependencies. Functional dependencies are the best-known class of database constraints and commonly accepted. They are one of the most important class of equality-generating constraints.

Given a type R and substructures X, Y of R.
The functional dependency $R : X \longrightarrow Y$ is valid in R^C if $o|_Y = o'|_Y$ whenever $o|_X = o'|_X$ for any two objects o, o' from R^C.

Functional dependencies carry at least five different but interwoven meanings. The notion of the functional dependency is thus overloaded. It combines different properties that should be separated:

Explicit declaration of partial identification. Functional dependencies typically explicitly declare a functional association among components of types. The left hand attribute uniquely identifies right side attributes, i.e. $X \xrightarrow{\text{Ident}} Y$.
Identification can either be based on surrogate or on natural attributes [1].

Tight functional coupling. Functional dependencies may also be numerical constraints. We denote such constraints by i.e. $X \xrightarrow{\text{Num}} Y$. Another denotation is based on cardinality constraints [18].

Semantic constraint specific for the given application. Constraints may be stronger than observed in usual life since the application has a limited scope and allows us to strengthen the constraint. In this case, constraints restrict the application only to those cases in which the left side has only one associated right side value, even though this restriction may not be valid for any application. We denote this case by $X \xrightarrow{\text{Sem}} Y$

Semantical unit with functional coupling.   *Semantical units* are those reducts of a type that are essential in the given application. Their components cannot be separated without losing their meaning. Semantical units may have their inner structure. This structure tightly couples dependent object parts with those that determine them [18]. We denote this coupling by $X \xrightarrow{\text{Unit}} Y$.

Structural association among units.   Semantical units may allow a separation of concern for certain elements. Their separation supports a more flexible treatment while requiring that the dependent part cannot exist without the determining part. If this dependence is functional we may represent such by the constraint $X \xrightarrow{\text{Struct}} Y$.

17.2.2 Concepts and Models

Concepts are the basis for conceptual models. They specify our knowledge what things are there and what properties things have. Concepts are used in everyday life as a communication vehicle and as a reasoning chunk. Concepts can be based on definitions of different kinds.

Thus, our goal for the development of a theory of conceptual modelling and of conceptual models can only be achieved if the conceptual model definition covers any kind of conceptual model description and goes beyond the simple textual or narrative form.

A general description of concepts is considered to be one of the most difficult tasks. We analysed the definition pattern used for concept introduction in mathematics, chemistry, computer science, and economics. This analysis resulted in a number of discoveries:

- Any concept can be defined in a variety of ways. Sometimes some definitions are preferred over others, are time-dependent, have a level of rigidity, are usage-dependent, have levels of validity, and can only be used within certain restrictions.
- The typical definition frame we observed is based on definition items. These items can also be classified by the kind of definition. The main part of the definition is a tree-structured structural expression of the following form:

SpecOrderedTree(StructuralTreeExpression
             (DefinitionItem, Modality(Sufficiency, Necessity),
               Fuzziness, Importance, Rigidity,
               Relevance, GraduationWithinExpression, Category))) .

- Concepts typically also depend on the application context, i.e. the application area and the application schema. The association itself must be characterised by the kind of association.

Concepts are typically ordered hierarchically and can thus be layered. We assume that this ordering is strictly hierarchical and the concept space can be depicted by

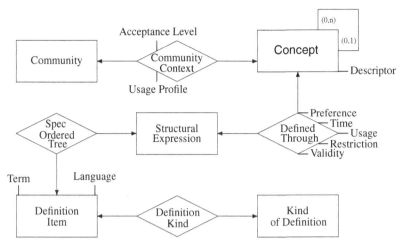

Fig. 17.9 The main schema for concept definition and formation

a set of concept trees. A concept is also dependent on the community that prefers this concept. A concept is typically given through an embedding into the knowledge space of users involved.

The schema in Fig. 17.9 displays the general structure for content definition. This schema also covers all aspects discussed in [13]. This schema extends the relationship between artifacts, representations and concepts introduced in Fig. 17.5.

Concept gathering can be understood as a technique that combines concept representation [5, 13, 19] and (algorithmic) learning approaches.

A concept gathering system is based on:

a *set of concepts and available experience* $\mathscr{C}$,
a *set of domain knowledge* $\mathscr{D}$,
a *set of representable meta-knowledge* $\mathscr{M}$,
a *set of learning goals* $\mathscr{G}$, and
a *set of representable hypotheses* $\mathscr{H}$.

The set of representable knowledge and concepts is denoted by $\mathscr{R} = \mathscr{C} \cup \mathscr{D} \cup \mathscr{M} \cup \mathscr{G} \cup \mathscr{H}$.

The concept gathering system $(\gamma, \lambda, \nu, \mathscr{C}, \mathscr{R})$ *consists of*

a *concept generator* $\gamma : \mathscr{C} \times \mathscr{R} \to \mathscr{C}$,
a *learning function* $\lambda : \mathscr{C} \times \mathscr{R} \to \mathscr{H}$, and
an *evaluator* $\nu : \mathscr{C} \times \mathscr{R} \to \mathscr{Q}$ where $\mathscr{Q}$ denotes set of quality characteristics.

A run of the concept gathering system *results in*

a *concept detection sequence* $C_1, C_2, \ldots, C_f$ with $C_i \in \mathscr{C}$ and
a *learning sequence* $R_0, R_1, R_2, \ldots, R_f$ with $R_i \in \mathscr{R}$ where R_0 denotes the initial knowledge and R_f denotes the final knowledge.

The run is typically recorded and is dependent on the concepts gathered thus far. Additionally, the concept gathering system *records*

the *background knowledge of the user* $\mathcal{B} \subseteq \mathcal{D} \cup \mathcal{M} \cup \mathcal{G}$ and
the *actual available knowledge* $\mathcal{B} \cup \mathcal{H}'$.

17.2.3 Information Exchange of Stakeholders Based on Models

Stakeholders such as the author of a model and the addressee for a model use models in a variety of ways. The main use of models is *information* (or knowledge) *exchange* among stakeholders. There are several definitions of "information":

- The first category of definitions is based on the mathematical notion of entropy. This notion is independent of the user and thus inappropriate in our project context.
- The second category of definitions bases information on the data a user has currently in his data space and on the computational and reasoning abilities of the user. Information is any data that cannot be derived by the user. This definition is handy but has a serious drawback. Reasoning and computation cannot be properly characterised. Therefore, the definition becomes fuzzy.
- The third category is based on the general language understanding of information: the communication or reception of knowledge or intelligence. Information can also defined as

  - knowledge obtained from investigation, study, or instruction;
  - intelligence or news;
  - facts and data.

  Information can also be the act of informing against a person.
  Finally, information is a formal accusation of a crime made by a prosecuting officer, as distinguished from an indictment presented by a grand jury.

All these definitions are too broad. We are instead interested in a definition that is more appropriate for the internet age:
Information as processed by *humans*,

- is carried by *data*
- that is perceived or noticed, selected and organized by its receiver,
- because of his subjective human interests, originating from his instincts, feelings, experience, intuition, common sense, values, beliefs, personal knowledge, or wisdom,
- simultaneously processed by his cognitive and mental processes, and
- seamlessly integrated in his recallable knowledge.

Therefore, information is directed towards pragmatics, whereas content may be considered to highlight the syntactical dimension. If content is enhanced by concepts and topics, then users are able to capture the meaning and the utilisation of the data they receive. In order to ease perception, we use *metaphors* or simply *names* from a commonly used namespace. Metaphors and names may be separated into those that support perception of information and into those that support usage or functionality. Both carry some small fraction of (linguistic) semantics.

The *information transfer* from a user A to a user B depends on the two users and on their abilities to send and to receive the data, to observe the data, and to interpret the data. Let us formalise this process. Let s_X denote the function used by a user X for data extraction, transformation, and sending of data. Let r_X denote the corresponding function for data receipt and transformation, and let o_X denote the filtering or observation function. The data currently considered by X is denoted by D_X. Finally, data filtered or observed must be interpreted by the user X and integrated into the knowledge K_X that user X has. Let us denote by i_X the binary function from data and knowledge to knowledge. By default, we extend the function i_X by the time t_{i_X} of the execution of the function.

Thus, the data transfer and information reception (or, briefly, information transfer) is formally expressed by

$$I_B = i_B(o_B(r_B(s_A(D_A))), K_B, t_{i_X}).$$

In addition, the time of sending, receiving, observing, and interpreting can be taken into consideration. In this case, we extend the above functions with a time argument. The function s_X is executed at moment t_{s_X}, r_X at t_{r_X}, and o_X at t_{o_X}. We assume $t_{s_A} \leq t_{r_B} \leq t_{o_B} \leq t_{i_B}$ for the time of sending data from A to B. The time of a computation f or data consideration D is denoted by t_f or t_D, respectively. In this extended case, the information transfer is formally expressed by

$$I_B = i_B(o_B(r_B(s_A(D_A, t_{s_A}), t_{r_B}), t_{o_B}), K_B, t_{i_B}).$$

The notion of information considers senders, receivers, their knowledge and experience. Figure 17.10 displays the multi-layering of communication, the influence of explicit knowledge and experience on the interpretation.

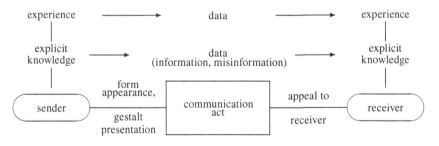

Fig. 17.10 Dimensions of the communication act

The act of communication is specified by

- the communication message with the content or content chunk, the characterisation of the relationship between sender and receiver, the data that are transferred and may lead to information or misinformation, and the presentation;
- the sender, the explicit knowledge the sender may use, and the experience the sender has; and
- the receiver, the explicit knowledge the receiver may use, and the experience the receiver has.

17.2.4 Mappings Among Models and Originals

17.2.4.1 Modelling Supported by Mapping

Thus far, two of the four main dimensions have been established. Let us now consider the mapping between two worlds: source world and target world. Examples of source-target pairs include:

- origins from the real world mapped to an artifact that is considered to be a model;
- elements of an artifact that serves as a model for a realisation of the artifact by an implementation; and
- elements of one model are mapped to elements of another model.

The first mapping (e.g., in Fig. 17.3) is typically based on a *description* of the origins that is represented by a model about these origins. The second mapping (e.g., in Fig. 17.4) is typically based on a *prescription* made by the model for a realisation of the model by a technical artifact. The third mapping has been used above for the association between the topographical model and the graph model for the Königsberg bridge problem on page 551.

We can observe other pairs of such mappings, depending on the purpose. For instance, documentation uses an artifact to be documented and another artifact that documents essential elements of the first artifact. It typically extends the first artifact for pragmatic rules for exploitation of the first artifact and by behavioural scenario as examples of deployment. It bases the documentation also on an idealisation of the first artifact.

A similar association may be developed for the other purposes:

- perception support for understanding the application domain;
- explanation and demonstration for understanding;
- preparation to management and handling of the original;
- optimisation of the application domain operating;
- hypothesis verification through the model;
- control of parts of the application;
- simulation of behaviour in certain situations; and
- substitution for a part of the application.

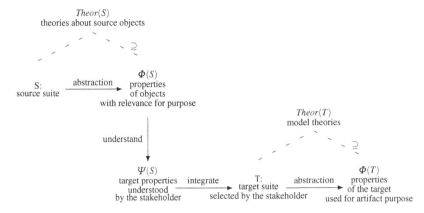

Fig. 17.11 Mappings between source artifacts and target artifacts

We may now combine these observations with the treatment of languages introduced in Fig. 17.5. We add to this treatment the logical framework. It defines for
a set of artifacts a language and a theory that can be used for reasoning on properties of the artifacts and for explicit consideration of postulates. In this case, we
need to consider two languages: the language of the origin of the mapping and the
language of the target of the mapping. Figure 17.11 displays the mappings between
the different artifacts.

Furthermore, we observe another important property of the mapping:

Principle of conservative stability of source properties.   The properties of the
   source are relatively stable. This results in some kind of target conservativeness:
   Any target artifact revision that cannot be reflected already in the current set of
   properties of the source is entirely based on explicit changes considered for the
   first artifact.

Principle of consistency of mapping.   Main properties of the source artifact should
   be stable for the target artifact.

These principles can be extended by other principles for mappings that are often
assumed but not necessary:

Conceptualization principle.   Only aspects of the source artifact should be taken
   into account when constructing the target artifact.

95% principle.   All the relevant aspects of the source artifact should be described
   in the target artifact. We notice that this principle is weaker than the classical
   100 % used in software engineering. It better reflects the engineering component
   of modelling.

Formalization principle.   Target artifacts should be formalisable in order to be re-
   alisable.

Semiotic principle.   Target artifacts should be easily interpretable and understandable.

Correspondence condition for knowledge representation.   The target artifact should be such that the recognizable constituents of it have a one-to-one correspondence to the relevant constituents of source artifact.

Invariance principle.   Target artifacts should be constructed on the basis of such entities detected for the source artifact that are invariant during certain time periods within the world of the source artifact.

Construction principle.   In order to construct a good target artifact, it is important first to construct relevant sub-artifacts and then to search for connections between them.

The main postulate for the mapping is however the

Postulate of purpose invariance.   The purpose of the modelling activity can be realised through the target artifact. It can be considered both for the source artifact as well as for the target artifact.

This postulate requires that the mapping must obey an invariance property for the purpose. It has several implications:

• The mapping is a realisation of an analogy property.
• It is possible to re-map properties observed for the target artifact to the source artifact if those are not caused by idealisation, distortion or amplification.
• The target artifact can also be used for other mapping with different intentions and goals.

We shall discuss specific forms of analogies below.

As an example, we may refine Fig. 17.11 to classical ER modelling, as displayed in Fig. 17.12. This figure allows also to reason on the advantages and on the disadvantages of the ER modelling approach.

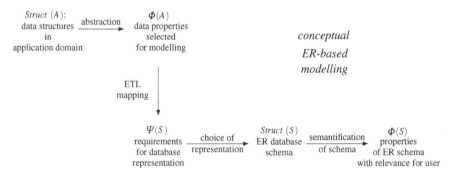

Fig. 17.12 The relationship between application domain world and Entity-Relationship modelling language world

17.2.4.2 Modelling with a Manifold of Models

Typical modelling follows a number of purposes. The UML is an example of model suites that are used at the same time. Class diagrams reflect the structuring of object sets and the functionality provided for the object sets. Object diagrams may be based on class diagrams. They may, however, also reflect things in the application domain as a combined set of class objects. Interaction diagrams reflect the message and control flow among objects in the first setting of object diagrams.

A similar picture is observed for models that are developed for different purposes. Consider, for instance, models that have been developed for construction of a technical artifact, for communication and discussion of properties among stakeholders, for documentation, and for analysis. Figure 17.13 displays the manifold of models developed for different purposes for an origin.

Figure 17.13 displays one pitfall of multi-language modelling. The models may consider different aspects of the origin, they may contradict and they may not be integratable. For instance, if we use class diagrams, statecharts, activity diagrams, time diagrams, component diagrams, interaction diagrams and others within a software development team, then integration of different aspects might become infeasible. Thus, we may apply two rather rigid modelling restrictions, which serve as the main principles for multi-language modelling:

Principle of coherence of models.   Models are coherent if their common reflection of the origin is consistent, i.e., sub-models that reflect the same properties of the origin can be injective mapped to each other.
Principle of origin property completeness.   Models partially reflect the same set of properties of the origin. None of the model uses properties that are different from properties that can potentially be used for another model.

Chapter 12 considered co-evolution of models and introduced a formalism to handle coherence. *Coherence* describes a fixed relationship between the models in a model suite. Two models are coherent when each change in one of the models is propagated to the other model. This change transfer implicitly assumes that the integrity constraints of the corresponding model types remain to be valid. Models are non-coherent if there is a random or changing relationship. We aim for an explicit specification of the association schema and use an explicit specification of the *collaboration* among models. For instance, the master-slave association or collaboration

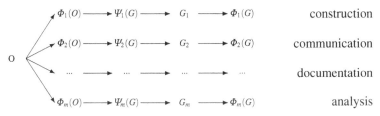

Fig. 17.13 Models reflecting different purposes

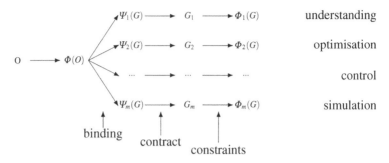

Fig. 17.14 Coherent models reflecting different purposes on a complete set of origin properties

propagates any change of the master to its slaves. Slaves do not have any right the change the master without consensus with the master.

If we enforce these principles, then the model variety can be handled in a simpler and feasible way. Figure 17.14 displays the advantages of a coherent set of models, based on a complete set of properties of the origin. It allows us to introduce a binding between these models. This binding can be mapped to a contract in the sense of Chap. 12. The contract may be used for the derivation of constraints the different models must obey in order to be coherent.

This approach directly results in a *coordination of models* on the basis of *separation of aspects*.

17.2.5 Development Phases That Use Models

17.2.5.1 Description Through Models and Prescription by Models

One of the main combined purposes of models is the description of an application domain that subsequently uses the developed model as a prescription for the realisation of a technical artifact. Conceptual modelling adds to the model a number of concepts that are the basis for an understanding of the model and for the explanation of the model to the user.

This two-phase development cycle of technical artifacts is the kernel of conceptual modelling of information systems and database systems. There are different other forms of this two-phase database system development. We may use the association between the model and the application for model refinement and model evolution. Models are typically parameterised. The parameters may be adopted to the actual or intended situation. Models are integrated during bottom-up modelling. They can be refined, optimised, validated, or improved before the realisation phase starts. Verification typically involves checking the properties of a model and the properties of a realisation. Testing checks the relationship between properties in the application domain and properties of the realisation.

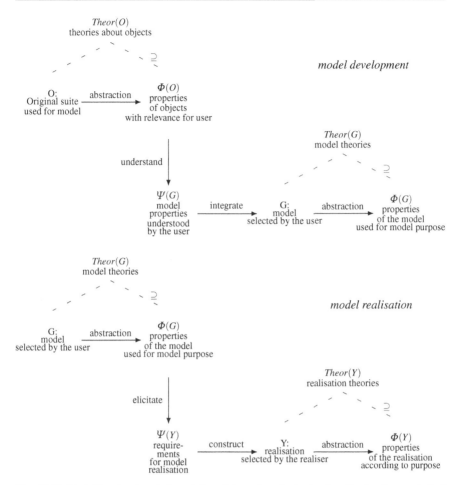

Fig. 17.15 Modelling for description of the origin and as the basis of realisation by a technical artifact

17.2.5.2 Reasoning Support for Modelling

Design science [7] has been aiming at an explicit support for the modelling process. This support includes an explicit consideration of the quality of the model, the modelling process, and supporting theories. We may combine the informal discussions with our approach and separate the modelling acts by the things that are under consideration.

Figure 17.16 displays the different ways of working during a database systems development. We use here the two-phase model: description followed by prescription.

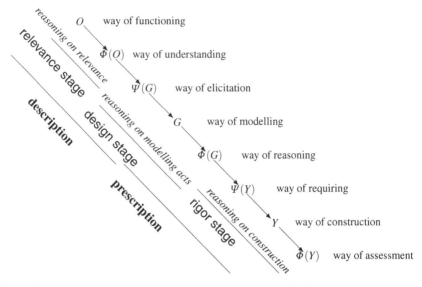

Fig. 17.16 Reasoning processes and reasoning support for description followed by prescription

These different "ways of working" characterise

- the *modelling acts* with its specifics; [20]
- the *foundation for the modelling acts* with the theory that is going to support this act, the techniques that can be used for the start, completion and for the support of the modelling act, and the reasoning techniques that can be applied for each step;
- the *partner* involved with their obligations, permissions, and restrictions, with their roles and rights, and with their play;
- the *aspects* that are under consideration for the current modelling acts;
- the *consumed and produced elements of the artifact* that are under consideration during work; and
- the *resources* that must be obtained, that can be used or that are going to be modified during a modelling act.

Consider, for instance, the way of requiring. It includes specific facets such as

- to command, to require, to compel, and to make someone do something with supporting acts such as communicating, requesting, bespeaking, ordering, forbidding, prohibiting, interdicting, proscribing;
- to ask, to expect, to consider obligatory, to request and expect with specific supporting acts such as transmitting, communicating, calling for, demanding;
- to want, to need, to require, to have need of with supporting acts of wanting, needing, requiring;
- to necessitate, to ask, to postulate, to need, to take, to involve, to call for, to demand, to require as useful, to just, or to proper.

The ways of functioning, understanding, elicitation, modelling, reasoning, assessment, and construction can be characterised in a similar form.

The rigor stage may be replaced by other stages that support different purposes.

We have concentrated on prescription and construction of new systems. Another application is *model refinement* similar to two-model representation of the Königsberg bridge problem on page 551.

Design science aims at another kind of model refinement by adding more rigor after evaluation of a model. This refinement is essentially *model evolution*. Another refinement is the enhancement of models by concepts. This refinement is essentially a 'semantification' or *conceptualisation* of the model. Experimentation and justification of models is a third kind of adding rigor to (conceptual) models.

17.2.6 Properties of the Models-Origin and the Models-Reflections Analogies

Figure 17.1 bases modelling on a quadruple of origin, model, author and addressee. The origin-model association, as well as the experimentation, construction or reasoning with models, is based on an explicit consideration of the notion of an *analogy* between the model and the origin or the model and its reflection in theories, constructions, hypotheses, or illustrations. Therefore we need a characterisation of analogies.

Analogies are statements of similarity, statements of adjustment, statements of emphases. They characterise the approximation made by the model. These characterisations can be given by:

Degree of *structural analogy.*   The degree of similarity of either the original with the model or of the model with its reflection.

Degree of *qualitative analogy.*   The degree to which the character and constitution is reflected.

Degree of *structural adjustment.*   The extent to which the structure is considered independent on the later use.

Degree of *qualitative adjustment.*   Characterizes what is going to be used for the later exploitation and what part is not going to be used.

Degree of *functional adjustment.*   Characterises the functions that are considered and the functions that are not considered.

Degree of *contrast and emphasis.*   Provides a means to specifically consider the distortion, amplification and idealisation made by the model.

Degree measurement is based on the ratio between the good or bad cases against all possible cases. We may consider a number of ratio measurements *Recall evaluation* relates the number of positive observations to the number of all possible observations. *Fallout evaluation* measures the negative observations against the number of all possible observations. *Precision evaluation* typically measures the relevant observations similar to recall observations. Measurement functions often use *metrics*. Another kind of measurement uses *model-checking* functions that are based on predicates that evaluate certain properties. These properties can be used to decide whether a work product is consistent and can be refined for work products at the implementation layer.

Additionally, we need an approach to provide *tolerance* of the results and deviations from the either the origin or the realisations.

We also need a logics that provides us with a means for reasoning on analogy and for using analogy for transfer of derived statements and properties into the other domain. This directly results in a *logics of analogical reasoning*. Such logics have been developed in artificial intelligence and logics research. We may use, for instance, derivation rules for a source object s and a target object t of the following form

$$\frac{t \approx_\alpha s, \alpha \ \Vdash \ \beta}{\beta(t) := \beta(s)} \ .$$

This rule allows us to conclude that whenever the source and the target object are analoguous based on a certain predicate α, and the predicate α entails another predicate β, then we may transfer the value for β for the source to the target.

Another such rule is:

$$\frac{t \approx_\alpha s, \alpha(s)}{\diamond\alpha(t)} \ .$$

If we know that s and t are α-analog and we observe the value $\alpha(s)$ then it is plausible to assume $\alpha(t)$.

We also may incorporate *lifting relations* or *bridge rules* between an origin and the model or the model and its reflections. These rules must consider a certain context for both the model and the origin, or both the model and its reflection. Therefore we use mappings between two languages with an additional context parameter for a context $\mathscr{C}$:

$$F : \mathscr{L}_1 \times \mathscr{C} \to \mathscr{L}_2 \ .$$

If we consider formulas α in context C_i the rules need to be extended:

$$\frac{(\alpha_1, i_1) \ldots (\alpha_n, i_n)}{(\alpha, i)} \varphi \ .$$

Such rules state that $(\alpha_1 \ldots \alpha_n)$ in their contexts $(C_{i_1} \ldots C_{i_n})$ imply α in the context C_i if the applicability condition φ is valid.

Such rules are considered in calculi of plausible reasoning that incorporate abduction and induction. Plausible reasoning uses inference pattern which can yield to uncertain conclusions even if the premises are certain. It is typical for situations in which the knowledge is incomplete. The modelling situation is based on incomplete information or incomplete knowledge.

The most important property for the analogy relationship is *adequacy*. Adequacy requires the satisfaction of the following four properties:

Similarity   between origin and model, or between model and reflection, in dependence on the purpose of the model is based on an explicitly given similarity relation that allows also to reason on the restrictions of similarity. That is, in the case of origin and model we may base similarity in subsets of properties $\Phi(O)$ and $\Phi(M)$ that are defining the similarity. Similarity supports the deployment of the model instead of the origin, or the reflection instead of the model, in all situations in which there is a similarity between the two sides.

Regulative factors   form a standardisation on the basis of exact rules which are given within a well-defined system. These rules permit one to derive the properties and do not result in exceptions that cover specific properties of the target that are not observed for the source.

Copiousness   is based on the capacity of the model. The model is a far better medium for reasoning about the origin or the reflection. It makes it simpler to draw conclusions, to reason about properties and to state postulates.

Simplicity   of the model is based on its concentration on the essential and relevant properties in dependence on the model's purpose.

17.3 Conclusion

The aim of this chapter has not been to develop a complete theory of conceptual modelling. Rather, our aim was to develop a programme for the theory. We described the general purpose of this theory, demonstrated how different paradigms can be selected, and showed which scope, modelling acts, modelling methods, modelling goals and modelling properties might be chosen for this theory.

The programme requires far more work. The theory needs a variable taxonomy that allows a specialisation to languages chosen for a given application domain, must be based on a mathematical framework that allows one to prove properties, must be flexible for coping with various modelling methodologies, must provide an understanding of the engineering of modelling, and finally should be supported by a meta-CASE tool that combines existing CASE to to a supporting workbench.

The following are the findings of this chapter:

- A model is a representation of something for someone's purpose somebody and developed by someone else.
- Each model is author-driven and addressee-oriented, is aspect-related, is purpose-specific, is limited in space, context and time, and is perspective.
- The model quality is also given by those elements that are not observed for the origin or not realised in the reflection or realisation.
- Due to amplification, distortion and idealisation, models cannot be used outside their purpose. If the purpose changes then the model should change as well.

- Models are similar to concepts; they are abstract and concrete; they associate worlds, e.g., the world of origins and models.
- Conceptual models are similar to other systems that are context- and utilisation-dependent. They have their value within the purpose range.

Models are imperfect and diverge from the real world. They are incomplete, have a different behaviour, and also exhibit other kinds of errors. Imperfection is based on exceptional states (events, time lags), on incompleteness to limitations of the language and consideration, and on errors either based on real errors and exceptional states or based on biases.

A theory of conceptual modelling can be based on a system of guiding principles. This paper shows that at least three guiding principles must be explored in detail:

Internal principles   are based on a set of ground entities and ground processes.

Bridge principles   explain the results of conceptual modelling in the context of their usage, for instance for explanation, verification/validation, and prognosis.

Engineering principles   provide a framework for mastering the modelling process, for reasoning on the quality of a model, and for termination of a modelling process within a certain level of disturbance tolerance (error, incompleteness, open issues to be settled later, evolution).

References

1. Beeri C and Thalheim B (1999) Identification as a primitive of database models. In: Proceedings FoMLaDO'98. Kluwer, London, pp 19–36
2. Börger E, Thalheim B (2008) A method for verifiable and validatable business process modeling. In: Software Engineering, Lecture notes in computer science, vol 5316. Springer, Heidelberg, pp 59–115
3. Chen PP, Akoka J, Kangassalo H, Thalheim B (eds) (1998) Conceptual modeling: current issues and future directions. Lecture notes in computer science, vol 1565. Springer, Heidelberg
4. Deppert W (2009) Theorie der Wissenschaft. Lecture notes for academic year 2008/09, Christian-Albrechts-University at Kiel, http://wolfgang.deppert.de
5. Fiedler G, Thalheim B (2009) Towards semantic wikis: modelling intensions, topics, and origin in content management systems. Inform Model Knowl Bases XX:1–21
6. Gregor S (2009) Building theory in the sciences of the artificial. In: DESRIST. ACM, New York
7. Hevner A, March S, Park J, Ram S (2004) Design science in information systems research. MIS Quaterly 28(1):75–105
8. Jackson M (2006) Problem frames. Pearson, Harlow, Essex
9. Kaschek R (2003) Konzeptionelle Modellierung. PhD thesis, University Klagenfurt
10. Mahr B (2009) Information science and the logic of models. Softw Syst Model 8:365–383
11. Mäkinen T (2010) Towards assessment driven software process mpdeling. PhD thesis, TUT Pori
12. Mittelstraß J (ed) (2004) Enzyklopädie Philosophie und Wissenschaftstheorie. J.B. Metzler, Stuttgart
13. Murphy GL (2001) The big book of concepts. MIT Press, Cambridge
14. Olivé A (2007) Conceptual modeling of information systems. Springer, Berlin
15. Simsion G (2007) Data modeling – Theory and practice. Technics Publications, Denville

16. Stachowiak H (1992) Modell. In: Seiffert H and Radnitzky G (eds) Handlexikon zur Wissenschaftstheorie. Deutscher Taschenbuch Verlag, Munich, pp 219–222
17. Steinmüller W (1993) Informationstechnologie und Gesellschaft: Einführung in die Angewandte Informatik. Wissenschaftliche Buchgesellschaft, Darmstadt
18. Thalheim B (2000) Entity-relationship modeling – foundations of database technology. Springer, Berlin
19. Thalheim B (2007) The conceptual framework to user-oriented content management. Information Modelling and Knowledge Bases, XVII:30–49
20. Thalheim B (2009) Towards a theory of conceptual modelling. In: ER Workshops. Lecture Notes in Computer Science, vol 5833. Springer, Heidelberg, pp 45–54
21. Thalheim B (2009) The conceptual framework to multi-layered database modelling. In: Proceedings EJC, Maribor, pp 118–138
22. Whorf BL (1980) Lost generation theories of mind, language, and religion. Popular Culture Association, University Microfilms International, Ann Arbor

Index